Joe McCarthy

ALSO BY ALAN H. LEVY
AND FROM MCFARLAND

*Tackling Jim Crow: Racial Segregation
in Professional Football* (2003)

*Rube Waddell: The Zany, Brilliant Life
of a Strikeout Artist* (2000)

Joe McCarthy

Architect of the
Yankee Dynasty

ALAN H. LEVY

McFarland & Company, Inc., Publishers
Jefferson, North Carolina, and London

Library of Congress Cataloguing-in-Publication Data

Levy, Alan Howard.
Joe McCarthy : architect of the
Yankee dynasty / Alan H. Levy.
p.   cm.
Includes index.

ISBN 0-7864-1961-X (softcover : 50# alkaline paper)

1. McCarthy, Joe (Joseph), 1887–1978.
2. Baseball managers— United States— Biography.
3. New York Yankees (Baseball team).
I. Title.
GV865.M293A3   2005   796.357'092 — dc22   2005003507

British Library cataloguing data are available

On the cover: Left to right, McCarthy in his first year with the
Yankees, 1931; McCarthy in command; McCarthy with the Yankees
(courtesy National Baseball Hall of Fame and Library, Cooperstown, N.Y.)

Manufactured in the United States of America

McFarland & Company, Inc., Publishers
Box 611, Jefferson, North Carolina 28640
www.mcfarlandpub.com

Table of Contents

Preface

Students of the national pastime sometimes think that virtually every subject in the history of the game has been studied. While there is almost always another way to look at a subject, few topics indeed have never been studied. Yet a perusal of the Internet and a careful check of the catalogues of the Library of Congress revealed for me a surprising fact — there has never been a biography of Joseph Vincent McCarthy, arguably the greatest manager in the history of baseball. The Library of Congress lists twenty books on Casey Stengel, none on Joe McCarthy. Ken Burns's famous nine-part television documentary on the history of baseball has significant coverage of such managers as John McGraw, Connie Mack, Casey Stengel, Billy Martin, and Earl Weaver. Joe McCarthy receives little attention, and the scant mention he does receive is largely in the context of the fact that Babe Ruth did not like him, which indeed he did not.

Joe McCarthy has certainly not been absent from works on baseball. All major books on the history of baseball in the 1920s, '30s, and '40s devote some pages to him. All significant books and articles on such baseball legends as Babe Ruth, Lou Gehrig, Joe DiMaggio, Hack Wilson, Rogers Hornsby and Ted Williams contain some discussion of McCarthy too, as do works on or by other baseball figures such as Tommy Henrich, Phil Rizzuto, Joe Gordon, Bill Dickey, Gabby Hartnett, and Lefty Gomez. McCarthy certainly has a presence in books about baseball managers, and in the histories of the major league teams he managed — the Chicago Cubs, the New York Yankees, and the Boston Red Sox. Indeed, the existing body of published literature in which Joe McCarthy receives some coverage is substantial. Still, it is striking that there has never been an actual biography of the man.

Several facts do render McCarthy less accessible to a historian. One simple matter is that unlike Connie Mack or John McGraw, McCarthy penned no set of memoirs. During his retirement years, he had lucrative offers to write such a book, but he felt neither a desire nor any pressing financial need to do so. This leaves many significant parts of his life somewhat mysterious. While much is known about McCarthy's work with the Cubs, Yankees, and Red Sox, most of the history of McCarthy's life in baseball before he became a major league manager has never been fully unearthed. McCarthy said little about it, or about his early life in general, and his pre–major league years, 1887–1926, receive at best a few paragraphs or even just a few sentences in the books and articles that mention them at all. In addition to

McCarthy writing no memoir, this paucity of coverage has been due to the fact that Joe McCarthy played only minor league baseball, and the records there are less substantive. McCarthy's never playing in the major leagues was something opponents and detractors regularly used against him when they tried to come up with points of criticism and derision. Many major league figures of his time, notably Babe Ruth, sniffed at McCarthy's mere minor league career. Indeed, McCarthy was the first baseball manager of any significance who never played in the major leagues. Such relative obscurity (and alleged unworthiness) is part of both the biographic and the bibliographic story.

An additional complication with McCarthy's legacy is the fact that a manager's work is often more obscure than that of the players. It is harder to discern, less visible to the eye. And among the fraternity of managers themselves, McCarthy had less of the flamboyance that has rendered others more famous, more accessible to writers, and of more interest to fans. Earl Weaver and Billy Martin were each ejected from more games in a single season than Joe McCarthy was in his entire career. John McGraw, Casey Stengel, and Yogi Berra were famous for their pontificating, and most others were usually affable and approachable. McCarthy, on the other hand, was known, and at times reviled, for his incorrigible silence. That was part of both his personality and his personal convictions. He was a hard man for journalists to grasp, and many were frustrated when they attempted to do so. He was rarely demonstrative with fans or umpires. Indeed in many seasons he was hardly ever seen on the field during a game. In the clubhouse he spoke little to reporters, and when he did he was often intentionally laconic. Yet (and here McCarthy would likely prefer "And") he compiled the best won-loss record of any manager in the history of the game.

Some likened Manager McCarthy to a kind of Buddha figure on a ball field. He sat quietly and saw absolutely everything. All matters flowed through him. Those around him knew what he wanted them to know. His players never even knew the signals he relayed to his coaches. He sought no notoriety and developed no media personality. After a key Boston Red Sox victory over the Yankees in late 1948, photographers were about to take McCarthy's picture, and he waved them off, telling them to take the players' pictures. McCarthy was not acting with false modesty, nor coyly "retreating into the limelight." He had a decidedly firm sense of his role, and that role was to be both thoroughly active and very quiet.

All these reasons combine with the great length of both his life (1887–1978) and his baseball career (1907–1950) to make the writing of his biography a task of no small difficulty and proportion. But when one considers the manager with the best record in the history of the game, a man who was called "an Einstein in flannels," the pilot who never managed a major league team to a second division finish and who had his team in the thick of a pennant race virtually every year he managed, and who, in a twenty-year span, won nine pennants and came very close ten other times, it certainly makes sense to consider what he did and how he did it.

The usually taciturn Joe DiMaggio once effused: "Never a day went by that you didn't learn something from Joe McCarthy." One Yankee pitcher, Joe Page, one of the few players McCarthy clearly mishandled (to the shock and consternation of all on hand), had every reason to comment negatively about the man. Yet he put it simply: "I hated his guts, but there was never a better manager." When the Yankees were in their absolute heyday in the late 1930s, a reporter asked future Hall of Fame catcher Bill Dickey what it is that makes the Yankees so successful. Dickey did not hesitate for a second. He simply pointed to McCarthy and said, "That man." After a 3000-hit career in the National League, Paul Waner put in a short stint with the Yankees during World War II. "I heard about him," Waner nodded, "but ... his work has been a revelation to me.... I would not have missed it for the world — I got such a belt out of watching him operate!"

Generally admired, sometimes resented, occasionally hated, always respected, Joe McCarthy was *the* manager. "Joe is a really remarkable person," Lou Gehrig once remarked. "He must have a dozen eyes.... Nothing on the ball field ever escapes him." A man who could look at the dents in his catcher's mitt to see how effective his pitcher was with his curve ball, a man who noted the velocity of foul balls that went back to the screen as a way of gauging the speed and hop of someone's fastball, a manager who saw everything, absolutely everything that was occurring on a ball field — how he did it; how he handled his men; how he chose and nurtured talent; how he developed strategies and decided upon tactics — it all makes for a fascinating study of a man who sat at the center of the nation's pastime for a quarter century and who quietly embodied success in an era when success seemed so tragically out of reach to so very many.

I would like to offer thanks to my colleague, Professor Charles Alexander, for his advice and encouragement as I began researching this biography. A thank you, as well, to Mr. William Burdick of the Baseball Hall of Fame and Museum in Cooperstown for his assistance with photographic materials. As with several other research projects I have undertaken on sports history, I am also greatly indebted to Mr. David Kelly and the rest of the staff of the Library of Congress for their kind help and expert assistance. Theirs is a truly grand institution.

1

Planning to Be a Plumber

A plain, working-class community; that was Germantown, Pennsylvania in the late 19th century. Since the mid–twentieth century, Germantown has become a lovely and wealthy section of Philadelphia, but the community in whose east side Joseph Vincent McCarthy was born on April 21, 1887, was not so well heeled. Germantown had originally grown in the eighteenth century as some of Pennsylvania's "Deutsch" ventured out there wishing to escape what they saw as the increasing worldliness of the city of Philadelphia to which they had emigrated to practice their firm social and religious ways. The separation and distance from Philadelphia were vital here, and the gap between Germantown and "Center City" was still very much in evidence when the McCarthy family lived there. Germantown was a community staunchly unto itself. Its attraction for immigrant and working class families like the McCarthys was simply that it was relatively inexpensive and close to jobs in the many local mills.

Joe McCarthy's father was apparently a typical hard-working member of the carpentry and building trade in the Germantown area. But the word "apparently" must be emphasized, as the nature of the man would be forever unknown to young Joseph Vincent, because his father died in a work accident when Joe was but three years old. He had fallen from a scaffold. Joe McCarthy thus had no real memory of his father. His relations with his mother and with his local East Germantown Catholic Parish (St. Vincent's) were always close. Armchair psychologists may make much of such points, but Joe McCarthy never showed any significant neuroses or dysfunction from this, or from much of anything else in his life. If anything, he grew to be a self-supportive individual at a level that many more insecure folks found unnerving. To the most extreme degree, he was always a man who kept his own counsel. Many a news reporter would indeed be quite frustrated at this closed feature of Mr. Joe McCarthy. Sports writers regularly commented on the distance McCarthy would keep, even from those he apparently respected and trusted. "Let me worry about that" was a phrase all reporters would hear from McCarthy again and again. Dealing with McCarthy, noted one always admiring reporter, "you reach what seems to be a thick plate of glass, through which you can see McCarthy, but beyond which he will not let you advance."[1]

From his earliest days, McCarthy's mother recalled, Joe was always a private person, someone who was not terribly close to many and who kept a decided distance from most. When Joe was a young adolescent, Mrs. Susan McCarthy married again, to a man named John Cassidy. Cassidy had children from a prior marriage. Mrs. McCarthy remembered no significant hostility between the step-siblings, but she noted that young Joe largely kept to himself, and was most adamant in the protection of his own personal belongings. Among the items of young Joe's private property, he most prized his various bits of baseball equipment. "He always liked baseball," recalled his mother. "He always had a ball and bat. He'd take them with him [to school or to work] or hide them to keep his older step-brothers from taking them, and he'd fight to get them back. Always out on the lots playing ball," Mrs. McCarthy remembered, "but that was harmless enough surely." Like all American boys of the late nineteenth century, Joe McCarthy grew up playing baseball. "I might have strung along with cricket," McCarthy once recalled,

> had not mother taken me to Snellenberg's store in Philadelphia for a new suit. It so happened that there was a special bargain that day, a suit with a bat and a ball. It cost slightly more than the others. Mother argued against buying it. I coaxed and finally won. We had hardly got out on the sidewalk when [a horse-drawn victoria bus carrying the New York] Giants started to pass. From that minute baseball became my life. I started to dream about the game — and have never stopped.[2]

McCarthy loved the game, and he was darned good at it. He liked other sports too, but baseball was his passion. One afternoon, while out on a sandlot, Joe may have badly banged his knee. Some have said he fractured his kneecap, and this may have held back his speed as a ballplayer for the rest of his days. "It left me with a loose cartilage which cut down my speed," McCarthy stated in 1937. "I didn't have that final quick step or two getting to first base. Then, it seems, with a bit of a twinkle he added, "but I didn't do so good against a curve ball either." In all the years McCarthy played minor league baseball, before he was a famous manager, no reporter made any mention of any knee problem, or of any problem of slow running being rooted in such a boyhood injury as a fractured kneecap. Reporters covering various minor league teams for whom McCarthy played actually commented specifically on his speed in the field. The knee injury may or may not have been real; it may have just been a story, from whomever it came, that was simply repeated over and over, one which the often taciturn Manager McCarthy felt no desire to clarify. It added to the image of a man who used hard work and mental agility to compensate for what may have been lacking in God-given physical skill. McCarthy's mother never mentioned any sort of injury when recalling her son's passion for the game. In the minors, McCarthy's foot speed was not what held back his playing career, it was his hitting. Given the repeated knocks McCarthy endured about never playing in the big leagues when he first managed in the majors, the kneecap story may have been a convenient rumor he cared to do anything but scotch.[3]

Young Joe was always a well-behaved lad in Germantown, never guilty of any delinquent behavior. "He was a good boy," his mother proudly recalled. He was apparently an able and diligent student in school, a good churchgoer, and a fanatic about baseball. He watched such Philadelphia Phillies stars of the late 1890s as Elmer Flick and Ed Delahanty. In 1901, when Joe was fourteen, the new American League's professional baseball team, the Athletics, began playing in Philadelphia. Young Joe became a rabid Philadelphia A's fan, especially after they won the American League pennant in 1902, and he idolized their manager, Connie Mack. Whenever he could, McCarthy would trolley down to the A's ball field at old Columbia Park. In those days, major league baseball teams ran on a shoestring, and they preferred to keep the baseballs that flew into and beyond the stands. Boys like McCarthy would gather outside the grandstand during the game in the territory where foul balls would often land. If someone caught a ball, he could trade it for admission into the park. McCarthy was good at listening to the crack of a bat, picking up a ball's flight quickly, and scrambling against the other boys to nab a free pass. Once in the ballpark, McCarthy would watch intently and often stay after the games near the clubhouse entrance to get a glimpse of Mr. Mack and sometimes follow him to the trolley station. "Connie Mack," he later confessed, "was my idol."[4] This admiration and respect for Mr. Mack was something McCarthy would onto hold for his entire life. Unlike other managers, notably John McGraw, Mr. Mack never yelled at his ballplayers. McCarthy tried to follow that example, and he succeeded, most of the time. He always held that Mr. Mack was the greatest of all baseball managers. At the home outside Buffalo, New York, where he lived for the last thirty-five years of his life, McCarthy maintained one room exclusively for all his baseball awards and memorabilia. In his main living room, however, there were no baseball items save for two signed pictures, and one was of Connie Mack (the other was of Lou Gehrig).[5]

While baseball was a joy, Joe McCarthy's boyhood in Germantown was anything but a mere light mixture of school and baseball. When he was not in school or at a sandlot playing ball, Joe was working. Like most families of their station, the McCarthy children went to work, and in the years before his widowed mother remarried, family finances were especially tight. Mrs. McCarthy worked as a child care nurse for a wealthy Germantown family named the Chews. (The Chew family had owned a mansion in the Philadelphia area that went back to Revolutionary times. George Washington had once made his headquarters there.) Joe did not finish high school; he had to work. He delivered ice in Germantown. He dug post holes for a fencer, what he later described as "back-breaking work under a broiling sun." And after grammar school, he worked as a bobbin boy at a Philadelphia yarn mill. Here his subsequently famous eye for detail was likely sharpened. The mill work likely magnified an already existing knack for being able to survey an expanse of activity and spot any problem as soon as it began to reveal itself. In the mill, he once recalled, "if you didn't catch the break in the yarn as it was spun out, the damage was considerable — and the boss gave you hell." With all such work he always brought money home. Pridefully he once confided to a reporter that at the mill he rapidly became the best and most dependable of the bobbin boys and gained for himself a promotion to "head tender," giving him a salary of $6.50 a week, $1.50 more than the other boys' weekly wages.[6] While never neurotically parsimonious, McCarthy would always be careful with his money and apparently never made a major financial error in his life.

McCarthy's mother and the family could envisage nothing unique for any of their children. They were of the working class and expected this future for their children. One of Joe's brothers, Maurice, worked as a truck driver for a stage company in Philadelphia. Sometimes Joe accompanied him when there was a lot of stage equipment to move. He was able to watch many shows, and this began what would be a life-long love of the musical stage. If he ever had any visions of performing, however, they were quickly dispelled: "One night an act failed to show up," he recalled, "so a pal and I filled in. We got a very rough reception. What a break for me," he laughed. "I might have been a song-and-dance man instead of manager of the Yankees."[7]

When Joe was a teenager, his mother recalled that it had been all arranged for him to be apprenticed to a local plumber whom the family knew. Without truancy laws in that era, McCarthy did not have to attend high school, and he did not complete it. It simply made sense, his mother felt, for her son to learn a useful trade. Plans were in the works for Joe to be apprenticed to a plumber. The plans would have gone forth but for the intervention of the family's parish priest. Joe McCarthy's ball playing was good enough to gain the notice of local priests, whose parishes provided some of the organizational structure for many of the youth baseball leagues, as well as their other athletic and social activities in and around Germantown. He had also been a standout with a local team in 1904 that was part of the Chew Athletic Association, named for the same well-heeled family for whom Mrs. McCarthy worked. They played at a ball field in the Chew Woods on the family mansion grounds. The family's parish priest suggested to Mrs. McCarthy that she abandon the idea of her son becoming a plumber and allow him to play more baseball with the distinct possibility that he could play ball for a Catholic college. "I had it all decided for him to be a plumber," recalled Mrs. McCarthy. "The man was going to take him as an apprentice and everything was all arranged. Then the priest of St. Vincent's Parish out in Germantown came to me and asked me to send Joe to Niagara to play on their ball team. It was a hard thing to let him go but I did it, so he never got to be a plumber; he kept on playing ball." Joe McCarthy would later laugh, his mother recalled, "about my wanting him to be a plumber, and I guess," she concluded, "it's a better thing that he isn't, though." Noting her son's job then of managing the Chicago Cubs, Mrs. McCarthy did hasten to add, "this is a harder job than plumbing." Mrs. McCarthy and the family acceded to their priest's idea, and with the Church's recommendation, young Joe later gained admission into Niagara College (now Niagara University) in upstate New York. In 1905, at age 18 with no high school diploma, Joe went off to college, something no one in his family had ever done. Mrs. McCarthy and the family would eventually be enormously proud of their son and his accomplishments in baseball, but his road to success would be long and circuitous indeed.[8]

McCarthy enrolled at Niagara in the fall of 1905. He was a dutiful student, although not an outstanding one. A boyhood friend and next-door neighbor in Germantown, Joseph M. Noonan, became a priest, and, by coincidence, later became President of Niagara University. McCarthy lived much of his adult life in or near Buffalo, and there Noonan would have occasion to chide McCarthy about his incurious academic record. He took high school-level "prep" classes. Outside of classes at Niagara, McCarthy took part in some student comedy theater productions (in black face), and, of course, he went out for baseball. Niagara, he later recalled fondly, was "the most picturesque spot in all the world to me." He took pride in the way the school supported him. "They are great for all kinds of sport at Niagara, but baseball," McCarthy learned, "has the first call." In the spring of 1906 he turned out for the college's varsity baseball team.[9] He immediately made the "Purple Eagles" starting lineup. Niagara's first outing was a rude awakening as to some of the competition they would face. They played against Cornell University, and Cornell's pitcher, Pete Deahon, blanked them with a no-hitter. The papers praised the play of Deahon and of several other Cornell players. The only thing from the Niagara squad to get any press mention were the "fine running catches by McCarthy," who played second base and filled in at left field in the late innings.[10] Subsequently, the team did better, albeit against generally weaker squads like Mt. St. Mary's College in Maryland, Bradford College in Pennsylvania, and Medina and Oberlin Colleges in Ohio. McCarthy quickly established himself as a fixture on the team. He batted cleanup and played second base, shortstop, and outfield, willingly filling in wherever his coach needed him. In one game against Mount St. Mary's, with the score tied, Mount St. Mary's had runners on first and third with two out. McCarthy quietly told the umpire to make sure the runner on first touched second base if there was a base hit. Earlier he had noticed a certain sloppiness in the player's running habits. It was like noticing a wobbly spool on a loom at the Germantown yarn mill. The next batter singled to right. One runner scored, with the other moving to third. McCarthy called for an appeal, and indeed the umpire ruled that the runner had not touched second. The game remained tied, and angry Mount St. Marys' student spilled onto the field. After order was restored, Niagara won. McCarthy showed he did not just have an eye for detail, but a knack for eyeing the right detail at the right moment.[11]

Later that May, a rude shock came to McCarthy and the team when they arranged to play against a professional team, the Baltimore Orioles of the Eastern League, who played a class of baseball just a cut below the big leagues. McCarthy and the Niagara team held the Orioles to a scoreless tie for four innings, and they were feeling pretty good about themselves. Then the Orioles stepped up and scored nine runs in two innings, eventually winning 10–2. Playing shortstop, McCarthy committed two of the Niagara errors that enabled the Orioles to score so freely. "The Niagara boys went into the air," noted a reporter sadly. McCarthy learned further something he would always teach about the value of consistent play and steady concentration. A week later, McCarthy and Niagara would play the Rochester Hustlers of the same Eastern League, and this time they would not be intimidated and won, 10–5. "McCarthy hit well," noted the papers.[12] The win over the Hustlers was a major coup for the college boys. Several years later, when he was playing professionally in Buffalo, McCarthy recalled, "We beat Rochester ... and the feat has never been forgotten. The deed is recalled when persons ask about Niagara's team."[13]

McCarthy seemed to have a good future ahead of him. He was in college, and he was an established leader on the baseball team. But McCarthy's ambitions in baseball ran wider than the collegiate level. He had played well against Rochester. He knew he was a more capable player than he had shown himself to be against the Orioles. Clearly he had deduced that he could compete at the professional level. The game, as he would later reflect, had gotten in his blood. In the summer of 1906 he played for a team in Dover, Delaware of the Peach League, then not an officially recognized league, but the forerunner of the Eastern Shore League that later produced Jimmie Foxx and Mickey Cochrane. By the time the next baseball season rolled

around, McCarthy had left Niagara. He had thrown his lot with professional baseball and would try to make it as a ballplayer. "I decided," he recalled, "that the family fortunes could not stand the luxury of a college education for Joseph Vincent."
He knew it would be tough, but he had to give it a try, and he ultimately found an
opportunity not too far from Germantown. He signed on for 1907 with a team in
Delaware, the Wilmington "Colts" of the Tri-State League. If he played well, he
figured a couple of good seasons could take him to the major leagues. He'd make it
to the majors all right, but it turned out to take a lot more than a couple of years.[14]

2

Starting Down at the Bottom

The Wilmington Colts began practice in the spring of 1907. While the wealthier clubs of the major and the upper minor leagues would travel deep into the South to train in good weather, the Wilmington team owners could afford no such luxury. They traveled South, but only as far as Virginia. In the Tidewater area of Portsmouth, Virginia, Joe McCarthy, still but 19, took his first stab at being a professional baseball player. Delaware sports reporters covered some of the team's exhibitions, and McCarthy gained some notice. In one game against a team from Portsmouth, "the features of the game," wrote one scribe, "were the fielding of ... McCarty [sic], while the manner in which ... [three others and] McCarty lined them was a wonder and admiration to the opposing players." Wilmington won that game 11–0, and in a return match three days later Wilmington won another, 5–4, and again "McCarty did great hitting."[1]

Life in the Virginia training camp, though certainly Spartan, was not all grim. Amidst coverage of a game against Norfolk the Wilmington papers announced that players "Harry Shortal, Joe McCart[h]y, and James McCusker have formed a trio and will sing selections prior to the opening game of the team in Wilmington." Wilmington won the game against Norfolk 9–8 in ten innings, with McCarthy getting two hits and scoring the winning run. After several more victories, a reporter sang praises of the young rookie: "McCarthy is one of the fleetest men on the team, and whenever any runs are required or it is necessary to have a hit, he is generally there with the goods." The only blemish came during a losing effort against Richmond when McCarthy was called for failing to touch second base when he hit a triple. Still, sensing the positive attitude the rookie displayed, the papers noted even in regard to McCarthy's miscue, "nobody regarded it worse than he did."[2] In later years, when McCarthy was managing the Yankees, some of the players used to chide him about his years in the minor leagues. It was a good thing that no one, especially Babe Ruth, ever got hold of the story of the base running error against Richmond. McCarthy would never have heard the end of it.

McCarthy never got big-headed about himself to the effect that he deserved to be playing at a higher level. He knew he had to work his way up, and he went about his business without complaint. One local scribe praised him: "He is one of the most reliable batters on the team and his work meets with favor from the spectators."[3] Still, the harshness of the conditions in which the Wilmington team trained must certainly have been obvious to him, as well as to all the players. In the two weeks the team spent in Virginia, there were only three days of good weather.[4] In subsequent times, when he was the manager in charge, he was always fastidious about arrangements for a good field and good training conditions, and when he could not have them, as was the case during the travel-restricted years of World War II, the memories of days like his "cup of coffee" with Wilmington were more than a bit depressing. One feature of the training may have been a bit odd to the Germantown-bred McCarthy. It was something that reporters indeed noted as "a novelty to the visitors." How McCarthy may have felt about it, or whether he simply did not give it much thought, he never said, but on April 8, at the Portsmouth, Virginia, ball park, the players from Portsmouth, Wilmington, and Binghamton (N.Y.) were given a "demonstration" as part of their running exercises. The papers described it thus: "Bill Smith, a Negro convicted of larceny and sentenced to three months, was given liberty at the ball park. He ran like a deer, much to the amusement of the ballplayers." The park officials then set a team of bloodhounds after him, with the players instructed, for the sake of exercise, to chase him as well. "The Negro and the dogs appeared to enjoy the exercise," noted the nonplussed reporter, adding with but a touch of concern: "had the Negro been unable to get out of the reach of the dogs, they would probably have torn him to pieces. In practice, however, care is always taken to give the Negro ample opportunity to take care of himself."[5] This was the Jim Crow South in which McCarthy and all ballplayers of the day trained. The sensibilities behind such practices, and the fact that almost everyone else shrugged and accepted them as part of life, was certainly a thread in the fabric that was professional baseball in that era, as the sport maintained rigid segregation during the regular season. McCarthy never commented one way or the other about such ways, nor would he ever speak out in any vein about the racial segregation that plagued the game during his heyday as a manager. He did, however, confide to his Yankee general manager, Ed Barrow, a certain antipathy toward Southerners, something he privately expressed when trading off some particularly unruly ones. Any sorts of "games" as he witnessed in Portsmouth were certainly never allowed in his presence on any ball club he managed, during spring training or at any other time. Professionalism had a deep meaning to him, for he would spend so many years seeing the very opposite, and those around him in later years had to appreciate this and behave accordingly.[6]

The Wilmington team came home on April 11, and 1000 fans turned out at the railroad station to greet them. Their victories in Virginia had sparked expectations for a good season, and local sports writers were busy fanning all the high hopes. The play of the rookie McCarthy was part of this rosy picture. Unfortunately in the first exhibition game back home in Wilmington, McCarthy sprained his ankle sliding into second base. As in Virginia, the game was played on a damp, sloppy field, and McCarthy's injury stemmed from the poor footing.[7] McCarthy missed the next two games, and without him Wilmington lost. He came back and starred with two hits and two runs in an important victory over another Wilmington professional team that played in the rival Atlantic League. Bragging rights were important, especially in a small town where the perception of who plays the better brand of baseball greatly affected gate receipts.

The high hopes for the Colts that greeted them upon their return from Virginia began to fade as they lost several more exhibition games, however. Still, 5000 came to several games, and Wilmington's Mayor attended opening day. McCarthy continued to receive some good press notices. "Sensational play at shortstop" was one description of him amidst a loss to Trenton, N.J. McCarthy was quickly regarded as a versatile and dependable fielder. He played well at second, third, shortstop, and in the outfield. In a game against Altoona, Pa., McCarthy "played his game of the season, and the manner in which he picked up the hot ones [at third base] was a revelation." McCarthy's hitting was less spectacular. In the batting lineup he was always sixth or seventh. After ten games he had seven hits in thirty-four at bats for a mere average of .206. Meanwhile the team was doing poorly. In early May, Wilmington's record was 1 and 9; they were in last place. The team's batting average stood at an anemic .182.[8]

With the preseason hopes having run as high as they had before the disastrous start, Wilmington's team president, William M. Connelly, began to worry. Fans were getting unruly. During one game on May 10, a dispute arose over whether a visiting player from Johnstown, Pa., had properly tagged up at second base before advancing on a sacrifice fly. The rhubarb between the players and the umpire was typical name-calling row, but this time, when one Wilmington player was ejected, he waved to the fans, urging they come onto the field. Some 500 did just that. As a result the police had to be called to supervise the rest of the game. (Wilmington's finest also had to remain with the umpire after the game. They kept him in the clubhouse until much of the crowd dispersed, and kept the remaining crowd at bay as they escorted the umpire to a hotel where they hid him until they could whisk him onto a train for Philadelphia.*) When fans behave like that, bad umpiring is often not the sole cause.[9] If the team had been playing good ball and contending for league leadership, fans' perspectives would have been more intelligently focused. The Wilmington Colts were inspiring anything but such maturity. Indeed, after describing the near-riots surrounding the Johnstown game of May 10, one reporter scoffed that aside from the extra-curricular excitement, "the game would [have] been scarcely worth witnessing," and "McCarthy," one scribe explicitly added, "played a poor game at third." He was at third amidst the tag-up play that prompted the near-riot in the first place. "Scarcely worth witnessing" are the last words a gate-receipt concerned team owner wants to read. McCarthy was the only rookie the Colts had kept up to that point in the season. He was considered the best of the prospects, but with lapses in the field and always mediocre hitting, the future did not look bright to McCarthy in Wilmington. The day after the crazy Johnstown game, McCarthy was benched. The papers, indeed, made explicit notice of it. Meanwhile, the team continued to slide. The day after they nearly lynched the idiotic umpire, the Colts got revenge on Johnstown with a win, but then they proceeded to lose their next seven games. On May 21 their record was 3 and 17; they were deep in the cellar, the laughingstock of the Tri-State League. Amidst all the losing, team president Connelly began to shift personnel, and

---

The umpire, George Bausewine, was apparently not one of the finest of baseball's officialdom. Wilmington papers reported that he had blown a similar tag-up call at a game in York, Pa. Ejecting the York club's manager amidst the ensuing argument, he was mobbed by fans and hit by a flying chair. Here the police had actually to resort to the firing of warning shots to restore order.

on May 13 the team announced "Joe McCarthy has been released and has gone to his home in Philadelphia." He had played in twelve games and hit .175. The Wilmington news report noted "he was a hard worker, ... the last of the youngsters who were tried out at the opening of the season to be let go." The paper added, with a positive though condescending spin, that young McCarthy "was evidently in too fast company."[10] (Wilmington's personnel changes did them little good. They floundered all season and finished in sixth place.)

The fact that the team made explicit announcements of McCarthy's benching and release did indicate that young Joe had gained some stature with the team and its fans. No other rookie's release gained such notice, nor indeed did any veteran's. This was hardly much consolation to McCarthy, of course, but it showed that he had made a decidedly positive impression in his first foray into professional baseball. With Jim Crow absurdities in the context of pre-season training, with fan riots against an umpire, and with cellar play in a low-level league, McCarthy's introduction to professional baseball could not have been much worse. It would not be hard to imagine him or his family leaning to his taking life in another direction. But baseball was in McCarthy's blood, and he was not going to give up. The question was, what he would now do? Would anyone else give him a chance?

3

Outlaw League

Intelligent baseball managers and owners keep tabs on prospects coming up throughout the various minor leagues. When the Wilmington Colts released McCarthy in May 1907, he headed back to Germantown, but within a month he received an offer from a Pennsylvania ball club out in the western end of the state in the town of Franklin. Other than his time at Niagara College, Joe had never lived far from the Germantown and Philadelphia environs. Franklin, Pa., was way out near the Ohio border. But the offer was legitimate, *and* the team said they would pay for his transportation. "They gave me a bus ticket to get down there and that was about it," McCarthy recalled, thinking of how little minor leaguers had to play for back then.[1] A bus ticket was certainly as good an inducement as young McCarthy could possibly expect, so he headed out to the wilds of Western Pennsylvania. On June 2, Franklin's team owner, L.L. Jacklin, signed McCarthy for $125 a month.[2]

Franklin was part of a circuit known as the Interstate League. It was considered an "outlaw" league in that they did not formally link themselves to other minor leagues or to any central administration that could help decide disputes and possibly assist during times of financial difficulties. They were a league purely unto themselves, and each team, like other minor league clubs, had to try to make it strictly through gate receipts. So the stronger the team (and the lower the players' wages) the better the owners would like it. The league was scouting for cheap young players. To that end, newspapers noted that after June 1, a number of college players would be seen in the Interstate League.[3] Back in the early 20th century, professional teams could be quite blatant about using college and other young players, despite some of their amateur standings. This was how Jim Thorpe would get himself in trouble with Olympic officials after he won gold medals in 1912. In 1906, the Philadelphia Athletics used an "Eddie Sullivan," who was then a student at Columbia University. His real name was Eddie Collins, and he would, of course, later be a Hall of Fame player, but at this point he was maintaining his amateur status while playing for the A's. McCarthy had no such amateur-standing issues, but he was of the age and price upon which minor league team owners shamelessly fed.

When it came to choosing teams on which to play, McCarthy's luck was not running well. The Franklin "Millionaires" (an odd name certainly, given the team and league's finances) were not doing much better than the Wilmington Colts. "We used to dress in the hotels," he later recalled, "and take the trolley down to the ballpark. Carried all our own stuff too. … They had the bats and balls in a suit roll. Players took turns carrying the suit roll." The Interstate League began play on May 15, and by June 3, Franklin was in last place with a record of 8 and 10. That was where Franklin stood when McCarthy first began to play for them on June 8. McCarthy was in and out of the lineup for a few weeks but soon became a regular, batting in the fifth spot by June 21. Franklin's fate did not improve much when Joe McCarthy was added to the daily roster, however. By June 24 they had dropped five straight and, as one paper caustically put it, they "seemed to have a mortgage on last place."[4]

That summer, finance and the weather conspired against the Franklin club, and against the entire league. Day after day, rainouts occurred. One local paper described a steady pattern of "chilling air and glum skies." According to the Pittsburgh papers, "Every team in the Interstate League is losing money with weather killing off games and attendance."[5] By July 1, Erie was the only club in the circuit not in debt.* Rainouts continued to frustrate the staging of games and promotion efforts. A Franklin "Booster Day," for example, was rained out twice before it was finally held. On July 15, a desperate Franklin club announced a street fair for the benefit of the team, with club officials admitting they needed quickly to raise $600. Umpires were not always paid. League games sometimes took place without them. By July 20, the clubs of Kane and Olean had disbanded.[6]

With two teams folding, the Interstate League set up an arrangement in which they declared a "first season" winner as of July 20 (DuBois won; Franklin was sixth) and started a "second season," with the two "season" winners to play off at the end. The teams absorbed players from the defunct Kane and Olean squads. The weather steadied; Franklin's attendance started to rise, and McCarthy continued to play every day, generally batting third and playing third base. DuBois and Punxsutawney did not fare as well as Franklin. They never got out of the red, and by August 4, they had both disbanded. The league was then down to four teams, but they kept playing, with thus a grand total of two games played in the league every few days. Somehow, the four teams limped through the next six weeks, playing one another plus a few exhibitions. On August 24, Erie actually played an exhibition game against the Cleveland team of the American League, and they won, 5–3![7]

Since DuBois had disbanded, second-place Oil City inherited the "first season" title. Meanwhile, Bradford was in a dogfight with Franklin for the second-season crown. Going into the final day of the season, Bradford was two games up on McCarthy's Franklin team. McCarthy had become Franklin's leading hitter. On that day each of the two teams was slated to play two games. Franklin had a chance to tie Bradford. They had to win their double header, and Bradford had to lose theirs. The prospect prompted a good crowd to turn out at Franklin for the doubleheader against Erie. Alas, Erie and Franklin split the twin bill, so the playoff berth went to Bradford. It would not be the last time McCarthy was part of team that faced the final day of the season with the possibility of getting into postseason play and coming up just short; "tough luck"— words he would hear 42 years later from the owner of the Boston

---

*At the outset of the '07 season, the clubs in the Interstate League were Bradford, DuBois, Erie, Franklin, Kane, Oil City, Olean, and Punxsutawney. Only four would survive the season.

Red Sox. In the 1907 Interstate League playoff, Oil City defeated Bradford, winning five games of eight. The day after its playoff victory, the Oil City team folded.[8]

For the twenty-year-old Joe McCarthy, the 1907 season could not have been a rougher introduction to the vagaries of minor league professional baseball. Having seen the depravities of Jim Crow while in spring training and an umpire attacked by an incensed crowd in Wilmington, McCarthy had made barely enough money to cover his meager personal living costs, and spent the summer with a team and a league that teetered unceasingly on the brink of financial ruin. Nevertheless, he finished the season with a solid reputation for his play at third base. Years later, he reflected on his early years, noting that he was "still not breaking down any fences, but already watching everything very closely." At the time, some baseball writers were not so deprecating. The Pittsburgh papers explicitly noted, "There were seven batters in the Interstate League hitting over .300. ... Though there are two men ahead of him, third baseman McCarthy is the next leader." McCarthy had batted .314 in 71 games. The figure of .300, then as now, holds sway with baseball people. Here was a twenty-year-old who could clearly field well and seemed to have found a batting touch. The Interstate League's second leading hitter, Harry Curtis of Bradford, had hit .327, and he was immediately signed by the New York Giants for $2000.[9] (Unfortunately, he would play only six games for New York that fall and never make it back to the big leagues.) McCarthy had some reason then to hope for a similar break. He was not quite so fortunate, but what he got was not that bad. He received an offer to play for the Toledo Mud Hens of the American Association, just one cut below the majors. He went back home to Germantown and worked to help out his family, full of hope that a good season with Toledo would open even bigger doors.

4

Mud Hens

"'Is that guy an outfielder?' asked [a player] … as Joe McCarthy clouted a line drive a mile over the head of … centerfield. 'If he is, we'll have to break his legs, eh?' continued [the player] as 'Mac' raced down to first like a streak."[1] Joe McCarthy made a decided impression on some of the Toledo veterans when they began training in Chattanooga, Tennessee in March, 1908. "He handles himself nicely at either position [of third base or the outfield] and hits the ball hard," noted a reporter.[2] The Toledo Mud Hens* had a core of veteran players. In 1907, they had contended for the American Association pennant with the eventual winner, intra-state rival Columbus, and all the fixtures of that summer's team were back. Still, observers noted that, despite his lack of experience, McCarthy had a chance to win a regular berth, and press reports certainly boosted his confidence. His versatility also stood him well, as even if some older players secured spots in the starting lineup, a young utility man would serve nicely, given the small bench strength that all ball clubs carried in those days. There were other youngsters trying to make the club, of course. A second baseman named Fred Merkle showed great promise, so much so, indeed, that in April his contract was purchased by the National League New York Giants.[3] McCarthy had reason to entertain hopes that such a fate would befall him too. The American Association was only one step from the majors. It had been a major league in the 1880s. Toledo's newspapers still smugly referred to the rest of professional baseball as "the minors." Players who did well in the AA "went up," as the saying went back then, all the time. There would be two pitchers in the AA that year, pitchers Joe Wood of Kansas City and Richard Marquard of Indianapolis, who would secure major league contracts and become stars. For a young ambitious player like McCarthy, such genuine prospects were certainly exciting. His salary at Toledo was $175 a month.[4]

While training in Chattanooga, Toledo played several exhibition games against major league teams, but McCarthy did not make the lineup. He was assigned to the "Colts," a squad of predominantly younger players who played intra-squad games

*The name "Mud Hen" refers to a bird that ducks under water just about the time the average hunter draws a bead on him, hence one smarter than the average bird. From the name's first usage by the Toledo baseball club, calls had come forth for "a more dignified cognomen" for the city's team. But in 1911, team President William Armour announced, "The name 'Mud Hen' is here to stick." (Toledo News Bee, April 7, 1911, p. 8.) It stuck.

against the "Regulars." The "Colts" won a few against their veteran teammates, but it did not seem to persuade the coaches and managers to make any significant changes in the lineup. McCarthy did make several errors in one of the exhibition games, and was described as having "played listlessly in several periods of the game." Meanwhile, Toledo's regular third baseman of several seasons, Bill Elwert, performed superbly.[5] The third base post remained his.

McCarthy got into his first game against a major league team on March 31. It was against the Chicago Cubs, then the defending World Series champions. The Cubs played mostly subs. Their famed infielders, Joe Tinker, Johnny Evers, and Frank Chance, for example, sat out the entire game. But McCarthy played, batted fourth, played right field, made one putout, and reached first once via being hit by a pitch; he later scored.[6] It was nothing spectacular, but it was his first time. The Mud Hens left Chattanooga on March 31, and Manager W. Reginald Armour split his squad in two—Colts and Regulars—for separate training. McCarthy was again assigned to the Colts, and they went off with an assistant coach to train in Fort Wayne, Indiana, and play some more exhibitions with major league clubs. McCarthy faced Eddie Cicotte and the Boston Red Sox. He faced Fred Merkle, now with the Giants, and he played against Ty Cobb and the Detroit Tigers. The "Colts" lost every encounter, but McCarthy's play was solid, both on the field and at bat. Meanwhile, veteran Bill Elwert could boast a spring batting average of only .177. On April 10, Manager Armour announced that "Joe McCarthy, the clever youngster ... would be retained this year as [a] utility man." The Toledo papers added: "McCarthy looks like a promising man and has a lot of experience in the outfield, as well as at third and short. He has played swell ball for the Colts and has been hitting the horsehide on the nose."[7]

While McCarthy earned a spot on the team, he was on the bench when the Mud Hens' season opened with a loss to Minneapolis on April 16. He first played on April 20 against St. Paul. Toledo won that contest, and during the game third baseman Bill Elwert tore a ligament in his knee. McCarthy was now the Mud Hens' starting third baseman. Elwert was out of action for a month, and McCarthy played every game in his place. His play was solid. In one game against St. Paul he threw high to first several times; however, he "atoned somewhat for his mistakes with a thrilling one-hand spear of a ... smash in the seventh." The catch came at a precipitous moment with runners in scoring position. They did not score, and Toledo went on to win 8–7.[8]

Going into early May, the Mud Hens jumped to first place with a record of 10 and 3. McCarthy hit .316 in this early stretch. The Hens even beat Kansas City's Joe Wood, despite the new pitching star's strikeout total of ten. The game went thirteen innings; Toledo won 6–5. "McCarthy," the Toledo paper chortled, "played a swell game at third, [making] two thrilling one-hand stops."[9] After reaching first place, the Mud Hens then went into a bit of a slump. They lost several, including a shutout to Indianapolis' Rube Marquard. The team's hitting fell off, including McCarthy's, his average dropping to .278. Indianapolis took over first place. McCarthy's batting slump occurred just at the point Bill Elwert was ready to play again. Hoping to give the team some spark, and noting McCarthy's drop-off in production at bat, Manager Armour reinstalled Elwert on May 17.[10]

McCarthy continued to play wherever Armour wanted him. He pinch hit. He played in the outfield. "The youngster is surely a find," heralded the Toledo sports writers, "and his ability to perform on either the infield or the outfield makes him a mighty valuable man. And he certainly can hit too."[11] McCarthy was proving his value. Unfortunately the rest of the team was earning such press descriptions as "Horrible!" and "Terrible!" Led by pitcher Richard "Rube" Marquard, Indianapolis was racing ahead of everyone. Toledo was not keeping pace. "Reg" Armour brought back some veterans. McCarthy's employment was not in danger, but he was not considered good enough to be the player who could lift the entire team. He continued to fill in where needed and do some pinch hitting. Armour was impressed with the way McCarthy stayed mentally in the game when he was not playing. This impression was significant enough that on June 4, Armour began to use McCarthy as a third base coach. This was certainly unusual for a twenty-one-year-old, but the papers wrote in approving tones, describing how "smart" and "reliable" a player this young McCarthy was. Then on June 10, Elwert was reinjured during a doubleheader with Milwaukee. This time he was spiked on the right foot. He had been hitting poorly since his return to the lineup anyway. McCarthy, the "popular youngster," was now both a regular and a coach.[12]

In mid–June, Toledo continued to contend with Indianapolis and Minneapolis for first place. McCarthy showed a lot of heady play. In a game against St. Paul, an opponent tripled. McCarthy noticed that the Saints third base coach had been gazing at the sun and at the women in the stands a bit too much. So he staged the hidden ball trick. While the coach, noted a reporter, "was getting an eye full of the sun scenery and fair femininity, the runner pranced off the pillow [with the coach] not there to say him 'nay.' McCarthy coyly tagged him with the ball." McCarthy would prove his headiness again and again. As the month progressed, however, McCarthy's hitting fell off. His batting average dropped from .293 to .266., and in one stretch he went one for twenty-two. He had to sit out a few games with a sore arm, and Armour then switched him to right field. His hitting continued to plummet. By July 4, McCarthy's batting average was a mere .239. The only regular on the Mud Hens with a lower average was Elwert. It was at this very time that the New York Giants signed Rube Marquard. (He signed on July 1, for $11,000!). It is possible that, had his play of May to mid June continued, McCarthy might have been given a serious look by a major league club. But his June/early July slump killed that. When he went two for three in a 5–0 loss to Columbus on July 3, the papers noted "Joe McCarthy played in his old form." This was hardly helpful. Still, McCarthy never griped. His attitude was always positive, and with that and his general braininess, Armour continued to use him as a coach.[13]

"Utility Joe," as he was now dubbed by the press, continued to struggle with his hitting. The June slump continued through the summer. Between July 4 and August 24, McCarthy's average wavered merely between a high of .236 and a low of .224. This was hardly going to make any big league scout take note. Cleveland Indians scouts Charley Somers and Ed Bernard made several trips over to Toledo to watch the Mud Hens. Philadelphia A's manager Connie Mack made three trips to Toledo in July and August. "Just who[m] he is after is not known," noted the papers, but no doubt it was not Joe McCarthy. In a doubleheader against Milwaukee, McCarthy made a "brilliant catch of a foul fly against the grand stand" that choked off a Brewers rally, but at the plate that day he went zero for six. "Good head, good glove, no stick" was no ticket to the major leagues. In addition to Marquard's record $11,000 signing (after which he won one and lost six for Indianapolis), several other American Association players "went up" that summer. The Boston Red Sox signed Joe Wood for $5000. Indianapolis Catcher Paddy Livingston, who had already played for the Cincinnati Reds, signed with the Red Sox for $6000. Two other Indianapolis Indians also struck gold: Chick Brandom signed with the Pittsburgh Pirates for $5000, and Owen "Donie" Bush signed with the Detroit Tigers for $10,000. It helped to be on the league-leading Indianapolis squad, certainly, but scouts were watching all the teams. The St. Paul Saints were lower in the standings than the Mud Hens, yet their catcher, Lee Meyer, hooked up with the Giants for $6000. As Joe McCarthy labored in his batting slump, he must have felt the world was passing him by. He was learning a lot of baseball, coaching as well as playing, but he wanted more.[14]

In September, McCarthy's hitting improved a bit. His average inched up to .246, higher than it had been at any time since early June. On September 1, he took part in a shellacking of Rube Marquard and his Indianapolis mates, 12–4. He made Marquard "mad enough to bite huge chunks out of the bench." If McCarthy could not go up, he and the Hens would at least get some sniggering jest in the besting of one who was. Indianapolis won the American Association flag that year. Toledo finished fourth, 11 games back. Reviewing the season, McCarthy's fielding won plaudits, and the papers explicitly noted "if McCarthy could hit all year as well as he did the last three weeks of the season, the fans would welcome him to a regular position on the club." Clearly, baseball people in Toledo saw some value in the young McCarthy, but a regular position with Toledo was not McCarthy's goal. So to be complimented with the notion that making the Mud Hens' regular lineup was a distinct possibility was hardly the kind of praise McCarthy wanted. But there it was. His first season with a significant minor league team seemed to have tagged him with the description of being a good fielder, an impressively heady player and coach, but an inconsistent hitter. There was nothing to do but keep trying.[15]

5

Still Can't Hit a Curve Ball

Life was grim for any ball player toiling in the minor leagues in the early 20th century. The pay was lousy, the conditions dirty. Players traveled sleeping two in a bed in the worst hotels, and the food was anything but gourmet. When a ballplayer saw the prospects of moving up to the majors growing dim, the cast of it all was even bleaker. In 1908–09, young Joe McCarthy was facing this. He lightened the mood a bit for himself by latching onto some local theaters wherever he went. That fall and winter, McCarthy and a Toledo catcher, Grover Land, hooked up with a group in Louisville, the Johnny Ray Theater Company. They did more than just sit in the audience; they landed temporary roles in the chorus. McCarthy used to chide Land, who apparently could not vocalize terribly well: "For Heaven's sake, Grover, if you can't talk, fire off a gun." When the baseball season was over, McCarthy joined up with the Johnny Ray Company. They traveled the South with the cast playing exhibition baseball games during the days and staging vaudeville skits at night. The troupe labored all winter and made a go of it financially. McCarthy starred at the baseball parts of the troupe's work. On stage he played the part of an Irish policeman, not much of a character stretch certainly. Jimmy Nagle, McCarthy's Toledo roommate in 1908, said that in anticipation of his postseason stage role, McCarthy would practice for hours in an effort to memorize and get the right tone for his one-line part as Chief Casey. All McCarthy had to say, in answer to a question "Who are you?" was "I'm Chief Casey." "He had an awful time getting that line right," giggled Nagle, "and I had to coach him time and time again." McCarthy got a huge case of stage jitters with the Johnny Ray Company and refused to appear on his debut night. "McCarthy," Nagle recalled, "is a clever dancer, and if it wasn't for his extreme modesty he might be able to get some easy money in vaudeville during the winter."[1] When the theater fun was over McCarthy headed back to Germantown.

That winter in Philadelphia, McCarthy hooked up with a singing and dancing partner. Toledo teammate Jimmy Nagle said they practiced together incessantly to get their teamwork down to perfection, but they never took it public. McCarthy said: "we weren't there."[2] McCarthy was probably right, although, as the likely weaker link of the two, he doubtlessly frustrated his partner. McCarthy was too much of a perfectionist and too shy to put himself on stage with something that could meet with any sort of derision. With such forays, despite their shortcomings, McCarthy maintained a love for the stage and for singing and dancing for the rest of his life. In Toledo he once actually appeared on stage with Harry Houdini. He apparently learned a few card tricks that he would enjoy showing to friends. In later years with the Yankees, George M. Cohan was one of his close friends. Like many of his generation, McCarthy would later grieve over the demise of vaudeville. His practice-practice-practice attitude toward his song and dance work was exactly what he brought to baseball. He clearly sensed he lacked the stage talent to do much professionally. The question was whether he had the talent to match his unremitting work ethic and keen mind to take himself very far in baseball. He did, but not quite in the way he first imagined.

The Toledo Mud Hens invited McCarthy back to spring training in 1909. His salary was up to $200 a month. Toledo had a new manager, Fred Abbott, and the city was constructing a new stadium, which they hoped to open by July 4. Amidst such spring time optimism, the papers opined that "McCarthy is regarded as likely to be retained as a utility man." He hit well in spring games, and reporters said "McCarthy knows the game a whole lot better than he did last spring, when he was practically 'green,' and stands up to the plate with a great deal more confidence." While noting that "Joe is clouting the ball as well as any man on the club," the reporter concluded with rather faint praise: "it begins to look as though the team would not be weakened much if he had to take the place of some regular, in case of an accident."[3] Such limp press notices hardly make major league scouts rush to the railroad station. Baseball people in Toledo had a sense of "utility Joe" which they normally held about a dependable old veteran — smart, doesn't beat himself, few errors. But twenty-one-year-olds get ahead with plaudits like "rookie sparkle" and "potential." No scribe ever penned such words in regard to Joe McCarthy. "Joe McCarthy, He's a Wise Gent" was the title atop another short piece about McCarthy in one Toledo paper. It told of how, at a pool hall, McCarthy feigned an inability to pick up six balls in one hand but then brazenly declared that he could pick up seven. One man bet McCarthy $5 that he could not do it. The bet was accepted, and the bettor gave McCarthy a maximum of five minutes to perform the feat. In five seconds, McCarthy had the seven balls in one hand and the $5 in the other.[4] Cagey minor league veterans make such bits of cash in pool halls. Meanwhile, more talented youngsters like Rube Marquard sign with the New York Giants for $11,000.

McCarthy played in a few of the Mud Hens' early games at the start of the regular season. The team got off to a flat 7 and 10 start, however, and from there they remained mired in the second division. McCarthy fielded well, both at third and in the outfield, but again, his hitting was poor. As of May 9, he had 6 hits in 27 at bats, for an average of .222. He was not the cause of Toledo's mediocre showing, but he was no bright light either. The team's main weakness was its pitching corps. Indicative of the strain of bad play, one pitcher, Bill Lattimore, was fined for umpire abuse ($10) amidst a doubleheader loss at Columbus, and later that same day got into a fight with a waiter at the team's hotel. As the team floundered that week against the equally pathetic Columbus Senators, a Toledo paper mocked: "Does Toledo want to win at Columbus? Why the Idea!"[5] The team appeared to be going nowhere. Reporters were already resorting to sarcasm, and with such a sad team McCarthy was but an intelligent utility man.

With the contagion of a dispiriting losing season in the works, McCarthy even committed what was for him a serious mental lapse at third base. In a game against Columbus on May 23, the Senators catcher, former Philadelphia Athletic Ossie Schreckengost, was on first. The batter grounded to second. The fielder first ran "Schreck" back towards first, then threw to get the batter, at which point Schreck ran to second. The first baseman pursued and caught him, but dropped the ball. Schreck, having overrun second, took off for third, and there McCarthy, thinking the runner was already out, nonchalantly took the throw with one hand and dropped it, thus giving Schreck third base. The Columbus bench snickered at it all. Toledo won the game, but such little-league escapades hardly did much for fan support, much less for the notice of big league scouts.[6] Two days later against Indianapolis, McCarthy's hitting gained further derision as the papers told of how the Indians pitcher "had a ridiculously easy time with McCarthy. ... The old curve ball had 'Mac' tied to the mast, and he whiffed as nice as you please." As of May 29, McCarthy was hitting but .202. "Elwert and McCarthy are about the only fast men on the club," complained one reporter, "and they are seldom on the bases." By the end of June, Toledo was in the cellar.[7]

On July 3, mired at the bottom of the league, Fred Abbott abruptly quit as the Mud Hens Manager. He was succeeded by a former American League home run champion, Ralph Orlando "Socks" Seybold. Socks weighed nearly 300 pounds, and people held hopes that his imposing physical presence might somehow intimidate and shove the Hens into showing some sort of life. It was certainly a listless atmosphere which then surrounded the completion of the ball park — Swayne Field. Nevertheless, the city held a grand opening as scheduled on July 4, and the Mud Hens actually won a game, defeating Columbus 12–11 in sixteen innings. No matter the new field, Toledo stayed in or near the league cellar through July and August. McCarthy, playing second, third, and outfield, never hit above .228. Despite the team's poor performance, one Toledo player, Karl Robinson, signed with Cleveland in September, so McCarthy knew that scouts were still regularly on hand. But, no matter a few press mentions about good fielding, McCarthy's hitting would earn him no serious looks, something he knew as well as anyone. Later in life, he would concede: "I wasn't much of a hitter." He also asserted that he "didn't have good speed either," but reporters of the day noted the opposite there.[8]

Playing out the string of an abysmal season, McCarthy finally lost his well-known mental control one day in September. In a game against Kansas City, McCarthy hit one to right. It seemed like a sure double. McCarthy slid into second. The papers said the K.C. second baseman missed tagging him. Amidst the meaningless game, the umpire had chosen not to leave his post behind the plate to cover the play, and he blindly called McCarthy out. McCarthy completely lost his temper, as did the first base coach. "McCarthy," noted a reporter, "is an orderly player as a general theme, and has never before attacked an umpire." He sure did this time. He could have been fined or suspended, but no fuss was made of the incident.[9] It seemed that summer McCarthy could not hit anything to great effect, with his bat or his mouth.

In the final week of the season, the Mud Hens did play the role of spoilers. They defeated second place Milwaukee, and this gave the pennant to Louisville. McCarthy batted .225 for the year, and the team finished in 6th place, six games under .500.[10]

He and some friends went off on a peanuts-paying barnstorming tour of Michigan. Returning to Germantown, McCarthy could root for Connie Mack in his pennant fight that fall. McCarthy's team lost that one too, as the Tigers won the American League pennant. A good utility man, yes, but a .225 hitter with a second-division minor league team; some future! During the winter, McCarthy maintained the grim minor league athletic atmosphere around him. He played some indoor baseball in a hotel league in Atlantic City, New Jersey. He was also involved in the fight game, as he had apparently been for several years, managing and "cornering" for some journeymen Philadelphia club fighters.[11]

In 1910, James William "Ducky" Holmes, who'd spent ten years in the major leagues, took over as manager of the Mud Hens. During spring training he commented about McCarthy: "Joe can tear around the infield with as much success as anybody, and this, with his outfield skill, makes it very plain to me why he has been called the best utility man in the American Association."[12] It is clear that McCarthy was appreciated. At training camp in Columbus, Georgia, Mud Hens owner Bill Armour, obviously trying to push up spirits during spring training, held forth to the press that McCarthy "was going to give some of those outfielders the hardest run they ever had for a regular job." The Toledo columnist concurred, adding "If Joe improves as much this year over his 1909 form as he did last summer over the previous season, look out for him." The key was his hitting. "All that McCarthy will have to do is to keep away from that curve ball, and he will be there."[13] Hitting that curve ball was a major hurdle for many young players who just could not quite get up to major league levels, however. Jim Thorpe had trouble with it (although John McGraw may have exaggerated his criticism of Thorpe along these lines), and McCarthy would later see many young prospects who were unable to surmount the same barrier. The problem in baseball is that once a player has a reputation for being unable to hit a curve, that is about all he is ever going to see at the plate. McCarthy was not about to give up, but he knew the sizable challenge that lay before him.

McCarthy usually came to camp already in good shape. Salary: $175 a month. Already trim, he would usually "round to" more quickly than most and hit well when others were still struggling to find their batting eyes and strides. In 1910, however, he came down with a sore arm during training, and this seemed to sap what hitting strength he usually had. Still his usual zest was apparent. When the Hens shortstop, Willis Butler, injured his wrist, McCarthy filled in there as the regular. Again, the praise came forth for McCarthy's work in the field. His only exhibition game "wobbles" were caused by the rough conditions on the fields where the Mud Hens toured. But the praise was as much a double negative as a positive: "Joe McCarthy ... will not handicap the club as long as Willis Butler is out." Meanwhile, over the course of the exhibition season, McCarthy hit .135, lowest on the team.[14]

The papers of all the American Association cities picked Toledo for the second division in 1910. With Willis Butler's wrist still keeping him sidelined, McCarthy opened for the Mud Hens at shortstop, or "short field" as it was still usually called then. He batted seventh on opening day and went 3 for 4 in a 5–0 shutout of Indianapolis. To all the prognosticators' surprise, Toledo ran up a 5 and 1 record in their first week and sat in first place. Then they took to the road and proceeded to lose 8 of their next 10. After one game at Columbus on April 21, the Toledo sports page headline read "McCarthy Spilled the Beans in the 9th Inning." With a runner on and a hit to the outfield, McCarthy took the relay and dropped it. The runner scored, and Toledo lost 2–1. Meanwhile, McCarthy's batting average for April, despite the 3 for 4 opening day performance, was .190. By then, Willis Butler's wrist had healed, and on April 25 he returned as the Mud Hens regular shortstop. McCarthy sat on the bench for nearly a month.[15]

Toledo played miserably in late April and early May. They lost one game to Indianapolis 18 to 3. By the middle of May, the Toledo papers were casting the Mud Hens game coverage in smaller print, figuring they could use the precious page space for more valuable things like professional wrestling and advertisements for cold remedies. McCarthy filled in a bit in right field, then sat on the bench again. In late May, the Mud Hens got things turned around. They ran off a string of 11 straight wins. McCarthy finally got into one game as a pinch runner, and that was the game that snapped the Mud Hens win streak. The winning streak put Toledo back in the middle of the American Association standings. Minneapolis and St. Paul had jumped out ahead of everyone, but Toledo had become a team ready to give the leaders some trouble. The Mud Hens kept winning, and as of June 14, only two games separated Minneapolis, St. Paul, and Toledo, with Indianapolis in fourth, a full 11 games behind. McCarthy, meanwhile, was hardly being used.[16]

While the Mud Hens were winning, Manager Ducky Holmes did not get along with meddling owner Bill Armour, and on June 4, he quit. Armour appointed second baseman Harry Hinchman to be the new manager. Under him the team kept winning. On June 28, Hinchman was spiked in the leg in a game against St. Paul. He tried to play with his foot bound and taped, but he could not do it, so he put McCarthy in his place. Joe played there for a week. He played very well at second. It would become his favorite position, but that week his batting average never got above .228. By early July, Hinchman's leg had healed, and McCarthy sat down again. Bill Elwert was out for a few days in late July, and McCarthy filled in at third. He hit three doubles in a weekend series, but Hinchman put Elwert back in the lineup as soon as he could. The Hens' hot streak of late May and June fell off in July, and the team again sank below .500. Save for a few pitchers, McCarthy's .185 average was last not only on the team but in the entire league.[17]

Owner Bill Armour pushed the idea of the Mud Hens giving more playing time to young players, and in August and September, McCarthy played in most of the Hens games at third and short. His batting average ended up at .214, but his fielding and leadership were both lauded. The team rallied too and began to climb in the standings. By mid–August, Toledo was again in third place, and in September they actually passed St. Paul for second place. The trouble was that Minneapolis was so far ahead of everyone that a run-up by a team like Toledo was bound to fall short. It did. The team finished with a respectable record of 91 and 75. Minneapolis', however, was 107 and 61. No one was going to approach that figure.[18]

Bill Armour kept Harry Hinchman as his manager for the 1911 season. McCarthy, having spent another winter with theater and fight people in Philadelphia, was invited back. Hinchman was from Philadelphia, too. They had spoken during the off-season. Despite his hitting, McCarthy was valuable in the eyes of both Hinchman and Armour. What continued to make McCarthy so valuable was the mental acuity he brought to the game. This was already apparent. He was only twenty-three but had developed an understanding of the game that some veteran major leaguers never possessed. In March, 1911, when the Mud Hens gathered in Chattanooga for spring training, Hinchman split the team in two. Wishing to make a little money, Armour had arranged for the Hens train and then tour as two teams, playing exhibitions throughout Ohio and Indiana. Hinchman was to manage one squad, composed largely of veterans. Joe McCarthy was to manage the other. Armour did not want to embarrass himself, and lose money, with bad, lopsided ball games, and he and Hinchman figured that Joe McCarthy could be trusted to run the second team in such a way that all the games would be respectable.[19]

McCarthy's boys held their own against the veterans. The tour was a success. McCarthy's team went off on its own and played some local Indiana and Ohio teams. They did well there too. McCarthy even "got into it" with an umpire in Terre Haute. The bases were loaded with two out for Toledo, and the umpire called the batter out on strikes. "Call 'em when they're over!" yelled "Manager" McCarthy. "G'wan, you fresh busher," snarled the ump, "'tryin' to show somebody up because Billy [Armour]'s in the stands?" McCarthy knew the ump. was referring to the team President/owner, but he decided to play it coy. "Billy who?" he shouted. "Billy goat, you mutt," snapped the umpire, "and if you say another word I'll have you thrown out of the park." McCarthy's young teammates kidded him about his "guying" the umpire. (He would do it a few more times in the years ahead.) But McCarthy was clearly learning knew how to go to work on an umpire when he felt the situation called for it. McCarthy's boys beat Terre Haute that day 8–0.[20] In praise of McCarthy, the Toledo paper opined:

> The youth has reached a point where he knows as much baseball as any man on the club outside of probably Manager Hinchman. Joe is a capital inside worker. He is a student of the game, and anytime there is a discussion of plays after or before a contest, 'Mac' is always there with his opinion. That's the reason President Armour and Manager Hinchman put him in charge of the second team.

The report went on describing McCarthy as a "swell base runner; pretty fast, and has the faculty for getting a good lead. He is keen on the fadeaway slide, and covers ground well, infield or outfield." McCarthy was also praised for other types of heady dependability: "Mac is a great man for getting the signs. He has the reputation among Toledo players of never having missed one since he has been with the team. As long as he is with the outfit," concluded the reporter, "the fans have no occasion to worry over the weakness of any particular position, except pitcher." However, sighed the reporter, he "still can't hit a curve."[21] All the tools seemed to be there, but "for what?" was something McCarthy and others had not fully grasped.

Having finished a surprising second to Minneapolis in 1910, Toledo fans had some aspirations for 1911. Alas, that spring the Mud Hens started miserably, and by the middle of May they were in last place. McCarthy did his usual filling in when regulars were hurt, and his batting average was also at its usual low — .179 as of May 13. The team picked up a bit in the last two weeks of May, and on May 30 they were hosting Indianapolis, a team faring even worse. The Indians had sustained several injuries in the early season. By the time they arrived in Toledo, they were using their reserve catcher in the outfield. They needed a player to fill the gaps, and they approached Hinchman and Armour about it. Result: on May 31, 1911, Toledo sold Joe McCarthy to Indianapolis.[22]

When minor league players, especially benchers, are sold, it seldom makes a ripple in the press. McCarthy's sale to Indianapolis, however, prompted the Toledo papers to give some specific explanations: "McCarthy was sold after a conference between Manager Hinchman and President Armour. McCarthy was a favorite with both his bosses, and no deal was made until his wishes were consulted. Joe was perfectly willing to go with the Hoosiers, for he felt that he didn't have much of a chance to break in here." McCarthy expressed sorrow about the trade but kept his thoughts positive: "It will be just like leaving home to quit Toledo, but there is some satisfaction in the knowledge that I will be playing regularly with Indianapolis." The Indianapolis papers were enthused about the deal: "Joe McCarthy for two years has been regarded as the best utility man that ever wore an American Association uniform," one wrote, "and since he has been playing baseball only about three years, there is reason to believe he has his best years ahead of him." "[Manager] Jimmy [Burke] has had his eye on the player for some time," informed another. Indianapolis maintained McCarthy's $175 a month salary. On the day he was sold, McCarthy started in left field for Indianapolis in a doubleheader against Toledo. He went 2 for 3 and 1 for 4 in the games. Indianapolis lost both games to Toledo, however, and with the losses, McCarthy found himself playing for a last place ball club.[23]

Within a week of purchasing Joe McCarthy, the Indianapolis Indians bought another player, Danny Hoffman from the St. Louis Browns. Hoffman had spent eight seasons in the American League, and he could hit a lot better than McCarthy, so after playing as a regular for a week, McCarthy's hopes for a steady playing spot in Indianapolis crumbled. He was back on the bench, and now with a manager, Jimmy Burke, who did not want his tactical input as had the people in Toledo. It was another depressing summer as a bench player for a tail-ender. Some games broke out in bench clearing fist fights. In Louisville, the fans showed their disgust with the play by hurling glass bottles all over the field. Indy lost one game to Milwaukee by a score of 20–1. McCarthy filled in for various infielders and outfielders wherever needed through the month of June. At the end of the month, his batting average was a mere .157, and the Indians were still in the cellar. McCarthy's reputation for light hitting was such that when he successfully pinch hit against St. Paul one afternoon, the fans actually gave him a mock cheer, and this was in Minnesota![24]

In mid July and August, McCarthy and Indianapolis seemed to break out of their lethargy. By mid September, McCarthy's average had climbed to a respectable .253. In the prior two months he had hit .322.* "Joe McCarthy is playing the game of his life," wrote one Indianapolis reporter, "Joe never had a fair chance to play at Toledo, but Manager Burke has persuaded him that he's an embryo Tris Speaker or Joe Jackson, and the way Joe was smiting the ball ... leads one to suspect that it may prove true." McCarthy's versatility and good fielding continued to win praise. Now that he could hit, the season was becoming fun. "Joe McCarthy Wins Game" ran one

---

*Of his 36 hits (in 142 at bats) with Indianapolis during his hot summer streak, however, McCarthy amassed only 41 total bases. He was hitting, but it was a very low accompanying level of slugging.

headline on August 26, after he doubled and tripled and scored two runs in a 7–6 victory over St. Paul. By September 3, the Indians had climbed their way into third place. Then some key injuries suddenly brought several Indians down, and in three weeks the team fell from third back to seventh place. It was a sad finish, but the late summer spurt gave Indianapolis and McCarthy some hope.[25]

Whatever the hope Jimmy Burke had for the 1912 season, it did not seem that McCarthy was to be part of his plans. While McCarthy joined the Indians for spring training, he played in but one exhibition game, and then only as a pinch hitter. Unfortunately that spring, McCarthy came down with a touch of malaria and was greatly weakened.[26] Burke figured that the light hitting and now physically weak McCarthy was of no use to him. When the team began the season 0 and 7 and finished the month of April at 2 and 12 and in last place, Burke and the Indians front office began to make plans for more changes. On May 9, while the team was heading for a series in Milwaukee, McCarthy was told to leave the train in Chicago and return to Indianapolis as the team "did not need McCarthy's services."[27] McCarthy could smell something was up, and after finally having had a respectable summer at the plate in 1911, this was a bitter pill. But, of course, he had no recourse with the Indianapolis management, and certainly none through the press. Back then a ballplayer had to take whatever came his way. Now his future ambitions in baseball were uncertain. Jimmy Burke released him. As for any hard feelings, McCarthy would later hire Burke to be one of his coaches with the Cubs and the Yankees. McCarthy was not one for grudges. In 1936 he paid tribute to Burke, calling him "a real gentleman, a real baseball master, a marvelous friend, [and] a wise head in all things having to do with the game."[28] In 1912, the question for Joe McCarthy was where he could now go.

6

Down to Wilkes-Barre

William ("Derby Day Bill") Clymer was a veteran baseball man and, like McCarthy, he was originally from the Philadelphia area. Clymer was a restless man who loved the race track; hence the nickname. On a baseball field he was the sort who just could not keep still. He was a peppery player, and as a manager he would coach first base and incessantly pace the baseline, talking, moving, clapping, gesturing. But he knew the game extremely well, so his manner was anything but silly or irritating. It usually infused a team with hustle and enthusiasm. Having played for Toledo back in 1900, Clymer knew the Mud Hens' owners, and he had seen Joe McCarthy for himself on several occasions. He liked heady ball players and thought he could make use of the young man on his club. Clymer's club was "down" (in class of baseball league) in Wilkes-Barre, Pennsylvania. He had moved to Wilkes-Barre, in part, because it was his wife's home town. And on Monday, May 13, 1912, that was where young Joe McCarthy was headed—*down* to Wilkes-Barre. Indianapolis' Jimmy Burke had sold McCarthy to Clymer. Joe was "on the way down." His only alternative was to go back to Germantown and take up another line of work, but baseball was still his passion, so there it was: off to Wilkes-Barre. The move seemed to be a step toward even further anonymity, but it turned out to be a good move, for on several occasions Clymer would prove to be the best personal connection the young McCarthy would have in the game.

The Wilkes-Barre "Coal Barons" played in the New York State League. The town was in Pennsylvania, of course, but along with the archrival Scranton "Miners," who pridefully took their laborer name vs. the elite "Barons" to add to the two-town rivalry, Wilkes-Barre sat close to the New York border and filled out a fiercely competitive league. The league also included the Utica Utes, Albany Senators, Elmira Colonels, Syracuse Stars (nicknamed "Twinklers"), Binghamton Bingos, and Troy Trojans. In 1911, Wilkes-Barre won the NYSL championship for the third straight time, and Clymer was their guiding force. In 1912, Manager "Bill Clymer," wrote one newspaper, "is supposed to have the highest salaried team in the circuit and one compliment of the best baseball artists who are not in the 'big show' itself."[1] Clymer was reputed to have a terrific eye for talent, and the purchase of McCarthy was heralded as another example of his intelligence. Here, the papers may have been kind to Clymer, as McCarthy was mistakenly credited for having hit .268 with Indianapolis. (A

30

catcher for Indianapolis in 1911 named John McCarty did hit for that exact average, so that was the likely point of confusion.) McCarthy joined the team on May 15. That day the Barons' second baseman was hurt, and McCarthy, still weak from his bout with malaria, immediately filled in and played every day for over a month.[2]

While the papers had rated the champion Barons highly in their preseason predictions, the early weeks of the season had not gone well for Wilkes-Barre. In April and May, no fewer than three infielders had each suffered a broken leg and were lost for the season. A fourth broke a bone in his hand. In June yet another infielder was seriously injured. Even an out-of-town newspaper conceded that "Manager Clymer of Wilkes-Barre had run up against more hard luck this season than the rest of the league has had in its history."[3] These injuries had prompted Clymer to go after McCarthy. When he joined the Barons, McCarthy again felt the malaise of a frustrated team battling to get out of the cellar. In late June, McCarthy was hurt and had to sit on the bench for a week. He had suffered a gash on his hand.[4] With all the injuries and losing, McCarthy witnessed more outbursts of frustration against mediocre umpires. In one game against Troy, a Wilkes-Barre Booster Day crowd of 6000 swarmed the field in the seventh inning when the umpire called a sliding Baron out at home. Fortunately, some policemen on their day off grabbed some bats and held the crowd back. In the next inning, Wilkes-Barre's pitcher was ejected after he protested a base on balls. The next pitcher yielded another walk and a hit which allowed Troy to score the winning run. The play at the plate was close. When the umpire yelled "safe," 2000 irate fans ran onto the field. Newspapers reported "threats of lynching." The constables again saved the umpire, this time beating through the crowd and holding the umpire in a locker room under siege for two hours until enough reserve policemen arrived to clear the mob.[5] The loss to Troy dumped Wilkes-Barre into seventh place. Nine days later they were in the cellar. Young Joe McCarthy felt that the clouds of losing had followed him from Wilmington, to Toledo, to Indianapolis, and now down to Wilkes-Barre.

At the very end of July, everything miraculously turned around for McCarthy and the Barons. McCarthy's hand was better, and he had recovered his strength from the malaria. Some of the other injured players returned. No other injuries plagued the Barons that summer, and they began to win, and win. In various games, McCarthy played all three outfield slots and put in time at first base, second base, third base, and shortstop. Even more significantly, when Clymer was ejected from a game, McCarthy managed the team. Wilkes-Barre sports reporters were steady in their compliments about Joe McCarthy: "A clever, resourceful player who knows how to play; ... snappy work at second, his baseball brains were in evidence; ... McCarthy is playing a great game at second and is hitting the ball when it is needed." So dependable was McCarthy, especially with men on base, that his third base coach would yell "press the button, Joe," and McCarthy would usually respond with a hit. McCarthy would later resent a label about "pushing buttons," but he certainly did not mind it here.[6]

As the Barons won, they steadily rose in the standings. By August 5, they were in fifth place; fourth place by August 7. By August 15, their record stood at .500 for the first time since May, and they kept up their torrid pace. In the entire month of August they were virtually unbeatable, and in August and early September they ran off a streak that gained press notices throughout the baseball world. On September 3, Wilkes-Barre defeated Scranton in the first game of a doubleheader to mark their 25th victory in a row! Their record stood at 76 and 54. Since July 22, the Barons had won of 45 of 55. Even independent of the 25-game streak, they had thus won two out of every three, and they stood in first place, one game ahead of Utica. They lost the afternoon game of the Scranton doubleheader to snap their streak.[7]

Clymer and the Barons actually complained that they had won one more game, as on August 28, the Albany Senators arrived late for a doubleheader. The tardiness caused one of the games to be cancelled, and Clymer wanted this to count as a forfeit. Albany's Manager, Jimmie Tamsett, claimed he had not been made aware of the schedule change which added the doubleheader to make up for an early-season rain-out. (Back then, such 24-hour decisions would often occur in the lower minor leagues.) At first, NYSL President John H. Farrell would not allow the forfeit. Then he upheld it. The custom of such game-day decisions would sadly come back to haunt Wilkes-Barre that month.[8]

Over the subsequent week in early September, Wilkes-Barre and Utica battled back and forth for the league lead. McCarthy made some key plays. He dashed home from second base on an infield hit. He saw a runner trying to score from second with an apparent winning run, noted the runner's failure to touch third base, and successfully appealed the play. He saw a runner on first fail to touch second on a two-out hit that appeared to score a runner from third and win the ball game for the opposition; McCarthy grabbed the ball, touched second, and the umpire correctly disallowed the run. This gave Wilkes-Barre an opportunity to win; they did. With such heady plays, the fans came to appreciate McCarthy very much.[9]

On the last weekend of the season, September 8–9, Wilkes-Barre and Utica were tied. On Sunday, Wilkes-Barre hosted Scranton, while Utica was scheduled to play Syracuse. Ten thousand turned out at the Barons' park, the largest sports crowd in the history of Wilkes-Barre. The Barons won. "Knowing" the Barons had at least tied for the pennant with their victory over Scranton, the story in the next day's newspapers made the entire city of Wilkes-Barre go berserk. The previous day, Utica had changed its schedule. They were slated to play one game against Syracuse. Instead, they played a doubleheader and won both games. Thus the final standings on Monday morning, September 9: Wilkes-Barre 81–57; Utica 82–57; as at Franklin in 1907, it was another final-day-of-the-season disappointment for Joe McCarthy. There would be others.[10]

Billy Clymer was fit to be tied. The schedule had called for twenty-one games between Syracuse and Utica, yet now it appeared they had played twenty-two times. Utica claimed one of these games was an exhibition, but Clymer pointed out that league rules call for no intra-league exhibition games during the regular season. Clymer wired representatives of each league team, calling for a special meeting to decide the pennant controversy. Both the Utica and Wilkes-Barre teams remained on hand for a possible playoff. On September 12, League President John Farrell's office released information that Syracuse and Utica had missed a game on May 6. It was supposed to have been covered by a doubleheader on Memorial Day, but that day darkness prevented the second game. Thus, said the League office, the second game of September 8 was a legitimate makeup. Considering that everyone would gain financially, why

Farrell would not call for a playoff game was never clear. Many felt he held a grudge against the peppery Clymer. With Farrell's ruling, Utica's two wins over Syracuse counted. Thus the League Office officially awarded Utica the pennant. Farrell wrote the Utica team a note of congratulations and actually went out of his way to call their pennant victory "untouched by the faintest suspicion."[11]

Clymer would not concede matters, nor would others in Wilkes-Barre. Pointing out that the two games between Syracuse and Utica took all of 69 and 58 minutes, the *Wilkes-Barre Record* made the blunt accusation that the Syracuse team had "laid down completely" and given the two games to Utica.[12] Clymer was seething. He and Farrell had had conflicts before. In 1910, when Clymer cut a player from Wilkes-Barre, Farrell ruled that he owed the player the remainder of his contract. The NYSL had a salary cap, and Farrell had accused Clymer of breaking it. In February of 1912, Farrell had sought to limit the number of players each NYSL team could have who had previously played in higher-level leagues. Clymer vigorously opposed this.[13] In the wake of the "stolen pennant," Clymer wrote that the unilateral decision by Farrell's office was beyond his purview as League President. He said it was a matter for the Board of Directors of the League to decide, and he called for a special League meeting. Farrell responded that there was no meeting scheduled, but Clymer retorted that there could be a special meeting at any time if representatives of at least four League teams called for one. Representatives from Troy, Elmira, Binghamton, Scranton, Wilkes-Barre (of course), *and* Utica all responded positively to Clymer's communications. Syracuse and Albany each offered no response. Believing he then had the possibility of six yeas and two abstentions, Clymer was ready to head off to Binghamton where the meeting was to be held, but within two days, many of the team representatives wrote that they could not attend. Farrell may have been back-channeling. He was an able politician, as he was not only head of the NYSL but also the Secretary of the National Association of Professional Baseball Leagues. Whether or not they were coming from Farrell, rumors were about that the bumptious Clymer wanted not merely to delegitimize Utica's pennant but to dethrone Farrell as well. The meeting was delayed for ten days. By then, as Farrell well knew, it would have been ridiculous to try to stage any sort of playoff game. Players had scattered. On September 25, representatives did finally convene in Syracuse. There they rejected Clymer's protest.[14]

Obviously unreconciled to what he saw as the New York State League's shenanigans with respect to Utica's pennant, Billy Clymer later quit as Wilkes-Barre's manager. He secured a better post for himself, managing the Buffalo Bisons of the International League. Clymer recommended a new manager to succeed him in Wilkes-Barre, and the Barons' owners agreed. The new manager of Wilkes-Barre for 1913 was the twenty-five-year-old Joe McCarthy. His salary would be all of $100 a month.[15]

After another a winter with Philadelphia fighters and theater people, McCarthy set off for Wilkes-Barre. While obviously young for a manager, he did not have to prove himself to his players, as they had known him from the grand, if bittersweet, 1912 season, during which he had managed whenever the quixotic Clymer had been tossed by an umpire, something which had occurred more than a few times. "Several reasons governed the selection of McCarthy," noted Clymer. "He is a clever ballplayer and one of the best inside men I ever worked with on a team. ... The spurt we made [in 1912] was in my opinion more due to the fact that McCarthy was on the job with his head up all the time than [to] anything else." The *Wilkes-Barre Record* added: "His all around work and loyalty to the team made him immensely popular with the fans." From afar, an impartial sports newspaper in Albany exemplified the enthusiasm of Wilkes-Barre when they announced that "Joe McCarthy, the fertile brained second sacker, has been selected" to manage Wilkes Barre.[16]

All Wilkes-Barre fans wanted redemption, and they looked to young Joe McCarthy to win it for them. The other seven teams in the league also had high hopes. Every manager was predicting a first division finish for his club. Perhaps they figured that since Utica had broken Wilkes-Barre's three-year monopoly on the NYSL pennant, and with Clymer off in Buffalo, the road was now open. "If they [all the League managers] all keep their word," joked one Syracuse reporter, "the circuit will go through the season without a second flight of championship contenders."[17]

The season did indeed prove to be a dogfight. McCarthy and the Barons were in the thick of it, and all through May and June they bounced about between first and fourth place. McCarthy was playing second base every day, and, as of June 9, he was batting .322. He was often placing himself eighth in the lineup, preferring to be in the dugout for any key moves to be made when the heart of the order was up. He made a few key trades, including one which brought ex-major leaguer and ex-Toledo Mud Hen Danny Hoffman to Wilkes-Barre. (Danny Hoffman, unfortunately, had been badly beaned by a pitch in a game in St. Louis in 1906, and he was never fully the same after the incident; he was now fully "on the way down" with his skills deteriorating from age and from the head trauma; indeed he would die in 1922 at the age of 42.) Hoffman may have cost McCarthy a regular job back at Indianapolis in 1911, but McCarthy would never let any personal feelings get in the way of his judgments of talent. McCarthy also paid little regard to other issues that were intensely personal to many baseball people at that time; while the Barons trained in April, for example, McCarthy scheduled exhibition games with the Royal Giants of Brooklyn and with the Cuban All Stars, each, the press tersely noted, a "colored team." (Wilkes-Barre split a double header with the Giants; the game with the Cubans ended in a tie.)[18]

In the early weeks of the season, pitching was the sore spot for McCarthy and the Barons. In early June, Wilkes-Barre lost five games in a row and fell to fifth place. But from there the pitching seemed to settle. McCarthy learned the value of resting his pitchers. One youngster, Dan Marion, emerged as a pitching star, and in late June the Barons ran off a 12 and 6 spurt. Into the summer, the Barons generally held second place, just behind league leading Binghamton. Amidst the good fortunes of June, McCarthy learned to appreciate good breaks. In a game against Albany on June 26, for example, Wilkes-Barre was at bat in the fifth inning. There were two out with a man on third. With a count of two and two, the Wilkes-Barre hitter swung and missed. The Albany players started for the dugout, and McCarthy and the Barons were grabbing their gloves and heading into the field. Suddenly the umpire ruled that there were only two strikes. Meanwhile the Wilkes-Barre runner on third had proceeded toward the Barons' first-base line dugout and stepped on the plate. The umpire ruled this to be a run scored. Of course, the Albany players and fans kicked up a storm. An Albany newspaper noted "even Joe McCarthy was surprised." After witnessing such umpire abuse as he had seen the previous summer in Wilkes-Barre, as well as earlier in Wilmington, Toledo, and Indianapolis (where he had been a participant), McCarthy certainly enjoyed being on the good end of an umpire blunder. He was also learning the folly of too much umpire abuse. It generally did not work, besides, he never saw Connie Mack lose his temper. Now, if only he could learn to hide his delight when a bum call went his way. (He loved the stage, but he knew he was a lousy actor.)[19]

Through July, McCarthy's team remained in the thick of the race. No one broke away from the pack. As of August 8, two games separated Troy, Binghamton, Wilkes-Barre, and Albany. (Meanwhile, on August 10, lowly Syracuse beat the New York Giants in an exhibition, heartening the League's fans as to the quality of the NYSL's play. McCarthy was in the stands, watching former opponents like Rube Marquard and rookies like Casey Stengel, and perhaps maintaining his own flickering hopes.) Albany papers referred to Wilkes-Barre as "Joe McCarthy's pesky Barons," a team that keeps coming at its opponent, that does not make many errors and somehow finds ways to win. McCarthy's Barons gained a reputation as a club against whom opponents had to earn runs and wins. Reporters referred to opponents caught trying to steal as having been "Joe-Joed," thrown out from catcher Joe Briger to second baseman Joe McCarthy. After a victory over Albany in which McCarthy went four for four at the plate, the Albany papers further conceded: "Manager Joe McCarthy is one sweet ball player. We have said so before, but this classy work of yesterday compels us to repeat it." W.R. Armour, managing owner of the Toledo Mud Hens, came to Wilkes-Barre to scout talent that summer, and he told a local reporter that back when McCarthy played for Toledo he "impressed me as being one of the most brainy and clever ball players in the association — a player quick to seize every opportunity." Armour thus expressed no surprise at the fact that McCarthy was doing well as a manager. After all, Armour noted, "he has made good in every other capacity."[20]

In late August and early September, Binghamton and Wilkes-Barre distanced themselves from the rest of the League's teams. Not coincidentally, they were the only teams to have kept the same manager for the season. Last-place Scranton had gone through three pilots that summer. By the second week of September, it looked like Binghamton had the pennant in its pocket. They were four games up on Wilkes-Barre with ten to play. Everyone else had faded. McCarthy's boys then proceeded to win each of their last ten games. Binghamton held on, however, winning seven of their last nine. The season ended with both teams at 84 wins, but with Wilkes-Barre three games down in the loss column. (The did not always make up rainouts back then, even when the games could have determined the outcome of the pennant; winning percentage was the deciding factor.) McCarthy's team, said one reporter, "were out after the honor, and they certainly did fight." It was another down to the wire finish for McCarthy — and another near miss.[21]

Wilkes-Barre was more than a little saddened, losing the pennant to Binghamton so narrowly, but they certainly could not fault their young manager. "Wilkes-Barre's hat is off to Joe McCarthy and his Barons," hailed the *Wilkes-Barre Record*. "They gave the fans a good run for their money." McCarthy kept the team battling, and his end-of-season winning streak got the whole town excited, as well as the whole

league. Reflecting on his first year of managing, McCarthy later wrote: "It was dur-
ing that season [in Wilkes-Barre that] I detected my first grey hairs." As a player,
McCarthy had batted .328 for the year. The Barons were also the only team in the
New York State League to finish in the financial black.[22] McCarthy's first foray into
managing a baseball team was an unqualified success. Maybe it was as a result of
McCarthy's good work, maybe it was also a way of getting back at the New York State
League, but after the 1913 season, Billy Clymer snapped up McCarthy with an offer
to play for Buffalo. A Southern League team in Memphis had actually drafted him,
but Clymer bought their rights to him. Joe was now on the way back "up."

7

A Snappy Little Second Sacker

Once again, McCarthy was playing for Billy Clymer. He would do "Derby Day" proud. Shortly after arriving at the Buffalo Bisons training camp in the spring of 1914, his "snappy infield playing," prompted one Buffalo reporter to declare it "a pleasure to watch." The same positive attributes about McCarthy's playing of previous years were apparent to the Bisons—his versatility, his on-field intelligence, slick glove work, *and* he showed he could hit, although he often got off to a fast start in the spring. Another solid performer who nailed down a starting position was Paul Kritchell, a catcher. (He would later serve as a scout for McCarthy with the Yankees.) Clymer had a large contingency of ballplayers on hand in training camp. The papers noted that it was indeed going to be a major task for the manager to cut the team down to the required number of players. But "surely," noted one paper, "Joe McCarthy must be retained." The scribe noted one day how McCarthy went into center field and, even though he was "unaccustomed to the place, made two fine catches. ... Besides this," the reporter added, "he poled one over the center fielder's head. [Conclusion:] He is a very handy man to have around a ball club." As opening day approached, it was clear that "Manager Billy Clymer has wanted to place Joe McCarthy in some position where his services could be utilized daily, for he is a very valuable man to any team, playing everywhere but the battery position, and has proven himself one of the most consistent and timely hitters the team possesses." During the spring training games, McCarthy led the team in total bases and runs scored and played first base, second base, third base, center field, and right field, "a heady player, a stiff hitter, and a good fielder—one that is liable to pull off something good at any minute."[1]

McCarthy started the season for the Bisons at second base, batting second. His pay: $300 a month. The opening day game took place in Baltimore against the Orioles. The Orioles started a young left-handed pitcher that their owner, Jack Dunn, had plucked out of a local Catholic industrial/reform school. His name was George Herman Ruth, and he was already being referred to as "Dunn's Baby," or "Babe" for short. In the game, Ruth showed some first-inning jitters. With one out, he walked McCarthy, and Joe took second on a wild pitch. The next batter flied to center field. The fourth batter popped between Ruth and first base. Ruth and his first baseman got mixed up as to who would take it. As the ball dropped in, McCarthy moved to

third. Here Ruth showed further signs of "skying," as he then hit the next batter, loading the bases with two outs. Ruth could have been in for a shellacking at that point,
as the next batter hit a hard liner which, had it gone through, could have cleared the
bases. But the second baseman made a good play on the ball in back of first base and
threw the runner out to end the inning. From there, Ruth settled. The Bisons did get
the bases loaded with two outs in the fifth inning, but the Bisons' batter, Roxey
Roach, grounded harmlessly to third. Opening the ninth inning, the Buffalo center
fielder, Delmar Paddock, hit one to the wall for a double, but no one could bring
him in. In all the other innings, young Ruth completely dominated Buffalo, allowing a total of only six hits. Meanwhile, Baltimore scored six runs and cruised to a
shutout. Aside from the first-inning walk, McCarthy went 0 for 4. Buffalo and
McCarthy remained hopeful for the 1914 season, but they certainly knew that the
Orioles would be formidable foes as long as this big, gangly left-handed rookie was
pitching for them. One Oriole coach added to the concern as he exclaimed: "you ought
to see him hit!" Two days later, indeed, Ruth pinch hit one inning against Buffalo;
he tripled and scored. Buffalo won the game 6–3, however, with McCarthy doubling
and scoring twice.[2]

The Bisons started the season weakly. On May 12, their record stood at 6 and 9,
but in late May and early June they ran off 22 wins in 25 games, including a streak
of ten in a row. The hot streak landed them in first place, but as anticipated, Baltimore was right behind them, with Ruth winning seven games in his six weeks and
delivering some key pinch hits. Meanwhile, McCarthy was fitting in well with Clymer and the Bisons. In 1913, the Bisons had had a popular second baseman named
Frank Truesdale. He had gone off to the New York Yankees, but "judging by the way
McCarthy is playing second base," noted one Buffalo reporter, "Frankie Truesdell
will not be missed. McCarthy has shown wonderful work with the willow, and he can
field too." In June, he was batting .254, and his fielding was marvelous. He was chris-
tened "the prize second baseman of the whole International lot, always with something up his sleeve."[3]

Reporters in minor league cities in these years were obliged to play up the
qualities of some players for the fans. Without radio or television broadcasting
the major leagues, fans followed their local teams more closely than would many
in later generations. Still, these fans read of the major leaguers in the newspapers
and magazines, so a little rhapsodizing by the local papers was useful to keep local
spirits from lagging. McCarthy, however, was not simply one of many Bisons to
get the shine of the Buffalo sports press. They often raved about him in particular,
and he had to have "the goods" to earn that. What was especially appealing about
McCarthy's play was apparent largely to people like the writers and players who went
to the park regularly and knew the game. McCarthy played "inside baseball." He
did all the subtle things well, seldom made errors, stole opponents' signs, and thought
strategically. Combine him with another youngster of pure talent like Ruth and
one would have the absolute best. Maybe the extra years in Wilkes-Barre had brought
McCarthy up to snuff as a hitter. If so, would a major league team now give him a
serious look?

OPENING DAY, BUFFALO AT BALTIMORE, APRIL 22, 1914 [Emphases added]

Joe McCarthy played second base for Buffalo; Babe Ruth pitched for Baltimore. Years later, when McCarthy was managing Ruth and the Yankees, a reporter found this box score for Ruth, and he chided McCarthy about his shutout.

Baltimore	A.B.	R.	H.	P.O.	A.	E.	Buffalo	A.B.	R.	H.	P.O.	A.	E.
Daniels, rf	4	1	2	3	0	0	Vaughan, 3b	5	0	2	1	2	1
Ball, 2b	3	0	0	1	0	0	**McCarthy, 2b**	4	0	0	0	1	0
Cree, cf	2	2	0	1	0	0	Murray, rf	3	0	0	0	0	0
Twombly, lf	4	1	1	1	0	0	Houser, 1b	4	0	1	10	0	0
Derrick, ss	4	1	3	1	5	0	Jackson, lf	2	0	0	1	1	0
Gleichmann, 1b	4	0	0	14	1	0	Roach, ss	4	0	1	2	5	0
Egan, c	4	0	1	4	0	0	Paddock, cf	4	0	1	2	0	0
Ruth, p	4	0	2	0	2	0	Kritchell, c	4	0	1	6	2	1
							McConnell, p	2	0	0	2	2	0
							*Stephens	1	0	0	0	0	0
Totals	33	6	10	27	11	0	*Totals*	33	0	6	24	13	2

*Batted for McConnell in ninth

Baltimore	3	0	3	0	0	0	0	0	*—6
Buffalo	0	0	0	0	0	0	0	0	0—0

Two-base hits— Daniels, Derrick, Kritchell, Roach
Stolen Bases— Ball, Daniels, Houser
Bases on Balls— Off Ruth 3, off McConnell 3.
Struck out — By Ruth 4, by McConnell 6
Passed Ball— Kritchell
Left on Bases— Baltimore 7, Buffalo 10.
Time — 1.50   Umpires— Nalfin and Carpenter

The trouble was his batting numbers were still not spectacular. Even the natural elements seemed to conspire against him here. The team slated exhibition games with the Giants, the Braves, and the Dodgers. Good play here could have gained notice from such managers as Wilbert Robinson and John McGraw, both of whom knew good inside baseball when they saw it, but rain cancelled both the New York and the Brooklyn contests. A three-run home run against Newark on August 11 was also wiped out by a thunderstorm which ended the game before it became official. The Bisons defeated the Boston Braves in mid–July, but Braves' manager George Stallings took no note of his opponents, he just grew furious with his own team. The Braves had fallen to last place in the National League, and Stallings, as McCarthy later recalled, "ripped into them. [As a result,] they were almost unbeatable after what happened here in Buffalo." The "Miracle" Braves moved from last to first place between July 18 and August 25. Later, they swept the World Series.[4] All McCarthy could do was keep playing his best and see what could happen.

Throughout June, Buffalo, Baltimore, and Rochester were nip and tuck at the top of the IL. In late June and early July, McCarthy was down with an injury, and the Bisons fell back to third place, seven and one half games behind Baltimore. When McCarthy returned to the lineup, Buffalo ran off six straight wins and pulled closer to first. The Orioles were still out in front, but in late July, Babe Ruth signed with the Boston Red Sox and left Baltimore. Now Baltimore was vulnerable. They had been in first place since June 12, but with Ruth's departure they fell off, and Rochester, Providence, and Buffalo were right there to overtake them. Rochester moved into first place on August 6, with Providence and Buffalo immediately behind. It remained that way for the entire month. On September 1, one game separated the three teams, with Ruth-less Baltimore fading fast.[5] In Buffalo's race for the pennant, McCarthy was a team leader. The "snappy little second sacker" came through with many key hits and defensive gems. The gathering war in Europe may have been getting the headlines, but for some folks up in little Buffalo, the fight of the summer was in the IL, and McCarthy was one of their heroes. (The infinitely more weighty issue of world war was, of course, on everyone's mind. Indeed, it penetrated the baseball talk. In a game between the Bisons and the Newark Tigers, for example, the Tigers' pitcher Wyatt Lee beaned three Buffalo batters in the first inning, including McCarthy. Manager Billy Clymer was yelling all over the field about it. Neither McCarthy nor his other teammates was seriously hurt, but in this era before batting helmets, head injuries from pitched balls were a major dread of the game. The newspapers simply mused that "Lee would make a fine artilleryman in the Kaiser's army.")[6]

The three-way race for the IL pennant continued through September. On September 17, Rochester and Providence were in a flat-footed tie, with Buffalo only a half game behind. Amidst the pressure-packed month, the Buffalo papers said "Roach and McCarthy are the reliables." It would, alas, be Providence that would run to the lead at the end. Buffalo finished second, just ahead of Rochester. For yet another season, McCarthy had been a leader on a team that stayed in the thick of a pennant race all season. He batted a respectable .266 for the year. Now it was time to do a little barnstorming and hope for a call from one of the "bigs."

No one from the majors gave McCarthy a call for a major league tryout in 1915. But staying in Buffalo as a starter and fan-favorite was hardly a sad consolation. In 1914, a new baseball league had formed, the Federal League. The Federals had seriously cut into the American and National Leagues' rosters. With the bidding for services between rival leagues, this situation had also driven up player salaries. McCarthy entertained hopes here that more good play in Buffalo might prompt a Federal League team to give him a look, or it could lead an American or National League team, particularly one depleted by Federal raids of their roster, to contact him. Connie Mack had won the American League pennant in 1914, but with a shocking 0–4 loss to Boston in the World Series and with Federal League pressures on his star players' salaries, he was forced to trade off much of his best talent to keep himself out of the red. What a thrill it would be for young McCarthy to earn a shot at playing for Mr. Mack and the A's. Whatever the prospects he thought about, there was certainly no reason for the twenty-seven-year-old McCarthy to quit or feel the slightest bit forlorn. Besides, up in Buffalo that winter, McCarthy had met a girl, Elizabeth Lakeman, a Dayton, Ohio, native who had spent most of her life in Buffalo. Joe certainly liked her. She seemed to appreciate his nature, that was at once so focused yet somewhat shy. They would keep seeing each other.

After the 1914 season, Billy Clymer left Buffalo to manage in Toronto. Former major league catcher Patrick "Patsy" Donovan succeeded him. There were rumors in Buffalo that the Bisons were trying to trade McCarthy. One of the first things Donovan did upon being hired as the manager of the Bisons was to quash any deal involving McCarthy. "Manager Patsy," chortled the Buffalo papers, "would have come in for some severe criticism on the part of the fans if he had allowed Joe to leave the herd. Joe," the paper rhapsodized, "is classed with the best players in the International League. Joe's graceful fielding, accurate throwing, fast base-running, hard and timely hitting, and his general all-around work in the region of second last summer, was one of the brightest spots on the team. ... One or two more infielders like Joe and there will be no worrying from any source."[7]

It was not just the press that sung McCarthy's praises. On April 15, 1915, McCarthy's Bison teammates honored him by electing him the team captain. In the first inning of a game on April 22, just as McCarthy was going to bat, play was halted. April 21st was Capt. McCarthy's 28th birthday, and the team chipped in and bought him a military dresser set and a gold fountain pen. A little ceremony took place right at home plate, and when it was over McCarthy promptly singled to left field. In a May 30 exhibition game against Niagara College, a similar event occurred upon alumnus McCarthy's first time at bat. Time out was called, and the college presented McCarthy with a gold locket watch fob as an acknowledgment of his success in baseball.[8] He was respected; he was liked; and he had a girlfriend. Life in Buffalo was not bad at all.

The 1915 season was full of stress for the Bison team owners, and for all the owners in the International League. The teams in Toronto and Montreal were deeply affected, of course, as Canada was in the war with the U.K. and France. Throughout the U.S., baseball ticket sales were down. Many attributed the war talk throughout the nation as a major factor here. The sinking of the *Lusitania* in May hardly stimulated a mood of "take me out to the ball game." For some cities in the International League especially, there was also keen competitive pressure from the new Federal League. Although it postured itself as a third major league and was paying some major league level salaries to various baseball stars, the Federal League was drawing some of its fans from minor league centers. In their first year, four of the eight FL cities were the homes of major league teams—Chicago, Brooklyn, Pittsburgh, and St. Louis, but the other four were American Association and International League towns—Indianapolis, Kansas City, Baltimore, *and* Buffalo. The major league cities did not like the competition, but with more resources and larger fan bases, they could hold on. The minor league cities were more nervous. In the American Association, Kansas City withstood the pressure. Indianapolis was hard hit, although the FL team there would subsequently move to Newark, another IL site, as the league hoped to muscle its way into the New York area market. In the International League, the Baltimore Orioles had to relocate in Richmond, Va. When the FL Indianapolis team moved to Newark, the IL Newark Tigers switched to Harrisburg, Pa. In Buffalo, the IL Bisons stayed put and fought for the fans' loyalty. It wasn't easy, and it preyed on everyone's mind all season. International League President Ed Barrow was angry about the FL's muscling, and he preached a policy of total non-cooperation. This meant no exhibition games (even though a Buffalo v. Buffalo game would have been an obvious crowd pleaser), and it meant that anyone who flirted with a jump to a Federal League team would be regarded as a traitor and excommunicated. President

Barrow was not someone to be crossed. There were constant rumors of top players on all the teams jumping to the Federal League, and in Buffalo some of the rumors concerned Joe McCarthy. Manager Donovan conceded that McCarthy "has received overtures from the Federals," but, proudly proclaimed the Buffalo papers, "McCarthy is no hurdler." Shortstop Roxey Roach, on the other hand, did jump to the Federal League — to the Buffalo team no less.[9]

The Bisons had a good season in 1915. As in 1914, they were in contention for the pennant all season. Meanwhile, the Buffalo "Federals," or "Buffeds" as they were sometimes nicknamed, spent most of their season in last place. They reduced bleacher ticket prices to fifteen and sometimes even ten cents. But the Bisons outdrew them consistently. The Buffeds manager quit in the middle of the season, and there was talk of the team moving to Boston.[10] Meanwhile, led by Captain McCarthy and outfielder Frank "Flash" Gilhooley, who led the team in both hitting and stolen bases, the Bisons were the only team to stay close to Providence through the summer. (Providence boasted one young pitching star named Herb Pennock, a future Hall of Famer.) On August 22, Buffalo was five games out of first; third place Montreal was fourteen games behind. The two teams kept battling. By September 11, Buffalo had whittled Providence's lead down to a game and a half. On the last weekend of the season, Providence lost two games, and Buffalo pulled ahead. Under Patsy Donovan, Joe McCarthy had at long last won a pennant. He had learned much watching Donovan work. He was particularly impressed with the way Donovan set his lineup and stuck with it, save for injuries. He saw the value in letting the regulars congeal into a smooth unit. He would not forget this lesson. It was his first pennant. There would be more.

8

A Flirt with the Federals
and Off to Louisville

In 1915, Billy Clymer piloted his Toronto team ahead of Montreal into third place in the International League. The Toronto management and fans were pleased, but only a week after the season had concluded, the always restless Clymer accepted another offer to manage the Louisville Colonels of the American Association for 1916. Clymer had played for Louisville in 1903, and he knew some of the team's management. Meanwhile, his friend Joe McCarthy contemplated where he could go. In 1915, he had hit another respectable .268, and with the offers from the Federal League flying all about among his friends, he figured something would fall his way. After the 1915 season, he would receive three possible offers. His teammate, Frank Gilhooley, had signed with the New York Yankees for $8000. McCarthy was offered no such bonus, but the Yankees did show some interest in him. McCarthy had been recommended to the Yankees by International League President Ed Barrow. He tried to persuade the new Yankee owners to buy both Gilhooley and McCarthy. (The IL would gain financially from the signing of one of their players in the American League. A Federal League signing yielded them nothing.) After the 1915 season McCarthy met with Yankee Manager Bill Donovan. The club expressed some interest, but they offered him no bonus, let alone one the size of Gilhooley's.[1]

At the same time McCarthy received an offer from the Federal League Brooklyn "Tip Tops." John "Popup" Ganzel, Brooklyn's manager, personally recruited him. McCarthy thought about it, and the simple thing was that Brooklyn offered him more money ($4000 a year, twice what he had been making in Buffalo). The Yankees were in a bit of turmoil, as the team ownership was changing hands. The Brooklyn Tip Tops seemed the more solid offer. Eager at long last to make it into a major league, McCarthy accepted their offer.[2] He did not know that while he was accepting the offer from Brooklyn, the magnates of the rival baseball leagues were secretly meeting to iron out their problems. The "Baseball Wars," as the papers were calling them, were getting out of hand. The owners, like most rich people, understood the idea of keeping the wealth in the family, rather than ruining one another in a bidding spree for workers. On November 27, the *Buffalo Express* sadly headlined in their sports page that McCarthy had "Gone Over to the Federals." John Ganzel of the Brooklyn Tip

43

Tops announced that he had signed "the best eight players in the International League," one of whom was McCarthy. McCarthy knew, of course, that the word of his jump to Brooklyn would come out. He did not know that Ganzel's move involved more posturing by the Federal League leaders as to how their position was strengthening as they were bargaining with the American and National League owners. Another FL owner, oil magnate Harry Sinclair, was simultaneously making noises about moving a FL team into New York City and building a new stadium on 145th Street and Lennox Avenue. Meetings had begun back in October during the 1915 World Series, but they had been kept secret. As late as October 29, indeed, Federal League President James A. Gilmore was denying any deal was in the works.[3] On December 16, a final deal was struck. (And it was during the intervening seven weeks that McCarthy had signed with Brooklyn.) The Federals had actually come to terms with the National League earlier, but everything was worked out with both the NL and AL on December 16.

The Federal League would disband. The American and National League had to assume some $385,000 of FL player contracts. Restaurateur Charles Weeghman, the FL Chicago Whales owner, was permitted to buy the NL Cubs, and he moved them to the new stadium he had built for the Whales on the city's posh North Side. Subsequently, Weeghman sold the team and stadium to chewing gum magnate William Wrigley. The FL St. Louis owner bought the AL Browns, and within a month he fired Browns manager Branch Rickey. Rickey stayed in St. Louis, however, going to work for the Cardinals. Other FL owners were reimbursed, and many FL players were sold back to the major leagues. In all the slick arrangements, the FL Baltimore Terrapins were left completely out in the cold. They folded, thus allowing the Orioles to return to Baltimore. The Terrapins ended up suing organized baseball, claiming the clique of owners were in violation of anti-trust laws. This case finally ended up in the United States Supreme Court in 1922. It was settled against Baltimore, with Assoc. Justice Oliver Wendell Holmes issuing his famous, and dubious, ruling that baseball was not a form of "interstate commerce" and was "exempt from anti-trust due to its peculiar nature."[4]

While Baltimore was shunned in the settlement of the baseball wars, so were the teams of the International League. League President Ed Barrow could, and did, legitimately argue that his league also had issues and financial concerns that any settlement should address. Fully half the Federal League teams, after all, had been competing primarily with his clubs. But no one cared to listen to Barrow very seriously. After the December agreement, there was a Peace Committee that formed. James Gilmore took part, as did two former FL owners, three representatives from the major leagues, and Ed Barrow. Whether he was jumping to conclusions prematurely or being perceptive, and few people ever found Barrow to be anything but utterly thorough in his work, Barrow quickly concluded the Peace Committee to be a sham. Within a week, he resigned. Any possible arrangements, such as the Buffalo Bisons working out a deal to use the park built by the Buffeds, or the reestablished Baltimore Orioles doing the same with the one built by the Terrapins, were quashed. Barrow's harsh mood with respect to any player who had jumped to the Federal League would then not be mollified. He had earlier been blacklisting any who had jumped, like Roxey Roach. The December settlement and Peace Committee nonsense hardened his views. While existing Federal League players were free to reenter the major leagues as best as they could, nothing was done for the protection of the little people of the minors who had switched to the Federals, much less for small fry like Joe McCarthy who had jumped after the 1915 season while the settlement deal was in the works. Forces way beyond his control had stuck McCarthy and others in limbo. The major leagues did not want them, and under no circumstances would Barrow let any of them back into the International League. McCarthy later recalled "that winter the International League voted to ban any player who jumped.... They put me in the class of a contract jumper." In addition to his previous recommending of McCarthy to the Yankees, Barrow had had hopes that the young man could manage in Jersey City. Billy Clymer had tried to broker a deal for McCarthy to join Jersey City as well.[5] Once McCarthy signed with Brooklyn, however, he was *persona non grata*. About all he had left in Buffalo was his girl friend. Elsewhere, he had one good baseball connection to whom he could turn — Billy Clymer. "Derby Bill" had moved to Louisville amidst all the baseball negotiations, and, as far as McCarthy was concerned, thank goodness he had done so. Finding himself otherwise at a complete professional standstill, McCarthy left Buffalo to rejoin Billy Clymer in Louisville. Back in Buffalo, he would keep in touch with Elizabeth, however.

Billy Clymer knew baseball talent, and he had none of the starchy, hidebound inflexibility of Ed Barrow. It mattered not one whit to him that someone had flirted with the now defunct Federal League. Flirtations and infidelity were not baseball issues as far as he was concerned. McCarthy's "defection" to the Brooklyn Federals, or his possible switch to Jersey City, was hardly a sin. To Clymer, Roxey Roach's mid-season defection to the Buffeds was not important either. Clymer brought them both to Louisville, along with a Cuban pitcher he had in Toronto, Adolfo Luque. The three would be very important parts of the team he would put together in Louisville. In fourteen years of baseball managing, Clymer had won five pennants and never finished worse than third. As far as he was concerned, Louisville was going to be another notch on his belt.

Louisville, Kentucky, was a city with a proud baseball history. Before 1900, the Louisville Colonels had been part of the National League, and they had boasted such stars as Honus Wagner, Fred Clarke, and Rube Waddell. Potentially embarrassing issues of overlapping management had prompted the National League to consolidate from twelve teams to eight after the 1899 season. Among the changes, the Louisville Colonels were absorbed by the Pittsburgh Pirates. (Cleveland merged with St. Louis, Baltimore with Brooklyn, and Washington was dropped.) Even though it lost its major league franchise, Louisville remained a fiercely rabid baseball town. The famous Louisville Slugger baseball bats were manufactured there, and after the dust settled on the National League consolidation and the year-later formation of the American League, the leading baseball cities of the Midwest formed the American Association, intentionally using the name of a circuit which had been a major league in the 1880s. Louisville was a charter member of the Association, and has remained a great baseball town ever since. During the early years of the Association, the Minneapolis Millers had been a dominant force. Baseball people in Louisville were tired of this. They wanted a winner, and their congenial owner, bourbon distiller Otha H. Wathen, hired Clymer to bring them one. Clymer hired Roach, Luque, and McCarthy to help him do it.

Luque quickly earned a spot on the pitching staff, and early into the pre-season training, Roxey Roach and Joe McCarthy clearly emerged as the "keystone combination." Luque became a mound fixture for Louisville and was a star in the Association. He had pitched a few innings for the Boston Braves in 1914 and 1915, and he would return to the majors after two seasons with Louisville and pitch splendidly for Cincinnati. In 1923, he would win a league-leading 27 games. (Like McCarthy, Luque would eventually manage, although only in his native Cuba. He managed to such notoriety that Ernest Hemingway's fisherman in *The Old Man and the Sea* would speculate as to who was the best Cuban manager of all time, "Dolf Luque or Mike Gonzalez.") As for Louisville's new infielders in 1916, one observer wrote "the way 'Roxey' Roach and Joe McCarthy work together around second makes double plays a trifling incident to a ball game." It was clear to all that Roach and McCarthy were in the starting line-up. Roach was elected team captain. The papers were quick to praise McCarthy's work. "McCarthy," wrote a reporter, "is like a streak of lightning around the keystone bag." Another wrote similarly: "Joe McCarthy is the same clever second sacker he was when in the [American] Association a few years ago. He covers a lot of ground and is one of the brainiest men in this circuit." His hitting, too, earned plaudits. Perhaps the Louisville reporters knew that some would be concerned about this, given Joe's batting record at Toledo and Indianapolis, so they made a point of noting: "The way Joe was meeting the ball ... was a source of gratification. He hit it the proverbial mile." Ten days later, another columnist wrote: "When Joe hits one squarely, it goes like a shot from a gun."[6]

The pre-season whoops of optimism proved to be more than mere vapor, as Louisville wound up the month of April with a first-place record of 10–1. McCarthy, meanwhile, was "winning his way into the affections of local fans." Respectfully referred to as "the mild-mannered Philadelphian, McCarthy endeared himself to the baseball knowing public of the city: "The devotees of the game like the way he goes after ground balls and wields his club. ... He and shortstop Roach make a lightning-fast team around hill no. 2. [Manager] Clymer," concluded the *Courier-Journal*, "knew what he was doing when he signed that pair of infielders to work for the glory of Louisville."[7] Louisville fashioned itself as a town of bourbon-drinking gents who knew their baseball and loved their city. They would be severe in their judgments of any who came there to play the national pastime, but for those like Joe McCarthy who passed the stern tests of both baseball and demeanor, the famous Southern hospitality would be warm indeed.

Nineteen sixteen was a pressure-filled year for Americans. The war in Europe was raging ever more tragically. Pancho Villa was raiding along the Mexican border. And national elections were coming that fall. Feeling pressures all about them, many Americans debated the issues, of course, but others appeared to try to avoid thinking about them. The *Brooklyn Eagle* ran a drawing of people seated on a commuter train, all with newspapers discernibly opened to sections like Fashion, Society, and Sports. Meanwhile, conspicuously strewn all over the car floor were the pages with coverage of the war in Europe.[8] The Louisville papers reprinted the *Eagle* cartoon. That summer, it seemed many folks just did not want to think about uncomfortable things. Baseball was a kind of touchstone for these people, as well as for the perennial fans. It harkened back to innocent days. When that urge coincides with a pennant race, as it did in Louisville, interest was going to be keen. Players who showed a kind of calm reserve would stand well with such citizens. Phrases began to pop up in the press here, referring to McCarthy as "the alert little Irishman" and the "thrifty Hibernian." The ease and rapid dispatch with which he and Roach snapped off double plays resonated nicely, as people enjoyed the notion that trouble on the horizon can be wiped away with a slick bit of infield skill. (One reporter noted that Roach and McCarthy dispose of runners "with the same degree of ease that Pancho Villa does a 'Greaser' he becomes suspicious of.")[9] McCarthy's emerging image as a sturdy little Irishman who did his job resonated well among those who invested into baseball both an interest in the fate of their local team and a denial of a world's troubles about which they preferred not to think.

In the summer of 1916, the American Association race largely involved four teams—Indianapolis, Minneapolis, Kansas City, and Louisville. On June 21, three and one-half games separated them. Milwaukee, meanwhile, was the worst team in the league that year. To cover sagging revenues, on June 22, they sold to Louisville, their big, if not terribly bright, first baseman, Jay Kirke. Milwaukee was left with former Olympian Jim Thorpe as their only offensive threat (and everyone knew he had trouble hitting a curve ball). Milwaukee went straight to the cellar, losing a staggering 110 games. But Louisville now had extra hitting. Kirke was an amazingly strong athlete. By several accounts he swung a 54-ounce bat(!); in seven major league seasons he hit .301. With Kirke playing daily, Louisville loomed an even greater threat in the American Association. McCarthy, unfortunately, fell into a batting slump in June. He had been hitting .280 and fell to .263 by the end of July, and by late August he was hitting only .248. Connie Mack visited Louisville on July 24, and there was McCarthy mired in a batting slump. Clymer shifted him from second to sixth in the lineup, but the slump continued. McCarthy "shone on the field," heralded one reporter after a key victory over Kansas City on August 22, a victory which put Louisville in the league lead by two games, "but [he] failed to deliver a safe punch." Still his fielding remained spectacular, and the papers were complimenting him for it: "because of his graceful fielding, [McCarthy] makes hard catches seem easy. He has made several almost impossible catches during games ... that with any other fielder would have brought forth ringing applause. Yet the fans thought it was but natural that Joe make the stabs."[10] To McCarthy, that was what being a good ballplayer was all about. He always liked the quiet, unflashy players, and when he was a manager, he liked them even more.

Along with McCarthy's and Roach's splendid defense, Roach and Kirke hit well through the summer. In September, Kansas City faded into the pack, particularly after Louisville swept them in a key series. Although Indianapolis was not so easily shaken, Clymer and the Colonels were not intimidated. Louisville took the pennant, and honors were lauded all around. Clymer received many gifts. Roxey Roach was named the team's most valuable player by the city's sports editors. However, noted the *Courier-Journal*, Joe McCarthy and [third baseman] John Corriden ran so close to Roxey that the Kendrick [jewelry] firm provided watches for both. McCarthy, quiet and unassuming," the paper hastened to add, "is the best second baseman in the league and has the smartest working brain in the association." Louisvillians knew their baseball; they appreciated the value of McCarthy, his batting slump notwithstanding. His fielding was slick. His hitting was especially keen in the clutch. His speed was good too. In the two years at Wilkes-Barre, the two at Buffalo, and the one at Louisville, he had stolen 101 bases. Casey Stengel once commented, indeed, that as a minor leaguer, McCarthy may have only been fair at bat and in the field, but he was an outstanding base runner.[11] Most others of the day praised his fielding. Kirke, McCarthy, Roach, and Corriden, said many, was an infield that could stand with those of most major league teams. In 1916 they played as a unit in 169 complete games. They would stay together for many seasons.

The Colonels headed out west after the 1916 season to play a set of games with the Omaha Rourkes, champions of the Western League. Louisville won. They tied the first game, 3–3 in 12 innings with darkness ending the contest. Omaha won the second game 11–7. The Omaha papers chortled that the Rourkes "made the Louisville Colonels look like a lot of ring tailed monkeys." Whether such statements angered the Colonels or not, they turned around and won the next four games to take the series. After insulting the Colonels, the Omaha papers graciously conceded after their fourth victory, "The 'Americans' easily and glaringly outclassed the Western Leaguers, and that was all there was to it." In the series, McCarthy got a hit in each game, two in the losing effort. He fielded errorlessly and scored two runs. The only conflict in the series came in regard to the arrangements for payment. The last two games were a doubleheader. The Omaha organizers cagily contended that the players were to be paid on a per-day basis, hence a doubleheader would earn the same as a single day game. The Colonels would hear none of that and threatened to leave after the first game. Matters were settled, but all through the last game McCarthy and the rest of the Colonels "acted more like a mob of rowdies than anything else."[12] McCarthy and his friends won their pennant, their "minor league world *serious*," and they got their money. McCarthy went home to Philadelphia, and, with his extra money, he could afford a few extra visits to Buffalo that winter.

9

War Years

As spring training was beginning for the Louisville Colonels in March and April, 1917, the realities of world events were impinging ever more upon any who preferred to think mere carefree, happy thoughts. Russia was in complete turmoil, as the Tsar had abdicated and the nation was lurching toward an unknown future. Even the Louisville papers printed a cryptic little story on April 15 about "Russian agitators, Nikolai Lenin and Zinovyof [sic] traveling through Germany in a sealed coach."[1] The exposure of the "Zimmerman telegram," and the revelations about German machinations in Mexico, the submarine warfare, the arming of American ships, continuing labor unrest, women's rights activities — such news stories were everywhere. Ball players were not immune from the news. They knew what was taking shape, and their opinions varied as much as did those of any group of people. There was nothing special about their perspectives, and reporters never asked them much about their views outside sports matters. Thus for the sports fans interested in "escape," ball players who appeared to do their jobs without reference to the day's troubling events seemed ever more a wonderfully serene break from all the hubbub. Socrates had always praised "the man who did his job," and in 1917, baseball seemed to represent that for some who preferred isolationism. Perhaps to a few such Louisvillians, the Colonels reinforced this Socratic ideal when they met for spring training — in Athens (Georgia).

Press coverage of the work of Joe McCarthy added to this sense of a solid man, bearing down on his job, no matter the whir of events around him. Roxey Roach was loudly complaining that the Colonels had refused to let him go to the major leagues and had cut his salary. Jay Kirke was famous for bragging heartily when he played well and always being ready with an alibi when falling short of perfection. ("Any time Jay can't come forward with an explanation that is convenient to Kirke," laughed one reporter, "the Ohio River will be full of sea lions.") Meanwhile, "Silent Joe McCarthy" continued to be the sort to let his work speak for itself, and even then do his work in an understated manner — "unpretentious but brilliant second baseman, ... he makes his chances look so easy that much of his work really is not fully appreciated. ... one of the brightest players in the ranks of modern-day baseballists."[2] Even where McCarthy spoke the tone was poignantly low-key. A newspaper relayed, for example, a "conversation" between McCarthy and the Colonels' jokester catcher, Hub Perdue (all in complete deadpan):

Perdue: Cy Perkins is dead!
McCarthy: Cy dead? How old was he?
Perdue: Ninety-five.
McCarthy: What caused his death?
Perdue: Same old story: wine, women, and song.
McCarthy: That's cut short many a life.
(And the two walked sadly into the hotel.)[3]

McCarthy always loved the stage. Perhaps he never realized that while he could not act or sing or dance, he had a future as a straight man. (And in vaudeville, the straight man of the comedy pair always got 60 percent). No matter the appeal of the play and temperament of the solid little *mensch*, no matter that the Colonels beat the American League Cleveland Indians that spring and were favored to repeat as American Association champions, no matter a tornado that killed 46 people in the nearby town of New Albany, Indiana, the significance of everything paled on April 6 when President Wilson officially declared the nation at war.[4]

A level of uncertainty shot through all of organized sports in the United States when the President and Congress declared war. Within a month, military conscription had begun, so the practical issue of available manpower emerged quickly. On May 1, the University of Kentucky announced the cancellation of all athletic activities, with virtually "every man on all the teams having enlisted or gone back to farms for more food duty." Until a government official said otherwise, or until a dropoff in demand for tickets made professional baseball a fruitless endeavor, teams would continue to play. But they did so with a different mood all about them. Just four days after the war declaration, for example, a fire broke out at the New York racetrack Belmont Park; immediately reports, typically using the passive voice in such instances, asserted "it is believed to have been set by German plotters." Quickly into the season, professional baseball games commenced with the raising of the American flag and the playing of *The Star Spangled Banner*. By May 5, there was talk from the office of the President of the American Association, Thomas J. Hickey, of a possible war tax of 10 percent on game receipts which could then shut down the league unless players took a voluntary cut in stipends. Before war had been declared, Hickey and International League President Ed Barrow had been arranging to have teams from the two leagues play one another in August and September. With the war, this venture was called off. For Kentuckians, perhaps the worst of all prospects appeared that spring on page one of the Lousiville papers—a possible wartime ban on whiskey![5]

The War also caused significant shifts in populations and neighborhoods, causing new levels of tensions in the nation's dysfunctional Jim Crow race arrangements. Baseball was not immune from these crossfires. In the previous season, McCarthy had witnessed a fight between his old Toledo friend, catcher Grover Land, who had been traded to Minneapolis, and his teammate, Cuban pitcher Adolfo Luque. Land had spat at Luque and called him a N_____-son-of-a-b____, offensive in itself, and, with the "b" word, even more so to a Hispanic.[6] On May 3, 1918, the manager of the Milwaukee Brewers, Danny Shay, was arrested for killing an African-American waiter in a restaurant in the English Hotel in Indianapolis, apparently because the waiter had failed to bring him a fresh bowl of sugar.[7]

Throughout all these new events and circumstances, McCarthy played steadily. The Colonels, nonetheless, were mediocre. Indianapolis got off to the best start. On June 7, when the 1916 Pennant of the American Association was officially raised at Eclipse Park in Louisville, the Indianapolis Indians defeated the Colonels to go up by four games in the standings. With the mediocre record of the spring, with the day's loss to Indianapolis, and with the world's pressing events, the raising of a 1916 pennant hailed a most distant memory. Other flags had become far more important.[8] Through June and July, the Colonels stayed close to Indianapolis. McCarthy's play continued to draw praise for the ease and grace of his defense and his hustle, and he was batting .280. With obvious reference to the events over in Europe, one paper effused here: "When a hit is needed to break up a battle or launch an attack that will put the enemy to flight, rely on Joe McCarthy to perform the job in an artistic and effective manner." Repeatedly reporters noted that "there are several second baseman in the major loops not half as clever as this ... hustling Hibernian."[9]

With all going well for McCarthy, in a game against Indianapolis on August 9, McCarthy was diving back to first base to avoid a pickoff. The first baseman stepped on his right leg and cut him with his spike. McCarthy had to leave the game for the first time in the season and remained out for two weeks. The spiking had strained a ligament in his knee. Just at the time of this injury, some major league teams were picking up the options of some minor leaguers to complete the season. No matter his recent press clippings, a convalescing Joe McCarthy would be of no interest to them. Before the game in which McCarthy was spiked, the Colonels were three and one half games behind Indianapolis. By the end August, they were seven and one half games out. And, noted one scribe, "without the level-headed Hibernian, old Derby [Bill Clymer] would be in an unenviable predicament." Even in a loss to Minneapolis, "the Philadelphian, as usual," came the report, "did more than his bit."[10] Over and over, such praise followed McCarthy. Still, no major league team gave a call.

Along with St. Paul, Louisville stayed at Indianapolis's heels through the season. But the Indians never faltered. St. Paul actually drew even with them for a day, after defeating Louisville in a key game, but they fell away from there. Indianapolis won the pennant, with Louisville and St. Paul tied for second, two and a half games behind. In March, Billy Clymer had proclaimed to the Wilkes-Barre papers that he was going to win a second pennant in Louisville. When Indianapolis clinched, he cabled back to Wilkes-Barre: "Somebody's fibbed."[11]

McCarthy had done everything asked of him. Without a pennant, and with a war on, there were no MVP ceremonies or any other post-season festivities, although the papers felt McCarthy a significant enough figure in the Louisville sports world actually to note his departure on September 20: "McCarthy," they said, "dotes on the Quaker City, hence a quick getaway." (He would go to Buffalo too.) In the major league World Series that year, the American League champion Chicago White Sox manager Clarence "Pants" Rowland had been regularly chided for having spent his entire playing career, as well as his pre–Chicago managing career, in the minor leagues. McCarthy noted that this mere "busher" had nonetheless guided the White Sox to the pennant and won the World Series.[12]

By the 1918 spring training, the nature of the American war climate had changed markedly. Specific war regulations had grown more fulsome and systematic. The scarcities of meats, grains, and vegetables were pronounced in many regions of the country. The sense of being on a war footing had fully penetrated the society. Man-power needs also took a decided shift late that winter. While troops were needed soon after the April, 1917 declaration of war, the sense of urgency among America's allies did not reach panic levels until the next year. Then, with the Bolshevik takeover of Russia, and their subsequent pull-out from the war, the Eastern front collapsed. Ger-many and Austria-Hungary no longer had to fight on two major fronts. As they could focus virtually all their military power on the West, the felt need for American troops became severe. (American casualties in the twelve months before April, 1918 were indeed tiny compared to the huge numbers in the last seven months of fighting.) Secretary of War Newton Baker had issued a proclamation that was popularly known as "Work or Fight." It meant that all eligible young men had either to be working in essential war employment or to be serving in the armed forces. Playing professional baseball was not considered essential. However, as would be the case during World War II, the maintenance of professional baseball was looked upon as useful for the sake of community and national morale. The point here was that if a young baseball player was called into military service, he had to go, but the teams could keep play-ing if they could come up with the players. They would just have to do the best they could as the war pressures bore down on them. In the spring and summer of 1918, many adjustments would have to be made. In Louisville and in many cities, game times were moved from 3:00 to 4:00 P.M. to enable plant workers to attend games (and not encourage anyone to slip away from work early).[13]

Still, with mills working constantly, attendance was down, despite low ticket prices. (In Louisville, a grandstand seat cost 54 cents, a bleacher pass was 27 cents, and men in uniform were admitted at half price.)[14] With highly industrialized cities like Buffalo, Baltimore, Rochester, Newark, and Jersey City among its chief mem-bers, the International League almost folded in 1918. (Ed Barrow left and became manager of the Boston Red Sox.) The American Association would not open until May 1, and it would cease play in late July. The American and National Leagues would cease in early September, and the World Series would take place a month early. At that point, for all the ball players of age, it was "work or fight." With no one know-ing how long the war would last, there was serious talk that organized baseball would no longer exist and have to start from scratch at some point in the distant future, if and when the war was successfully concluded. In the spring of 1918, no one knew what to expect.

"Ball players inclined to complain of meatless and wheatless hotel meals the coming season," ungrammatically warned the *Louisville Courier-Journal*, "should have a care about talking too loud. You can never tell these days who may wear a secret service button under one's coat."[15] Ball players, major and minor league, were facing Spartan times. Many teams, including Louisville, did not travel South to train. In Louisville, Roxey Roach, however, still tried to hold out for better pay.[16] Amidst all these pressures, Louisville began its season. McCarthy was there, dutifully play-ing second base every day, as were his infield mates John Corriden, Jay Kirke, and Roach. While losing the opener, the Colonels proceeded to win their next eight and took first place. After the week of winning, they actually risked disrupting their momentum by calling off a game on Saturday, May 11. War, morale, winning streak, it didn't matter, it was Derby Day. "NUF SED," explained the *Courier-Journal*. Most

Louisvillians were probably surprised the paper even explained that much. There went the Colonels' momentum, however. They lost their next game and soon fell back into a pack with Minneapolis, Columbus, and Kansas City. As of June 1, two games separated first and fourth place.[17]

Through the month of May, baseball teams were losing players right and left. Some were drafted. Others, fearing the draft, went off to War Department–approved essential jobs. For some this was easy if they came from a productive family farm. Others hustled and found work in shipyards and steel mills.[5] Shoeless Joe Jackson, for example, left the Chicago White Sox and worked in a Bethlehem Steel–owned shipyard in Wilmington, Delaware.[18] Many players who did this were subject to ridicule, but they did it anyway. Grover Cleveland Alexander, on the other hand, left the Chicago Cubs, to whom he had just been traded by Philadelphia, and served in Europe. Most famously, Christy Mathewson, nearly 38 years old, his pitching days just over, volunteered for the service and suffered gas inhalation in a training exercise. The effects led to his untimely death in 1924. Less nobly, Roxey Roach left Louisville in June. He headed home to Windber, Pennsylvania, claiming the drafting of employees was imperiling his family's business. This did not end his susceptibility to the draft as he had hoped, so he took a job in a steel plant outside Harrisburg.[19] Joe McCarthy endeared himself to Louisville by continuing to play ball and tutoring the replacement players. When Roach left, the players elected McCarthy captain.

The American Association was wavering. Attendance was down. Some owners were calling for the league to disband for the war's duration. Toledo teetered on bankruptcy. Louisville owner Otha Wathen was instrumental in keeping the season going. He argued that disbanding would be bad for work morale in the various cities of the league. He asserted that any such move would have to be unanimous, and he cagily added that if teams did disband, he and other owners would be free to contract with unemployed players, leaving the disbanded teams with nothing upon which to build after the war. Led by Wathen's urgings, as well as by his threats, the Association did not disband.[20]

Baseball people in Louisville were feeling an extra bit of pressure on their ball club that summer. It was not just the war pressures. After the 1917 season, Thomas Chivington had left his post as the President of the American Association and became general manager of the Louisville Colonels. As is often the case in such managerial situations, the person in a new, and lower, position will tend to micro-manage some of the affairs around him. Chivington did just that, much to the frustration of the already highly strung Colonels field manager Billy Clymer. In July, two Colonels pitchers, Ralph Stroud and Fred Beebe, fearing the draft, bolted the Colonels and took jobs in steel plants in Pennsylvania. ("Another player will follow them," not so cryptically wrote the *Courier-Journal*, "This is a most capable infielder, and his loss would be a severe blow." They sure liked Joe.) Upon leaving Louisville, Stroud and Beebe chose to sound off to the papers. Beebe pointed out that when Clymer was in charge "there was never the least trouble. Now every time we drop a game, Chivington is around at night to tell us how we should have played the game. As long as he is in charge," predicted Beebe, "there will be little harmony prevailing, and I'm afraid that Clymer will have a hard time getting the best out of the players, although all of the men are for him strong." Stroud agreed: "The problem is General Manager Chivington. On the road Chivington is the boss. He runs the whole show, or, rather, attempts to do so. With all due respect to Mr. Chivington, who was once President of the American Association, I must say that his knowledge of the game is rather limited." Stroud expressed further frustration, as had Beebe, about how Chivington felt he could tell team members how to play baseball. Stroud asserted that it was Chivington's meddling that drove Roach off the club and that "Clymer cannot get the proper results when he is compelled to take orders from the business office." He predicted that Clymer would soon resign under such circumstances.[21]

When Roach left, Chivington ordered a young player named Art Kores to play shortstop. Clymer wanted to secure another player, via trade or sale, but Chivington, wishing to face no financial consequences from Roach's departure (which he may have caused), insisted on Kores, and pointed to "evidence" of Kores's experience at shortstop — in high school! When upper level managers, no matter how out of touch they are, insist they are right about something and use evidence that amounts to nothing more than self-delusion, respect dies all around and dissension ensues. The Louisville papers snickered at Chivington here. They told him to put himself at shortstop. Meanwhile, Louisville lost six of their next seven games.[22] Some writers tried to downplay the matter, declaring that Beebe had been having a bad year, which was true, and that neither Roach nor Stroud "was capable of playing under the big tent."[23] Stroud had actually played briefly with the Giants and the Tigers, and Roach had played for the Yankees and the Senators, but these facts were less important than was the fact of dissension all about. Amidst the troubles, McCarthy impressed the team's supporters with the way he carried on. He certainly understood what was taking place between Chivington and Clymer, and made mental note of it all. As a field manager he would never suffer such meddling from a general manager.

Contrary to the predictions of the papers, McCarthy did not leave the team. He also spent many hours trying to tutor the hapless Kores at shortstop, and he never spoke to the press about any of the controversies. In no way did McCarthy have to bite his lip here. Such was his natural tendency anyway, and the press respected him for his ways (something that would be very different in later years). He always was one to try to make the best of whatever situation fell upon him. On July 21, Louisville stood in fourth place, only four games behind first-place Kansas City. That morning the papers announced that the season would end — on that day! Billy Clymer went to the ballpark that afternoon, suited up, and waited, wondering where everyone had gone.[24]

With baseball seemingly about to become nothing but a memory in Louisville, the newspapers could not resist getting in one more swipe at Chivington. "Chivington, old sport, it is tough luck that you didn't have an opportunity to show your hand … and," they dead-seriously challenged, "we doubt your ability as a short fielder" (the term of the day for shortstop). The column went on to urge Otha Wathen to get rid of Chivington when baseball returns to Louisville. Meanwhile, the *Courier-Journal* went out of its way to lavish praise upon one Louisville player. "To honest Joe McCarthy, the sturdy field captain of the Colonels," they wrote, "local fandom owes a debt of gratitude for his loyalty." Admitting that several newly forming leagues which were emerging around some war-work industrial plants had tried to lure Joe, the *Courier-Journal* went on: "Being a man of integrity, the Philadelphian lived up to his contract ... and stayed on the roster until the American Association clubs sounded taps. By his manly attitude, Joe McCarthy returned to his native hea[r]th carrying the heart felt esteem *and* whole-hearted respect of every true lover of fair play. May his future be as bright as his record is honorable." (emphasis theirs)[25]

Louisvillians were bidding good-bye to McCarthy in a manner not unlike so many families seeing their sons go off to the war. Their affection and respect for the man was truly remarkable.

McCarthy went home to Philadelphia. Under Baker's "Work or Fight" edict, ball players had until September 1 to make arrangements within that law. (A special dispensation was made for the American and National League pennant winners, respectively Boston and Chicago. The season ended at the end of August, with the Red Sox and Cubs playing a premature World Series. The Red Sox won, the last World Series Boston would win, until 2004.) In regard to the army, McCarthy had a hardship status, in that he was working to support his mother. He needed work, and the steel mills in Eastern Pennsylvania were going full blast. Meanwhile, he wanted to maintain his baseball skills. This was, of course, a big question for all ball players. The major leagues were closing. A few teams were still playing out West, but there was no real future there, and they were scraping by with lesser and older players. Pitcher Joe McGinnity, for example, who had not played in the major leagues since 1908, was pitching in the Pacific Coast League at age 45. Even the assuring talk about the game's future did not sit well with players. "The game will not suffer if war ends within the next two years," opined one sports reporter. Ball players knew that such lengths of time could see a significant erosion of skills, and for a player in his early thirties like Joe McCarthy, such a prospect would likely mean an erosion that could not be recovered. He needed money for his family, and he felt he had to keep playing if he possibly could. A solution here was clear: join up with the steel plant leagues whose people had been contacting him that summer anyway. In August, McCarthy began working at the large Bethlehem Steel Plant in Steelton, Pennsylvania, just outside Harrisburg. On August 20, he played his first baseball game for them. He played second base, with his old Louisville sidekick Roxey Roach at shortstop.[26]

The Bethlehem Steel Corporation was a giant manufacturer for the nation's war effort. In Delaware, Maryland, and Pennsylvania they maintained six enormous steel mills and shipyards. The Pennsylvania plants were in Steelton, Lebanon, Bethlehem, and Fore River; the Delaware shipyard was in Wilmington; and the Maryland plant lay just east of Baltimore in the town of Sparrows Point. These were huge concerns before the war, and with the war, they became virtually round-the-clock operations. Employment at these plants shot up, with new numbers of workers flooding into the towns, living in whatever crude arrangements that were available, in some cases tents. Under such harsh conditions, said the manager of the Bethlehem's Steelton plant, Frank H. Robbins, there was a tremendous amount of wasted time. Employees, he said, seemed intent to gather as much money as possible without doing any more work than necessary, at times side-stepping work altogether. Education/propaganda programs did not seem to cure the malaise. The way out of the trouble, he said, was to furnish forms of relaxation for the employees. Sports and amusements were the unanimous choices here as the means. Bethlehem thus set up a series of baseball leagues within each plant and cap-stoned the effort with games between their plants, at which, of course, each used its best players. These games between the plants quickly gained rabid followings among the workers. Robbins concluded here: "We have experienced much better results since the introduction of sports, mainly baseball, in our local plant. The workmen seem to feel that they are doing a patriotic duty and that they are working for more than mere dollars and cents." In regard to the inter-plant team, he added "Interest runs high throughout the entire plant, from the native born American to the immigrant, and, just as sure, if the Steels suffer a defeat, a cloud of gloom is temporarily cast over the entire works." Robbins went on to suggest that the government use similar means to maintain morale within its ranks of workers and military personnel.[27]

Believing "baseball was the right thing" for plant productivity, and that winning teams were the best for the plants, the Bethlehem plants went about recruiting ball players. (And there were no objections from the Federal government.) This was how Roxey Roach had hooked up with Steelton as well as how "Shoeless" Joe Jackson had landed in a Wilmington, Delaware shipyard. Several other baseball stars were also employed by Bethlehem Steel, among them, the Washington Senators' Joe Leonard, who played for Fore River and George Dumont, who played with Joe Jackson in Wilmington, along with the White Sox' Claude "Lefty" Williams. The New York Yankees' Allen Russell played for Sparrows Point. The Chicago Cubs' George Pierce, the St. Louis Cardinals' John Beall, and the Philadelphia Athletics' Jack Knight and Eddie Plank all played for Steelton, as did Roach and McCarthy.[28]

With language and arguments that were similar to subsequent years' debates over universities admitting athletes to bolster their intercollegiate teams, and with the stakes obviously much more in earnest, some athletes in uniform, and some military people in general criticized Bethlehem Steel, as well as other corporations engaged in similar practices. Lieutenant Harry "Moose" McCormick, formerly of the New York Giants, was serving in the trenches. He claimed that many of the soldiers were bitter about the news of ballplayers landing jobs in industrial plants. "If the ball players knew what the boys who have gone ... to fight think of them, they would not want to play.... They would want to turn in their bats for guns and get into the real contest." The staging of the World Series in September was part of the story that apparently angered some soldiers, and the Army newspaper *Stars and Stripes* barred the printing of the box scores of all baseball games. It seemed, McCormick said, "that the baseball people were thinking more of their game than of their country." In France, McCormick met with Major T.L. Huston, then half owner of the New York Yankees, as well as with other big leaguers now in uniform. These men expressed similar sentiments, despite, in Huston's case, the large fortune he had invested in the Yankees which the war had imperiled.[29]

While the baseball issue certainly touched some raw nerves, the plants were permitted to operate with their little baseball leagues as long as the government did not object. A Harrisburg editor begged to point out that "It is true in some cases," he conceded, "that big league ball players hopped into the Bethlehem Steel League and other industrial leagues ... as a means to evade military service." He concluded that they "should be given no exemption and are rightfully panned by the soldiers 'over there.'" But he said "it is hardly fair to point the finger of scorn at all the representatives of such teams." Some, he said, were legitimately working to provide for their families and/or aged parents, with the steel plants being one of the few avenues available to them. The players, meanwhile, were "punching the clock" like all the other workers. Many were on posts that required few machine skills. Others were in unskilled "Social Welfare" work, but it all contributed to the plant's output, as defined and accounted for by the corporation, by its managers, and by government officials who oversaw all contracted war work.[30] The War Department wanted the maximum productivity out of the plants, and if the plants' managers felt that a little baseball would increase productivity, the Department was not going to make any issue, as long as players were legitimate hires. McCarthy was a legitimate war worker, and he spent the rest of the war working and playing ball for Steelton. He did his job.

The specter of the industrial plants and shipyards hiring ball players may have caused more strife and dissension had the war lasted longer than it did. As it was, it remained intensely difficult for some to read about Steelton defeating Sparrows Point while Yale's star track and field athlete, Johnny Overton, was killed in action on August 23. Meanwhile, in the late summer of 1918, the Steel League was one of the few sports that the public could follow. It made little impact outside the Pennsylvania, Delaware, and Maryland region where the games were played, but there was strong fan support in the little industrial towns, and perhaps this did help morale and productivity and help win the war.

Steelton played the various Bethlehem Steel teams, as well as those from other plants and shipyards. It finished the league's season tied with Bethlehem, and the corporate/league officials decided to have a best-of-three playoff for the "Schwab Pennant," Charles Schwab having been one of the founders of Bethlehem Steel. Bethlehem won the first game, Steelton the second. There was then talk of staging the final game in Philadelphia's Shibe Park, with hopes of a big crowd and the receipts going to a Soldiers' Fund. These arrangements could not be made, so the deciding game took place in Steelton. 100 percent of the proceeds from the game were given to the Soldiers' Tobacco Fund. The Harrisburg papers' headline for the game's story ran: "Joe McCarthy's Triple in the Tenth Frame Gives Steelton Possession of Steel League Pennant." Everyone cheered, and immediately went back to work.[31]

The Steel League had been a success. The plant managers felt it had propped up morale. As its profile was not terribly significant, the dismay it may have engendered among soldiers, fairly or unfairly, was not great. The league even kept some statistics. Not surprisingly, Joe Jackson led the league in hitting with an average of .393. McCarthy only batted .105. There was talk of expanding the league in the next season. In late September, Babe Ruth was going to work at the Lebanon plant.[32] Then the fighting in Europe suddenly ended on November 11. Not realizing the geographic narrowness of the circle in which the league had operated, pitcher Eddie Plank expressed hope, after the war had ended, that the league could continue.[33] Somehow few other baseball men felt that the confines of Ebbets Field and Shibe Park would yield to the charms of Lebanon, Pa. and Sparrows Point, Md. But no one ever accused Plank, as great a pitcher as he was, of being Rhodes Scholar material. In 1919, baseball returned to business as usual. Joe McCarthy headed back for Louisville, via Buffalo of course.

10

Now Managing for the Colonels

With the Armistice of November 11, 1918, all talk about baseball dying with the War instantly vanished, as did the idea of the professional game having to start *tabula rasa* whenever the war would end. As the 1919 spring training season approached, the major and minor baseball leagues simply returned to business as usual. Any charges people could have fairly or unfairly raised about Joe McCarthy or many others playing in the Steel League never arose. For McCarthy this was especially so back in Louisville, where he maintained a reputation not just as a fine ball player but as a man of integrity. He had stayed with the club when others were bolting for the industrial plants, and he had been above the fray when General Manager Thomas Chivington was meddling in the work of field manager Billy Clymer. By March, 1919, team owner Otha Wathen had gotten rid of Chivington. Clymer had been "turned adrift" as well, and he took a job managing Seattle in the Pacific Coast League. Wathen's new GM was "Captain" Billy Neal. In Clymer's place, Wathen hired Patrick "Patsy" Flaherty, a man with nine years of part-time play in the majors and who had been managing in Mobile, Alabama in the Southern Association. Flaherty seemed like a good choice, but some players and fans had been advocating "time and again," according to the *Courier-Journal*, in favor of Joe McCarthy getting the job.[1]

The team assembled for training in Dawson Springs, Kentucky. McCarthy showed some muscle soreness but quickly "rounded to," performing some "mid-season stunts" at second base in some early exhibition games. Earlier the Louisville papers had extolled McCarthy's standing as a second baseman, with discussion focusing around the question of why he was not a major leaguer. Writers pointed out that aside from the Chicago White Sox' Eddie Collins, who was past his peak anyway, there was not one outstanding second baseman in the major leagues. The overrated Johnny Evers had retired, and he was famous largely for a poem previously penned about him as part of a Chicago Cubs' double-play combination. Pittsburgh's Bill McKechnie was just about to retire. Cleveland's Billy Wambsganss and Pittsburgh's George Cutshaw were certainly solid, but not outstanding. The second basemen on the rest of the major league teams read like a list of nobodies, and the *Courier-Journal* named them explicitly: Morgan, Pratt, Gedeon, Young, Grover, Baumann, Barry, Maisel, Janvrin, Lawry, Rawlings, Niehoff, Doyle, Miller, Herzog, Pitler, Smith, Betzel, Shean, Massey, and Dugey. Surely, Louisvillians argued, the Colonels' Joe McCarthy is at least in the class of these players.

He probably was, but in April, McCarthy turned thirty-two. His weak hitting with Toledo and Indianapolis had hurt his chances when he was young. His Buffalo work perked some interest, but then came the Federal League complications. He won lots of praise in Louisville, but the war years discombobulated the significant planning of everyone in baseball management. Now it was 1919, and McCarthy was old. Thirty-two year-old men were simply not considered "prospects." The only people of that age who were given a chance at the majors were usually former big leaguers who a club in the thick of a pennant race felt could come back and provide some key contributions. While Louisvillians lamented this situation for McCarthy, their expressions of lament were also voiced as statements as to how fortunate the Colonels were. No one knew it at the time, but before the 1919 season was over, McCarthy would be contributing a lot more to Louisville baseball.[2]

The season began with Louisville needing a shortstop. Roxey Roach was gone. His replacement, Mike Ciresi, was not as good. One reporter remarked that "if Mike Ciresi had two months of preliminary training under Joe McCarthy he would fill the bill." Meanwhile, McCarthy was hitting and running well, and his fielding was winning plaudits as usual.[3] The Colonels started well, but they hit a patch of bad luck in mid–May. In one week they lost three straight extra-inning games. By May 27, they had fallen to fifth place. Meanwhile, St. Paul was running ahead of the entire Association. Shortstop was a gaping hole in the Colonels' defense. Manager Flaherty experimented, switching McCarthy to shortstop. From there into June, the Colonels played steadily, with McCarthy pulling duty at the two positions. On June 16, having run off a six-game winning streak, Louisville pulled to one and one half games behind St. Paul. Accounting for the success, the papers proclaimed: "Joe McCarthy ... is playing a great game. The value of a man like McCarthy to a team is beyond calculation. For the figures fail to record his achievements. ... McCarthy's defensive work saves many a ball game. ... McCarthy's worth is inestimable." Into mid–July, the Colonels stayed right on St. Paul's heels. On July 9 they were just percentage points behind, two up in wins but two down in losses. Then they lost four in a row, remaining in second place, but giving St. Paul more breathing room than they had had in over a month.[4]

While the Colonels' front office/field relations were much calmer than they had been in the days of Chivington and Clymer, Manager Flaherty and General Manager Neal were apparently not on the best of terms. The making of trades is often the spot where the business and field sides of baseball management duties can collide. This apparently occurred with Neal and Flaherty. Amidst such tensions, and with the team falling off a bit in the race with St. Paul, Patsy Flaherty suddenly resigned. It was a surprise to every baseball person in Louisville, but Flaherty was upbeat about it all, simply saying it was for the good of the team. On July 22, General Manager Neal announced that with Flaherty's resignation, he would appoint a new manager — Joseph Vincent McCarthy.[5]

"Of course I am pleased with my promotion," acknowledged McCarthy to the press. "How would he do with the team?" he was asked. "I am fortunate in having a good team," he nodded. "The boys can play ball and they are in there fighting every minute. I won't say that we will win the pennant, but we will be mighty close to it if we don't win it." With such a firm but careful prediction, McCarthy, having managed the one season in Wilkes-Barre, began a managing career that would last another 40 years, and in almost every one of those 40 seasons he would indeed either "win the pennant ... [or] be mighty close to it."

A child's baseball novel about a manager taking over a team at midseason might cast the club suddenly catching fire and blazing into first place. In the real baseball world, the appointment of a new manager often prompts weak teams to get into a winning spurt. Under McCarthy, however, the Colonels actually lost seven of their next ten games. McCarthy's appointment was not the cause here, for it was a popular choice with the players. They knew McCarthy had a grasp of both the game and the team. They trusted that his judgments would be sound, and indeed with the initial string of losses, there was no ensuing malaise.[6]

When things are not going well and for no apparent reason, a standard ploy for a manager is to try changing the batting order. McCarthy did a little such tinkering. Significantly, he moved himself from second to sixth in the lineup, showing his players that he was not above his own relegation. This way, as he had in Wilkes-Barre, he could also be on the bench making key moves when the heart of the order was batting. By the middle of August, the Colonels had begun winning again. They won seven of ten, on a road trip no less, and drew a bit closer to first-place St. Paul. "Manager McCarthy has his men going at full speed at present, and they are playing the best game they know how." Given the previous troubles in the Colonels' management, the *Courier-Journal* took pains to note, "Business Manager Neal did not accompany the Colonels on the trip, and they are solely under the managership of McCarthy." After the seven of ten spurt and the accompanying praise in the press, the Colonels lost their next five, however.[7]

The problems here involved injuries to several pitchers and to some starting players, including first baseman Jay Kirke and catcher Bill Meyer. Although he did not admit it until the next spring, McCarthy himself was hobbled by a "charley horse" during much of the summer. One pitcher, Frank "Lefty" Graham, quit the team claiming the wildness of the game "disheartened" him. At this point, the papers made repeated references to the team as "McCarthy's Cripples" and noted how the new manager "is in a bad way for twirlers ... and [is] forced to continue using a twirler in the outfield." Facing the final weeks of the season, the *Courier-Journal* conceded, "Repeated injuries to players have caused the Colonels to abandon hope of a pennant this season. ... McCarthy was never able to present his strongest lineup." But, they added, "McCarthy has kept his men on their toes even when the lineup was well plastered with substitutes." While some sports reporters were thus despairing, McCarthy was more positive: "We have had a lot of bad luck, but of course we have to take things as they come. The boys have played 'up to the handle' from start to finish. It is the gamest team I have ever played on. When things broke worst for us, they were not discouraged for a minute, and that spirit saved many games. Now that bad luck has cost us our chance for the pennant, we are going to fight just as hard to finish as high as we can, and it looks like third place is our goal." At that point, the Colonels' record stood at 74 and 66. At the end of the season, they record was 86 and 67. They had won twelve of their last thirteen games, including a run of ten straight, and they did it on the road. For the last few weeks of the season, McCarthy's Colonels were thus playing the best baseball in the Association. McCarthy finished third, as he had projected, and he was but two games behind second-place Kansas City, with the same number of wins. No one was going to catch St. Paul that season. They finished eight games ahead. (St. Paul lost a series to the Pacific Coast League champions, but at least it was a more honest series than the one the big leagues staged that October.)[8]

Since first managing the Colonels on July 23, McCarthy had won at a rate of 55.5 percent. He had overcome injuries and maintained the loyalty and respect of his players and fans. Billy Neal immediately rehired him for the 1920 season, a move greeted with unanimous support from all Louisville baseball people. In mid-October, after taking the Colonels on a little barnstorming tour around Kentucky and Indiana, McCarthy left Louisville for Germantown. During the winter he joined with former teammate Roxey Roach, running a string of pool halls and amusement emporiums around Philadelphia. He also made a few trips back to Louisville to confer with Neal. He was in earnest about his role as manager, and Neal quickly knew that he was working with a real pro.[9]

11

First Full Season at the Helm

In March, 1920, McCarthy took the Colonels down to Mobile, Alabama, to train for the season. Perhaps it was the memories of the rainy March and April days back in 1907, training with the Wilmington Colts, or perhaps it was the recent years training with Louisville in the cooler climates of Dawson Springs, Kentucky, but whatever the memories, McCarthy wanted to train in good weather. When teams do not train properly, he believed, they get off to slower starts and are more susceptible to injuries, and after the rash of injuries the Colonels went through in 1919, he wanted to do all he could to prevent any repetition of such misfortunes.

The Louisville squad of 1920 had several "question marks." It was, conceded the *Courier-Journal*, "not the best looking ball club in the league at this point." Louisville's best outfielder and leading hitter of 1919, Tim Hendryx, had "gone up" to the Boston Red Sox. The Red Sox had some cash, as a result of selling Babe Ruth to the Yankees that winter, and they saw Hendryx as a possible "find" to succeed Ruth. This hardly proved to be the case, and some say Boston has yet to recover. The validity of "the Curse of the Bambino" notwithstanding, the Red Sox would be a perennial second-division team for a full generation after selling Ruth. Their subsequent later rebuilding and agonizing near triumphs would ultimately involve McCarthy, but that was in the distant future. For the moment, Boston's spending was robbing his Colonels of some needed talent.[1]

Another question being asked about the Colonels concerned second base. At the end of the 1919 season, McCarthy had intimated that he would manage from the bench in 1920. Would McCarthy continue to play? His answer in the spring of 1920 was emphatic: "Me a bench manager, I should say not, 'never felt better. I expect to have one of the best playing years of my career." McCarthy was insistent that he was going to continue to play second base, and given what he had implied months before, he was a bit defensive. He went so far as verbally to single out one who may compete with him for the post: "If Bruno Betzel or any other member of the team thinks he can beat me out of my position at second base, he is badly fooled." Whether McCarthy was objectively better than Betzel, or whether a newspaper reporter or another player felt one way or the other, no one was going to say anything about it to McCarthy. This was an uncharacteristic sort of expression from McCarthy. It caused people to be hesitant, something he never liked. Rarely did he single out a player by name to the press in such a negative context. In almost every other instance, McCarthy was acutely aware of the distinction of what was fit to say before the press and public, as opposed to what was either kept within the team or strictly as a matter of one on one conversation. Here he slipped because his ego about himself as a player was still at stake. He needed to work this out, and it would take a little time.[2]

The Colonels had other problems too, little and big. Jay Kirke, always ready with an alibi or a complaint, moaned loudly about the food at the hotel in Mobile: "a fellow can't hit on grub like that." More serious was the problem of unsigned players and the meager numbers then reporting to training camp. In 1920, the constraints of the war were obviously gone. Money was now being spent on amusement and recreation. Ball players grasped that they could take advantage of the situation and hope to bargain for higher salaries. In the spring of 1920 this problem hit many major league teams, as well as some of the upper minors like Louisville. In mid–March, many of McCarthy's players remained unsigned. When it came time to have a practice game in Mobile against a local team, McCarthy arranged for the Colonels to play the Mobile YMCA — in a basketball game. "At its present make-up," he quipped, "the club undoubtedly would do better at basketball than baseball." McCarthy would never be one to sit still. As a manager he would make positive use of any situation before him, although he was hardly pleased at having to train his team on a basketball court, and he came to believe that basketball playing could be harmful in the training of a ball player, as several players pulled up with muscle strains playing "the indoor game."[3]

Once the exhibition games started, as he had firmly predicted, McCarthy played himself at second base. The sports editor of the *Courier-Journal*, Sam McMeekin, did write here: "Any hesitancy McCarthy felt at inserting himself in the lineup has been removed by the manner in which he has been playing at the training camp." Still, whenever McCarthy miscued, and it was rare, people could not help but note it. In an exhibition against a team from Akron, Ohio, McCarthy made an error which cost the team a run. Louisville won, nevertheless. That April, McCarthy managed for the first time against some major league teams. The American League champion White Sox beat him 6–3. (They played a lot better than they had against Cincinnati during the World Series.) McCarthy's team beat the Philadelphia Phillies 7–2, with McCarthy himself going two for four, including a shot to right center which center fielder Cy Williams and right fielder Casey Stengel let drop between them.[4]

With hard practices and the eventual signing of his players, McCarthy rounded his team into condition. The sports editors of the American Association city papers picked Louisville to finish second to St. Paul. Even the hometown *Courier-Journal* picked it this way, but they hastened to add: "This will be McCarthy's first real opportunity as manager of the Louisville club. When he took over last year there were too many tattered ends, and that McCarthy got them together was shown in the last string of games [12 wins in 13 games]. McCarthy is a smart ball player and a smart manager, and it is a certainty that he will get the utmost out of his club."[5]

The opening day for McCarthy had a special poignancy. It was not only his first opening day as a manager, the game was also against Columbus, and the Senators were now managed by none other than Billy Clymer. McCarthy always liked Billy, and the friendship and respect was mutual. Clymer had given McCarthy the managerial reins at Wilkes-Barre. He had brought him up to Buffalo, and he signed him at Louisville when he had nowhere to turn. Clymer, meanwhile, had a score to settle with Louisville, even though Chivington was long gone. "A triumph for McCarthy over his former mentor today," mused the *Courier-Journal*, "would not be without satisfaction." Unfortunately, it did not work out that way. Louisville lost 6–1, giving up four runs in the ninth inning. McCarthy himself committed two errors, including one during the four-run deluge in the ninth. He did beat Clymer the next day, however.[6]

In early May, McCarthy and the Colonels were 6 and 6, in third place. As expected, St. Paul had quickly taken the lead. Although he committed no more errors, McCarthy actually sat himself down for much of May, even during a series against St. Paul, and reporters noted that his replacement, former St. Louis Cardinal Bruno Betzel, "played second like Eddie Collins." McCarthy apparently felt no conflict. He had too much else to worry about. In one of the games against St. Paul, the whole Louisville team was in an uproar about an umpire's call at first base. The papers said it "looked like he called it wrong." Earlier, the umpire had apparently made two bad calls against St. Paul. McCarthy came out to argue and accused the umpire of "trying to even up," i.e., make a bad call against Louisville deliberately to make up for the earlier mistakes. McCarthy was ejected.[7] This was the first time this had happened to him. It would not be the last, although it would not happen very often.

Louisville played just under .500 ball during May. As of June 1, they were in fifth place. A key for the Colonels' mediocre showing was a lack of reliable pitching. "The season is well under way," snapped the *Courier-Journal*, "and if the management desires to be up in the running, it behooves it to get a move on and obtain a pitcher on whom McCarthy can depend to win ball games." A headline on June 11 read "What is the Matter with the Louisville Baseball Club?" McCarthy, the paper said, has been denied the authority to buy and sell players. One paper mentioned that McCarthy pointed Neal to the opportunity of acquiring Frank Gilhooly, who had been the leading hitter with Buffalo in 1915, adding that Neal had done nothing with the suggestion. As McCarthy was "little more than a field captain, [William] Neal," accused the papers, "is responsible for the show of the team." McCarthy, the paper angrily argued, "may be a good manager or a bad one, but ... he has not been given an opportunity to display his ability or lack of it in a managerial role. The players know that McCarthy is the 'flunky' ... and while he is popular with his men, their morale is not benefitted by the condition."[8] It is difficult to imagine any ball player considering Joe McCarthy to be anyone's mere flunky, but the papers were calling the Colonels' general manager and owners to task, and they were certainly giving McCarthy a little comfort room in regard to the team's early-season mediocrity. Of course, McCarthy had no comment on any of these matters.

The month of June went little better for the Colonels. On June 16, after losing three in a row, the Colonels had found themselves in last place. Bruno Betzel did run off a 19-game hitting streak, but the team played mere .500 ball (17 and 17), and this only occurred because of a decided upswing at the end of the month. Aside from two pinch-hitting roles, McCarthy played in only two games. July was little better. The team was on the road most of the month, and that made matters tougher to turn around, although Betzel did have another streak, this time of 17 games. Reporters noted that when G.M. William Neal was away, the team played better. When he went off on a scouting trip, the Colonels won four in a row. Still, the pitching corps was weak, although one pitcher, Tommy Long, threw a no-hitter against Toledo. Aside from one pitcher, McCarthy had no one hitting .300, not even Kirke. Of course, big Jay had an excuse.

Meanwhile, St. Paul had the pennant virtually locked. On July 26 they were sixteen and one half games up on second-place Indianapolis. "McCarthy's cripples," as they were again called, were out of the race in the pack with the also-rans.[9] The team seemed outclassed, and there was no help from the front office. Could Manager McCarthy work any kind of magic here?

When the Boston Red Sox acquired Tim Hendryx from Louisville they sent down an outfielder named Bill Lamar. Into the 1919 season, Lamar had been a bench player for the Yankees. He played regularly after being traded to Boston in the summer and had hopes that in 1920 he would be a Red Sox starter. Then came the Ruth and Hendryx deals, and Lamar was off to Louisville. Lamar was a solid player, and he had started most of Louisville's games that season in center field. His nickname in Boston had been "Good Time Bill," but he showed anything but that sort of personality in Louisville. He always maintained a distance from the rest of the team. He resented being sent down and felt he was above the level of the American Association. Then and later, McCarthy was never one to "rah-rah" a sulking player. Their personal emotions and lives were their own business as long as they gave their best on the ball field. Lamar seemed to do just that until a game on July 29. That day Louisville was playing St. Paul, and during the game, right fielder Roy Massey had simply told Lamar to shade a bit more his way. It was hardly a big issue. No hits had fallen in, but the little incident somehow cut Lamar to the quick. Amidst a mediocre season and in the July heat, Lamar's resentment at his "busher" teammates presuming to give him orders boiled him over. Right there in the outfield, he suddenly rushed at Massey and began fighting. The left fielder ran over and much of the Louisville team also spilled onto the field to break up the fight. McCarthy sat Lamar down, of course, but once on the bench Lamar began fighting with others. McCarthy immediately sent him to the showers. The incidents created a crazy mood among the Louisville fans. In the ninth inning, a St. Paul runner was called out at the plate, and he went after the umpire. Fans swarmed the field. The police had to restore order, and the St. Paul players had to be kept in the Colonels' owners' office until the crowd cleared.[10]

Lamar may have been a valuable player, but McCarthy knew that no one could be allowed to get away with that sort of behavior. He suspended Lamar for the season, and Lamar immediately left Louisville. (He actually broke back in with the Brooklyn Dodgers for a few games late that season. He played a few more games for Brooklyn in 1921 and then finished his career playing four seasons with the Philadelphia A's.) The next day, reporters noted how the fans cheered Roy Massey when he came to bat, how they applauded the umpire who had called the St. Paul runner out, and how "the entire team seemed to take a new lease on life after Lamar had left the line up." With Lamar gone and with Betzel hurt three days later, the team was stretched. McCarthy returned himself to the lineup, and the papers noted some "fast fielding by the manager."[11]

With Lamar gone and McCarthy back in the lineup, the Colonels snapped off three wins in a row. Still, the pitching corps remained weak. Indeed, by August 8, the team was carrying a grand total of 13 active players. On August 10, only 10 men were in uniform. Sometimes McCarthy played second base, sometimes left field. "No matter where he plays," praised the *Courier-Journal*, "McCarthy is in the game up to his ears every minute, and he never gives up until the last man is out in the final inning." The club may have been depleted by injuries and by the termination of Lamar, but, the paper went on, "every man on the club is doing his best for (Manager McCarthy), and there is not the least bit of dissension among the players. There never was," concluded the report, "a more popular leader of the Colonels than McCarthy, and he is invariably given a big hand by the fans every day. ... When a manager can get out and win ball games with such little playing material on hand, he deserves a great deal of credit."[12]

A storybook ending would have a team like Louisville going on a winning tear from there, but real world of 1920 minor league baseball was different. On August 12, McCarthy's Colonels lost to St. Paul 27–5! It could have been worse; St. Paul stopped all scoring after the fourth inning. Louisville committed seven errors. Bruno Betzel was still injured. McCarthy himself was nursing leg cramps. The pitching staff was full of sore arms. The papers continued to harp on the lack of support the team was getting from the front office. McCarthy and the Colonels actually beat St. Paul the next afternoon, but they lost three of the next four. William Neal went off to Alabama and came back with one outfielder, claiming he could find no pitchers. The papers pointed out that no less a team than the Pittsburgh Pirates went to Birmingham a week later and signed a pitcher. Their simple conclusion to Neal: "Figure it out!" McCarthy was doing all he possibly could, and the Colonels front office did announce on August 29 that McCarthy was to be retained as Louisville's manager for 1921.[13] At least Neal knew this was the right move. He may have grasped that his safety would have been in jeopardy if he had chosen to do otherwise.

No one was going to catch St. Paul that season. On September 4, they were 21 games up on second-place Minneapolis. On September 6, Louisville was still mired in sixth place with a record of 61 and 73. On September 1 they had lost another crusher, this time to Toledo, 20–5. At such a point in the season, most managers would simply "play out the string," but that was never McCarthy's nature. With Bruno Betzel returning to the lineup, Jay Kirke hitting well again, and some of the pitchers' arms coming back to life, Louisville ran off a record of 16 and 1 between September 6th and 18th. From there through the remainder of the season they went 9 and 5. McCarthy was battling all the way. On September 13, two successive pitchers for Columbus brushed him back, and after the second one flew at his head McCarthy charged the mound. His players had to cool him off. (Less than a month before, the Yankees' Carl Mays had beaned and killed Cleveland's Ray Chapman; brushbacks were never taken lightly, especially in the late summer of 1920.) In another game against Toledo, McCarthy waited for a strategic moment to call attention to the fact that the Mud Hens were batting out of order. The call killed a Toledo rally, and Louisville won. McCarthy's battling mood was infectious. Louisville finished 88–79. They had raised themselves from sixth to second place, albeit 23 games behind St. Paul who had won an incredible 115 games. No one could accuse McCarthy and the Colonels of lacking heart. As the *Courier-Journal* summarized at the season's end:

To the manager of the Colonels is accorded full credit for the finish of the club in second place. McCarthy's never-say-die spirit kept the team playing when the outlook seemed hopeless. McCarthy has won his spurs as a manager. If Louisville owners will give him absolute control of the team, local followers of the club believe they may hope for even better things next season.

The growing popularity of McCarthy and the Colonels came forth after the season too. The usual week of barnstorming turned into nearly four weeks of daily games in towns like Hazard, Campbellsville, Cynthiana, and Elizabethtown. Everybody "out back" had heard about the Colonels and their feisty little manager and were willing to turn out and watch 'em a spell. Inquiries kept coming into the Colonels' business office arranging for more and more exhibitions. Irvine, Paint Lick, Lebanon Junction, Bloomfield, Winchester, Jackson, — on and on it went. Few of the towns had hotels, so wherever they went, McCarthy and the players stayed in local homes. They were delighted with the hospitality.[14] McCarthy and the boys made a little more money than they expected, and everyone looked forward to the next season. On October 30, McCarthy officially signed his contract to manage in 1921. Surely the personnel issues would be solved. If that occurred and the team got an even break on injuries and sore pitchers' arms, how well could they play? Folks in and around Louisville figured it was "worth a look see to find out."

12

Winner

Towards the end of the 1920 season, Louisville was playing St. Paul. A St. Paul runner, Bert Ellison, was caught in a run down between first and second. Jay Kirke, Louisville's big-hitting, 54 oz. bat wielding, constantly alibi'ing, clumsy-fielding, slow-running, and even slower-thinking first baseman, had the ball. He was trying to tag Ellison. Ellison was heading for second, where McCarthy was covering. With McCarthy screaming for the ball, Kirke delayed tossing it. Then he grew panicky and finally threw the ball—extra hard and a trifle wild. The ball caromed off Ellison, hit McCarthy in the jaw, and bounced into right field, leaving the runner safe and McCarthy steamed. McCarthy later took Kirke aside and let him have it. "Why you big kraut-head," he yelled, an especially harsh and new insult of the World War I era, "what made you do a stupid thing like that? That's the dumbest play I ever saw in my life! Why didn't you give me the ball sooner?" Always one to try to shift the blame in such instances, and Kirke found himself in many of them, the large, lumbering first baseman slowly eyed McCarthy and retorted: "I guess you're right, Joe. But you know, you ain't looked so good to me yourself lately."

Many players of subsequent years who served under McCarthy would have cringed at the thought of anyone talking back to McCarthy in such a manner, but McCarthy possessed an integrity few managers ever had. Jay Kirke may not have been the brightest bulb on the tree, but he had a point, and McCarthy acknowledged it to himself, although not without a little insult of his own within his thoughts. "I knew," he mused, "that if the time had come when I didn't look good to Jay Kirke, the only thing for me to do was quit."

McCarthy certainly did not mean that he would quit baseball. What he meant was that he had to face the fact that as he was now in his mid 30s, he had to give serious thought to how effective a player he was. At the time Kirke talked back to him, he was batting .232. McCarthy did not completely hang up his glove at this point, although some have mistakenly said he did, but from then on he would only be a spot player. "Me a bench manager?" he intoned once again in the spring of 1921, "well I should say not a regular, but I'll be right there to step in at a moment's notice whenever the opportunity prevails." McCarthy would keep himself ready to play, but he was now more exclusively a manager. In retirement, forty-nine years later,

McCarthy was answering a young fan's letter. Asked "What made you quit playing and start managing?" McCarthy simply answered: "Age 35."[1]

Meanwhile, the next time Kirke learned that Joe McCarthy wanted to talk to him, this time for missing a sign, he brought along his priest: "Joe, I thought you would be glad to meet Father Monohan. He's a great admirer of yours." Kirke could be a pain, but in 1921 he knocked out 282 hits, batted .386, and struck out only three times. McCarthy knew to be flexible when he had to be, ever more so in the company of a priest.[2]

The Colonels assembled again in Mobile for spring training. This time, there was no raft of holdouts. To reporters the team appeared "just rarin' to go." They joked that McCarthy looked a little overweight. McCarthy held the team to a single three-hour workout per day. He did not like the double workout system, feeling it wore people out and risked injuries. The schedule gave the players a lot of free time, and they were largely free to do as they pleased. As would always be his way, McCarthy spent virtually no time checking up on players or enforcing hours. Their performance on the field would reveal everything he needed to know. When the hotel threw the team a free dinner on April 1, Jay Kirke missed it. McCarthy only shrugged: "looks like you missed another play, Jay." One shipping entrepreneur from Paducah, Kentucky named John O'Leary tried to bring the Colonels over to Florida for a series of exhibition games. A striking feature of his offer here was that he offered to *fly* the team over to Florida. O'Leary was obviously thinking about the publicity the flying would bring to the games he was staging. McCarthy was all for it. He would later have misgivings about flying during the regular season, but at this point in his career, he was willing to "stretch." Meanwhile, the Colonels' General Manager William Neal was not so sure, and the flying plans fell through. The Colonels did play a few games in Pensacola, but they traveled by train. O'Leary and his Pensacola colleagues knew what they were doing in their promotion efforts, as the next season, the Colonels would hold their spring training there.[3]

As the 1921 season was approaching, American Association followers were predicting a closer fight for the pennant. Two stars of the 1920 St. Paul Saints— Goldie Rapp and Bubbles Hargrave — had left for the major leagues. Still, a consensus of the Association's sports writers picked St. Paul. With its strong finish in 1920, Louisville was picked for second, and two of the poll's writers had picked them for first. One was from Milwaukee and the other was not from Louisville but from St. Paul! That writer knew something about the Saints, as well as about McCarthy. McCarthy also mentioned that he did not think St. Paul would be able to run away with the pennant as they had in 1920. He would rarely make such preseason statements to the press.[4]

In preseason exhibitions, McCarthy's Colonels defeated the Boston Braves and the Pittsburgh Pirates. On opening day, McCarthy again faced Billy Clymer, who was now managing the Toledo Mud Hens. The friendship was still there, but the moment had far less teacher-pupil tonality now. McCarthy not only won the opener this time, he swept the four game series. The team's good start continued against Columbus. Here McCarthy's sly thinking played a major role. Two players on the Columbus Senators had been batting out of order. McCarthy could have called the matter immediately, but he waited until it was useful. The game was tied and went into extra innings. In the tenth inning, Columbus had one run in, two men on, and two out. The out-of-order batter stepped in, and as soon as he did McCarthy brought the line-up card to the umpire. The batter was immediately ruled out. A smirking Louisville team scored two runs in the bottom of the inning to win. "When it comes to brain work," chortled the *Courier-Journal*, "you sure have to hand it to Joe."[5]

The Colonels started the season fast, but in May they settled into "the pack," as a few players came down with minor injuries. McCarthy had to fill in at shortstop and second base in several games. He had to do so again in June when Bruno Betzel went out, this time not with an injury but because he punched an umpire.[6] Ever more, McCarthy was recognizing the destructiveness that comes to teams with players that lose their heads. The Lamar incident of the previous summer was an obvious example, but whenever people crossed a line beyond a rhubarb or being sent to the showers for the day, McCarthy felt it was completely unnecessary. Increasingly, he idealized players who, over and above their talents, never beat themselves mentally.

While Louisville had settled into the pack in early 1921, the difference in this season was that most of the Association was part of "the pack." As a few insiders had suspected, St. Paul was not so strong this year. They started the season 4 and 12. By early June, hapless Columbus was in the cellar, but otherwise only three games separated first-place Indianapolis from seventh-place Milwaukee. Everyone was in contention. For the first three weeks of June, Louisville had an extended home stand. It was an opportune time for a winning streak, and the team came through. Minneapolis kept pace with Louisville, but no other team could. By June 25, the Millers and the Colonels had opened a five-game lead over the rest of the Association. The next day McCarthy inserted himself as a pinch-hitter in the bottom of the tenth inning in a game with Toledo. He knocked in the winning run. He tried the same thing the next day and struck out, but Louisville won anyway, and with the win, they were in first place by themselves. The fans were ecstatic. Louisville had the best attendance in the Association. When the league held a special exhibition game to raise money for the widow of an AA umpire who had suddenly died that spring, they held the game in Louisville, so confident were they of the fans' enthusiasm. The game raised $1085.10.[7]

One afternoon, Bruno Betzel stroked a double to right field. Betzel legged the smash into a triple, and as he was speeding around second, a woman jumped up in the stands and yelled "Ride, Mooney, Ride!" (A jockey named Roy Mooney was booting home a lot of winners at Churchill Downs that summer.) Her cheer caught on, and "Ride, Mooney, Ride!" became a war cry in Louisville that summer as the Colonels continued to stretch their lead. In a big series with Minneapolis in mid–July, Louisville won four of five. This pushed their league lead to seven games. Life looked great, but McCarthy then learned, or relearned, the lesson of being too confident. He lost five of six to Kansas City and two of three to Milwaukee. In the final game with Milwaukee, he was up 7–1 in the eighth inning and still lost. At the beginning of August, Louisville was still in first place, but they were only a game up. In subsequent years, whenever he was managing a team that was running out front, McCarthy always guarded against complacency. He knew that mid summer leads were not safe, and that any mood of celebration can render the status yet more fleeting. Louisville's July spin was hardly the first, let alone the only lesson here for him here, but it was the first time he experienced it as a manager.[8]

In addition to getting bad breaks or becoming too confident, other factors such as injuries can bring a team down quickly. Louisville righted itself with some key wins in August against Minneapolis. They continued to hold a narrow lead. Then second baseman Bruno Betzel went down with a broken ankle, and he was gone for the season. McCarthy filled in. This time, the Colonels' front office stepped up too. They picked up Charley "Buck" Herzog to shore up the infield. Herzog had thirteen years of major league experience. He was two years older than McCarthy, but McCarthy felt anything but peeved or threatened by the move. He was the manager and was seeing his role in just that context.[9]

On August 15, he New York Yankees came to Louisville for an exhibition game. This was a normal occurrence in major league seasons, an opportunity for teams to pick up a little extra money during travel dates. The Yankees had yet to win a championship, but they now had a decided aura because of the presence of Babe Ruth. McCarthy had only seen Ruth when he pitched for the Orioles back in 1914. Ruth, of course, had been converted into an outfielder in 1919. In 1920, after being traded to New York, he had romped through an incredible season, and in 1921 he was in the midst of completing an even better one. Ruth's 1920–21 consecutive season slugging percentages of .847 and .846 and home run marks of 54 and 59 marked a two-year power pace that few would ever even approach. Beyond his on-field exploits, Ruth had become a media idol, not only like no other in baseball, but like virtually no other in cinema, other sports, music, politics or anything else. So powerful was his charisma, when he and the Yankees came to Louisville, it seemed the whole town had turned out. Ruth toured the city, and thousands followed him. He paid a touching visit to St. Xavier's College and its Louisville Industrial School, a Louisville counterpart to the St. Mary's School he had had to attend in Baltimore. When it came time for the ball game, a record 12,081 paid to get into Eclipse Park, and hundreds of kids climbed over the fences as well. McCarthy was certainly impressed with it all, but not enough to affect his managing, as the Colonels won the day 3–1. But the bigger issue was a sense of the new excitement that Ruth had brought to the game in the new era that *was* baseball and America in the 1920s. McCarthy still had hopes to make it to the big leagues, not as a player anymore, and the sense of what that big time was like was made all the more real to him as he and the Colonels entertained Ruth that day in August. Meanwhile, the next morning it was back to the pennant race in the American Association.[10]

After the Yankee game, McCarthy and the Colonels would leave Louisville for a full 30-day road trip. Some said part of the reason they were able to lead the other clubs in much of the summer was that they had the longest home stands. Could Louisville hold its lead on the grind of the minor league road circuit? Up to Chicago they shared the train with Ruth and the Yankees. Ruth cavorted; McCarthy kept to himself. The Yankees disembarked in Chicago, while the Colonels proceeded onto Milwaukee and St. Paul. Here they split each series evenly, and the standings remained unchanged between Louisville and Minneapolis. Then the Colonels headed over to Minneapolis for a key series with the Millers. They lost the first game, and McCarthy protested that the Millers were using an illegal player they had just picked up from the White Sox. The question was how late in the season can Association teams use discarded major leaguers. League President Thomas Hickey ruled the Millers' player eligible. McCarthy may have lost that round, but he certainly showed his players and his opposition that he was leaving no stone unturned.

The Colonels' bad luck did not stop with the one loss in Minneapolis. The night after that loss, McCarthy went down with an attack of ptomaine poisoning. McCarthy's first-string catcher, Bill Meyer, managed in his absence for one game, one which the Colonels lost too. Against advice, McCarthy came back for the next game, and perhaps his presence reversed his players' anxieties over losing. Whatever the cause, Louisville won that day 15–1; they won the next day too. In the final game of the series, Louisville was down 4–2 in the eighth inning. They came through with three runs to win. McCarthy held forth to the press: "Tell the folks back home we'll win the pennant. ... The fight is still on," he said, "but the Colonels from now on must be considered heavy favorites." McCarthy was always careful in his statements to the press, and such boasting was then not mere braggadocio. McCarthy wanted to sustain the confidence of his team and put a little extra pressure at the right moment on his rivals. At this point in the season he had no more games in Minneapolis. For the rest of the trip he faced lower teams, who could perhaps be intimidated. Meanwhile, Minneapolis could do nothing directly about McCarthy's comment but snarl to themselves, and perhaps be thrown a bit off their game as a result.[11]

Louisville began the road trip two up on Minneapolis, and that was how it stood when the road trip was over. Back home, the Colonels did not falter. On September 19, Minneapolis came to town four games down, eager to even things up. Louisville took the first two games, at which point the papers started to dare using the word "pennant." Minneapolis won the final game and kept their hopes up, but they next went up to Indianapolis where they lost a doubleheader. The same day, September 25th, Louisville swept St. Paul. The pennant belonged to the Colonels. Manager Joe McCarthy had won his first championship.[12]

Several Louisville pitchers had had excellent seasons. Jay Kirke had batted .386 with 282 hits. The papers noted all this, but most of the praise went to McCarthy. With all the injuries in 1919 and 1920, McCarthy proved that he could take a struggling team and win. He did the same thing in Wilkes-Barre in 1913. Some managers are good at propping up weak teams, usually for but a short time (then their pressuring ways usually burns a team out). In 1921, McCarthy proved he could manage a winner. Reporters wrote of the fighting spirit he instilled in his players. More specifically, they noted the "inside baseball" the Colonels played under McCarthy. Their fielding was tight. Outfielders always hit the cutoff man. Infielders made double plays at key moments. Few baserunning errors wiped out good hits. Such a pattern indicated not only a smart manager, but one who could infuse that intelligence into his players. It was all apparent to the astute observer, and they lauded McCarthy accordingly. On October 1, Louisville held a big parade for the Colonels. Thousands marched, and anyone who gussied up a car could drive in the parade. One thousand decorated automobiles toured the city that night. (After clinching the pennant, Louisville actually had six more games to play, and they lost five of them.)[13]

The season did not end for the Colonels with the winning of the American Association pennant, and it was more than mere October barnstorming that lay ahead. The Baltimore Orioles, champions of the International League, were awaiting them to play the "Little World Series." The Orioles were an excellent team. They had shocked St. Paul in the 1920 series, defeating them 5 games to 1. In 1921 the Orioles compiled a record of 119 and 47. (With 100 wins to its credit, Rochester had come in second, 19 games behind, probably the greatest margin of loss for any baseball team in triple figures.)

The clash of Louisville and Baltimore had an added edge for some, as these were two teams that before 1900 had been in the National League. Such efforts to convey a major league appearance were then all part of the hype, and it certainly drew fan interest. Baltimore seemed full of confidence. The Orioles owner/president/manager, Jack Dunn, was boasting that "victory was sure," although insiders admitted that he was not taking Louisville the least bit lightly. One reporter for the *Baltimore Sun* sniffed at the Colonels: "A good pitcher having one of his effective days can make the [American Association] leaders at times look very cheap." Another stuck in a few other digs, which the Louisville papers reprinted: "Buck Herzog is the real brains of the team. Kirke at first base is a big fellow with no brains. Ballenger at shortstop is [also] one of this species. ... The outfield cannot be compared with the 1920 St. Paul trio." Still, one Baltimore scribe did state the Orioles "will be meeting a club that is superior to the 1920 St. Paul team." Baltimore had excellent team speed. They had a brilliant all-around player named Jack Bentley who played first base and outfield, hit well, and had an 11–1 record as a pitcher. They also had three other pitchers who had each won more than twenty games, including their ace Jack Ogden, who had won 32, plus a twenty-one year old fastball whiz from Maryland named "Robert Groves." He would, of course, be soon known as Lefty Grove. McCarthy, meanwhile, was not to be outdone when it came to pre-series propaganda. "We are just as confident of winning the series from Baltimore as we were of finishing first in the American Association this season. My players never talked of anything but pennant all season, and now all you can hear them say is 'beat the Orioles.' I am positive that I have the best club and will prove it in the coming series."[14]

McCarthy certainly proved to be right in game one. A silent film actress, Hope Hampton, attended the game in Louisville. She was in town for a stage appearance and was specially invited to the game by the Colonels. In New York, Babe Ruth considered her good luck, as he once had his picture taken with her before a game and then went out and hit two home runs. She wrote that "the Louisville boys seem to possess as much snap and vim as the Yankees." As for McCarthy, she added after meeting him, "Manager McCarthy's roguish smile ... seemed to carry with it a sort of determination and tenacity which made me feel as though he was pretty confident that his team would come out on top."[15] Miss Hampton was quite perceptive.

Bob Groves started for the Orioles. Two days before the game, Groves had been hit on the ankle by a line drive during a team practice. Whether or not that was a factor, his start in game one of the series for the Orioles proved ineffective. After Louisville touched him for five runs in the third inning, Dunn yanked him. In the next inning, Buck Herzog was on third. McCarthy had noticed the long, deliberate windup of the new Orioles pitcher, Harry Frank, and he signaled Herzog to steal home when Frank went into a full windup. Herzog was safe at home, the Orioles were demoralized, and Louisville won 16–1. "I am surprised at the ease with which we whipped the Birds," McCarthy acknowledged, "but not at the fact that we won the game."[16]

In game two, thirty-two game winner Jack Ogden "lived up to his reputation," as the *Courier-Journal* conceded. But it was not an easy win. McCarthy started Cherokee Indian Ben Tincup (actress Hope Hampton absolutely adored his name). The game was simply a pitchers' duel, one which Ogden won 2–1. The Orioles' two runs came via a critical error by Buck Herzog. In the last of the ninth inning, the Colonels had a runner on. Ben Tincup, an excellent hitter, cracked a hard liner to center. The Orioles center fielder raced for it and leaped to grab it as it was about to clear the fence. If he caught it, the game was Baltimore's; if he missed it, the Colonels had another win. It was the first game Tincup lost all year.[17]

McCarthy's team was not the least bit discouraged with the tough loss in game two. They had stood toe to toe with the Orioles' ace and, but for an uncontrollable break, had the game as easily as not. The next day they turned around and pounded Baltimore pitching to win 14–8. The Series had been organized for eight games (with an extra game in case of a tie). The first four were to be in Louisville; the rest in Baltimore. Louisville's management had decided upon an unusual ploy in the selling of tickets. Believing that interest in the Series was sufficiently keen, they sold passes only for all four games, no single-game sales, not even if someone who bought one four-game pass wanted a few other single tickets for friends. This did not sit well with the fans, who felt their enthusiasm was being exploited. The result was that attendance at the first three games was light — merely 3253 on opening day, 3,209 at game two, and 2,957 at the third. The Baltimore papers criticized this, adding that most of the fans in the "race horse town" read the daily race forms as assiduously as they watched the ball game. For the city's final game, the Colonels' management changed the ticket rule. They obviously had no choice, although no one could figure out why they did not do it sooner. Allowing single-ticket sales on the final day, attendance more than doubled to 6569, but the legacy of management's ticket gambit had left a bitter taste, and the crowd at game four seemed most unruly. Since they felt they were being regarded as a lower-class bunch, the fans would act accordingly.[18]

As the Colonels did not play well in the fourth game (the Orioles won 12–4), the crowd's unruliness grew more obvious as the game progressed. In the fourth inning, shortstop Tim Ballenger protested a strike call. The umpire ejected him. Then, oddly, he allowed Ballenger to return. This gave the fans an even greater sense of entitlement as to how they should and could bend customs and do more than merely watch the game. In the Colonels' half of the fifth, with two out and a man on second, the batter hit one down the third base line. The Orioles third baseman, Fritz Maisel, fielded it but then threw wildly. Only after the throw did the field umpire rule the ball to be foul. Again the fans started jeering loudly. After another disputable call in the seventh inning, the fans out in the bleachers stormed the field, causing a ten-minute delay. Then all hell broke loose in the Baltimore half of the ninth. Baltimore was already way ahead, in part, the fans felt, due to the umpires' calls. With two men on base, the Orioles' next batter appeared to swing at a 3 and 2 offering. The umpire awarded him a walk. With the bases loaded, the next batter singled, scoring two. With the score 11–4, the Baltimore batter hit a grounder and was ruled safe on a close play at first. Another run scored, and the fans erupted. Seat cushions and soda bottles began flying all over the field. Players on both teams rushed for cover. Fans began to spill onto the field amidst not-so-humorous yells of "kill the umpire." McCarthy ran onto the field and rushed to the side of the two umpires. He escorted them through the dugout to a safe place. (One of the umpires, Bill McGowan, would later umpire in the American League when McCarthy was with the Yankees. "Whenever I meet Joe off the ball field," McGowan noted in 1938, "he usually takes his hat off, wipes his brow, and says: 'Hey, Mac, will you ever forget that Baltimore game in Louisville?' All I can ever reply is 'You're asking me?'")

With the riot, officials of the two leagues immediately declared the game to be over. It was officially recorded a 9–0 forfeit in favor of the Orioles. The *Courier-Journal* lamented the whole catastrophe as a "shameful spectacle [which] will stay a long time as a blemish on Louisville sportsmanship."

McCarthy was chagrined at the whole affair. The ticket sale controversy had nothing to do with his job. Mediocre umpiring always infuriated him, but he knew how to handle it (generally). He had now an ever more fulsome sense of how the game of baseball should be managed; if he could only get to a place where it could be done the way he wanted. He had held major league aspirations as a player. Now he was forming them as a manager.[19]

Tied two games to two, the teams headed to Baltimore. The Baltimore papers warned their fans that they were going to "see a smart ball club in action." McCarthy told them, "I am confident my club will win the series." Louisville reporters made light of the Baltimore stadium's small dimensions. They laughed that Jay Kirke would hit 75 home runs if he played in Baltimore. In game five, however, Kirke did little, and Jack Ogden was again strong for Baltimore as they won 10–5. Louisville's Ben Tincup won the next game, however, beating Bob Groves 3–0. The seventh game was the best of the series, with Louisville winning 7 to 6. During the game the booing Baltimore fans proved just as dissatisfied with the umpires as their counterparts had been in Louisville. Even the odd calls that went in Baltimore's favor drew derision, a further indication of just how poor the umpiring was that McCarthy was enduring. Up by a run in the ninth, Louisville again faced the Orioles' Jack Ogden, this time in relief. Ogden set the Colonels down 1-2-3, but the Orioles failed in the bottom half, and the day belonged to McCarthy. In what proved to be the final day of the series, the eighth game was anti-climactic. Louisville won easily 11–5 and took the Series championship. In Baltimore, McCarthy received over 100 telegrams of congratulations from fans in Louisville and from all the managers of the American Association. On the train back from Baltimore, the Colonels treated McCarthy and the team to a six-course banquet.[20]

Catcher Bill Meyer was given much praise after the series. The speedy Orioles were held to only two stolen bases in the whole series. Kirke, Meyer, and others had hit well. But, gloated the *Courier-Journal*: "To Joe McCarthy goes the credit of winning the series." McCarthy's "shrewd headwork," the Louisville reporter went on, "proved the undoing of the Oriole contingent." McCarthy had used a youngster named Tommy Gaffney as a first base coach because he was good at needling opposing pitchers. It worked, especially against young Bob Groves. McCarthy's leadership had steadied the team after such debacles as the riot of game four. Most of all, McCarthy had been smart about his pitching choices. From all about the minor league rumor mills McCarthy had heard talk that the Orioles murdered right handed pitchers but could not hit lefties. "I was badly informed as to the strength of Baltimore [against right vs. left-handed pitching]. When I saw [righty] Tincup throw past the batters, I knew."[21] As players, reporters, and fans would come to know ever more, whenever Mr. McCarthy "knew" something from his own observation, he *knew* it. While some would see this manifest itself as arrogance, what he actually had was a supremely secure sense of his own powers of discernment. He kept his own counsel, and when he made a decision, no matter any tide of opinion against it, he had no second thoughts. McCarthy's successes led his players more and more to have complete confidence in his judgments, and the sense that they were operating with a special knowledge and insight behind them provided a further boost to morale and planted seeds of doubt in the opposition. This was one of McCarthy's special gifts as a manager, one that could not be simply copied. It was a product of all facets of his powers of intellect, memory, knowledge, discernment, and character. Back in Louisville the Market Street Merchants' Association presented McCarthy with a cup. On it they inscribed: "With best wishes to a fighting leader of a fighting team."[22] No mere manual for managers can earn someone such gifts. With McCarthy's victory, some major league teams began to take more serious note of his talents.

13

Ups and Downs

McCarthy stayed in Louisville for a few weeks, enjoying the town's many celebrations after winning the Little World Series Championship over Baltimore. Here McCarthy, in a somewhat grandiose state to be sure, held forth with his "Ten Commandments of Baseball." So popular were McCarthy and the Colonels among Kentuckians that copies of the Commandments were printed by the thousands. While McCarthy did not always follow the ninth, the Commandments resonated well among baseball people, as well as among church and community leaders; pap, to be sure, but useful in their simplicity, especially with children:[1]

1. Nobody ever became a ballplayer by walking after a ball.
2. You will never become a .300 hitter unless you take the bat off your shoulder.
3. An outfielder who throws back of a runner is locking the barn after the horse is stolen.
4. Keep your head up and you may not have to keep it down.
5. When you start to slide S-L-I-D-E. He who changes his mind may have to change a good leg for a bad one.
6. Do not alibi on bad hops. Anybody can field the good ones.
7. Always run them out. You can never tell.
8. Do not quit.
9. Do not find too much fault with the umpires. You cannot expect them to be as perfect as you are.
10. A pitcher who hasn't control hasn't anything.

McCarthy was the toast of Louisville after the 1921 championship. His Commandments added a regal sense to the hoopla. Louisville had a vibrant stage and screen life in the early 1920s, and the now celebrated McCarthy added to the life here. That October, McCarthy was a regular attendee at the Fountain Ferry Theater, the National, and McCauley's, as he had been during the baseball season whenever the schedule permitted. Joe McCarthy did not have many diversions or hobbies. The cliche fit: Baseball was his life. Musical theater was a joy for him, nevertheless. Friends said he knew the tunes and lyrics of many of the era's show tunes as well as he knew most opponents' batting averages. He loved the stage, and the theater managers loved his presence, especially that fall as ticket sales likely went up. Later in the fall, McCarthy returned to Germantown, but he was still paying visits to Buffalo, more than ever.

In February of 1922, Joe married Elizabeth Lakeman, the woman he'd met back when he played for the Buffalo Bisons in 1914 and 1915. They were married in Buffalo in a modest family gathering. (Some sources listed Mrs. McCarthy's birth name as "McCave," but the Louisville papers, who McCarthy told of the nuptials, quoted her name as "Lakeman," as did the Buffalo newspapers fifty years later in her obituary. Mrs. McCarthy once wrote of her father being a descendent of the McCave family, and there was the confusion.) The Louisville papers did not even learn of the marriage until McCarthy told them at the beginning of spring training. "Babe," as Joe would always call her, and this had absolutely nothing to do with Babe Ruth, had strong ties to her family and to the Buffalo community in which she lived. Thereafter with Babe, Joe would spend virtually all of his off-season months in Buffalo. They settled in amidst Babe's family and friends and began to search for a suitable permanent home, eventually purchasing a house on Gates Circle in a residential neighborhood in downtown Buffalo. They would live there for over 20 years. They would later buy land outside Buffalo, build a home, and spend the rest of their years in the Buffalo area. The marriage would last until Babe's death parted them in 1971. They had no children. While Joe was managing in Louisville, they leased a home on the corner of 20th Street and Broadway. In Louisville, Mrs. McCarthy apparently enjoyed the theater nearly as much as her husband.[2]

With purchasing a home on his mind, McCarthy dickered with the Colonels about a new contract. At this time, the Colonels management was itself in a bit of flux. Earlier, the team's former sole owner, Otha Wathen, had sold one-sixth of the club to another bourbon distiller, William E. Knebelkamp, the original blender of "Old Grand-Dad" Bourbon. In the off season, Mr. Wathen sold $8/15$ of the club, a controlling interest, to Knebelkamp. (To underscore the unity here, Knebelkamp actually named his newly born son Wathen Knebelkamp.) In addition to having the purchase of a home on his mind, McCarthy may have wanted to start off strongly with his new chief and thus made an issue of salary. He and Knebelkamp tussled a bit over salary specifics. As of March 1, when the newspapers began to write of spring training and the coming of a new baseball season, they noted that McCarthy had yet to sign his 1922 contract. This certainly perked fan interest. McCarthy wanted $6,000 a season. Knebelkamp first offered him $4,500, with an additional $500 if he continued to play as well as manage. (At the top of the major leagues at that time, Rogers Hornsby was making $25,000 with the St. Louis Cardinals that year; Babe Ruth made $32,000 with the Yankees.) Salary scales of subsequent generations make such issues as McCarthy's seem so utterly absurd. Nonetheless, McCarthy and Knebelkamp squared off, but they settled amicably. McCarthy signed his new $5,000 contract on March 7, 1922.[3]

Having been effectively courted by Kentucky-born businessmen in Pensacola the previous winter, McCarthy and the Colonels did their 1922 spring training in Pensacola, Florida. With Knebelkamp now in charge, reporters noted a changed tone in the running of the ball club. The meddlesome power of William Neal, who had driven Billy Clymer to Seattle several years before and who had appeared to stymie some of McCarthy's effectiveness in 1919 and 1920, had all been curbed. "It is said," declared the *Courier-Journal*, "that no player is added to the Louisville club without the sanction of Joe McCarthy." Neal apparently handled the details of the trades, but McCarthy had full initiating and veto power. Neal had thus become more purely a business manager. McCarthy was in charge of all things baseball, and during spring training, Knebelkamp announced to the press that McCarthy could stay as manager of Louisville as long as he wanted. Such control and expressions of confidence certainly pleased McCarthy, but it came with a price. He now had to review lots of correspondence, some of which was downright idiotic. Many young men wrote asking for tryouts, for example. One pitcher wrote that he could throw a great spitball — "dry or wet." Another offered a tip on the greatest outfield prospect in the Western League — the young man was playing in Chattanooga. The job of batboy was open, and McCarthy actually had to review fifty applications. When Frank Robinson became the manager of the Cleveland Indians in 1975, he said that one of the unpleasant surprises of the job concerned the amount of paper work he found himself doing. McCarthy could have warned him. The days, and the nights, were long. Meanwhile, of course, McCarthy could never pull himself away from any of the field activities that were central to running a ball club. Anyone with arm trouble was to report to McCarthy immediately. Every day in practice he would be on the field running with the team to make sure no one loafed, and he hit grounder after grounder to infielders as they incessantly practiced the double play under his watchful eye. "McCarthy," complimented one reporter, "is everywhere on the ball field." He still planned to play in some games too: "While I am no longer a player-manager with the Colonels, I am far from being all in, " he commented. "I still believe I am good for a few more years as an active player."[4]

The decision to train in Pensacola was one of the last major decisions that General Manager Neal made before Knebelkamp took over the club. It proved anything but a good legacy. With the order that anyone with a sore arm was to report to the manager, McCarthy found a lot of people reporting to him. Pensacola's Maxent Park was sufficiently close to the Gulf of Mexico that it was often swept by stiff breezes. This caused many players, especially the pitchers, to get chills while working out. In addition to the sore arm problem, the highly sandy nature of the Park's infield slowed ground balls and blunted attempts at fast fielding practice. It caused a different paced game than the Colonels wanted or would play in the Association. In addition to these troubles, Bruno Betzel's ankle, broken in August of 1921, was still giving him trouble. It may have healed improperly. To top it all, on the night of March 29th, someone broke into the Colonels' clubhouse and stole most of the team's mitts and bats, including Jay Kirke's huge 54 oz. club. McCarthy was anything but pleased with the camp, and the Colonels did not return to Pensacola. By the time the team left Florida on April 2, the *Courier-Journal* lamented that, with the possible exception of Toledo, the Colonels were in "the worst shape of any club in the American Association."[5]

There was one bit of good news out of spring training. This involved the play of one rookie, a native of Richmond, Kentucky named Earle Combs, who had just graduated from Eastern Kentucky State Normal School. McCarthy was very impressed with him, although he did try to work on the rookie's habit of hopping in the air as he caught a fly ball. This, he said, slowed the boy's ability to return the ball quickly to the infield. Combs' early moments in practice under McCarthy's eye illustrate both the force of personality which McCarthy could already bring to the field, and the confidence he had in his own judgment of a prospect's potential. "The first day," Combs recalled,

> he put me in center field. I was so nervous. I could hardly see straight and I muffed the first ball that was hit to me. Joe never said a word to me when I went to the bench at the end of the inning, and he didn't say a word when, a couple of innings later, I booted a single into a couple of extra bases for the hitter. Finally in the 8th inning, with the score tied and a couple of men on the bases, a hitter singled to center. As I saw the ball coming to me, I said to myself, "I will stop this ball if it kills me." Well it didn't kill me. But it went through my legs to the fence. As I went after it, I was tempted to keep right on going, climb the fence and not stop running until I got back to Pebworth [Kentucky]. But I couldn't do that. I had to get the ball, throw it in, finish out the game, and then go to the club house and get dressed. But my mind was made up. I was through. If McCarthy didn't fire me, I'd quit.
>
>   He didn't say anything to me until I reached the clubhouse after the game. I guess he could tell how I felt by the way I looked. He came over to me and said: "Forget it. I told you today you were my center fielder. You still are." And then he laughed and said: "If I can stand it, I guess you can." I think I can say that from that moment on I was a ball player.[6]

Combs proved to be what would later be called "a McCarthy kind of player." He talked of nothing but baseball. "He would," noted one reporter, "rather get a solid base knock than a love letter from his girl in Richmond." (He would marry her that October, nevertheless.) As for a solid base hit, Combs himself said: "My that's a great and glorious feeling." Combs proved to be McCarthy's best "find" in Louisville. The Colonels had picked up an outfielder named Lyman Lamb from the St. Louis Browns. As a former major leaguer, Lamb certainly seemed like a good bet to play solidly in the outfield. After Combs had worked out a few weeks, McCarthy cancelled the Lamb deal with the Browns.[7]

    With the less than satisfying spring training behind them, McCarthy and the Colonels proceeded to lose most of their preseason games and this, said one reporter in hindsight, "took the edge off their confidence and they never regained the snap that characterized the play of their championship year."[8] Warily they faced their opening day contest against Minneapolis. They were the defending champion, but they hardly felt like it, and no one was picking them to repeat. They lost the first game in 11 innings and completed the month of April with a decidedly mediocre record of 7 and 7. With all the sore arms from Florida, the pitching was definitely lacking, and the team, said one reporter, appeared generally to "have not hit their stride." As early as May 7, the usually positive *Courier-Journal* was blunt: "The Colonels don't look like pennant winners." By the middle of May, Louisville was playing below .500. Only Toledo had a worse record. On May 17, the Colonels scheduled a ceremony to hoist their 1921 pennant. Baseball Commissioner Kenesaw Mountain Landis was supposed to attend. For the seventh-place Colonels, it all seemed rather distant and hollow. Fittingly, it rained that afternoon, and the ceremony was postponed. Jay Kirke was batting .381, and Earle Combs was batting .462, but there was little else to rejoice.

When the pennant ceremony was finally held in June, its meaninglessness was even more pointed. They lost that day to Milwaukee, and by that juncture in the season the *Courier-Journal* could only toss it off with a de-articled shrug of a headline: "Flag raising precedes usual local defeat." When rain held up another June game, the paper dryly commented that for the crowd at the park, "an hour and ten minute wait with the team idle is the least of what they have had to endure recently."[9]

In mid July, the team ran off a surprising eight-game win streak. Then they went on the road and won ten of their next eleven. But as quickly as they rose, in late July the Colonels went 3 and 15 and returned to seventh place. Even Combs' batting average fell from .462 to .329. (Big league scouts did not lose interest, however.) Such a frustrating season will strain anyone's patience, even Joe McCarthy's. He had before never witnessed such an epidemic of lame pitching arms, and he certainly grew determined not to let that happen again. During a (losing) doubleheader with Toledo, McCarthy's frustrations got the better of him. The Mud Hens pitcher turned to pick off a Louisville runner at first. When he turned, he found no fielder at the base, so he stopped and, in a second motion, strangely rolled the ball to first. The pitcher must have somehow thought that this would save him from a balk call — and on this day it actually did! McCarthy was never one to get agitated often, but he would when the situation involved a hard and fast rule rather than a matter of judgment. "Fathead" was one of his favorite words in such situations. Since the pitcher's first gesture had not resulted in a throw to first, it was a balk. McCarthy was absolutely right, and he spent the rest of the afternoon being right — in the clubhouse. The umpire, meanwhile, was hit by "a fusillade of cushions, pop bottles, and lemons." Unlike the previous October's Oriole-game riot, McCarthy did not lift a finger to aid the umpire this time. He just trudged to the showers. The umpire endured more cushions at the end of the game too. Such are the frustrations of an abysmally losing season. No one was hurt in the melee.[10]

At the outset of the season, hopeful Colonels fans wondered about the quirk in the schedule which had Louisville playing its last home game on September 2 and being on the road for the entire last month of the season. What would this do to their pennant chances? By the time September 2 actually arrived, most folks were relieved. Playing out the string on the road, some games were nearly cancelled due to poor attendance. Some days reminded people of Billy Clymer's arrival at the park in 1918 and finding no one there because the Association had closed for the duration of the war. At one game at Toledo, 600 people came, and that was an afternoon when ladies were admitted free! The Colonels completed the season in sixth place with a record of 77 and 91. McCarthy later wrote: "That year I got a few more grey hairs."[11] After the season finale in St. Paul, McCarthy did not even return to Louisville. The Colonels barnstormed without him. McCarthy headed straight to Germantown, and Babe met him there. They visited McCarthy's family and then went to Buffalo. No other Joe McCarthy-managed club would ever play below .500 or fail to finish in the league's first division. If McCarthy did not already fully grasp the value of good training and the heading off of injuries, he sure did now.

During the off-season, several changes occurred for the Colonels. In October, they traded Jay Kirke to Indianapolis. Kirke was thirty-four, and with the lousy 1922 season, an emphasis on youth certainly seemed in order. McCarthy never commented, but it is possible that Kirke's less-than-heady brand of baseball was not to his liking. Certainly the Colonels must have figured that his still considerable batting prowess (.355 in 1922) would be valuable in trade and best be used before it was too late. It proved a good move, although for sad reasons, as early into the next season with Indianapolis Kirke fractured his wrist and never played well again.[12] The other major event of the off season was that the grandstand at Eclipse Park, from which Louisvillians had watched the playing of Honus Wagner, Fred Clarke, Rube Waddell, and Joe McCarthy, was razed by fire in the wee hours of the morning of November 20. A carelessly discarded cigarette was the probable cause. The new park, which was to be called Parkway Field, would take some time to complete. With the money needed for the construction, less could be spent on spring training, so the Colonels were once again relegated to do their March work in nearby Dawson Springs. This all surrounded manager McCarthy's pre-season planning with a lot of "ifs."[13]

In March and early April, Dawson Springs, Kentucky cannot be depended upon to have good weather. 1923 proved no exception. The day that the Colonels arrived there a thunderstorm not only cancelled practice, it damaged the ball field. For the next month, rainy days cancelled practice after practice. Aside from having more time to hone his skills at the harmonica, which he played both in his hotel room as well as in the lobby, McCarthy just had to sit through it like everyone else. Indoor calisthenics and running amidst puddles on the road was about all he could organize. The team moved to the town of Maysville. There they were hit by more rain. The bad luck with the weather, of course, made everyone remember the ill fortunes of the previous season.[14]

Kansas City and St. Paul were the writers' picks for the Association championship that April, but Louisville surprised everyone that month. Their new park was not to open until May 1, so their first weeks of the season were all on the road. After the first 10 days, their record stood at 7 and 1, although the one loss was by a score of 15–2. The fact that they could endure such a loss yet bounce back was itself a good sign as to the team's toughness, as well as of McCarthy's leadership. When the team returned to Louisville, the opening of Parkway Field was a major event. It always works well in Louisville to have any such celebration occur around the time of the Kentucky Derby. For the Park opening, a number of the city's businesses declared a holiday. The major service clubs— Lions, Kiwanis, Rotary, etc.— all turned out.

In total, 18,000 fans came to the opening game. It was not only the largest baseball crowd in the history of Louisville, it was the largest in the history of the American Association. One problem was that while the stands were ready for occupancy, the field was hardly ready for play. No grass seed had been planted, and no sod had been laid. The games were played on dirt. Louisville won their opener. The next day, however, they (and the fans) came back to earth. Toledo beat them 19–3 before a mammoth crowd of 1300. After two more losses, McCarthy found himself getting more than a trifle frustrated. He protested a call and was tossed from a game. The team was still in first place, but their play was looking as ragged as the unfinished diamond on which they performed. Another marketing ploy with the new stadium also diverted the team's focus in their new park. Owner Knebelkamp decided one Monday to let all children enter for free. The result was that 3500 kids came to the park. They chipped wood off the seats, broke soda bottles, and began throwing the scraps of wood and glass all over the park and onto the field. It seemed the shoddy field invited such vandalism. If the field did not respect the game, why should the kids? With the vandalism that day, play had to be halted.[15] Such extreme highs and lows with the new stadium opening, the harsh spring training conditions, the inconsistent play, and the childish vandalism, were all matters McCarthy knew, now better and better, to be avoided. Steadiness of play and emotion were ever more among his ideals.

After being ejected from a game, McCarthy returned to good behavior, at this point for added reasons. Evangelist Billy Sunday, a former ball player, came to Louisville on May 6, and the next afternoon he took in a game at the new ballpark. Rev. Sunday not only played, he umpired and batted once, grounding to the pitcher. How all this meshed with American Association rules was never fully addressed, but obviously some felt that Rev. Sunday went by a higher set of rules anyway. Visiting Columbus was not going to protest anyway, as they won the game 5–3. While McCarthy acknowledged the entertainment value of what transpired that day, it was a further indication to him of the ideal of complete professionalism, something his spring training and new ball field were not affording him.[16]

While McCarthy would have ideally wanted tighter control over matters like the ball field and spring training sites, some things he recognized to be beyond human control. This was made quite clear to him that same week in May, as a freak snowstorm hit the Midwest. One game was cancelled, and on the next afternoon Louisville played before a shivering "crowd" of 255. Amidst the cold, several pitchers complained of sore arms. The initial home stand reversed the good fortunes of the team's surprising opening. By mid May their league leading 7–1 opening had turned into a third place 13–8. With Kirke gone, Earle Combs was the offensive leader of the club. McCarthy had him in the fourth spot, of course, and he was batting .377. Unreliable pitching continued to plague the team, however, and by mid June, Louisville's record stood at a flat .500 (25 and 25). When the Colonels actually won a doubleheader, the *Courier-Journal* smirked: "Can this be Louisville?"[17]

Other than Combs, McCarthy's best player was an outfielder Merito Acosta. On the day of the doubleheader victory, Acosta went down with a sprained ankle. At first it appeared that he would be out for a few weeks. The next day the doctors told McCarthy that Acosta's ankle was not merely sprained but fractured. He was gone for the season. Combs continued to hit and field superbly. McCarthy began to maintain his pitchers differently. He had them throwing, lightly but much more often between starts. It seemed to work, as the team began to pick up. After falling to .500 in mid June, the Colonels ran a record of 13 and 5. They held third place. The trouble was that neither leader — St. Paul or Kansas City — showed any sign of slipping. McCarthy had put his team on an even keel, but even the papers were nodding that their fight was for third place. As of July 4, they were in third, nine games out.

Amidst the heat and frustration, McCarthy was hit by another ejection. Another balk call was in question. McCarthy advised the umpire that he needed to be accompanied by a dog and a tin cup as he wandered about in public places. The remark not only prompted an ejection, it led American Association President Thomas Hickey to suspend McCarthy for one game. Hickey's integrity had just undergone an attack, by St. Paul manager Mike Kelly, in regard to another matter. That matter went all the way to Commissioner Landis, who chose to suspend Kelly. Hickey suspended McCarthy after the Kelly matter and may have been more harsh than normal as a way of asserting his authority to the other American Association players and managers.

Whatever the backdrop, it was the only suspension McCarthy would ever have imposed on him in all his years in baseball. He would not lose his temper often, but when he did, it could be a real steamer. During his one-day suspension, Joe sat in the stands as the team played Kansas City, and the K.C. fans rode him hard. Joe showed no sign of it fazing him at all.[18]

After the suspension one Kansas City sports editor, Edward Cochrane, was complimentary of McCarthy, and he noted the effects of McCarthy's leadership on the Colonels: "Joe McCarthy's club," he declared, "is not beaten until the last man is out." In the series, he said, the Louisville squad "put over every smart play that he [McCarthy] knew, and," the reporter added, "he knows plenty of them." Neither Association President Hickey nor Commissioner Landis could not do anything about a sportswriter like Cochrane. Judge Landis was anything but a champion of civil liberties, but he could not reduce to the press to his domain, much as he would have liked to.[19]

Louisville's solid, but definitely third-place standing continued through August. On August 17, a run of eleven wins and two losses drew the Colonels only to seven games from the lead. Then they lost eight of their next nine. At that point some saw double meaning in the black armbands the team wore in honor of the recently deceased President Warren Harding. Throughout, McCarthy maintained the team's mental state as best he could. During the losing streak, Earle Combs made two errors in one inning, in a game which Louisville lost to St. Paul 24–6. When Combs returned to the dugout, McCarthy did not take him to task. "Forget it," he shrugged. Subsequent stars, like Lou Gehrig, noted McCarthy's mastery of psychology in handling players. With Combs, here and when he first practiced in the spring, McCarthy showed his knack, with the sparest of words, for taking a load off a player's shoulders who he knew would rebound with time and encouragement. With lesser players, McCarthy might not have gone out of his way to say or do anything, other than look into how he could most profitably trade them. When he recognized talent, and he seldom erred in that vein, McCarthy knew how to nurture it, both with physical pointers and with a psychological nudge. At this point, mired in Louisville with a mediocre team, such managerial talent hardly seemed well utilized.[20]

With Kansas City battling St. Paul for the pennant in September, Louisville's role could only be that of spoiler. When Louisville lost three games to Kansas City in late September, the *St. Paul Dispatch* sent Knebelkamp a telegram, criticizing McCarthy's use of rookie pitchers and the team's playing "otherwise indifferent baseball." Louisville won the next game, and neither McCarthy or Knebelkamp responded to St. Paul's charges, but the Saints' slight paranoia did indicate a level of respect they implicitly held for McCarthy, as they believed he could readily make the team play better if he wanted to.[21]

Knebelkamp released the telegram to the *Courier-Journal*. Louisville fans enjoyed the controversy. As St. Paul had lost in the postseason after their two pennants in 1920 and 1922, and Louisville had won in 1921, Colonels fans felt that the Saints might not be the best representative of the Association, and that they, Louisvillians, were eminently qualified to make such declarations. Towards the end of the season, Louisville crowds cheered the postings of Kansas City victories and of St. Paul defeats. All this certainly touched raw nerves among proud St. Paul fans, whose second-city status *vis a vis* neighboring Minneapolis was always an irritation anyway. And when Kansas City nosed out St. Paul for the pennant, with Louisville beating St. Paul in a key game down the stretch, Saints' rooters were even more angry.[22]

McCarthy could only smirk and shrug at the controversy, as he did with regard to another seat-cushion throwing incident which caused a forfeit of a late-season contest against Minneapolis.[23] 1923 was yet another disappointing season, better than the disaster that was 1922, but "a solid third place" followed by a few weeks of low-paying barnstorming around rural Kentucky, Indiana, and Ohio was hardly satisfying. He felt he was in a rut. His weak hitting back in his days with Toledo and Indianapolis had likely cost him a shot with the big leagues. Could he make it to the big show as a manager if he steadily guided mediocre teams to similarly solid, but mediocre finishes? It was hard at this point to be optimistic.

14

That Boy Is a Wonder

"Many baseball enthusiasts in Newark, New Jersey," wrote the Louisville Courier-Journal in March of 1924, "believe that Lou Gehrig will eventually become a rival to Babe Ruth." The paper went on, prognosticating that Gehrig is "not a whale of a first baseman and may never be a star at that position, but that he is going to be a sensational hitter is a foregone conclusion."[1] Lou Gehrig had recently graduated from Columbia University. In 1923, he had been playing under a New York Yankee contract, a bit with the Yankees but mainly in Newark and up in Hartford, Connecticut. Earle Combs was another hot prospect at this time, and in 1923 the Yankees were among the many teams who sent scouts to Louisville to evaluate him. Like everyone else, they were impressed. When the Colonels and the Yankees were negotiating over Combs, McCarthy and the Colonels first asked the Yankees to trade young Gehrig to Louisville in exchange for Combs. The Yankees would not accept the offer. The Yankees were also interested in the Colonels' pitcher Wayland Dean. Yankee Manager Miller Huggins phoned McCarthy and asked his advice about the two. McCarthy told him: "Take Combs. He's a sure thing. Dean isn't as level-headed." Later McCarthy recalled that "the Yankees would have taken both ... if I had not held out for Lou Gehrig." Combs went to the Yankees, and a few years later Combs and Gehrig would both be playing for McCarthy in New York. (Dean would make it to the majors, but he played only four seasons, winning just twenty-four games. Then, sadly, he died of pneumonia at age 28.)[2]

Combs signed with the Yankees at the close of the 1923 season. The Colonels received $50,000 and a player named Elmer Smith, a nine-year major league journeyman who was three years older than McCarthy. (The Colonels subsequently sold him to the Cincinnati Reds for $15,000.) McCarthy wanted nothing but success for Combs, but now he was facing a season without his star player. Such was often the fate of minor league managers. Meanwhile, after Combs had worked out with the Yankees for a few weeks, Miller Huggins commented to the press that "McCarthy must be an exceptional manager, for every time the coaches tell Earle anything he says, 'Yes, I know that. McCarthy taught me that.'"[3]

Over the winter of 1923–24, Joe and Elizabeth McCarthy bought their home at #55 Gates Circle in Buffalo. At the end of the 1923 season, he also signed a contract for two more years with the Colonels. McCarthy, celebrated the papers, is "considered one of the shrewdest managers in baseball." One of his players from 1923, Nick Cullop, had spoken similarly. Cullop would play with the Yankees, Indians, Senators, Dodgers, and Reds, and he was not one "given to idle words." McCarthy, he said, "is undoubtedly the most efficient manager I have ever played under. He knows more baseball than anybody of my acquaintance and knows how to impart the knowledge to his players. I can't understand why some major league club hasn't grabbed him. He is much superior to several managers now in the majors." In hindsight, many baseball people in Louisville have commented about McCarthy's tenure as manager of the Colonels to the effect that "everyone knew that he was destined for the Big Show," but in the spring of 1924 neither McCarthy nor any of his Louisville fans had any inklings of his future in the major leagues. In 1918–19 people were commenting that he was as good as or better than most of the second basemen in the major leagues. Now they were saying the same thing about him as a manager. The question was whether he was destined for yet another bad break of neglect.[4]

McCarthy drove down from Buffalo to Louisville for spring training. The team's budgetary constraints were again such that once more the team convened in ole' Dawson Springs, Kentucky — good mineral water, good hotel accommodations, lousy weather. This March, however, rain actually did not prevent terribly many practices; snow did. After a week in snowy Dawson Springs, McCarthy's team had yet to set foot on a baseball field. All they could do was work out in the hotel basement. Amidst the snow and sleet, the Colonels did announce, at long last, that future spring training camps would be in the South. About the only consolation here was that none of the players could spend any off-time playing golf. Like many baseball managers, McCarthy did not want any of his men to play golf. He felt it developed bad batting habits. A golfer, he mused, "is said to have hoof and mouth disease. He hoofs it all day and talks about it all night."[5]

Finally out on the ball field, various Colonel pitchers exerted their arms overly and quickly developed soreness. When a buzzard flew over Dawson Springs Park one cold afternoon, McCarthy was heard ruefully quipping: "He must be after one of our dead arms." Cold weather plagued all the weeks at Dawson Springs, and it followed the team as it tried to play exhibition games in Tennessee and Kentucky. Merito Acosta's broken ankle of 1923 had healed at least, but otherwise the Colonels were hurting. "Cold weather," sighed McCarthy, "is on our trail. [infielder Bruno] Betzel is limping, [catcher Bill] Meyer has a crippled arm, [pitcher Nick] Cullop is in bed with a deep cold, [pitcher Ben] Tincup is out with a smashed nose [he had been hit by a line drive], and half the team is sneezing and coughing."[6]

Bad springs had led to bad starts in the regular season several times for McCarthy. In April he had reason to worry. In four major league exhibitions with the Boston Red Sox and Pittsburgh Pirates, the Colonels lost all four games, including one to an underhand thrower named Howard Ehmke. (McCarthy would meet him again.) Aware of their condition and of their loss of Earle Combs and Wayland Dean, few American Association sports writers picked Louisville to do well that spring. The *St. Paul Dispatch* picked the Colonels for seventh place. The *Toledo Times* predicted they would wind up in the cellar. Kansas City was the consensus favorite. Fittingly, McCarthy would not engage in the forecasting: "Excuse me from a prophecy. I promise to do the best I can, and to keep on doing it all the time."[7] He kept his word.

Despite all the gloom, 13,200 turned out on opening day in April and saw Louisville beat St. Paul 6–4. McCarthy was happy, both with the game and with the new American Association rule of three umpires rather than two. After the opening win came three straight losses, leaving the Colonels indeed starting the season at the bottom of the league. McCarthy gave the team a lift the next day against Minneapolis. The score was tied. Louisville was batting with a runner heading for third. In the play, the ball got away from the Minneapolis third baseman. He turned to locate the ball. McCarthy, coaching at third, immediately pointed to the right side of the dugout. The fielder took the bait. Of course, the ball had gone in the other direction. Even though it was Sunday, the fans could more than forgive McCarthy's little white lie. The Louisville runner scored, winning the game and snapping the losing streak. The next day, however, Minneapolis won 16–2. There was nothing McCarthy could do to save that one. A week later, when Milwaukee also beat Louisville 16–2, a reporter earnestly declared: "That 16–2 ball game last Monday was no fluke."[8] It hardly bodes well when, still in the month of April, a ball club is the butt of wise cracks from its home town newspaper.

Since he had been able to do so little training in the bad weather of March, McCarthy had been forced to regard the month of April as part of the team's spring training. In early May, his record was thus a mere 7 and 9. From there, McCarthy turned the team around. He cut a few players and held extra practices. By May 16, the team was in fourth place with a record of 13 and 12. "Joe McCarthy has whipped them into a snappy fighting team," happily announced the *Courier-Journal*, "if they continue to play this brand of ball they will be heard from." Later in the month, the paper was singing similar praises, conjecturing that with the "alert baseball" the Colonels were now playing, they "seem to have a fair chance for the pennant." This was quite a change from the sarcasm of late April. The question was whether there was sufficient depth in the pitching corps to last the season.[9]

The New York Yankees came to town again that June for another exhibition, and Babe Ruth did not disappoint. He visited orphanages and glad-handed his way all over town. Up at Parkway Field, in the ninth inning, he hit "the mightiest home run in the history of Kentucky baseball." Ruth took the headlines. McCarthy and the Colonels took the game, 7–6. Whether it was the victory over the Yankees, or just McCarthy's working the kinks out of players who had trained insufficiently in the cold of March, by mid–June the Colonels had risen into contention for the league lead. On June 19, after sweeping a series from St. Paul, they were one game out of the lead. From there they continued to win, reeling off nine victories in a row. From the day of the victory over the Yankees until June 23, Louisville's record was 15 and 5. The league had settled into a three-team race—St. Paul, Indianapolis, and Louisville. Having predicted the cellar for Louisville; Toledo had it for themselves. Minneapolis' Manager Mike Kelly observed here: "Joe McCarthy is a big league manager in a minor league."[10]

In another series with St. Paul, the papers gave credit for Louisville's first-game victory strictly to McCarthy. He had judged at the very outset that the St. Paul pitcher had no control. In the first inning, he thus ordered his batters to take. The result: three walks and seven runs in the first inning. The papers' conclusion: "McCarthy is no ordinary manager." Louisville won the next two games, but they lost the final game of the series, and in that game disaster struck. On a play at the plate, a St. Paul runner, Johnny Neun, collided with Louisville's catcher Billy Meyer. In the collision, Meyer broke his leg in two places. "The boys will hustle," McCarthy assured, "we're not licked yet." But everyone knew how hard it would be to contend with the starting catcher out for the year. The team went 2–5 over the next week and fell out of first place. The *Courier-Journal* headlined simply: "Help! Help!" McCarthy and the Colonels did not fold that month, however. Observing Louisville's continued winning, the *Kansas City Journal* acknowledged: "With one of the smartest managers in the league, ... the Louisville Colonels look right now to be the best bet. McCarthy has the knack of keeping his team in the race despite the loss of star players. ... That is the kind of manager who will win."[11]

Still, without their starting catcher, it was difficult to sustain any winning. Indianapolis took a series from Louisville in late July, and the Colonels fell to third place. The next day Toledo beat them 22–1. In August, Louisville's next catcher, Ernie Vick, who had played well in place of Meyer, broke his jaw and was lost for the season. A key pitcher, Tony Brottem, was down with a broken finger. Grumblings grew in Louisville, not at McCarthy but at Knebelkamp for not purchasing the necessary talent to plug the holes. Describing the team as "a battered lot in third place ... [with] the depressing handicap of no help from the business office," reporters exclaimed: "The magic of McCarthy can work wonders, but the business office must provide some ammunition other than blanks." Knebelkamp responded with a lot of talk about how he wanted Louisville to beat Baltimore and then go out West and beat the Pacific League champions. Folks wondered how much hooch from his own bourbon distillery Knebelkamp was consuming. He was dreaming about October while everyone wanted him to help the team win in August and September. McCarthy learned ever more about the need to work with a good business manager.[12]

Sounding like a national war leader, McCarthy promised "we'll fight them for the honor until the very last," and the team did just that. In September *another* catcher went out with an injury, but the team never went into a losing streak. With all the injuries, however, the team could not overtake St. Paul or Indianapolis. Down the stretch, they lost two games which they had led going into the ninth inning. These losses killed their hopes. On the final days of the season, Indianapolis was in Minneapolis, and Louisville was in St. Paul. Even though they had just been mathematically eliminated, Louisville beat St. Paul in the series, but Indianapolis could not sweep the Millers. St. Paul thus won the pennant. Both teams left the Twin Cities on the same train, and on route to Indianapolis, the Indians insisted on buying drinks and dinner for McCarthy and the Colonels. Louisville's gameness had won the respect of the league. Danny Boone, captain of the St. Paul Saints, told the *Courier-Journal*: "We weren't afraid of the Hoosiers, ... [but] we were a bit afraid of you fellows." Indianapolis Manager Donie Bush said "Joe McCarthy should be covered in medals for his achievement. ... Nobody should get any more honor out of the race than McCarthy. That boy is a wonder."[13]

15

Made Me Blush for the First Time in My Life

When McCarthy arrived in Louisville from Buffalo in early March, 1925, he was full of optimism. In 1924, his Colonels had proven they could stay in a pennant race despite an incredible rash of key injuries. Presuming, hoping for, a relatively normal rate of injuries, McCarthy told the papers: "I am very much pleased with our prospects. ... I am sure the Colonels will be a factor in the pennant." He had reason to be optimistic: he was actually heading South for the month of training. Spring training, 1925 was going to be in Mobile, Alabama, and on March 12 the Colonels arrived there amidst what McCarthy described as "mid-season weather." They went right to work. Knebelkamp's budget was still tight, so the Colonels could go South, but not for too long. McCarthy had persuaded him that a few hard weeks in Mobile would be enormously preferable to a more leisurely stay at Dawson Springs. He was right. The weather cooperated, and McCarthy made the most of it, drilling his players intensely. They left on April 2, fit and ready.[1]

The consensus of the American Association reporters had Louisville finishing second, just behind Indianapolis. (St. Paul had lost several players, including their star shortstop, Mark Koenig. He had joined Gehrig and Combs with the New York Yankees, who were certainly building an impressive squad.) The *Courier-Journal* was talking pennant. "Louisville," they chortled, "with a neatly balanced ball team and a managerial genius, Joe McCarthy, in charge of it, seems to have the best chance."[2]

From the outset of the season, McCarthy felt his squad had a shot at the pennant, and he managed accordingly. They started well, with St. Paul and Indianapolis right there with them as usual. On April 21, the Colonels were up 7–4 on Minneapolis. The Millers scored six runs in the ninth inning to win the game. McCarthy called a meeting and took everyone to task. He rarely went after a team whose prospects were not good, but this was different. He was going to make this Colonels team play up to its ability. Two days later a Miller pitcher threw three fastballs at pitcher Nick Cullop's head. The Louisville bench cleared, and McCarthy was right there with them. McCarthy had given the team a unified, fighting spirit, and neither he nor they were going to let anything damage it. Another fight broke out at the end of the month between Louisville and Minneapolis players over an allegedly too rough slide into third base by one of the Colonels. The Louisville player, Joe Guyon, was a Creek Indian, and that racial element may have been part of the backdrop; especially since Cullop was also part Indian. (Overly aggressive base running by "colored" players often prompted violence. Along with brush-back pitches, hard sliding was point of physical contact in the game that jangled nerves, and where such incidents involved "coloreds," the many racists in the game would be vengeful. It happened Jackie Robinson, and later to Frank Robinson. Back in the 1920s in the days of segregation, Native American players were often the targets.) With this Minneapolis-Louisville fight, matters boiled over. The field umpire was a small man. He could not break up the situation and had to call for the police. The constables restored order on the field. Several players, including Guyon, were ejected. When these players headed for the clubhouse, they recommenced the fight in the dugout tunnel under the grandstand. No one was seriously injured. Each city's newspapers claimed their side had won the fisticuffs. Such incidents brought McCarthy's team together even more.

Minneapolis had a new manager that year. His name was Mike Kelley, and he considered himself the best manager in the Association. (In 1899 he had actually played for the Louisville National League club.) "You just watch my smoke," he bragged, "I'll put out pennant winners just as fast as the years roll by." Reporters did acknowledge Kelley's strengths. Indeed some said that he was the only manager in the circuit who could rank with McCarthy. Kelley may have been intent on brushing back and fighting with McCarthy's men in hopes of establishing an edge of intimidation. But if he thought the tactic would make McCarthy even think of folding his tent, he was quite mistaken. After the second fight, Louisville won two straight from Kelley and the Millers. As opponents would always learn: Joe McCarthy never needed to act as though he was not intimidated; he simply never was.[3]

After the run against the Millers, Louisville let down a bit with three straight losses. Again McCarthy took action. On May 6, he called a morning team meeting in his hotel room. Reporters were not allowed, so McCarthy's actual words were not made known, but according to one reporter who witnessed the team that afternoon: "Something ran through the entire squad that inspired it to better ball playing." McCarthy apparently wanted to get beyond the point of the snarling unity that the team showed against Minneapolis. He wanted crisp, professional baseball execution, not just a bunch of brawlers. The team then began to win consistently. Playing on the road in much of May, Louisville kept pace with St. Paul and Indianapolis. Through the month, the three were never apart by more than three games.[4]

Back home in June, Louisville began to win. For the first time in years, McCarthy found himself with a good pitching staff. Nick Cullop pitched a no-hitter against Columbus until one out in the ninth. Then a liner down the right field line fell fair by three inches. That runner died on second, and Cullop had a one-hit shutout. The next day against Columbus, McCarthy added to Louisville's sense of bravado in regard to its opposition. With the Colonels up 4–2, a Columbus batter doubled. McCarthy went out to the mound and instructed his pitcher to pay no regard to the runner. The runner stole third and then scored on a sacrifice fly. McCarthy's strategy here was defiantly to allow the run while giving the opposition no opportunity to build a rally. It worked. Louisville held its lead and won the game.

The added point here was that McCarthy was serving notice on the opposition that Louisville was always going to be so confident in its strength that a single run here and there would not matter to them. McCarthy would not employ such a strategy with a weak team, but with a good team such a demonstrated outlook can make them play with even more confidence, psychologically push the opposition a bit, and perhaps unnerve them. He would employ such a strategy in future years as well. Some managers excel at taking a mediocre team and making it good. But taking a good team and making it very good involves different skills. Not everyone possesses them, but McCarthy sure did, and his team was now playing with an even stronger level of confidence.[5]

McCarthy's ploy worked in the games against Columbus and against the rest of the league. Louisville went on a tear. Nick Cullop continued to pitch well. Another pitcher, Ed Holley, struck out 13 in one game, and Ben Tincup was pitching effectively as well. Kansas City released a "hopelessly ineffective" pitcher named Roy Wilkinson. McCarthy picked him up, and he began throwing well too. This was another of McCarthy's strengths—an eye for the kind of talent that could contribute in a specific role within the team. The Colonels won the rest of the week's games to nose ahead of the St. Paul on June 8. The next day, St. Paul came to town for a six-game series with the Colonels. When the series was over the *Courier-Journal* gloated: "When the Saints hear the pathway call to Heaven, they will not route their progression by Parkway Field." Louisville had won all six games![6]

Many a high-flying team comes down to earth as quickly as it soars. McCarthy showed another management skill in avoiding this. His leadership had simply put the team on a higher plane, one that could be sustained. In all, Louisville won 13 straight in early June. On June 17, against the now hated Minneapolis Millers, a Minneapolis player bounced one off the wall in left field. The umpire ruled it a home run. The normally calm McCarthy argued, to no avail of course. But he came back to the bench with an anger that was apparent to all. Down 5–3, the Colonels came back "spurred by adversity," as one reporter observed it, and won the game. So much for Mike Kelley's "smoke." By June 30, the Colonels had won 29 of their previous 31 games. No one could keep pace with them. They had made a farce of the pennant race. On June 30, last-place Milwaukee stood 10 games behind second-place Indianapolis, while Indianapolis was 11 and one half games behind Louisville. The team led the league in batting, fielding, double plays, and fewest errors. Attendance actually declined in the American Association that summer as everyone knew what the outcome would be. Future McCarthy teams would engender the same such sense of total annihilation.[7]

On July 1, catcher Bill Meyer came down with a case of pleurisy. But McCarthy stood ready. Reserve catcher Gus Redman filled in capably. Out in Baltimore, Orioles chief Jack Dunn expressed concern about Louisville. With a thirteen-game lead on July 4, with speed, hitting, reserves, and pitching, there seemed to be no weakness. Moreover, Dunn noticed, "the club seems to be one that shows its best when under fire." Billy Meyer rejoined the club on July 10. That week Rudy Hulswill, a scout for the Boston Red Sox, came to Louisville to look at some prospects, especially Colonels' outfielder Ty Tyson. To McCarthy he exclaimed: "I came here expecting to see a team of baseball players, and what you've got out there is a pack of wolves. Nobody can beat a bunch of fellows who relish their work like the Colonels do. Never have I seen such spirit on a professional ball field."

One cannot instill such spirit in mediocre players. The air will spurt out of the balloon as fast as it goes in. Talent has to come first, and McCarthy knew both how to spot it and how to develop it. Once he had that in position, McCarthy showed he knew how to make the most of it over a full season. He would later show how to sustain such excellence over successive seasons.[8]

With McCarthy's rise to complete dominance of the American Association, several surprising developments were grabbing the sports headlines in the major leagues. The New York Yankees were having a shockingly abysmal season. Babe Ruth was in the hospital with acute indigestion and flu; the team floundered and would finish next to last, by far the worst Yankee season from World War I until 1966. Meanwhile, in the National League the Chicago Cubs, with a proud tradition of winning going back to their glory days of the early 20th century, were playing terribly. Their manager, Bill Killefer, quit in early July. Veteran player Walter "Rabbit" Maranville succeeded him. Maranville had a reputation for hard playing and even harder drinking. Cubs President Bill Veeck, Sr. wagered that giving Maranville more responsibility would temper him and thus bring the whole team into line. The new responsibility deterred neither Maranville's destructive habits nor the Cubs'. Two days after being named manager, Maranville was arrested at Times Square in New York on charges of disorderly conduct. He was enraged at a cab driver for allegedly overcharging him. Maranville's undisciplined ways did not stop there. During a Cub road trip, he ran through a Pullman car spraying spittoon juice on all the passengers. He did promote first baseman Charley Grimm and catcher Charles Leo "Gabby" Hartnett to full starting roles. Otherwise, the only guidance he seemed to be able to give his men was how to get to the nearest speakeasy.

Maranville did not even finish the season with Chicago. He resigned in early September. George "Moon" Gibson managed for the last 26 games. The Cubs were completely dispirited and finally sank to the National League cellar. The day the Cubs appointed Maranville as manager, McCarthy and the Colonels were en route to Milwaukee to play the Brewers. The Louisville papers noted that McCarthy left the team when the train stopped in Chicago and rode up to Milwaukee later in the day. Some people began to wonder. Years later, McCarthy told the *Christian Science Monitor* that a Cub scout, Jack Doyle, had been in touch with him inquiring as to his availability.[9]

While a few in Louisville thought about McCarthy's stopover, the team kept winning, and McCarthy continued to keep the team fired up. In the first game of a doubleheader at St. Paul, Louisville was up 3–1. In the bottom of the eighth inning, St. Paul had two on base. The next batter was hit by a pitch. This appeared to load the bases, but McCarthy stepped on to the field with one of his tricks. The batter just hit by the pitch had been batting out of turn. He was in his usual spot in the lineup, but the manager had erred filling out the lineup card. McCarthy noticed this and, as usual, made no issue of the violation until it could be of use. Rather than have the bases loaded with a rally brewing, St. Paul went quietly in the eighth, lost the game, and lost the nightcap too. Louisville's lead was now 14 games.[10]

In a game on July 19, second baseman Bruno Betzel made an uncharacteristic error. He had been receiving congratulations, as he had just gone 21 consecutive games without making an error. It was the second-best such mark ever set by a

Louisville Colonel. The Colonels' record for consecutive errorless games, noted the papers, was 25 — by Joe McCarthy. A few more rumors began to circulate about McCarthy's day in Chicago, so much so that McCarthy actually commented to the papers: "I flatly deny considering managing another team. It I were considering it," he conjectured, "you know the Chicago newspapers would have had something about it by this time." McCarthy could have been challenged here. As McCarthy was hardly known among Chicago reporters, their non-coverage was not significant. The Louisville papers' concerns were more the issue. Cubs President Bill Veeck and owner William Wrigley, Jr. certainly did not want any controversy, as they did not want any further problems in an already terrible season. Now they knew they could trust McCarthy's discretion, and they saw that he could keep his head on his Louisville business and deftly finesse the press. Veeck and Wrigley scheduled a meeting with McCarthy in Indianapolis, but on the appointed day, McCarthy wired them that the Colonels had a crucial set of games and he felt he had to stay with the club. Bill Veeck, Jr. later revealed that this "made a very good impression on my dad." As he tended to baseball matters in Louisville, McCarthy made note especially of two players in the league who impressed him. One was Riggs Stephenson, who played the year with Kansas City and Indianapolis. The other had recently been sent down from the New York Giants to Toledo. He was a short, stocky outfielder from Pennsylvania named Lewis "Hack" Wilson.[11]

In early 1926, Casey Stengel, having just completed his major league playing career, wanted to become a manager. His first managerial post came with the Toledo Mud Hens. Looking over his team's and the Association's performance of the previous season, Stengel asked many players on the Mud Hens, as well as a few on other teams, why it was that the Louisville Colonels so dominated the league in 1925. From the players he repeatedly got snarls of how "damned lucky" the Colonels were. Stengel later recalled that those answers were not good enough to satisfy his curiosity. He set about to scour the box scores and statistics and learn more. What he found was that Louisville's "luck" was really a matter of execution. They had the fewest errors. They had the most double plays. They thus gave away the fewest runs and games, and, perhaps most important, snuffed out the most rallies. "Double plays," said Casey, "meant the ball was being pitched in spots and that the fielders were being placed right." This, he reflected, was not mere luck or even a simple matter of talent. It was a result of the work of their manager. McCarthy indeed had the Colonels running perfectly.

In 1926, Stengel also picked up a player from Louisville named Tommy Gaffney. Several Toledo players told Stengel that Gaffney never played in Louisville, and that McCarthy just kept him on the bench because, like McCarthy, Gaffney was a native of Germantown, Pa. Stengel soon discovered "Gaffney was one of the shrewdest observers I ever saw in baseball." Gaffney knew the league intimately, how to pitch to each hitter, where each would hit a ball if it was pitched to certain spots. McCarthy never let sentiment get in the way of a personnel decision; there was always a sound reason for each of his actions. In Toledo, Stengel held onto Gaffney and began relying on his judgments.[12]

In the summer of 1925 the question around the league was whether anything could derail Louisville. Something nearly did, and quite literally. En route from Minneapolis to Indianapolis, the Colonels train encountered an oncoming freight train whose engineer — Ed Woolman — pulled to a siding to let the passenger train pass. As it passed, Woolman saw sparks fly from one of the cars, and he immediately signaled the passing engineer to begin braking. As the passenger train began to decelerate, within 100 yards one of its cars jumped track. Fortunately, it was at a reduced speed, and no major problems ensued. At high speed such a derailment could have been tragic. The Colonels were soon on their way to Indianapolis, and there they kept winning. Amidst the pennant drive, McCarthy never chortled. When the team was a mere 15 games ahead he still said: "The pennant race is too close to suit me, and I'd still be a bit nervous if we were 23 games out front."

"What do I think of Joe McCarthy?" snapped Jimmy Burke, manager of the also-ran Toledo Mud Hens, "why I think he would take a dead fly from a blind spider."[13] It would be a great source of irritation to opponents over the years, but no pennant race lead was ever too wide for McCarthy's comfort. He would bear down even against the weakest teams. That year against Jimmy Burke's Mud Hens, for example, Louisville won 17 of 19. That was part of why McCarthy was so successful. In order to be truly intense with a 6 game lead, you have to be the sort who is still nervous with a 15 game lead, otherwise that 6 game lead will more easily evaporate. To have that kind of intensity without being self-destructively volatile is quite rare.

The papers were full of praise for McCarthy as the Colonels steamed towards the pennant, which they wrapped up on September 11 with a victory over Jimmy Burke and Toledo. Toledo's President Joseph O'Brien said he would rather have McCarthy than any other manager in baseball. This did not make Manager Burke feel terribly well, and he was let go after the season. O'Brien could not get McCarthy. That was when he settled on Casey Stengel. On September 20, the city of Louisville proclaimed Joe McCarthy Day. It rained at Parkway Field that afternoon, yet 5,260 came anyway. "Louisville," the papers proclaimed, "owes McCarthy a deep debt of gratitude for his ten years of loyal and efficient service to the ball club." McCarthy received $500 and a silver service. Mrs. McCarthy was given a bouquet of roses. McCarthy later said the gifts "knocked him cold. ... 'made me blush for the first time in my life; the goodness of everyone simply stunned me.'"[14]

There were other aspects of Louisville which gave McCarthy similar delight. The theater life was a joy, as was the general camaraderie of the community. This camaraderie was particularly noticeable at the ball park. One fellow from the town of Lynch, out in the hill country of Eastern Kentucky, J. W. Greaver, was known as the Colonels' biggest fan. The papers said that he out-rooted all of Baltimore in the Little World Series of 1921 and that many Baltimore fans came to the final game that fall just to hear Greaver. Greaver's rooting was considered so significant that when he asked if his local Lynch team could play the Colonels in an exhibition, McCarthy agreed. "The mountain folks asked for the game so they could determine how their players compared with city slickers." They slated a game just before a scheduled Saturday contest with Minneapolis, and made Kelley and Millers wait a bit; a nice new touch of irritation, undoubtedly. Louisville won 6–4, but the mountain boys "gave a good account of themselves."[15]

If he ever felt the slightest bit downcast, McCarthy could regularly turn to another rabid Colonels fan named Claude Silbernagel. After a game, McCarthy could ask Silbernagel such a question as what he thought of the liner that Betzel grabbed. Silbernagel would often respond by correcting the question: "That was no liner to Betzel. That ball went to him on the first hop. Anybody could hear that!" "Hear" was the proper word; Claude Silbernagel was blind! But he could hear a baseball game from the stands almost unerringly — "the struggle of the fielder for the ball as he hears it hit, and the fielder's struggle to get that ball to first ahead of those pattering feet — the suspense," Silbernagel proclaimed, "is glorious." McCarthy once wagered that Silbernagel would miss fifteen plays in a Colonels game. McCarthy lost the bet by a mile; Mr. Silbernagel missed only four. In April, 1924, after being away for the winter, McCarthy approached Silbernagel before the first game in Louisville and, with a high-pitched voice he had rehearsed for a week, said "How do you do, Claude, I hope everything by you is all right." Silbernagel calmly retorted: "Why hello, Joe, what's happened to your voice through the winter?" McCarthy declared respectfully: "He can see more than any man on my ball club."[16]

With such truly extraordinary people in his work and throughout the community, McCarthy must have felt some strain as he corresponded privately with the Chicago Cubs about the possibly of becoming their manager. By late August, the Chicago rumors had increased. McCarthy continued to deny he had signed with Chicago, which was true. "Any information to the contrary," he declared, "is pure bunk, flattering, I'll confess, but nevertheless, pure bunk." It wasn't. While he had not signed, McCarthy had previously met with Wrigley and Veeck in Chicago, and in September he again met again with Veeck in French Lick, Indiana.[17] Meanwhile, Louisville had more to think about; they had to prepare for another series — with the Baltimore Orioles.

The Orioles had won the International League pennant for the seventh straight time. They had beaten St. Paul in the previous October series, but they had a score to settle with Louisville. With their run-away-and-hide pennant win in the American Association, Louisville had to prove that they had not just thrashed a weak league. The series started in Louisville on September 30. In game one, the Orioles were up 7–4 as Louisville batted in the bottom of the ninth inning. The Colonels rallied for three runs. Then with one out, the Colonels had runners on first and second. McCarthy signaled for a double steal, and it worked. With runners now on second and third, the next batter hit a grounder. Without the steal, it would have been an inning-ending double play. But the runner scored from third, and the game went to Louisville. After a rainy day, Louisville won again, but the Orioles knotted the series, taking the next two. The teams were then off to Baltimore.[18]

Louisville had a third baseman named Pelham Ballenger, who was a hot head. He batted .302 for the Colonels that season, but he lost his temper in arguments with umpires on several occasions. McCarthy always wanted intense players, but he was always distressed at those who could not control their tempers. Their influence, he felt, was disruptive. Ballenger was one such player. McCarthy later recalled: "He had too much guts for his own good."[19] Ballenger also liked to drink, although that was hardly unusual for a ball player, but alcohol was another thing of which Ballenger "had too much ... for his own good." Back on August 25, Ballenger's father suddenly died. McCarthy and the Colonels gave him leave to attend to the funeral and see to his family for a few days, of course. When he returned, he was more temperamental, but with the pennant a virtual lock at that point, there were few circumstances that pressured any major emotional outbursts. Then amidst the tight series with Baltimore, Ballenger snapped. On the train to Baltimore, Ballenger arrived in the club car where McCarthy was playing cards. Ballenger was wearing nothing but his underwear. McCarthy simply said: "Go Now!" Ballenger, obviously drunk, immediately grew obstinate: "I'll go when I'm ready." McCarthy firmly repeated: "You'll go right now." Ballenger again yelled: "Not until I get good and ready." A round of name-calling ensued.[20]

When the train arrived in Baltimore from Louisville, McCarthy had the Colonels traveling secretary give Ballenger a return ticket to Louisville and immediately ordered him off the team. President Knebelkamp, who was in the club car during the altercation, made a statement to the press:

> Never again will Ballenger play as a member of the Colonels. I'll sell him if I don't get anything for him but a baseball hat. He is hard enough to get along with when he is sober, and when he is drunk he is a menace to everyone. This well cost me a lot of money because nobody will want him ... but I would rather lose the money than lose my respect through letting him stay.[21]

Joe Guyon, speaking for several of the players, went to McCarthy, asking him to let Ballenger play. Ballenger had hit .437 in the first four games of the series. McCarthy refused, saying: "It is better for us to lose with our heads up than to win with our heads down." Ballenger chose to stay in Baltimore. He went to one of the Colonels' coaches, Tom Estell, asking him to appeal to McCarthy and promising to swear an oath on the Bible that he would adhere strictly to all team rules. McCarthy was adamant. American Association President Thomas J. Hickey was completely supportive of McCarthy here. The Colonels may lose to the Orioles, he said, but he added: "the Association will win the ever-lasting respect and gratitude of the nation which ever is ready to uphold clean athletics." The sports world was still reeling from the 1919 World Series scandal, Babe Ruth's misbehavior was not winning much admiration, and college football was also rocked with some scandals. Hickey may have inflated the significance of the American Association in the nation's sports world, but clean appearances were paramount to him.[22]

McCarthy substituted Shanty Gaffney at third base in game five. He did not get a hit, but he fielded his position perfectly, and Louisville won easily 7–1. The next day everything began coming unglued for the Colonels. Baltimore won game six by a score of 5–3. Meanwhile, the Chicago papers announced that McCarthy would be the Cubs manager for the 1926 season. The Louisville *Courier-Journal* learned of the Chicago press releases and headlined the Chicago news with a sigh of disbelief: "Here It Is Again!" Still, all the Chicago papers had the story. The Cubs office was silent, but the *Chicago Tribune* attributed the story to "an intimate friend" of McCarthy. Of course the stories were true, and two days later McCarthy officially signed with the Cubs. His seasonal salary would be $7,500.[23]

In the Baltimore series, meanwhile, other events were grabbing the fans' attention. In game six one Oriole, Maurice Archdeacon, physically attacked one of the umpires. The other umpires requested that Archdeacon be disciplined. Baltimore Manager/President Jack Dunn would do nothing; neither would any official of the

International League. They did not even offer a statement. This prompted the *Courier-Journal* to snort about the International League officials being completely in Dunn's pocket. In Baltimore's Emerson Hotel lobby, Dunn had a verbal altercation over the matter with AA President Hickey. At this point, with Archdeacon starting game seven, McCarthy made a move of somewhat strained logic. He chose to reinstate Ballenger. It did not exactly follow to assert that if Archdeacon was going to play, so was Ballenger. In any case, it certainly contradicted the posture of "better to lose with our heads high…." Perhaps McCarthy was making a gesture to his players, many of whom wanted Ballenger back. By then, the players all knew that McCarthy was leaving, so he may have thought it best not to be so stiff at this point. Archdeacon took the field, and he did apologize before the game. The Baltimore fans actually booed the gesture. The Orioles won the game 10–9. Ballenger hit a single and a double, but he committed two costly errors. The next day the Orioles won again, 5–2, thus winning the series.[24]

The events of the '25 series certainly gave an odd cast to the sports mood in Louisville. The Colonels lost the series. They had retracted their noble stance in the disciplining of an errant player. The plans for the team to head West and play the Western and Pacific Coast champions now had a certain hollowness about them, as they were not the champions from the East as they expected to be. They did play in Omaha and Kansas City. Then they played a series with the San Francisco Seals, led by a young star named Paul Waner. In San Francisco, Louisville went down one game to four in the series. Then they battled back to 4–4, only to lose the deciding ninth game 9–8. Knebelkamp managed the team.[25]

Most disturbing about the month's events to Louisvillians was of course the loss of Joe McCarthy. McCarthy traveled with the Colonels as they went out to play Omaha. But he left the team in Chicago. With all his friends and colleagues in Louisville, it was a difficult move. But virtually everyone in Louisville did nothing but wish Joe well. With his surprise at the way the city's baseball fans had honored him on McCarthy Day, McCarthy certainly knew the feelings the Colonels had for him. He learned it even more upon leaving. Louisville fans were simply happy for his new attainment and expressed no bitterness. After all, as Louisvillians later acknowledged: "Everyone knew he was destined for the big show." That he was once one of theirs was more than enough. The Louisville years were happy and productive for McCarthy, and he would always enjoy return visits. "I don't mind saying," he later noted to a hard-bitten New York press when he was managing the Yankees, "I have a particularly warm spot in my heart for Louisville. Here I was given my first real opportunity in baseball. The fans there were always kind to me, and it [visiting there] is like coming back home."[26]

16

Don't Forget the Cubs

When McCarthy arrived in Chicago, several sensations struck him. Years later, McCarthy recalled: "When I finally got to the big leagues I thought, 'Well, I've got it made now.' But once I got up there and had a look around, I realized my work had just begun. I was starting all over again."[1] In 1925, Chicago baseball was in miserable shape. Ever since the exposure of the 1919 White Sox World Series scandal, the city had suffered in a state of baseball gloom. Since 1920, the White Sox had been terrible. Uptown, the Cubs had not been much better. Given what some their city's players had done to the integrity of the game in 1919, some Chicago fans may have felt deep down that they deserved this. It was quite a comedown for the Cubs, a team which had had such a strong run in the early twentieth century, winning three pennants in a row and being in the pennant race, never finishing below third in every season from 1903 to 1913. In 1925, they hit bottom, losing on the last day of the season to "clinch the booby prize" of last place, as the *Chicago Tribune* ruefully described it.[2] Landing in the cellar on the last day was in some ways even worse than languishing there for much of the season. For here there was no getting used to it or making jokes about it in compensation. It was almost as if the Cubs had finally attained the elusive damnation which the baseball-evil city deserved. As the city's poet Carl Sandburg had once written: "They tell me you are evil, and I believe them...."

The last-place Cubs had gone through three managers in 1925. Team spirit was dead. Discipline had completely eroded. The team still had a few things going for them, however. They had an amazingly strong fan base. They had a capable front office with owner William Wrigley and President Bill Veeck. Veeck was a completely knowledgeable baseball man, and as long as people would chew gum, Wrigley would have plenty of money. There was no question that the Cubs would need a new manager for 1926, and in the summer of 1925 they were looking in earnest. One of Veeck's field scouts was former Louisville Manager Patsy Flaherty. Veeck himself had begun his career as a journalist in Louisville, so he had many sources there. Veeck also took advice from John B. Foster, editor of the *Spalding Baseball Guide* and club secretary of the New York Giants. A strong field manager was the obvious solution for the Cubs, and Flaherty, Foster, and Veeck all reported great things to Mr. Wrigley about Joe McCarthy. (Mr. Wrigley himself had also grown up in Germantown.)

The only stumbling block for the Cubs' appointment of McCarthy involved a matter of tradition. Baseball had developed a long tradition of hiring the manager off the bench. The undisputed team leader among the players always appeared to be the logical choice to be the manager when an appointment was to be made. McCarthy was not the first to be selected differently, but he was one of the most conspicuous. It would be an enormous challenge, and not only in the simple winning of the players' respect, for McCarthy would do this in short order. The Cubs' appointment of McCarthy marked a kind of professionalization of the post of manager. This was something a tradition-bound set of institutions that ran America's pastime would not too readily embrace. To many Americans in the 1920s, baseball was perhaps the most supreme symbol of past times of innocence, to which they were then clinging with an unprecedented level of nostalgia and sentiment. Anything that tampered with that would encounter resistance. Of course there was one obvious answer to any such misgivings—winning.[3]

Chicago was a city with a large measure of civic pride. The decline of baseball there in the early 1920s wounded people deeply. At the end of the disastrous 1925 season, Wrigley commented on how the fate of the Cubs was more than a mere baseball matter to him:

> In 1896 I was traveling. I was bragging about Chicago being "the greatest town on earth." A fellow in Cincinnati stopped me cold one day. "Why that town of yours doesn't even own its own ball club." That was right, and to rub it in I learned that the team [then called the White Stockings] was owned by Cincinnatians ... I resolved that some day I would give Chicago a ball team of its own. ... Yes, they're in the cellar, those boys of mine, [but next year] we'll have the ability. I'll shoot another quarter million dollars.[4]

Joe McCarthy as the manager of the Chicago Cubs. The Cubs had fallen to last place in 1925. McCarthy was hired out of Louisville to turn them around, and he did just that. Chicago contended for the National League lead every year he managed them, 1926–1930, winning the pennant in 1929. Troubles involving owner Phillip K. Wrigley prompted Chicago to dismiss him in 1930. (The *Washington Post* would later wonder: "How did they let him get away?") Within weeks of his dismissal, the Yankees hired him. (National Baseball Hall of Fame Library, Cooperstown, N.Y.)

Such a promise certainly made Chicagoans chew lots of gum. Wrigley had only bought the Cubs in 1918. He thus had little to show for his years in charge. With the collapse of 1925, he was prepared to do whatever it took to make a positive change. As for a new manager, Veeck had conferred with McCarthy over the winter prior to the 1925 season, but at that point McCarthy had rejected any notion of quitting Louisville. Contrary to the denials during the 1925 season, McCarthy had indeed met with Veeck and Wrigley during the summer. When the Cubs fell into numerous turmoils in September — Manager Rabbit Maranville's drinking escapades, his resignation, and the team's fall to last place — the hiring of McCarthy for 1926 was sealed.

When McCarthy formally signed in October, the press reaction was positive. The *Chicago Herald and Examiner* described him as "a high class baseball man [who] knows the game from A–Z and on top of that is a gentleman. He has all the qualities." John C. Hoffman of the *Chicago Daily News* predicted: "Chicago will like McCarthy. He knows baseball ... and he will be extraordinarily popular with the fans here.... He is congenial, although firm, and thoroughly capable of handling ball players." William Wrigley also expressed great confidence: "We have a man who knows baseball with us and don't forget that." Still, there came the obvious question that lots of people talked about in the city's barber shops, restaurants, and drinking establishments, which sports writer Irving Vaughan first voiced in the *Chicago Tribune*: "The man becomes a major league pilot without ever having played in the big show."[5] There it was, right off the bat — McCarthy had never played in the major leagues. Vaughan's use of the word "pilot" was especially shrewd, as the sense of what it takes to run a major league team could make some people nervous when "the wheel" was given to someone who had never been "up there" before in any capacity. Cast in that manner, the hiring of McCarthy seemed almost irrational. Obviously, he was going to have his chance, but in the event of any mishaps, the "I told you so's" were going to be ready.

Assembling a team and getting them ready were McCarthy's priorities for 1926. He was obviously excited about the upcoming challenge. Back in Germantown, McCarthy's family and friends threw him a send-off party. Connie Mack came to wish him well. That meant a lot to Joe, as he had idolized Mr. Mack since he was a boy. At the dinner, McCarthy expressed hopes of having "the pleasure sometime soon of meeting him in a World Series."[6] Everyone laughed that evening (and three years later it happened). The prospects of what he had available for spring training could only make McCarthy smile broadly. While in Louisville, he had had to struggle with cold-weather sites, short training times, and limited budgets. With Mr. Wrigley's team, matters would be quite different. William Wrigley owned much of Catalina Island off the coast of Southern California. The Cubs would train on his property. Time was not an issue. The Cubs would gather in Chicago to go out to California in mid–February, and they would stay out West nearly two months. For McCarthy, this was nirvana. If he could not ready a team for a baseball season under these circumstances, he was not worth his salt as a manager.

Assessing the needs of the Cubs after the 1925 season, various Chicago writers pointed to many areas of weakness. (That was not hard to do.) But a recurring theme concerned how light-hitting an outfield the team had.[7] The 1925 regulars, Mandy Brooks, Cliff Heathcote, and Arthur Jahn, hardly constituted a Murderers' Row of flycatchers. Jahn was a big, raw-boned Iowa farm boy with some potential, but in that last place outfield there was certainly room for someone more talented. In the second half of the 1925 American Association season, McCarthy, always studying his opposition, noticed a new player with the Toledo Mud Hens, Lewis "Hack" Wilson. People nicknamed him "Hack" because he looked like a famous wrestler of the day named George Hackenschmidt. Wilson had played three games for John McGraw and the New York Giants in 1923. In 1924 he was with them for most of the season, and he hit .295. He fell off in 1925, however, playing in only 62 games and hitting but .239. Wilson had shown some behavior problems (drinking and fighting), and McGraw decided he needed to mature a bit. He sent him to Toledo. One Chicago reporter claimed that McGraw had pronounced Wilson "unfit for the big time." McGraw spoke of the matter with a little more respect. "I let Wilson go," McGraw proclaimed, "not because he was not hitting for me. He went wild for a while, but then he went to pieces.... The club wasn't going, and the number of players had to be trimmed. I couldn't afford to hold him."[8]

Years later, McCarthy had a somewhat different memory of the situation. At that time when a major leaguer was "sent down" his former team could maintain rights to him, provided they filed the appropriate "waiver" claims with their league office. McCarthy said that McGraw and the Giants failed to do this with Wilson. Informed of this, and never one to miss a trick, McCarthy thus grabbed Hack Wilson for the Cubs for a simple waiver price. McCarthy recalled:

> We stole him from the Giants. ... They had sent him to the minors and then forgot to recall him, a clerical mistake. So he was unprotected when the draft came around. The Cubs finished in the cellar the year before, so we had first pick. We took Wilson for $5000. McGraw hit the ceiling when he heard about it.[9]

Earlier, McCarthy's recollection of the procurement of Wilson had given credit to Veeck: When Veeck asked McCarthy if he wanted to get Hack Wilson, McCarthy said he "told him Wilson was the property of the Giants and couldn't be had. But Veeck said he thought he could be, and he was right. So we got Wilson." McCarthy was being kind to Veeck. McCarthy knew Wilson was unprotected from waivers. It was Veeck who thought Wilson was McGraw's property; McCarthy was the one who knew better. Mr. Wrigley had said that he was willing to spend a lot of money to rebuild the Cubs into contenders. Some said he had staked McCarthy $250,000 to build up the club. With this key move by McCarthy, Wrigley did it on the cheap. Everyone in baseball knew that Hack had great talent. The question was whether any manager could keep him from self-destructing.[10]

When the team assembled to work on Catalina Island, Chicago reporters were there to observe McCarthy and his methods. Bill Killefer, the Cubs' manager of the previous spring, had been a friend to his players. He mingled, kidded, and drank with them. McCarthy was anything but that sort of man, and the players quickly realized it. There was a standing joke among the Cub veterans to tell rookies about the "bowling alley" on Mr. Wrigley's yacht that took them from the California coast to Catalina Island. Awed by stories of Wrigley's wealth, a couple of rookies took the bait and went all through the ship's lower decks, looking for a bowling game while the veterans and crew chuckled. No one thought for one second about trying to pull that one on McCarthy. He had already made an impact even before arriving in camp, and he would have never fallen for the story anyway.

When the team traveled by train, particularly on long treks like the ones to and from the West Coast, the players regularly sang songs. Killefer would always sing with them. McCarthy never did. He was, noted one scribe, "a more sober-minded fellow who is going to keep them on the jump all the time." Still, the writer hastened to add: "After they get to know him a bit better, they will discover that he is a pretty fair gentleman to work for." The point was that McCarthy was not there for the players, or for the press, to get to know, let alone like. What was learned about him would be learned *en passant*, for the whole purpose in his being there was to prepare a ball club for a new season. McCarthy was simply "business at all times, and on the practice field [he] talks to his men only when issuing an order or giving a pointer. [While] Killefer depended on friendship, ... McCarthy apparently believes respect is more efficient." "No loafing, no time for play;" these were the sorts of reports about which Chicago fans read in February and March. "All business;" twenty-two years later, Ted Williams would say much the same, as would everyone else in the intervening seasons.[11]

Chicago's baseball scribes noted McCarthy's reserved nature. He "keeps decisions to himself until he has fully decided." "McCarthy evidently is one of those individuals who believes actions speak louder than words." Phrases like "the mystery pilot," "his usual reticent self," and "Silent Joe McCarthy" began to appear. But they were all written with respect and good humor. One reporter jokingly complained that McCarthy is "ignoring entirely the most important phase of this Spring Training racket — the noble ballyhoo. Concerning himself only with athletes, most of the correspondents have nothing left but their typewriters." In an age where deference was still a social grace, a manager like McCarthy could win complete acceptance and respect while keeping a discreet distance at all times. People would bow to Wrigley, but expect him to provide them with a winner. They yielded to and expected the same of McCarthy.

In subsequent generations, reporters would approach their work with much more of a sense of entitlement. McCarthy would see more and more of this as his career progressed. News people have increasingly taken as a given the notion that they are there to be served by the sports figures they cover, believing their coverage to be an integral part of the game. In the 1920s the media operated with a keener awareness that their work lay on the periphery with respect to the central activities of the players and managers. If a manager like McCarthy then chose to be relatively silent with the media but appeared to be whipping his charges into good shape, the silence would simply be attributed to and rationally accepted as part of the man's nature. Even when a manager was worse than silent, reporters would respond with respect. When the Cub regulars lost some intra-squad games to the reserves, games pitting the "Spearmints" vs. the "Doublemints," McCarthy was queried about the light hitting. He snapped: "What of it?" The *Tribune* reporter noted the comment with a chuckle: "You have to admire his attitude."

Later generations of reporters would take umbrage at such dismissals. At this time reporters were no less analytical but far less egocentric. They regarded McCarthy as a "dandy little leader ... [who has] made a most favorable impression with the war correspondents," noting that "these war scribes sometimes are critical birds." Back then, a good reporter had to know the intricacies of baseball, and he had to be able to judge a man's character through discreet observation. Perceptive reporters came quickly to appreciate McCarthy. Among the Chicago reporters all talk of "never played in the major leagues" quickly vanished. Fans in opposing ballparks would yell things — "Hey busher!" "I hear you were a big shot in Wilkes-Barre!" "How does it feel to sleep in a lower berth?" In the first few weeks, particularly since he was coaching third, McCarthy was also especially susceptible to "Busher" barbs from opposing fielders. Throughout, McCarthy was not the slightest bit fazed, and in Chicago players and reporters took very little time to recognize the quality of what was there before them.

Baseball was full of veteran big league managers in 1926. Seven were star player-managers, including Ty Cobb, Tris Speaker, Eddie Collins, George Sisler, Rogers Hornsby, and Bucky Harris. Others had years of playing or managing experience like Wilbert Robinson and Bill McKechnie. And of course there were John McGraw and Connie Mack, who between them had already managed over 50 years. McCarthy was the only new manager in the majors that spring, and with no big league experience, his rookie status seemed all the more stark. But after a few weeks of spring training, no one in Chicago felt the least bit of apprehension. "In two months time," wrote one paper, "McCarthy has accomplished more in the training season than seemed possible. The team resembles the Cubs of last year only in that they wear similar uniforms."[12]

Another recurring set of references came forth about McCarthy that spring. Reporters saw the tough physical regimen through which he put his players. He drove them hard, harder than any manager the reporters or the players had ever seen. No one complained, for they quickly saw it was working. Still, reporters could not resist. In addition to "Silent Joe" and "the mystery pilot," writers described the training camp with references to the ante-bellum South. "Cub boss plays Simon Legree," was a *Chicago Tribune* lead in to a spring training article. When the light hitting from regulars began to show improvement in intra-squad games, a reporter relayed that "McCarthy has promised to show his slaves his first smile of the season." Amidst such Southern plantation allusions, one nickname stuck with him for his next twenty-five years of managing, and for the rest of his life — "Marse Joe." The name was first coined by Harry Neily of the *Chicago Evening American*. Political sensitivities of later generations readily attach racism to any such allusion, and in 1926 some who bandied about such a name with respect to McCarthy undoubtedly harbored such prejudices, but the nickname stuck, not because of any racism of the times but because McCarthy was indeed the Master. He ruled.

There was no doubt as to McCarthy's authority or his confidence. That spring, Wrigley and Veeck had picked up a hot prospect from Salt Lake City of the Pacific Coast League named Francis Joseph "Lefty" O'Doul. In 1925, O'Doul had hit .375, clouted 24 home runs, and knocked in 191 runs for Salt Lake. McCarthy cut him, claiming he was not yet ready for the majors. It would prove to be one of the few times a player that McCarthy cut became a star. (O'Doul batted over .300 in five straight years, including a phenomenal .398 season with the Phillies in 1929.) This would later bother Wrigley, but for the moment, Marse Joe was in charge; Wrigley accepted it. O'Doul would never forgive McCarthy for the slight. A few years later, he played some of his best baseball against McCarthy. Even as late as 1948, with O'Doul having retired for fourteen years and then managing in San Francisco, he would still angrily hold forth to the press that McCarthy could not appreciate talent. The rest of the men, however, played for him with complete faith in his mastery of the game, as well as with a touch of fear as to what could befall anyone who was foolish enough to doubt him, let alone stand up to him.[13]

Spring training went very well for McCarthy and the Cubs. The team rounded into good condition. With a sardonic headline in one paper of "Extra! McCarthy Talks About The Team," McCarthy expressed confidence: "Pick us last like everyone else seems to be doing and get fooled with all the rest of them," he proclaimed. "We've got a ball club here that's going to be the surprise of the league. ... Anybody who tells me I have an eighth place outfit doesn't know anything about baseball." The Cubs had been hapless in 1925. Rebuilding with a rookie manager did not give baseball people in other league cities much basis to be optimistic about Chicago, and the spring predictions showed it. McCarthy's words, in their optimism and even more in their pugnaciousness, certainly resonated well with Chicago fans and reporters. "Mr. McCarthy still bears up nobly now that he has learned the worst and belligerently insists that his Cubs are not as bad as people insist."[14]

The only significant mishap of the spring concerned the team's famous veteran pitcher, Grover Cleveland Alexander. He suffered a sprained ankle. McCarthy could and did little about this, although he may have been irritated by Alexander's well-known tendency to "dog it" during spring training. When he noted that the team was in good shape he explicitly noted, "with the exception of Alex."[15] His attitude was, logically, that there was little he needed to teach Alexander anyway. Alexander had already won 315 games in his career, so there was nothing he missed in spring training other than the time to get in shape. McCarthy just had to let Alexander mend and let him know when he was ready. Alexander was 39 years old, two months older than McCarthy. His pitching was still great. His record in 1925 was 15 and 11, and several of the losses were one-run affairs in which he'd had little offensive support. In 236 innings he had walked but 29 batters, and several of them intentionally. He was a marvel, but there were questions. One was the obvious one — how would his ankle heal? That was going to be a matter of time. The other question concerned how Alexander would fit into McCarthy's team and system. Alexander had been given a free pass by most of his managers throughout his career, especially Killefer, his former catcher and drinking buddy. Alexander drank, and he did not keep good hours. Still, when a man can win 300 games an intelligent manager is not likely to try to tinker too much. For McCarthy, with Alexander injured, there was not much to consider, at least not yet.[16]

After the Catalina training, the Cubs toured the West, playing some teams in the Los Angeles area. Wrigley also owned the L.A. Angels of the Pacific Coast League. From there they headed back to Chicago playing some games in Texas and Kansas City on route. The team nearly lost Hack Wilson in El Paso. There he ventured across the border into Juarez, Mexico. He caroused heavily and was nearly prevented from reentering the US because he had stayed across the border too long. When he finally got back to the hotel, after the drinking and the stress with the border officials, Wilson got sick in the lobby, in front of several reporters and McCarthy. McCarthy said nothing until the next day. Then he told Hack to come up to his hotel room. As he boarded the elevator, Hack confessed to a reporter, "I'd rather face a firing squad than go up there." McCarthy simply told Wilson that he picked the wrong place to get sick. Years later, McCarthy reflected: "What could a manager say to such a loyal player with a weakness he could not handle?" Most managers would have tried to put some sort of shackles on Wilson for his behavior. Many did, and with them Wilson played poorly. Only McCarthy would get Hall of Fame play out of Hack.[17]

On April 10, the team arrived in Kansas City, and McCarthy called the team together for a 10:00 A.M. meeting at the Muehlebach Hotel. Since several of the 1925 Cubs had been traded, notably Maranville, McCarthy wanted to work out a new set of signals. As he was proceeding with the meeting, Alexander sauntered into the room, obviously late and even more obviously drunk. He had probably been out all night. As McCarthy was speaking, Alex lit up a cigarette, and just as McCarthy said "Now suppose we get a man at second base...," Alexander interrupted and joked loudly, "You don't have to worry about that, McCarthy. This club will never get a man that far." The room was silent for a moment. No one chuckled, and McCarthy responded by maintaining complete composure. He icily continued: "Well, Alex, we're going to try anyway." There was a certain pall cast about the room at that moment. It was not as though Alexander was seeking any sort of player rebellion forcing teammates to choose "him or me." This was just Alexander the loose cannon. He had been noticeably vocal when McCarthy first came to the Cubs, calling him "a bush league manager." McCarthy could ignore Alex., provided the rest of the team continued to give him their respect and attention. It could work, and everyone hoped that Alexander could once again pitch superbly, but in the long run such a player-manager mix could certainly set up a showdown. After the morning meeting in Kansas City, no one was going to be surprised if such a clash occurred.[18]

On the morning of opening day McCarthy published a short article in the *Chicago Herald and Examiner*. In it he asked, dared, and warned the fans "not to say too much about the 'hopeless' Cubs. [For] before this race is run," he predicted, "they'll wish they hadn't." Starting his article to the city with such Irish bravado, McCarthy then took a more considered pose: "We do not start tomorrow in a dash after the pennant. We are going out to prove we are a ball club that is capable of playing intelligent baseball and of taking advantage of every opportunity that comes our way. We may not be the best ball club in the National League," he nodded, "but we are a long way from the worst. This we will prove, perhaps before the week is out. ... The Cubs will be a fine team, and they will be one that will worry all opposition. ... Pay all the attention you want to the contenders. But don't forget the Cubs."[19]

The Cubs' opening weeks proved euphoric. On April 21, 33,000 fans turned out for the home opener against Cincinnati. The city was excited. In the previous week, at Easter time, the city had been hit by a freak blizzard. Now the snow had melted; it was 78 degrees at game time, and the Cubs were opening with a new spirit. It had been a long time since the city's fans felt this good in April. "An almost operatic ovation was accorded at the first official appearance of Joseph McCarthy in our midst as manager of the Bruins," wrote the *Chicago Daily News*. "Chicago's athletic prestige is partly in his hands." The memories of 1919 and of the Cubs' five-year fall were all there for McCarthy to shoulder. The city was more attuned to the moment than ever, as this was the first year that Cubs games were broadcast on radio. WMAQ, a station owned by the *Daily News*, carried the games. Hal Totten was the first announcer. McCarthy accepted a good-luck floral wreath, and the Cubs proceeded to defeat the

Cincinnati Reds—in three straight games. Wrigley was rhapsodic. After the third win over the Reds he proudly proclaimed: "Our boys looked defeat in the eye a half dozen times, but they were never licked. ... I think we've got the team. We've certainly got the manager." In the eighth inning of the second game, the Cubs got a man on first. Coaching third, McCarthy signaled for a steal. The Reds catcher's throw to second was wild, and on McCarthy's direction, the runner took third *and* home. "Joe's work again," smiled Wrigley. "He's some manager." The next day, the Cubs won 18–1, a tribute, smirked one reporter, to "the unkindly spirit of McCarthy's boys." From Cincinnati, the Cubs traveled to Pittsburgh to play the defending champion Pirates. The Cubs won 4–3. Hack Wilson scored the winning run on a squeeze play in the eighth inning. In the next week against St. Louis, Wilson doubled to open the fourth inning. The next batter walked. Cardinals third baseman Les Bell was playing back on the grass. McCarthy noticed it and immediately called for a double steal. It worked. At this point, Chicago reporters confessed they were unaccustomed to clacking out such terms as "squeeze play" and "double steal." Everyone recognized the changes to be the work of McCarthy. Rogers Hornsby, player-manager of the Cardinals, had obnoxiously opined that the Cubs lacked "the punch that is necessary to make a fight all season." He predicted that Chicago would thus lose a lot of close games. After his double-steal call and a Cub victory over the Cardinals, punched over by another Hack Wilson hit, McCarthy sneered to a reporter, in obvious cognizance of Horsnby: "Let me answer those who have doubted the Cubs' punch—they have it!" After the same game, another reporter asked Hornsby if he now had any revised comment about the "punchless" Cubs. Hornsby snapped: "Get the hell out of here!"[20]

It was still quite early in the season, but the Cubs' good start excited everyone. Two of three victories over the Giants in early May proved most gratifying, and not just to Hack Wilson. Like Hornsby, John McGraw also asserted that the Cubs, although they will "be knocking around up there and cause a lot of trouble," do not "have the punch." While, for obvious reasons, McCarthy would never show any sympathy for such views, in private conversations with Veeck and Wrigley he had been saying much the same thing. Indeed in late May the Cubs did lose a number of close ones, just as Hornsby and McGraw had predicted. The Cubs were holding on to second place then, but they slipped to third after losing six of eight in early June. At that point, McCarthy made a significant personnel move, wrapping up a deal with his friends in Indianapolis. He sent the Indians a reserve outfielder, Joe Munson, and infielder Maurice Shannon, who he had brought to the Cubs from Louisville but who had not delivered. In exchange for these two, the Cubs received infielder Harry Schreiber and an outfielder named Riggs Stephenson. "Stevie" was the man McCarthy wanted, and he proved to be quite a catch indeed. The St. Louis Cardinals were hot after him too. Hack Wilson and Riggs Stephenson would bat fourth and fifth in McCarthy's lineup for many years. With them, the Cubs' "punch" would be much improved. Before the season, Wrigley had staked $250,000 for McCarthy to spend as he endeavored to build up the ball club. After picking up Wilson and Stephenson, McCarthy returned $200,000. "I can't use this," McCarthy explained. "The only players I want to buy can't be bought, and there isn't any sense in spending your money on players that won't do the club any good."[21]

While the acquisitions of Wilson and Stephenson were huge personnel moves for the Cubs, at the moment, a more pressing personnel issue needed to be addressed. Grover Cleveland Alexander had continued to be a loose cannon. His ankle had healed, but his drinking and poor hours had not. That spring, he developed the first major sore arm of his career. His pitching had been decidedly mediocre. In June his record stood at a mere 3 and 3. On May 28, he had one dizzy spell on the bench which required medical attention. Like everyone in baseball at that time, McCarthy did not fully grasp the degree to which Alexander's problems were due to epilepsy. There was no question that he had a drinking problem, one which did his epilepsy no good, but whatever the mix of alcohol and illness, McCarthy was growing impatient. He did not mind players drinking (Wilson sure did, and McCarthy himself appreciated a good scotch), but everyone had to come to the park ready to work. Alexander had not always done this. Several times McCarthy called on Alexander, and Alex replied: "I'm not ready." Meanwhile, Alexander was a beloved figure in Chicago. He had been with the Cubs since 1918 and twice won 20 games for them. In May, the Cubs had hosted "Alexander Day," at which various Cub boosters showered him with gifts, including a new Lincoln. Young Charlie Root, a rookie pitcher with the Cubs, was also having arm problems in May and June. With this trouble, McCarthy's early run in the standings was imperiled, and Alexander's seemingly self-imposed problems were not helping one bit.[22]

In mid–June, the Cubs were off on a trip around the East. It marked McCarthy's first appearance in Philadelphia in any capacity as a professional baseball man. It had been a long road traveled since heading off from Germantown to play for Wilmington in 1907, but here he was a big league manager. Germantown could not have been more proud. June 14 was declared "Joe McCarthy Day" in Philadelphia. Before the Cubs-Phillies game McCarthy "was all grins and flushes" as the St. Xavier Boys Band paraded about Baker Bowl. A boyhood friend, Frank Foster, marshaled the band. A Germantown Boy Scout troop brought in several trunks from which McCarthy was given such gifts as a travel bag, a wardrobe trunk, and a grandfather clock encased in Mahogany, all from donations from people in Germantown. The Cubs players bought him a new watch for the occasion, "fully establishing Joe as a big leaguer." With his family and friends sitting on the first-base side that afternoon, McCarthy switched his coaching duties to first base. Otherwise he was business as usual, as his mother commented: "he doesn't like this fuss." In public, McCarthy did not care to show much emotion. But the gifts were deeply appreciated. When interviewed at his Buffalo home twelve years later, he still had the grandfather clock. He proudly proclaimed: "Mrs. McCarthy and I will have this clock as long as we live." They did.[23]

The hoopla of his triumphal return to Philadelphia was a fine, especially since the Cubs won 9–7. If the occasion raised any hint of sentimentality in McCarthy, he sure did not show it. The very next day, indeed, he made a bold move. He suspended Grover Cleveland Alexander. So much for sentiment! That afternoon a group of reporters asked McCarthy "Any news?" McCarthy deadpanned: "Nothing except that I have suspended Alex indefinitely." "McCarthy," quipped one of the reporters, "seemed surprised at the haste the reporters made to get to the telegraph office." McCarthy may have been composed before the newsmen, but he knew the significance of his move and was in absolute earnest about it. On June 15, McCarthy said Alexander had arrived at the Phillies' Baker Bowl "out of condition," i.e. drunk. McCarthy refused to let him dress for a team practice or even enter the Cubs' dressing room. "This isn't the first time by any means," McCarthy mentioned. "This is the sixth time it has happened in the last nine or ten days. He can't hope to get his arm cured by such things as he is doing, and those things don't fit with my plans to build up a team. I absolutely refused to allow him to disrupt our ball club and will not have him around in that condition. Any player," noted McCarthy, "may drink and get away with it if he is winning. ... but no player can get away with it if he isn't winning. I refuse to stand for it any longer."

McCarthy said he was not going to let "one man ruin all the work I am doing in attempting to build up this club. All the players saw his condition this afternoon, and they'll think they are privileged too if I pass over his condition as it was out there. ... There had to be a showdown, and here it is." McCarthy would not blink in such a circumstance. The papers were supportive of his move. No one wrote in sympathy of Alexander. Wrigley telegraphed McCarthy directly: "Congratulations. For years I have been looking for a manager who had the nerve to do that." Alexander returned to Chicago. If he imagined any sort of groundswell of fan support, it did not come forth. If anything, the exposure of his behavior engendered a feeling of betrayal, especially after the gifts they gave him in May. Alexander sought a meeting with Veeck, but Veeck refused to see him. Veeck issued a statement to the press:

> I do not see what purpose Alex would serve in seeing me. I have the utmost respect for McCarthy's judgment. It is sound and it is good. He had plenty of provocation for what he did in the Alexander case, and you can say for me as plainly as you want that I will back McCarthy's judgment until hell freezes over. McCarthy is the manager of the ball club and will continue to manage it. The sooner all persons get that idea in their heads the better off all will be.[24]

Alexander had become a kind of Romantic figure among Chicagoans. Amidst the naughty days of Prohibition, such devil-may-care athletic figures as Babe Ruth and golfer Walter Hagen had their appeal. But Babe Ruth had just come off his most disgraceful year, and a young golfer of impeccable behavior named Bobby Jones was eclipsing Hagen for supremacy in much of the country club sports world. In Chicago, as well, the Prohibition thug Al Capone certainly had his followers, but many others in the city had turned their idealism toward lawman Eliot Ness. Given the Cubs' failure to produce in their freewheeling days, McCarthy was as welcome a figure in sports as Ness was in law enforcement. Meanwhile, Alexander had no grasp of how he may have outworn his welcome. For many years, Alexander had been the batterymate of Bill Killefer, with both the Phillies and the Cubs. They had come to the Cubs together in a single trade. When Killefer became the manager of the Cubs, Alex enjoyed a special place on the roster, and he never really adjusted to McCarthy. Upon his suspension and with the rebuff from Veeck, Alex suddenly professed a new understanding and penitence. He said he would go back to the ballpark and start working himself back into condition. But McCarthy and the Cubs would not relent, and a week later they sold Alexander to the St. Louis Cardinals. (There he pitched well. He was reunited with Killefer, now a Cardinals coach. That fall he won the final game of the World Series for St. Louis in dramatic style. He won 21 games the next season, then faded to a 9 win season with St. Louis in 1929 before retiring after unsuccessfully attempting one more season with the Phillies. Needing the money, he still sadly knocked around the minors a few years thereafter.) In later reflections, McCarthy would be generous. "'Did Alex follow the rules?' Sure he did, but they were always Alexander's rules. ... But he was a nice fellow. Alex was all right, 'just couldn't keep to the rules, that's all." The Cubs had finished last in 1925, and in June of 1926 McCarthy felt "If last again, I'd rather it was without him."[25]

The Alexander trade left the Cubs with even deeper concerns about their pitching. Young Charlie Root had a sore arm. Aside from him, they had only two reliable starters—Guy Bush and "Sheriff" Fred Blake. The pitching roster was thin, but the papers were forgiving: "Chicago fans will regret the passing of Alexander, but Chicago fans also regret his actions that forced Manager McCarthy to discipline him." In the area of hitting, Wilson and Stephenson performed well. McCarthy's young catcher, Leo "Gabby" Hartnett, was rounding nicely. When Killefer brought him up in 1925, Hartnett had had a spectacular first half-season, but he had fallen off thereafter. McCarthy was guiding him into becoming more of a contact hitter and swinging less for home runs. It would work, but it would take time. Meanwhile, Hartnett was proving to be one of the best defensive catchers in the league, with a throwing arm few base stealers would dare to test. By the end of June, the Cubs did not look like pennant contenders, but there was no doubt that a new era had begun, and equally no doubt as to who was in charge.

Back during spring training on Catalina Island, McCarthy had stated that "the Cub teams of the last two or three years have burned out by the end of June, and that is what I want to avoid." Here it was the end of June. He had two excellent hitters, and his pitching strength was meager. A game against St. Louis, and Alexander, on June 27 showed they were not going to quit. Given Alex's recent release, the game was full of tension. All afternoon, McCarthy was in the coaching box, twenty yards from the mound as Alex pitched. St. Louis fans were wildly cheering: "Make him like it, Alex." "You never saw pitches like that at Wilkes-Barre!" The game was tight all the way through. Alexander was effective, but so was Chicago's Bob Osborn. With the score 2–2 in the tenth, St. Louis scored an unearned run to win. The Cardinals had won, but McCarthy and Chicago had stood their ground, and they beat the Cardinals in their next two games.[26]

McCarthy had some of his old heady tricks for the other National League managers that summer. In a game with Cincinnati, McCarthy noticed that their catcher "Bubbles" Hargrave was batting seventh, ahead of shortstop Frank Emmer, instead of his usual eighth spot. He was batting in his usual spot simply because Reds Manager Jack Hendricks had filled out the lineup card incorrectly. Hargrave went hitless through the game, and McCarthy said nothing. Then with two out in the eighth inning and the Reds up 3–0, Hargrave knocked in a run. McCarthy lodged a protest, which was upheld, thus ending the Reds' half of the inning and depriving them of a run. Still down 3–0, the Cubs rallied for two in the ninth and had a runner on third. Alas, McCarthy's old Louisville teammate Adolfo Luque struck out Gabby Hartnett to end the game. Luque was not surprised at McCarthy's display of cunning. He had seen it years before. As the 1926 season rolled by, the National League was growing less and less surprised too. The Cubs won the second game of the doubleheader that day, 9–4.[27]

Into July that season, Cincinnati had been the surprise of the National League. On July 8, the Reds were in first place, four games ahead of Pittsburgh. Right there with Pittsburgh stood Brooklyn, St. Louis, and the Cubs. Only two games separated second from fifth place. The Pirates, Dodgers, and Cardinals were living up to expectations. The Cubs' showing was a shock. Dodgers' Manager Wilbert Robinson commented: "I certainly admire Joe McCarthy, and you can't make that too strong. He's shown some of the older managers how to run a ball club. His tactics are right; he won't stand for any foolishness. He's going to be a highly successful manager." Some of the very same things Casey Stengel discovered down in Toledo, when he researched why Louisville had been so successful in 1925, were part of the Cubs' new success under Joe McCarthy. As of mid–July, the Cubs were first in the National League in fielding percentage. They had committed the fewest errors, and they had turned the most double plays. As for the offensive punch that Hornsby said was lacking, Stephenson and Wilson were both batting above .330, and Wilson was leading the National League in home runs. On July 21, after clobbering the Giants 16–2, the Cubs were just three games out of first place.[28]

Inexplicably, the Cubs fell away from the lead in late July, losing most of their games to such lowly teams as Philadelphia and Boston. Noting how most of the losses were one-run affairs which could have gone either way, McCarthy lamented: "It is certainly enough to keep you awake nights." After losing another game in Boston, the *Herald and Examiner* eulogized: "Somewhere under the dank and unkept corridors of this dingy park, Mr. McCarthy could install an epitaph in commemoration of the burial of the pennant hopes: 'Here lie the Cubs of '26. Their aims were high; Their hits were nix.'" The fact that the Cubs fans and correspondents had taken the word "pennant" seriously in 1926 was quite an accomplishment in itself. But McCarthy was hardly in accord with the press here. He was distressed about the losses, "wearing a dark scowl," as one scribe noted, but he knew there was still time. This was a problem McCarthy had with lots of reporters. They needed to exaggerate, even distort, in order to frame a story. He saw little reason to feed this any more than he had to. If the team could put together a decent winning streak, he noted, it was still possible to climb back into the race.[29]

Many players and managers had been predicting that the Cincinnati Reds would not be able to hold on to first place. In August, this proved correct. The Reds faded, as St. Louis and Pittsburgh picked up the pace. The Cubs moved forward too. From August 2nd to the 30th they won 18 of 26 games, 10 of the last 11. On September 2nd, they were in fourth place, five games behind the now leading Cardinals, and that afternoon they hosted St. Louis in a doubleheader. Thirty-four thousand came to the park, the largest weekday baseball crowd in Chicago history. Alexander would start game one. It was his first appearance in Chicago since being sold. Alex won his game, and the Cardinals won the nightcap too. The next day's sports headlines ran: "Alex Shatters Bruin Morale." "It's all over now," wrote one scribe, "but," he savored, "for one afternoon Chicago knew the excitement of being a pennant contender." This time, indeed, the reporters were not being premature. Rogers Hornsby had praise for his opponents that day. The Cubs, he opined, "aren't a championship ball club, but McCarthy has done such a fine piece of managing that he's made them look that way at times." St. Louis remained in first place, although the Reds briefly drew even with them in mid–September. Whatever faint chances the Cubs may have had vanished when Hack Wilson was knocked unconscious in a beaning against Philadelphia. He was out, Stephenson had a pulled leg muscle, and the Cubs lost five in a row. After that, and with the pennant hopes gone, McCarthy chose to rest Wilson for the remainder of the season.[30]

St. Louis went on to clinch the pennant, nosing out Cincinnati by two games. Defending champion Pittsburgh took third, and the Cubs were in fourth, two games behind them. Fourth place marked a first division finish. This meant the Cubs were "in the money;" each player getting a small cut of World Series revenues ($600). This was a big deal in an era when many players were making well under $10,000. Cub fans could only be pleased with the 1926 season. They came in fourth; more importantly, through the summer and into the month of September, they had been legitimate contenders. McCarthy had brought them all the way back from last place into complete respectability. Warren Brown of the *Herald and Examiner* wrote at the season's end:

> To baseball writers I ask, 'What do you think of the Cubs?' Over and over the answer: 'I have yet to see them play a BAD ball game.' That estimation of the Cubs is an appreciation of the managerial art of Joe McCarthy. When a club makes rivals admit that it looks like an organization even in defeat, then it is A ball club. Though he won no pennant in his first year of major league duty, Joe McCarthy can rest on his laurels. I know he will not. He has proven he can scare the dickens out of an entire league by getting the organization idea into the heads of a collection of ordinary ball players." [emphases his][31]

McCarthy had constructed a system. With the complete backing of William Wrigley and Bill Veeck, he had made it work. He had gotten rid of Grover Cleveland Alexander. He had worked his team into believing in him and in one another. The Pittsburgh Pirates were troubled by dissension, as General Manager Fred Clarke openly second guessed Manager Bill McKechnie. The New York Giants had much disharmony. Some St. Louis Cardinals chafed under the know-it-all leadership of Rogers Hornsby. The Cubs had none of this. McCarthy had ironed out all the details in the creation of a smoothly running organization. While he coached third base and Jim Burke coached first, McCarthy installed a third "bench coach," Mike Doolan. This was a baseball first. Doolan guided players on defensive pointers and sign stealing and was there to keep the players on edge. Doolan's personality was perfectly suited for this, something else McCarthy's attention to detail had encompassed. McCarthy even changed the bat boy assignments. He preferred the personality and character of the visiting team batboy, Eddie Froelich, and switched him to his side of the field. No stone had been left unturned. McCarthy gave an improved cast to everything. The Cubs then played heady baseball; their league lead in such areas as fielding, fewest errors, and double plays showed it. They did not beat themselves. They were the first team, in an era of tiny gloves, to have more double plays than errors. Such strong organizations tend to do well in the long run. With such a base, the question was whether Joe McCarthy could keep his pitching in shape and find the extra "punch" that Rogers Hornsby and others had said he needed.[32]

17

McCarthy's Scrappers

"A little of the same old stuff, both morning and afternoon." That was McCarthy's simple description of the regimen for the team as it assembled on Catalina Island to begin training in 1927. (It was also, smiled one reporter, "an almost record breaking speech for McCarthy, at least so far as length was concerned.") After the showing of 1926, no one doubted McCarthy or his system. "Marse Joe" seemed indeed a most appropriate sobriquet. That February a new spirit and enthusiasm surrounded the Cub team. People had gone from despair to hope and now to expectation — that they would have a genuine contender in their midst. Amused reporters noted how many more people in the Cubs' offices found excuses to make the trip out to California that spring, at Mr. Wrigley's expense, of course.[1]

The players arrived in generally good shape, and with McCarthy's two drills a day the few excesses of winter storage quickly vanished. "We could start the season in two weeks," nodded McCarthy. Despite the calls for more "punch," the Cubs fielded pretty much the same people who completed the 1926 season for them. The big change elsewhere in the league involved pitcher Jimmy Ring and infielder Frankie Frisch being traded from New York to St. Louis in exchange for Rogers Hornsby. Baseball people wondered two connected things here: what would Hornsby do for the Giants, and how would he and John McGraw get along?[2]

McCarthy drilled his players on the fundamentals. One of his repeated bits of advice to his pitchers: "Don't let go of the ball too soon; get the body in front of the pitch." Such coordination gets the full body into the pitch. The opposite forces a reliance upon just the arm for pitching velocity, with the usual result of sore arms. McCarthy wanted to avoid another round of those at all costs. Charlie Root, Sheriff Blake, Guy Bush, and Percy Jones were to be his rotation. If they remained healthy and pitched as McCarthy felt they could, the Cubs would have a chance. Some still reminisced about Alexander, but McCarthy did not give the matter a second of thought. The team looked a little ragged in some games against West Coast teams. It was unusually hot in Southern California that winter, and that could have affected some players. In a doubleheader against the Hollywood Stars, McCarthy actually missed an opponent batting out of turn. "That mistake will never happen in the regular season when I am on the job," promised McCarthy, and, in reference to the system he had constructed, McCarthy confidently added, "If I don't catch a bobble like that [coaches] Jim Burke or Mike Doolan will."[3] For Cub fans there was a touch of humor in the revelation that Marse Joe could actually make a mistake, and even more reassurance in the point that his system would not.

Whether or not the California heat affected McCarthy, it certainly got to Hack Wilson one day, and McCarthy knew why. One Sunday morning McCarthy was up and heading off to early Mass. He saw Wilson pass him by in a car with a group of local rowdies, obviously having been out all night. That afternoon the Cubs played the Pacific Coast League Los Angeles Angels. With the heat of the afternoon and in the usual course of a spring training game, McCarthy juggled his lineup, using many subs. He kept Hack Wilson in the game, however. Hack never loafed that entire afternoon. He never did. When he hit a home run in the seventh inning, Wilson could barely circle the bases. As fatigued as Wilson was at the end of the day, McCarthy hoped the message would sink in when he said to him: "better go in now, Hack. You're liable to be too tired to go out automobile riding tonight."[4]

McCarthy always liked Hack Wilson. He never kept track of his or any of his players' hours or their off-field habits, and Wilson had some hellacious habits. Beyond his drinking, he would get in fights. He was arrested on several occasions. He once had to be pried loose after he got stuck trying to squeeze out of a men's room window during a raid on a speakeasy.[5] McCarthy knew all this, but he cared only about a player's condition and performance at the ball park. At game time, Hack could always be depended upon to deliver, no matter what he had been doing the night before. Any discussions as to how drinking could shorten a player's career were never something upon which McCarthy cared to offer an opinion. It touched upon the life of a man off the ball field, and that, he always felt, was none of his business.

McCarthy tried a few experiments that spring. He had several outfielders to whom he wanted to give a chance, especially Earl Webb, whom he had managed in Louisville. Meanwhile, third baseman Howard Freigau was a question mark. In 1926 he had made several key errors and hit but .270. McCarthy decided to try outfielder Riggs Stephenson at third base. Stephenson had hit .338 in 1926. There was no question that he had a place in the 1927 Cubs lineup. One view to which McCarthy held was that a third baseman was more important for his hitting than his fielding, as the number of fielding chances he would have per game would usually be low. If Stephenson could become reasonably fluent with the basics of the position, this could allow a stronger hitter in the lineup than Freigau. He felt it was worth a try, and in the first few exhibition games, it seemed to work.[6]

On April 13, the Cubs opened against St. Louis. A capacity crowd of 35,000 came to the Cubs park, now for the first time officially called "Wrigley Field." Ten thousand more had to be turned away. Commissioner Landis was in the stands. Grover Cleveland Alexander was on the mound for the Cardinals. The Cubs won 10–1. Earl Webb hit two home runs. Riggs Stephenson went three for four, had one infield assist, and made no errors at third. With the victory over the champion Cardinals, and with a seemingly successful adjustment by Marse Joe, Chicago fans were wildly optimistic. Webb, wrote one reporter, "will remind many a Chicago fan of [former White Sox star] Joe Jackson." The experiment with Stephenson at third only lasted a week. Right fielder Cliff Heathcote went out with an injury, so McCarthy put Stephenson back in the left field and shifted Webb to right. He preferred the left-handed Webb in right field anyway. McCarthy always wanted a right-hander in left and a lefty in right as the natural curve of the each's throws would then not be away from the field but into it. This, he felt, could make a difference in a close play at the plate. It was one of a myriad of subtleties to which he was always attuned.[7]

The beginning of the season was decidedly mediocre for McCarthy, and he was not the least bit happy about it. Into mid–May, the team was playing mere .500 ball. Aside from Wilson and Stephenson, no one was hitting well. Worse, the team had the seventh worst fielding percentage in the league. After one 5–4 loss to the Giants in which the Cubs committed four errors, the *Tribune* headlined "Cubs Poor at Bat; Worse in Field." The only thing holding the team at .500 was the pitching. McCarthy kept juggling the lineup, trying to find a chemistry that produced. In late May he seemed to find it. He settled on an infield with Charlie Grimm at first base, Clyde Beck at second, Elwood "Woody" English at shortstop, and Sparky Adams at third, sometimes shifting Adams to second and inserting Eddie Pick at third. The pitching continued to be strong, and the team's fielding went from seventh to first. Maybe it was contagion from all the hoopla of Charles Lindbergh's solo flight to Paris, but the Cubs started winning. On the road in the East they won five in a row and were 9 and 12 on the whole tour. "McCarthy's scrappers," as they were now called, seemed to be playing every game with a desperation that excited fans and unnerved the opposition. On May 22, the Cubs found themselves percentage points ahead of the Giants in first place. For the first time, aside from meaningless times at the season's outset, Joe McCarthy had a major league team in first place. It was also a first in many years for the Cubs. Down on the South Side of Chicago, the White Sox were showing some spunk, at one point drawing to four games behind the league-leading Yankees. The Chicago clubs' performances were nearly rivaling Lindbergh in some of the city papers' headlines.[8]

The Cubs attainment of first place in May was so euphoric it actually spawned some adolescent pennant talk. Meanwhile, the Giants, Cardinals, and Pirates were right behind them. In early June, Pittsburgh ran off a ten-game winning streak of their own and took over the lead. McCarthy's pitching began to falter a bit. Now he was losing as many close ones as he had been winning. On June 8, McCarthy made a personnel move, trading reserve shortstop Jimmy Cooney and pitcher Tony Kaufmann to Philadelphia for veteran pitcher Hal Carlson. In 1926, Carlson had gone 17 and 12 for the lowly Phillies. McCarthy was positive Carlson could do better with his team. The very next day, Carlson went the distance, defeating Brooklyn 3–2. Carlson's only quirk appeared to be that he liked often to get a rubdown from the team trainer. McCarthy did not object, although he did not believe in rubs. (The trainer, "Doc" Lotshaw, used to apply Coca-Cola as a magic salve. No one told Carlson.) Bolstered by Carlson's presence, and enjoying the comforts of an extended home stand, McCarthy's Cubs proceeded to run off twelve wins in a row, with wins two through eight of the streak each by a one-run margin. Chicago fans were ecstatic. For game eight of the streak, against the Giants, 45,000 came to Wrigley Field. The streak did not put much distance between the Cubs and Pittsburgh, however. The Pirates were hardly ever losing either. The result was Cubs and Pirates found themselves a clear notch above St. Louis and New York. Then, of all the ways to end a winning streak, the Chicago lost two to lowly Philadelphia, leaving them two games behind Pittsburgh, just as the Pirates were coming to town for two games. Wrigley had installed some extra seating out in the bleachers, and whatever he put in was filled and then some. Thirty-seven thousand packed into Wrigley Field for the first game. Charlie Root pitched his 12th victory of the season, as the Cubs pulled to one game behind, drubbing the Pirates 14–7. Fittingly, the next afternoon's second Cubs-Pirates contest was the only game scheduled in the entire league. It was as though everyone in baseball had known this was going to be a big game. Again, the stadium was filled, and radios were tuned in all over the city. Pittsburgh took a 4–0 lead. In the ninth, however, the Cubs had the bases loaded with one out; the fans were screaming — and then they did nothing. Their home stand was over, and they were two games out of first.[9]

On the road, McCarthy would recall the old adage of not getting too low or too high. They were swept in St. Louis. With decided relish, Alexander defeated them in one game. In another, showing the strain of not holding first place, Hack Wilson lost his head and was ejected arguing a called third strike. This occurred in the first game of a doubleheader, and in the second game when Wilson received a strike call and, merely looking back at the umpire, was again ejected. McCarthy blew up at this, and he was ejected too. As the Cubs were swept by St. Louis, the White Sox were also falling in the standings. In the American League, the pennant had quickly turned into a foregone conclusion as the Yankees appeared to be lapping the field, but the National League flag was still up for grabs. After the Cardinals' series, McCarthy knew not to despair, and on the train out of St. Louis he told as much to his players. The train was headed for Pittsburgh. Two days and two wins later, Chicago was right back in the thick of it, and at the end of June, one and one half games separated Pittsburgh, St. Louis, and "McCarthy's scrappers."

Even the heavens seemed at work on behalf of the Cubs that summer. With a seven-game winning streak on the line and playing in Pittsburgh on July 7, the papers were calling for all Chicagoans to haul out their "horseshoes and rabbit's feet." In the game the Cubs were up 2–1 in the ninth. The Pirates scored one run and had two men on. As Pittsburgh was ready to clinch the win, rain began "coming down in sheets." The umpires called the game. The score reverted to that of the eighth inning, and the Cubs again found themselves in first place. The next afternoon, Charlie Root threw a 1–0 shutout. This was front page news in the *Tribune*. It was the first time McCarthy had been in first place for over a day. National League sports writers were complaining that McCarthy has no outstanding stars; how can he be winning. Such words as "lucky" and "mystery" came forth repeatedly. "The Cubs have been called a 'mystery' team," noted one Chicago reporter, "but when the fans remember McCarthy a great deal of the mystery is dissipated."[10]

The battle for the lead continued through July. Chicago held the lead that month for ten days. Then Pittsburgh moved past them. St. Louis was always lurking. So it remained, back and forth, with eight lead changes in one two-week stretch. McCarthy knew to keep his team loose. He made sure his pitchers got rest and religiously monitored their practice regimens. "Those who are still unable to account for the ritzy position of the Cubs and who believe that a crash is inevitable," lectured a *Tribune* columnist, "are advised to take certain things into account. First of all, and of greatest importance is that Mr. McCarthy, while business like at all times, is not a slave driver of the McGraw type. Mr. McCarthy issues his orders in a gentlemanly tone. His players appreciate his methods so give their best ... there is no discord, and [there] has not been at any time since McCarthy put on his robes of office." Still, McCarthy's tone could be severe when he felt it necessary. In one game in July, for example, one outfielder finished an inning in the field and chose to sit along the fence rather than come in to the bench for the Cubs' half. He had just batted the previous inning. McCarthy sent out his trusted batboy Eddie Froelich to call the player in, and when he arrived in the dugout, McCarthy ordered him to the showers. McCarthy later told the squad that the player in question "took off his uniform today because he didn't come into the bench. You fellows," he admonished, "aren't going to learn my methods while you're sitting along the fence. You may learn something on the bench." That incident received no publicity until the following spring (and its exposure had a tone of respect for McCarthy even more pronounced than the supportive coverage which accompanied his release of Alexander), but the players sure knew about it. Marse Joe was in charge. The Cubs retook the league lead on August 2, and they held it for the entire month.[11]

On August 15, Chicago's lead reached five full games. At that point they began a 19-game road trip. Chicago fans thought the pennant was in reach. "The minions of Joe McCarthy can now be regarded as practical certainties for top honors," predicted one smug scribe. "It is still possible that they may stumble over their own ambitions or that one of the other contenders will put on a record-breaking burst of speed, but neither is probable." McCarthy did not like this sort of opining any more than he like premature defeatism. To say anything against such pomposity would obviously be too negative. Yet he knew that such childish effusions could backfire. There was just too much time left and too many things could happen. But this was the time when lots of Chicagoans were enthusiastically investing in both the Cubs' pennant and the stock market. While doing his utmost for the pennant, McCarthy was financially out of step with many of his fans, quietly saving his money to buy land. The Cubs' road trip began in Brooklyn on August 16. Against the lowly Dodgers that afternoon, Charlie Root first won his 22nd of the season with a 3–0 shutout. All looked rosy.

The next day, the Cubs were up 5–2 in the ninth. The Dodgers scored two, and with two out had runners on second and third. Brooklyn's weak-hitting second baseman, Chuck Corgan, was on deck. A better hitter, Bob Barrett, was up. McCarthy chose to pitch to Barrett. He singled, and both runs scored to give the game to Brooklyn. The next day it rained, and the Cubs had time to ponder the tough loss. The following afternoon, two key errors gave Brooklyn another win. Going up to Boston against the weak Braves should have then been a reprieve. Again, with a 5–2 lead, and with Charlie Root pitching no less, the Cubs gave up four runs in the ninth inning and lost. Meanwhile, Pittsburgh beat Brooklyn, reducing the Cubs' lead to only three games. The Braves won again the next day, with the Cubs committing five errors. That same day, the Commonwealth of Massachusetts executed convicted murderers Nicola Sacco and Bartolomeo Vanzetti. They seemed to have little sympathy up there in New England.[12]

For the first fifteen games in the Eastern part of the road trip, the Cubs went five and ten. Heading back West, McCarthy arranged for an August 31 exhibition game against his old team, the Buffalo Bisons. Even though he was resting his veterans, McCarthy's boys lost to the Bisons that afternoon. The game obviously did not count, but it hardly put any wind in anyone's sails, and from Buffalo, the dispirited Cubs were headed for Pittsburgh. Pittsburgh swept them. Then Cincinnati swept them. The losing streak not only took the Cubs out of first place, it shoved them down to third. The Giants, who had gotten hot while sweeping Chicago just before the Buffalo loss, had continued to win and were now pushing the Pirates. The Cubs' train at last arrived in Chicago, with the Cardinals waiting there to play them. 38,000 turned out the next afternoon to try to revive the team. One fan got into a fight with Grover Alexander before the game. The Cubs lost it 2–1 and lost two of the next three, including a disastrous 13–1 defeat in the finale, with Alexander pitching. In the weeks since the Eastern trip had begun, the Cubs won 6 and lost 16. The newspapers were sounding "Taps," but again "McCarthy's men would not quit." On September 9, with a defeat of St. Louis, the Cubs were still only two games behind Pittsburgh. Then the Giants came to town. They split the series, and it was one of the nastiest series of the year. Questionable umpire calls led to showers of pop bottles flying out of the stands. Fans remembered the "scrappy old days on the West Side" when John McGraw and Frank Chance went at it, and fisticuffs were a daily event. "Well, the boys are at it again," grinned one old reporter. It was spirited play, to be sure, but with no real movement in the standings, time was slipping away. Brooklyn followed New York into Chicago that week. When they beat Chicago as Pittsburgh won a doubleheader, a sports headline sadly read: "Mr. Flag Hope Packs His Bag and Waves Good-Bye."[13]

The "recently interred pennant contenders" played out the string in September. Mr. Wrigley graciously bought each player on the Cubs a ticket to the Jack Dempsey — Gene Tunney rematch of September 21. The gesture proved symbolic in at least one respect. The Cubs' seats were so far back in the Soldier Field stands that they could not see anything. That was pretty much where they had gone in the pennant race. In the fight, famously, the scrapping Westerner Dempsey knocked down the Easterner Tunney, but in his haste at the moment of the knockdown, Dempsey failed immediately go to a neutral corner, causing a delay in the beginning of the count, which some say would otherwise have put Tunney out. Tunney recovered and won the "long count" fight. The Cubs had also knocked down some opponents, but in the long run of the season they needed more to sustain themselves, and a few such umpire calls as they had gotten against the Giants added to the frustration.[14]

The Cubs again finished fourth in 1927. Pittsburgh won the pennant. Fourth place was pretty much what people had predicted back in April. Commentators were positive in their end-of-season retrospective comments. The Cubs had certainly given a good account of themselves. They did not lose so much as Pittsburgh had won with a great team. But McCarthy was hardly content. He had had a pennant in his grasp. Some bad umpire calls and, even more, some bad infield play had hurt at key moments. His hitting had improved. Riggs Stephenson, Hack Wilson, Charlie Grimm, Gabby Hartnett, and Earl Webb had all hit over .300. Charlie Root had won 26, and Hal Carlson had won 12 since joining the team in June. The elements were there. Fourth place may have lent a feeling of satisfaction among some baseball people, but it was hardly a good feeling to McCarthy. "Joe always knocks [at the door] before entering home," Mrs. McCarthy divulged to the *Herald and Examiner*. When discouraged over the team's play, "he knocks in a world-weary funereal fashion. But ... when he feel certain his team is in A-1 fettle he knocks like the King of England, the President of the United States, and the Emperor of China rolled into one."

Through September of 1927, his knocking was certainly world-weary. When Babe tried to console him after a tough loss by saying "you still have me," Joe supposedly responded, "Yes, but today I would have gladly traded you for a sacrifice fly." The McCarthys were so close that they could make such jokes. Joe's door knocking would rebound to a regal level, but not for a while.[15]

18

Aggressive Even in Repose

When the 1927 season ended, McCarthy immediately left Chicago. He had contracted with the *Chicago Herald and Examiner* to write articles covering the World Series between the Pittsburgh Pirates and the New York Yankees. The Yankees, with Babe Ruth, Lou Gehrig, et. al., had just completed a season in which they utterly dominated the American League. They were never out of first place. The had won 110 games and finished 19 games ahead of second-place Philadelphia. Some said it was the greatest team of all time; some still do. McCarthy picked the Pirates to win the series, however. He believed that the rest of the American League was a weaker circuit, hence that the Yankees would not be accustomed to facing such competition as the Pirates would give them. Pittsburgh, he felt, had played against stronger opposition all season and would be accustomed to the pressure. The Series obviously proved him wrong, as New York swept Pittsburgh. Analyzing the Series, McCarthy believed that the Pirate pitchers threw the Yankees too many fastballs. Once they saw what hitters like Ruth and Gehrig could do with their offerings, the Pirates, he said, should have adjusted. They did not and paid a heavy price. Still, it would not have made much difference, as McCarthy noted, "the Yankees get better as they go along." McCarthy thus conceded: "I am willing to admit now, this Yankee organization is the greatest one I have ever seen put together," concluding: "I extend my sympathy to the American League managers who are required to compete with them."[1]

McCarthy had a range of qualities that made him so outstanding as a manager. Recognizing his own mistaken judgments was but one. The 1927 World Series was McCarthy's first in-depth observation of the Yankees. Like everyone, he was impressed. The fact that his praise focused on their "organization" was significant. His eye was trained on what builds winning not just for the moment but for the long haul. A man with such an eye could contribute perfectly to such an team, and he would.

After the Series was over, McCarthy returned to his home on Gates Circle in Buffalo. He stayed in regular touch with Veeck, of course, discussing possible deals to improve the Cubs. One matter virtually fell into their laps. It concerned a top-notch outfielder with the National League champion Pirates named Hazen "Kiki" Cuyler. Cuyler had then played four seasons with Pittsburgh. He hit over .300 each season. Twice he led the league in runs scored, and once in stolen bases. In October, a reporter asked Veeck his opinion of Cuyler, and he responded with the obvious: "Cuyler is a fine player, and we would like to have him." During the 1927 season, Cuyler had run into several problems with the Pirate organization. He had had a salary dispute with Pittsburgh's owner Barney Dreyfuss. Rumors circulated of bad blood between Cuyler and Pirate Manager Donie Bush. Cuyler had supposedly objected to batting second in the lineup. He had broken rules when he brought a friend into the clubhouse. In August, he had once been benched for failing to slide, supposedly ignoring a signal to do so. Most conspicuously, Bush kept him on the bench during the entire World Series. How all these elements precisely weighed among the Pirate brass, they apparently wanted to trade him. The Cubs offered a swap, Cuyler for their starting infielder Sparky Adams and reserve outfielder Pete Scott. The Pirates accepted. To even the most casual baseball observers of the era, the deal hardly seemed even, and no one in Chicago was complaining. Mrs. McCarthy said that in all their years together, she never brought up a baseball subject with Joe except once, and that was over the Cuyler deal in the winter of 1927–28. "I was very curious," she recalled, "why Pittsburgh was letting Kiki Cuyler go if he was all he was cracked up to be. So," she said, "I asked Joe. 'Babe,' he retorted, giving me a long penetrating glance, 'let's go skating.' And so we did."[2]

With Kiki Cuyler destined for the Cubs' starting lineup, the prospects for 1928 looked yet more favorable for Cub fans, as well as for McCarthy. The club that assembled on Catalina Island in February had about it a more mature air. They had gone from a hopeful, rookie-like outlook, to one of optimism. Now they had among them a more confident sense of having been through the battle. Nerves were not going to be such a factor as they apparently were in the late summer of 1927. McCarthy's only problem appeared to be Charlie Root. He had won 26 games in 1927, but at the season's end, after 48 games and 309 innings, his weight had dropped from 190 pounds to a mere 160. To prepare for such depletion in 1928, Root decided to bulk up over the winter, and he did so mainly by eating. He arrived in California weighing over 200 pounds. "Charlie Root is about the same as before," reassured the *Tribune*, "except that there are two of him." McCarthy appreciated Root's value to the team and brought him into playing condition slowly. As for the rest of the Cubs, McCarthy philosophized: "I don't know whether all work and no play will make by Cubs dull boys or not, but I do know that no work at all is sure to." The Cubs worked very hard that spring. They mowed down their exhibition season opposition, winning 16 of 18. Opening day saw them healthy and ready, although Hack Wilson had twisted his ankle in one of the last exhibition games in Terre Haute, Indiana. The meat of the 1928 batting order, nos. 3–7, certainly made a few opposing pitchers swallow hard — Kiki Cuyler, Hack Wilson, Riggs Stephenson, Charlie Grimm, and Gabby Hartnett. With such a lineup, "the chin of Joe McCarthy," chuckled one reporter, "is aggressive even in repose."[3]

As the season began, nothing but good signs lay before the Cubs and their fans. Papers praised the "team" of Wrigley and Veeck and even more the "fearless, unhampered, and original" leadership of McCarthy. The start was rocky, however. In April and early May, the team played under .500 ball. Only the lowly Phillies had a worse record. Team errors were numerous. McCarthy's "indisposition" was up. Pitcher Hal Carlson was suddenly out sick, and Hack Wilson reinjured his sprained ankle, only the problem proved to be more than a sprain. Wilson had actually broken a small bone. Asked by reporters here about the medical specifics—that he had a small fracture of his internal maleolus—Wilson just glared: "All I know is that it hurts like hell." Wilson had to sit out a few weeks, and this upset him no end. "I ought to be able to pinch hit or something," he cried. "I'll die if I have to stay in bed for twelve days." McCarthy heard Wilson at that point and sourly interjected: "You won't die, but you'll weigh a ton."[4]

Wilson actually got back in the lineup in a week. They day he was due to return, 46,000 came to Wrigley Field. Scalpers sold tickets at twelve to twenty-eight times their face value, and on the afternoon Wilson went four for four and hit two home runs. McCarthy certainly did not approve of the ways Wilson handled his private life, but he sure admired his fighting nature. Wilson was only 5'6" but weighed 190–200 pounds (his shoes were a size 5; his shirt collar, size 18). His short stature seemed to invite people to test him, but, as McCarthy noted, people would test Hack, but they would only do so once. The fans loved him too. He was from a working-class mining community in Ellwood City, Pennsylvania. His stature, his pugnaciousness, his always dirty uniform made him the hero of the folks in the cheap seats. At a game in Wrigley Field that June, Wilson grounded to second in the ninth inning. This marked two outs and a loss seemed inevitable. A fan seated near the front row named Edwin Young began yelling at Wilson, "Why don't you bench yourself, you fat so-and-so?" The fan, whom McCarthy described as "obviously drunk," went on to yell at Wilson with what McCarthy later termed "unprintable language in every breath." Wilson jumped into the stands and began fighting with him. Young was actually arrested and later convicted for inciting a riot. (The fans had spilled out onto the field, and the final out was held up for ten minutes.) Young apparently thought about suing for $50,000, but he got nowhere. Would any jury of late '20s Chicagoans ever side against Hack Wilson and the Cubs?[5]

A standard move for a manager when his team is in a slump is to juggle the line-up. McCarthy began doing that in early May. On May 1, he used sixteen players in a game against Pittsburgh. Nothing was working, however, and various injuries still nagged, including Wilson's. Pittsburgh took three in a row. McCarthy mused to reporters about "a ballplayer who got himself in bad by throwing a bureau, some chairs, and a table out of a room on the top floor of a hotel. I never could understand," said McCarthy, "how a man could get that way until just now." When a reporter asked McCarthy if he had contemplated resorting to such actions, McCarthy replied ruefully: "My room is on the first floor." The underlying point here is that McCarthy would talk about such things, smile, and not do them. Other players would act out, and he would have no truck with them. After the Pittsburgh series, McCarthy instituted morning practices, and the Cubs started winning again. Of course, with the next series against Philadelphia, this seemed not too difficult. But the successful Phillies series started something, and between May 4th and 19th the Cubs won 13 in a row.

The ninth victory, against the Giants, had an added sweetness. New York Manager McGraw not only lost the game, he then went out and "lost" an encounter to an automobile on the corner of North Clark and Addison Streets. (He was not seriously injured.) The Cubs' streak came with a price, however. During the 13th win,

Catcher Gabby Hartnett injured his hand and was expected to be out for a month. The May streak jumped the Cubs up to first place. Then they lost four, fell from the lead, and lost Riggs Stephenson to the flu as well. The ups and downs were hard on the nerves. McCarthy revealed the strain himself in early June. In an important game against Pittsburgh, the Cubs were up, with McCarthy out at third coaching. The Cubs appeared to be starting a rally. Then on a play at third, in which the runner easily appeared safe to McCarthy, umpire Albert "Dolly" Stark yelled "out!" "Boss Joe probably never has been madder in his entire career," acknowledged one reporter. He not only yelled at Stark, he appealed to the other two umpires, and when they would not listen he screamed at them too. The three umpires threatened to carry McCarthy off the field. McCarthy was ejected, naturally, along with one of his players. Usually taciturn with the press, McCarthy later poured forth: "I try not to be an umpire baiter, but some of the men who are trying to officiate in the National League," he declared, "are downright terrible." The league levied a $100 fine on McCarthy for his outbursts, but he felt it was money well spent. The result of all the scrapping was that the Cubs were in the race as everyone had expected. On June 6th they were in fourth, three games behind leading Cincinnati, with New York and St. Louis just ahead of them.[6]

As most baseball people were predicting, Cincinnati could not hold its lead. By July, they had faded, and the race came down to St. Louis, New York, and Chicago. With McCarthy keeping the team on its edge, the Cubs stayed in the race that summer. Charlie Root, who, when fatter, had pitched poorly in the early season, slimmed down and found his stride in the summer. Pat Malone pitched well too. Before the season, the Cubs had picked him up from Minneapolis. They agreed to pay $2,500 up front and had until June 1st to decide to keep him. As of June 1st, Malone's record was 0–7. Yet McCarthy had a feeling and told Veeck to keep Malone, hence to pay the rest of the $25,000 purchase price. Malone won 18 games the rest of the way. Other pitchers on McCarthy's staff were not as strong, however. Hal Carlson won only three games all season. McCarthy tried his old Louisville friend Ben Tincup, but he did not pan out. Cuyler was battling a slump for the first three-quarters of the season; he had collided with the outfield wall in Wrigley and was less than 100 percent much of the time. Meanwhile, first baseman Charlie Grimm, shortstop Woody English, Gabby Hartnett, Wilson, and Stephenson were all injured at one time or another, and in late August, Stephenson went home to Alabama to tend to a serious illness of his father. This cost the Cubs more than a few games. As of September 1, Chicago was in second place, four and one half games behind St. Louis. "It's evidently going to be a real hot fight until the last game," predicted McCarthy, "and you can put it down that we'll be in the thick of it all the way down the line." The Cubs did indeed stay in the race. After August 14, Kiki Cuyler broke out of his slump and hit .357 the rest of the way. The Cubs won 90 games for the first time since 1912, an impressive total, often enough to win a pennant. But this year it only earned them a third-place finish, four games behind St. Louis and two behind New York. Again the papers praised to the team's quality, its front office, and its field management. Two Cubs— catcher Gabby Hartnett and center fielder Hack Wilson — were voted as the best at their positions in the major leagues.[7] Phrases like "should hold their heads high" were all about Chicago. But all the fans knew how they really wanted to feel.

Reflecting on the season and on the team, fans and reporters knew the Cubs outfield of Cuyler, Stephenson, and Wilson was one of, likely the best, in baseball. No changes there seemed in order. Hartnett, of course, was the best at his position. McCarthy later said he was absolutely the best catcher in the history of the game.[8] The infield was where the questions lay. Sparky Adams had gone on to Pittsburgh in exchange for Cuyler and set a record for 207 fielding chances without an error. Some Cubs fans and reporters thought the infield had been the weak link in the Cubs lineup. Still, noting the improvement in the infield under McCarthy's guidance in 1928, the *Tribune* predicted that changes even there "are not probable unless the possessers of some established star get hungry for a big bag of gold." Mr. Wrigley had the gold, and the lowly Boston Braves had Rogers Hornsby. After the 1927 season, the Giants had traded him there. On November 7, after sending five players* and a $150,000 "bag of gold" to Boston, the Cubs suddenly had Rogers Hornsby at second base for 1929. Hornsby was an incredibly egocentric and abrasive man, but he was also a sensational hitter, the highest average in baseball for the decade of the 1920s. The question was whether he could help push the Cubs to the top. Privately, McCarthy had not favored the trade. He feared Hornsby would not fit in well with the squad. With the trade, Hornsby was brimming with confidence: "I feel sure I can give the Cubs the punch that will put them over in next year's race." Knowing the predictions that were immediately coming forth about his potential conflicts with such a strong personality as McCarthy, Hornsby spoke reassuringly. Noting that he indeed had experienced problems in New York and St. Louis, Hornsby dusted these off as "personal matters." "If people take a dislike to you or you to them," he shrugged, "it is something that can't be avoided. ... There is no need to worry about cooperating with McCarthy. We have been friendly as long as he has been in the league, and I regard him about the slickest manager I have ever encountered." Such problems as he had in New York and St. Louis, he said, "will not occur in Chicago because it is not that kind of organization." Hornsby proved both right and wrong here. Success would come to the Cubs, but the results would not leave everyone terribly happy. There was a baseball dictum of the era: "He who lives by Rogers Hornsby, dies by Rogers Hornsby."[9] With Wrigley having made the trade, McCarthy was going to put that theory to the test.

The five players were Fred Maguire and Percy Jones of the Cubs, and minor leaguers Bruce Cunningham, Louis "Doc" Leggett, and Harry "Socks" Seybold.

19

Don't Blame Hack

After the Cubs' strong showings in both 1927 and 1928, and with their acquisition of Rogers Hornsby, baseball people all over the National League were picking Chicago to win the pennant. Other than Hornsby, it was basically the same team. McCarthy did add a new coach — Grover Land, his old vaudeville buddy from the Toledo Mud Hens. Babe Ruth predicted the Cubs would win the NL flag. Wall Street betting parlors set the odds for a Cubs pennant at 11–10. New York, St. Louis, and Pittsburgh were each given a 5–2 chance. Chicago fans had equally high aspirations. They were not hoping. They were expecting. As the team gathered on Catalina Island, some players expressed similar sentiments. Hornsby said "this ball club … ought to win a pennant this year if it is ever going to win." The fact that Hornsby was making such pronouncements was an indicator of his well-known sense of self-importance. He was obviously a great player, and he had managed the Cardinals to a World Series victory in 1926. Now he was playing for McCarthy and the Cubs. But his sense of being a special player never subsided. On the boat over to Catalina Island, the players were free to wander about Mr. Wrigley's spacious yacht, but there was an unstated protocol: that no one, not even McCarthy, went up to the bridge where Mr. Wrigley maintained his command. Hornsby did.[1]

The Detroit Tigers, also training in the West, played ten exhibition games against the Cubs in various parks in and around Los Angeles in March and early April. Chicago won eight of the games, and Tigers manager Bucky Harris called the Cubs "the greatest club I ever saw." The training had indeed gone well. For McCarthy there was a bonus: most of the baseball writers were involved in a labor dispute, and fewer made the trip out to California. McCarthy always hated needless diversions, and the questions from reporters, day after day, was something he never grew to like, especially in the preseason when the questions were always the same. About the only problem that arose during spring training occurred after one of the games in Los Angeles. A storm had just blown in, making the seas very choppy. Catcher Gabby Hartnett always got sick on the boat to Catalina. This day everyone did. The next morning was the only day McCarthy cancelled practice. He was looking a little green himself.[2]

The series of games between Chicago and Detroit prompted some writers to consider some comparisons between the teams, especially between managers McCarthy and Harris. Many of the Tigers had not been out West before, and that spring Harris found himself having to deal with several discipline problems. There were the usual late hours, carousing, and drinking, which had the added problem then of being illegal amidst Prohibition. Several Tiger players also went off with some rodeo troupes, trying their hands at bronco and bull riding. Harris was only 32. He had been a player/manager for several years, and he considered many of the players to be his friends. He had always hoped to this point in his managerial career that his friendship could be a source of good camaraderie on his teams, hence that discipline would take care of itself with all voluntarily joining in the team spirit. McCarthy, writers noted, never took this approach. He was more distant. He had a set of rules, and any who broke them, like Alexander, learned of their inflexibility. The result was that since he established himself, "no manager gets greater respect from his own players or from the opposition than ... McCarthy." Harris's ways, on the other hand, "left his gallery of Tigers wondering." No one wondered about leadership on a McCarthy team, and the players could (and had to) focus on nothing but their playing. As for the possible challenge of the great Hornsby, who had certainly been troubling to other managers, he appeared to "join in" with the players and newsmen by taking everyone out — for ice cream. "That," enthusiastically laughed a senior Chicago writer, "is the sort of hell-raiser this Hornsby has turned out to be." All the signs were there for a championship season. After the Cubs won two of three, opening against Pittsburgh, and won the two by scores of 13–2 and 11–1, the *Herald and Examiner* headlined with a nod: "The March is On!" With this team, pennant talk in April seemed anything but idle or inappropriate.[3]

McCarthy was always secretive about his plans for his teams. With all the talent on the Cubs' starting roster, reporters were repeatedly asking him about the lineup and what the batting order would be. Throughout the training season, McCarthy would not say. Here some took offense — "for the 1000th time Boss Joseph refuses to make a guess on his probable batting order." McCarthy was trying different schemes, and obviously did not want to make any promises or needlessly hurt any feelings among his players by saying anything prematurely. At the outset of the season, the prestigious cleanup spot went to Hornsby. Hack Wilson appeared disgruntled. Some writers then tried to make something of a supposed rivalry between Wilson and Hornsby. McCarthy expressed a bit of frustration. With Wilson batting after Hornsby, he shrugged: "So he'll drive in more runs. He's going to find either Cuyler or Hornsby on base nearly every time he comes up. Many times he'll find both." As for Riggs Stephenson then being dropped to sixth, McCarthy smiled: "It makes no difference to Stevie, first, fifth, or last. Stephenson ... will never be credited with his full value to the ball club." McCarthy liked Stephenson's sort of understatement. He wanted players to subsume their personal ambitions to those of the teams. The fact that such players often failed to win plaudits in the papers served to reinforce McCarthy's disdain for many reporters. As for Stephenson's underrated status, McCarthy was prophetic here, as Stephenson remains, other than Joe Jackson, the player with the highest lifetime batting average — .336 — not enshrined in the Hall of Fame.[4]

All managers should have such problems as McCarthy's lineup questions of 1929. As McCarthy predicted, Wilson would constantly stand in with men on base. He led the league with 159 RBI's. Hornsby was not far behind with 149. Cuyler and

Stephenson each topped the 100 mark as well. Wilson batted .345, and his was the lowest average of "the four aces." Cuyler hit .360; Stephenson, .362, and Hornsby batted .380. The team had it all, except for one problem — the all-important position of catcher. At the end of spring training, Gabby Hartnett's throwing arm began to feel sore, and the soreness would not abate. If he played, runners would steal on him with abandon. He had to sit down. Veteran reserve catcher Mike Gonzalez stepped in and played capably, but on April 24th in a game against St. Louis he was spiked in the hand. In came the third-string receiver, Earl Grace. Two pitches later he was out with a split finger. That left the Cubs with only a completely inexperienced catcher named Tom Angley. They immediately picked up a journeyman named John Schulte from Columbus in the American Association, who had previously played a bit for the Cardinals and Phillies. Five days later in a game against Cincinnati, Schulte was spiked and so severely that he had to be taken to a hospital. This put Tom Angley back in the game, and left the team more than a little nervous. "Oil" Grace's finger was mending, and he and Angley split the duties starting the next day in Cincinnati. The two were roommates on the road, and that night in Cincinnati someone robbed their hotel room. An obvious feeling of being snake-bit behind the plate began to displace some of the April euphoria. McCarthy was still showing confidence, however. When the team embarked from Cincinnati on a swing around the East, he was asked if the pitching would break down under the strain of the catching troubles and of being on the road. McCarthy wisecracked that if the team does break down, "it will be from a train wreck, not from the hitting of those [Eastern] teams." McCarthy knew better than to motivate his opposition, but when he had such talent as he possessed this season, he knew that such arrogance would only put more pressure on them. He was in the driver's seat, and he wanted to let everyone know it; it was yet another part of his tactical arsenal. He had already shown he could take a mediocre team and make it good. He was now showing that he knew how to take a potentially great team and maximize its considerable talents.[5]

Amidst the Eastern trip, Gabby Hartnett took leave from the team and paid a visit to the Johns Hopkins Hospital in Baltimore. His physician there, Dean Lewis, pronounced his arm 100 percent. Three days later, Hartnett found himself back in the hospital, not for his arm but this time to be treated for tonsilitis. McCarthy had originally slated Grace for the minor leagues, but "Oil" was doing fairly well. Still, the team hit a bit of a slump. In twenty games on the road trip, they went but 8 and 12. Wilson's left ankle was bothering him. Hornsby was not hitting well. Cuyler was out for several games with a pulled muscle. Stephenson came down with the flu, and there were the constant worries about catching. Perhaps it was the combination of such pressures, but McCarthy lost his usual reserve during a game in Pittsburgh and was ejected. The Cubs never fell to more than three games out of first place, but the early season was a pennant fight and not the easy walk so many had breezily predicted.[6]

In June, the team began to gather momentum. Barring any more injuries, their talent could simply not be held back. Mike Gonzalez's hand had healed, and he and Johnny Schulte shouldered the catching load. As for Gabby Hartnett, the doctors said his arm was healthy, but he still could not throw well. Hartnett could serve as a pinch hitter, and he did so with some effectiveness. He maintained a good humor about his predicament, and this helped team morale. Hartnett was always good for a wise-crack. When aviator Amelia Earhart came to a Cub game, he went up to her and said "so you're the little girl that flies over oceans. I fly often myself." Earhart was intrigued. "Really?" she asked. "Yeah," cracked Gabby, "out to right field." His wit was always a great asset when it came to handling pitchers, and in 1929 it was a nec-essary element on a team which otherwise could have frayed with the mix of such more serious sorts as Wilson and Hornsby. First baseman Charlie Grimm ("Jolly Cholly") served a similar role. Indeed the press referred to the meat of Chicago's order — Cuyler, Hornsby, Wilson, Stephenson, and Grimm — as the "Four Aces and a Joker in McCarthy's hand." On July 4th, the Cubs, four aces et. al., had forged ahead with seven straight wins. They swept a key series with St. Louis to knock the Cards back from contention. The Pirates were the only team to stay with them. It looked like the '29 juggernaut was now rolling as expected, despite the absence of Hartnett.[7]

On July 4th came trouble. The Cubs hosted Cincinnati in a holiday double-header. The teams had been going at each other for most of the year. Earlier in the season, it was the Reds who had spiked catcher Johnny Schulte. In the first game of the July series, Riggs Stephenson had taken out Cincinnati second baseman Hugh Critz with a hard slide. This angered Reds Manager Jack Hendricks. For the rest of the series, the two teams were then "sliding high" at one another, and the bench jock-eying was vicious.

In the second game of the July 4th doubleheader, the lid blew off. Hack Wilson singled to start the sixth inning. The Cincinnati bench was on the first-base side, and as Wilson stopped at first, the Reds began taunting him. Pitcher Ray Kolp, whose nickname was "Jockey," "in a pointed manner questioned the origin of Mr. Wilson's ancestors." He went on to call Wilson "yellow" for not sticking up for himself. Upon hearing that, Wilson took one look at the Reds bench, picked out Kolp and charged the dugout. He pushed aside a half dozen Cincinnati players who tried to block his rush. He got to Kolp and landed "two solid swats" before he was pulled away. Some fans tried to climb onto the field to help Hack, but the police held them back. The plate umpire fought his way through the players, separated the two combatants and ejected them both from the game. Wilson went to the showers and then watched the rest of the game from the stands. As Wilson took his seat in the stands, he was greeted with "a thunderous ovation."

The two teams split the day's doubleheader, and that evening both arrived at Chicago's Union Station to head East. On the platform, another Cincinnati pitcher, Pete Donohue, encountered Wilson. Wilson was looking for Kolp to demand an apology. Donohue told Wilson that Kolp was already on the train. Then Donohue taunted Wilson to the effect that if he entered the Reds' car he might not come out alive. Wilson whacked Donohue in the chin. Donohue fell, and when he got up Wil-son hit him again.[8]

Wilson's fights were front page sports news all over the country. To Cincinnati fans, Wilson was nothing but a bully. To Chicagoans, Kolp and Donohue merely got what was coming to them. Wilson was the Cub fans' most beloved baseball figure, and he acted, they said, in self-defense. Within twenty-four hours, a local Goodyear Tire dealer, showing obvious entrepreneurial spirit, ran an advertisement in the

Tribune claiming their tires could provide "Safety for Cincinnati." Printing a picture of Hack Wilson, the Goodyear advertiser wrote next to the photo: "'Hack's' Goodyear Double Eagle Tires STAND UP Under His DRIVES Without Going FLAT — We Recommend Them for Cincinnati" [emphases Goodyear's].[9]

Talk of Wilson's pugilistic talents was everywhere. Several people sent him boxing gloves as gifts. Still, it was not all fun and games. While the Cincinnati and Chicago sides each had their slants on the fights, National League President John Heydler read an official report from the game umpire, Cy Rigler. Heydler slapped Wilson with a $100 fine and three-day suspension. Wilson accepted it without a word. Cincinnati Manager Jack Hendricks then began complaining. He made references to Wilson's fight with Edwin Young in 1928 and said Wilson had no right to assault Kolp or Donohue. He argued that Wilson's suspension should be not three days but 30, and he went on to predict "something doing for a certainty" when the Cubs were next scheduled to appear in Cincinnati on August 25. McCarthy had been silent about the matter until Hendricks mouthed off. But since one manager had spoken, he certainly felt it proper to respond. McCarthy called Hendricks's statement absurd. He came feistily to Wilson's defense:

> Hack nailed Kolp in the Cincinnati dugout and he'll do it again if that loudmouthed pitcher doesn't quit abusing him in the kind of language he used Tuesday. ... Hack has stood for more abuse and razzing than any other man on the club and has taken it like a true sportsman. Any time a fan or opposing player calls him the names that Kolp did, ... Hack is going to give them action, and I, for one, am right behind him.

As for the reference to the fan, Edwin Young, whom Wilson had hit in 1928, McCarthy accounted for the fellow being drunk and using such ridiculous language that "finally Hack could stand it no longer." McCarthy noted as well that Young had previously "been in jail for disorderly conduct." While McCarthy was not at the train station (he had gone ahead to stop in Buffalo while the team went to Boston), he said of the fight there: "Donohue was looking for trouble. He got it." Years later, McCarthy reflected about Wilson: "I guess people picked on him because he was small [5'6"]. They never did it twice, I can tell you."[10]

With Wilson out of the lineup and with third baseman Norm McMillan hurt too, the Cubs lost three games in Boston, allowing Pittsburgh to take over first place. Meanwhile, Hendricks persuaded Cincinnati Reds President C.J. McDiarmid to call upon National League President Heydler to punish Wilson more severely. Clearly, Hendricks was trying to derail the Cubs' roll towards the pennant, and getting Wilson out of the lineup for an extended period of time could certainly do that. His agitating could upset the Cubs too. McCarthy pointed out that Hendricks had made several bold predictions at the outset of the season that the Cubs could not win the pennant, and McCarthy joked that Hendricks did not want his analyses to appear foolish. (He may have been hinting at suspicions that Hendricks had laid down some bets, which, in the wake of the 1919 World Series, was the worst of sins for anyone in major league baseball, especially in the eyes of Commissioner Landis.) Various newspapers chided Hendricks for behaving like a crying schoolboy on a playground. Nonetheless, when the Cubs left Boston for New York to play the Giants, Heydler held hearings. Two Chicago City officials, Thomas Bowler and Dorsey Crowe, went on record, stating they were ready to organize a City Council Commission and fly to New York should character witnesses be called (and it was not even an election year!).[11]

In the hearings, Hendricks told President Heydler that Wilson had attacked Donohue from behind. This led some of Wilson's friends to ask how, then, it was that Wilson was able to hit Donohue in the lip. Hendricks also said that Wilson had hit several Cincinnati players in the dugout besides Kolp, yet no Cincinnati player corroborated. Cubs' pitcher Guy Bush testified that Donohue took the first swing at Wilson. Overall, Hendricks looked foolish, and Heydler closed the matter of Wilson's first and second fight, stating "a severe reprimand and nothing more is warranted." As for the train station altercation, Heydler asserted: "The men passed insults, and Donohue should have been prepared to defend himself." McCarthy termed the whole affair "a great big laugh," and chortled that Hendricks "knows where he stands now for all his shouting." Wilson was relieved: "Great stuff. I'm no troublemaker. Maybe I do deserve a reprimand. But Heydler had the right dope. Those Cincinnati fellows didn't fool him any." A slick New York boxing promoter, Humbert Fugazy, tried to organize an after-season match between Kolp and Wilson, the "Dempsey of the Dugout," as he was now being dubbed. Fugazy sent Wilson a set of gloves, and Wilson joked "Maybe I'll be fighting [Max] Schmeling one of these days." McCarthy, in earshot of this, snapped at Hack: "Shut up; I can lick you myself in a pinch." Wilson shut up.[12]

McCarthy wanted Wilson to cease all thinking about the fights and focus on baseball. The team had lost in Boston, although McCarthy picked up a sorely needed spare catcher there named Zack Taylor. From Boston, the Cubs had next gone to New York. Crowds at the Polo Grounds cheered Wilson every time he came to the plate, but the Cubs could only split the series and then found themselves three games behind Pittsburgh. Once the Wilson decision had been put behind them, the Cubs began to win again. They won three of four in Philadelphia and swept Brooklyn to complete the road trip. In one of the Brooklyn games, the Cubs infielders got a case of "scatter arm." They committed three wild throws, but each throw hit an umpire, preventing any runner from advancing. "Of all the luck!" yelled Dodger Manager Wilbert Robinson. McCarthy chortled: "Not at all; we've been practicing that stuff for weeks, Robbie. I always tell my players that if they have to throw the ball around always to hit something. Even if it is only an umpire." Robinson was anything but mollified, of course. But McCarthy knew how to rub it in when he was on a roll. After the Brooklyn sweep, back in Chicago, the Cubs reeled off nine in a row. Hack Wilson had hit in each of the previous 38 games in which he had played. Guy Bush had won 10 straight. On July 24, the Cubs retook the lead from the Pirates, and by August 6 they were solidly in front, seven games ahead.[13]

Pennant talk began to rise in earnest again throughout Chicago. Some players were already making deals with various newspapers to write articles for them about the World Series. They did not dare tell Joe McCarthy about this. McCarthy still held to the view that anything can happen. Still, while McCarthy did not "count his chickens" he did reflect a bit on his blessings. Zack Taylor, the catcher McCarthy had picked up from Boston, drew such words that few ever heard from McCarthy: "Rarely does one man win a pennant for you, but here's a fellow who is a great catcher and who fitted into our club like a cog. He has the spirit. That's what you have to have to win the pennant. And when the day comes that the Cubs have it in the 'bag,' don't forget one fellow that helped as much as anyone else. That's Taylor." Having started the season on the bench with the lowly Boston Braves, all Taylor could say about suddenly playing for the Cubs was "I am happy as a kid with a new toy." As for McCarthy, few ever heard him speak with such optimism. Perhaps one reason he rarely did so ever again was that the very next afternoon, first baseman Charlie Grimm cracked a bone in back of his left thumb while chasing a foul ball. He would be out for much of the remainder of the season. McCarthy knew he could protect his ten-game lead, but Grimm would be missed. He was the only significant left-handed hitter in the lineup.[14]

Three days later, August 24, the previously heralded rematch with Cincinnati took place, the first encounter since Hack Wilson's brawls. It brought out a crowd of 35,432. Those hoping to see a fight were disappointed. (Since Cincinnati was in last place, fans could not hope for much more.) Perhaps Heydler had done some things behind the scenes; in any case, there was no sign of Ray Kolp at Crosley Field that day. The Reds won the first game. Hack Wilson played and went 0 for 4. There was some yelling from the stands when he stepped up for his first at-bat, but that was it. Pete Donohue pitched the second game and lost it 10–1. Wilson cracked one hit off him. When the Cubs returned to Chicago the next day, one fan, Miss Harriet Davis, presented Wilson with a cake she had baked for him. Chicago was 14 games ahead.[15]

The Cubs could coast into the pennant in September, and that was pretty much what they did. They played mere .500 ball for the month. They clinched the pennant with a Pittsburgh Pirate loss while they were losing their fifth game in a row. "The 'Whoopee' [is] lost to fans when the Cubs back into the flag mathematically," lamented one paper. Wrigley reassured, claiming the team was just a bit tired at this point. McCarthy tried to keep the worries down. For obvious reasons, he aired none of his concerns. Hack Wilson had to tape both his ankles for every game. Guy Bush, who had pitched superbly all summer, seemed to have lost his edge. Riggs Stephenson was playing with a special brace, hobbled by a groin injury, and his throwing arm was bothering him. Charlie Grimm was out with his thumb still on the mend, and Gabby Hartnett's arm was still no better. Hartnett "is quieter," wrote one reporter, "and has acquired a wistful earnestness that is heart-breaking to the friends who have known him through all his years of fiery and eager catching." McCarthy's only words to the team about any possible slipping were spare and to the point: "Give everything you've got. If you do and we're beaten again, I won't have anything to say. If you don't hustle, I'll have plenty so say." Elsewhere, he tried to keep a light touch. McCarthy actually took himself out of the third-base coaching box for two games in late September. They were the only Cubs games he ever managed from the bench. In the last week he also allowed the baseball writers to choose the pitcher for the final game. They chose the batting practice pitcher Hank Grampp. He lost. It was all in good fun, and McCarthy's view of it was that it was fine if people were a little diverted, just so they refocused themselves when the World Series began. He had every reason to believe they would. The Cubs had won the National League pennant by the greatest margin in over ten years. While McCarthy's role in the triumph certainly gained notice, some players felt he actually deserved even more credit. Years later, for example, Charlie Grimm raised a point few realized about McCarthy until later — his knack for handling diverse personalities. "The Cubs," recalled Grimm, "were a tough bunch to handle — about twenty different, clashing personalities. But they played ball and enjoyed it, too, under McCarthy — played pennant ball."[16]

The city of Chicago was all a-flutter over the coming World Series. It had been a long hard road for the city. Yes, they had won a pennant in the war-shortened season of 1918, but otherwise, until the McCarthy era, they had been down since 1914. For the Series, Wrigley installed extra seating beyond the outfield walls along Waveland and Sheffield Avenues. Traffic had to be rerouted, and the city's motorists enthusiastically obliged. Wrigley Field's capacity was now 50,740. McCarthy had brought Chicago back to the edge of the promised land, and now they were in the World Series.

Their opponents were the Philadelphia Athletics, and they were quite a team too. While the Cubs had such stars as Cuyler, Wilson, Stephenson, and Hornsby, the A's had Jimmie Foxx, Al Simmons, Mickey Cochrane, and Lefty Grove. The prospect of facing the A's was a real thrill for McCarthy. "All my life," he wrote, "I've waited for this hour. I've schemed and dreamed of the day when I would lead a major league team into the World Series against Connie Mack. And here it is, all come true." As a boy, McCarthy had rooted for the A's, and he had greatly admired Mr. Mack. In 1925, when friends in Germantown had thrown him a dinner to celebrate his being named manager of Cubs, Mr. Mack's presence was a thrill, and McCarthy fondly recalled how he "went out of his way to predict great success for me." Still, McCarthy was not going to let sentiment get in the way of the tasks before him. He pronounced his team fit and ready (they were not fit, medically), and he predicted a Cub victory, but he knew he was facing a formidable foe.[17]

Game one was in Chicago. Every seat in the stadium was sold, including those in the extra seating Mr. Wrigley had installed. Over 50,000 fans jammed into Wrigley Field. Much speculation had been raised as to who would be the pitchers for game one. McCarthy went with Charlie Root. Everyone expected Mr. Mack to start either of his aces George Earnshaw or Lefty Grove. Mack never told anyone, but Grove had recently been sick and, still weak, could not be counted on to pitch for a long stretch, and he never started a game in the entire Series, but the Cubs were still mentally preparing to face him.

Instead of starting either of his aces, however, Mack made a move that became the stuff of legend. He turned to a 35-year-old veteran named Howard Ehmke who McCarthy had faced back in World War I. While Grove had won 20 games that season, and Earnshaw 24, Ehmke had pitched only eleven games for Mack that season. His record was a mere 7 and 2. This seemed befuddling to everyone, but as befuddling as was the choice of starting Emhke, equally befuddling proved the task of actually hitting him. Mr. Mack figured that the Cubs would be gearing themselves up for the speed of Earnshaw and, even more, of Grove. The change of pace, he thought, could work wonders, particularly from someone like Ehmke who threw both right-handed and underhanded, something with which all the Cubs' mighty right-handed hitters might have trouble. They did, although at several points it was definitely touch and go.[18]

In that afternoon's paper, the *Chicago Daily News*, Chicagoans first read how

"Connie Mack, the wily old leader…, dragged Mr. Ehmke right up to the spotlight, and the old-timer with his speed gone and supposedly laboring with a dead arm handed up a lot of the slowest, sloppiest but most tantalizing assortment of curves that Joe McCarthy's men of murderers' row have gazed upon this season, and the murderers' row didn't function at all." Ehmke had supposedly been in Mr. Mack's doghouse for many weeks. He had indeed not played all September but had actually been spending some of the time out scouting the Cubs. Mr. Mack had told Ehmke to let him know when he was ready again to pitch up to his ability, and before game one he told his manager "I will win the game for you. Don't worry." He won, but Mr. Mack worried plenty.

The game was not a one-sided handcuffing by any means. Charlie Root was in many respects the stronger pitcher that day. He held the A's to no runs and just two hits through six innings, while on several occasions the Cubs seemed ready to break the game open. With no score in the third inning, for example, the Cubs had one out and men on second and third. Then, amidst huge anticipation among Chicago fans, and with Lefty Grove hastily warming in the A's bullpen, both Rogers Hornsby and Hack Wilson struck out. Some said that inning cast a pall over the entire Series. In the seventh, with the A's up by one run, the Cubs again put runners on second and third with one out. The next batter flied out. McCarthy sent up Gabby Hartnett to bat for Charlie Root. He struck out. In all, 13 Cub batters struck out that afternoon. Ehmke's mark stood as a World Series record until 1953. Mack, reflected McCarthy, "knew what he was doing. Our club was loaded with powerful right-handed hitters, and Ehmke had a way of pitching to right handers that was tough on us." The decision to start Ehmke made Mack look like the smarter manager.[19]

McCarthy sent Guy Bush into the game to relieve Root after Hartnett's pinch-hitting. Root had pitched well, and Bush did too, but the A's scored two runs in the ninth inning, both unearned, due to two errors by shortstop Woody English. Down 3–0, Hack Wilson stepped up to start the bottom of the ninth. He hit a shot that struck Ehmke in the stomach. Ehmke recovered, threw out Wilson, and stayed in the game. Cuyler grounded to third, but the throw to first was wild, and Cuyler went to second. Stephenson singled him home. Fans started to stir. Charlie Grimm, his bad thumb having largely healed, singled. The next batter grounded and Grimm was forced. With two on, two out, and the winning run at bat, pinch hitter Charles "Chick" Tolson struck out, setting Ehmke's record number at 13.

The game made Philadelphia fans rejoice. Like Chicagoans, they too had had glory years in the early 20th century and had since then spent a long time "in the wilderness." They felt just as "due" as Cubs fans. Someone had to win the first game, and whoever lost would just have to pick up and come back the next afternoon. What gave Philadelphia fans an extra bit of chortle and the Chicago faithful an additional cringe was the sense that Manager Connie Mack seemed to have outsmarted everyone. The Howard Ehmke gambit would loom over Chicago Cubs fans for decades. Perhaps only game four of the '29 World Series would be a worse memory for them.[20]

Shocked or not by Ehmke's win, the Cubs had to go out the next day and face George Earnshaw. He could obviously be formidable under any circumstances, and on this day he certainly was. He held Chicago scoreless for five innings. Meanwhile, the A's jumped out with 6 runs in the third and fourth. When the Cubs finally came to life with 3 runs in their half of the fifth, Mr. Mack simply inserted Lefty Grove. He held the Cubs scoreless from there while the A's scored 3 more, coasting to an easy 9–3 win. Between them Earnshaw and Grove posted another 13-strikeout win for the A's. About the only Cub to receive praise in regard to game two was McCarthy. "Who was the Cubs hero in the second game — Joe McCarthy," wrote the *Tribune.* "Despite the score he stayed on the coaching line all afternoon. Any other manager would have gone home in disgust after the fourth inning." Perhaps McCarthy's not quitting was noble, but when the local sports reporters have to turn to the stolid figure of a manager standing in the third-base coach's box, they are certainly revealing how little they can find about which to cheer. McCarthy may have looked noble, but it was Mr. Mack who looked wily.[21]

The Cubs had the travel day to contemplate their situation. McCarthy held no team meetings. There was no need to "rah-rah" the likes of Hornsby, Wilson, Cuyler, and Stephenson. They knew what they had to do. McCarthy was deliberately coy with the press as to who would pitch for him the next day. He was obviously trying to put a little mystery into his choice as Mr. Mack had done with Ehmke. His could not be a significant ploy, however, as the A's knew all the likely starters for the Cubs. McCarthy chose Guy Bush. Earnshaw went again for the A's. They both pitched well. Earnshaw had one bad inning, yielding 3 runs on 2 hits. That was all the Cubs would get, and it was all they needed. Bush, as McCarthy said, "pitched splendidly," scattering nine A's singles, as the Cubs won 3–1. Now matters felt better. "Look Out Now!" hailed the *Herald and Examiner.* "As long as we're swinging we're dangerous," warned McCarthy. A 2–1 lead is indeed no crisis, although the fourth game is critical, for afterwards one will either be even up or down almost insurmountably.[22]

On the day of the third game, the rumors were starting to grow about how Ehmke had been sent out in September not to Mr. Mack's doghouse but to scout the Cubs. The sense of being outsmarted a few days earlier was hardly something about which Cubs fans wanted to read or think any more at this point in the series. It came out that from August 15th to September 15th, Ehmke had been at virtually every Cub game. Mack had also met with players on the Chicago White Sox who had seen the Cubs several times. The four, Tommy Thomas, Ted Lyons, Red Faber, and Moe Berg, gave him added tips as to various players strengths, weaknesses, and tendencies. (Catcher Moe Berg certainly appreciated the value of Mr. Mack's sly espionage, as he would later spy for the U.S. Government during World War II.) In addition to Ehmke doing some scouting, Mr. Mack had also apparently sent reserve catcher Ira Thomas to scout the Cubs in a series against the Giants. There Thomas smartly diagramed every position in which John McGraw posted his men against each of the Cubs' hitters. The further news of such crafty maneuvers by Mr. Mack gave Cubs fans a certain discomfort as they approached the all-important game four.[23]

Game four, Saturday, October 12, 1929, a date which will live in infamy—for Cubs fans. At first it all went so smoothly for McCarthy and the Cubs. McCarthy started Charlie Root, and he proved as effective as he had been in game one, only this time the breaks went with him. For six innings he held the A's scoreless, while the Cubs ran up a huge lead of 8–0. McCarthy later recalled ruefully: "It looked like we had the series squared at two victories apiece."[24] Fans in Shibe Park were shrugging, figuring the game was lost, and the series would be a fight to the end. Then came the seventh inning, an *inning* which will live in infamy — .

Al Simmons led off with a towering home run that hit the roof of the left field pavilion. Oh well, sighed Cubs fans, there goes Charlie Root's shutout. Jimmie Foxx was next up, and he singled to right field. Then Bing Miller popped an easy fly to center field. In the early fall, Shibe Park's center field was a murderous sun field, and on this afternoon the skies could not have been clearer, even though the weather service had predicted clouds. As a result, Wilson simply lost the ball in the sun. No one blamed him. The official scorer did not even tag him with error. McCarthy later reflected about Wilson: "If he had caught Miller's short fly which came early in the seventh..., Root would have gotten out of the inning." But Wilson did not catch it, and now there were two on, none out, and one run in; hardly a time to panic with the lead still at seven. Then: Jimmy Dykes singled to left, Joe Boley singled, George Burns popped out, and Max Bishop singled. McCarthy pulled Charlie Root for Art Nehf. The score was now 8–5. Nehf faced George "Mule" Haas. Nehf was a left-hander, and, as McCarthy knew, Haas usually had trouble with lefties. Haas hit a fly ball to center field. McCarthy recalled: "It looked like an easy catch for Hack Wilson, but Hack lost the ball in the sun, and it rolled to the bleacher wall for a home run." Score: tied! Philadelphia fans were going nuts. Nehf was rattled, and he walked Mickey Cochrane. McCarthy pulled Nehf and brought in Sheriff Fred Blake to face Al Simmons, batting for the second time in the inning. Simmons, as McCarthy grimly described, "hit a perfect double play ball right at [third baseman] Norman McMillan.... Just when McMillan appeared to be set to clean out the inning, the ball took a freak bound and shot over his shoulder into left field for a safe hit." Then Foxx singled, scoring Cochrane. McCarthy again went to the pen, bringing in Pat Malone. Anarchy was loosed upon Shibe Park. Rattled from the moment he took the mound, Malone hit Bing Miller with a pitch, loading the bases. Jimmy Dykes doubled, with Stephenson having trouble with the ball in the sun. Foxx and Simmons scored. 10 runs, 10 hits, still one out. Remarkably, the next two batters struck out. McCarthy shuddered, "I have never lived through another such inning." No one had ever come back from an eight-run deficit in a World Series game, let alone do so in one inning. The A's were jubilant; the Cubs were in shock. Mack sent in Lefty Grove to pitch in the eighth. The shaken Cubs could do nothing with his blazers—a grounder to shortstop, and two strikeouts in the eighth; two strikeouts and a pop fly in the ninth. Game four to Philadelphia, 10–8.

One afternoon earlier that season, McCarthy's Cubs were pouring it on the hapless Boston Braves. Judge Emil Fuchs, the Braves owner, yelled to McCarthy out at the coach's box, pleading with him to "have a heart." McCarthy would not let up, however, and told Fuchs that some day he would answer why. Fuchs attended the '29 World Series, and after the Cubs' 10–8 loss to the A's, he went to the Cubs dressing room to offer condolences. McCarthy took one look at Fuchs and said "there's your answer, Judge." Upon leaving the stadium, an unconfirmed story went, McCarthy encountered a boy who asked him for a ball. McCarthy allegedly turned to him and sighed: "Come back here tomorrow and sit beside Wilson, and you'll be able to pick up all the balls you want."[25]

What could anyone say about such a debacle? Charlie Root was emphatic: "Don't blame Hack." Rogers Hornsby said the same: "Don't go bearing down on Wilson. If you think those breaks weren't excusable, go out there yourself and see how much of a baseball you can see in that sun." (Later, Hornsby would opine that McCarthy erred when he brought in Nehf to pitch to Haas, yet if he felt Haas's fly could have been caught but for the sun, why was Nehf's insertion a mistake?) Wilson did not hide or put on a long face. He talked willingly to reporters both in the clubhouse and in the hotel. Over and over he put it simply and honestly, "I couldn't see the balls." Recalling that the weatherman had predicted a cloudy day, Wilson lamented, "if he'd only been right." McCarthy defended Wilson: "They may want to blame Wilson, [but] you can't fasten it upon him. The poor kid simply lost the ball in the sun, and he didn't put the sun there." As for the game, McCarthy sighed: "when you cannot hold an eight-run lead ... there isn't a great deal to be said on the subject." It was better left at that, but the fans were starting to speculate, asking such questions as why McCarthy left Root in as long as he did. Everyone in Chicago was mad, and everyone had an opinion, and McCarthy's seventh-inning management was high on the list of complaints.[26]

With the Cubs down three games to one, even the *Chicago Tribune* was lamenting about "the record whiffing Cubs," and no one threw any rocks at the *Tribune* office windows later that day. Teams had come back from such a deficit, but it was hard not to be a little down. To add to the sense of a cold slap in the face, before the fifth game Commissioner Landis came to both managers and told them to cut out all the bench jockeying. Neither side was worse than the other here, but it was getting out of hand. A's third baseman Jimmy Dykes recalled that you could hear the profane language all over the park. Mr. Mack never used such language, and McCarthy was usually silent. But each accepted it as part of the game and understood that a high-tension situation like the World Series would prompt more of it. Judge Landis was going to have his way, however; he always did. So the managers relayed the message. Anyone who used foul language would forfeit his entire World Series share! The A's Mickey Cochrane took his position at catcher at the beginning of the game and, knowing the orders from on high, yelled to the Cubs, "Come on out boys. Put on your bib and tucker. We're serving tea and cookies today." The little event may have been insignificant, but the fact that the A's were the ones taking the psychological initiative at this juncture certainly demonstrated who was up and who was down.[27]

McCarthy selected Pat Malone to start the game. Connie Mack decided to put out Ehmke again. The two kept the game scoreless for the first three innings. Then in the fourth, the Cubs came up with a two-out rally and pushed over two runs. Ehmke was relieved. The Cubs scored no more that inning, but Malone continued to hold the A's scoreless into the ninth inning. Philadelphia fans were getting restless. President Herbert Hoover was in the stands, and, in protest of Prohibition, fans began chanting "We Want Beer!" As the ninth inning progressed, their attention turned back to baseball. Malone struck out the first man. Then he gave up a bad-hop single to Max Bishop. Mule Haas again stepped in and hit a home run, tying the game. McCarthy did not relieve Malone, and he got Cochrane out on a grounder to second. Al Simmons then doubled. McCarthy chose to walk Jimmie Foxx and bring up Bing Miller. He still had faith in Malone. Miller doubled, Simmons scored, and that was the game and the Series. Mickey Cochrane encountered Commissioner Landis in the locker room after the game and announced: "we're not serving tea and cookies today." The next day, the sports headline in the *Chicago Daily News* simply read "Cubs Tell How to Get Refunds for Tickets to 6th Series Game."[28]

"What can I say," sighed McCarthy, "without violating the rules of the losing manager's union? But," he added with a little verve, "I'll be damned if I'll say the best team won. I wish it was ethical for me to say the A's had more luck than I've seen in twenty-one years of baseball. I don't mind today's game so much, but I'll never believe what my eyes saw in that bad dream Saturday [game four]." Later he mused more ruefully: "No excuses, the A's took our best. The A's are a great ball club, though I'll not say, taking the results into consideration, that we were happy to have made their acquaintance."

McCarthy was never much for philosophizing at length with the press. Some managers could make a memorable joke about such a loss, but that was not McCarthy's nature. Fans were then left more with the bare bones of defeat. Questions about Wilson were obvious, and silly. The question of why the Cubs struck out 50 times in 5 games could only underscore the quality of the A's pitching. Questions began to come forth about McCarthy, however. Why was he allegedly slow with the relief pitching decisions in game four? Why did he stay with Malone in game five? Why had Connie Mack seemingly outsmarted him with the Ehmke move? Warren Brown of the *Herald and Examiner* heard a lot of this and quickly responded with a bit of sarcasm: "The real trouble with the Cubs, as everyone knows," he chuckled, "is that William Wrigley and Bill Veeck had the old-fashioned idea of letting one man manage the ball club. Since game one, I have encountered at least 100 persons who insist that they were better managers than Joe McCarthy."

Brown may have helped some folks set a few feelings aside, but the grumbling remained, and it would linger through the next season. Wrigley seemed unable to get over the loss. McCarthy was not patient here. The off-season would not be pleasant. In December, one columnist for the *Tribune* did express praise for McCarthy's exceptional understanding of men and "his ability to keep all hands fighting for the common cause." Otherwise the mood was glum, on the streets and in Wrigley's office. The only happy news for Cub fans was that the Cincinnati Reds fired Manager Jack Hendricks. Otherwise it was bleak. The stock market crashed, and the economy began to falter badly. What little compensation sports can bring to such a picture had no impact on Cubs fans that winter. That December, McCarthy was in Chattanooga scouting minor league pitching prospects. One wag grabbed McCarthy and told him he had a prospect who "has everything, more than any hurler in your league." McCarthy had heard such bragging many times and was hardly impressed. Nevertheless, he told the man to bring the prospect to his room. A few minutes later in walked the "prospect" with a big grin. It was Howard Ehmke! McCarthy managed a weak smile. Twenty-one years later, a reporter wrote: "It was a long time before any reporter who valued his friendship with McCarthy dared to mention to Joe the subject of that 10-run rally. Marse Joe paled and the very recollection of it." Forty years later, McCarthy did nod, with animation still in his voice: "Boy what a lesson Connie taught me in that Series! I've never forgotten it." He would not cash his '29 World Series check until June 7, 1930.[29]

20

Fractured Ankle, Fractured Season

The day the Cubs lost the World Series to Philadelphia in 1929, McCarthy looked at some reporters and asked, "I wonder what time the train leaves for Catalina." Obviously he wanted to convey that as far as he was concerned, the 1929 season was over, and it was time to focus on the next one. He wanted, he demanded, that his players adopt the same attitude when they met at Chicago Union Station to head off to Catalina in February, 1930. The day they left, 1000 automobiles crowded around Union Station as folks gathered to see them off. Many brought Cubs players gifts and wanted to let them know that the city's spirit was still strong. Once out at Catalina, Hack Wilson showed a similarly positive, foot-forward outlook when he fielded, as he had all winter, the endlessly repetitive questions about the fly balls in the seventh inning of game four of the World Series. His repartée was always the same: How did you miss that ball in the sun? What ball? Do you mean to tell me that you did not see the ball in that sun? What sun? As in later times, athletes had to deal with the same questions from the press, over and over, and if they showed temper or expressed exasperation *that* would become news. One simply had to have the utmost of patience. It was all part of why McCarthy held a certain disdain for the press. The only other questions with which Hack Wilson had to deal in 1930 concerned his fighting. The Kolp/ Donohue matter had been laid to rest, but there was actual talk in Chicago of Hack fighting professionally. One Chicago promoter, Jim Muller wanted to stage a "Chicago championship" fight between Wilson and White Sox first baseman Art Shires. Shires, the previous summer, had punched out both the team's traveling secretary, Lou Barbour, and his manager, Lena Blackburne. (Blackburne had actually suffered a broken jaw.) Muller offered Wilson $15,000 for the appearance, which was more than Hack usually made in a year. Odds makers were taking wagers, declaring Wilson a 7–5 favorite. To McCarthy's utmost pleasure, Commissioner Landis prevented the event from occurring.[1]

Whether the events of October, 1929, baseball and otherwise, were going to cast shadows over the 1930 Cubs, McCarthy knew the best thing was to push ahead and pay no heed. The Cubs had the same squad as 1929, with the addition of an excellent new third baseman, Les Bell. But while spring training had been so smooth in 1929, with the notable exception of Gabby Hartnett's chronically sore arm, the spring of 1930 gave rise to many problems. Bell came down with a sore arm. Woody English and Charlie Grimm each had badly pulled leg muscles. Most important, Rogers Hornsby had a nagging problem with a bone spur in his heel. This had been bothering him in 1929, and in the off season he underwent a minor operation. In the spring it still gave him trouble, however. While the '29 team had blazed through the spring exhibition games, the 1930 Cubs exhibition record was decidedly mediocre. Perhaps there were some ghosts from the World Series. Some of the 1929 memories certainly had a way of worming their way into the news coverage. Reporting a game in Kansas City, for example, one paper went out of its way to describe: "There were runners on first and third, and none out, when the batter lifted a long fly to Hack Wilson. It was in the sun, but Hack caught it." During the 1930 season, opposing players and fans tried to goad the Cubs any way they could. Wilson, for example, was nicknamed "Sunny Boy." It never got to him, however. He would have a sensational year, one of the greatest in the history of the game.[2]

No matter the memories and nagging injuries, the Cubs were still the favorites to win the National League pennant. Bookies in New York had them at even money, and despite the loss in the World Series, some Chicagoans were waxing poetic about what a truly great team they had. Some reporters saw potential problems, however. Kiki Cuyler was the only player on the club who had any speed. The pitching staff could be inconsistent. It was a club that could clearly match anyone's offensive power, but that spring the National League had introduced a new, much more lively ball. This would, indeed, offset some of Chicago's power. The entire league would hit .303 that year; the last-place Philadelphia Phillies hit .315. The Cubs were, then, a team that would both hit and get hit. McCarthy thus had on his hands, said Warren Brown of the *Herald and Examiner*, "a club that is made to order for second guessing. The World Series," he said, "proved that and developments this Spring [like the injuries and the mediocre record] have added to the proof."

Noting how difficult it could be to win consistently if both Grimm and Hornsby miss a significant number of games, Brown observed with intentional understatement "that there is more in the job of Joe McCarthy than putting uniforms on nine or nineteen men and sending them out on the playing field." Brown was one of McCarthy's admirers, and he saw how fans, other reporters, and players would jump at him when anything went awry and regard successes as simply a matter of putting great athletes out to play. (In future years, many others would raise the same criticisms about McCarthy.) The trouble, here and subsequently, was that people's tendencies to blame the manager, and to think they could do his job as well or better, were not going to abate just because of the words of one news columnist. A lot of fans grumbled about McCarthy. That was no major issue, but in 1930, one Cubs player would do a lot of second-guessing too. That would be a big problem.[3]

Gabby Hartnett was back behind the plate when the Cubs opened the 1930 season. This was a great joy to the fans. But Rogers Hornsby's heel continued to give him trouble, and he had to sit out a few games in April. Riggs Stephenson also missed some early games with a muscle pull. Into early May, the Cubs were playing just around .500. The pitching, observed one writer, "has been terrible." Stephenson has missed half the games, and Rogers Hornsby has been "hitting viscous pop flies to first base." Fans maintained an optimism that the return of a healthy Hornsby and Stephenson would turn everything around. McCarthy gave the team a neat lift in a game against the Giants. Down 5–3 in the eighth, the Cubs put men on second and third. Stephenson stepped in, with the pitcher due up next. McCarthy sent the injured Hornsby to the on-deck circle. Hornsby knelt, conspicuously swinging three bats, *à la* Ty Cobb. With first base open but with Hornsby to follow, Giants' Manager McGraw elected not to give Stephenson an intentional walk. Stephenson promptly doubled, tying the game. McCarthy withdrew Hornsby, who could not play anyway, and let pitcher Hal Carlson hit for himself. Carlson actually singled, scoring Stephenson with the winning run. An injured Rogers Hornsby is of little value to a team, but McCarthy could use him in such a state. The Cubs ended up winning eight in a row that week and briefly took over first place.[4]

In May, Stephenson's throwing arm continued to bother him, and Hornsby was in and out of the lineup. After their little winning streak, the Cubs fell off with a 4 and 11 slump. By May 27, their record had fallen back to 19–19. St. Louis and New York were then proving the strongest teams in the league. Brooklyn was also surprisingly good. (Surprising to all but McCarthy, anyway; during spring training, McCarthy was the only manager in the league to predict that Brooklyn would be tough.) Cubs fans remained optimistic. They still thought of their strong personnel and remembered that in 1929 they had to scramble in the early stages of the season, too. The next day, however, genuine tragedy struck the team: pitcher Hal Carlson died. Carlson, aged 38, had served in World War I and suffered phosgene inhalation at the Battle of the Argonne Forest. Weakened by the gas attack, Carlson had developed tuberculosis in 1928. This was exactly what had happened to Christy Mathewson. Carlson outlived every doctor's prediction, battling the illness as best he could. In 1929 he pitched well, winning 11 games, and he even won 4 in 1930, one as late as May 10. But the illness proved too much for him. McCarthy eulogized at Carlson's funeral. He may have been speaking literally or metaphorically. People took it as they wished: "When you're in one of those games, with first place at stake, Carlson's the pitcher. He can come up with those 1–0 and 2–1 victories. He knows what he's doing out there. He knows how to protect himself." Regrettably, it would not be the last time McCarthy would have to maintain a team and show a deft combination of heart and brains amidst the tragedy of a dying ball player. It would indeed be sad for him to learn just how much skill he had in handling such situations. The day Carlson died, McCarthy and the Cubs went out and beat Cincinnati.[5]

Carlson's death was a blow like no other for any team. But while other mere baseball matters were dwarfed by the tragedy, the Cubs' misfortunes did not stop with Carlson's death. Two days later against St. Louis, Rogers Hornsby, still in and out of the lineup testing his heel, hesitated on a slide into third base. McCarthy's Fifth Commandment of Baseball was: "When you start to slide S-L-I-D-E. He who changes his mind may have to change a good leg for a bad one." Sure enough, as Hornsby hesitated, he caught a spike and broke his ankle. His leg was put in a cast. Doctors said he would be lost for at least two months. (On the same day that Hornsby broke his ankle, Connie Mack released Howard Ehmke. In 1929, folks had said he was washed up; they were just a trifle premature in their judgment.)

On June 1, Rogers Hornsby received the award for being chosen the Most Valuable Player in the National League in 1929. He was the first person to receive the award twice. (The award was discontinued at that point because the game's parsimonious magnates felt that it could increase various salary demands.) Hornsby accepted his award on crutches. The occasion was thus a grim illustration to the fans of the state of their team's affairs. In 1929, it was Hartnett who was out the whole season. This year it would be Hornsby. To fill the void in the infield, McCarthy inserted second-year player Clarence "Footsie" Blair. Naturally, no one expected him to be another Hornsby. Blair hit decently, .273, but the fact that the mark fell over 100 points below Hornsby's 1929 average spoke to the significance of Hornsby's injury.

Warren Brown wrote that the Cubs should go after a hot young prospect currently playing for the San Francisco Seals in the Pacific Coast League. His name was Frankie Crosetti. The Cubs did not seek him. McCarthy had actually hired Cincinnati's manager Jack Hendricks as a scout. (Marse Joe did not hold a grudge.) Hendricks recommended a journeyman infielder named Eddie Farrell, who did fill in some games that year.[6]

Hornsby was gone, and the injuries kept coming. Les Bell missed 80 games that season; Riggs Stephenson missed 45 games. The load fell to Gabby Hartnett, Kiki Cuyler, and Hack Wilson. They were certainly up to the task. Hartnett hit .339, Cuyler .355. Wilson's year was phenomenal. He hit .356. He hit a National League record 56 home runs, a league mark that stood for 68 years, and his 190 RBI's was the most anyone ever hit and few have even approached. In June, Wilson was carrying the team. The team ran off another winning streak of nine games. It left them one game behind Brooklyn on June 7. For the rest of the month they battled for the league lead and were in first place when the month ended.

With Hornsby's ankle and other injuries, McCarthy had his hands full. When the Cubs were in first place, he received a fair amount of credit. When the credit came from Chicago reporters, people could chalk that up to hype for the fans and for general team morale. But some praise was coming from out of town. With the Cubs in first place on July 1, George Barton of the *Minneapolis Tribune*, for example, wrote "Joe McCarthy once more is proving to the baseball world that he is one of the greatest managers of modern times. ... Along with being a strategist, he is a natural leader of men." Noting Carlson's death, Hornsby's broken ankle, others' illnesses and injuries, and pitcher Pat Malone's drinking, Barton concluded, "It requires real managerial ability to accomplish what Joe McCarthy has done this season."[7]

As Hornsby was recuperating, rumors began to fly about the league that he was not getting along with the Cubs management. He was supposedly mad at McCarthy for not playing him more in May as his heel was getting better. On July 8, the *Cincinnati Enquirer* reported that a rift had developed and the Cubs were not going to play Hornsby again, even when his ankle was better. McCarthy would not dignify the report with a comment. Veeck joked that "we haven't reached the point where we are trying to get rid of .375 hitters." Like any injured player, Hornsby was bound to go through a "down" period. Hornsby was always one to scrutinize the play around him and voice his opinions, and apparently he was giving his opinions to Wrigley, who some said had still not recovered from the World Series debacle. The report out of Cincinnati brought forth nothing but denials, but Hornsby's opinionated nature had plenty of time on its hands, and he had apparently found a sympathetic ear.[8]

Through July and into August, the Cubs remained in the pennant fight. Brooklyn did not fade, and New York and St. Louis were in the thick of it too. By late August, the Cubs had a five-game lead. McCarthy proved his worth throughout the many tensions of the summer. In a game against the Giants on August 24, the score was tied in the ninth inning. Cubs' outfielder Danny Taylor was on third base with two out. McGraw chose to walk the next two batters to get to the pitcher, Guy Bush. McGraw preferred to make the pitcher hit, or force McCarthy to go to a pinch hitter, as, if unsuccessful, it would take Bush out of the game and oblige McCarthy to dip into his tired bull pen. McCarthy let Bush hit; and with a count of 0–2, he signaled for Taylor to steal home. It worked; the Cubs won. (And if it had failed, he would have had Malone on the mound in the next inning.) Asked about calling for the steal of home, McCarthy demurred: "I'd rather you talk to Taylor about that." Reporters knew who deserved the credit. "As great managers of the game go, McCarthy is earning a place besides Mack and McGraw," wrote one scribe. Arch Ward of the *Chicago Tribune* reflected:

> Whether the Cubs hold their lead ... or not, they have made a valiant fight. And much of their success is due to J. Vincent McCarthy. ... The Cubs, with all their injuries, have needed a pilot more than any team in the league. They have players of various mental abilities and personality traits, and it has been no mean task to weld them into an efficient and concerted machine. It has taken a strength of human nature as well as a baseball mind to take a last place club, like the Cubs were when McCarthy came [and] build them up to title contenders and eventual league champions. And it has been even harder to hold that level.

Ward's references to "mental abilities and personality traits" likely referred to Hack Wilson and Rogers Hornsby. Wilson was always hard to handle, yet no one brought out his talent like McCarthy, especially in 1930. The personality of Rogers Hornsby was a more difficult matter. As Hornsby's ankle was healing, he grew more restless, wanted to get back in the game as soon as he could, completely confident that he could contribute and give the Cubs another pennant. In late July, McCarthy stated "Hornsby's broken ankle may have mended, but even if it has, I doubt it he could get into the game for another two to three weeks. It doesn't seem possible that Hornsby is again able to play and unless he is in top shape, I wouldn't dare take a chance on crippling him again." Hornsby possessed an utterly overweening ego. He may have egotistically felt that McCarthy was using his expressed concern as a way of keeping him out of the lineup, believing that McCarthy was in some way jealous of the potential threat his presence posed to his leadership. (If this was inherent in McCarthy's makeup, he would likely have bragged about his call to have Danny Taylor steal home against the Giants.)

There was a lot of projection and ambition in Hornsby's views. They were all very much part of Hornsby's nature. If McCarthy was deliberately holding Hornsby out of the lineup for any reason other than a medical one, it would be the only time in all his years as a manager, before or after, that he ever did such a thing. But Hornsby was upset, and he was grumbling about it to Veeck and Wrigley.[9]

On August 28th and 29th, the Cubs split a pair of games with the Cardinals. Although the results amounted but to little mathematically, the contests proved highly significant. The first game, which the Cardinals won, lasted 20 innings, and the second went 13 innings. Over the two days and 33 innings, McCarthy used *all* his pitchers. Ten years later, he sadly recalled: "... that was the end of the Cubs. The pitching staff was shot. Charlie Root, our ace, developed a disastrously sore arm. [Fred Blake came down with a bad back, and Hack Wilson pulled a muscle on his left side.] I couldn't get any replacements. ... If we had lost (the two games) in nine, we would have won the championship." The importance of the two games with St. Louis was such that ten years later, McCarthy's usually infallible memory had it that the first game went 23 innings and ended in a tie, with the next day's "replay" going 13 innings. This was not so, but it showed the anguish McCarthy felt over the games. Meanwhile, one part of his memory was dead on target. His pitching was now in dire condition. As of September 1st, the Cubs, having just lost a doubleheader to lowly Cincinnati, stood four games ahead of New York and St. Louis.

With some talk of the Cubs folding under the pressure, Hack Wilson yelled: "We'll beat all those guys regardless of what anyone else says. All this hooey about anybody stopping us makes me sick." McCarthy smiled: "Nine fellows like that Wilson [and] we'd never lost a ball game." Wilson was certainly pulling his load and then some. Sheriff Fred Blake had been nursing a bad back and in September was out with a torn stomach muscle. Charlie Root had a pulled muscle in his pitching arm. Riggs Stephenson had been out three weeks. Hack himself had been nursing sore ribs but playing anyway. And there was still the question of Hornsby. McCarthy inserted Hornsby back in the lineup on September 4th. He had first baseman Charlie Grimm shade a bit toward the middle of the field, as he knew Hornsby would still be slow, but he hoped his bat would be strong. In the first game, Hornsby went 0 for 2. Two days late, in a rather wild 19–14 victory over Pittsburgh, Hornsby committed two errors, and McCarthy took him out of the lineup. Again, Hornsby felt miffed.[10]

In mid–September, St. Louis and Brooklyn proved to be the hot teams of the National League. After the Cubs lost three to Brooklyn, the Dodgers and Cardinals had moved to half a game behind the Cubs. "Help! Help!" headlined the *Herald and Examiner*. On September 13th, the Cardinals beat the Cubs, and the Dodgers won their ninth straight. Now the Cubs were out of the lead for the first time in nearly two months.

With two teams to surmount, the Cubs headed to Philadelphia and New York. One thousand two hundred World Series ticket orders still came into the Cubs' ticket office that week. Knowing they had to win against the lowly Phillies, the Cubs merely split a doubleheader on September 15. In the first game, which the Cubs lost 12–11, Lefty O'Doul knocked in the winning run for the Phillies with a pinch-hit home run. The Cubs dugout was on the third base line and as he rounded third, O'Doul made a decided finger gesture right at McCarthy. McCarthy had cut O'Doul back in 1926, feeling he was not yet ready for the majors. Wrigley and Veeck had wondered about this move, but they yielded to McCarthy's judgment. O'Doul was steamed about it, as he languished in the minors for two more seasons. He played for the Giants in 1928, and in 1929 and 1930, with Philadelphia, he was arguably the best hitter in baseball, leading the league with a .398 average in 1929 and batting .383 in 1930. His feeling of revenge against McCarthy with his home run at such a key moment in the season was especially sweet.

McCarthy may have been right as to O'Doul needing more grooming in 1926, but Lefty was the only player McCarthy would ever discard who later blossomed into a genuine star, and at that point in the 1930 season, the sense of McCarthy's error was truly irritating to Wrigley. In 1926 he had played a personal role in O'Doul's recruitment. O'Doul's subsequent stardom made Wrigley lament, "Oh, no! ... my O'Doul!" Meanwhile, Wrigley had already been hearing complaints from Hornsby, and all this combined with his anguish over the World Series to make him even more upset.[11]

In New York the Cubs faced young Carl Hubbell, who proceeded to strike out ten and yield but three hits en route to a 7–0 shutout. The Giants, in John McGraw's last real pennant effort, had faded with injuries of their own and were "delighted to encounter a team more miserable than themselves." Wrigley was in New York on business, and he was conspicuously absent from all the Cubs games. The Cubs split the series with the Giants. Hornsby played only as a pinch-hitter. Meanwhile, the Cardinals had gone into Brooklyn and taken two from the Dodgers, putting them two up on both Brooklyn and Chicago. The *Tribune* lamented "It's About Over Now."[12]

McCarthy was certainly not conceding defeat. The team went up to Boston. Kiki Cuyler went into a terrible 4 for 26 slump that week. In Boston, the Cubs split a pair of games. Brooklyn lost, but St. Louis did not. As of September 21, the Cubs were three down with six to play. Having been absent from many Cubs games, Wrigley spoke to the *Tribune* lamenting the troubles the Cubs had experienced that season with Carlson's death and with the many injuries to Hornsby, Stephenson, Bell, Grimm, Blake, and Root. Wrigley was asked about a matter which, placed in print for the first time, shocked many Chicago readers: what of the rumors about firing McCarthy?(!) Wrigley's response was rather icy.

> I've heard them for several weeks, but I can't reply to them. ... I will not say McCarthy will be manager next year. Neither will I say he will be offered a new contract. We have no way of knowing what McCarthy might demand in the way of salary. He might ask for $100,000 a year. Or maybe McCarthy might not want the job any longer. He might feel that by failing to win a pennant he had placed me in an embarrassing position.—Ask Veeck. Whatever he says or does, I will second.

This was a bit of a bombshell, coming as it did with the pennant race still on. If there were rumors around Wrigley, they could obviously be more than mere rumors. And for him to raise such a ridiculous figure as $100,000 and to speak of himself being placed "in an embarrassing position" revealed a certain self-absorption that has not been the mark of good American sports team owners when they behaved in a civic-minded way. Meanwhile, McCarthy would offer no comment.[13]

Years later Bill Veeck, Jr. said that his father had told him that William Wrigley had never gotten over the loss in the 1929 World Series, especially the eighth inning of the fourth game. "My dad," recalled Veeck, "was all against making the change. [Wrigley and Veeck] argued about it for a long time, my dad saying 'No,' but in August of 1930 Mr. Wrigley made the decision to let McCarthy out." Then came the question of how and when to tell McCarthy of his termination. Veeck, Jr. said that "my dad didn't want to fire him in the first place and didn't want the job of telling him. So [he and Wrigley] kicked that around until finally they agreed to toss a coin."

Veeck lost the coin toss. On September 22, the *Chicago Herald and Examiner* headlined: "McCARTHY WILL LEAVE CUBS." McCarthy was out, and not just at the end of the season, but right then and there! The new Cubs manager — Rogers Hornsby. (Hornsby quickly got rid of Jack Hendricks as a scout; he did hold grudges.)[14]

Like everyone, Rogers Hornsby knew that Wrigley remained upset about the 1929 World Series. He implied to Wrigley and Veeck that McCarthy had let the team celebrate too much after securing the pennant, with the obvious implication that he would never have allowed such a lapse to occur. Here Hornsby may have also convinced Wrigley that McCarthy was also too lax with Hack Wilson, again implying that he would hold him in line better. (Wilson would never play well under Hornsby.) Hornsby conveyed to Veeck and Wrigley that McCarthy needed to play him more, particularly in the crucial September games when the team faded from first place. Meanwhile, Hornsby did miss a team meeting and claimed he was exercising in the bullpen. McCarthy restrained himself and did not make a big issue of it. Hornsby had supposedly mouthed off about Cuyler and English being "all washed up." He flatly denied this, claiming that Cuyler was one of the greatest outfielders and that English "will be the greatest shortstop next year," with the "next year" implying that he, and not McCarthy, can make him better. Wrigley claimed that all the rumors forced his move. "We were planning to tender Hornsby's contract after the season," he said, adding, "We didn't want to embarrass McCarthy." They didn't. At the Cubs' next home game against Cincinnati, Hornsby came out of the dugout smiling and went over to Wrigley's box to shake hands. The boos were enormous, and the only question among the people concerned at whom the boos were more fully directed.[15]

Wrigley was a wealthy man, fully accustomed to having his way, especially in close situations. When McCarthy brought the Cubs back from obscurity, the fourth-and third-place finishes were not embarrassments; quite the contrary. But 1929 and 1930 were different. Wrigley was expecting a winner, as were all Cub fans. When this did not happen he somehow could not accept that in sports humans can manage the details only up to a point after which factors like chance take over. No one could do better than McCarthy at bringing a team close, but issues like chance, and injuries, are beyond anyone's control. Wrigley could apparently not be persuaded that something more could not have been done, and Hornsby was in the perfect position to convince him that his leadership could have made the crucial difference.

Thus came such statements to the press as "Wrigley wants a winner, 'not sure McCarthy can give it to him." Wrigley also mouthed the absurd banality: "McCarthy lacked enough desire for a world championship." Rich people and out-of-touch administrators can spout off such cliches, and they usually surround themselves with people who will nod and earnestly "harrumph" at their "keen insights." When leaders of any organization let their egos get in the way of sound decisions, they usually get the results they are seeking to avoid. Hornsby's private words to Wrigley or Veeck resonated against this wealth of frustration, ego, embarrassment, and entitlement. Hornsby's tactics worked, at least insofar as he got McCarthy's job.[16]

As far as being the one to put the Cubs over the top, Hornsby was completely unsuccessful. Hornsby was not a winner, and none of the Cubs particularly liked or respected him. Most were indifferent; a few genuinely hated him, and after he became manager many more came to. He regularly berated players in front of others when they did not measure up, and often got less out of them as a result. He also "hit up" many Cubs for loans to feed his gambling, a compulsion/addiction as strong as Wilson's alcoholism. When McCarthy left the Cubs, Hack Wilson never played as well again. One reason here (besides Wilson's lack of sound self-management) provides a good example of the differences between McCarthy and Hornsby as managers.

In 1931, Wilson's batting average dropped from .356 to .261. His home run/RBI totals dropped from 56/190 to 13/61. Two factors unduly load the comparison here. One point is that Wilson missed 40 games in 1931; the other is that Wilson's 1930 season was so phenomenal that virtually no one could duplicate it. But for Wilson there was one significant contrast between the two managers. Under McCarthy, whenever Wilson had a 2-0 or 3-1 count, he had the option to swing. With either of those counts under Hornsby, Wilson always had orders to take. The mathematics which dictate that a batter take on 2-0 or 3-1 are obvious to all baseball people, and McCarthy followed the percentages *most* of the time, but with Wilson he knew there was something special at hand. Hornsby was too egotistical, too compulsively desirous of being in control, to see where it was wise to bend. That was a major difference between the two.[17]

Under either manager, players fully knew who was in charge. With Hornsby, they were made to know it more fully because of the hierarchical fact he had the power given to him by the team owner. He wielded power and appeared to enjoy finding weaknesses in players he berated. With McCarthy command was no less beyond question, but he needed far less to lead with any implicit or certainly explicit threat, and his ego was such that he did not ever need to revel in the fact of him possessing such power. Players could come to him with ideas and he would listen. If the idea was good he would take it, and if he thought it bad he would certainly say so. Under Hornsby, players knew they simply best do what they were told. All thinking was his domain. He even tried to call individual pitches.

Hornsby certainly knew his baseball, especially hitting. But from the time he took over the Cubs, he was never very successful as a manager. He had had one great year as a player/manager of the Cardinals in 1926. But the 1931 Cubs fell to third place and were never really in the pennant race, finishing 17 games out. During the 1932 season, the team played well but Hornsby's constant irritations led Wrigley and Veeck to fire him (and without him they took the pennant). From there Hornsby managed the hapless St. Louis Browns and later the Cincinnati Reds. He never finished higher than sixth. He simply did not know how to handle people, and ball players generally did not perform well under him.[18] McCarthy would do just a little better.

As for the rest of the 1930 season, the St. Louis Cardinals would not be headed. They kept winning, and the Cubs finished two games behind. In the World Series, Connie Mack and the A's were again the American League champions. They beat the Cardinals too. With Hornsby set to manage the Cubs in 1931 and McCarthy out, some Chicagoans felt something certainly should be done as a token of thanks to the manager who had rescued their Cubs from last place, made them contenders in one year and won the pennant in four. As the season was ending, Edson White, President of the Armour Meat Company, held a ceremony for McCarthy in the Board of Trade Building. From the Cubs, only Charlie Grimm and coach Jimmy Burke attended. McCarthy received $2000 worth of silver, including flatware, a tea set, and a pitcher that, people noted, could have come in handy during the pennant fight of the previous weeks. Along with the silver and best wishes came a telegram: "I would rather lose a World Series to you than play anybody else." It was from Connie Mack, and he meant it. McCarthy was most appreciative and thanked everyone. Then he simply boarded a train and left for Buffalo. His only reflection to the press: "I have been treated very nicely, and I'm not going to do any squawking." Wrigley and Veeck honored the rest of his contract, and forwarded him his share of the Cubs' second-place money from the World Series. Meanwhile, the unemployment of Joseph Vincent McCarthy would be rather short-lived. McCarthy attended the 1930 World Series in Philadelphia. There he spoke with Commissioner Landis. Judge Landis told McCarthy "I want you to get the best job in baseball." McCarthy replied, "I can't," and when Landis asked "why not?" McCarthy smiled: "Because you've got it." Landis laughed. "Then get the next best," he said. McCarthy would do just that.[19]

During the 1930 season, the New York Yankees had fallen to third place. Connie Mack's defending champion A's held a wide lead all season, but the Yankees' owner Jacob Ruppert and team president Ed Barrow were not satisfied that a team with Babe Ruth and Lou Gehrig could not make a better showing. The big factor here was that the manager from their glory days in the 1920s, Miller Huggins, had suddenly passed away just at the close of the 1929 season. A coach, Art Fletcher, finished out as manager for the few remaining games of '29. Then former Yankee pitcher Bob Shawkey was hired for 1930. Invidious comparisons to Huggins were inevitable, and with the A's so strong on top of it all, it was nearly impossible for Shawkey to look good under such circumstances. In many such situations in sports, and elsewhere, it is hard to be the one who succeeds the immortal. It is far better to be the one succeeds the one who succeeds the immortal.

By September, 1930, the Yankees leadership was interested in a new manager. Barrow was displeased with Bob Shawkey. Shawkey had been the teammate of some of the Yankees. He knew them. He socialized with them. As a result, there seemed to be little discipline. The team seemed more like Babe Ruth's fraternity house. A mere third place finish in the socio-economic circumstances of a rapidly deepening depression made that adolescent image no longer light and lively to many fans. Attendance was off, and Ed Barrow and Jacob Ruppert wanted a more mature, stable atmosphere. Back when Huggins fell ill, Yankee scout Paul Krichell had mentioned to Barrow to "keep that man McCarthy in mind. If anything should ever happen to 'Hug,' McCarthy would make a mighty good skipper for the Yankees."

In early September of 1930, Barrow privately contacted Warren Brown of the *Chicago Herald and Examiner* to make discreet inquiries about McCarthy. They met in New York at a boxing match. Brown informed Barrow of the troubles that were brewing for McCarthy and the likelihood of his being replaced in Chicago. Barrow told Brown that the he and Ruppert were not happy with Shawkey. Brown told him: "You'll never get anyone better than McCarthy." Joe Vila, sports editor of the *New York Sun*, had also told Barrow that McCarthy would be leaving the Cubs. (It was McCarthy himself who had secretly told Brown that it looked like he would not be with the Cubs after the 1930 season. Brown kept this confidence secret until 1944, a fact which

explains why Brown was one of the small minority of journalists McCarthy admired.)
Before a September game, Brown was in the dugout and he casually asked McCarthy,
who was watching his team in their pre-game workout, "How would you like to man-
age the Yankees?" McCarthy did not hesitate. He glanced over at Brown and snapped:
"Who wouldn't?" Brown relayed this to Barrow. Brown had sent an intermediary,
George Perry, to Jacob Ruppert to ask the Colonel if he was interested in hiring
McCarthy. Ruppert was enraged, ordering, some say chasing, Perry out of his office.
Baseball owners had learned a lesson from back in the early days of player raiding dur-
ing the Federal League's time and before that such raiding ultimately hurts everyone.
Ruppert, moreover, regarded William Wrigley as a friend, and he would not cross him.
Perry was later able to convey to Ruppert that McCarthy was available. Ruppert con-
tacted Wrigley, just at the time the whining of Hornsby, the O'Doul home run, the mem-
ories of the 1929 Series, and the failure of the 1930 season were all weighing upon him.
Wrigley told Ruppert that he had no difficulty with the Yankees contacting McCarthy.[20]

With Ruppert's approval, Ed Barrow got in touch with McCarthy when he
returned to Buffalo. He asked McCarthy to attend the St. Louis–Philadelphia World
Series in October. There Krichell contacted him. They privately met with Barrow and
Ruppert the night before game one. Later that month, McCarthy, taking a separate
train from any Yankee personnel, went to the Hotel Commodore in New York. From
there Krichell took him to a meeting with Ruppert and Barrow at the Colonel's 5th
Avenue office. McCarthy was tough in the negotiations, telling Ruppert "You sent
for me; I didn't ask to see you." At one point McCarthy stood up and began to leave
the room. Ruppert liked this kind of toughness. He knew it made for a good field
manager. They worked out all the details. McCarthy would manage the 1931 New York
Yankees. (Barrow later asked McCarthy what he would have done, when he threatened to leave the meeting, if Ruppert had not called him back. McCarthy confidently
responded: "I would have kept on going. I started out of there, and I could not have
done anything else.")

McCarthy, Barrow, and Ruppert met with the New York press to make the
announcement. As they were stepping out to make the announcement, Bob Shawkey
had just arrived. "I was heading for Barrow's office," he recalled somewhat bitterly,
"when the door opened and Joe McCarthy came walking out. I took one look and
turned around and got out of there. I knew what had happened." Shawkey was angry.
When he had earlier asked Ed Barrow about a new contract, Barrow had told him
they would take care of it during the winter. "It was a dirty deal," Shawkey snarled.

At the first meeting with the New York press, McCarthy was so nervous that he
referred to Ruppert as "Col. Huston." Colonel Tillinghast L'Hommedieu Huston had
formerly been co-owner of the Yankees with Ruppert. Ruppert had bought him out
in 1923, under less than friendly circumstances. With McCarthy's slip, everyone
laughed, including Ruppert. The signing was being filmed for the newsreels, and
Ruppert had the cameraman do a retake. Ruppert subsequently took center stage
and jauntily said "I hope 'McCardy,'" as he would always pronounce his new manager's name, "will be around here long enough so he will get to know me better." He
would be.[21]

McCarthy had been considering other bids for his services that month. The
Boston Red Sox were keenly interested in him. Their President Robert Quinn

declared: "It is time that the Red Sox regained their place in the baseball sun." Quinn hoped that McCarthy could take the last place Red Sox and repeat what he had done with the Cubs. He told McCarthy that his club would match and eclipse any offer received from the Yankees. He promised McCarthy complete autonomy with on-field matters and with trades. He also raised the point to McCarthy that Babe Ruth would likely displace whoever the Yankees named as their manager. McCarthy turned down the Boston offer and stated frankly, "It's not a question of money. I want to go where there is the most opportunity." Quinn was a trifle bitter about his failure to nab McCarthy: "After conferring [with McCarthy] for more than two hours," Quinn noted, "he impressed me with the fact that he preferred to pilot a ready-made ball club that required little or no handling than one that needed attention." The 1926 Cubs had hardly been ready-made, but Quinn's mood was obviously such that facts and logic were not important. The Red Sox would have to wait, and Quinn would soon sell the team to a young South Carolinian named Tom Yawkey. For McCarthy, there was no question where the better opportunity lay. The Chicago firing was, as McCarthy recalled, "a bitter blow, but I landed on my feet." When the option was there to become the manager of the New York Yankees, he took it. As he had said to Warren Brown only a month before: "Who wouldn't?"[22]

21

"Don't Like to Finish Second"

"McCardy," intoned Jake Ruppert, "I finished third last year. I realize that you are confronted with problems that will take you a little time to solve, so I'll be satisfied if you finish second this year. But I warn you, McCardy, I don't like to finish second." Unhesitatingly, McCarthy responded, "Neither do I, Colonel." Ruppert was being as flexible and magnanimous here as anyone ever knew him to be. He was a man who always wanted to win, be it in business, card games, or baseball. His club president, Ed Barrow, was equally uncompromising. This management combination could intimidate many a field manager. McCarthy felt right at home with it, however, and knowing the quality of the men above him in the Yankee organization, he had every confidence in his prospects.[1]

As the team began to assemble in February of 1931, the differences between managing the Yankees and the Cubs became increasingly clear to McCarthy. Most of the Cubs would assemble in Chicago and travel together out to California, where everyone would board Mr. Wrigley's yacht to Catalina Island. The sense of the players all being part of a parent organization was thus conveyed immediately. The Yankees trained in St. Petersburg, Florida, and they arrived via their own means, usually one or two at a time. There was much more an in-the-course-of-other-events milieu surrounding the opening. Out on Catalina Island, aside from a few reporters, the team was completely on its own. With no diversions, training could be the only focus. In St. Petersburg, there were all the usual diversions of a tourist town, and baseball fans were there in droves every day, wanting to watch the players and ask for their autographs. This could all make the establishment of a new managerial aura more difficult. Still, McCarthy was upbeat. "When I left the Cubs," he enthused, "I tumbled into the best baseball job I ever had. ... I thought it was pretty nice at Catalina Island, where the Cubs used to train. But Catalina certainly has nothing on this place." Fans flocked to St. Petersburg, and among the players the fans came to watch and hound for autographs, one player utterly dominated the crush and cast a shadow over the issue of the Yankees having a new manager — Babe Ruth.[2]

By the first week of March, all the Yankees had reported, including Ruth. The only holdouts were catcher Bill Dickey and infielder Tony Lazzeri. Reporters asked McCarthy about the two, and McCarthy casually replied: "It'd be kind of a joke to open the season without 'em, wouldn't it?" Reporters immediately jumped on this statement, filing reports to the effect that McCarthy says that Dickey and Lazzeri were unexpendable to the team and worth their salary demands. Ed Barrow was upset, and McCarthy learned a valuable lesson. Thereafter he held the New York press at greater length and would come to have but a few friends among its ranks.[3] The New York team McCarthy inherited presented him with a marked difference from the post-1925 Cubs. The Yankees were hardly a tail-ender. They had not won the pennant since 1928, but, undeniably, they were contenders with established stars. In Chicago, the only real star McCarthy had inherited was the aging Grover Cleveland Alexander, and he soon got rid of him. Charlie Grimm and Gabby Hartnett were just beginning to achieve prominence, and McCarthy himself had brought up Riggs Stephenson and Hack Wilson. With the Yankees, McCarthy had, among others, Dickey, Lazzeri, Joe Sewell, Earle Combs, Herb Pennock, Red Ruffing, George Pipgras, and, of course, Lou Gehrig and Babe Ruth. Contending with established egos at such a grand scale was a new challenge for McCarthy. In Chicago, McCarthy had only had one such problem in the person of Rogers Hornsby, and the results were not all to his liking. Matters like salary holdouts among prominent players were relatively new to him. In regard to his new manager making flippant comments on such matters, Barrow would learn that McCarthy was never one to make the same mistake twice. In regard to field matters, Barrow would stay out of McCarthy's way. He was present at McCarthy's first spring training. Thereafter, he made a point of spending the month of March in ninety miles away in Sebring, Florida, the training site of the Yankees' Newark, New Jersey farm club.[4]

When asked what his general formula would be for the Yankees that spring, McCarthy quipped: "All work and no play"; that was it. McCarthy knew that the Yankee offense would take care of itself. He was frank about where he felt the problems lay. "Last year," he wrote, "the Yankees made enough hits to win a pennant in any league, and scored more runs than any other team in the majors. ... In team pitching last season," he noted, "the Yankees were seventh, ... and no better than sixth in club fielding." Pitching and defense would then occupy his primary focus.

Quickly he began his usual drilling and drilling, at a level the Yankees had never seen. The infielders worked endlessly on double plays, and the pitchers practiced their fielding, taking hundreds of grounders and repeatedly throwing to each of the bases. McCarthy would often have the shortstop and second baseman trade positions, so they could more fully grasp what the other had to do in a double play and gain a more precise sense of where it was best to toss the ball. He would have outfielders practice at shortstop and second base to accustom themselves fully to the fielding of fast moving grounders. Meanwhile, the pitchers all ran in the outfield, chasing flies during batting practice. Watching the way McCarthy went to work, one reporter noted confidently, "The man seems to have all his baseball buttons about him." Recognizing that he is "something of a disciplinarian," the scribe added, "but one that is tactful, just, and gives his orders in an ingratiating way."

McCarthy hated mental errors, but any such mental miscues prompted one-on-one discussions. McCarthy never criticized a player in front of others. Stars or newcomers, the Yankee players quickly learned that McCarthy was all business. "A ballplayer," he declared, "has only two hours of concentrated work every day, and if he cannot attend to business with the pay high and working conditions so pleasant, something is wrong with him, and he ought to go somewhere else." The *Daily News* put it simply: "McCarthy'll do."[5]

McCarthy's all-business impact had reporters turning to their history books, recalling the famous story of Napoleon encountering a proud officer after a successful day in the field: "Fine; what do you propose to do tomorrow." McCarthy imposed that sort of "never satisfied" attitude upon the Yankees. In an exhibition game against the Boston Braves, the Yankees won 17–9. One young infielder, Lyn Lary, asked McCarthy, "Well, Boss, how did you like that?" McCarthy replied: "All right, but we should have scored more runs." A gasp fell over the players gathered around at that moment, and, noted one reporter: "Those nearest looked to see if he was in earnest and decided he was." Miller Huggins had never really worried about wins and losses in the exhibition games, but the players quickly learned that McCarthy was one "who wants to win all the time."

McCarthy simply wanted 100 percent effort at every moment, and to him that was a habit that had to be maintained without any letup. Lou Gehrig said to Bill Dickey here: "You know, Bill, I think this man's going to be all right. I like him. I like his attitude." Dickey agreed: "So do I. He's our kind of guy." Entering the clubhouse in early March, McCarthy heard a group of players discussing matters of golf and bridge. McCarthy turned to all of them: "You know how to make all the shots in golf, and you can take a bridge game apart. But you're making your living as ball players, and it might not be a bad idea for you to give as much time to studying baseball as you have to golf and bridge."

Later that spring, the Yankees trounced a minor league team in Nashville, scoring 23 runs. Again a player, infielder Jimmie Reese, was foolish enough to ask McCarthy what he thought of the team's performance. McCarthy shot right back: "You should've made 50 runs against that kind of pitching." Anyone can adopt that sort of "never satisfied" pose. Such a person can easily come across as a pompous martinet and actually generate less productivity as a result. The key question in understanding success-

McCarthy in his first year with the Yankees, 1931. As he had in Chicago and Louisville, McCarthy managed and coached third base. After 1931, he was exclusively a bench manager. He brought the Yankees back from the slight fall they experienced in 1929–30. They were strong in 1931 and won the World Series in 1932. (National Baseball Hall of Fame Library, Cooperstown, N.Y.)

ful management concerns how someone like McCarthy made his attitude work. One key was that the attitude was not a mere pose. He truly meant it, and he imposed the same demands upon himself. Further, the Yankees quickly learned what a Chicago reporter had written soon after McCarthy had come to the Cubs: "Because McCarthy is reserved, some say he takes himself too seriously.... But when you get to understand him you can see that he considers baseball and not himself seriously." This was a crucial matter, and the players quickly grasped it. There was little or no ego in McCarthy asserting his ways. Never, for example, in virtually all his years with the Yankees, nor earlier, did players address McCarthy by any name but "Joe." This may strike some as terribly odd, but there was no contradiction here. McCarthy needed few personal protocols to impose the legitimacy of his leadership. He knew the game at a level few others did, and his ways would carry their own inherent force.

"He isn't the nagging type of manager who tears at his players' nerves with a rasping voice," wrote Frank Graham of the *New York Sun*, "but it is almost impossible to satisfy him. That is why in every managerial job he has ever held he has been a builder of winning teams. ... He demands the most that any given situation possibly can yield. He makes no excuses and accepts none from anyone else. Surface appearances do not satisfy him. He wants to know what's underneath or behind everything that goes on."

From the start, Yankee players grasped this, and McCarthy never changed. Eighteen years later, in his last years managing Boston, McCarthy impressed the Red Sox exactly the same way. (Catcher Birdie Tebbetts asked: "How many managers do you know who ever cut anything so fine?") McCarthy also paid incessant and meticulous attention to detail, showing "that infinite capacity for taking pains that is said to be the mark of genius and his ability to impart his own enthusiasm to his ballplayers."[6] Back in New York, folks were reading such stories out of Florida and beginning to anticipate a return to the great days of the past. If the nation's economy could not bounce back, maybe at least the Yankees could.

While McCarthy did not "nag" and generally led in a quiet, firm way, he could be gruff when he had to be. One player was not getting himself in good shape. McCarthy sat him down and went straight to the point (not knowing a reporter was in earshot): "You're not kidding me and I'm not going to kid you, so listen attentively and believe what you hear. You are going to get one more chance. If you don't behave yourself in the future I won't simply fine you $100 and let it go at that, nor will I release you. I'll put you on the bench, and every day you sit there will cost you a day's pay. Now you may go, for that is all I have to say." The young man hunkered down from that point on and quickly got himself into playing trim. On another occasion, McCarthy chewed out a player who was late for practice. Normally, McCarthy confronted a behavior situation one on one. On this occasion, veteran Tony Lazzeri overheard it while going back to the bench to get a bat. Lazzeri looked at McCarthy and after the delinquent player was gone said to his manager: "That was a fine thing to do." McCarthy reacted instantly:

> I'm glad you were here, Tony. I'm glad you heard what I had to say to him. Now I want you to understand why I said it. I know the boy doesn't like me. I'm not interested in whether he does or not. But I am interested in him as a ball player. He could be one of the best in the league, but he isn't because of his attitude. He thinks he is

getting away with something around here just to spite me. But he hasn't. I took this opportunity to tell him so because I hope that, by scaring him — as I thought I did — I can wake him up. I didn't like to do it that way. But I made up my mind it was the only way. I wasn't in here by accident when he came in an hour late. I was waiting for him. Do you understand now what it was all about?

McCarthy's leadership with a key veteran player was at stake at that moment. In effect he was potentially putting his success at Lazzeri's disposition. Lazzeri responded: "I do, Joe. I've known all along how he felt about you, and how some of the others feel. I didn't know just how I felt about you myself. But I do now. I want you to know that from now on, I'm on your side." This was a critical hurdle for McCarthy. There were factions on the Yankees, the key one with which McCarthy had to contend involved those who felt Babe Ruth deserved a chance to manage. Lazzeri was no longer with Ruth, and his prestige on the club was critical. McCarthy's exchange with Lazzeri was not publicized in the papers. It only came out later. The fans knew only how tough McCarthy could be when he felt it necessary, and how he seemed to be instilling a new hustling spirit in the team. With Lazzeri, he had achieved something much more vital and elemental that ball players do not share with the fans and the press. Lazzeri and others began genuinely to trust McCarthy's leadership.[7]

Babe Ruth would remain a problem, however. Ruth wanted eventually to be the manager, and he clearly resented McCarthy and his martinet ways. Ruth still had a few good playing years left, so the conflict did not come to its full intensity, but Ruth would never like McCarthy. Meanwhile, Babe continued to play well. Indeed, about the only time anyone saw an actual smile come to McCarthy's face in St. Petersburg that spring was when Babe Ruth took batting practice, although Lou Gehrig's hitting certainly pleased him too. McCarthy always tried to be diplomatic when speaking of Ruth before the press. He noted, for example, that when he first managed with the Cubs in 1926 people were saying that Ruth was through. But "look what has happened," McCarthy exclaimed, "He has played his finest ball in the last several years, breaking among other things his own home run record [59 in 1921] — something everyone agreed would never be done."

Reporters noted that Ruth was slowing, but McCarthy would not even hint at the fact that he may have agreed with them. Ruth did arrive at camp on time and in pretty good shape — 227 pounds, three pounds under his weight of 1930. He was 36, but he still saw himself as a player with a few good seasons before him. His ambitions to manage the Yankees were not yet foremost in his mind. He lightly kidded McCarthy about never having played in the big leagues, bringing up the fact that he had faced him as a pitcher way back in 1914 when the Baltimore Orioles opened against the Buffalo Bisons. To Ruth, McCarthy was yet another Yankee manager, the fourth since September, 1929. He made a few wise cracks about why the Yankees had to go over to the National League for a manager. In the back of his mind, Ruth maintained the simple belief that when his playing days were over he would manage the Yankees. Always more than a trifle childlike, Ruth entertained no doubts about this. For the moment, McCarthy was the manager. And in spring training under McCarthy, approvingly noted a reporter, "Babe has had to keep pace with the rest of the squad."

McCarthy appreciated Ruth's talent, obviously, and he knew very quickly that he could always count on Ruth's desire to help the team win. Even when tensions later arose between the two, McCarthy never lost sight of that essential point: Ruth could always be counted on to do his best on the field. Meanwhile, McCarthy shrewdly met Ruth's expressions of antagonism without any direct comment. He would never deviate from this strategy. If Ruth did not want to eat meals with the team, or if he wanted to travel with an entourage, McCarthy stirred not one bit. On this matter, he cared only how Ruth played. McCarthy showed a hint of "edge" that spring when a reporter asked him to talk about the greatest all-around player in the game. McCarthy said that Honus Wagner was the greatest player ever (Ed Barrow agreed), and that among active players Frankie Frisch was the best. Some took this as a swipe against Ruth. McCarthy would not comment on that. There was some fallout from McCarthy's statement. Later that summer the *Philadelphia Public Ledger* polled twelve prominent baseball people, asking who was the greatest of all ballplayers. Among the polled were John McGraw, Connie Mack, Walter Johnson, and McCarthy. Ty Cobb received seven votes. Honus Wagner garnered three, and Babe Ruth got two, one of which was McCarthy's; the vote was a shrewd tactic.[8]

A significant issue facing the Yankees that spring concerned the lineup. Bob Shawkey had shifted some personnel around, especially in the infield, so matters of Huggins' vs. Shawkey's setups left confused expectations at the time of McCarthy's arrival. There were some rookies in the mix too. McCarthy cast a blank slate. "Everyone on the squad has a chance to make the team, and I want them all to realize it." During practices and in exhibition games, he tried many combinations, noting "when the pennant race is going on, experiments are sometimes costly." There were certain fixtures. Ruth would play right field. Gehrig would play first base. Dickey would catch. (And Dickey and Gehrig would be roommates, while Ruth would have a room to himself.) Shawkey had switched Tony Lazzeri to third base, claiming he was a bit slow on double-play work. McCarthy observed Lazzeri, worked with him, and thought about putting him back at second base. Joe Sewell could go to third base. Lyn Lary looked like he would win the job at shortstop. McCarthy also had a young infielder of great promise named Ben Chapman. He knew he had to put him somewhere in the starting lineup.

In the outfield, aside from Ruth, there were several questions. Shawkey's left fielder had been Earle Combs. He had moved him over there from center. Earle Combs, of course, knew McCarthy from Louisville. "Well, Earle, at last I've caught up with you," said McCarthy when he first saw Combs in St. Petersburg. "Yes, and I'm darned glad of it," Combs replied. Shawkey had switched Combs to left field and moved him back a few notches in the lineup. Combs never outwardly complained, but he did not like it. He was supremely confident with McCarthy at the helm. He believed his old boss would make all the right moves. Combs's confidence had a positive effect on some other Yankees. McCarthy quickly put Combs back in center field and pushed him up to the leadoff spot. Asked why he put him there, McCarthy glared at the reporter and asked pointedly: "Do you know of a better one?"

As for pitchers, McCarthy had his veterans, George Pipgras, Red Ruffing, and Herb Pennock. Shawkey had tried out a young left-hander named Vernon Gomez in 1930, but Gomez seemed a bit quixotic, and Shawkey sent him back down to St. Paul. McCarthy kept him. Gomez's first start that year was poor, but McCarthy had faith in his own judge of talent. Gomez would win 87 games over the next four seasons.

That season, McCarthy had Gomez room with a 35-year-old veteran named Cy Perkins, with the idea that the veteran could be a steadying influence on the rookie. After a very tough win in Cleveland, McCarthy told Perkins "You're doing a good job with the boy." Perkins confessed, "Joe, I ain't doing a thing. All he does is sit at the phone and talks by the hour to some doll named June, eat a tomato sandwich, and go out and throw the ball." McCarthy nodded and replied: "Maybe we're under-estimating the power of tomatoes. Don't change his diet, and let's hope he keeps the same girlfriend."[9] Gomez later married June O'Dea.

In April, as the Yankees returned to New York to start the season, expectations were high. The lineup questions were still to be resolved, and everyone knew that Connie Mack's two-time defending champion Philadelphia A's were still completely intact and would be difficult if not impossible to beat. Still, the sense of how McCarthy had reformed the squad gave a certain hope. "The Yankees may not win the pennant this year," wrote one sports writer, "but Manager Joe McCarthy at least will keep them on their toes, hustling forever." In 1930 it appeared to most reporters and fans that by June, as the Athletics ran out in front of the league, the Yankees shrugged at the situation and more or less went through the rest of the season on idle. Reporters wrote angrily of this, and to depression era-fans, the idea of ball players getting pay-checks while merely going through the motions was not pleasing and did not moti-vate many to go to the Stadium. Ruppert and Barrow recognized this and were infuriated. This was a major reason they wanted to get rid of Shawkey. They believed McCarthy to be the sort of manager never to let this occur.

The intense spring training gave every indication of this. Another writer also sensed that the "inferiority complex of last year has given way to new found ambi-tions." There seemed a startling change in spirit. A year before, various Yankees had dodged discussions of their chances. In 1931 they were courting interviews on the subject. "McCarthy has roused lagging ambitions and has fired the imaginations of even those who have had their share of pennants and World Series and the roar of the crowd. And all this," he wrote, "is not pep talk, m'lads. ... McCarthy can revive lagging stars. ... [Take his] ability to handle men, enforce discipline, and compel respect for his baseball knowledge an you have a worthy successor to Miller Hug-gins." The Yankees had just commemorated their St. Petersburg stadium as "Miller Huggins Field." To be named Huggins' "worthy successor" in such an atmosphere was quite significant. Bob Shawkey could not escape Huggins' shadow. It is indeed better to be the one who succeeds the one who succeeds the legend.[10]

A feeling that the new manager had put things back on track—that was all for which Col. Ruppert, President Barrow, and all New York baseball people could ask as the season began. As for the players' feelings, one reporter noted: "Those Yan-kees have always been the most clannish gang in the majors, but Manager Joe has made the grade with them." When the team traveled, McCarthy required all players wear coats and ties. When Red Ruffing got in trouble for wearing a polo shirt, the rest of the team knew McCarthy was serious. Players had to carry their own bags, or tip a porter out of their own pockets. As McCarthy had always done in the minors, the players were also responsible to carry the bats, secured in a suit roll. "Nobody was too good to share the bats," McCarthy recalled. Breakfast was at 8:30, although McCarthy begrudgingly gave Babe Ruth some leeway here. In the clubhouse there was to be no radio playing, smoking, shaving, or card playing. If a player needed to shave, he was to do so before coming to the ballpark. Players could smoke, but not in the clubhouse. McCarthy forbade pipe smoking altogether. Players could also drink, but any public display of drunkenness could bring an immediate fine. McCarthy advised against any excess of beer, believing beer can "go to the legs." As for the card playing, the old clubhouse table was removed. There were rumors that McCarthy had ordered his clubhouse manager, Fred Logan, to chop the table to pieces with an axe. "Do your card playing in your homes. When you come here, I want you to have your minds on baseball." The story of the axe may have been apocryphal, but the popularity of the rumor reflected the new, out-with-the-bad, in-with-the-good outlook that McCarthy was instilling. There was no more country clubhouse atmosphere. Players' minds were to be completely on baseball.[11]

With all the infield and outfield assignments not completely set, but with greater optimism than they had held in several years, the Yankees began the 1931 season. After ten games, their record stood at 7-3. This included winning two of three from Philadelphia. All three losses were by one run; two were extra-inning games. "McCarthy has the machine functioning in high," wrote one reporter. They "show more fire and dash. ... Before, they never ran unless there was a fire; now ... you should see them sprint at the drop of a ball." "See them" is exactly what people did. Nearly 70,000 came to opening day; over 200,000 attended the first five games. All signs were good, but several injuries quickly struck, and all within two weeks. Pitcher George Pipgras went out with a bad arm. Red Ruffing came down with the flu, a more serious matter in his case as he had gone through a bout of pneumonia that winter. Lefty Gomez was sick for a few weeks— after he had eaten a mothball someone had hid in a bowl of after-dinner mints at a hotel. Bill Dickey had a pulled leg muscle. Outfielder Sam Byrd strained his back in a near-collision with shortstop Lyn Lary. Another outfielder, Myril Hoag, had a strained right shoulder.

Outfielder Dusty Cooke suffered a terrible injury, displacing his clavicle while diving for a fly ball in a game with the Washington Senators. (The doctor who treated Cooke at St. Vincent's Hospital in Washington, Edward "Bunny" Larkin, was a former ball player. He had managed the DuBois, Pa., team in the Inter-State League in 1907 when McCarthy played for Franklin. McCarthy remembered him. He told him he would like to leave Cooke in his capable hands but felt it best to take him back to New York. Cooke was out for much of the season.) Most conspicuously, Babe Ruth went down in a game in Boston. He had turned an ankle while rounding third and was then knocked down by Boston's catcher, Charlie Berry, while trying to score. He stayed in the game, but in the bottom of the same inning he collapsed in the outfield while chasing a fly ball. He had to be carried off the field. There was no bone fracture, but he had badly strained the ligaments in his right knee. McCarthy shook his head and ruefully mused that with all the injuries his players were photographed more for x-rays than for news pictures.[12]

The sense of how April's hopes seemed to be unraveling came forth during the game in Washington in which Cooke displaced his collarbone. Late in the game, with two out Yankee shortstop Lyn Lary had walked. Lou Gehrig then hit a home run into the center-field bleachers. The ball hit the seats and caromed back to the field where Senators' outfielder Harry Rice caught it. Lary, rounding second, looked to the outfield just at moment Rice caught the ball. Gehrig's shot was a home run, but as he saw Rice catch it, Lary thought it was the third out. So when he crossed third he headed for the dugout. Gehrig rounded third and was, under the rules, called out for passing the runner ahead of him, getting credit for but a triple. The Yankees lost the game, and Gehrig lost a home run and two RBI's from his season totals. McCarthy was frustrated about the injuries, and he was upset with Lary, as well as with himself (he was coaching third).[13] Under most circumstances, McCarthy would have sat Lary down for such a mental lapse, but with all the injuries he had no choice but to leave him in.

McCarthy had to make other personnel shifts. One of them proved fortuitous. Infielder Ben Chapman was extremely valuable in the lineup. He hit .315 that season, and he led the league in stolen bases with 61, an incredibly high total in an era when such a style of play had gone out of fashion. Here McCarthy showed some of his remarkable savvy. When Chapman was on base McCarthy did two things. One was to give Chapman the green light to steal whenever he felt he could. The other, when he explicitly called for a steal, was to have the batter move back in the box a few inches. This usually made the catcher shift back just a bit. As most successful steals occur by fractions of a second, McCarthy's little adjustment at the plate made the difference in many of Chapman's steals. When some opposing managers saw what McCarthy was doing, they adjusted by having their pitcher throw a fastball. McCarthy anticipated this, of course, and told his batters to be ready for it. In the 1950s, Baltimore Manager Paul Richards credited McCarthy's innovativeness here.[14]

While a terror on the basepaths, Chapman did not play well in the infield. He had a scatter arm, a problem some infielders incur, one that often starts with slight errors in throwing mechanics and quickly becomes as much a mental block as anything else, resulting in wide and high throws from medium to short distances. Another single incident with Chapman appeared to stick with McCarthy, and eleven years later he claimed to recall it vividly. In a game at Boston, with the score tied in the ninth, the Red Sox had runners on first and third with one out. McCarthy narrated:

> Either of two plays would help us, one at the plate cutting off the winning run or a double play via second base which would retire the side. I pulled the infield in a little to set up either play. The ball came to Chapman [at second base]. He could have worked either play, but I could see right away he would gum it up. He did. He tried to tag Muddy Ruel, the runner coming from first. Muddy stopped running and dodged. Ben could still have made the double play by forcing Ruel at second and then getting the ball back to first. Instead he threw to first base. ... Ruel was trapped between first and second but meanwhile the winning run had crossed. The game was over, and Chapman was still out there trying to tag Ruel. There wasn't much I could say when I got Chappy in the dressing room. I called him over and just told him: "Okay Ben, from now on you're an outfielder."[15]

The newspaper coverage of the Yankees' 1931 games relays no such incident. However this exact ninth inning situation and miscue did occur in a loss to Detroit on August 17, 1935, but it was second baseman Jack Saltzgaver who made the mental error, not Chapman.[16] McCarthy confused the specifics of the incident in his memory. In any case, he wanted to get Chapman out of the infield and projected his desires into his recollections.

With Chapman's speed, and with so many injuries to his outfielders, McCarthy switched Chapman to the outfield. The move worked out very well. Tony Lazzeri and Jimmie Reese would share second base duties, and Joe Sewell, and occasionally Lazzeri, played third base. This set the lineup for McCarthy amidst the injuries. As players came back, he did not alter matters terribly much. Babe Ruth was back in two weeks. He could hit, but he could hardly run. In one game against the Senators, Ruth hit a ball 450 feet to the deepest part of left center field in Yankee Stadium. All he could get out of it was a double. McCarthy first used Ruth at first base, switching Lou Gehrig to the outfield. Then Gehrig suffered an injury to his right thumb and strained his right calf muscle. He did not come out of the lineup, of course, but he did go back to first base. Ruth returned to right field, where for the next several months, he would often play five or six innings, with McCarthy inserting Myril Hoag or Sam Byrd for the rest of the game. At most games, when Ruth went out about a third of the people headed for the exits.[17]

Throughout the rash of injuries and mishaps, McCarthy not only kept his composure, he kept the Yankees winning. On May 4th he was initiated into the "Rites of the Tough Club" on West 14th Street. On May 7th, the team headed out to Chicago for their first Western trip. With all the injuries, the *Daily News* referred to the troupe as the "Hospital Train." McCarthy made sure team trainer Dr. E. V. Painter was well stocked with supplies. When the Yankees arrived in Chicago, various clubs and organizations had arranged to commemorate his return. Wrigley and the Cubs may have held some ill feelings, but many other Chicagoans felt very much the opposite way. Indeed, for many White Sox fans to give laurels to McCarthy at this point was a way of "sticking it" to their detested North Side rivals anyway. Before the first Yankees—White Sox game at Comiskey Park, McCarthy received many presents. He was given a gold membership card to the Midland Club, and he was presented with "enough flowers to send a Chicago gangster into the great beyond in magnificent style." Before the game, McCarthy was informed not only of the ceremonies in store for him but of the fact that a French boxing team was attending that day. Knowing the boxers might be unfamiliar with baseball, McCarthy, the old corner man that he was, went out to the box where the Frenchmen were seated and explained the game to them — in perfectly good French, much to the surprise of players and reporters. Then the Yankees proceeded to beat the White Sox 13–9, a victory which put them in first place by a half game over Philadelphia.[18]

After playing Chicago, the Yankees moved on to St. Louis. There several days of rain left the team idle. Will all their injuries, they needed the rest, but that week the Athletics won several games and took over first place. The feeling of helplessness was discouraging, and the team could do little but sit about the hotel lobby. As it happened, the hotel was the site of a funeral that very week, and the lobby was filled with various appurtenances for the solemn occasion. McCarthy sensed the depression into which the team was falling, and he decided to do something about it. He gathered the team about him on the morning of May 13 and gave them his orders:

I want you fellows to make a beeline out into Forest Park. You've been hanging around this hotel looking at caskets and shrouds till you've all got the jimjams. You're quaking in your boots and don't try to tell me you ain't. You should have sense enough to light out without being told and get your mind off these sights. You act like you were going to a funeral. The Browns will bury you unless you snap out of it pronto. I have the antidote for your case of nerves. What you need is a few giggles to liven you up. So I'm sending you over to the Forest Park Zoo. … All ballplayers like animals, or they should. Go over and spend a few profitable hours limbering your arms throwing peanuts to the monkeys. Spare no expense. There will be an extra handout of meal money to cover the situation. See that the monkeys are well rationed. Buy yourselves toy balloons if that will help bring you up. Have a jolly May day out in the sunshine. And then go to the ball park without returning to the hotel. I don't want you to look at those caskets again until after the game.

The trip was a success. McCarthy tipped off the zookeeper that the boys were coming. (The zookeeper was Cub Charlie Grimm's father.) Lou Gehrig filched a couple of eels and had them broiled by one of the Sportsman's Park hot dog vendors. They were not as good as his favorite pickled eels that his mother regularly prepared for him, but they proved a more than satisfactory lunch nonetheless. Lefty Gomez developed a new half hitch in his windup from observing the ways the monkeys wiggled their tails. The Yankees beat the Browns that afternoon, with Lefty Gomez winning in relief, baffling the Browns with his new windup. They won the next day too, 14–2. Then they headed off to Detroit and won five straight. McCarthy had once again demonstrated his genius in his handling of men. The winning went on in Cleveland and Washington, with McCarthy's "touch" continuing to be in evidence. Against Cleveland, he felt Ruth was ready to be left in for a full game, and he responded with a double, triple, and home run. In a 7-6 win over Washington, McCarthy signaled a double steal and a squeeze bunt. Both worked, and he successfully called for a steal of home by Ben Chapman. This was all, said one paper, "astonishing to New Yorkers not used to brainy baseball."[19]

As the road trip was closing, the Yankees' record stood at 19 and 10. They had been winning, but so had Philadelphia. The A's had taken over first place during the Yankees' rainouts in St. Louis, and they had not relinquished it. The A's record stood at 21 and 7. After the exciting victory in Washington, the Yankees next stop was Philadelphia, a "'Croocial' Series," headlined the *New York Sun*, one that "will go a long way toward deciding the American League Pennant." It was a little odd for baseball pundits to be writing about pennant deciders in May, but it showed how much excitement McCarthy's new Yankees had generated. The players had certainly been won over. Veteran pitcher Philip "Lefty" Weinert put it simply: "If you can't play ball for Joe McCarthy, you can't play ball for anybody; he's my ideal of a baseball manager."[20] The Yankees had indeed been a clannish crew. But McCarthy the strategist, the tactician, the logistician, the personnel director, the spotter and honer of talent, the psychologist and zoo-keeper had been most impressive.

There was only one question left: could the Yanks haul down the A's? In 1931, the answer was simple: No. In late May, the A's won five of six games with the Yankees. Whatever McCarthy could put forth that season, often in spite of all the injuries, the A's could match it. Earle Combs had hit in 34 of the Yankees' first 36 games, including 27 games in a row. Meanwhile, the A's Al Simmons put up a 26-game streak of his own. Gehrig and Ruth would put up home run and RBI numbers, so would Simmons and Jimmie Foxx, although Ruth's and Gehrig's would be a little better. Lefty Gomez would win 21 that season; Lefty Grove would win 31. Bill Dickey hit .327 and caught brilliantly; Mickey Cochrane was equally strong behind the plate and hit .349. Connie Mack had simply put together one of the best teams in the history of the game, and when they inexorably pulled ahead of the league in May, no one was surprised. With the A's expected show of muscle, the question was whether the Yankees would again fold their tent as they had previously.[21]

Other than Dusty Cooke's clavicle, most of the Yankees' injuries had healed by June, so there were no excuses. Ruth still stepped out of the late innings of many games, but Gehrig was healthy. Gomez felt better and was eating normally. Dickey was fine. Ruffing was stronger. The only Yankees down in June were Col. Ruppert and Ed Barrow. (Barrow was actually quite ill and had to be hospitalized for a time.) McCarthy knew winning was the one thing he could do to make his two bosses feel better, but, as sometimes occurs in baseball, while the Yankees had run up a good record despite the injuries in May, they fell off in June despite being healthy. Their record for the month was a mere 15 and 14. That was hardly going to keep pace with the A's, much less cut away at their lead. At the end of the month the A's were eleven games ahead, and the Washington Senators were in second place to boot. Ruth and Gehrig were hitting well. Ben Chapman was stealing bases like crazy, but aside from Lefty Gomez, the pitching was proving especially undependable.

McCarthy made some moves. Lefty Weinert may have liked playing for McCarthy, but the feeling was not mutual. McCarthy shipped him off to Louisville. He brought up a new infielder, a Dartmouth College graduate named Robert "Red" Rolfe. He also made some efforts to trade Tony Lazzeri, whose batting average had fallen to .200. Word leaked of the efforts to make a deal for Lazzeri. Mrs. McCarthy said the Lazzeri rumors prompted her to get 26 phone calls about the story in one evening at their upper 5th Avenue residence. (She nearly burned a tray of muffins as a result.) Although Mrs. McCarthy divulged nothing, there was something to the rumors. McCarthy met with the Washington Senators' owner/president Clark Griffith in Wilmington, Delaware, hoping to pick up some pitching strength in exchange for his star infielder. McCarthy rejected the deal, however. He sensed that Griffith was a bit too eager to grab Lazzeri and decided it best to keep him. Jimmie Reese, his other second baseman, soon came down with back spasms, and Lazzeri, more secure in his position, began to play with more of his old consistency. No other team proposed any deals for McCarthy. The only inquiries McCarthy received were about the availability of Lefty Gomez. McCarthy had a simple reply to all seven American League clubs that wanted his young pitching ace.[22]

June was an unhappy month. The winning was inconsistent. With no strong right-handed pitching, opponents stacked their line ups with right handers. Fortunes further turned against New York when they made a Western swing in late June, just at the point of a heat wave in the Midwest. Many of the games that month were played in 100-degree heat. Back in May, McCarthy had sent a down club to the zoo to perk up, he took a very different tone with his team amidst their June doldrums. On June 21st, the team lost a doubleheader to the St. Louis Browns, and they lost the next day too, by a score of 14–11. The losses left them thirteen games behind Philadelphia and ten behind Washington. The *New York Daily News* was using such terms as "shameful ... disgusting ... awkward ... inexplicable.... Suffering Mackerel! ... [and] HELP!" McCarthy met the team the next morning and upbraided them unceremoniously:

> Why you blankety-blank so-and-so's. So the A's and the Senators have you licked just because they've grabbed a good lead? You're licked, and you act like you like it. You ought to be ashamed of yourselves, folding up this way before the Browns. ... I can't stand looking at your antics any longer. I'm leaving tonight. I'm going over to the American Association territory where they have some teams that fight for ball games. ... The White Sox [the next opponent] will know there's a Santa Claus after all when you limp into Comiskey Park.

McCarthy was in earnest about looking over some talent. He went to Columbus and watched one strong prospect, infielder Jack Saltzgaver of the St. Paul Saints. He would later sign him. McCarthy never tipped his hand to the team as to how much or little of a personnel overhaul he had in mind. But given that he was in his first year, the team was not performing well, and with the A's appearing to be a team that would not weaken for years, a major shift of personnel did not seem too far-fetched an idea. The economic conditions of 1931 made the prospect of being released put quite a bit of fear into many players. They went off to Chicago and took five games in a row. If he could not salvage the pennant chances, McCarthy could certainly motivate his players' to salvage their jobs.[23]

The flat play in June was troubling to McCarthy, because so many of the games were against the weaker teams of the West. After the Chicago series he was going to have to face two weeks of games with the A's and the Senators. That was obviously going to be a tough stretch, so he had wanted to have a strong showing in June as a cushion. Now he had to win, and he did. The Yankees swept the Senators in Washington and took two of three from Philadelphia. Returning to Yankee Stadium, they again beat the Senators and found themselves only three games out of second place. Everyone knew that the A's were not going to be taken down. By July 18, Lefty Grove had already won 19. But New York baseball people wanted to see good baseball, and after June the *Sun* gladly declared the Yankees "much improved; McCarthy has them stepping."[24]

The problem was still the pitching. In one game against Cleveland, the Yankee pitchers yielded eleven walks, including four straight with two out in the fifth inning with the bases loaded. Bill Dickey was also hurt again. He had a split finger and incurred a bone chip on the ring finger of his right hand. He strained his neck in a taxicab accident in St. Louis and a few days later was hit in the neck by a late-swinging batsman. As with all great catchers, it took a lot to get Dickey out of the lineup, but McCarthy had to rest him, and the team's performance suffered. Some papers were pronouncing the '31 Yankees dead. McCarthy noted that such words were written by the same reporters who would subsequently criticize any mere "going through the motions" if they saw it. McCarthy was not going to tolerate any perfunctory performances, and he would tolerate no such eulogizing so early in the summer. The Yankees were leading the league in home runs and in stolen bases. They could score in great spurts, and McCarthy believed he should be able to find a way to make this offensive punch more consistent. In a five-game series with Chicago, for example, the Yankees scored 63 runs, yet they only won three of the games. One reporter joked about McCarthy's hopes here as joining the "Auto Club — there 'auto' be a way to parcel out runs more evenly and get more wins."

McCarthy had tried to motivate gently and through fear. He also tried simple logic. In a doubleheader against Philadelphia on July 9th, the Yankees had won the first game. Before the second game McCarthy called the team together and simply pointed out that on July 19, 1928, the A's were fourteen games behind the Yankees, and on September 9 they were a half game ahead. "In short," he said, "they had gained 14 games in 51 days. We have a better club than they had three years ago. What do you say?" Unfortunately, the A's won the next game in fourteen innings. Again it was the pitching that did not hold up. Reporters commended McCarthy for his optimism, but some could not stop themselves from lamenting — "Here lie the Yankee pennant hopes of 1931. They died of extra innings." Other scribes turned to sarcasm: If the Yankees and the A's "continue at their current gait, the Yankees will overhaul the A's by September — September, 1932." McCarthy would never concede defeat. It was his own Seventh Commandment. He could not control the newspapers. He did not want to try. But he would be furious at any sort of feelings, let alone statements, of concession from his players. In a sense, McCarthy was planning for 1932. He was training his players as to the only attitudes he would tolerate.[25]

No one was going to overhaul Philadelphia's drive for their third successive pennant. But McCarthy showed all New York fans that as long as he was leading the team, Yankee efforts were never going to lag. He had put his stamp on the team in his first year with them. With this, fan interest did not wane. Babe Ruth and Lou Gehrig battled for the league home run lead. They both wound up with 46. (Gehrig would have had 47 were it not for Lyn Lary's base running boner in April against Washington.) Ben Chapman's 61 stolen bases made him one of the most exciting players in the league. In September the Yankees played the Giants in an exhibition game, with all the profits to go for badly needed New York City unemployment relief. Over 60,000 came to the game, including such Broadway and musical stars as McCarthy's friend George M. Cohan, Fred Astaire, and Kate Smith, who, as one paper irreverently noted, "occupied two box seats, gnawing hot dogs and swigging down soda pop." In most in-season exhibition games, all managers, including McCarthy, used lesser pitchers so they would not waste their best throwers. In this game, McCarthy used Lefty Gomez for the whole game. There were some things more important than baseball, and McCarthy never lost touch with this. The Yankees won 7-3. The city's relief fund had a check for $59,642.50. Two weeks later McCarthy's Yankees took part in another baseball exhibition. This one took place at the Polo Grounds, and there were two games. The Giants beat Brooklyn; the Yankees beat Brooklyn; and the relief fund received a check for $52,125.[26]

The year 1931 was a terrible year for hundreds of thousands of New Yorkers. Even if any of the New York teams had won a pennant (St. Louis won in the National League and they beat the A's in the Series), the relief that such entertainment as major league baseball could bring to the sufferings of the Great Depression would have been merely illusory. In a certain respect, McCarthy's work with the Yankees was an example of what was best done in the name of recovery and reform. Relief was something with which he could and literally did help via the September exhibitions. Reforming the Yankees and helping them recover their winning traditions would take more time. In instilling a sense that there was a steadily optimistic attitude at the top and by steadily pushing such an attitude into the clubhouse, and excluding everything else, McCarthy restructured the sensibilities of a team, so that older vestiges of defeatist or lackadaisical thinking and habits would never again infect them.

In August, he picked up some new talent for the next season, signing infielder infielder Frankie Crosetti from San Francisco and Jack Saltzgaver and pitcher Johnny Murphy from St. Paul. The Yankees they would join in 1932 would be a decidedly different one than McCarthy first took signed on to manage back in October of 1930. That Yankee team had folded its tent in June. In 1931, the Philadelphia A's wrapped up the pennant on September 16, yet in those weeks when the A's were assured, the Yankees ran off a ten game win streak and took second place from the Senators. Second place was what Ruppert had told him would be satisfactory. There was more work to do, but when McCarthy arrived back at the Hotel Croyden residence on 5th Avenue he looked at his wife and said: "It's all right now, kid. Put an extra thick steak on the fire." "Pete," the family canary, loudly chirped in agreement.[27]

The Yankees, wrote Joe Williams of the *New York World-Telegram*, "did better than they figured to ... in large measure [due] to the new manager. ... Mr. McCarthy is inventive and daring ... blending speed with power in a way that made the games doubly interesting to watch." McCarthy's first year yielded him much the same results and respect as had in his first year with the Cubs. There was no question he had done a superlative job. But in New York there was one person who was not happy — Babe Ruth. McCarthy's free use of Ben Chapman and his stolen base tactics, prompted Ruth to scoff that such a style of baseball had gone out of fashion. Ruth was sarcastic about this one day when, with Gehrig at bat, Chapman was caught stealing and Gehrig then homered. Ruth snorted: "Somebody ought to tell that guy McCarthy base stealing went out of style when Ty Cobb quit." McCarthy offered no response. Base stealing was the very style of baseball that Ruth's unprecedented slugging had superseded. With Chapman in 1931, the tactic worked far more often than it failed. The broader team issue was that tensions were building between Ruth and McCarthy. Still, as long as Ruth could still play effectively the rivalry would remain on medium heat, and in 1931 Ruth played well, hitting 46 home runs and batting .373. The tension would have to be confronted in the future, and McCarthy was well aware of it. The question facing McCarthy in 1932 was whether he could take the team to the highest place, the place which Yankee fans had previously enjoyed and to which they wanted, and felt they deserved, to grow accustomed.[28]

22

The Fewest Rules,
the Most Discipline

The tough winter of 1931–32 gave few people much cause for optimism. No one knew worse times. A cadre of well-heeled Democrats could at least rejoice at the prospects of defeating the Republicans in the 1932 elections. Franklin Roosevelt was their emerging hero. In the baseball world, Joe McCarthy was having a similar impact in the world of sports, at least in New York. McCarthy had made quite a hit in the city's baseball circles. He seemed to bring together the right combination of knowledge, personality, and discipline that won the trust of both players and fans. The Yankees' prospects for 1932 seemed one of the few bright topics for New Yorkers during that hard winter of cardboard shacks in Central Park and massive hunger and unemployment.

With the financial hardships in which he grew up in Germantown, McCarthy certainly grasped the troubles that lay all about him. Mrs. McCarthy and he were in good shape financially. McCarthy never invested wildly. He saved his cash, and his only major purchases were in real estate. He also had no great ambitions to be in the public eye. Other than going to some of his beloved Broadway musicals, he was never one for the New York nightlife. He and Mrs. McCarthy were never apart. "The only time you don't see the two of them together," noted a reporter, "is when McCarthy is in the coaching box."

He never traveled much, other than where his baseball duties took him. When one reporter was visiting him at his upper 5th Avenue residence at the Hotel Croyden, he asked if they frequented the nearby Metropolitan Museum of Art. Mrs. McCarthy virtually swooned at the mention of the Museum. Joe responded: "I'll take you tomorrow. I understand it doesn't cost anything anyway." Sensibilities of later generations could eagerly cast Mrs. McCarthy as stifled, but there was no evidence of anything but a loving relationship in regard to the McCarthys' marriage. Mrs. McCarthy rarely gave interviews. Neither she nor Joe wanted their private life to be grist for reporters. She did write one short piece for the *New York Times* in 1933. There she stated how she felt that too many wives delegate details to others. She preferred to tend to household matters herself, especially the cooking. Joe's favorite was fried chicken with homemade noodles and chicken giblets. More than good cooking and

maintaining a "well-ordered household," Mrs. McCarthy contended the most important element in married life was "a real sense of humor." As for baseball, Mrs.
McCarthy said she attended few games. "I get so nervous. They get me all excited,
and if we don't win I feel even worse than does Joe about it." So Mrs. McCarthy generally stayed home. But one afternoon, shortly after the '31 season, she and Joe did
go to the Metropolitan Museum. Then they spent their usual winter at their Gates
Circle home in Buffalo.[1]

Throughout the winter, rumors continued to circulate of the impending trade
of Tony Lazzeri, possibly to the Senators for a pitcher named Fred Marberry. En route
to Florida in February, McCarthy did conspicuously stop in Washington, but no
trade occurred. There was also talk of the Yankees trading outfielder Sammy Byrd.
This also never came to fruition. McCarthy was never hasty in his trading. As with
money, he was a careful investor with talent, too. Pennant talk surrounded the Yankees throughout spring training. Virtually everyone was back; there were no major
contract disputes. Babe Ruth, having fallen a bit in his hitting, did take a cut from
$80,000 to $75,000. Feeling financial matters more satisfactorily under his control,
Ed Barrow nodded confidently to the press: "No one will ever make $80,000 again!"
(His words were about 60 years ahead of their time, although their meaning then
would be decidedly different.) Only pitcher Hank Johnson was out. He had come
down with acute appendicitis and was expected to be out until May or June. In 1931,
Johnson had given up the most walks on the staff anyway. Lou Gehrig had actually
been injured in the off-season. He and Babe Ruth went on a baseball tour of Japan
that winter, and Gehrig actually sat out several games while on tour there. But in
March he was back at the Yankees camp. One reporter predicted, in view of Gehrig's
winter injury: "He'll only play 154 games."[2]

McCarthy seemed to be suffering from an embarrassment of riches that spring.
He had an outfield "problem" in that he possessed Babe Ruth, Ben Chapman, Earle
Combs, Myril Hoag, Sam Byrd, and a new arrival, a former professional wrestler
from Canada named George Selkirk. Perhaps, with all that talent, McCarthy could
have thought about switching Chapman back to the infield, but there he had Gehrig,
Lazzeri, Lyn Lary, Joe Sewell, Ed Farrell, plus two younger talents who received a lot
of press attention, Jack Saltzgaver and Frankie Crosetti. That March, Crosetti proved
to be "the most talked about American Leaguer in the spring camps." He seemed the
best shortstop prospect anyone had seen in years, "the gem of the lot," as one writer
termed him. Yankee outfielder Tommy Henrich later said that McCarthy loved
Crosetti's competitiveness. It was, said Henrich, "the only kind of attitude McCarthy
wanted." Back in 1926 the arrival of shortstop Mark Koenig along with Tony Lazzeri
had excited the team and the city, and with them the Yankees returned to greatness,
winning three straight pennants. People had much the same in mind with the flutter
over Saltzgaver and Crosetti.[3]

McCarthy handled the 1932 talent situation as he had before; aside from Dickey
at catcher, Gehrig at first, and Ruth in right, the field was open. Whoever played
the best ball that spring would get the job. This turned out to pose McCarthy another
problem, because in early 1932 virtually everybody played good ball. The Yankees
beat almost all their opponents in Florida, and in March and April they won a
series of routs in a tour throughout the South. Lazzeri, Hoag, Selkirk, Combs,

Crosetti, Ruth, and Byrd all hit over .300. Byrd, who batted only .270 in 1931, actually hit .593 and *had* to be put in as a starter, noted one writer: "It would take an injunction to keep Sammy Byrd out of the lineup." On a team with Ruth and Gehrig, Byrd had naturally tried to copy their ways, including the use of an extra heavy bat. Ruth still swung a 48-ounce bat, and Gehrig's was not much lighter. Byrd had been swinging a 38-ounce bat, and it was McCarthy who saw the problem. He switched Byrd to a 34 ouncer. His wrists could now snap more freely and fully, and up went his average. McCarthy actually had to sit Earle Combs on the bench, despite a spring average of .333. Combs was such a perfect team player that there was no hint of complaint from him.

The pitching also appeared to have no weak spots. Red Ruffing and young Lefty Gomez were throwing as well as ever. Veterans George Pipgras and Herb Pennock still seemed to have a few miles left in them, and another new face, Johnny Allen, impressed everyone and seemed as certain to be retained as Crosetti. McCarthy was also impressed with Selkirk. Reflective of his deep confidence in his ability to develop talent, McCarthy noted about the big 24 year old, "I wish I had had him a few years ago. He might have been another Combs." Selkirk hit .321 that spring, but he would have to labor in the minors before he could meet McCarthy's exacting standards and play with the big club. Dartmouth College graduate Red Rolfe also had to stay in the minors. Rolfe and Selkirk played the year in Newark. This was a club for which Red Rolfe and George Selkirk were not yet good enough — McCarthy certainly had his problems that spring, and reporters did note that he was smiling a lot more.[4]

On the Yankees' spring tour of the South, they stopped in Louisville to play the Colonels on April 4th. The town's baseball fans turned out with yet more "local boy makes good" pride than they had shown when McCarthy visited there with the Cubs. Before the exhibition, they held a grand ceremony for McCarthy. McCarthy received a gold watch fob, many bouquets of flowers, and lavish testimonials of esteem. The predictably cynical *New York Daily News* described the gifts as being "as useful to [baseball] performers as lawn mowers are to sailors." Such a response noted the contrast of sensibilities between the worlds in which McCarthy found himself. He shared none of the hard-bitten, street-gang anger of the *Daily News*. He had much more spiritual content in his nature. Yet his talent was such that he belonged in the "big time" of New York baseball, a world that used a *Daily News* perspective to filter out the maudlin. For McCarthy, as it was for Col. Ruppert and Ed Barrow, the logical recourse here was simply to keep his own counsel and let his own inner circle provide the personal comfort that he needed and enjoyed, while producing the best in his profession amidst the most brutal, hard-boiled of all worlds. Barrow and Ruppert could keep their distance from New York's journalistic free-for-all whenever they wanted. McCarthy had to deal with it daily. Here he would never show the New York writers much of his sentimental side, and he would seldom let their harsh veneer get the better of him.[5]

The Yankees' 1932 schedule had them playing most of the first half of the season against the Eastern teams, while traveling West or hosting the Western teams more in the second half. This repeatedly pitted the Yankees in the early season against the two teams they expected to be their chief rivals— Washington and Philadelphia. The way that so many players wielded such hot bats in the spring thus proved fortuitous.

While the press was constantly hounding about the Yankees' lineup, McCarthy kept quiet, telling reporters the same refrain that became an ever more famous line from McCarthy: "Let me worry about that."

The season-opening series was in Philadelphia. Chapman, Byrd, and Ruth started in the outfield. Saltzgaver got the nod over Lazzeri at second. Lary kept his position at shortstop, and McCarthy tried the rookie Crosetti at third. The press was especially interested in why McCarthy put Crosetti at third. McCarthy would not say. The opening game was an offensive display. Babe Ruth hit two home runs; Sam Byrd hit two; Gehrig only hit one, and they were all off of George Earnshaw. New York won 12–5. Five home runs in the first game was quite a start, and the power display continued. After five games, as the Yankees were holding their home opener (against Philadelphia), the team had already hit fifteen home runs. At home, Ruth hit another one to defeat the A's 8–3. This time Lefty Gomez bested Lefty Grove. With 16 home runs in a six-game stretch and with an average of two home runs per game in April, the papers were already referring to the lineup as the "New Murderers Row," the most famous having been the great 1927 crew. The papers were full of praise: the power was the best in the league; Gomez had bested Grove, and Bill Dickey had eclipsed Mickey Cochrane as the game's best catcher. Virtually every day, another Yankee was an offensive standout. Meanwhile, Gomez, George Pipgras, Red Ruffing and Johnny Allen were all pitching well. Yankee pride and Yankee chauvinism were back in full force. For Yankee fans amidst the Depression, there was a sense that 1929 had been the end of everything. The stock market crashed, and the Yankees' greatness had fallen to the A's. The hoopla over the Yankees' return to greatness was thus tied to a deeper wish that other, more important, things would turn around, too. The economy would sadly not turn around so nicely, but the Yankees were indeed rolling (and no one would have sacrificed to make the opposite case more than McCarthy and the Yankees).[6]

Invariably, some Yankees would come down with brief slumps. In early May, Babe Ruth's average dropped from .378 to .308. Gehrig, playing on a sprained ankle, also fell from .444 to .342. McCarthy simply switched Byrd to cleanup, and when he finally came down to earth, Earle Combs went back into the lineup. Lazzeri began to hit so well that he took his second base post back. Crosetti also fell off a bit, so Joe Sewell went back in at third. Reporters made much of this, thinking that Crosetti would be another bonus baby gone bad. (The Giants had a similar situation. They had shelled out $75,000 for a youngster named Len Koenecke, who turned out to be a bust.) McCarthy had more faith in Crosetti and made sure the rookie's morale remained good, the press's guffawing here providing him with yet more of a basis to hold them at a disdainful arm's length.

McCarthy pepped up Crosetti by telling him that Lou Gehrig was getting a bit languid at first, and it would help if he fired his throws to Gehrig extra hard. Lefty Gomez recalled, "You'd hear Gehrig's glove pop all over the park every time Frankie threw to him. But Joe wasn't worried about Gehrig." It worked. Meanwhile, through April and May, when the hitting did not come through, the pitching did. Gomez, Pipgras, Allen, and Ruffing all pitched at least one shutout. As of May 16, the Yankees' home record stood at 13 and 1.[7]

It all looked rather easy. So many signs pointed to success. That May, for example, Amelia Earhart flew the Atlantic. It seemed it was once again OK to have faith in some risk-taking. Detroit Manager Bucky Harris was already saying that the Yankees were going to win the pennant, although he was likely saying so to play a psychological game. With the winning, the home run hitters and the star pitchers were getting lots of praise. McCarthy was receding from the news stories, but it was McCarthy who strategically juggled the lineup. With the pitching, McCarthy was willing more and more to go to a reliever rather than let a starter tire, and he brought in Cy Perkins as a coach to work with the pitchers. Perkins had been with the Philadelphia A's. He had refined Lefty Grove from a fireballer into a true pitcher, and had worked as well with George Earnshaw and Rube Walberg. Each had his greatest seasons with Perkins. With the Yankee staff, Perkins taught Pipgras a better curve ball. He taught both Ruffing and Gomez how to throw a changeup, and he tried to work with Johnny Allen on keeping his composure, which repeatedly got the better of him. All this added to the sense that McCarthy was simply delegating. But the point was that McCarthy was constructing an organization and a system. He could do as each of his coaches was doing, and he had done it. Now he was not simply instituting a system, he was cultivating one not from a blueprint but within his own managerial personality and fully governed by his own baseball knowledge. At the end of May, the McCarthy Yankees stood at 28 and 11, five games ahead of Philadelphia, Washington, and surprising Detroit.[8]

On June 1, some Yankee fans began to get a bit nervous. June had been a troubling month for the team in the previous two seasons, and on this day the team lost a doubleheader to Philadelphia, while the Senators also won two. The Yankees had tied the first game with a home run in the ninth inning, but they lost the game in the sixteenth inning, 8–7, and lost the second game 7–6. Losing such close ones is often the mark of a team starting to hit a bad patch. In the first game, furthermore, Lyn Lary was spiked. He would be lost for at least a week. McCarthy inserted Crosetti back in the regular lineup. The next day, Gomez righted matters with a victory, but in the game Joe Sewell cracked his chin after two collisions with the Shibe Park wall while chasing pop fouls. (In both cases, Babe Ruth kept yelling to him "lots of room.") Now McCarthy chose to move Tony Lazzeri over to third base, and he put Jack Saltzgaver at second.

Feeling on thinner ice, the Yankees' power stepped up. The very next afternoon, in Philadelphia, June 3, Lou Gehrig hit his famous four home runs in one game. He actually hit four home runs in a row, the only player ever to do that. He was up two more times that day and hit one that might have gone out as well but for a good leaping catch in the outfield. It wasn't terribly breezy that day, but there was something in the air, for in addition to Gehrig's blasts, Combs, Ruth, Lazzeri, Foxx and Cochrane each homered as well. Combs', Ruth's and Gehrig's third homer all came in the same inning. After Gehrig had hit three, Connie Mack relieved starter George Earnshaw with Lee Roy Mahaffey. As Earnshaw headed for the showers, Mr. Mack said: "Wait, George, I want you to see how Mahaffey pitches to Gehrig." Gehrig hit Mahaffey's first pitch, a high fastball, for his fourth homer. "I see," nodded Earnshaw to his manager, "may I go now?" The Yankees won the game 20–13. (Gehrig got very few headlines for his feats, for on the same day, up in New York, John McGraw resigned in ill health and ended his 30-year career of managing the Giants.)

Such was often the fate of Gehrig's standing in the press, but he never whined, and McCarthy respected him all the more for it. The Yankees' display of power may have shown many managers that any such a slip as the they may have been experiencing was nothing about which to be worried. But McCarthy was never one to be complacent. In September he reflected that splitting the June series in Philadelphia after losing the first two was the pivotal point in the season for the Yankees. With two more wins, he noted, the A's could have pulled perilously close.[9]

The day after the slugfest in Philadelphia, McCarthy completed a deal with the Boston Red Sox. It was McCarthy's first trade as Manager of the Yankees. New York traded three reserve pitchers, Hank Johnson, Paul Andrews, and Tony Freitas (whom they had just purchased from Philadelphia) to Boston for Danny MacFayden. Mac-Fayden had won 16 games with the lowly Red Sox in 1931. His record to that point in 1932 was 1–10. Writers were wondering what would lead McCarthy to want someone like MacFayden. With four starters pitching well there seemed no need, but McCarthy wanted a stronger pitcher in reserve. Herb Pennock was 38 years old. He needed long rests between appearances, and when he lost it seemed to affect morale. Hank Johnson, although recovered from his appendectomy, had a history of yielding walks in tight spots. MacFayden would win seven for the Yankees that summer. He did not set the league ablaze, but he was effective in spots, a lot more effective indeed than his 1 and 10 record that made some scoff at the trade in the first place. On June 15, the Yankees had to cut down to the required 24 players, so the three-for-one deal made further sense. A week later, with Lyn Lary recovered from his spiking wound, McCarthy put him back at shortstop. Lazzeri returned to second base. Jack Saltzgaver had had his chance at second, but he hit only .128. McCarthy cut him. Joe Sewell went back to third base too, and Crosetti again sat down, but McCarthy kept him. The power display in Philadelphia seemed to carry the team. By June 15, the Yankees lead was seven games. In a victory over Cleveland on June 13, the Yankees were down 6–5 in the seventh inning. The bases were loaded with two out. McCarthy signaled for a triple steal. It worked; indeed the runner from second scored on an error during the play. His tally turned out to be the winning run. McCarthy's only response was to call the team together at their Cleveland hotel and yell at them about winning games by close margins that should be won going away. He was not going to let anyone get too happy or complacent.

By the end of June, the Yankees were up by nine games. The *World-Telegram*'s Dan Daniel asked McCarthy about the team's pennant chances, given their nice lead. McCarthy, chewing on a pencil, simply said: "More double plays; only four double plays on this Western trip. We are not manufacturing enough of that commodity." Crosetti soon replaced Lary at shortstop. With Lazzeri and Crosetti now at the heart of the infield, the Yankees began "churning out double plays with pleasing frequency," and New York City's Sons of Italy began turning out in droves at Yankee Stadium. They would have even more to cheer about in years to come.[10]

A good reserve catcher can often prove a most valuable piece of property to a team. McCarthy well remembered the contribution Zack Taylor made to the 1929 Cubs. On July 1, McCarthy mentioned to Frank Graham of the *New York Sun* how valuable a man Arndt Jorgens was as a backup to Bill Dickey. His praise proved to be prophetic. On July 4, the Yankees were hosting the Senators in a doubleheader.

Lefty Gomez lost the first game. It was only his second loss of the season against 14 wins. In the second game, Senators outfielder Carl Reynolds was caught in a rundown between third base and home. Bill Dickey had the ball and, in a planned maneuver, deliberately overthrew the third baseman with the left fielder positioned to take the throw and relay back to home to cut down the runner. As Reynolds was heading for home, he chose to slam into Dickey. (Reynolds had just knocked down Joe Sewell at third base.) He jarred the ball loose, missed the plate, walked back, touched it, and was called safe. Dickey was usually a most even-mannered player, but here he lost his temper. As Reynolds returned to touch home, Dickey took a swing at him. The benches cleared. Fans threw firecrackers. Dickey's single punch actually fractured Reynolds' jaw.

Senators President Clark Griffith was enraged. At his urging, American League President Will Harridge suspended Dickey indefinitely. Dickey expressed regret over the incident, but he maintained that Reynolds had no business barreling into him as he did. McCarthy and the Yankees figured that Dickey would probably get a ten-day suspension. Instead, Harridge chose to suspend him 30 days and fine him $1000! (Dickey's 1932 salary was just under $20,000, thus the fine alone was the equivalent of a top major league catcher in the early 2000s like Ivan Rodriguez being fined over a half million dollars.) The Yankees were livid. Col. Ruppert said the "severity was absurd and unwarranted." Dickey wrote that he had been hit and spiked several times during the season. He said a catcher can only take so much and had to protect himself. Yankee fans paralleled Reynolds' tactics with those of Ty Cobb.

McCarthy spoke out, too. He pointed out that Reynolds had previously used such rough play with the White Sox when they played the Cubs in the 1931 postseason city series, which McCarthy had attended. (McCarthy had quite a memory, as everyone knew.) He claimed that Griffith was exaggerating both the incident and the degree to which Reynolds was hurt. He openly stated: Reynolds "is entirely to blame, and there are no excuses for him." Dickey, he said, had been getting rough treatment for weeks and received no protection from the umpires; he had to take care of himself and "just had the hard luck to sock a bird with a glass jaw."

This sort of "sensitivity" was not going to score many points with the American League offices. It was not one of McCarthy's better arguments with an official. Indeed, McCarthy stated openly, "the Yankees need Dickey at this point of the race, and I feel sure that when President Harridge has weighed the facts he will lift the suspension." Harridge obviously had to judge the punch regardless of from whom it came — the league's MVP or a rookie in a game for the first time, this could not be allowed to matter. McCarthy's plea thus came across as the mere protection of a highly valued player. Harridge would not lift or reduce the suspension; Dickey would be gone for the month. Although it was not exposed until October, Col. Ruppert continued to pay Dickey's salary and paid the fine. Several days later, with McCarthy's encouragement, Ben Chapman spiked Reynolds.[11]

With the various slumps and injuries in the infield and outfield that season, McCarthy had skillfully juggled his players. He was fortunate to have Combs to go in for Byrd, Hoag for Ruth, Crosetti for Lary, etc. Dickey was another matter. McCarthy would rest him, as he always would rest his catchers, but when Dickey went down, McCarthy's lineup strategies would be strained. Arndt Jorgens was capable, but the position of catcher, played day after day, wears down anyone. McCarthy picked up two minor-league receivers, Ed Phillips and Joe Glenn, but Jorgens carried most of the load. Jorgens was a lighter hitter than Dickey. (He batted .219 that season.) The key was whether the rest of the team could make up for the loss. Gomez's effectiveness was markedly diminished in Dickey's absence. More than for his bat, Dickey was indeed missed for his ability to handle the pitchers. The Yankees' record was 50 and 21 on the day Dickey punched Reynolds. For the next month, their record was 18 and 12, not as good, but the Senators were fading, and the A's merely kept pace. Perhaps the infestation of Japanese beetles at Shibe Park that summer stymied any A's advances. On July 31, the Yankees' lead remained at eight games. The loss of Dickey did not put the Yankees behind, only a bit less far ahead.[12]

One bit of good news came to McCarthy in early August. Out in Chicago, McCarthy's former team was in a race for the pennant with Pittsburgh. On August 2, with the Cubs five games behind the Pirates, Wrigley and Veeck suddenly fired Rogers Hornsby. The papers were full of comparisons with McCarthy. In contrast to McCarthy's performance, "it is not unfair," opined one New York reporter, "to say that Hornsby has failed to come up to the expectations of Windy City Fans." Reporters pointed to how poorly Hornsby judged talent and how badly Hack Wilson performed after McCarthy left Chicago. By September, 1931, Hornsby was ready to release Wilson. Reporters wrote of Hornsby's abusive ways with his men. The *Daily News* brought out the nasty little fact that, at the point of his firing, Hornsby had amassed $6000 in IOU's to Cub players which he had built to fuel his compulsive racetrack betting. New owner Philip Wrigley (William Wrigley had passed away in 1931) paid off all the IOU's and deducted them from Hornsby's salary, which he continued through the duration of his contract.) McCarthy made no comment, but the news of Hornsby's demise came at the very point Bill Dickey returned to the lineup. It seemed a good sign, and it was definitely a good feeling.[13]

With Dickey's return to the lineup, there seemed to be nothing that could derail the Yankees. In a game with Detroit on August 1, one of McCarthy's old tricks came back at him. McCarthy had reversed Lazzeri's and Chapman's names on the lineup card, and they batted out of order. Tiger manager Bucky Harris protested. Unlike McCarthy, Harris did not lodge his protest at a key moment in the game, however. No such moment ever arose, as the Yankees won 16–3. Instead Harris waited until the game was over. It thus first appeared that Harris had no case, but Harridge upheld his protest and ordered the game to be replayed.[14]

Major tensions also arose over Dickey and the Yankees' first appearance in Washington after the Reynolds incident. There had been talk of a lawsuit. The Yankees and Dickey had received many threatening letters from Washington fans. No one knew what to expect — tomatoes, soda bottles, rocks? News of this prompted New Yorkers to send counter-threats to Washington, telling them if anything happens in Washington, Yankee fans will…. McCarthy actually consented to have Dickey come into Washington's Union Station disguised as a baseball writer. (He dumped a bunch of cigarette ash on his coat and tie, and walked "carrying a typewriter and a mashie-niblick [a seven iron].") As it turned out, there was no furor at the Station. The next afternoon at Griffith Stadium, several policemen were on hand, and President Harridge sat conspicuously in the stands. No incidents occurred. Perhaps knowing that he had fanned the flames of the situation back in July, Griffith went out of his way to claim that he had saved Dickey. He said that he had dissuaded three Washington judges, all Senators fans, who had urged Dickey's arrest. Griffith also bragged about rushing Dickey into a taxi after the game.

Whatever Griffith's contributions, there were no incidents during or after the game. Like the situation, the game was tense but devoid of action. It was a scoreless tie until the tenth inning. All the players seemed to feel themselves in a surreal world amidst the tension. Then Babe Ruth stepped up and slammed a home run to win the game. From Washington, the *Daily News* laughed: "Mr. Ruth's skill has made the celebrated Dickey case deader than a session of Congress." For McCarthy it was a nonevent similar to Hack Wilson's first appearance in Cincinnati after his fights with the Reds in 1929.[15]

By the end of August, there was a general sigh of relief in New York. Franklin Roosevelt had secured the Democratic nomination for President. Playboy Mayor Jimmy Walker had finally resigned under scandal-driven pressure. And the Yankees had the pennant all but sewn up. An oddity in the Yankees' schedule that year had their last home game on September 7. The pennant was not yet mathematically clinched, but McCarthy actually relaxed his relentless guard a bit. In an exhibition game up at Binghamton, where he had not visited since his Wilkes-Barre days, he started a young pitcher named Charlie Devens. Devens was from a wealthy, Social Register Boston family. His mother was a Vanderbilt, and he had graduated from Groton and Harvard, where he was a member of the Hasty Pudding Club. When he signed with the Yankees earlier that summer, the papers gave it great coverage. It illustrated the pride people felt in how truly democratic was the game of baseball. Here was Devens (as well as another prospect, Red Rolfe, an Exeter and Dartmouth grad) playing with Frankie Crosetti, whose Italian immigrant father worked as a garbage man in San Francisco. McCarthy's way of judging talent regardless of the person's background (he never had the chance to do so with any African-American player) reinforced this tradition, a tradition that seemed to give people a needed bit of confidence in their nation's culture amidst the troubles of the Depression. The fact that African-Americans were excluded amidst this shared pride spoke to how deeply that racist wound struck, well beyond the purview of such a mere game as baseball. McCarthy and the Yankees would not have the chance to address that matter. In 1932, the mixing of the children of immigrants and the Social Register was as far as they could go. Devens won his outing in Binghamton. He expressed great excitement to the press over pitching and over the fact that Babe Ruth called him "kid." Devens took Babe's word as a show of affection. Newsmen sadly informed him that Babe Ruth called everyone "kid," and usually because he could not remember anyone's name.[16]

The Yankees clinched the pennant with a victory in Cleveland on September 13. New York fans were all celebrating. Some players whooped it up; McCarthy was "quietly elated." He went out of his way to praise Connie Mack who, he said, despite injuries kept his team hustling and "probably came as near to four straight flags as any American League entry ever will." When McCarthy won his fourth in a row in 1939, no one reminded him of this. The New York reporters commented about McCarthy being the first manager to win a pennant in both leagues. Otherwise, most focused their coverage on the play of various Yankees. Amidst their raves about the team's many standout players, *New York World-Telegram* columnist Dan Daniel begged to point out to Yankee fans that, "one of the salient factors in the success … is a man who has had less publicity than any other winning leader of the past decade — Joe McCarthy." McCarthy's system, he said, brought about "the regeneration of Joe Sewell. It has given new life to Lazzeri and Earle Combs. It has made Gomez a great pitcher; Ruffing more proficient that ever. And it has started Crosetti toward the heights."

Noting McCarthy's often strained relations with reporters, who then refused to give him much credit for the Yankees' success, Daniel shared none of the ego that colored many of his fellow writers' analyses. McCarthy told him: "I don't want to tell a man one thing and then do something else. I don't like to stick to first impressions. I want to be guided by changing circumstances. Your ideas at 6:00 in the evening may be knocked into a cocked hat by noon the next day." McCarthy felt baseball questions were to be answered in earnest. Reporters wanted a full analysis every day, and McCarthy felt this could tie him down needlessly. It would cause too much back-checking and second-guessing. Other managers would use humor or rely on personality to keep the reporters occupied while they ran their teams. (Casey Stengel would make it an art form.) McCarthy was not a soothing, fireside chat sort of person. Some reporters could not understand this and simply saw him as hostile. At times he certainly could be, and reporters knew to give him a wide berth, especially after a loss. Mediocre reporters equated his treatment of the press as somehow indicative of the way he treated his players. Dan Daniel knew how wrong this was. McCarthy never dressed his players down in front of others, and after a loss he waited until the next day before going over details that needed attention and correction.

Contrasting McCarthy's system with those of the other clubs in the game, Daniel also noted "The Yankees have fewer rules than any other club in the majors. And discipline is keener that it is

McCarthy with the Yankees. His clear, unchallengeable generalship was something his players respected, and his opponents feared. (National Baseball Hall of Fame Library, Cooperstown, N.Y.)

on any other team." This was a key distinction. A team with genuine discipline did not need a lot of rules. The felt need for too many rules was an admission that discipline would break down without them. McCarthy would later state: "I have very few rules that my players must observe, and they are simple ones as regard to keeping in condition. The hours of work for a big league player are easy, and it is up to my players to be in shape to work two or three hours a day. If they cannot do that, I would rather some other club had them." This was the McCarthy system that was only just beginning to work. It started with his eye for spotting talent. It grew with his knack for developing it, his ability to handle and motivate a variety of personalities, his mastery of details, his ability to use the right bits of stored knowledge, both as a game tactician and as a short and long-term strategist. With someone like that at the helm, it was impossible for any player to want to do anything but contribute all he could.[17]

It is often difficult to maintain a team's momentum in the weeks between the wrapping up of a pennant and the World Series. Some said McCarthy had failed at this in 1929. McCarthy actually received many telegrams advising him about what to do. McCarthy had one crisis anyway. Babe Ruth came down with what some feared to be an attack of acute appendicitis. He missed much of September, rested with ice packs, and ate nothing but soup. He lost seven pounds, but otherwise the crisis passed; no operation proved necessary. McCarthy rested some other players, especially his pitchers. Gomez had won 24 games, and some wanted him to get his 25th, but McCarthy would not push him. McCarthy even rested Lou Gehrig for a half a game. This he would never do again. Gehrig was so nervous: "You'll play me Friday, won't you boss. I can't afford to get rusty like this loafing on the bench. I simply don't know what to do with myself." McCarthy relented: "I can't have you fuming and fussing on the bench. The bench being what it is, I can't stand another neurotic." Coach Jimmy Burke begged to differ. With Gehrig, he said, "It ain't a neurosis, it's the pickled eels" he always eats. McCarthy took the point, but added that a pickled eel "doesn't explain Gomez." No one argued with that.[18]

Ever since the pennant was clinched, fans had clamored for an appearance by Charlie Devens with the Yankees in an actual league game. The sensibilities of subsequent generations may huff in consternation at the idea that working-class New York Yankee fans would root for a rookie out of Boston's Social Register and Harvard's Hasty Pudding Club, but Devens was a fan favorite in 1932. The fans were from the same sorts of neighborhoods and families as Joe McCarthy's. He appreciated the appeal that Devens had among the faithful, and he started the young pitcher in one game in late September — in Boston. He started some other rookie pitchers that September too. In the Boston game, Devens gave up six hits and won 8–2. The Boston fans gave him a big cheer.[19]

For McCarthy that September the pressing matter was to prepare for his National League opponent in the World Series. The race in the National League remained tight for much of the month. The results made McCarthy smile, for the Chicago Cubs edged Pittsburgh by four games, securing the flag in late September. In early August, Charlie Grimm had replaced Hornsby as the Cubs' manager. "Jolly Cholly's" manner was a welcome relief from the Hornsby dictatorship, and the Cubs' responded. A critical factor in the Cubs pennant drive involved their pickup of shortstop Mark

Koenig. Their regular shortstop, Billy Jurges, had suffered a gunshot wound in July. Grimm picked up Koenig in August. He played in 33 games, fielded superbly, and batted .353. His contribution was enormous. Yet after the Cubs wrapped up the pennant they voted Koenig a mere half share of World Series money. (Hornsby was voted zero shares, some said because Wrigley was paying him the remainder of his $40,000 contract.) While the Cubs voted only 20 full shares, the Yankees voted 26 full shares. Charley Devens received a half share. Hank Johnson and Paul Andrews, who'd been traded to Boston for Danny MacFayden, were even voted $500. Newspapers noted the contrast of generosity and parsimony between the teams, and the Yankees tucked the matter away in their heads. McCarthy said nothing about it. Meanwhile, people thought he needed to do little scouting of the Cubs, since he knew most of them. "I know a lot about the Cubs," he intimated. "Grimm certainly has a fast, hustling team. There isn't a quitter in the lineup." Never one to take undue risks, and always willing to learn from prior mistakes, McCarthy nonetheless hired someone to scout the Cubs—Howard Ehmke![20]

The Yankees impressed the writers as the favorites for the series. The always-cautious Ed Barrow predicted the series would go six games. McCarthy would make no game predictions. He spoke only of the fact that the team had not let down in September. They had won every series on the road in September and finished a full 13 games ahead of second-place Philadelphia. The only question was Babe Ruth. Since coming back from his appendix problem he had gone only 3 for 16 at the plate.[21]

Back in October of 1930, when McCarthy signed with Col. Ruppert to manage the Yankees, McCarthy openly stated "It is my ambition to build up the Yankees into a pennant winning team and meet the Cubs in the next World Series. It may only be a dream, but if I could beat the Cubs with my new team, I would be willing to jump off the Brooklyn Bridge." It took one more year than McCarthy had hoped, but now he had his chance (at the Cubs).

The World Series opened in New York on September 28. The Cubs arrived in the late morning and began to practice as the Yankees assembled in the dugout. Cubs' shortstop Mark Koenig was a former Yankee, 1925–1930. Some of his former teammates ran out to greet him with an outward show of camaraderie. The Cubs did not take kindly to this. The Yankees expected that and pompously chided them: "Hey, once a Yankee always a Yankee." The Yanks left the field, but then they started in on the Cubs. Babe Ruth led the verbal charge, and he had the voice to do it. "Hey Mark, who are dem cheapskates you're playin' with?" Shouts of "Chiselers!" and "Yellow Guys!" spewed forth. Reminders about Hornsby's zero-share came forth too. The mentions of Hornsby may have had little impact, but the rest of the bombardment focused on Koenig, and it hit home squarely.

McCarthy never stopped any of the bench jockeying. Sam Byrd, Ben Chapman, Lefty Gomez, and coach Art Fletcher were all quite good at it. Back in the 1929 Series, Commissioner Landis had ordered McCarthy to quash all the bench yelling, but that was due to obscenities. The money knocks against the Cubs were nothing Landis was going to touch, and the Yankees piled it on. Landis would intervene in the series, but not till later, and it would have nothing to do with Series shares. McCarthy may have been glad to see some of his former players, but he would not interfere with the psychological edge his Yankees were forging. The remaking of old acquaintances would have to wait. Throughout the Series, the bench jockeying was fierce. With their incessant reminders of how they had shortchanged Koenig, the Yankees definitely got under the Cubs' skins. The Cubs had no such leverage, but there was no paucity of effort with the standard list of taunts. It was as bad a verbal battle as any World Series ever witnessed. Chicago fans took part where they could. When the Series was in Chicago, the Yankees were rudely jeered at the La Salle Street Railway Station and at their hotel. Babe Ruth was spat upon, and McCarthy remembered how the team "had to run the gauntlet of a double line of women fans at the Edgewater Beach Hotel."[22]

Other than Sam Byrd spelling Ruth in the field at the very end of the final game, McCarthy used the same eight men in the field throughout the series. He had worked out his lineup by midseason, and he was saw no need to change it — Combs, Sewell, Ruth, Gehrig, Lazzeri, Dickey, Chapman, and Crosetti. Chicago's pitching proved a problem for the Cubs. Chicago scored in the first inning of every game, but McCarthy was not impressed, and when the Cub pitchers began giving up walks (23 in four games) McCarthy was content to let the Yankee offense do the work. Knowing Hartnett's throwing arm and wanting to let the bats do the work, McCarthy held back Ben Chapman and all others from any stolen base attempts. The hitting came through. The Yankees won the first game 12–6 and the second 5–2. "The Cubs appear outclassed," wrote Grantland Rice, and he went on, suggesting what would become a point of comfort, or chagrin, for many baseball fans throughout the harsh decade in which they found themselves: "In bull markets and bear markets, in times of luxury and times of want, the Yankees continue to maul."[23]

When the teams traveled to Chicago, Babe Ruth added to the Yankees' intentional obnoxiousness. He bad-mouthed Wrigley Field as puny, as he and Gehrig put on a murderous display of power in the Yankees' first batting practice. "I'd pay half my salary if I could hit in this dump," chortled Ruth. Chicago fans threw lemons at him during practice and while he was in the on-deck circle. McCarthy stayed below the headlines but did some important things. One general point was that he maintained a feeling of calm and confidence. It was no mere act, the antics of the Cubs fans had no impact upon him, and that was how the rest of the team then dealt with them too. Several weeks before the series, McCarthy had bought a supply of National League baseballs so the Yankees could do some batting practice with them and get used to any subtle differences each player might see. As in so many other contexts, McCarthy always thought of and intelligently addressed details that never crossed the minds of most other managers.[24]

Some Yankee fans had been worried about Ruth's apparent slump after his appendix problem in September. Their fears were proving baseless. Gehrig even commented on how Ruth was in one of his hot spells, adding that when he was in such a groove there was no stopping him. In game three, with New York Governor Franklin Roosevelt smiling in the stands, Ruth and Gehrig each hit two home runs. It was in the fifth inning that afternoon that Ruth supposedly "called his shot." What actually happened was that with two strikes on him, the Cub bench was erupting with every insult they could hurl. Ruth motioned at them with two fingers, meaning that he had two strikes on him and had one more coming. He supposedly yelled at pitcher Charlie Root: "I'm going to knock the next pitch right down your god-damned throat." He then hit the next pitch to the very deepest part of the center field bleachers.

Rounding the bases, he mocked the Cubs, motioning to them with three fingers. The Cubs and their fans were completely stunned. Franklin Roosevelt loved it, of course, but he kept his composure, as he badly wanted the Illinois vote in the next month's election. Lou Gehrig hit the very next pitch down the line for another home run that put the Yankees ahead to stay.

The myths of Ruth calling his shot grew from there, and Ruth did nothing to dissuade them. Two days after the supposed called shot, the *New York Herald Tribune* ran a story about a boy in a New York hospital on a respirator with a lung disorder. The boy supposedly grew so excited at the news of Babe Ruth's home run that his natural breathing was at last restored: "Physicians credited 'Dr.' Ruth with an assist as well as a hit and a run." This became the basis of the famous myth that Ruth had promised a home run to a boy he had visited in the hospital. Ten years later, Ruth was in Hollywood making the movie *Pride of the Yankees*. Charlie Root was there too. Root asked Ruth whether he really had called his shot that day. Ruth laughed: "No, but it made a helluva story, didn't it?" One of Ruth's knacks, that rendered him such a perfect hero for his age, was his instinctive sense for juicy journalism. It made him both legendary and wealthy. McCarthy had no such instincts for journalistic sensation, but he knew how not to get in the way of others. When asked about Ruth allegedly calling his shot, he said, "I don't know, I was looking elsewhere at the moment he gestured." That may have appeared an evasion, but forty years later he maintained the same thing. He later admitted, however, that the "called shot" was fiction, adding simply, "Babe went along with it. He was a great showman, you know."[25]

With Ruth's and Gehrig's awesome display of muscle in game 3, the Cubs seemed beaten. Going into the bottom of the ninth, they were down by two. Then Gabby Hartnett hit a home run, and the crowd began to stir. McCarthy took out George Pipgras, and rather than use Ruffing or Gomez, he inserted old Herb Pennock. Pennock held the Cubs from there, and McCarthy thus appeared to add to the psychological victory. He wanted the Cubs to know he was so sure of victory that he felt no worry about graciously giving an appearance to a 38-year-old. There was another factor in McCarthy's thinking too, something he did not make public for 34 years. When Pipgras was still pitching, the Cubs' pitcher was due up next. Manager Charlie Grimm sent Mark Koenig to the on-deck circle. Koenig was a switch hitter, but McCarthy knew he was more dangerous from the left side, particularly on this afternoon, with a stiff wind that had helped lift the four homers of his big lefties Ruth and Gehrig. Against Pennock, McCarthy knew Koenig would swing from the right side and be less of a threat. Grimm knew it too, and when Pennock took the mound, Grimm recalled Koenig and sent out a young reserve catcher named Rollie Hemsley. Pennock struck him out.[26]

After such an insult as the insertion of old Pennock, the Cubs were angry, and McCarthy obviously hoped their anger would take them out of their game. One thing did interrupt some of the Yankees' momentum. The bench jockeying, first directed at Mark Koenig, had grown to such coarse levels that Commissioner Landis told both managers to have their teams stop it all. McCarthy read the order, and, as Joe Sewell recalled, "we sat there like mummies." While the players' yelling stopped, their feelings were still in evidence. In the first inning of game four the Cubs' anger came forth with a vengeance. Cubs pitcher Guy Bush challenged Ruth to a fight, and he hit him with a pitch in the first inning. Ruth laughed at him, however. After he had trotted down to first, he just flicked the spot on his arm where he was hit like he was shooing a mosquito. Then he yelled down to Gehrig: "Don't look for nothin', Lou; he ain't got it."

Even though Root could not ruffle Ruth, the Cubs did not fold. In the bottom of the first, they jumped all over Yankees' rookie starter Johnny Allen for four runs. Down three games to none, it was hard to be too optimistic, but the Cub fans did their best to rally the team. McCarthy again made a move as much psychological as purely tactical. Rather than turning to Ruffing or Gomez, he brought in 35-year-old Wilcy Moore, who had pitched but 25 innings that season. The move worked. Moore ended the Cubs' rally, and he was strong from there. The Yankees then turned around with a 19-hit barrage, including a home run by Earle Combs and two by Tony Lazzeri. The result was 13 runs. When the Cubs pushed over a meaningless run in the ninth to cut the Yankees' lead to a mere seven, McCarthy relieved Moore. Again he turned to old Herb Pennock. Pennock throttled the Cubs from there. That was the Series, as completely overwhelming a victory as could be imagined. As the *Daily News* asked: "Is That Fun?" The Yankee arrogance of the 1920s was reborn.

Meanwhile, the Cubs certainly had not avenged their 1929 humiliation, but Manager Joe McCarthy sure had. "That was the Series, above all the others," he later acknowledged, "that gave me the big thrill." Babe Ruth went over to McCarthy in the clubhouse and shook his hand. For the next weeks the Yankees toasted at New York's finest clubs. Mr. and Mrs. McCarthy immediately returned to Buffalo, of course. McCarthy had actually developed a nose infection and had to undergo a minor operation. Joe Glenn, Lefty Gomez, Sam Byrd, and Bill Dickey all got married that month, and McCarthy had to miss all their weddings because of his surgery. Later that month, Col. Ruppert offered him a new three-year contract. McCarthy signed immediately.[27]

23

Watch Out for Those Senators

As McCarthy and the Yankees gathered in St. Petersburg in March, 1933, several circumstances had changed, and some key issues were ongoing. In McCarthy's infield there remained the rivalry between Lyn Lary and Frankie Crosetti. Lary had been the regular shortstop in 1931; Crosetti had held the job for most of 1932. With both young and healthy, McCarthy was going to have to choose. His strategy here was to leave the position open to both: "I'm going to let [the two]... fight it out down here, and it would not surprise me if Lary staged a grand comeback and regained the job he held so successfully in 1931." McCarthy was not tipping the scales in favor of Lary here. He was seeking the motivate the non-incumbent Lary and also serve notice on Crosetti. Crosetti would win the job. McCarthy would later be uncharacteristically sarcastic about Lary. Lary was a bit of a wisecracker, and he enjoyed the New York nightlife a bit too much for McCarthy's taste. A bigger issue for McCarthy may have been that Lary was close to Babe Ruth. Ruth was godfather to Lary's son. Crosetti, on the other hand, was not in Ruth's circle, and McCarthy always liked him anyway.[1]

Lary's situation touched upon the most delicate problem for McCarthy and the Yankees that spring — the future of Babe Ruth. Ruth was now 38. He was slower, and his numbers, while still impressive, had declined. After the 1932 World Series, Ruth made more noise about wanting to manage. But Ed Barrow was fully convinced that Ruth could not handle a ball club. Barrow had given McCarthy a three-year contract. (Ruth had been getting some managerial feelers from other American League teams; the White Sox, the Tigers, and the Red Sox all contacted him, but at this point he only wanted the Yankees.) Always brutally frank with the numbers, Yankees President Ed Barrow presented Ruth with a new contract, calling for a cut from $70,000 to $50,000, with the softener of offering the salary for both 1933 and 1934. Ruth balked, and the negotiations were on in earnest. While Barrow could, and did, talk about Ruth's declining statistics, Ruth pointed to the numbers in the stands which would undeniably dwindle if he was not on the field.

McCarthy never involved himself in contract matters. Publicly he said he looked for Ruth "to have a great year." To a young reporter in Nashville, McCarthy insincerely described Babe as "spry as a cat, good for five or six more years." Perhaps seeking to give a subtle nudge on Barrow's behalf, McCarthy said elsewhere: "If Ruth should require a little more help, Sam Byrd will be on the job." The word "more" was especially poignant, as it presumed that Ruth was already in need of a little assistance, which indeed he was, but it was not something Ruth cared to read.

Ruth and Ruppert came to terms ($52,000) on March 22nd. In the deal Ruppert also promised to return the $5,000 Manager Miller Huggins had fined him back in 1925. Ruth had a victory here. But he did not realize that his concern with something which had happened a decade ago, the general acrimony that his publicity instincts brought to the negotiations, and the lavish penthouse scene in which Ruth staged the signing all reinforced for Ruppert and Barrow their conviction that Ruth was fundamentally immature and definitely not management material. The only more compelling point of proof for them here was the quiet, thoroughly effective manner of their current field manager. While Ruth had a victory in 1933, he thus set himself up for bigger disappointments later. Meanwhile, his relationship with McCarthy remained cool, and McCarthy was certainly not going to be the one to make any overtures. Mrs. Ruth and Mrs. McCarthy were not speaking either. Meanwhile, Ruth's relationships grew ever cooler with the clearly identified McCarthy men on the Yankees, notably Gehrig.[2]

When Ruth signed his contract, Ruppert said to the press gathered in Ruth's Florida penthouse: "Well it's all fixed up. Ruth has signed.... Now if the President signs the beer bill, everything will be jake."[3] March, 1933 marked the beginning of Franklin Roosevelt's presidency. The country was anxiously awaiting what he would do about the Depression. So many of his programs and instituted bureaucracies would have enormous long-range consequences. In the immediate circumstances of the era, however, one of the key questions on many Americans' minds concerned beer and the possible end to Prohibition. Since 1920, a baseball game was certainly one place where many had lamented losing the pleasure of (openly) enjoying a beer. For Colonel Ruppert, this was especially important, not just because he owned the Yankees but even more because he also owned the Knickerbocker Beer Company. Roosevelt, of course, did repeal Prohibition. Baseball fans rejoiced, and Knickerbocker Beer became the largest-selling beer in the country for the rest of the decade.

Next to the availability of beer in the ballparks, perhaps the biggest change in the American League before the 1933 season concerned the Philadelphia Athletics. Back in 1914, after the A's had won their fourth pennant in five years, Connie Mack was compelled to break up his team. Competition with the outlaw Federal League was driving up player salaries to a point that Mack and the A's could not make ends meet. He sold off some of his greatest stars and had to start building again. The A's spent many years mired in the second division, but they finally reemerged as a powerful team in the late 1920s and won three straight pennants from 1929 to 1931. With the Depression, Mack faced a similar problem to the one he had faced in 1914 — high-priced star players and salaries amidst severe economic pressures. After the 1932 season, Connie Mack again began to dismember a great team, expecting to be able to bounce back as soon as prosperity returned. It didn't, and he didn't. Before the 1933 season Mack began the process, selling Mule Haas, Jimmy Dykes, and Al Simmons to the Chicago White Sox. Later, he would sell Mickey Cochrane to Detroit and Lefty Grove and Jimmie Foxx to Boston. With Chicago in 1933, Simmons led the league in batting. Before the Chicago deal, most baseball reporters were expecting the A's to challenge the Yankees' hopes of repeating as league champion. With the departure of Haas, Dykes, and Simmons, no one took the A's as seriously. Connie Mack himself admitted that his club was not the contender. "The Yankees," he said, "look like the toughest club, but," he added, "watch out for those Senators."

Washington had made some strategic trades. They already had Joe Kuhel, Buddy Myer, Ossie Bluege, Heine Manush, and Joe Cronin, now their player-manager (and owner Clark Griffith's son-in-law). They added Goose Goslin, Fred Schulte, and Luke Sewell. Other than Sewell and Bluege, all these players would hit above .295 in 1933, and Sewell and Bluege would be especially valuable on defense. They also picked up three new pitchers, Earl Whitehill, Lefty Stewart, and Jack Russell, who would win a total of 49 games that year. Connie Mack knew his business; the Senators would be tough. McCarthy knew this. In Nashville he predicted the Yankees would win, adding "Washington will be our roughest competition. They['ve] got a good young manager in Cronin."[4]

McCarthy had no new faces of any significance to study in St. Petersburg. He had the competition among the infielders, and he had to decide which reserve outfielders to keep. The team did not tear through the Florida exhibition schedule as it had in 1932, nor did it appear so overwhelmingly powerful on the tour through the South. Nevertheless, McCarthy received another grand welcome in Louisville. "I don't mind saying I have a particularly warm spot in my heart for Louisville," he admitted. "Here I was given my first real opportunity in baseball. The fans there were always kind to me, and it is like coming back home."

George Selkirk still could not make the ball club that spring. Sam Byrd remained as Ruth's late-inning substitute, along with rookie Fred "Dixie" Walker. But the starting outfield remained as it had been with Chapman, Combs, and Ruth. The infield was still Gehrig, Lazzeri, Crosetti, and Sewell. Dickey remained the catcher, with Arndt Jorgens his backup. The pitching staff was the same too. Charlie Devens pitched some exhibition games but spent most of the season in the minors. There seemed no compelling reason to change, and when the Yankees opened the season with seven straight wins, fans and reporters were chortling. At first McCarthy could only nod, "I really have no complaints." When he heard that some reporters were actually using the word "pennant" in the wake of such a start, McCarthy yelled: "Don't talk like that! Some of the players might hear you. Besides, don't think for a moment that the race is going to be a pushover for us." He thought a bit about the victories and pointed out: "We've been playing good ball lately, but we've been getting some breaks too ... a few timely singles by the opposition might have changed the whole picture." Indeed four of the seven victories had been one-run games, and McCarthy acknowledged: "we've just scraped through to win practically all of them."[5]

The Washington Senators ended the Yankees' undefeated streak with two one-run wins. As McCarthy well knew, those types of wins do have a way of evening themselves out. The Senators certainly held high hopes for themselves that spring. Knowing the Yankees would be their obvious rivals and remembering the Dickey-Reynolds incident of the previous summer, they geared up for the encounters. The two April victories were thus quite special to the Senators; they silenced all those who were talking about New York running away with the race.

The next day, the tensions and rivalry between the two teams again came to a boil. In the top of the fourth inning, Gehrig led off with a single. Ben Chapman then singled, with Gehrig going to third. Tony Lazzeri was next up, and he grounded to shortstop Joe Cronin. Conceding Gehrig's run, Cronin went for the double play. As he tossed the ball to second baseman Buddy Myer, Chapman sped into second with a hard slide, trying to break up the double play. As Chapman slid, he spiked Myer. Myer fell, got up, and kicked Chapman. The two began to fight, and both team's benches cleared. As it was Chapman who had spiked the Senators' Carl Reynolds the previous summer after the Dickey fight, the Senators had held a grudge against him. Cronin grabbed Chapman just as the umpires arrived and restored order. Chapman was ejected from the game. The umpire escorted him to the tunnel that connected to the visitors' dressing room. In Griffith Stadium, there was only one tunnel, and its entry point was at the end of the Senators' dugout. Chapman thus had to pass by the Washington bench, and as he did, pitcher Earl Whitehill yelled at him, calling him a "fatheaded _____." Chapman turned and hit Whitehill, whereupon several Senators jumped on Chapman. Several hit and kicked him. The entire Yankee team then rushed across the field to help Chapman. As they did hundreds of fans jumped onto the field. Fights broke out, and the District police had to be summoned. Dixie Walker, Ben Chapman's roommate and fellow Alabaman, hit several players and fans. Lefty Gomez hit a policeman. Ruth and Gehrig grabbed and subdued several Senators. Fights broke out in the stands, with five people eventually arrested. The Yankees won the game 16–0. After the contest, the Yankees required police protection. They proceeded directly to Union Station and left town. Chapman required some medical attention for his lumps and cuts.[6]

American League President William Harridge issued an immediate suspension of Ben Chapman, Buddy Myer, and Earl Whitehill. Neither Dixie Walker nor anyone else was punished. Claims and counter claims dotted the newspapers. Myer claimed "Chapman had it coming to him. He tried to spike me last year. I had to stop him before he ended my baseball career. … I'm all through taking it from him." Chapman countered: "The idea that I intended to spike Myer is silly," and, Chapman added, "Myer has tried to spike Gehrig several times." McCarthy weighed in claiming the suspension of Chapman was "uncalled for." Chapman, he held, "was not to blame for doing what he did after Myer deliberately kicked him while Chapman was on the ground." The only thing McCarthy said Chapman was guilty of was "aggressive base running, something every ballplayer should do." As with the Reynolds case, neither McCarthy's nor anyone else's claims would have any effect on Harridge's decision. Chapman, Myer, and Whitehill were each fined $100 and suspended for five games. Clark Griffith was mad at the equality of the punishments. He said "Chapman should have been fined twice as much as my players and [suspended] twice as long."[7]

Two days after the fight, the season schedule happened to have the Senators coming to New York for another series with the Yankees. Twenty-five thousand came to the Stadium on a weekday afternoon to watch the rematch. Sam Byrd played in Chapman's place that day. The game went off without incident, and the Senators won 4–3 in ten innings. The next day the Senators won again, 6–3, and the Yankees seemed dispirited. In the ninth inning, with one out and one run in, Walker and Gehrig were on first and second. Lazzeri hit a liner to right center. Gehrig waited until the ball dropped, then took off. Behind him, Walker was running all the way, and they rounded third and headed for home but a yard apart. In the outfield, McCarthy remembered, the turf was soggy, and "the ball took a freak bounce straight up into [centerfielder Goose] Goslin's hands. He turned and threw to Cronin, who made a perfect relay to the plate." The catcher then tagged *both* runners, ending the ball game. One newspaper joked that the Yankees were looking like the Brooklyn Dodgers, the worst of all insults to a Yankee fan. McCarthy was furious. This was a mental lapse, something he could not stand. "Hell, this isn't baseball," yelled a fan behind McCarthy, "it's a nervous breakdown." McCarthy agreed, later referring to the old saying, "uneasy lies the head that wears the crown." McCarthy recognized, as he later reflected, "It wouldn't happen again in a hundred years— two runners put out at the plate on a single throw." But the mishap convinced him further that the team's mental focus had been diverted. He blamed the Chapman incident.

Outwardly McCarthy did not blame Chapman for what had occurred in Washington, and he was certainly not excusing Myer and Whitehill, but he was growing more convinced that while he demanded that players hustle with the utmost intensity, a line should not be crossed beyond which a player loses his poise. This sort of balanced intensity is not an easy thing to strike, let along maintain. But McCarthy grew increasingly demanding of it. He would thus grow more impatient of players who tended to boil over in rage, like Ben Chapman and pitcher Johnny Allen. Their uncontrollable tempers, he felt, not only held down the level of their own play but affected the whole team, too.[8]

After their runaway at the beginning of the season, the games with the Senators brought the Yankees down to earth. After the early winning streak, the Yankees played .500 ball into mid–May. By the end of May, as Connie Mack had predicted, the Senators and the Yankees were the two leading teams in the league. It remained that way through the entire season. Being the same Yankees as in 1932, some of the team was showing signs of age. Detroit Manager Bucky Harris declared: "I cannot believe they are as good as they were a year ago." Combs and Sewell were approaching 35; Ruth was 38; and Pennock was 39. Pennock was hardly used, winning but seven games that year. Ruth, Sewell, and Combs were still playing every day, and in each case not up to the level at which they had once performed.

There was not much McCarthy could do at this point. He regularly sat Ruth down in the late innings, but the three were the best at their positions. "I've played percentage baseball all my life and shall continue to play it. ... This is the only sensible way to go about winning ... [and] most of the time I have been right ... the batting order was carefully arranged on a percentage basis, each in the position where he figures to be the most effective. Why should I tinker?" McCarthy did not tinker when the team soared in 1932, and he was not going to sound any alarms over any slumps in 1933. The percentages dictated that making any adjustments would likely make the situation worse.

One adjustment McCarthy did make during the season was to take himself in and out of the coach's box. Ideally, he preferred now to manage from the bench, but when the team play turned in any way ragged, he went back out. This reinforced what the league's teams already knew— the Yankees were not riding as high they had in 1932; they were beatable. They were certainly tough, but, as one New York paper lamented, they "seem to lack the 'fire' of old."[9]

The most obvious illustration of the Yankees' vulnerability was the fact that Babe Ruth was in decline. He was still *the* gate attraction, both at home and on the road, but his productivity was dropping. When McCarthy judged Ruth needed rest and sat him down, Ruth grew resentful. He was "spelled" in the late innings of many games, and he missed 15 full games as well. In 1933 he hit 34 home runs and batted .301. He had been the game's greatest player; now he was merely a very good player. In a *New York Daily News* poll taken in regard to the upcoming first baseball All-Star Game, scheduled for Chicago that July, Ruth was not the top vote-getter, even among outfielders. The top pick was Al Simmons of Chicago, the league's leading hitter. A *Daily News* cartoon depicted Babe Ruth holding a tiny little baseball bat over his big shoulder while reading a newspaper. On the baseball bat was the label "'33 Home Run Record." The newspaper Ruth was reading announced "President Roosevelt pleas for armament reductions." The cartoon's caption said "I'm with you FDR!!" The images that had made Ruth famous and infamous in the 1920s were somehow less resonating in new economic circumstances. The diminished level of Ruth's performances was not there to back up the old swagger any more.

The Yankees still treated Ruth specially. They let him travel with his wife. The couple stayed in a separate hotel suite, and took their meals in their room. Ruth entertained visitors wearing silk pajamas and green satin slippers, holding forth to his guests while drinking and smoking a cigar. It was all very grand, but now just a trifle pathetic. In April, six orphans from New Jersey had helped avert a train wreck when they waved down a train heading towards one stalled on the tracks ahead. In May, Ruth brought them to Yankee Stadium as his guests. Ruth brazenly promised them he would hit two home runs for them that day. He went hitless, and the Yankees lost to the Browns. When an athlete can showboat and back it up with his play, the results are grand, as they defeat the opposition mentally as well as physically. When a showboating athlete's skills start to deteriorate, his brazen antics can backfire. The opposition is often awakened to play better as well, and his teammates can readily be diverted from their proper focus.

Ruppert and Barrow had always sought to accommodate Ruth. They knew it was good business. Now they were going to have to face the inevitable fact of his aging. They may have entertained a naive hope that Ruth would pull back gracefully, but, understanding his nature, they knew that was unlikely. For the moment, the Yankees' management thought it best to let the matter rest. McCarthy knew that he could only make the best of the situation. Ruth grew ever more resentful at McCarthy for the times he sat him down. When Ruth played well when McCarthy put him back in the lineup, it showed McCarthy that Ruth could play well if intelligently rested. To Ruth, a good performance showed that he should not have been benched in the first place. Ruth mouthed off to reporters, including Dan Daniel and Frank Graham, both of whom liked McCarthy. Ruth asked them if they thought McCarthy was a good manager. They said yes. Ruth then fumed: "Well I don't. I think if we had a good manager we'd win this year." Reminded of his own slow play, Ruth yelled even more: "I don't care. I still say he's a lousy manager. If you can't see what's going on around here and see how he's f_____ everything up, I don't know what the hell you've been looking at." All this obviously added to the tensions over Ruth's aspirations to manage, although it certainly did not move Ruppert or Barrow one iota. Meanwhile,

McCarthy would never confide any frustrations to his players here, and he certainly would not do so to the press. Unless he wanted to quit, he simply had to bear it. And that is exactly what he did. Later, as Ruth's McCarthy-or-me fuming continued, McCarthy did offer Ruppert his resignation. Ruppert refused him. "Don't worry," he counseled, "You're the manager." McCarthy never forgot such an act of loyalty.[10]

Whether it was Babe Ruth, the temper tantrums of Ben Chapman, or just the pressure of a tight pennant race, McCarthy himself showed signs that matters were getting to him. On June 10, amidst losing a doubleheader to the now more mediocre Philadelphia A's, McCarthy was thrown out of a game for the first time in the season. Four days later, Lou Gehrig protested a call at first. When he could get nowhere with the umpire, he threw his glove in the air in disgust and was ejected. This was highly unusual for Gehrig, but McCarthy had been trying to get Gehrig to be more demonstrative and assert more on-field leadership. When Gehrig was tossed, McCarthy started out onto the field, and he was immediately tossed. In addition to the game ejection, league President Harridge slapped McCarthy with a three-day suspension. The Yankees complained that managers had certainly protested calls a lot more vehemently than McCarthy and received nothing more than a game ejection. On May 31, when Lou Gehrig had hit a home run which Senators Manager Joe Cronin said was a foul ball, Cronin had yelled and screamed for fifteen minutes, yet there was no suspension. Perhaps McCarthy had yelled certain words to the umpires as he was stepping out of the dugout which the umpires reported to Harridge; perhaps it was the fact of two ejections in four days; in any case, Harridge's ruling stuck. It seemed an overreaction, but there was again nothing to do but bear it. In early June, the Yankees were six games up on Washington. On June 23, they were virtually tied. That day the Senators beat Chicago. The Yankees won the first of two in St. Louis. In the second game, with the Yankees up 4–2 in the eighth inning, St. Louis rallied for three runs, the third due to a bobble and throwing error by Lazzeri. The Yankees could not score in the ninth. St. Louis won. Washington took over first place, and, as one newspaper noted, the "furrow in McCarthy's brow deepened."[11]

The Yankees were in the pennant fight, but everyone knew they were vulnerable. Their offense was potent, but not as potent as it had been. This gave opposing pitchers greater confidence. Meanwhile, the Yankees' pitchers were not performing up to past standards. Herb Pennock and Wilcy Moore were old, but Lefty Gomez, Red Ruffing, and Johnny Allen had no such excuse. They were just not terribly effective. Gomez was regularly weakening in late innings. From May 28 to June 24, he had no complete games. Johnny Allen was continually losing his composure. In a game in Detroit, amidst 100-degree heat, Allen protested a bad call at second base. Rather than just yelling, Allen thumped the umpire with his shoulder. He was ejected, of course, and the league suspended him for five days. McCarthy did not comment on Allen. (How could he defend anyone actually striking an umpire?) Since McCarthy had just suffered a suspension, albeit of dubious validity, he knew better than to say anything anyway. But, as with Ben Chapman's fights in Washington, McCarthy was increasingly distressed with players who lost control of themselves. It was doing neither them nor the team any good.[12]

The Yankees finished a Western road trip in early July. They were a half game behind the Senators. On July 4, Washington came into Yankee Stadium for their usual holiday doubleheader. A crowd of 77,365 turned out for the game. After it was over, a *Daily News* sports headline simply sighed: "Oh Well." In the first game, with the Yankees up 5–2 in the eighth, Tony Lazzeri collided with Joe Sewell, letting a popup drop and a run score. Two wild pitches by Gomez helped Washington stage a two-run rally in the ninth inning to tie the game. Then they won it in the tenth. In the second game, Babe Ruth hit a home run that almost hit the right field roof, but no one else did anything; Washington won 3–1.

There was no return match in the series, for then the leagues broke for the first All-Star Game. Recently retired Giants Manager John McGraw led the National League. Connie Mack managed the American League, and he chose McCarthy and Yankee coach Art Fletcher to be his coaches. The game raised $58,000 to help former ball players left indigent by the depression. The American League won the game, and Ruth hit a home run. It was all good fun and for a noble purpose. But for McCarthy the pressing issue was how to regain momentum and catch Washington. He was "at his wits' end about the team's pitching." Ruffing and Gomez were down. Johnny Allen had been nagged by effects of the flu most of the season. Ruth was inconsistent, and complaining. And there were critical lapses in defensive play. "McCarthy," observed one reporter, "is not sleeping well."[13]

Considering Washington's good play, a frustrated Lou Gehrig fumed: "It can't keep up." In July the Yankees appeared to retake command. In one stretch New York ran off nine straight victories while the Senators seemed to prove Gehrig right, falling back with a mediocre stretch of three wins and seven losses. Then, however, the Yankee pitching began to stagger again. McCarthy tried bringing up some pitching talent from the minor leagues. Don Brennan and Charlie Devens started a few games in July, but they did not fare terribly well. A newspaperman listed Devens as "Ph.D., LLD, MA, and AOBE(Always Out Before the End)." For the rest of the month Washington and New York remained close, and the race was strictly a matter between them. On August 1 they were tied, with Philadelphia in third, fourteen games behind. If Franklin Roosevelt's New Deal was marking the beginning of Washington's challenge to New York as the center of political and economic power in the nation, the American League race showed a definite symbolism that summer.[14]

On August 4, the A's Lefty Grove blanked the Yankees 6–0. It was the first time McCarthy's Yankees had been shut out since August 2, 1931; 308 consecutive games with at least one run. This was a new record. The team had unfortunately grown conscious of the record. Just a few days earlier, McCarthy had commented that he "wished we didn't have that scoring record." With Grove's shutout, the pressure was off. The question then was if the Yankees could get some sort of streak going. They would find out soon, as two days later the Senators were due into New York for four games. The first two took place on a Monday afternoon doubleheader, August 7. The Yankees won both games, leaving them but one game behind. Yankee fans were anticipating their team finally rising to the top and driving to the pennant from there. Instead, Washington won the next two. The federal government's new National Recovery Administration had a motto: "We do our part," with companies that took part displaying the "Blue Eagle." After the losses to Washington, the *New York Daily News* ran a "letter" to President Roosevelt in which they told FDR that he "should let the Yankees wear Blue Eagles on their sleeves—[as] they are doing their part—to establish the World Series in Washington." Four days later, in another game in Washington, down 4–3 in the ninth, with Lazzeri on third and two outs, Dixie Walker stepped in as a pinch hitter. He stood there and "made a pretty statue of a man holding up a piece of wood." Strike one, strike two, strike three went his turn at bat. After the loss, Arndt Jorgens passed a baseball-style pinball game in the lobby of Washington's Shoreham Hotel and ruefully asked a reporter: "I wonder if we could win a game on that one." Morale was not good, and the only thing Babe Ruth was talking about was how McCarthy was not managing properly by taking him out of the lineup from time to time.[15]

That summer the Yankees just could not overhaul Washington. They headed off on another tour of the West. On route, they stopped in Pittsburgh for an exhibition and lost to the Pirates, 10–2. A boy trying to get to Pittsburgh to see Babe Ruth tried to jump on board a freight train outside the town of Oil City, near Franklin where McCarthy had played in 1907, and fell beneath the train and lost a leg. Such events, over and above their tragedy, seemed to show how nothing could fully come together for the Yankees that summer. Ruth, McCarthy, and the Yankees felt horrible about the accident, of course. When Babe Ruth learned of the tragedy, he sent the boy an autographed ball. Obviously it was not enough, but the point was: what could the Yankees do? The anguish was terrible.[16]

The first stop on the Western tour was St. Louis. There was an added bit of tension in this series, since the Browns had just hired a new manager on July 25—Rogers Hornsby. Hornsby and McCarthy had not spoken or shaken hands since the Cubs' change of managers in 1930. McCarthy and Hornsby treated the event as just another game. There were no words between them. The Yankees won the first game of the series. The next two outings marked Lou Gehrig equaling and then eclipsing the all-time consecutive games played record (1307). Meanwhile, St. Louis won both of the games. The second game was especially difficult, as the Yankees were up 6–5 in the ninth inning. Hornsby inserted himself into the game in the bottom of the ninth and hit a home run to tie the game, with the Browns winning in the tenth. Meanwhile, Washington swept a series in Chicago, and the *New York Sun* declared, "It becomes increasingly obvious the Yankees are not going to win the pennant." This sort of "quitter" journalism usually enraged McCarthy.

The next day it seemed the accumulation of the failures in the race with Washington, the games with Hornsby and the Browns, the news of the boy in Pennsylvania, Babe Ruth's issues, and the constant nagging of reporters all took their toll. At the hotel in St. Louis, the Yankees had to summon a doctor. Manager Joe McCarthy had taken ill. Papers variously said it was an attack of stomach colic and/or gall bladder trouble. It may have been one of those, but at the very least it was aggravated by the glasses of White Horse Scotch that McCarthy regularly drank. This problem would come and go with McCarthy, especially when the pressures of a tough season bore down on him. The doctors in St. Louis gave him a pain injection, and he missed the final game there. Art Fletcher managed in his absence. During the game Babe Ruth went down, hit by a pitch on the right ankle. While the Yankees were mired in all their troubles in St. Louis, Washington swept their series with Chicago. In two weeks their lead over the Yankees had grown from one game to nine. Several weeks later, the *New York Sun* concluded: the Yankees "fell out of the pennant race in St. Louis."[17]

For the rest of the Western tour, many fans applauded Babe Ruth as though he was retiring and making his final appearance before them. This only added to the sense of the season being over. Meanwhile, McCarthy was under orders to get as much rest as possible. He missed no more games, but the Yankees needed more of his leadership, and he was under medical orders to go easy. Johnny Allen had a row with Lou Gehrig. Rumors again flew that Lazzeri was to be traded. Arndt Jorgens and pitcher Russ Van Atta were out sick. McCarthy had recovered as the Yankees returned home on September 7, and over the next two weeks, he righted matters. The Yankees won thirteen of their next fifteen games. It was not enough to catch Washington, but it did restore some respect with the fans and press.

McCarthy made Washington earn their pennant. More important, he cut away the conflicts within the team. In an amazing feat, the Yankees defeated the Red Sox 6–5 on the final day of the season, with Babe Ruth playing the whole game — at pitcher! Fundamentally, no matter Ruth's complaints about not managing, McCarthy always respected Ruth because of his fanatical desire to win. McCarthy conceded: "Ruth was an institution according to himself, and I tried to treat him accordingly. I would have been silly to try to curb him in any way. Besides he was a great team player. ... One thing you could count on: [his] desire to win." He said this later, in hindsight. Even if he had said it at the time, Ruth would not have been mollified. He felt he deserved to manage the Yankees, and no other position was acceptable to him.[18]

Now that New York's taverns were again serving beer, talk of the Yankees was loud and long. Some were blaming McCarthy for "the Yankees flop" of 1933. One problem was a pitching staff of people who had each had bad years. Some said that McCarthy needed to relieve his pitchers more quickly. Another big problem was that some of his key players — Ruth, Sewell, Combs, Pennock — were simply getting old. McCarthy could not be expected to have any remedy for this. The issue of Babe Ruth's continuing disdain for McCarthy weighed on some. Here there could be no middle ground. To Ruth's supporters, the Babe deserved to manage, ever more since McCarthy did not win. To Ruth's detractors, his history of childish behavior was proof that he was not management material. This was ultimately a matter for Barrow and Ruppert. They were very much on McCarthy's side and believed he was doing the best possible job under tough circumstances. Still, the Ruth question was out there, and it could not be resolved quietly. Meanwhile, the Senators lost the World Series to the Giants. This was a bitter pill for Yankee fans, for it meant they had not merely the second best team in the league but the second best team in New York.

24

Second Place Joe

The same questions which had been plaguing McCarthy and the Yankees throughout the 1933 season were staring at them throughout the winter of 1933–34. Like the Depression, the Yankees' hopes for a rapid recovery had proven false. What could make the pitching come around? Besides Gehrig, who are going to be the starting infielders? What, if anything, should be done with Babe Ruth? Which outfielders should be kept in reserve? As spring training began in St. Petersburg, reporters continually nagged McCarthy with these questions. A few reporters had learned not to ask, but there were so many and such a turnover of new scribes that McCarthy could never fully get his point across with his general silence.

Of the issues McCarthy and the Yankees were facing that spring, the question of Babe Ruth was receiving the most public and journalistic attention. More than ever, he wanted to manage the Yankees. For McCarthy there was little to say. He expressed confidence that Ruth "will give 100 percent all the time," and he was totally sincere when he said this. Ruth had struggled with illness and injury during the 1933 season, and McCarthy had come to appreciate his toughness as well as his obvious, if ebbing, talents. But for McCarthy the situation was like the previous year's, simply a question of judging how much playing time and rest to give his aging star. The fact that there were going to be dozens of reporters asking him about every such decision he would make about Ruth was not going to have the slightest effect on the decisions themselves. Reporters scoured every nuance of every statement and situation, and they began to use their own preoccupation as a point of evidence — there must be a problem here, otherwise why would reporters be focusing on the matter? (Senator Joseph McCarthy would use the same such logic.)

The *New York World-Telegram*'s Tom Meany tried to settle the matter with common sense: It falls to McCarthy to "make the decision just when the Babe's 40-year old legs make his fielding such a liability that his powerful hitting will be offset"; meanwhile, there are the constant rumors that "Ruth is to take Joe's place as manager." That was pretty much the situation. But it was so easy, and it made such juicy journalism, to highlight the personal feud that was at work. To the degree there the matter was personal, it never affected any of McCarthy's managerial decisions. Ruth was hardly speaking to McCarthy. He tried to rally others into a clique who would also shun him. This was not easy to do. As a result, Ruth would not talk to some players he knew to be "with McCarthy," notably Gehrig. Were they in any sort of analogous situation, many reporters and fans would not have behaved with McCarthy's professionalism, and it was difficult for many to avoid projecting their own shortcomings into such a highly publicized situation. But McCarthy knew it best to ignore the Ruth "situation" as much as possible. Ruppert and Barrow understood fully. With no contract issue before them, they had little to say as well.[1]

One major change for the '34 Yankees was that Joe Sewell had retired. He had been McCarthy's regular third baseman for three years and had batted .282. Of hidden value, although not to McCarthy, was the fact that Sewell had struck out a grand total of 15 times in the three seasons. Sewell would not be easy to replace, but here McCarthy still had the many infield contenders—Lazzeri, Crosetti, Saltzgaver, Lary, plus two youngsters, Red Rolfe and Don Heffner. McCarthy focused on the basics, the same ones he always stressed in spring training. Drill the infielders on the mechanics of the double play. Bring the pitchers along slowly. Drill them on their fielding duties too. As he observed to one newspaperman: "There is no way of going into the records and finding out how many good pitchers had good defensive teams in back of them. I'll venture to say, however, that any pitcher with a good double-play combination and a fast outfield is twice as good as a pitcher with a wobbly defense." Rolfe and Heffner executed seven double plays in a string of five exhibition games. Heffner was not hitting, however, but Rolfe was—fourteen hits in eight games. If he earned a start, where would McCarthy put him? McCarthy decided to begin the season with Rolfe at shortstop (his position at both Dartmouth and Newark), Lazzeri at third base, and Heffner at second. Elsewhere it was the same lineup with Combs, Chapman, Ruth, Gehrig, and Dickey.[2]

McCarthy voiced optimism about Rolfe and Heffner—"Those boys can made a double play, and boy how that helps the pitchers!" Still, McCarthy was not overly enthusiastic in his most private thoughts about his new infielders. This was why, despite the efforts of some teams to make trades, notably Cleveland, McCarthy would deal away neither Lyn Lary nor Tony Lazzeri. It proved a wise choice, as he would eventually replace Heffner and bring back Lazzeri. McCarthy noticed that Heffner played a "deep" second base, on the edge of the outfield grass. This worked well on the sandy spring training diamonds in Florida and about the South, but McCarthy quickly realized that Heffner's tendency would not suit the American League's regular infields. As for Rolfe, McCarthy found that while he had great quickness and deft hands, Rolfe did not have the range he wanted at the position of shortstop, especially going to his left. As he had shown a few years before when he switched Ben Chapman to the outfield, McCarthy's deftness, his genius some said, came forth when he decided to make Rolfe a third baseman. While mulling over his infield, McCarthy was still faced with pitching troubles. Johnny Allen remained a problem with inconsistency and temper tantrums. Danny MacFayden also continued to disappoint. He even had a nickname, "Dismal Danny." Just two weeks into the season, McCarthy had to start juggling his lineup as well, as Red Rolfe went down with a leg injury. Over the season, McCarthy would be doing a lot of injury-driven lineup juggling.[3]

McCarthy was never one to make specific predictions about any season, but in April he did let one thought slip: "Detroit is going to be tough." Further dismembering his great, but expensive team, Connie Mack had sold catcher Mickey Cochrane to Detroit for $100,000. (He also dealt Jimmie Foxx and Lefty Grove to Boston. The A's would finish fifth that season.) Cochrane not only became the Tigers' new catcher, he was their manager. In addition to himself, Cochrane had Charlie Gehringer at second base, pitchers Tommy Bridges and Lynwood "Schoolboy" Rowe, and a young first baseman named Hank Greenberg. Greenberg was a native of the Bronx. He grew up a Yankee fan and had very much wanted to play for the Yankees. But he was a first baseman, and with Lou Gehrig a fixture playing every game, the Yankees could have no use for him. (Several years before, the same fate had befallen another possible Yankee first baseman. His name was Bill Terry, and he hit .401 for the Giants in 1930.)[4]

Through the first two months of the season, four teams vied for the league lead — New York, Detroit, Washington, and Cleveland. Rolfe had returned to the lineup, and by mid–May McCarthy had to trim the team roster. He could not option Lyn Lary to the minors, as another club could legally grab him for a mere waiver price, so on May 15 he traded Lary to Boston for another infielder, Fred Muller. Muller was optioned to Newark, and he never made it back to the majors. As in 1933, the Yankees were in the thick of the race, but they were not head and shoulders above the other contenders. There was no great Yankee mystique intimidating the opposition.[5]

The good news that spring was that Lefty Gomez appeared to have regained his earlier form. McCarthy had learned it wise on occasion to relieve him in the late innings, and Gomez responded with 26 wins. McCarthy had also learned to deal gingerly with Gomez. To say the least, Lefty Gomez had a quirky nature. He was a complete extrovert, seemingly without self-doubt or inhibition in his words and actions. Reporters nicknamed him "El Goofey," but McCarthy knew there was more to Gomez than that. Some managers, like Rogers Hornsby, have to be such complete martinets that they impose the same system on everyone. McCarthy was driven by no such ego needs. To squelch such a personality as Gomez's would affect his play. McCarthy knew it was best to adjust, and when someone can win 26 games in a season, even with relief after seven innings, it certainly made sense to try.

McCarthy allowed no smoking in the clubhouse (not for health reasons; players could smoke elsewhere, and McCarthy himself smoked cigars daily). The rule was part of McCarthy's desire to have players in the clubhouse focus on nothing but baseball. Gomez would regularly sneak out to the nearest phone booth. McCarthy caught him a few times, but he never fined him. When McCarthy once caught Gomez smoking in a phone booth in Boston's Fenway Park, whose short left-field wall was hellish for left-handed pitchers, Gomez pleaded that he was trying to acclimate himself to the dimensions of the Boston park. McCarthy sort of chuckled, then quickly ordered him back in the clubhouse. During games, Gomez would occasionally stand on the dugout step, turn away from the field, grab the top of the dugout and do pull-ups. The rest of the team would just shake their heads and smile until McCarthy yelled, "Gomez, get the hell out of the way!"

There was no sense of "teacher's pet" nor any resulting dissension. It was indicative of the depth of respect that the Yankees had developed for McCarthy that the ways he chose to bend his own rules were accepted as part of their manager's purview and wisdom. When the weak-hitting Gomez was once picked off at second base, McCarthy snarled at him, asking "Why?" "How should I know," replied Gomez, "never been there before." No other Yankee would dare talk that way to McCarthy.

The few times McCarthy was away, Gomez would instinctively push at the edges a bit more. In early June, 1934, for example, McCarthy had been ejected from a game in Boston, having once again employed his favorite term "fathead" when discussing his perception of an umpire's aptitude. It was the only ejection McCarthy sustained that season, but it earned him a three-day suspension and a $50 fine from league President Harridge, largely because he had not left the bench after the umpire ejected him. (He honestly thought the ump had just told him to go back to the dugout. Harridge was not impressed.) The next afternoon, Gomez pitched. Without McCarthy's presence, Gomez was more audacious pitching to Jimmie Foxx, and Foxx responded by belting two home runs. When Foxx came up late in the game, Gomez shook off several signs from Bill Dickey. Dickey then called time and went out to talk to Gomez. He asked Gomez what he wanted to throw, and Gomez said "Nothing; let's just wait and see if he gets a phone call." He would have never tried this with McCarthy on the bench. McCarthy chuckled at a rock Gomez kept in his locker on which it said: "Please turn me over," and on the other side said "Thank you." Once when a game was heading into the night and the Yankees were winning, Gomez came out to bat and handed the umpire a lantern. McCarthy was actually amused, ever more so when the umpire soon called the game on account of darkness.[6]

McCarthy was right about the Tigers' toughness that season. Cleveland and Washington faded from the race in June. (Washington fell all the way to seventh place.) In 1934, the pennant was strictly between New York and Detroit, and in June and July the two teams were pretty much stride for stride. For two tense months, one was never ahead of the other by more than two games. At the end of July, Detroit was up by one game. During these weeks, the Yankees sustained a bizarre quantity of injuries and illnesses. Ruth was bedridden several times, and he hurt his elbow in a collision with the fence. Bill Dickey played while suffering from the flu. Tony Lazzeri had a displaced cartilage in his right knee. Earle Combs went down for a week with a sprained ankle. Then on July 24 he was hurt again, this time badly. He had collided with the outfield wall in St. Louis while chasing a fly ball and suffered a concussion, a fractured skull, a facial fracture between his left eye and ear, injuries to both his knees, and a broken left collarbone. He was in a coma for a short time and was certainly done for the year, some suspected for good, although that turned out not to be the case.

Lou Gehrig fractured his big toe, was hit in the leg by a line drive, and suffered severe back spasms from lumbago. He kept playing, of course. (Gehrig actually missed a game in 1934, an exhibition game in New Haven on June 4. It was the only in-season exhibition game he ever missed.) With Gehrig banged up, McCarthy did do one thing to accommodate Gehrig's streak of consecutive games played. On July 14 in Detroit, McCarthy wrote Gehrig into the lineup starting the game leading off and playing shortstop. Jack Saltzgaver played first. Gehrig got a hit in his leadoff at bat, and McCarthy immediately put in a pinch runner. In the game the Yankees had an 11–8 lead going into the bottom of the ninth. Detroit rallied with four runs to win and retake first place. The next day, Gehrig was back in the lineup and hit three doubles and a single. There was no lack of heart on the Yankees that summer, but for many other body parts were just not up to the task. For Yankee haters, it was cause for a bit of a smirk. The Feds had caught up with John Dillinger that July, and the fates, it seemed, were nailing the damned Yankees too.[7]

In early and mid–August, the Yankees ran off ten wins in fourteen games, and they gained a grand total of a half a game on Detroit. As the Yankees then tailed off a bit, Detroit ran off a streak of their own —fourteen wins in a row from August 1 to 15.

The Yankees broke the Tigers' streak, but even with that victory, Detroit's lead by then was six games. Never one to whine, McCarthy did shake his head and blurt out to the *New York Sun* just after the Yankees snapped the Tigers' win streak: "They haven't run into a slump this season, and they haven't had any injuries." For McCarthy to talk like that shows he was feeling more than a bit of frustration. The Yankees kept the heat on Detroit. In mid–August they won fourteen of seventeen games. This time their spurt gained them one whole game. Then injuries hit again. Babe Ruth, Dixie Walker and Don Heffner were all down; more important, on August 23, Bill Dickey fractured a bone in his throwing hand, and he was lost for the season. McCarthy picked up Zack Taylor from Syracuse. Taylor was now thirty-five years old. McCarthy may have been hoping for a repeat of the pickup Taylor gave the Cubs in 1929 when Gabby Hartnett was out. It did not occur, although not for any lack of effort by Taylor. He just was not as effective as he had been when he was five years younger. McCarthy could have picked up Hack Wilson for the outfield. Brooklyn had released him on August 10, but McCarthy would not touch him. George Selkirk was finally able to come up to the big club from Newark, and he made the most of it, batting .313.

The Tigers were just too strong. Schoolboy Rowe won a league record sixteen games in a row. Greenberg and Gehringer were each hitting above .340, and, as McCarthy had moaned, they suffered no injuries. Later, amidst a cold Buffalo winter in 1938, McCarthy sat by his fire and remembered with a touch of anguish, "Detroit would never have beaten us out a few years ago if Dickey hadn't broken his finger."[8]

By early September some of the newspapers were already writing about how the Tigers would fare in the World Series, but McCarthy did his best to keep the pressure on. With all the injuries, he made adjustment after adjustment. Finally he settled on an infield with a healthy Lazzeri back as second base, Frankie Crosetti back at shortstop, and Red Rolfe moved over to third base. It seemed to work, although Rolfe had been hit in the face by a bad-hop grounder on his first play at third. He was discouraged; McCarthy was not. Then Babe Ruth got hurt again, and Selkirk went down briefly with a pulled thigh muscle. Still, on September 13th the Yankees were only three games behind the Tigers. Then they lost two in Cleveland, while Detroit beat Washington. New York then went into Detroit for a weekend series needing a sweep. They could only split the four games. Detroit had its first pennant in a quarter century. Then St. Louis beat them in the World Series.[9]

When the Yankees were playing on the road that September, fans again turned out as always to see Babe Ruth. This time people knew they were seeing him for the last time. On many occasions the Yankees' train was delayed as crowds compelled the engineer to stop in scores of the small towns between the major cities. Everyone loved Babe Ruth, but his career truly seemed over. Lazzeri later recalled: "I never knew [in 1934] when to go back for a short fly or when the Babe was going to make up his mind to come in after it. We were always getting mixed up in our signals." This was not the kind of baseball Joe McCarthy wanted. Ruth had missed the latter part of 100 contests in which he took part that year; he missed 29 full games as well.[10]

As Ruth sat on the bench more, the non-speaking friction between McCarthy and him only grew. Ruth batted but .288 that year, and his home run total dwindled to twenty-two. The player leadership of the team had clearly shifted to Lou Gehrig, who, despite his injuries and ailments played every day *and* led the league in batting, home runs, and RBI's. (Babe Ruth had never won the triple crown.) A spat between Ruth's wife and Gehrig's mother had caused a rift between the two, and no one could mediate it. Mrs. Ruth and Mrs. McCarthy were still not speaking either. Meanwhile, Mrs. McCarthy and Mrs. Gehrig were good friends. Had Ruth been a younger man, there might have been more of an impetus for someone to try to mend all matters. But everyone knew that 1934 was Ruth's last as a player with the Yankees.

The biggest trouble was that after the season Ruth expected to move from player to manager. As his playing had dropped off in 1933 and 1934, he had been more vocal about his expectation to manage. Here he ran into the most bitter of disappointments. Col. Ruppert and Ed Barrow were not going summarily to dump McCarthy, in whom they still had the greatest confidence. In early 1934, Ruppert had stated: "McCarthy is certain to run the Yankees through 1935, and if he proves that he deserves to continue on, he will remain the manager indefinitely." When asked if he had changed his estimation of Ruth's potential as a leader, Ruppert calmly responded: "My ideas on Ruth as a manager have not changed since 1930." In the early 1920s, one of Ruppert's biggest conflict with his former partner, Col. Huston, concerned pressures to fire Manager Miller Huggins. Ruppert stood by Huggins then, and the Yankees subsequent championships vindicated him. Now he felt in an analogous situation standing by McCarthy. McCarthy had offered to resign. Ruppert had refused him.[11]

Ruppert and Barrow understood Ruth's aspirations to manage and offered him the post as manager of their farm team in Newark. Ruth was insulted. He was a major leaguer and saw no reason to be expected to step down in such an undignified manner. Ruth was still of the school, the very one that McCarthy had challenged when he first signed with the Cubs, that believed managers should come from the ranks of the best players. McCarthy disproved that, certainly not to everybody, but to many bright baseball people, including Ruppert and Barrow, and at this juncture their views were the only ones that counted. Ruppert held out the Newark offer; Ruth would not take it. So in February, 1935, Col. Ruppert dealt Babe Ruth over to the National League Boston Braves, then commonly called the "Bees." "I wish Ruth all possible luck," waved McCarthy, pointedly adding, "and that is all I will say about the deal."

Ruth may have had the opportunity to manage the Tigers, but after the 1934 season he elected to travel and play exhibitions in Hawaii, leaving him unavailable to any owner. Detroit's Frank Navin wanted to negotiate with him, but at that point Ruth only wanted to manage the Yankees. Given McCarthy's eventual success, history vindicates Ruppert and Barrow's decision not to switch to Ruth. If there was an unfairness in Ruth's never managing, it lies less with McCarthy not being fired and more in the fact that no other team ever gave him a chance, neither then nor even later.

The Boston B's hinted to Ruth that they might make him their manager, but they were intentionally deceiving him. Their sole interest lay in the gate he would bring. Certainly there were concerns as to how well Ruth could handle situations involving personnel issues, defensive shifts, the calling of bunts, hit and runs, and other plays. But certainly Ruth's enormous contributions to the game — he saved it from possible death after the 1919 World Series scandal — earned him a chance, and the matter of how his presence could sell tickets adds further to the point that the game's clique of owners treated him (as well as their own wallets) unfairly. McCarthy could not be blamed for any of this, however. If Ruppert and Barrow had wanted Ruth, McCarthy would have been gone immediately. McCarthy was well aware of the pressures on Ruppert and Barrow, and he would never forget their loyalty to him.[12]

The sale of Ruth caused no dissension among the Yankees. By 1933–34 he had few real friends left. All Ruth's Yankee followers in his after-hours life were long gone. Joe McCarthy had long won the respect of all, even from the veterans who had played with Ruth in the Huggins era. Now the press would have to find another utensil with which to stir the pot. None would have such an impact as had the Babe Ruth controversy, but as long as the Yankees were not winning pennants they would find something about which to complain. After falling just short in three of four seasons, newsmen began to hang McCarthy with the nickname "Second Place Joe." McCarthy never complained, although he did not like it one bit. There was only one way to get past that name, and everyone knew what it was. Until then, the name would not go away. There would be only one nickname that McCarthy would ever loathe more.

On the train down to St. Petersburg in February of 1935, McCarthy called some reporters into his compartment. He said to them: "Come on in 'fellers,' and meet the new manager of the Yankees." (The only other person in the compartment was Babe — Mrs. McCarthy.) That was the only comment McCarthy ever made that year in regard to the absence of Babe Ruth. Some writers still touched upon the issue at the outset of training camp — "at last he is the undisputed boss of the club"; McCarthy is "easier in mind than at any time since taking over." As usual, McCarthy was all business at camp. But the Ruth issue lingered, especially since Ruth's new team, the Boston Braves, happened also to be training in St. Petersburg. Not one player on the Yankees went out to meet Ruth's train when he arrived in Florida. It was not a snub done out of fear of McCarthy, nor did it really indicate any deep resentments at Ruth. It was simply that the 1935 Yankees wanted to get on with the business at hand. Ben Chapman did note that Ruth's departure "sorta puts Joe on the spot this year. Well," he concluded, "we've just got to go out and win for Joe."

The Yankees played some exhibition games against the Braves, and the players were intent on treating them as practice games like any others. The Ruth issue was more a media concern than a players' matter. Ruth was upbeat. He predicted he would hit fifty home runs with Boston. As for no longer being with the Yankees he said: "I'm sure I'm going to miss those fans in the right field bleachers in Yankee

Stadium. Tell Bill Dickey, the two wops [Crosetti and Lazzeri], and the rest that I'll be reading the daily box scores and pulling for them." One New York State Assemblyman, James Stephens of Harlem, did introduce a bill officially expressing "deep regret" at the Yankees' loss of Babe Ruth. It never came to a vote. Ruth played miserably with the Braves, although one Sunday afternoon in Pittsburgh that May, he hit three home runs in one game. On June 2 he retired. The Yankees would not hire him to manage, nor did any other team — ever.[13]

There may have been some sentimental regret over Ruth's departure, but in 1935 no one in New York missed the Babe Ruth of 1934. Writers noted a new peppery spirit on the Yankees. With Red Rolfe, Dixie Walker, Myril Hoag, George Selkirk, Ben Chapman, and rookie Jesse Hill, the Yankees had a great deal of speed. With the new youth, and with Ruth gone, there was a sense of a page now fully turned. McCarthy seemed to have resolved the infield questions which had occupied so much attention in past years. The combination at which he arrived in late 1934 — Gehrig, Lazzeri, Crosetti, and Rolfe — seemed to work, and he determined to stick with it. In the outfield, Ben Chapman was a fixture. George Selkirk, having labored in the minors so long, earned a starting role in Ruth's old position. McCarthy even had him wear Ruth's #3. (There was no such thing as retiring numbers back then.) Perhaps sensing the concern about the departure of Ruth, McCarthy was unusually effusive in his praise of Selkirk: "He has shown me everything — punch, speed, defensive strength, enthusiasm. ... I am going to give him every opportunity to prove he deserves to be out there every day." The only outfield question was whether Earle Combs had recovered from the broken bones he incurred when he struck the St. Louis outfield wall the previous July. Revealing of the level of sentiment McCarthy brought to much of his decision making, that spring McCarthy had refused to re-sign Combs, his protege from Louisville, until he proved he still had some of his old form.[14]

Pitching would prove the chief question for McCarthy. He always fretted about pitching — their training, their health, their fielding, their rest, their knowledge of opposing hitters, their techniques; everything was crucial. Perhaps more than any other manager, McCarthy knew how to spot a pitching prospect. Unlike many, he knew to look beyond the mere matter of speed. One rookie in 1935, for example, Clifford Melton, was as fast as anyone on the team. He had done well with the Baltimore Orioles, so the Yankees decided to invite him to training camp. McCarthy cut him, concluding to a reporter: "What good is a fast ball, no matter how fast, if it's straight as a string? It's got to have something on it, like a hop, or it must do something like sail or sink. You can't fool batters in this league with just speed." Melton never forgave McCarthy for that, and he would later have a chance at revenge.

Perhaps most important of all matters to McCarthy within the complexity of pitching were the psychological issues. McCarthy had as good feel for this as any manager. By not over-disciplining, he could even get the most out of Lefty Gomez. Most others were kept on a short leash. But, as he had once mentioned with a sigh, "anybody who thinks he understands pitchers and women is a sucker!" Pitchers were fundamentally a puzzle to such a precise baseball mind as Joe McCarthy's. There was one pitcher written up that spring in the *New York Daily News*. His speed, they said, "is like Dizzy Dean, except he is faster, [and] his curve is like Carl Hubbell's, only more so." The pitcher's name was Leroy Robert "Satchel" Paige. If McCarthy had any leanings to hire African American talent, he never commented one way or the other. If he ever did wish to move positively here, Ruppert and Barrow would have nullified him. (And even if they were willing, Commissioner Landis would have squelched the effort and denied his ever doing so.)[15]

After losing two exhibitions to the Boston Braves, the Yankees beat them on March 19. Upon returning to the Yankees Hotel in St. Petersburg, McCarthy received word that his mother, Susan McCarthy, had died at the age of seventy-nine. McCarthy left immediately. Art Fletcher ran practices in his absences. The death of his mother was not easy for McCarthy, since she was the only parent he ever knew. Joe McCarthy had always been one to keep his own counsel. With his mother gone, this would only deepen. McCarthy returned to camp four days later. People offered condolences. McCarthy nodded, accepted, and conveyed one simple message in return: thank you, now let's get back to work.[16]

As opening day approached, McCarthy was right to the point. "Detroit is the team for us to beat." To another paper he commented, "barring injuries and unforseen bad breaks, we have the best team we have had in years." He predicted the Yankees should win the pennant. Selkirk had hit .348 in the spring and earned his spot in the starting lineup. Dixie Walker was praising McCarthy for turning him into more of a pull hitter, making him more effective against left handers. Ben Chapman also said that McCarthy's converting him into an outfielder saved his career. McCarthy, he said, "has been the chief figure in such success as I have had in the American League."

McCarthy broke a long-standing tradition on the Yankees that had gone back to 1922. Babe Ruth had been the team captain in 1922. One day that season, Ruth had run into the stands after a taunter. Miller Huggins had fined him and then deposed him as captain. Since then, there had never been a Yankee captain. With Ruth gone, McCarthy wished to emphasize the notion of a page turned, and he had the players elect a captain. They chose Lou Gehrig. Gehrig was the perfect player for Joe McCarthy. Before, McCarthy had had to give Babe Ruth leeway in regard to such matters as sleeping and breakfast hours. He knew he had to yield, as enforcement efforts would cause even more commotion. Now his #1 player was one who gladly conformed to all the rules, so he could demand complete conformity from the rest. He did, and he got it. It was all part of a new way that was impressing everyone about a team intent upon moving ahead. From then on, McCarthy demanded total team discipline. He also showed extreme displeasure when anyone on the team made a mere positive comment about Babe Ruth. The pursuit of discipline, Tommy Henrich later noted, "created an air of professionalism we brought to our clubhouse, our train rides, our hotel stays, and everything else we did as New York Yankees. And it's why we won." When the Yankees won ten straight preseason contests in April, everyone knew the "new" signs could indeed be more than just window dressing.[17]

The opening weeks of 1934 had gone very well, but despite a successful preseason, the opening of 1935 was not easy for McCarthy and the Yankees. That April, some players inexplicably fell into anemic hitting slumps. Earle Combs was hitting .066. Jesse Hill and Myril Hoag each batted .200. Hoag was caught stealing several times, and McCarthy told him to stop attempting. "Why," complained Hoag,

"Crosetti does it." "Crosetti makes it," McCarthy icily replied. Ben Chapman's batting average was so pathetic (.121) it prompted one reporter to crack: "Let Gomez hit for him." (Gomez was a notoriously weak hitter, even by pitchers' standards.) Several pitchers were sick, including Ruffing and Gomez, and George Selkirk seemed to fall flat before the fans in Yankee Stadium. McCarthy tried to treat Selkirk's problem straight away: "You are letting that 'Ruth's successor' and that number '3' on your back get the best of you," he told him. Years later, McCarthy acknowledged, "taking over Ruth's No. 3 and his old spot in right field, ... no player ever had a tougher assignment." McCarthy offered to change Selkirk's number. Selkirk said no, so McCarthy just urged him bluntly: "You will never be a star player as the Babe was, so get down to business." The day after his conversation with McCarthy, Selkirk hit a single and a home run against the Red Sox. McCarthy could not solve the other problems on the Yankees quite so quickly, but the team began to pick up, winning six straight in late April, early May.[18]

At the end of April, just as the team seemed to settle, McCarthy encountered some troubles of his own. At the very time he was snapping Selkirk out of his doldrums in Boston, McCarthy caught a bad cold. He thought little of it and continued to manage and coach third base. In those weeks, the spring weather in Boston, Philadelphia, and New York was especially cold and damp. Exposed to such conditions, McCarthy's cold worsened. He stopped coaching on April 29th, and managed from the bench wrapped in a windbreaker. That night he was quite feverish. The next morning, Mrs. McCarthy summoned two doctors to their Hotel Croyden residence. It was serious; McCarthy's temperature had reached 104 degrees. Reports of his condition varied between pneumonia and influenza, some said it was aggravated by a gall bladder condition. In any case it was not just a drinking issue, and in an era before penicillin and other antibiotics such illnesses could be very serious. While McCarthy was a difficult patient to keep at rest, between the urgings of Mrs. McCarthy, Ed Barrow, and his doctors, he stayed indoors for nearly two weeks. When the Cubs came to New York to play the Giants at that moment, a number of the players went to the Croyden to see McCarthy. He was particularly feverish that evening, and some of the Cubs feared the worst. They wanted to sit up the night in the Croyden lobby, but Mrs. McCarthy sent them away. Joe wanted to be sure they faced the Giants the next day with a good night's rest. The players left, at least knowing that McCarthy's spirit was still strong. The Yankees went 3 and 6 during McCarthy's absence. He returned on May 16, and the Yankees won twelve of their next fourteen games.[19]

With a doubleheader victory over Washington on May 30, the Yankees took over first place. Not one player in the regular lineup was hitting above .300. But McCarthy was juggling his regulars and his bench quite effectively. With the Yankees somehow sustaining first place, the *Daily News* referred to the Yankees as "Hitless Wonders!" No one was wondering who was responsible for the victories. In one of the victories over Washington, reserve catcher Arndt Jorgens felt he had tagged a runner on a close play. When the umpire yelled "safe!" Jorgens leapt up and, in his anger, made contact with the umpire. The umpire ejected Jorgens immediately, of course. McCarthy ran out and began taunting the umpire. "You didn't put him out of the game, did ya? ... All he did was give you a little push—like that." And he tapped the umpire! Then McCarthy tapped him again, repeating his point: "That's all he did." The umpire was none other than Bill McGowan, the man McCarthy had saved from the rioting fans during the Louisville-Baltimore series of 1921. McCarthy knew he could get away with such little antics with McGowan, up to a point anyway. McGowan recalled: "I realized I should have chased him the first time. So chin-to-chin we started walking back to the Yankee dugout. We were talking plenty fast and using not a living-room word in the crop. 'Go on, show me once more what the kid did,'" McGowan challenged. McCarthy did not oblige. He returned to the bench with a big grin on his face. He wanted to turn the loss of Jorgens into something that would make the team smile a bit and keep them on a winning track. It worked. McCarthy had a wonderful sixth sense as to just how far he could push a situation. He never overplayed his hand.[20]

Despite the light hitting, the Yankees held onto first place through June and into July. In July, conscious of Babe Ruth's recent retirement from the Braves, Col. Ruppert signed McCarthy for two more years. McCarthy expressed thanks then turned immediately to the issue of the pennant race. It was a good tactic from both McCarthy and Ruppert. Had Ruth yelled at this juncture, he would have looked like a self-serving crybaby. As for the pennant fight, McCarthy emphasized all along that Detroit had "the pitching, the hitting, and the fielding" and would be the team to beat. As usual, McCarthy was right. In late June, Bill Dickey went down after being hit on the right hand by a pitched ball and then beaned behind the right ear his next time up. He was out cold for five minutes. Batting helmets were just starting to be introduced. McCarthy was neutral about the matter, letting players make up their own minds about wearing them. In June, Detroit and New York rose ahead of the rest of the league. In early July, Detroit won twelve of thirteen to trail by a game and a half. As in 1934, the two then remained nip and tuck for several weeks. In the last two weeks of July, Detroit won nine of fourteen, including two of three over the Yankees. New York's record for those weeks was only four and nine. On July 27, Detroit took the lead and never gave it back.[21]

In 1934, an incredibly bad string of injuries had depleted the Yankees' strength. It was not quite so bad in 1935, although Gehrig had a bad back (lumbago) which continually plagued him and Crosetti tore a ligament in his left knee that would require surgery in the off season. In late August, Earle Combs again injured his shoulder and collarbone. He was again out for the season. This time, as it turned out, it was the end of his career. Beyond these injuries, the key was that many players simply had poor years. Only Gehrig and Selkirk hit above .300. Ruffing was the team's best pitcher with all of sixteen wins. Gomez victory total had dropped from twenty-six to twelve. Gomez was a skinny fellow, and in 1934, while winning 26 he had often tired in late innings. So he thought some extra weight could increase his stamina, and he came to camp in 1935 fifteen pounds over his playing weight. No good came of it. Paradoxically, the extra pounds tired him out as the season dragged on. He won the All-Star Game on July 7 but won no more until August, during the very weeks when the Tigers took first place. His only victories after that came against second division clubs. (There were rumors that the Tigers had figured out how his preparations tipped off his various pitches.)

Other pitchers also proved disappointing. McCarthy had picked up Pat Malone, who had pitched for him with the Cubs. Col. Ruppert paid $15,000 for him. He had won 101 games in six seasons with Chicago. With New York in 1935 he won all of three, losing many key games with leads going into the late innings. One reporter pronounced Malone "a flop," and words like "corpse" were also creeping into various articles about the Yankees after Detroit started to pull away. After a hard loss to Detroit, the *Daily News* ran a cartoon, depicting a broken-down jalopy stuck in a ditch, marked "second place," with Joe McCarthy standing to the side, scratching his head, not knowing what to do.[22]

While Detroit did build up a six-game lead by mid–August, McCarthy would not permit his team to stop scrapping. Fights broke out in Detroit when Tony Lazzeri and Tigers' third baseman Marv Owen tangled after a collision at third base. Fans threw bottles and fruit. (Chapman and Selkirk threw it back at them.) The next time Owen batted, Gomez beaned him. This brought the police out to restore order. The game ended in a disheartening fashion for McCarthy. Tied in the tenth inning, Detroit loaded the bases with one out. There was a ground ball to Jack Saltzgaver at second base, and for some strange reason, he simply threw the runner out at first — no play at home, no double play. Detroit won. It further confirmed to McCarthy how hustling and intensity, taken beyond the point of control, is ultimately counterproductive to the team's focus. He wanted players who could draw that important line, yet never ease off. McCarthy was so concerned with such temper-induced mental lapses that seven years later he retold the story but erroneously blamed the infield error on Ben Chapman. It was indicative of how much he had come to believe that Chapman's uncontrollably bad temper was hurting the team. It also showed the play made him so mad that if affected his memory.[23]

Detroit continued to win, and there was not much the Yankees could do about it. Lefty Gomez and Bill Dickey developed an interesting idea. Privately they practiced a quick-pitch maneuver they wanted to use against Hank Greenberg. With two strikes, Dickey would call time. He and Gomez would then walk towards one another, pretend to have a brief conference, and walk back to their positions, having precisely rehearsed, measured, and counted the required steps and seconds. Their plan was to reach the mound and plate at exactly the same time, at which point Dickey would whirl around and Gomez would immediately throw a fastball and strike out Greenberg. Naturally, they did not dare trying this in a game without first checking with McCarthy. McCarthy listened to their idea and watched them rehearse it. Then he looked at them and asked: "Fine, but how are you going to get two strikes on Hank Greenberg?" McCarthy was not just being funny. He knew that having such a plan in mind could lead to a loss of focus and intensity beforehand, something that would be disastrous with such a hitter as Greenberg. Gomez and Dickey never tried to pull the stunt in a game.

McCarthy himself did pull one trick on Greenberg, however. In Detroit, McCarthy learned one day that the Tigers were having the visitors' clubhouse boy eavesdrop on the Yankee locker room conversations. McCarthy then intentionally called a meeting and loudly told the pitchers to throw knockdown pitches at Greenberg every time he was at bat. Greenberg admitted "I was nervous every time I stepped up there in that series."[24]

At the end of August, Detroit was nine games in front. McCarthy continued to press for team hustle. New York won nineteen of twenty-seven in September, and closed with a seven-game winning streak. They ended the season only three games behind, but it was not really that close. There were no miracles in the American League that September. Some wrote of parallels between the Yankees' hopes and the concurrent fate of the Ethiopian army against Mussolini. (The New York fans of Crosetti and Lazzeri did not care much for such allusions.) There were miracles in the National League, as McCarthy's old friends in Chicago ran off twenty-one wins in a row to nose out the Cardinals and the Giants for the pennant. (Detroit beat them in the World Series.)

For McCarthy it was another second-place finish. The damned nickname was sticking. He went to Col. Ruppert and voluntarily took a $7,500 pay cut. Before spring training the next winter, the *World-Telegram* ran a cartoon, "A Diet of Dust," depicting McCarthy standing in a whirl of dirt left by the pennant winners of the past years. Boston was improving with all the talent young Tom Yawkey was buying. Cleveland was looking better with veteran star Earl Averill and a young talent, Hal Trosky. Detroit would again be strong. It was obvious to any good baseball observer that McCarthy was a good enough manager to take any reasonably talented team and bring them into contention. But with such growing talent facing them, the question was whether the Yankees could come up with something or someone to put them up a notch. (Oh, how they would!)[25]

25

One Bounce, Not on the Fly

Throughout the 1935 season, particularly as the pennant was slipping into Detroit's hands, the New York papers often mentioned a young player out in San Francisco who the Yankees had signed and who everyone said was a sure thing for future stardom. His name was Joseph Paul DiMaggio. Many clubs had been interested in him, but in 1934 he had badly strained some ligaments in his left knee when hopping of a San Francisco bus. Despite this, the Yankees remained interested. Others did too, but DiMaggio went with the Yankees. With the San Francisco Seals of the Pacific Coast League he had previously set a record that has never been topped in professional baseball: he hit safely in 61 consecutive games. In the 1935 season he hit .398 and had thirty-five throwing assists from his right field post. DiMaggio later said he would have gotten more assists but for his arm getting sore in the late season amidst the cool San Francisco nights. In February of 1936, Frankie Crosetti and Tony Lazzeri met DiMaggio out in San Francisco, and together they drove across country to St. Petersburg. (After they had gotten on the road, Crosetti and Lazzeri learned that DiMaggio did not have a driver's license.)[1]

From the moment of his arrival in St. Petersburg, DiMaggio was under the close scrutiny of reporters, and of his teammates. McCarthy was also badgered with questions from reporters as to how he felt about the rookie and what adjustments he would have DiMaggio make in his hitting or fielding. McCarthy's response surprised all but the most thoughtful baseball people. "It would be dangerous," he noted, "and an injustice to the boy, to attempt to change him in any particular way. If, under the stress of American League competition, he indicates that he needs some alterations in style, there will be time enough then."

Good teachers know how to find and form talent. The very best also know, when working with the rarest of talent, the wisdom of not over-managing. McCarthy would not treat a typical player with such distance; indeed he freely altered players' batting stances and throwing habits. But with a few like DiMaggio, he knew it not best to tinker. Many other managers fail to make such fine distinctions. Rogers Hornsby's mishandling of Hack Wilson was such an example. DiMaggio himself recalled the particular way that McCarthy welcomed him and brought out the best in him and in the other rookies. McCarthy felt DiMaggio "was a little timid when he broke in." DiMaggio remembered that McCarthy had some methods all his own for making rookies feel at home, for taking the pressure off them. He acted on the theory that the only good ball players in the whole country were wearing his team's uniforms and that once players put on his club's uniform you automatically became a better ball player. Maybe this sounds like kid's stuff to a professional psychologist, but all I know is that it worked. ... You'd be surprised by the lift a rookie gets from the McCarthy treatment. It impressed you right off the bat that you're a professional now; you're in the majors and it's up to you to act like a Major Leaguer not only on the ball field but away from it. ... He stresses dignity, which may sound out of place among ball players, but which is definitely a morale lifter.

The sorts of pep-talk phrases that McCarthy uttered would indeed come across as mere banalities coming from most other managers and coaches. But as with other truly great coaches, and with such leaders in general, the nature of the example they set made the fact of the words coming from them resonate deeply among those who heard them. Such command of respect is anything but "kid's stuff," to a psychologist or anyone else. Soon after training camp had started, McCarthy announced that DiMaggio would be one of his starting outfielders. This took further pressure off the highly scrutinized rookie.[2]

Aside from DiMaggio's presence, several other issues lay before the Yankees that spring. McCarthy had traded pitcher Johnny Allen to the Cleveland Indians. Allen was a talented pitcher, but McCarthy had grown weary of his flaring temper. He felt Allen's uncontrollably quixotic nature not only held down his own performance but affected the team's play as well. For Allen, New York received two pitchers, Steve Sundra, who would amount to something but not for a few years, and Monte Pearson, who would win 19 that year with the Yankees. Fans and reporters were wary about the trading of such a talent as Allen, but McCarthy was supremely confident in his judgment of pitchers, and of all other baseball talent besides.

The other chief concerns for McCarthy and the Yankees that spring involved outfielder Ben Chapman and pitcher Red Ruffing. Each was holding out for more money and thus not training with the team until they signed. McCarthy was irritated about this. He intervened with Ed Barrow on behalf of Bill Dickey. Because of Dickey's 1935 injuries, Barrow wanted to cut his salary. McCarthy persuaded him to keep Dickey's salary the same. Otherwise, McCarthy did not involve himself directly in the year's contract and financial matters. With Ruffing and Chapman, who wanted actual raises, McCarthy was squarely with Barrow and pronounced to the press: "If you win a championship, increases are in order, but when a team finished second after having a good lead, hollering for salary rises is unreasonable." About Ruffing, McCarthy had other specific concerns. Some players come to camp ready to go. Others need the routines and specifics of training, and McCarthy felt Ruffing was one of the latter such players: "a man who needs an early start in training as badly as does Ruffing every year only bites off his nose to spite his face by hollering for the impossible and lingering on the sidelines." Chapman stayed home in Alabama and worked out on his own. Ruffing stayed in Illinois and worked out at a gym at the University of Chicago. Apparently he caught the eye of the baseball coach there. The coach made inquiries as to whether the young man could possibly play for Chicago. Apparently the coach's eye for talent was better than his recognition of faces.[3]

DiMaggio proved to be everything he was cracked up to be. His speed and outfield coverage were spectacular. He threw out tagging runners at home from deep center field. At the plate, swinging a 36-inch, 40-ounce bat, he hit .600 and knocked in seven runs in four exhibition games. Then on March 22, he was sliding into second in a game with the Boston Bees. The Bees' second baseman, Joe Coscarart, stepped on DiMaggio's left ankle. DiMaggio suffered a slight sprain, and the Yankees' trainer, Earle "Doc" Painter, prescribed treatment for the injured ankle with a Diathermic lamp. Diathermy was a form of heat treatment. In more recent decades, trainers have largely abandoned the use of any form of heat in the immediate treatment of sprains, but this was a different era. (Painter was also advising tepid salt water for indigestion and laxatives for players who claimed to be constipated from exercise.) In addition to heat not being a terribly good treatment for a sprain, Diathermic lamps pose an added danger of users burning themselves all too quite easily.

DiMaggio did just that. Holding his ankle under the lamp too long, he gave himself such a burn that he blistered his skin. Painter hypothesized that DiMaggio's high blood sugar made him sensitive to the lamp treatment. McCarthy was not mollified. A doctor lanced and drained the blisters. This is something else more recent medical practitioners are less willing to do, for the very reason of what then happened to DiMaggio—his surgical wounds soon became infected. As with McCarthy's bad cold of the previous spring, in an age before penicillin, such an infection could be serious. DiMaggio was ordered to a New York hospital for immediate treatment. McCarthy was none too happy with his trainer. He never involved himself in the specifics of injury treatment and always wanted any such matter he delegated to be handled with competence. When it was not, he had little patience. Some said he never regarded "Doc" Painter with the same trust thereafter.[4]

The spring training and the exhibition tour of the South gave McCarthy additional headaches that year. The spring of 1936 saw incessant rain in the South and East. Flooding was especially bad in many areas that March, most famously in Johnstown, Pa. but in many areas of the Appalachians besides. Many of the Yankees came down with colds. The tour of the South, lamented the *Daily News,* was nothing but "pneumonia, grits, and fried food." Everybody was either sick or sore. The weak spring performances did not pick up when Chapman and Ruffing finally signed, and the season began on a dispirited note. "Without the propelling force of Mr. Joe DiMaggio," wrote one reporter, "our Yankees are just another American League entry." The press was already attaching enormous attention to DiMaggio, even though he had yet to play in the regular season. McCarthy was still a bit worried about his star rookie being placed under such pressure.[5]

In late April, DiMaggio had yet to play, Lazzeri was hurt, and Chapman had come down with a case of pleurisy. The outfield play of Roy Johnson, Dixie Walker, and George Selkirk looked "ragged." Fans in the bleachers were free with their opinions. They were already upset about having to crowd into the right field cheap seats, as the club had closed the left field bleachers to make repairs. Other fans were also steamed that the window view of the Stadium field from the 161st Street Subway Stop had been painted over. With bad moods from many vantage points, winning was the obvious solution. The early weeks of the season brought out a lot of Bronx cheers, but not the kind McCarthy wanted. DiMaggio began to test his ankle and work out at the Stadium on April 24, and that afternoon the Yankees began a decent spurt, winning seven of eight, including three wins over Cleveland, one of which was over a revenge-minded Johnny Allen. McCarthy's Yankees were showing a collective mental strength, not letting any emotional pressures get to them. Ben Chapman also returned to the lineup during the upswing. Perhaps more importantly for the Yankees' chances that year, Detroit's Hank Greenberg suffered a broken wrist on April 29. He would be out for the season.[6]

DiMaggio was ready to play on May 3. The day before, McCarthy sold Dixie Walker to Chicago. With the trade, with the team winning, and with Greenberg's injury, it was as though the baseball world was opening the door of success for the rookie, with the full expectation that the young man would walk through with a real bang. With all the pressure on the young man, McCarthy strategically picked the St. Louis Browns and a starter named Elon Hogsett to be DiMaggio's first opponents. DiMaggio would not disappoint, and, as McCarthy would ultimately learn, DiMaggio did not need to start first against the lowly Browns. After his first game, the *Daily News* headlined "DiMaggio Smacks Three Hits in Debut." DiMaggio had indeed hit two singles and a triple, but the two singles were actually a bit lucky. His first single involved a mere ground ball to the pitcher, Hogsett. Frankie Crosetti was on third, and he feinted a dash for home. This unnerved Hogsett. He threw wildly, and DiMaggio easily made it to first. The second single was a popup that simply fell in between fielders. In the sixth inning, however, he stroked a legitimate triple off the center-field wall. Ben Chapman went four for four that day. Lou Gehrig went four for five and knocked in five runs, but New Yorkers seemed interested only in the play of one man.

McCarthy took DiMaggio aside to counsel him about dealing with all the press attention. He had seen it badly affect Lyn Lary when he first came to the Yankees, and McCarthy felt Lary never really recovered from headiness of all the attention. With DiMaggio, the attention was even greater. Phrases like "the successor to Babe Ruth" were pretty heady stuff indeed. Joe DiMaggio bluntly told McCarthy not to worry about it. He would not let it affect his focus on the game. In the next game DiMaggio went three for five, and this time all the hits were solid shots. McCarthy stopped worrying so much. He especially enjoyed his star rookie having such a day against the Browns, still managed as they were by Rogers Hornsby. The next day, in a 14–2 victory over Detroit, DiMaggio went two for four and was hit by a pitch. The *Daily News* was already running a special insert in its sports section—"At Bat with DiMaggio." McCarthy had no reason to be concerned. The day DiMaggio hit his first home run, Babe Ruth was at the game. Ruth came to the Yankee dressing room and greeted him with "Hello, Joe." Lefty Gomez was in shock. Ruth called veterans "Doctor" and all rookies "Kid." "You're the first guy," Gomez exclaimed, "I've ever heard him call by name."[7]

If people thought DiMaggio had made his mark with his bat in his first games against St. Louis, what he did in the game two days later against Detroit made all other feats pale in comparison. At bat DiMaggio was only one for four on the afternoon, and this lowered his batting average to a mere .474. Playing left field that day, he made seven putouts, and, said one paper, "no chance was easy," especially his shoestring catch of a liner off outfielder Pete Fox. But the big play came in the ninth inning. The Yankees were up 6–5. Pete Fox was on third base with none out. Fox was one of the fastest men in the league. Second baseman Charlie Gehringer stepped up and stroked the first pitch deep to left center. DiMaggio caught the ball less than fifteen feet from the wall, turned, and winged a perfect strike on the fly to Bill Dickey who tagged out the sliding Fox. After the double play, the next batter, Goose Goslin, grounded harmlessly to second base, ending the game. The fans were screaming at DiMaggio's play. With Goslin's groundout, the noise grew and grew, and by the time DiMaggio arrived at the dugout, fans had swarmed the field and the noise was deafening. As he entered the dugout, however, DiMaggio felt only silence. McCarthy was there, calmly waiting for him. He looked at DiMaggio in the eye for but a second and then calmly asked: "What are you trying to do Joe, show me how strong you are? You're supposed to throw the ball on one bounce to Dickey, not on the fly!"

McCarthy could not have been in greater earnest, and DiMaggio knew it. DiMaggio later said that he intended to bounce the throw but had miscalculated the distance, but he never told this to McCarthy. "It would have sounded like an alibi, and no manager wants to hear alibis." If McCarthy had learned that he need not worry about the press and fan adulation unbalancing DiMaggio, at that moment DiMaggio learned just how peripheral was the roar of the crowd to McCarthy. With players like DiMaggio on his team, there was a kind of baseball he wanted and upon which he would insist. This was one of McCarthy's knacks that separated him from so many excellent managers. Not only could he make a middling team stronger, when he had great talent, he knew how to maximize it. And a great player like DiMaggio knew how to respond with a new level of demands being placed upon him. He was ennobled, as he knew that he was playing for someone who could take him to a new plateau. The two now knew exactly what to expect of and appreciate in one another. With the spurt of winning just before DiMaggio's entry into the lineup, the Yankees had moved to half a game behind first-place Boston. On May 10, the day DiMaggio hit his first home run in a win over Philadelphia, the Yankees took first place. They never relinquished it, neither that season, nor in any meaningful way for the next four.[8]

During Babe Ruth's heyday with the Yankees, there could be a certain feeling of rivalry between players, especially if anyone seemed to be grabbing the limelight from the Babe. Gehrig's good press could bother Ruth. It was part of the tiff between Mrs. Ruth and Gehrig's mother that caused the two men not to speak. McCarthy hated this sort of friction, but he knew he had to wait for Ruth's star to fade before he could assert himself here fully. With DiMaggio dominating the newspapers, McCarthy discovered there was little he needed to do. Lou Gehrig was the obvious person to become jealous, but Gehrig was simply not the kind of person to vent any frustrations about a teammate's media attention. DiMaggio himself may have disliked others getting much press attention, but as a fresh rookie he was not going to say a thing. Later in his career he would show such concerns, but that may have then been a consequence of knowing and being a trifle depressed over the fact that his career was on the wane with age and ailments catching up with him. In his early days, DiMaggio never voiced anything negative about others' status with the fans and media. If he had, he certainly knew that he would earn the displeasure of McCarthy, and that was something he genuinely did not want to do.

DiMaggio never respected and liked any manager as he did Joe McCarthy. He praised McCarthy for simply wanting nothing but players giving their absolute best.[9] To many, that sounded like a bland cliche, but DiMaggio understood just how deeply McCarthy dug into a player and a team to fashion the composite of what "best" really meant. McCarthy's understanding and appreciation of the nature of his prize rookie also revealed itself in the road-trip roommate assignments. DiMaggio roomed with Lefty Gomez. He was the only man who could get away with needling Joe DiMaggio. Gomez was as extroverted and DiMaggio was withdrawn. To the extent that they both wanted glory was something they could accommodate in one another, as each respected the other's ability and recognized that they both put personal achievements beneath those of the team. And whenever there was a chance of that perspective being lost, there was the presence of McCarthy. After Gomez suffered a hard loss, DiMaggio sat with him on the train and tried to cheer him up, tweaking his nose and making sounds like a banjo. Gomez began to laugh. Then McCarthy came out and yelled at them, though only for a few seconds. They needed to let off a little steam, but McCarthy wanted them to keep more than a little inside too.[10]

The trade of Johnny Allen to Cleveland had been another step toward the kind of mature excellence that McCarthy wanted. Whenever he faced the Yankees in 1936, Allen would be keyed up. McCarthy did not want the Yankees to be keyed up especially for Allen. He wanted a level of consistency that held a higher level than the norm through the peaks and valleys that would come with the tempestuous emotions of someone like Allen. Ballplayers were often a cursing, snarling lot, and harnessing this was the key to many past managers' successes. John McGraw was famous for it. In the 1930s the "Gashouse Gang" St. Louis Cardinals had been highly successful with it. Even Connie Mack accepted it with various personalities he knew best to tolerate. What McCarthy was after had never really been envisioned, much less achieved.

On May 17, the Yankees faced and easily beat Johnny Allen and the Indians. But McCarthy sensed something afoot, and he did not like it. In the next game, with the team having apparently been so keyed up facing Allen and all his yelling, the Yankees played a mentally ragged game. They argued with the umpire on several occasions. (In one argument, the umpire was surrounded by Lazzeri, Crosetti, and DiMaggio. As they yelled at him, the ump said he felt like Haile Selassie encircled by Mussolini's troops in Ethiopia.) Ben Chapman got himself ejected for his bursts of temper. When DiMaggio took a throw in the ribs as he tried to break up a double play, the benches cleared. The Yankees won the game easily, but McCarthy was further confirmed as to the disutility of players losing their heads. With this in mind, on June 14 McCarthy made a key and controversial move. He traded Alabaman Ben Chapman to the Washington Senators.[11]

"They're all moonshiners back there in cornpone country," McCarthy exclaimed to Ed Barrow, "they are just naturally against the law. They seem to resent any kind of rules or discipline." McCarthy was indulging himself in a bit of hyperbole here. He had worked effectively with many Southern players. With the Cubs he had Mississippian Guy Bush and Alabaman Riggs Stephenson. Among his Yankees, Bill Dickey was from Arkansas. Johnny Allen and Ben Chapman were hotheads. There was no question about that, and McCarthy came to the conclusion that their personalities were on balance not helpful to his team. As a Northerner he may have easily seen the tone and accent in which they acted out their anger, but it was not the geography or accent that bothered him. Years later a fan asked him "Did you ever have trouble with a player, and how did you handle it? McCarthy's response: "Got rid of the player." The trade of Ben Chapman was not something McCarthy did in haste. If he had acted so, it would have been a contradiction in regard to the kind of team McCarthy wanted to forge into which he felt Chapman did not fit. "Chapman," said McCarthy, "should be the best player in baseball, but his temperament is all wrong." As many ball players acknowledged, one of McCarthy's true gifts was his ability to handle various temperaments and personalities. He had full faith in his own abilities here that when he could not handle someone, he knew it was best to trade him. He traded Johnny Allen, and as Tommy Henrich later reflected, "I don't think anybody was ever able to handle Allen." With Ben Chapman it was much the same. McCarthy felt, with both Allen and Chapman, that their tempers would always hold them back, and while both continued to play in the major leagues, neither had any terribly distinguished seasons after their years with the Yankees.[12]

In late May and early June, the Yankees opened a comfortable lead for themselves. A big problem loomed on May 26, however. On a play at the plate, Red Sox infielder Eric "Boob" McNair crashed into Bill Dickey with elbows up. Dickey had to be taken to a hospital with injuries to his kidney and spleen. He would be out for a month. If anything, the loss of Dickey may have prompted McCarthy to want to keep Chapman because of his batting, his speed, and his fighting nature. But McCarthy had more in mind. He had Joe Glenn, as well as Arndt Jorgens, to replace Dickey, and, as it worked out, according to one reporter: "Glenn performed so ably [that] Dickey isn't missed." In exchange for Chapman, the Yankees got Alvin "Jake" Powell. Chapman was probably a better player than Powell, although at that point Powell was having a better season. McCarthy had made inquiries about Powell during the previous winter. Chapman's spring holdout had not endeared himself to the Yankee management. His batting average in 1936 had fallen to .267, and, while having once let the league in stolen bases, he had stolen only one base all year, slowed as he was by a strained thigh muscle. But Chapman was an established talent and only 27 years old, so his lower production was something most managers could readily choose to ride out. Indeed such slumps in performance were not central to McCarthy's choice to trade him.

As with Johnny Allen, McCarthy's reasons centered on Chapman's nature. Many managers love players like Chapman, believing they ignite everyone else. With earlier Yankee teams, McCarthy may have felt the same way. But now he was developing a new team, one he believed could do some remarkable things. With Chapman as a Yankee ace in 1931, McCarthy terrorized the league with stolen-base, Ty Cobb-style baseball. It was Chapman who also had terrorized teams with his brawling. (Ironically, it was the Senators who were among his biggest enemies here.) McCarthy felt that Chapman's hot-headedness would ultimately get in his way, and, after five seasons, he felt sure of his sense that Chapman was not going to change. In 1936 McCarthy felt, on balance, he no longer needed the kinds of contributions a man like Chapman would make to a team. He was after a style of play from which a Chapman would detract. In his first week with the Yankees, Powell gave a teammate a hot foot. McCarthy took him aside: "You're with the Yankees now. We don't do those things."[13]

As for who would then play center field now that Chapman was gone, that was easy — Joe DiMaggio. Yankee Stadium's left field was a difficult sun field for DiMaggio; besides, he had the anticipation and the speed to chase down flies in center field better than Chapman. McCarthy later recalled that DiMaggio "never would have become the great outfielder he was if I hadn't moved him. He needed that room to roam in Yankee Stadium. That's the toughest center field in baseball, and only the really great ones can play out there." Meanwhile, with Selkirk and now Powell, plus Myril Hoag and Roy Johnson as outfield reserves, McCarthy believed the Yankees would not skip a beat. He was right, and two days after the Chapman trade Bill Dickey was back as well.[14]

The Yankees were never seriously challenged that summer. One young pitcher for the Indians, Denny Galehouse, pitched several strong games against them. McCarthy was impressed. In August, Cleveland brought up another young pitcher, Bob Feller. McCarthy was impressed with him too. But that summer, the Yankees were simply overpowering. By July, the team's batting average was .310 (against a league average at that point of .289), and they led the league in home runs and every other offensive category. Aside from Dickey's hospitalization in May and early June, there were no such major injuries as had incapacitated the team in previous years. In an exhibition game that summer against Pittsburgh (inter-league play was rare, but if it was mutually convenient both sides were certainly willing to make extra money), former Yankee pitcher Waite Hoyt pitched for the Pirates. Asked to size up these new Yankees, Hoyt opined "the trouble with the Yankees is [that] there aren't enough real Yankees on the team."

Hoyt had played with Babe Ruth in the halcyon days of the late 1920s. The Yankees of 1936 were indeed a different sort of team than the Yankees that Hoyt fondly remembered. To the present day, every great Yankee team has had to endure comparisons with the 1927 squad. When baseball experts are asked to name the greatest team of all time, the '27 Yankees always enter the discussion. For Hoyt, so soon after 1927, and with none of the eight Yankee teams since then ever measuring up, including '32, it was easy to brush off any notions of the 1936 squad rivaling the '27. As with all the comparisons of boxers of different eras, such debates can never be resolved, but the team McCarthy put together in 1936 has since been compared to the '27 squad. The '27 team set the stage for two straight championships. The '36 Yankees were the first of four championships in a row, and the first of seven pennants in eight years. Hoyt was still looking at the Babe Ruth model — the hard drinking, hard driving gang that bowled over everyone, and did it laughing and fighting. McCarthy's best teams did not get into fights, even though they would if they had to. And they did not so much laugh at their opponents as sneer.[15]

Before the '36 season began, columnist Dan Daniel of the *World-Telegram* had declared that a missing ingredient from the Yankees was "a Holler Guy." Some writers had noted this alleged deficiency ever since Babe Ruth left. Without Ruth, wrote one, the Yankees "were as exciting as watching a master plumber tighten a joint." Dan Daniel noted that pitcher Johnny Allen had been such a "holler" person. The question in Daniel's mind was who was going to take up that important role.

McCarthy had an answer — no one. No good manager can envision such a team in the abstract and then expect his players immediately to conform to his vision. McCarthy could only develop such a sense of what the Yankees could attain after he had taken years to understand the personnel he had and take them through the various levels of attainment of which they were capable. He had shown the major leagues various things he could do — take a bad team like the Cubs and make it a winner; handle tough personalities from Hack Wilson to Babe Ruth to Lefty Gomez; use the speed of a Ben Chapman, discover and develop great talent. Now he had great personnel, and he would do more with them than others similarly blessed had ever done. McCarthy had trained to be a plumber, and he was often drawn to the kind of work that was boring but highly dependable. Some journalists and fans may have felt that the Depression era called for excitement as an escape from the harshness of the times. McCarthy's Yankees would prove to be not so much an escape as an exemplification of how to succeed, be it in depressed or in prosperous times. For some, even though it did not provide as exciting a release from day-to-day woes as other more quixotic outfits like St. Louis's Gas House Gang, McCarthy's formula would be quite ennobling. His success over the next years would be unprecedented.[16]

McCarthy in command. When Joe McCarthy managed a team there was only one person in charge, and everyone knew it. (National Baseball Hall of Fame Library, Cooperstown, N.Y.)

The Yankees not only won the pennant that season, they clinched it on the earliest date ever — September 9. Col. Ruppert was still nervous about the season all the way up to the date of clinching. McCarthy shared some of Ruppert's sensibilities. Through late August, reporters joked that McCarthy was actually willing to predict that the Yankees would likely finish in the first division. It was an instinctive cautiousness that made for a wonderful owner/ manager relationship, and Ed Barrow blended perfectly with the mix as well. After the pennant was secured McCarthy admitted to the players: "As soon as I sized up the squad at St. Petersburg, I knew we had the flag." Here he may have been trying to deflate some of the exu-

berance over the pennant and keep the team hopping for the World Series, something he may have felt he could have done better in 1929. To this end, he also wrote
an article in *Liberty Magazine*, frankly predicting the Yankees would win the World
Series.[17] He did not want his Yankees to come to the Series merely "happy to be there."
Such careful planning by the Yankee management was a perfect symbol in the Depression era of how success can indeed come, not despite but because of an ever-present
concern for the worst that could happen. Col. Ruppert and Manager McCarthy were
acting no differently about the '36 pennant than President Roosevelt was about the
'36 election, although predicting victory was not the right method in politics. But
no leader can really relax with his colleagues until the results were final. The Yankees' final margin in the pennant race was nineteen and one half games over second
place Detroit. In that era, no margin of comfort could be too great. Lou Gehrig was
the league's Most Valuable Player. DiMaggio was the league's top rookie. McCarthy
had shown a deft touch with the pitching. Ruffing did win twenty. The key, however,
was that he had no single ace but seven pitchers who combined for 99 wins. He developed a number of dependable arms, thus giving him the means of using pitchers of
one strength or another against particular teams, batters, and situations. He could
also make sure his many pitchers could each get necessary rest.

The World Series of 1936 was especially enticing to Yankee fans that fall. For
one thing, the Yankees had regained ascendency in the American League and could
now prove they were better than the National League winner, a matter which had
added importance in that the National League had won that summer's All-Star Game,
a contest in which Joe DiMaggio did not play very well. The additional factor concerned the Yankees opponent that fall — the Giants. This was the first time since 1923
that two New York teams played for the title. The excitement here may have riled,
or bored, many other parts of the baseball world, but it lent an element of vicarious
reassurance to many, especially in New York. The era of the Great Depression
unhinged so many elements of faith, economic and otherwise, in the nation. Part of
the struggle during President Roosevelt's New Deal, beyond the actual efforts at economic recovery, involved the attempt to convince people that solutions could work
and that life's traditions could rebound. For New Yorkers, the Yankees' return to
greatness was a most positive message. It had come with a mix of some components
of past grandeur plus many new elements, drawn significantly from all rungs of society. The fact that the Series was to be decided strictly within New York also served
to demonstrate that the city had not lost its dominance. New York had obviously
maintained three major league teams in these years, but the seasons since 1929 had
shown but spotty dominance indicating a loss of status. Efforts at economic revital-
ization, much like the building of the Empire State Building — an ambitious project
which gave the city a great structure left grossly underutilized for a full decade — had
not borne many results. The success of the Yankees and Giants in 1936 conveyed the
sense of the reestablishment of an old order. In the fall of 1936, all was hardly right
with the world, but in the semi-illusions of politics the imminent reelection of FDR
by overwhelming landslide lent a sense that the nation had fully come together under
a genial leader. In fantasies that surround the world of sports, the sense that all things
had come back to their proper place marked a similar emphasis that things were getting back to normal, here as well under another commanding but fatherly figure. For

Yankee fans there was then one added hope — that a victory over the Giants would provide the final exclamation point on a happy proclamation.

Game One of the Series was a simple matter really. The Giants' ace pitcher, Carl Hubbell, had been mediocre in the early season, compiling a record of 10 and 6. Then he won his next 16 consecutive decisions and was a major force in the Giants' drive over St. Louis for the pennant. He continued his ways against the Yankees, besting Red Ruffing 6–1. The victory, of course, heartened the Giants and gave them room to chortle as to their apparently overrated opponents. McCarthy and the Yankees showed themselves not the slightest bit downcast, however. The usually modest Lou Gehrig laughed: "Oh, that's just one we gave 'em to make 'em feel good. You wouldn't want us to beat Hubbell and win four straight would you. He's a great fellow. I'm glad to see him win."

McCarthy noted that it had been raining in New York for several days, and hence "the first game was not a fair test for either club. Sooner or later," he said, "one team was going to be beaten by the mud and slime and it was our tough luck to have it happen to us." In regard to Hubbell, McCarthy acknowledged: "He's a great pitcher, no doubt about that. I'd say he's the best there is — but we had a great chance to lick him today. And we would have done it if we had gotten the breaks." The Yankees had hit Hubbell, but several key balls had gone right at a Giant fielder. After the game, indeed, McCarthy turned to Joe DiMaggio and lamented: "Tough luck, Joe. Every time you hit one on the nose it goes right at somebody." (In the eighth inning, with runners on first and third, DiMaggio hit a hard liner that happened to go straight to second baseman Burgess Whitehead and resulted in a double play and nearly a triple play.)

At one point in the game, with runners on first and second, McCarthy called for a double steal. The runner was out at third. Some questioned McCarthy's call, especially with a left-hander at the plate, thus making the catcher's throw to third easier. But McCarthy insisted it was the right call. Giant third baseman Travis Jackson, he noted, "made a great play on that ball." This was how McCarthy incessantly managed: press the offense in such a way that it requires a sparkling play by the opposition to beat you. There are never guarantees, but the percentages are with you with such tactics. In the seventh inning, with the Yankees down 2–1, Jake Powell was on first, and McCarthy did not call for a bunt, letting Tony Lazzeri hit away. Many complained he should have bunted, but McCarthy seldom played for one run. Better to take the chance and try for a big inning. When he had less offense he would play for the steal and the bunt, but not with this team. The Giants scored four in the eighth, and they won the game 6–1. McCarthy was not worried.[18]

The one Yankee run in the first game came via a home run by George Selkirk. McCarthy congratulated Selkirk and expressed sorrow that his effort was wasted. "Do it again tomorrow and it won't be wasted," he admonished. Then McCarthy immediately turned to Lefty Gomez: "You're ready for them tomorrow, aren't you, Gomez?" He was, and so were the Yankees, and so were their fans, among them President Roosevelt. In the game the Yankees pasted the Giants 18–4. No one had ever scored more than 13 runs in a World Series game. Every Yankee in the lineup got at least one hit; even Gomez got a hit in the ninth (in the whole season he'd gotten only ten hits and batted .145). Like Brutus's stab, mused one reporter, this was the "cruelest hit." Whatever euphoria the Giants may have had after Game One, it was now a faint memory. Mark Koenig, who had been the butt of so much Yankee bench jockeying in the 1932 Series, was now with the Giants. Feeling sweet revenge, he had been quite vocal in game one. Now he had little to say. McCarthy was uncharacteristically ebullient: "It would not surprise me now if we went right through the Giants." Even acknowledging that he would have to face Carl Hubbell again, McCarthy said he was confident of victory over him.[19]

The third game was the best of the series, with the Yankees squeezing out a 2–1 win. Gehrig had hit a home run in the second inning. The Giants pulled even in the fifth. The key play occurred in the Yankee half of the eighth inning with runners on first and third. McCarthy called for an apparent double steal, with the runner on third to go when, or if, the catcher threw to second. The batter, Frankie Crosetti, hit the pitch, however. It glanced off the pitcher's glove. The second baseman charged it, but he was late. The key was McCarthy's call for the steal. It had forced the second baseman to take several strides toward second, and this made him several steps late for the ball as it rolled off the pitcher's glove. This was again part of McCarthy's "always in motion" tactics—keep the pressure on the opponent with a steady stream of intelligently selected maneuvers and the percentages are that the breaks will fall in your favor. Here they did.

It was a heart-breaking loss for Giant starter Fred Fitzsimmons, who pitched a great game. A reporter told McCarthy, "I was rooting for you, as you know, but I felt sorry for Fitz." "To tell you the truth," commented McCarthy after the game, "I did too." A year later McCarthy conceded to Grantland Rice that the ball that glanced off Fitzsimmons' glove was a lucky break. Fitzsimmons, he said, was "one of the best fielding pitchers in the game, ... and nine times out of ten he would have stuck the ball in his hip pocket." But the victory was New York's, and it had strategic importance in an additional respect. Up two games to one, McCarthy knew his next opponent was to be Carl Hubbell. McCarthy had forced Manager Bill Terry to bring back his ace a game sooner than planned.[20]

McCarthy had said he was confident in his Yankees beating Hubbell the next time they faced him. McCarthy took an alleged risk, naming Monte Pearson as his starting pitcher. Pearson had been a trifle ill, but McCarthy used him anyway. Perhaps McCarthy was remembering Connie Mack's use of Howard Ehmke in 1929. Perhaps it was merely a hunch, something McCarthy freely admitted to be the basis of many managerial decisions, especially when it came to pitchers. It was the choice to start Pearson that became one of the chief bases of the story that McCarthy believed he was psychic. Asked how he got such "psychic" messages, McCarthy chuckled, "Prepaid; that's the best part of them." All such stories served McCarthy well, as they added to his mystique and gave him an added edge with other managers and players. In Pearson's case, McCarthy knew full well that Pearson was a notorious hypochondriac and was more than capable of pitching. He further knew, indeed, that such an ego as Pearson's could soar with such a story as stepping forth from death's door to pitch in the World Series against Carl Hubbell. McCarthy thus did nothing, at the time or afterwards, to dispel the image that he had yanked Pearson out of a sickbed any more than he curbed the talk about him being psychic.

In the actual game, Gehrig homered; the Yankees scored three runs in the third inning and were never headed. Pearson was effective, scattering seven Giant hits yielding two useless runs. With the final score, cheers and shreds of paper were flying about Yankee Stadium. After the game, when the subway leaving the Bronx passed the Polo Grounds' 155th Street Exit someone shouted "All off for the graveyard!" McCarthy was unusually smug: "I told you that I was sure we would beat Hubbell the next time. This was not boasting. I knew that Hubbell needed more rest than he was likely to get." Against a team that can beat you, it is seldom a good idea to rile them, but with a team against whom one is confident of victory, such arrogance can put more pressure on the opposition.[21]

McCarthy liked to needle Giants manager/first baseman Bill Terry. Terry smoked a pipe, and whenever he could McCarthy chided Terry about pipe smokers being overly complacent. (Word of this got into the press, and several Yankee players who smoked pipes, including Gehrig and Rolfe, grew a little nervous about puffing on their briars when McCarthy was around.) McCarthy's chiding always got under Terry's skin, and that was McCarthy's real aim with his pipe thoughts. Riled and pressured, the Giants were snarling the next day. Coach Art Fletcher added to the needling that fall. Fletcher was one of the best bench jockeys in the business, and he "got on" Terry something fierce. While McCarthy had the pipe issue, Fletcher cut more to the bone. Terry had refused to join the major league Players' Association. In a time like the Great Depression, such displays of arrogance and superiority rubbed many the wrong way. Fletcher did not like Terry, and he knew he could salt any "union" wounds among the Giants with his barbs. It worked, but the risk was that the angry Giants would play harder and better.

It certainly looked that way at the outset of game five. The Giants scored three runs in the first inning off Red Ruffing. The Yankees came back with a rally in the third inning that nearly broke the game open. They scored one run and had the bases loaded, but they could get no more across that inning. They tied the game in the sixth inning, however, and the game remained tied into the tenth. Then, with a runner on third and the count two and two, Bill Terry took a controversial ball three. Many, including McCarthy, believed the call was wrong, but of course it stood. Terry hit the next pitch for a sacrifice fly. The Giants won, and Terry enjoyed his pipe. Tony Lazzeri yelled that the umpire's two and two call was "plain robbery." McCarthy was asked about the call. He just took a puff on a cigar, looked at the reporters, and smiled: "Well you saw it as well as I did, what did you think?" McCarthy knew better than to add to any team anger. All that would do was make the Giants feel they had gotten a psychological edge. He would never give them that.[22]

McCarthy had Lefty Gomez for the sixth game. The game was close throughout. Up 5–3 in the seventh, the Giants scored a run and had runners on first and third with one out. McCarthy relieved Gomez with Johnny Murphy. Murphy got the next batter to pop up. Then he struck out former Yankee Mark Koenig. The two teams each scored a run in the eighth. Then the Yankees exploded for seven runs in the top of the ninth. That was the series. McCarthy was euphoric but a trifle humble. He spoke to the team: "Great work boys, all of you." To reporters he nodded: "I'm glad that's over. I musta' lost ten pounds today. Those Giants don't know when they're beaten — a fine club that — full of fight. ... I wasn't fooled by the talk that they had been lucky to win the National League pennant."[23]

The day after the World Series, in obvious reference to his victory of 1932, McCarthy wrote: "Often a manager takes a World Series with a team which he knows cannot hope to go on for another season and must be revamped. But this Yankee outfit [of '36] still looks good enough for me." McCarthy knew he had put together a team that could sustain winning, and not just for another season. (Starting in 1936, the Yankees would win 22 of the next 29 pennants.) It was with the World Series victory over the Giants in 1936 that some newspapers were proclaiming Joe McCarthy the greatest manager in baseball. Having written a series of articles for the *Buffalo Evening News*, McCarthy confidently concluded to his readers: "Now so long until October '37. And I hope the Giants are in it again." He did not say he hoped the Yankees would be there too. He did not need to. Over the next years, people (and McCarthy himself) did not hope for great things from the Yankees; they expected.[24]

A few months after the victory over the Giants, the New York Young Men's Board of Trade held a ceremony in which they gave out their annual award to the man who sets the finest example to the boys and young men of the city. Criminal investigator Thomas Dewey had won the previous year's award. This year the award went to Lou Gehrig. It was the first time such an award went to a New York athlete.[25] McCarthy was delighted at the news and was utterly convinced that it was well-deserved. It moved him deeply that an athlete could be recognized as such an example to young people. It confirmed to him what he had been seeking with his team. The Yankees of Babe Ruth's time had become symbols of the roaring age of fast cars and speakeasies. The nature of the hero worship and enjoyment of the exploits of Ruth was not unlike the pleasure some got at the successes and sprees of Al Capone. Youth organizations do not award such people for the example they set.

The Depression marked a vastly different era, of course. For some, the hardships of the time pushed people to right and left-wing extremes in politics and prompted a romanticizing of such criminal types as Bonnie and Clyde. In baseball, St. Louis' Gas House Gang symbolized the raucousness that was the devil-may-care response to the Depression. (And McCarthy never liked their sloppy uniforms.)[26] But while some Americans may have indulged in some spiritual dabbling in nostalgic, romantic, and radical expressions, the majority huddled tenaciously around earnest values of stolidity and patriotism. McCarthy's Yankees became a perfect symbol of this no-nonsense line that was the bass tone of the tough era. Their successes and the examples their people set affected more than just the sports world. Coat and tie dress, proper behavior, no card playing, supposedly no pipe smoking and genuinely no excessive contentment, no emotional outbursts, a weeding out of all the quixotics, 100 percent effectiveness at the job every day, even when danger seems more distant — this was a set of values to which Americans in the Depression turned. People like Lou Gehrig and Joe McCarthy gave them proof that it worked, and not just in baseball. Sadly, just a few years later, other events would further prove to Joe McCarthy and everyone else that, as great a ballplayer as he was, Lou Gehrig was indeed an even greater human being.

26

A Ten-Game Lead Is Never Safe

I don't know, sir, you'd better ask Mr. McCarthy.
— a Yankee rookie's response to a reporter
who asked him if he was married.

After the 1936 season, the nickname "Second Place Joe" was certainly dead and buried. Looking at the prospects for the 1937 season, everyone in the sports world favored the Yankees to repeat. The prospects seemed so overwhelming that reporters had to result to superstition and numerology to find some basis for doubt — it was, for example, the 13th time the team would train in St. Petersburg. McCarthy was not impressed. If anything, McCarthy had one numerical sign that pointed in the opposite direction. It was his 7th season with the Yankees.

McCarthy did have one real problem in early March — a quarter of his players were still haggling over salary matters. But as usual he consigned most of those issues as Ruppert's and Barrow's purview and stayed out of Yankee business matters. In 1936 he had intervened for Bill Dickey, while leaving Red Ruffing and Ben Chapman to their own devices, and in 1937 he intervened in only one case. Lou Gehrig, the American League's most valuable player of 1936, wanted $50,000. In 1936 he had made all of $31,000. On his own, McCarthy phoned Gehrig. "Come on now, Lou," he admonished, "let's get down to work. How much do you want?" Gehrig came down to a request for $40,000 a year for two years. McCarthy took it to Col. Ruppert. Ruppert was adamant, and a little peeved. "Sorry, I won't give him a cent more than $36,000, and it will be on a one-year basis. I'm sorry you called him." Gehrig phoned McCarthy with a proposal for $36,750. Ruppert agreed but insisted the contract had to read $36,000 with a $750 bonus. Late 20th, early 21st-century salary levels make such haggling look utterly comical, but Gehrig was in deadly earnest, as was Ruppert. For McCarthy to intervene was also quite a step. It showed that he certainly knew he had credibility with Col. Ruppert, that he could exercise, albeit carefully. He only did so with the few players who were most valuable to him like Gehrig and Dickey. The others were on their own. Tony Lazzeri made $16,000; Frankie Crosetti made $13,000.[1]

McCarthy had his usual embarrassment of riches in both the infield and outfield. His infield would not change. Like his old infield in Louisville of Kirke, Roach, Corriden, and himself, the Yankees' Gehrig, Lazzeri, Crosetti, and Rolfe was so good that it made no sense to tinker. Lyn Lary was long gone. Jack Saltzgaver would have virtually no playing time. A new arrival from Boston, Ellsworth "Babe" Dahlgren proved versatile enough at all the infield positions that he was kept on the bench for some of the season, although he spent a lot of the year in Newark. With Dahlgren in the wings, McCarthy dispensed with Don Heffner. As in 1936, he thought of trading Lazzeri, but nothing yet came of it. In the outfield he still had DiMaggio, Selkirk, and Powell, plus Roy Johnson, Myril Hoag, and newcomer Ernie Koy. Joe Glenn and Arndt Jorgens remained as backups to Dickey. As for the pitchers, with Ruffing, Gomez, Murphy, and the rest of the staff, McCarthy had a machine in full operation. Murphy had fully emerged as a relief specialist, something for which few before McCarthy had ever fully employed a pitcher. It seems such an obvious idea to subsequent generations of baseball people. In hindsight, sometimes the greatest innovations appear utterly simple. To most managers, a starter, like Gomez, who tended to weaken by the seventh inning was a pitcher to be traded or sent down. McCarthy's way won more games. Meanwhile, down in Newark he had a solid corps of prospects.

One major adjustment McCarthy made with his outfield in 1937 concerned George Selkirk. Over the winter Selkirk had "bulked up" fifteen pounds. (Apropos of Selkirk's new physique, McCarthy was actually doing advertisements that spring for the New York Bureau of Milk. "I always try to get every man on my team to drink plenty of fresh milk. It tones up the system, sharpens your reflexes, so you think faster, act faster. And milk helps to prevent you from going haywire when you're under pressure." He still let his players drink other beverages.) McCarthy felt the newly strengthened Selkirk now had the muscle to be more of a pull hitter. This was important, because throughout 1936 McCarthy had used Selkirk almost exclusively against right-handers. Against left-handers McCarthy now had Selkirk shift his body a bit more towards first base and use his arm strength to pull the ball. The move worked quite well. Selkirk could now hit against any pitcher. Until he hurt his shoulder that July, Selkirk would lead the league in home runs. McCarthy was very good at spotting where such adjustments could be made, and in engineering the subtle mechanics for working them out. New York's Columbia University actually wanted him to teach some of their newly established sports courses in their summer curriculum.[2]

One young player with the Cleveland Indians system, Tommy Henrich, had been playing in their farm system. As they shuttled him from the New Orleans Pelicans to the Milwaukee Brewers, Henrich felt the Cleveland organization was unfairly holding him down in the minors. Billy Evans, the business manager of the Red Sox, wrote an article about Henrich's situation. Henrich tried to break his contract with Cleveland, and the matter went to Commissioner Landis. Landis was always harsh with the owners on their farm system and how they used it to restrain some players from getting ahead. On this score, Landis was immensely popular with the players. Illustrating the players' attitude, the St. Louis Cardinals' extensive system that Branch Rickey had built was commonly referred to as "The St. Louis chain gang." Good players were sometimes making as little as $100 a month down there. Landis upheld Henrich's appeal, leaving him free to negotiate with any team. He signed with the Yankees. He showed some hitting difficulties and was soon assigned to Newark.

A glance at the '37 Newark club showed New York's prospects looked as bright in the distant future as they did in the immediate. Among the starters for Newark that year were Babe Dahlgren, outfielder Charlie Keller, just out of the University of Maryland, infielders Joe Gordon and Billy Knickerbocker, catcher Buddy Rosar, and pitchers Marius Russo and Steve Sundra. All would eventually play well for the Yankees. Now they had Tommy Henrich too. The rest of the league could only sulk.[3]

Expectations about continued Yankee success lay not just among Yankee rooters. They were present among their opponents, players and fans. The intimidation was part of the success formula. The team had built such an organization as the game had never before seen. Col. Ruppert was obviously willing to spend the necessary money, and he had the wisdom to choose good people for various key posts. Ruppert had surprised Ed Barrow back in December of 1931 when he fully bought the Newark club of the International League. But it certainly proved the wisest of moves. George Weiss, another extremely thorough and able man, ran the Yankees' farm system. Oscar Vitt managed the top farm club in Newark, New Jersey. McCarthy's former Louisville catcher Bill Meyer managed Kansas City, and he took over in Newark after Vitt was hired by the Cleveland Indians. Scouts Paul Krichell, Johnny Nee, Bill Essick, Steve O'Rourke, Gene McCann, and Joe Devine were the best in the business. The organization involved people who not only knew how to win, but how to sustain winning. This was not done by decree, nor even by mere money. Ruppert had plenty of money, to be sure, but so did other owners, notably Tom Yawkey of the Red Sox. Yawkey spent lavishly and certainly improved the Red Sox. But he never won.

By 1937, the Yankees were starting to win with such a regularity and style that some people found it irritating and boring. But just as the best athletes always make their performances look easy to the untutored, the same is so of those who are successful in management. Personnel was obviously the key, and McCarthy knew better than anyone how to find and develop it among ball players. Ruppert and Barrow knew the same with regard to the rest of the organization. McCarthy was also a master at game tactics, and always used his marvelous personnel to his greatest advantage here. He did little things well too. After his illness had sidelined him in 1939, Lou Gehrig entertained thoughts about managing, so he sat near McCarthy during games. He later commented about the experience to a reporter: "This fellow amazes me the way he operates. I learn new things every day. What amazes me most are the seemingly little moves he makes that turn out to be so vitally important. I kick myself that I can't see them at the same time, but then I guess there's only one McCarthy."

Beyond game tactics, McCarthy attended to other subtleties with the same care. He had the Yankees wearing uniforms cut just slightly larger. He also ordered the caps designed with a slightly more square design, all to the effect of presenting an ever so slightly more intimidating aura. Just the sight of the uniform, or the simple name "New York" on the road outfits, could be enough to make many opponents go a little dry in the mouth. And with a McCarthy team always "in motion," ready to pounce upon the slightest letdown, that was often all it took to touch off a big inning and a win. All such attention to detail was part of McCarthy's success. He was blessed with incredibly talented men, but many managers have failed with such personnel or have succeeded only for a short time. No one could sustain winning like McCarthy. As the editor of *The Sporting News* put it: "Even though his players were giants among their contemporaries, McCarthy was a giant among dugout executives."

It was in 1937 that McCarthy and the Yankees let the American League know that they were going to be around for a long time. As McCarthy knew even when he dispensed with Ben Chapman, fighting can win games. But playing above such a merely scrappy level, can take even that combative tactic away from an opponent and keep his Yankee team from experiencing too many ups and downs.. The Yankees could take on any fight if they had to, but opponents came to see no point in even trying it. It was quite an achievement to make the Ty Cobbs of the era resign themselves with a "what's the use" shrug.[4]

The Yankees toured the South before the '37 season and won 13 straight. They began the season in a somewhat disappointing manner, staying in the pack with the other leading teams, Detroit, Cleveland, Boston (who now had Jimmie Foxx, Bobby Doerr, Pinky Higgins, Joe Cronin, and Lefty Grove), and surprising Chicago. DiMaggio was down for a bit. Doctors decided that he needed to undergo the removal of his tonsils, adenoids, and an infected tooth. For the second year in a row, he was lost for the last exhibition contests and for the first games of the season. McCarthy said he "never put much stock in those doctors who advised removing tonsils and teeth if an arm ached." But he conceded, "there must be something to it after all," for by late April DiMaggio seemed fine. Meanwhile Red Ruffing was still holding out, and the fans were yelling for him at the Stadium. There was talk that he was to be traded; McCarthy denied it. Without Ruffing, and without DiMaggio's bat, the pitching fared not so well, and after the good spring in Florida, McCarthy was perplexed about his pitchers. They did not seem to be responding to the usual training regimen. As McCarthy had earlier proclaimed, "anybody who thinks he knows anything about women and pitchers is a sucker."[5]

McCarthy's sense of pitchers resonated well among many baseball people. It certainly made sense within the Yankee organization. Lefty Gomez, for example, continued to be a source of consternation for McCarthy and the rest of the club. McCarthy always felt rubdowns were bad for pitchers' arms. Gomez loved them, however, and he would often sneak into the trainer's room for a rub. One day, Gomez walked into the trainer's room. Bob Feller happened to be visiting there too. Gomez took off his shirt and waited until Feller was done. Then McCarthy suddenly walked in with Feller still on the table. A bit angry, and perhaps with a nip of whiskey in him, he asked Feller if he "believed in this rubdown stuff." Feller replied that he did not really know but added that "it might have some psychological value." McCarthy suddenly barked: "Psychology! I had a pitcher on my club who majored in psychology in college. 'Sent him to Newark last week." McCarthy then asked Feller how old he was. Feller respectfully replied "Twenty, sir." McCarthy responded: "Twenty, eh? Well take a look at Gomez over there. He's about thirty and never been on a rubbing table in his life, have you, Lefty?" Gomez immediately snapped to. "No sir," he responded, quietly putting on his shirt. Lefty later confessed: "That was the only rubdown I had to pass up all year."

Gomez regularly hid such things from McCarthy. He smoked where McCarthy disallowed it. He once hurt his foot fouling off a pitch in a sandlot game he had joined walking to a game at Griffith Stadium. Such extra playing was forbidden because of the possibility of injuries, but Gomez was too much of a free spirit to conform. He persuaded Washington Manager Joe Cronin to confirm the story he told to McCarthy — that he had tripped on the dugout steps. McCarthy may have suspected, but Gomez was so good that McCarthy knew it best to give him a wide berth. He knew Gomez well enough to know it did not pay to try to understand too much.[6]

On May 3, McCarthy had been suffering from a severe cold and was ordered by his doctor to remain in bed. He refused; "I'll feel better when that gang of mine starts hitting," he said. At the moment, he mused, "they couldn't hit me if I ran across the plate."[7] He made a scheduled trip with the team out to Detroit where they proceeded to win two in a row. During that time, on behalf of Ruppert and Barrow, he sat down with Red Ruffing, who was still holding out for more salary. McCarthy could appeal to team spirit in a way that Ruppert and Barrow certainly could not. The heart-to-heart worked; Ruffing signed for $15,000; this for having won 20 games in 1936 and batting .291 (he was one of the best hitting pitchers ever). To some it may be a wonder that McCarthy was able to forge such a spirited team given the sternly parsimonious nature of the team's general management. McCarthy's leadership was remarkable, and the sad fact was that virtually all the other clubs were being run by their general managers and owners in exactly the same niggardly way.

The two wins in Detroit put the Yankees in first place, but then they lost four, including one of several that year to Cleveland's young Denny Galehouse. (Over the years, McCarthy had a winning record against Bob Feller, but Galehouse often gave him trouble.) After the fourth loss, McCarthy walked into the clubhouse in Chicago in a very crusty mood. There he overheard outfielder Roy Johnson complaining to a teammate: "What, does McCarthy expect us to win every game?" McCarthy detested any sort of complacency. He liked the fact that he had to tell Red Ruffing to slow down in the hustling way he chased down fly balls during outfield practice. But he would not stand for such a mediocrity-inducing attitude as Johnson's. Within 24 hours, Roy Johnson had been sold to the Boston Bees. "I don't care who you get," McCarthy fumed to Ed Barrow. "Just get him out of here." (Barrow only got the waiver price for Johnson.)

With Johnson gone, McCarthy told Barrow: "Get me that kid at Newark." "That kid" was Tommy Henrich. Earlier that season, Henrich had been up with the Yankees, but he had been having trouble with inside curve balls from right-handers. McCarthy had been blunt with him. "Lay off that pitch. The pitchers are making a sucker out of you," McCarthy said. After another week of missing curve balls, the very pitch McCarthy himself could not hit in Toledo, Henrich got another earful from McCarthy, including what Henrich called "the Yankee threat:" "I told you to lay off that curve. Either you do it now, or you'll learn to hit in Newark." To Newark he went. After all the fights with the Cleveland Indians, Henrich was exasperated, and he protested. McCarthy simply said, "Son, I can *ask* you to go to Newark. Or I can *make* you go." Henrich went, but because of Roy Johnson's little gaffe, he was back with the Yankees in ten days. Roy Johnson was playing in Boston, and Tommy Henrich stopped swinging at inside curve balls.[8]

By mid–May, McCarthy's cold was better, and perhaps the unloading of Roy Johnson lit a fire under some people. Whatever the reason, in late May the Yankees won nine of ten and took over first place. They never relinquished it. During the spurt, one tragedy occurred. The Yankees were hosting Detroit. In the fourth inning manager/catcher Mickey Cochrane had hit a home run; in the next inning he came up again and was hit by a pitch from Bump Hadley. Hadley had thrown a pitch high and inside. Instead of falling backwards, Cochrane attempted to duck, and the pitch struck him in the head. Cochrane was not wearing a helmet. The event reminded people of the incident in 1920 when Yankee pitcher Carl Mays fatally beaned Cleveland's Ray Chapman. Fortunately, Cochrane did not die, although at first some feared he would. He did suffer a major concussion, however, and his skull was fractured in three places. He never played again, and Detroit's chances in the pennant race fell precipitously, although the Tigers did bring up a young catcher named George "Birdie" Tebbetts who played solidly. For the Yankees there was the task of accepting such an incident and still playing their best. They did so, and some opposing fans then came even more to see them as cold, ruthless enemies. For McCarthy, who felt as badly as anyone about Cochrane's injury, it was part of the discipline involved in being a professional athlete. The Yankees won the game and kept on winning.[9]

Led by their wisecracking, feisty manager Jimmy Dykes, the Chicago White Sox proved the Yankees' most pesky foe that summer. In June they actually drew even for a day. But the Yankees seemed always to have the necessary reserve to pull ahead whenever the least bit pressured. Opponents like Dykes resented the Yankees' strength, but the season was by no means easy for McCarthy; it only appeared so. As the Yankees were so good, it was natural for people to see the job of McCarthy as enviably easy. In mid July, as Grantland Rice later commented, "everyone was asking why the American League simply didn't enter the Yankees [in the All-Star game] and let it go at that." In the All-Star Game this almost came to pass. McCarthy managed, and he started five Yankees—Gomez, Rolfe, Dickey, DiMaggio, and Gehrig. Gomez pitched three innings; the other four played the entire game. McCarthy was roundly criticized for this, but the American League won 8–3 (and they had lost the previous summer).[10]

The easy road everyone felt was McCarthy's managerial course that season was indeed not as simple as it looked. Pitcher Johnny Broaca came down with a bad arm that would not respond to treatment. Broaca apparently grew depressed over this, and in July he abruptly deserted the team (as well as his wife). McCarthy made no effort to find Broaca, but he and the Yankees did see to it that Mrs. Broaca was provided with means. Elsewhere, DiMaggio had, of course, been out at the beginning of the season, and there was a rash of injuries among the other outfielders. Myril Hoag and DiMaggio collided on a play, and Hoag suffered a concussion. Tommy Henrich twisted his knee. Jake Powell pulled a leg muscle. Then he came down with appendicitis. George Selkirk also pulled a leg muscle. He played with his bad leg for the month of June and played very well. As of July 2nd Selkirk was the American League home run leader with seventeen, but that afternoon he injured his collarbone and shoulder. Within a week his injury had not healed, and doctors pronounced it worse than they had originally diagnosed. He wore his arm in a sling for over a month and played little thereafter that year. Henrich and Powell played hurt. Red Rolfe had a calcium deposit on his leg that was pressing on his thigh muscle. From the previous season, his batting average dropped from .320 to .278. He played in constant pain, but he was never out of the lineup.

Neither was Gehrig, of course, but he was beaned in an exhibition game in Norfolk. The day after the beaning, from which he had been out cold for five minutes,

Gehrig's head was so swollen that he had to borrow Babe Ruth's old cap; it was the only one that would fit. McCarthy told Barrow that he wanted no more exhibition games that season. There were four on the schedule, and Barrow cancelled them.

Effectively juggling his injured players, McCarthy and the Yankees put on another spurt starting in late June. From June 15th to July 22, they won 28 of 33 games and ran up a seven game lead on Chicago. "Ashes to Ashes, Dust to Dust," wrote a bad poet for the *Daily News*, "If Dimag. and Gehrig don't get you, Dickey must." Beyond the lead, the best news McCarthy learned that summer was that Rogers Hornsby had lost his job as manager of the St. Louis Browns. To make it even sweeter, the last day Hornsby managed in St. Louis he lost a doubleheader to McCarthy's Yankees. About the only bad news of the summer came via a telephone call McCarthy received in his Chicago hotel late one night in early in August. The caller claimed to be U.S. Post-master Jim Farley, and he was asking McCarthy to get him a couple of tickets for the next afternoon's game at sold-out Comiskey Park. McCarthy curtly told the caller to get in touch with the Yankees' traveling secretary and hung up the phone. 'Turned out, it *was* Jim Farley at the other end of the line, and he had to secure his tickets from another source.[11]

In August, Chicago faded from contention. Despite the loss of Cochrane and bad arm trouble for Schoolboy Rowe, Detroit rose in the standings, as did Boston. But the Yankees' lead had grown to 10 games, and no one was going to get near them. McCarthy was never complacent, however. Indeed he was often nervous. The Roy Johnson trade had taught a lesson to anyone inclined to doubt McCarthy's jitters, let alone be even the slightest bit lackadaisical. "Second-place Joe" had been replaced by a new, somewhat lugubrious name among reporters: "Joe 'A Ten-Game Lead is Never Safe' McCarthy."

Wanting to keep a fierce Yankee image, even against rival Detroit, no matter the terrible injury to Mickey Cochrane, McCarthy ordered his players to stop the sportsman-like act of picking up the opposing team's catcher's mask after pop fouls and other such plays. A St. Louis reporter noted further how Red Rolfe was once chasing a foul popup. Rolfe caught the ball at the edge of the St. Louis dugout and was about to tumble into the bench as two St. Louis players reached out and caught him before he hit the concrete. Several days later the Yankees were in Cleveland. Late in the game the Indians' catcher was chasing a foul popup and approached the Yankee dugout. As he was making the catch, he fell into the dugout and dropped the ball. No Yankee attempted to break his fall. Only after he had dropped the ball did the players intervene. They solicitously helped him up, dusted him off, slapped him on the back, and sent him on his way. (The reprieved batter subsequently doubled, two runs scored, and the Yankees won the game by one run.) This was a bit of the Yan-kee edge that made New Yorkers smirk and the rest of the league gnash their teeth.

McCarthy always strove to maintain such a team focus, no matter the breadth of their lead, and that summer the Yankees produced much about which to boast. DiMaggio was proving his rookie splash was anything but a fluke. He batted .346, led the league with 46 home runs, and had hitting streaks of 19, 21, and 22 games. Gehrig had his last great season, batting .351 and knocking in 159 runs. Gomez and Ruffing won 21 and 20 games respectively, the only pitchers in the league to win 20. Again, McCarthy had made it look easy. Reporters noted the mature atmosphere he had created on the team — no rules, no curfew hours, no checking up. He had brought a team to a level he conceived, one that others could not duplicate but only envy. The Yankees won the pennant by 13 games. They led the league in home runs, RBI's, earned run average, and even in stolen bases. To top it all off, Newark won the International League by a whopping 25 games. Some papers printed stories that the Yankees were utterly blasé about the pennant. Fifty movie cameramen were all set to film the Yankees' celebration in St. Louis the day they clinched the pennant. Unfortunately, the Browns did not cooperate with the plans. They beat the Yankees that afternoon, so the cameramen caught a team that was anything but jubilant. Later in the day, the Tigers clinched the pennant for New York by losing, so the dispirited Yankee clubhouse scene was all that was on film. The camera crews were hardly happy about it, and they did nothing to scotch any rumors about the Yankees being blasé.[12]

As McCarthy had hoped the previous October, he would again face the Giants in the World Series. McCarthy was taking no chances. After the Yankees had wrapped up the pennant, he left the team in the hands of Art Fletcher for a series in Washington and stayed in New York, scouting the Giants. McCarthy decided that lefthanders would start against Carl Hubbell. He figured Hubbell's screwball was more like a righthander's curve ball. The move proved wise. Over the summer, as the teams anticipated another Series, the "talking" between the squads had grown during the season, especially as each approached the league pennant. The Giants had a pitcher, Cliff Melton, who had tried out for the Yankees in 1934. McCarthy had cut him, and Melton had never accepted it. (Melton had a good fast ball, but McCarthy said it had no movement to it, so it would not be effective.) Melton had pitched well for the Giants in 1937, and this confirmed his view that McCarthy had made a mistake. He announced to the press that the Yankees were going to lose. Their problem, he held, was that they were a team of "more brawn than brains." Melton's characterization fed National League chauvinists' view that the Yankees had bludgeoned a weaker league and would come up short against a team that could handle their power and present them with a level of finesse and cunning they had not seen in the regular season. All such generalities are fine in coffee shops and bars, but they have meaning among players on the field only insofar as the players let themselves be affected psychologically. This was not going to happen to a McCarthy team. Earlier that September, McCarthy conceded to Grantland Rice that he was worried about Selkirk's shoulder and Henrich's knee still giving them trouble, but as always his focus would be tenacious.[13]

The first game proved who had the psychological edge. The Giants were yelling a lot from the bench, and McCarthy told his bench to return fire. "Get on those Giants," he demanded. In the game, Carl Hubbell was pitching against Lefty Gomez. In the top of the fifth inning the game was scoreless. The Giants put runners on first and third base with none out. Throughout the season, the Giants always figured a one-run lead was all that was necessary when Carl "the Meal Ticket" Hubbell was pitching, and they figured the Yankees knew it too. McCarthy, however, decided to weigh in with a bit of his own psychology. He chose to play his infield back, concede the run, play for the double play, and avoid the possibility of a big inning. So the Giants had their run, but they had to internalize the point that these Yankees had no problem giving it to them. They had never had to contend with such confidence in an opponent in the regular season. As the Yankee half of the inning was about to start, as Lou Gehrig later recalled, McCarthy announced to the team: "Hubbell is going to walk our lead-off man. Let's get ready for an inning to win this game." Hubbell did just as McCarthy predicted, and the Yankees exploded, pounding Hubbell for seven runs. It was like a boxer deliberately and arrogantly taking his opponents' "Sunday punch," just smiling at him, and then delivering a knockout blow. The final score that day was 8–1. The game and, more important, the mental edge belonged to the Yankees. The Yankees had ground up Hubbell and the Giants in the very way no National League team would have dared even to attempt. Joe McCarthy is a tough man, wrote one reporter, "Even as a kid he never knew how long a lollipop should last because he always chewed it." McCarthy was proud of his tactics. When the World Series was over he beamed, "Not once ... did I pull my infield in." Many years later McCarthy told the newly appointed Washington Senators Manager Ted Williams, "as a manager you must never believe that one run will beat you." His prediction of Hubbell walking the leadoff man in the sixth only added to the McCarthy mystique that gave the Yankees an added margin over all his opponents.[14]

In game two, the Giants scored one run at the top of the first inning and thus took the field with a lead. Their pitcher was on a mission. It was Cliff Melton. He held the Yankees scoreless for four innings. Then in the fifth inning he faltered. The Yankees chased him with four straight hits and two runs. His relievers fared no better, and the Yankees again won 8–1. Game three was pretty much the same, except that the Yankees took the early lead and were never headed — 5–1. No team has ever come back from a 0–3 deficit in a seven-game series in any sport. The Giants were not going to quit, however, and Carl Hubbell salvaged game four for them. But now he had to rest.

The next afternoon, Melton had a chance to redeem himself. McCarthy had some choice words for the occasion of Melton's second start: "That's not a bad ball club the Giants got; their relief pitching looks good!" Melton gave up home runs to Myril Hoag and DiMaggio in the second and third innings, but the Giants tied the game in the bottom of the third. In the fifth inning, however, Tony Lazzeri singled home another run, and Gehrig then knocked him in with a double. Meanwhile, Lefty Gomez was breezing along, and it seemed nothing could stop him. Something actually did stop Gomez that afternoon, but it was not the Giants. With two runners on in the seventh inning, and a count of 3–0 on no less a hitter than Mel Ott, a biplane flew over the Polo Grounds. Gomez enjoyed flying and had a pilot's license. He stopped completely, stood there on the mound, and followed the flight of the biplane with his hands on his hips, utterly oblivious to the game and to the thousands in the stands. McCarthy came out. Gomez looked quizzically at McCarthy and exclaimed "That was the damnedest looking crate I ever saw." "Never mind the crates," snapped McCarthy. "Keep your mind on the ball game. This is the World Series!" Gomez shrugged: "Hell, we're just playin' the Giants aren't we?" McCarthy returned to the bench; Gomez shut out the Giants from there, and the Yanks were again the champs.[15] (Years later McCarthy cast the event a little differently: "I've been asked many times if I reprimanded Lefty for gawking at that airplane in the World Series game. I asked him in a kidding way what was happening out there and ... if he liked what he saw. 'Nothing can happen, skipper,' he replied. 'The batters can't hit the ball as long as I have it in my hand.'") Whatever were the actual words at the time, the fact was that McCarthy had a deep faith in Gomez. And Lefty never lost a World Series game for him.[16]

Gomez played the kind of baseball McCarthy wanted. When once asked about what pitcher he wanted "in the game of his life," McCarthy nodded, "you had to take Lefty in the clutch because he was always so loose. … [He] was never awed by any batter." Gomez had all the ability and confidence; he could just be a little odd at the edges. Even though no opponent ever unnerved him, he actually had a genuine phobia of lightning. Gomez's "edges" were the very places where many mediocre managers would focus if they had him, thinking they could impose some useful discipline. McCarthy had a more precisely honed sense of what was useful and important. He later admitted that

> Lefty really got on my nerves sometimes. He was no trouble on the days he was pitching. In fact he was nice to have around then. … But he was really something on days when he was sitting on the bench. He'd keep walking up and down in front of me until I'd nearly fly out of my skin. Finally I'd send him down to the bullpen. That helped until [pitching coach] Fred Schulte complained. He started to get on Schulte's nerves too.

Other managers might have done more than send someone like Gomez out to the bullpen, particularly in his early years. McCarthy was usually able to see past his own irritations. When Gomez and Selkirk staged some 50- and 100-yard races (for $1), McCarthy told them if they did it again it would cost them each $50. "We had a lot of fun then," Gomez remembered, "but we didn't do much laughing when Joe McCarthy was around."

McCarthy tried to nudge Gomez toward saner ways more gently, but it seldom worked. At dinner after an off day on the road, McCarthy told Gomez about a plane he had seen. "Lefty," he earnestly relayed, "I'm sorry you missed seeing some nut in a plane today. Had you been able to see what he was doing you would realize just how frighteningly dangerous flying is." Gomez asked if the plane was red, and McCarthy acknowledged that it was. Gomez then explained to McCarthy: "Skipper, I know how dangerous it was. I was in that plane." McCarthy could only sigh.[17]

While some reporters had great fun with the Gomez story at the end of the '37 World Series, McCarthy spoke of other highlights. Aside from the moment when the Series was clinched, McCarthy said his biggest thrill was the catching of Bill Dickey. "In every one of the five games," noted McCarthy, "he did a rare job. Not once did he lose sight of the scheme we had arranged for every hitter. And here and there he ordered little variations from the book which proved uncanny. Bill," he concluded, "used excellent judgment and proved a tremendous help to our pitchers." Some managers leave too much of the pitching tactics to the catcher. Other hyper-controlling managers, intent on showing how tough and "never satisfied" they were, could have used Dickey's independence of judgment as a point of remonstration. Rogers Hornsby would have likely done so, for example. The fact that McCarthy made a point of praising Dickey for his judgment exemplifies the golden mean that he had achieved with the team. McCarthy tended to all details. Virtually nothing missed his eye. He developed a regimen to which all had to adhere. But the system he forged and the men who were part of it were such that McCarthy felt enough confidence in its operation to let others use and develop their baseball sense as they saw fit. His system was thus not rigid. It was not infused with his own ego, so the players could grow and thrive within it. Few other managers could or can create such a creative balance. They either lacked the knowledge and ability or were too self-centered.[18]

When the World Series was over, Giants Manager Bill Terry did not, as was customary, come over to the Yankees' locker room to congratulate McCarthy, something McCarthy obviously noted. In late January that off-season, at the annual Baseball Writers Dinner in New York, McCarthy encountered Terry and offered him a cigar. The writers thought it was a peace offering. They forgot that McCarthy always chided Terry about smoking a pipe, as he claimed that pipe smoking made one too complacent. Just over a month before, at a winter meeting in Chicago, McCarthy had further needled Terry about his pipe smoking. Rumors flew that Terry and McCarthy actually got into a fight at the Chicago meeting. It was not true. The cigar offer was a true story, however. It was McCarthy's little reminder as to how his New York rival could "improve." McCarthy saw no need to be humble with Terry. In case they met again in a World Series, McCarthy wanted to maintain a psychological edge. Terry did not take the cigar, and he never won another pennant.

Several years later, McCarthy would rub this in a bit. McCarthy put in a rare appearance at a New York nightclub, Club 81. The club owner, Jack White, was a diehard Giants fan. Standing at the club microphone, White acknowledged the rarity of McCarthy's presence in New York's nightlife and asked him to say a few words. McCarthy agreed and announced to White that "I came here to your club because I never see you at the World Series any more." White may not have directly relayed the quip to Terry, but columnist Walter Winchell was on hand, and he clacked it into his Broadway column.[19]

There were no more doubts about McCarthy and the Yankees. The day the Yankees clinched the Series, McCarthy went immediately to see Col. Ruppert. "Do it again next year" were the Colonel's only instructions. Four days before the Yankees finished off the Giants, Newark won the Little World Series from American Association champion Columbus—in a four game sweep after losing the first three. Twenty-one year old Charlie Keller led the International League in hitting with a .355 average.[20] He would still have to wait in the minors. He could not crack New York's lineup, and the Yankees were not about to trade him. Proof of how little doubt existed about the Yankees' future was shown by the fact that some reporters actually tried to come up with tidbits of criticism to show some sort of flaw somewhere. The extent of their "reach" was revealing. Some reporters claimed that Joe DiMaggio couldn't bunt. McCarthy's response was perfect: "I'll never find out." (Gehrig never bunted for McCarthy either.) DiMaggio remembered: "McCarthy would not let me bunt, but I once tried anyway. I fouled the ball off so it tipped my nose. I almost decapitated myself. I said: 'That's it for bunting.'" (DiMaggio always concluded that McCarthy knew best.) McCarthy also held DiMaggio from stealing bases, although he had speed. McCarthy knew not to waste resources. As the 1938 season approached, the only question in reporters' minds concerned by how many games the Yankees would win. Col. Ruppert restored the $7,500 pay cut that McCarthy had taken after the second-place finish in 1935.[21]

McCarthy and his fellow managers, March, 1938. Gathered after dinner are, left to right, seated: Bill McKechnie, Cincinnati; Mickey Cochrane, Detroit; McCarthy; Casey Stengel, Boston Bees; and Frankie Frisch, St. Louis Cardinals. Standing: Bill Meyer, Kansas City; Burleigh Grimes, Brooklyn; Johnny Neun, Newark; and Steve O'Neill, Cleveland. Newark and Kansas City were Yankee farm teams. As he often did, McCarthy picked up the tab that evening. (National Baseball Hall of Fame Library, Cooperstown, N.Y.)

Among the better players on the Newark Bears in 1937 had been their infielders, Joe Gordon, Bill Knickerbocker, and Babe Dahlgren. As the Yankees organized themselves for the 1938 season, the question of the infield had to be settled. To some degree it was settled before spring training when McCarthy and Barrow traded away Jack Saltzgaver, who had never really cracked the lineup, and veteran Tony Lazzeri, who was finally dealt to the Cubs. Right after the World Series, McCarthy had spoken about the possible shift at second base. With uncharacteristic candor, he told one of his few reporter friends, Dan Daniel of the *New York World Telegram*, "I would say that Joe Gordon is ready to go to second base. But I will have to see him in the spring training before making definite arrangements." No one said much about trading Saltzgaver, but the Lazzeri trade was a significant move. New York's Italian community was not pleased, certainly, and it put added pressure on the young players from Newark. McCarthy, however, had faith in his own sense of the team's new talent, especially Joe Gordon's.[22]

Such wealth of personnel was a major part of what made many baseball fans and Yankee opponents resent McCarthy so much. It was a natural reaction to someone who seems to have it all, a reaction that would naturally be at its sharpest in a time of economic depression. Yet McCarthy was so much more than a mere collector of talent. In the previous season, a rookie pitcher, Spud Chandler, was about to start his first game. As game time approached, Chandler naturally developed a case of butterflies. McCarthy called him into his office. Chandler recalled McCarthy giving him a stern look and asking him sharply: "What are you playing baseball for?" Chandler responded that "I am playing baseball because I love it and because it is my livelihood." Later on, Chandler confessed that he "did not know what in the world he [McCarthy] was driving at." But McCarthy went on sharply asking: "Do you think you're any good?" Chandler said he thought he was. McCarthy sniffed: "You do, huh?" Chandler said "yes" and grew more irritated. McCarthy pressed: "Do you think you're going to win today." Now Chandler was raising his voice a little: "There is only one way to tell," he snapped at McCarthy. "Get your uniform on and come on out and we will see!" Reflecting on the exchange years later, Chandler noted: "McCarthy got my mind off my nervousness by getting me irritated. He had a way of sticking the ice pick in you when it was real cold. But he had a reason for it. He always had a reason for everything he did." That afternoon, Spud Chandler pitched a four-hit shutout, as the Yankees won 1–0.[23]

While McCarthy was weighing the reconfiguration of his 1938 infield, the chief question with which the press was pestering him concerned Joe DiMaggio. Back in October of 1936, right after the World Series victory and DiMaggio being named rookie of the year, Ed Barrow had cagily tried to sign DiMaggio to a three-year contract at $15,000 a year. DiMaggio had refused it, saying he wanted to go home to San Francisco and reflect on matters before signing any contracts. He signed a one-year deal and obviously demonstrated his worth with the season he had in 1937. Right after the 1937 World Series, Barrow tried the same maneuver, offering his star center fielder a quick deal amidst the euphoria after the second Series win over the Giants. Again, DiMaggio would not accept any offers. In February, DiMaggio said he wanted $40,000; Col. Ruppert's offer was $25,000, obviously a greater gap than the paltry sums which had held up the previous years' signings of Gehrig and Dickey. In '38, Gehrig was at a short impasse with Ruppert over salary too. He wanted $40,000; Ruppert offered $39,000. They actually haggled over this! McCarthy persuaded Gehrig to accept the $39,000. DiMaggio's situation was not so easily resolved. Ruppert would not budge. McCarthy spoke to Ruppert, and with Ruppert's permission he spoke to DiMaggio, but there was nothing he could do with such a wide dollar gap. One reporter editorialized that Ruppert should break the $25,000 barrier, give DiMaggio $26,000, and let him sign and save face. Neither McCarthy nor the press could do anything. Ruppert would not budge, and DiMaggio would not leave San Francisco. McCarthy spoke for the exasperated Ruppert as well as for himself when he declared: "The Yankees can get along without DiMaggio. And the $25,000 is final."[24]

DiMaggio's holdout clouded everything for McCarthy and the Yankees that spring. One reporter noted a "lack of devastating drive" with DiMaggio absent and their "lack of real cohesion as champions." New York's March exhibition game record was a mediocre 9 and 7, and just before opening day they lost two straight to Brooklyn. This obviously would not do. McCarthy tried a strained bit of humor over DiMaggio's absence: "I don't know whether we can win with him. He can't pitch." Elsewhere he was frank with his concern that his players "have been at their peak for several years and are bound to pass the high point some time. When that time will be," he wondered, "I don't know. It may come slowly, or it may burst on me like a clap of thunder. I hope it isn't this year." Noting that his job was "to keep the boys on the jump … [and] stop any easing off." McCarthy put the pressure on the players here. In effect he was giving them an excuse to play like any other team, while banking on the notion that he had instilled enough pride that they would show him what he expected deep down — that they would sustain their peak level of play.

The team opened with a loss to the Red Sox on April 18. Two days later DiMaggio signed for $25,000, minus $162 for each day of training he had missed. There was a sense of relief, but there were, according to the irreverent *Daily News*, "almost as many hoping to see Joe flop as there are others joyfully welcoming him back." McCarthy welcomed DiMaggio. "How do you feel?" he asked. "You look like you've been sitting under an umbrella all winter." McCarthy did not immediately insert DiMaggio into the lineup. DiMaggio had kept himself in good shape, but McCarthy wanted to be sure. McCarthy had him work out with the team but kept him on the bench. He hit well, and McCarthy noted: "That guy could get out of bed on New Year's morning and hit home runs."[25]

With DiMaggio still out a bit longer, McCarthy had to continue to turn to a greater amount of platooning. Given the choice, McCarthy always preferred to have a set lineup, but if the situation necessitated juggling he could do it as well as any. In a late April series with Washington, McCarthy engaged in what one reporter described as a "masterminding battle between [himself] … and [Washington Manager Bucky] Harris." It was a series of chess games with pinch hitters, pinch runners, relief pitchers. McCarthy used twenty-eight players in the series, and he swept all three games. Whatever style of management was called for, McCarthy was the master.[26]

The Yankees finished the month of April three games behind Cleveland, now managed by the former skipper of the Yankees' Newark club, Oscar Vitt. (There were rumors about that the two managers were feuding, yet when New York was in Cleveland or vice versa, the two often had breakfast together.) DiMaggio had yet to play. Jack Smith of the nasty *Daily News* accused him of sulking in the dugout. Meanwhile, DiMaggio had other troubles, as the papers announced that Commissioner Landis was investigating DiMaggio's connections to a man named Joe Gould, a boxing manager and racetrack owner who Landis feared to pose at least the impression of a connection to gambling concerns.

It seemed to some a time for falling heroes. The economy, having rebounded a bit, had fallen backward. President Roosevelt had been sullied by his scheme to pack the Supreme Court. The enthusiasm for the New Deal seemed to be waning. The European powers were then disgracing themselves as they allowed Hitler to seize Austria and Czechoslovakia. In the sports world, the German tennis player Gottfried von Cramm received a one-year jail sentence because of an improper relationship with an eighteen-year-old, the punishment from the Nazis likely coming as much because the boy was Jewish as for the relationship being homosexual, although neither was at all popular among German officials.

In baseball, besides DiMaggio, pitcher Lefty Gomez's childishly goofy image was being severely tarnished as his wife, former Broadway showgirl June O'Dea, was suing him for divorce. Rumors were flying that he had locked her in a room, had hit her, and had even threatened to kill her. (All rumors came to naught. Mrs. Gomez dropped her suit, and they reconciled.)[27]

The world had gone from devil-may-care prosperity to utter depression. The trauma of depression had brought forth a desperate search for heroes, a yearning which brought political disaster to some nations. By 1938, amidst a little more stability for some and with a failure of the economy to improve significantly, it indeed now seemed a time for heroes to be debunked. The general public certainly appeared willing to think some worse thoughts. While baseball was more purely symbolic in such dynamics, the fate of DiMaggio's image, although it would go through many more ups and downs, was a part of this symbolism. For DiMaggio's and the Yankees' actual work, there was only one recourse, something upon which McCarthy was very good at getting them to focus—stick to baseball matters, and ignore the fickle winds of journalistic and popular opinion.

McCarthy started DiMaggio on April 29 in a game against Washington. The crowd greeted DiMaggio with an even mixture of cheers and jeers. He got a hit, and the Yankees won the game 8–4. A new problem cropped up for McCarthy that day, as DiMaggio collided with rookie second baseman Joe Gordon on a short fly. DiMaggio was fine, but Gordon was injured. Meanwhile, shortstop Frankie Crosetti was in a slump, and Lou Gehrig, hitting .122, was playing worse than anyone had ever seen him. Ruffing, Dickey, and Selkirk all had nagging injuries. More juggling was needed. McCarthy dropped Gehrig to the sixth spot in the lineup. Billy Knickerbocker replaced Gordon at second base. Back in St. Petersburg, Knickerbocker had bragged that "if someone is hurt and I get into the lineup they'll never get me out." After playing for a week, Knickerbocker seemed true to his word. McCarthy admitted: "The way that fellow has been hitting and fielding, I can't take him out. Gordon is ready, but Knickerbocker has the job." Despite the injuries, the slumps, and the bad press surrounding DiMaggio which was reportedly causing friction with his teammates, the Yankees began winning. Briefly, they held first place, although Cleveland held the lead for most of May. At the end of the month, the Yankees were still three games out.[28]

McCarthy held Gordon out of the lineup, but he was able to maintain the rookie's confidence, reflecting further his unique skills as a handler of men. It was an unwritten rule among the Yankees that no one sat near McCarthy during a game, let alone next to him. Yet while Knickerbocker was playing, McCarthy instructed Gordon to sit right next to him. It may have been a trifle startling to the rest of the team, but that was no issue to McCarthy. He counseled Gordon on some of the finer points of strategy, but more than anything he boosted Gordon's confidence just by the fact that he had him sit with him. While watching the Yankees play Detroit, McCarthy observed the play of the Tigers' second baseman Charlie Gehringer. When Gehringer committed an error, McCarthy asked Gordon: "Don't they say that's the best second baseman in the game?" Gordon acknowledged with a nod. Well, McCarthy observed with total seriousness, "You'd've fielded that ball with a catcher's mitt." Knicker-bocker's hitting tapered off a bit in early June, and on June 9, Gordon was back at second base. He had fully absorbed the specific pointers from McCarthy about their favorite position of second base and was now playing with a new excellence and confidence. He had been having trouble hitting balls high and inside, but he was now comfortable with these pitches, and opposing pitchers learned it best not to thrown him there. Some said it was all due to McCarthy's patient teaching. (Others said it may have also been due to Gordon's eloping to Elkton, Maryland, one night and marrying his University of Oregon girlfriend.) Knickerbocker traded off a bit with Crosetti at shortstop, but he was largely relegated to the bench.[29]

Lou Gehrig had picked up his hitting in late May. From May 3 to 25, his bat-ting average had risen from .122 to .272. On June 1, while the Yankees defeated Boston 12 to 5, Gehrig marked his 2000th consecutive game played. Gehrig had been beaned three times, suffered a bone chip in his elbow, broken the little finger in his glove hand four times and every other finger in that hand once. He had broken several toes, suffered torn muscles, and, since 1933, dealt with chronic back troubles. Yet he kept playing. "Since I have been manager of the Yankees," commented McCarthy, "one player on whom I have depended most and who has never let me down is Gehrig. In running up his record he has never taken it easy so he could extend it. He is the great-est player of all time." Later McCarthy reflected: "When you needed a lift, you'd look to him, and he seldom failed you." At that time there seemed no reason to believe the 35-year old Gehrig would not play superbly for several more seasons. The event of Gehrig's 2000th consecutive game served to demonstrate to the Yankees the wis-dom of putting team issues first. Potential diversions had resolved themselves. Selkirk and Gordon were over their injuries. The cloud over DiMaggio from the Commis-sioner's office passed quietly, and the booing which accompanied his stepping to the plate faded—for the moment. In June and July, the Yankees record was 36 and 16. In the month of July they lost only five games. Cleveland remained their chief rival.[30]

On July 25, the Yankees took over first place, but Cleveland was still in con-tention. From August 5–7, the Indians hosted the Yankees for a crucial three-game series. Cleveland's cavernous lakefront stadium was filled each day. Bob Feller pitched the first game. Johnny Allen, always keyed up to face the Yankees, squared off against Lefty Gomez in the second. The Yankees won both. In the first game, everyone was expecting to see McCarthy send out Gomez face Bob Feller, yet McCarthy beat Feller with a journeyman starter, Bump Hadley. A key here was that McCarthy rested Hadley for a week before the key game, and in practice Hadley appeared razor-sharp. The defeat of Feller with the mere Hadley gave the victory added psychological dimen-sions. Cleveland Manager Oscar Vitt was in shock over it, and his reaction con-tributed to a rift between him and some of his players. Word also shot about the league of McCarthy's choice of starter having come to him in the wee hours of the morning. McCarthy indeed liked to cast himself as a bit of a psychic. He confessed that he made many key decisions at 4:00 A.M. For many people, the mind is simply clearest at dawn. But McCarthy did not care to clarify anything about the "psychic" image; left standing with a bit of mystery, it added another edge to his and the Yan-kees' mystique that intimidated the rest of the league.

With regard to Hadley's victory, another practical point was that McCarthy always saved a pitcher to work against Feller, and he was the only manager to have a career winning record against him. Some managers refused to waste talent against Feller and virtually conceded the games with lesser starters. McCarthy never would; of course he had "the horses," but even more, he always had the knack for finding a special way to win. He was the same over the years against Lefty Grove. Standard managerial thinking said load the lineup with right-handed hitters against him. But McCarthy saw that right-handers would try to pull the ball, and that was futile against such an artist as Grove. He batted left-handers and had more success.

Meanwhile, back in Cleveland, in the third and final game of the key August series, Red Ruffing pitched a two-hitter. Gehrig hit a triple and a home run. The Yankees won 7–0. On June 22, the Indians had held a lead of four and one half games. On August 7, at the end of the Cleveland series, the Yankees' lead was five and one half games. They never looked back. From August 2 to 21, their record was 18 and 3, and the spurt left them eleven games ahead. There would be no more pennant fever in Cleveland for a long time. By the middle of the following season, one Cleveland newspaper was printing the standings of only the second through eighth place teams in the American League.[31]

By early September, another pennant was secured. With injuries, and with divorces and salary controversies plus lots of gossip in the New York media, McCarthy's players had started slowly, with many writing them off as "a once great Yankee team," as Jack Smith of the *Daily News* had declared. McCarthy had been patient. His demeanor was always cool, and he expected the same of his players. When pitcher Wes Ferrell first joined the Yankees in the summer, having been released by Washington, McCarthy called him into his office. "We've got one rule around here," Ferrell recalled McCarthy telling him. "We don't second-guess the manager." No one did. McCarthy was at the helm in a way like no other. On every other team, for example, the players could see the signs their manager was relaying to the third and first base coaches. The Yankees never knew McCarthy's signals. Lefty Gomez tried sitting near McCarthy to see if he could figure out the signs. Two things happened. One was that Gomez could not figure out the signs. The other was that McCarthy quickly figured out what Gomez was up to and snarled at him: "Gomez, pay attention to the ball game. You can't get my signs." Years later, in an Old Timers Game at Yankee Stadium, Tommy Henrich queried McCarthy about his signals: "Joe, have you told anybody what your signs with Fletcher were?" McCarthy merely responded, "No, why should I?" One man was in charge, and everyone knew it.[32]

That summer in 1938, McCarthy juggled lineups and skillfully used lots of substitutes when he had to. His pitchers remained strong through the season, and unlike other all other managers of the day, McCarthy never used starters in relief that summer. Chandler, Ruffing, and Gomez thus remained effective. When various starters regained their health in midseason, McCarthy forged lineups that were murderous. Hoag and Powell started in the outfield with DiMaggio against left-handers. Opposing right-handers would have to face DiMaggio, Selkirk, and Henrich. (One day in Boston that summer, however, the Yanks faced right-hander Jim Bagby. McCarthy benched Selkirk and Henrich and went with Powell and Hoag. The wind was blowing out to left, and McCarthy felt that a right-handed lineup would work that day no matter who was pitching. Result: Powell hit a pop fly home run that the wind took over the left-field wall, and the Yankees won.) In the infield, Rolfe was the fixture at third, Crosetti at shortstop, and Gordon played second. Gehrig of course played every day at first, and, despite his slow start, he had raised his average to .295. With such talent, it was inevitable that one day to the next, one or two players would star. Meanwhile, six pitchers won a total of 86 games. Ill-tempered players like Chapman and Allen had been discharged. The team was on a murderous even keel.[33]

McCarthy always held his temper, and he had forged a team in his own image. To say that McCarthy wanted and forged a team of non-fighters would be erroneous, however. Jake Powell, Chapman's replacement, got in several fights, including one on Memorial Day with Boston Manager Joe Cronin, somewhat at McCarthy's prompting. Lefty Grove had been pitching a bit wildly, and he brushed back several Yankees. McCarthy needled Powell: "Do you see what he is doing to us? ... Are you going to let him get away with that?" When Powell was next at bat Grove had been relieved, and the new pitcher hit Powell with one high and inside. Powell rushed the pitcher; Cronin jumped between them. Powell and Cronin fought, and both were ejected. Then they starting fighting in the dugout tunnel. This cleared both benches, an unusual event in the baseball of that era. McCarthy defended Powell. Unlike Chapman's or Allen's, Powell's rage had a logical focus and was not just about himself.

There was one way Jake Powell was like Alabaman Ben Chapman, however: he was an open racist. Powell once wise-cracked to reporters that during the off-season in Dayton, Ohio, he liked to serve as a policeman. When asked on a pre-game radio program what he liked about police work, he blatantly declared, "what I like to do is go around beating those N____'s on the head." Commissioner Landis suspended him for ten days. McCarthy and Barrow ordered him to visit a series of clubs in Harlem and offer apologies. Powell did as he was ordered. At that point, McCarthy ordered the rest of his players to do no more pre-game radio interviews. Powell was one who would always dedicate himself to the team, and for that McCarthy respected him and wanted him on his roster. McCarthy said if someone on the team had to sleep in the baggage car, Powell would oblige. He never squawked about things like hotel food, and he would crash into many a fence to catch a fly ball. "If selling peanuts will help," said Powell, "I'll sell peanuts."

Joe Gordon was similar. McCarthy noted how Gordon never knew his own batting or fielding average or his RBI total; the team's record was all he knew. "All he cares about is beating you," smiled McCarthy. It was a team of attitudes and not just abilities that McCarthy had built. Chapman was a hothead McCarthy could not control. Powell was a dog that attacked only on command. McCarthy used him judiciously, and the occasional Powell incident often sparked a Yankee rally. As long as Commissioner Landis and the team owners were barring African Americans from the game, all related tinges of racism would not have to be expunged. Many were not even exposed.[34]

Amidst the endless debate about the greatest baseball teams, one era to the next, Ed Barrow said that the 1938 Yankee team was the greatest. Two opposing managers, Connie Mack and Jimmy Dykes, felt the same way. In various times, journalists and baseball people have speculated (endlessly) about the greatest baseball teams of all time. Various Yankee teams obviously figure strongly in the discussions. People often point to the teams of the late 1990s and to those of 1927 and 1961. What gets over-looked in these discussions are the Yankee teams of the late 1930s, as well as those of the early 1950s. The teams of those years won with a steady success like no oth-ers. They had amazing talent and no weaknesses. In the critical months of June, July, and August, the 1938 team won 75 percent of its games. Only the greatest teams have won 70 percent.

Wes Ferrell noted McCarthy's role here: "When you got up there, you saw why the Yankees were winning all those pennants. They were all business, all baseball. ... You didn't see guys running around all night and then kicking your game away the next day." Ferrell had seen a lot of that in Cleveland and Washington. McCarthy had ended such behavior when he was in Chicago, and of course he did the same with the Yankees. It was not that other managers would not try to demand their players behave intelligently, they just did not seem to have the requisite force of personality and will. How McCarthy could muster and convey his demands is not a matter that can be summarily copied via some management manual, it has to come from the heart. Part of how McCarthy did it was perhaps captured by one reporter who later wrote: "When McCarthy became angry, there was always the feeling that not only jobs or careers were at stake, but also arms, legs, jaws, and possibly life itself." Such outbursts of anger were rare, and that was certainly part of their effectiveness, as a steady stream of rage merely dulls the senses of all concerned. Still, the effectiveness of an occasional, well-timed outburst can only be explained in the context of the rest of McCarthy's managerial ways. Red Rolfe, himself later a manager, reflected that "the most important thing McCarthy does is make his players feel important. As a matter of fact, he insists upon it."

Joe DiMaggio encountered that in his rookie season. He brought out the best in his men, and impressed upon them that he expected nothing less all the time. Once he established that outlook, his own players would handle any necessary enforcement. Indeed by 1938, the veterans did a lot of the work to impress the rook-ies with the ways that McCarthy's team comported themselves. Tommy Henrich recalled: Dickey would take you aside. Gehrig and DiMaggio would just glare at you. Crosetti would yell at you in front of the team, as would Selkirk, Red Rolfe, and Johnny Murphy. By 1938, McCarthy's imprint was so fully imposed upon the Yan-kees that no one would dare even think of doing anything but play 100 percent, the way he knew McCarthy wanted. Surrounding this, as Rolfe reflected, one "never saw McCarthy give way to fear." He could be "worried or upset, or just plain mad. But," Rolfe recalled, "I don't think I ever observed fear in him or any sign of defeatism. He communicates that steadiness to his teams, even as an inferior manager will pass along a feeling of insecurity."

That was McCarthy's Yankees; they did not merely act like they feared nothing, they genuinely did not, and the rest of the league knew that full well. Attempted postures to the contrary from any opposition merely reinforced what everyone knew was the real state of affairs. McCarthy's team was simply the best, and McCarthy had made sure everyone knew it. The reporters certainly knew it, and it addition to praising the greatness of the Yankee players, columnists were starting to acknowl-edge that after three pennants McCarthy was truly one of the all-time best man-agers.[35]

After they wrapped up the pennant that September, the Yankees fell off a bit. They were fifteen games up when they secured the flag. McCarthy then rested several starters and gave some opportunities to younger pitching talent. In the end, the Boston Red Sox, who had surged past Cleveland, were nine and a half games behind. In reality, it was not even that close. Nevertheless, McCarthy was anything but content. In November he mentioned to a reporter: "Do you know what was the worst punishment I took all this year? It was the last three weeks of the season, after we had clinched the pennant and when everybody was pushing us around! Those weeks were agony for me. ... I wanted to raise hell in the clubhouse, ... but you can't bawl out a club that has given you your third straight pennant." Doubtlessly, some of the players grasped McCarthy's mood anyway. They would take the unspoken hint into the World Series. McCarthy earned Manager of the Year.[36]

While the Yankees seemed to be making the American League race a boring matter of *deja vu*, sports readers, who were not checking elsewhere in their papers on what Hitler was up to, were more interested in the National League. (They were also intensely interested in whether Hank Greenberg could break Babe Ruth's home run record; he fell just short with 58.) The Giants were in the thick of the National League race, but New Yorkers' hopes for another Yankees-Giants clash would not come to pass. The Giants were strong, as were the Cincinnati Reds, but each was eliminated in late September. Pittsburgh had played well all season, but it was the Chicago Cubs who, as in 1932, came on strong at the end to nose out the Pirates and win. The Cubs were ten games out of first on August 20, but they won twenty-one of their last twenty-five, with a streak of ten in a row in late September.

While he had not meant it as a statement of arrogance, although he would not have objected to it being taken as such, McCarthy minimally scouted the Giants before he faced them in the World Series. He was confident in his existing knowledge of the opposition. Moreover, he was supremely confident in the makeup of the team he was fielding. Others may have wanted to scout the Yankees, but the other way 'round was unnecessary. With the prospect of facing Chicago, McCarthy felt the same way. Two Cubs, Charlie Root and Gabby Hartnett, were former McCarthy Cubs. Tony Lazzeri was on the Cubs too. Generally, McCarthy felt secure in his sense of the team without additional reports. The Cubs fans were trying to come up with some basis to give them a sense of hope. They did have great pitching and defense. Some Chicagoans turned to history; in 1906 it was the mighty Cubs who were the overwhelming favorite going into the Series against the seemingly vulnerable White Sox. The "Hitless Wonder" White Sox shocked the baseball world by winning, so now it was time for the Cubs to pull such an upset. That was how far fans and reporters had to turn to find something positive. Every way one analyzed it with respect to power, speed, experience, coaching, management, confidence, arrogance ... the Yankees had the edge. Even in the Cubs' forte of pitching and defense, the Yankees were at least their equal. To make matters worse, one of the Cubs' best players, outfielder Augie Galan, was hurt at the end of the season and could not play in the Series. McCarthy freely commented on the Cubs situation to add to the pressure: "A ball club does not hold its form after a race like the one the Cubs have just finished," he proclaimed. "A team should have a week in which to let down after clinching the pennant. The situation which develops is mental as well as physical. Our boys have had a good vacation. They let me down too much to suit me. But they did it in 1937 too." McCarthy was in the driver's seat. In previous years, he showed everyone how well he could hang in the thick of a fight. Here he was showing everyone the finer points of maximizing one's position as a front-runner.[37]

McCarthy arrived at the train station in Chicago for the opening of the World Series. He waved off any predictions about the Series. He simply walked with Mrs. McCarthy and shook his head "No, No!" and left. Lots of Yankee fans were predicting a sweep, remembering New York's 1932 sweep of Chicago. Also in recollection of that series, the Yankee players came up with a similar source of bench jockeying. In 1932 the Cubs had given their late season acquisition Mark Koenig only a half share of Series money. This year, former first baseman Charlie Grimm had managed the Cubs for over half the season. In July, Grimm was fired and replaced by catcher Gabby Hartnett. The Cubs voted Grimm a zero share. A late-season pickup pitcher, Vance Page, won five games for the Cubs, and he was given a half share. So the decision to give Grimm nothing was something Yankee bench jockeys could not resist, especially since rubbing in the Koenig matter had been so effective in 1932. Of course, in 1932 Koenig was present amidst the jockeying while this time Grimm was not there.[38]

Some say that in a short series it is better to be lucky than good. But when a team is both lucky and good the results can be demoralizing to the opposition. In the first game the Cubs Bill Lee pitched as well as Red Ruffing, but two hits, a walk (the only walk of the game), and a Cub error gave the Yankees two runs in the second inning. Each team pushed over a run from there. The Yankees won.

The second game became famous in baseball lore. At the outset of the 1938 season, the Cubs had picked up Dizzy Dean. Dean had been one of, if not the, best pitcher in baseball from 1932 until the All-Star Game of 1937. In those five and one half seasons he had won 133 games. But his famous effort to continue pitching after breaking the big toe of his left foot in the All-Star Game had forced him to alter his throwing motion. Against all advice, he continued to pitch and the changed motion caused both muscle soreness and the onset of bursal inflammation. His arm was never the same. His Cardinals team was then willing to deal him away, and the Cubs were willing to give him a chance. He won seven games for Chicago in 1938, including an important one down the stretch against Pittsburgh. Although that September win against Pittsburgh was critical, it was the only game Dean had pitched since August 20. Nevertheless, Manager Gabby Hartnett decided to take a chance and pitch Dean against Lefty Gomez, a man who had never lost a World Series game. After seven innings, Dean and the Cubs were up 3–2. Dean had none of his famous fastball. He was pitching on guile, using change-ups and varieties of motions to keep batters off stride. It was working.

Then in the eighth, Crosetti hit a home run with one on base. Joe DiMaggio did the same in the next inning. As he had so often in the season, McCarthy wisely relieved Gomez with "Fireman" Johnny Murphy, as he was now popularly known. Murphy held the Cubs scoreless, and the Yankees won again. After the game, with genuine admiration in his voice, McCarthy said of Dizzy Dean while patting his heart: "That fellow has one of these." McCarthy admitted the Yankees had been fortunate to win the two games in Chicago. He had been so keyed up and nervous about the outcome of the first game that he tripped over the step of the clubhouse entrance and bruised himself. But while the Yankees had been lucky for two days, the Cubs had been the lucky ones over the prior two weeks. Baseball teaches that these things do have a way of evening out, however cruelly.[39]

The teams traveled to New York for the next games, and as the Cubs entered Yankee Stadium, one reporter described their gait as being "like a condemned man walking his last mile." A reporter asked McCarthy who was going to pitch game five, and McCarthy scoffed at him: "What in the hell are you talking about?" McCarthy was unusually effusive in his praise for his team. To Grantland Rice he exclaimed: "I'll tell you why this is a great team. It's a team — not a collection of individual stars [which is what the 1932 squad had been]. I know they are all for me — and they know I am all for them. They are not merely a team of sluggers. They are as strong defensively as they are offensively." Ed Barrow had said that the 1938 Yankees were the greatest. He elaborated on his claim by pointing to how balanced the team was. There was greatness at so many positions. Day after day, one player or another starred. So it was in the Series with the Cubs. Ruffing won the first game. Homers by Crosetti and DiMaggio won the second game. In the third game, it was Joe Gordon and Bill Dickey who stepped up. Each hit a home run as the Yankees breezed 5–2. In the fourth game Tommy Henrich hit one out. Henrich's homer, along with the now demoralized Cubs giving up a key error and two wild pitches, gave the Yankees an 8–3 romp. As in '32, it was a four-game sweep over Chicago. No one had ever won three straight World Series before, and the succession

McCarthy leaving his office at Yankee Stadium, 1938. The Yankees had just won their third straight World Series, and he was obviously quite happy about it. Reporters rarely found him so jolly. The confidence of McCarthy's Yankee teams of the late 1930s was enormous, and appallingly so to opponents. In 1938, the players bought McCarthy a silver platter as a Christmas present. On it each of their names was inscribed below the heading: "World Champions, 1938." The purchase of such a platter did not show confidence, save for the fact that the players ordered and paid for it in August, seven weeks before the season had been completed. (National Baseball Hall of Fame Library, Cooperstown, N.Y.)

of the margins of victory — 4–2, 4–1, and 4–0 — made the achievement yet more fearsome. Asked if his was the best team ever, McCarthy affirmed with a nice diplomatic touch: "Connie Mack says so, didn't he?"

The Yankee players certainly felt that way. That Christmas, the team gave McCarthy a plaque, with each player's signature inscribed in silver and on top were the words "1938 World Champions." There was nothing unusual about the gift, except the fact that the Yankee players had ordered it in August (and McCarthy knew it). Meanwhile, Newark again won the International League. In 1937, Charlie Keller had led the IL in batting with an average of .353. In 1938 he raised his average to .365, but it was only good enough for second place that year. Catcher Buddy Rosar led the league in hitting. He also played for Newark. Newark actually lost the Little World Series to the American Association champion, Kansas City. Even there no Yankee hater could find a touch of comfort. The Kansas City club was a Yankee franchise too.[40]

Two things McCarthy permitted in the Yankee clubhouse after a World Series victory that he permitted at no other time. One was that the players could sing "Roll Out the Barrel." The other was that Barrow could enter the room. So it was for the third year in a row. With Barrow there, the players sang. Amidst the festivities, one reporter was talking to Bill Dickey. Noting the way that different stars had come forth in the various games, from Crosetti to DiMaggio, to Gordon, to Henrich, the reporter asked what became of his roommate Lou Gehrig. Some reporters had noted that Gehrig's play seemed to be falling off a bit in the late summer. McCarthy had been unwilling to talk about it. Dickey dusted off the question. Gehrig had hit .286 in the Series, and Dickey told the reporter, "The only thing I have against Lou Gehrig is this: He never even had a cold in his life. He's too healthy."[41] Such were the "complaints" of the Yankees at the end of 1938. McCarthy himself had a complaint. After winning the World Series he went to Ruppert and asked for a raise. Ruppert said he could not give him one, as his incessant winning was making everyone so blasé that ticket revenues were down. McCarthy gave up.[42]

For Yankee detractors, the victory over the Cubs, especially the defeat of Dizzy Dean, seemed a cruel crushing of a heroic individual effort. For Yankee fans, the organization McCarthy had forged was the better alternative to mere individual heroics. Many individuals had soared in the '20s. The Depression era needed different models to resonate truly. McCarthy's did. McCarthy recognized, indeed, that he had, at times without realizing it, altered his ways over the years. In Louisville and Chicago he had led more scrappy, fighting sorts of outfits, very much in the John McGraw model. With the Yankees of the late 1930s everything was different — both the times and the players. To a reporter, Fred Lieb, he reflected:

> It has been said that I was tougher in my early years as a manager, especially in my early years in Louisville. Ballplayers were different, and I suppose I have changed. I guess I used to blow off steam a little oftener [sic]. It seems to me that the time when a manager used to talk to his players as though he was driving a bunch of mules is pretty well past. Present day players no longer stand for it. If they do not openly resent it, such a bawling out leaves a mental sore spot. An older generation of players shook off those clubhouse oaths like water off the back of a duck. But you can't run a present day club by using systems of the 90s any more than you could run an industrial plant by using 1895 methods with your hired help.

Some managers never could adjust to changing circumstances. Great players like Ty Cobb and Rogers Hornsby had come up short of expectations as managers because of this, as well as because of their arrogant ways with most of their players that failed to bring out the best in their men.[43] McCarthy had been an effective manager in the 1920s. In a very different era, he became even more successful. "The Yankees," remembered Tommy Henrich,

> never took the field with the attitude that the other team had to roll over and play dead because we were the mighty Yankees. ... Our attitude was: 'We're ready to play; let's go.' ... We weren't cocky, but we knew we were tough. We knew we had good players, and we knew McCarthy was going to make sure we played together as a team and not as nine individuals out there for their own glory.[44]

McCarthy's Yankees won and won (and American League attendance was indeed falling everywhere but Yankee Stadium; the main times other clubs had good home gate was when the Yankees were in town).[45] Looking forward to 1939, everyone, including McCarthy, knew that, barring a calamity, they would win again. They would win, but it would be in spite of calamities, one of which would shake McCarthy and all the Yankees to their very cores but which brought out the best in them, not only as ball players but as men.

27

There'll Be Nobody Again
Like You in 100 Years

After the four-game triumph over the Cubs in 1938, McCarthy went directly from the Stadium to the home of Colonel Jake Ruppert on Fifth Avenue and 93rd Street. (His Hotel Croyden residence was nearby anyway.) Ruppert had not been at the Stadium to watch the game. Since April he had been ill with phlebitis and several resulting complications including a serious liver infection. By October it was difficult for him to get out of bed. Col. Ruppert had, of course, listened to the games on the radio, and when McCarthy arrived, Ruppert smiled and said "Fine, fine 'McCardy,' now do it again next year." McCarthy would do just that, but Col. Ruppert would not live to see it. On January 4, 1939, he suffered a heart attack. Nine days later he was gone. The Yankees were devastated, and McCarthy felt the loss as much as anyone. It was Ruppert who had hired him. When McCarthy met with the press after being hired and nervously referred to Ruppert as "Col. Huston," Ruppert's former partner, the Colonel immediately showed his kindness and confidence by laughing off the matter as an inconsequential joke.

Ruppert had steadily supported McCarthy during the four second-place years, and his loyalty never wavered during the controversies over Babe Ruth's desire to take over as manager. Ruppert had allowed McCarthy to intervene in a few holdout situations, and he had been McCarthy's biggest fan amidst all the pennants and World Series victories. McCarthy lamented to the press: "He will be missed by all, especially by those who were connected with him, as he was very loyal. His place will be hard to fill." Now Col. Ruppert was gone. For the immediate future, Yankee matters looked unchanging. Ed Barrow would continue to run the business affairs of the team, and he, and three others* were given financial control of the ball club.[1]

With Barrow still in charge of the Yankees' business management, the personnel and salary matters of the club did not change. McCarthy wanted no trades. Several clubs in the American League offered as much as $125,000 for Newark star Charlie Keller. All overtures were summarily rejected. More generally, there was some talk

---

*The four trustees were Barrow, George Ruppert (Col. Ruppert's brother), H. Garrison Silleck (the Colonel's brother-in-law), and Ruppert's attorney, Frederick E. Grant.

in baseball that something should be done about the Yankees. Previous three-pennant teams like the Baltimore Orioles, 1894–96, and the Philadelphia A's, 1929–31, had been broken up. Barrow remembered the fact that two three-time Yankee winners had flopped in 1924 and 1929. Reporters reminded McCarthy of this, but it hardly worried him. Most of the pressure was to "break up the Yanks." Rationale here was based on the idea that better balance in the league would prompt higher attendance and profits for all. Col. Ruppert had always rejected such ideas. No one had helped him by curbing the AL leaders in 1915 when he and T.L. Huston had bought the downtrodden Yankee team and began to build it. Barrow and McCarthy would honor that legacy. Others were free to copy their methods, but no outside agency would exert control over them, at least insofar as they could control matters. "My team is set," McCarthy told a Buffalo newspaper. "It's a great one, probably the best ever assembled. We'll not break up this team. We're on top now, and unless the other clubs do some tall hustling before next season, we'll be right there again."[2]

While the political rationales of pure capitalism had been in retreat amidst the struggles of the Great Depression, America's solutions to economic woes had not involved any radical shifts away from a free market's essential foundations, no matter how much the right wing may have criticized the levels of welfare and regulation, nor how much the doctrinaire Left yearned for more systematic alternatives. Within the little world of baseball, the triumph of the Yankees provided a kind of happy proof, at least from the standpoint of New York fans, that a free market can repair itself and come back in triumph. True, this was only baseball, but the game, especially then, could resonate among the population as a powerful metaphor for the broader workings of the society, far more that it would by the late 20th and 21st centuries.

In the late 1930s the nation was still in tough economic shape, and other problems loomed on the horizon, but the triumph of the Yankees symbolized just how well a tightly run organization could still perform brilliantly. American League fans in cities like Philadelphia or St. Louis may have felt victimized, but any claims that there was something unfair in the way the Yankees steadily beat them could not convincingly out-word the straightforward fact that McCarthy and the Yankees simply had the best-run business in the game.

While once a sneering critic of middle America in the 1920's, novelist Sinclair Lewis penned a fundamentally patriotic argument in the 1930s, *It Can't Happen Here*. In his title he meant that the wholesale abandonments of democracy and capitalism that were occurring in many nations during the Depression were things Americans would successfully resist. Whether or not the sense of superiority was true, it was an outlook that appealed to, and indeed deepened, the strongly patriotic elements in the society which survived the Depression. Baseball in '30s America was as significant an artifact of culture as anything in that era, and the ascendency of McCarthy's Yankees gave fans an added source of national as well as community pride. They were a team of players from of both poor backgrounds, like DiMaggio and Crosetti, and elite backgrounds, like Red Rolfe and Charlie Devens. There were college graduates like Gehrig, Rolfe, Devens, and Charlie Keller, and many with no such education. Their fandom similarly spanned all classes. The total domination of the Yankees in these years could certainly provide the basis for opposing political arguments which sneered at the ongoing power of corporate giants.

The articulation of this view would require someone who was, in effect, both a socialist and a Philadelphia A's fan, and such radicals were outvoted even within their own ranks. One radical critic of the era, James T. Farrell, for example, was an ardent Yankee fan. When he watched his Yankees play Cleveland one afternoon in 1940, Cleveland first baseman Hal Trosky hit a home run. Farrell was not pleased, and he puckishly expressed fears that some of his left-wing colleagues might be angry at him for not rooting for someone whose name was but one letter away from that of one of their heroes (Trotsky). The radicals' critique of monopolies certainly had cogency, but few radicals cared about applying their theories and energies to "opiates" like sports anyway. And the few who chose to consider such matters, like Farrell, were too busy enjoying their hot dogs and rooting for Joe DiMaggio and the Yanks. The argument was there to be raised, but the nation's radicals were not terribly interested in the political implications inherent in the plight of the St. Louis Browns. And most smart baseball people, right wing or left, knew even the Browns and their fans would likely benefit less from any outwardly imposed restructuring of the game than they would simply from better management from within, like the management practiced by such a man as Joe McCarthy.[3]

When the Yankees gathered again in Florida, the media's and many of the players' eyes were on the rookie Charlie Keller. Had he been with any other team, Keller would have already been playing in the major leagues for several years. The Yankees could afford to "season" him in Newark, where he batted over .350 in two straight seasons. Keller had an impact. He hit for power. That combined with his hulking appearance and rather "hairy" features led his teammates to nickname him after a big ape in a movie then making the rounds in New York and the nation—"King Kong." McCarthy did not care about nicknames, but he did see in Keller, as he had with George Selkirk, such considerable physical strength that could enable some adjustments in the player's stance and hitting. Like many left-handed hitters, Keller was stronger against right handed pitching. McCarthy had Keller turn his stance slightly forward and more toward right field and instructed him to pull the ball. With those little adjustments Keller could muscle pitches and be less at the mercy of any left-hander's finesse. McCarthy later admitted that he ordered his batting practice pitchers to throw inside to Keller so that he could more readily pull the ball and thus gain confidence with the new way McCarthy wanted him to hit. "You see," McCarthy mused, "there are a lot of things managers never talk about that people think just happen. But things don't just happen. I don't want to sound like I'm bragging; I'm just explaining the way things work."

As with Selkirk, the little adjustment worked well. Keller made the club, as did catcher Buddy Rosar, who'd led Newark and the International League in hitting in 1938. The only other newcomer was Joe Gallagher, the best hitter on the Kansas City club the previous summer. McCarthy was especially pleased about the additions of Rosar and Gallagher, for each was from Buffalo. Otherwise there were no vacancies in the starting lineup or on the bench. Other promising hitters had to stay in the minors.

There would be one other possible vacancy on the club in 1939, one that caused the sports world the utmost of anguish. This matter concerned the health of Lou Gehrig. In the spring, there was no way that McCarthy could bring himself to make any adjustments here. Some things are more important than baseball, as McCarthy and the Yankees would show they knew all too well.[4]

While rookies like Keller, Rosar, and Gallagher were making their marks, the troubles of Lou Gehrig quickly grabbed everyone's attention. "Father Time Scouting Gehrig" was the headline in the *New York Sun* during the first week of spring training. Gehrig was not hitting. His fielding was unsteady, and his running was downright painful to watch. When he played golf, he wore sneakers so he could slide his feet. Lifting them was too difficult. No one knew what was wrong. Some did pinpoint the fact that whatever was wrong was not just a typical slump, or even an extremely bad one. One writer, James Kahn, noted how in a slump one normally sees a batter swinging a split second early or late, or never quite meeting the ball squarely. In Gehrig's case, the timing appeared exactly right. He would hit the ball as squarely as he ever did, but it was just not going anywhere. Writers were loath to say too much about it. People attributed the downturn to "stiffness" and to the strain of having played so unremittingly for so many years. McCarthy obviously saw what everyone else saw, but he said nothing. "Wise old Joe," noted DiMaggio, "didn't try to jolly Lou along, for he knew Lou would see through it." Reporters, let alone players, all knew better than to raise any questions with McCarthy about it. McCarthy's only words to the press here were brusque: "He'll come around."

McCarthy with Yankee catcher Bill Dickey at spring training. When a reporter asked Dickey "What makes the Yankees go?" Dickey calmly pointed to McCarthy, and responded "That man." Dickey was Lou Gehrig's roommate and best friend. He played in more games under McCarthy's management than anyone else, and he ultimately succeeded McCarthy as the Yankees' manager when McCarthy stepped down in 1946. (National Baseball Hall of Fame Library, Cooperstown, N.Y.)

Gehrig's exhibition season batting average was .132. In one game with Kansas City, McCarthy played Tommy Henrich at first base. A few questions arose, but McCarthy belittled them, gently saying that he had told

Gehrig that the springtime rounding into shape simply takes longer as one ages. In a game in Norfolk, actually Gehrig hit two home runs, and the press tried to seize upon the performance as proof that Gehrig was OK. In another game, Gehrig scored from first on a double; the *Daily News* proclaimed "Gehrig CAN Run!" McCarthy, however, knew the Norfolk field had a "short porch" in right where Gehrig had popped his two home runs. He also knew of the fielding error which had allowed Gehrig to score from first. In another game, Gehrig hit what appeared to be a clean double but was easily thrown out coming into second base. McCarthy had no problem with the papers trying to put a happy face on matters, but he was not going to pretend to himself the problem was going away. Some reporters pressed McCarthy about Gehrig, but he would give them nothing. Just before opening day, McCarthy broke his silence here and announced that "Lou will open the pennant season at first base even if he has to hobble around on one leg. If by some mischance he is not able to retain his form, Lou will be the first one to recognize that fact and take himself out."[5] That was all.

Gehrig was suffering, of course, from a disease of which virtually no one outside the medical community of the day had ever heard — amyotrophic lateral sclerosis; ALS, since then commonly referred to as "Lou Gehrig's Disease." At the time of the opening of the 1939 season, no one knew this. McCarthy did not have to instruct anyone to keep silent. Gehrig's roommate, Bill Dickey, simply declared: "Oh, leave him alone. He'll snap out of it." The team maintained what one reporter eerily described as "a dead calm." It was not that McCarthy and the team were in denial. They had only seen Gehrig since March. Given the incredible toughness of the man, they could not help but believe that he could pull out of whatever the problem was. Gehrig was not maintaining any sort of artificial optimism. He brooded. Everyone could see it, especially McCarthy. People avoided meeting Gehrig's eyes, and among the players there was a genuine fear of some sort of emotional outburst. In early April, McCarthy did speak to reporters. The context had to do not with Gehrig but with yet another journalistic discussion as to who was the greatest player of all time. Debate focused on Ty Cobb, Honus Wagner, and Babe Ruth. McCarthy added a new name to the mix. "What about Lou Gehrig?" McCarthy asked:

> What could Cobb do that Lou hasn't done? Run? Yep, that's right. He could run faster. But it hasn't been much of a running game since Gehrig broke in. It's a hitting game. ... Just look at the way Gehrig has gone along year after year. Look at the runs he's scored and the runs he's driven in. Look at his extra-base average. Look at his consecutive game record. Then figure his disposition, his willingness and his steadiness — and a good fielder too. Don't let anybody kid you about that. Gehrig's been quite a guy around that bag.

Although it is not at all far-fetched to place Gehrig in the company of Cobb, Ruth, and Wagner, McCarthy may have been "laying it on" a bit thick here, but the situation that spring was such that he desperately needed to use every possible device that he could to try to buck up his ailing star. No one was a better psychologist here than McCarthy, as Gehrig would soon note. Alas, Gehrig's condition could not be treated with mere psychology.[6]

Gehrig played in the first eight games of the regular season. McCarthy had second baseman Joe Gordon shade noticeably to his left to compensate for Gehrig's limited range. At the plate, Gehrig actually got four hits in twenty-eight at bats. Seeing that Gehrig's reflexes were shot, McCarthy was most afraid of Gehrig being hit by a pitch. He wanted to rest him but nervously left the matter with Gehrig. In the eighth game, against Washington on April 30, Johnny Murphy entered the game as a relief pitcher. He ended one inning with a simple pitcher to first baseman ground out, one requiring only the most basic coordination between the two fielders. As became a famous story, Murphy approached Gehrig in the dugout after the out and said "Nice play, Lou." That was when Gehrig decided to take himself out of the lineup.

After the game in Washington, the Yankees headed out for their first trip "around the West." Their first stop, after a day off, was Detroit. As he often did, McCarthy took the travel day to make a trip home to Buffalo. When he rejoined the team at the hotel in Detroit on May 2, there was a message awaiting him from Art Fletcher that Gehrig had asked for a meeting. At noon the two met in McCarthy's hotel room. Gehrig said he believed he should be out of the lineup. McCarthy wanted to go over all points thoroughly and asked: "You mean you're ready to break your streak?" Gehrig said the streak did not mean a thing if he had ceased being an asset to the club. McCarthy asked Gehrig what made him decide, and when Gehrig began to mention Murphy, McCarthy was ready to hit the roof. But Gehrig stopped him with the point that it was a compliment from Murphy that did it. Gehrig said Murphy "meant it to be kind, but it was worse than any bawling out I ever got in baseball." McCarthy was moved. "I'm sorry it has to be this way, Lou. We'll see how it goes and maybe you'll be back in there later." With Gehrig having said that he felt he was not contributing, McCarthy added: "You shouldn't feel badly about this. You've played this game like a man. There'll be nobody again like you in 100 years."[7]

Later that afternoon, McCarthy inserted Ellsworth "Babe" Dahlgren into the lineup at first base. When the Detroit stadium announcer told the fans that Gehrig was not playing that day, as McCarthy later remembered, they "all got to their feet and gave him the damnedest ovation I ever heard." With regard to Dahlgren, McCarthy said: "I'm going to give Babe every chance to prove he can hold the position. I believe he can. I'm not even thinking what I'll do if he doesn't prove satisfactory." It was highly unusual for McCarthy to reveal how he had not thought through a personnel situation. It certainly revealed how deeply disturbing was Gehrig's situation to him.

McCarthy had another problem. The day before Murphy's "nice play" took Gehrig out of the lineup, Joe DiMaggio tore a muscle in his right leg. At first people feared he had broken a bone. He hadn't, but the torn muscle he had incurred was hardly good news. DiMaggio would be out for several weeks. McCarthy still had Henrich, Keller, Selkirk, Powell, and Gallagher to share the outfield chores. But the sense of how the Yankees, so fully expected to repeat, would fare without Gehrig and DiMaggio was daunting. What the Yankees would do from there would indeed be daunting—for the rest of the league.[8]

Still not knowing what exactly was wrong with Gehrig, the Yankees had to handle the bench presence of their fallen captain. It took the beloved extrovert, Lefty Gomez, to speak up. Tommy Henrich recalled the day Gehrig told McCarthy to take him out of the lineup: Gehrig was the team captain, so he still turned in the lineup card to the umpire. After he did so, he came back to the bench with tears in his eyes. With Gehrig openly crying on the bench, no one knew what to say or do. Gomez finally called out to him: "'What the heck, Lou, now you know how we feel when we get knocked out of the box.' Everyone laughed," remembered Henrich, "including Gehrig, and that broke the tension." The Yankees won the series in Detroit and took over first place. McCarthy kept the team spirit on the same level. The next day the Yankees were in Cleveland and faced Bob Feller. "No doubt about it," nodded McCarthy, "Feller is better than last year. He has better control, which means, however, we'll get more hits off him." The Yankees chuckled at their manager's needling, and they beat Feller and the Indians 10–6.[9]

Another strategic McCarthy move helped the team's coping with the loss of Gehrig. In 1938, just after Jake Powell had gotten into a fight with Joe Cronin, Powell had made some rash racist statements to the press before a game. This had gotten him in hotter water with league officials and with Commissioner Landis, who suspended Powell for several games. McCarthy decided that his players would not speak to the press before any games. This had several benefits. It emphasized that the issues of Gehrig, and of most other team matters, were strictly private. Thus McCarthy enhanced his team's pride and kept all intrusions at arm's length. The fact that Gehrig's situation was much more than a mere baseball matter made untenable any potential press criticisms of McCarthy's policy, and McCarthy would not have listened to, let alone heeded, any newspaper criticisms anyway. As the team won ball games, the efficacy of McCarthy's ways grew all the more apparent to the team. They would privately shoulder their own problems, whether it was Ruppert's passing, DiMaggio's injury, or Gehrig's condition. McCarthy once explained to the press: "A single bad actor on your club can ruin it. First thing you know he's buzzing his roomie. Then his roomie turns into a bad actor. The two influence the others, and before you are aware of it, your whole club is grumbling and completely split into two or three factions." McCarthy had forged a club as utterly devoid of any hint of such behavior as any team, ever.

As McCarthy had constructed and defended them, the Yankees were a force completely unto themselves, and from the point of Gehrig's departure from the lineup until May 28, they compiled a record of 20 and 3, including a streak of 12 wins. On May 27, DiMaggio put in his first appearance as a pinch hitter. He doubled, knocking in two runs. The Yankees finished the month of May six and one half games ahead of Boston. Before every game, Gehrig took out the lineup card, and every Yankee (as well as the opposition) could not but take a moment of meditation and reflection. If anyone's spirit was ever lagging, all he had to do was look down the bench at Gehrig. Meanwhile, to the degree any opposing teams could rally themselves with "damned Yankees" hatred, the presence of Gehrig further routed it. Some praised the Yankees of 1939 for keeping Gehrig on the team and thus winning with one less contributing player. McCarthy knew nothing could have been further from the truth. Gehrig's presence on the bench was worth that of several players.[10]

DiMaggio was fully back in the lineup on June 7. He began to hit at a .400 clip, and the Yankees continued to win. They actually fell off a bit; in May their record had been 23 and 4; their June record had "fallen" to a mere 20 and 7. After a victory over Washington on June 30, the Yankees' record stood at 50 and 14. Second-place

Boston came in the next day. McCarthy made what one newspaper called "a magnificent gesture of contempt toward the rest of the American League." He had just brought up a new pitcher from the minors, Marius Russo. He had sold Joe Gallagher to the St. Louis Browns and released Wes Ferrell unconditionally to make room for him. Ferrell had developed arm trouble, so there was no controversy there. With Gallagher, some reporters were arguing that he was better than Charlie Keller, but these were some of the same people who had doubted that Joe Gordon could adequately succeed Tony Lazzeri. McCarthy always trusted his instincts. Second-guessing in the press would never have any impact on Joe McCarthy. (In St. Louis, Joe Gallagher joined former Yankees Myril Hoag and George McQuinn in the Browns' starting lineup, now one third ex–Yankees.) The Yankees were twelve games up on Boston, and while the Boston fans were hyped about the upcoming series with the Yankees, McCarthy sent Russo out to pitch the opening game with young Buddy Rosar as his catcher. Sustaining the team's incredibly high pitched pace, but nonetheless keeping it on an even keel was paramount in McCarthy's mind. The Red Sox actually took two of three in the series. McCarthy was not worried, however. He and the Yankees had something more important on their minds anyway.

Back on June 2, the Yankees had announced that Gehrig was going to go to the Mayo Clinic in Minnesota for a complete examination. "We hope it's nothing serious," McCarthy said, adding "though he doesn't look good now." It was the only direct comment McCarthy ever made about Gehrig's deterioration, something about which the team, and the papers, had continued to make no statements. Gehrig sat on the bench at every game with the Yankees over the subsequent ten days. From June 9–12, the team played a series in St. Louis and then traveled to Kansas City for an exhibition. Gehrig put in an appearance for three innings in Kansas City. Then he took a train to the Mayo Clinic where he spent a week. The report from the Mayo Clinic examination came forth in the newspapers on June 22. It was the first time the general public had ever heard of "amyotrophic lateral sclerosis." The Clinic's report was full of technical terms, but within days, thousands of fans, reporters, and most of the Yankees who had seen their personal physicians had been able to ask someone capable of interpreting the report. A sense persisted that Gehrig's condition was akin to that of President Roosevelt's infantile paralysis, hence one that would end his baseball career but not his life. Those who listened to any competent doctor learned this was not so. Gehrig's condition was steadily degenerative, irreversible, and fatal.[11]

The news of the true gravity of Gehrig's condition prompted the Yankees to organize an appreciation day for him. They chose to have it on July 4, as a between-games ceremony during a doubleheader with the Washington Senators. On June 18, they had a pre-game ceremony, the first to be held before a game and simultaneously broadcast over the radio. This one was to honor McCarthy for being Manager of the Year in 1938.[12] Thirty-five thousand came to the Stadium that afternoon. The ceremony for McCarthy was a complete success, and everyone expected the July 4 ceremony to be its equal. That morning the *New York Times* called the event "an occasion which gives promise of developing into a momentous day." The day indeed proved momentous, but its most memorable moment came within a whisker (and a McCarthy nudge) of never occurring. Yankee greats, past and present, were on hand, including Babe Ruth, who stepped over the old rift between his wife and Gehrig's mother, and made peace (with Gehrig not completely comfortable with it). Also present were many of the city's prominent citizens, including Mayor LaGuardia and Postmaster General Jim Farley. Gehrig had indeed weakened enormously, as ALS sufferers always do, and he could not even hold the gifts presented to him. He stood during the entire ceremony. The emotions were overwhelming, and even independent of any such emotional depletion, it was very difficult for Gehrig to maintain himself at a standing position for too long.

McCarthy stood near Gehrig the whole time. He quietly told Babe Dahlgren to stay nearby as well to be on the alert and "catch him if he starts to go down." Every few minutes, as Gehrig swayed on his shaky legs, McCarthy steadied him with words of reassurance. McCarthy spoke briefly: "It was a sad day in the life of everybody when you told me you were quitting because you felt you were a hindrance to the team. My God, man," exclaimed McCarthy, "you were never that!" There was not the slightest bit of hyperbole from McCarthy here.

After all the presentations and speeches, Gehrig was supposed to speak. He first whispered something to the master of ceremonies, *New York Journal-American* columnist Sid Mercer. Mercer then turned back to the microphone and announced to the crowd: "Ladies and gentlemen, Lou has asked me to thank you all for him. He is too moved to speak." Mercer then began taking the microphone away, and all the players and guests assembled on the field began moving, believing the wonderful ceremony had concluded. But the crowd started to chant over and over: "We want Gehrig!" Mercer had no response and merely continued to move the microphone.

It was Joe McCarthy who stepped forth at this point. He walked the few steps with Gehrig up to the microphone and gave him a gentle tap. "Go on, Lou," he whispered, "You don't want to disappoint the fans." Gehrig may have planned a speech, but he discarded it and stepped forth with a "count your blessings" peal from the heart which, in its utter authenticity, still resonates, in the annals not just of baseball but of American letters.

Telling the crowd how lucky he was, Gehrig cited his associations with teammates, past and present, and with his opponents. "Sure I'm lucky!" he professed. "Who wouldn't consider it an honor to have known Jacob Ruppert ... Ed Barrow ... Miller Huggins ... and," he emphasized, "to have spent ... nine years with that smart student of psychology — the best manager in baseball today, Joe McCarthy." Many films and fictionalized versions of Gehrig's speech fail to convey how his expressed sentiments actually drew the crowd into vocal involvement:

> When the New York Giants [and the crowd boo'ed loudly here] a team you would give your right arm to beat, and vice versa, sends a gift — that's something [and the boo'ers then cheered]. ... When you have a wonderful mother-in-law [and the crowd boo'ed again] who takes sides with you in squabbles against her own daughter [the cheers returned] — that's something. When you have a father and a mother who work all their lives so you can have an education and build your body — it's a blessing [more cheers]. When you have a wife who has been a tower of strength, and shown more courage than you dreamed existed, that's the finest thing I know.

Now the crowd was absolutely silent. Gehrig then concluded, "I might have had a tough break, but I have an awful lot to live for. Thank you." The fans erupted. Many wept. Joe DiMaggio did, so did Mrs. Eleanor Gehrig and Mrs. McCarthy, who were seated together. Mrs. Gehrig said to a reporter: "I'm glad Lou was able to walk out there and make his little talk over the microphone. I knew he wouldn't let the fans down."[13] Joe McCarthy also knew Lou couldn't let them down, and posterity is the richer for his knowing it.

When the ceremony was over Gehrig turned to Bill Dickey and said "Bill, I'm going to remember this day for a long time." Baseball had never seen a dedication of such emotional depth and intensity. Less than a half hour later, Gehrig was back on the bench, and the Yankees went out and beat the Senators 11 to 1. The Yankees would actually begin a slight slump, going 3 and 9 in the first half of July. It may have indeed been an emotional letdown after the July 4 ceremony. It was their only slump of the season. Boston beat them five straight and closed to six and one half games behind. McCarthy grew a bit irate: "Just who the hell are supposed to be the world champions, us or the damned Red Sox? We're a whole lot better than Boston."

With McCarthy at the helm, five Yankees played the entire All-Star game. The AL won, but some criticized McCarthy again for the apparent favoritism. Unaffected, the Yankees reacted to the sniping by snapping out of their July slump. They finished the month with a record of 14 and 5 and followed that with a spurt from August 1 to 25 in which they went 21 and 8. In the last nine games of that stretch, they scored 104 runs, finishing the month with a lead of 13 games. At this point, one newspaper in Cleveland was listing only the second through eighth place teams in their daily printing of the American League standings. They did not wish to publish what was all too well known. Other dynasties have dominated the game; no other ever prompted such a sign of complete concession. Yankee fans bore some of the burden in regard to the American League becoming so blasé. Their fourth-straight pennant winning Bombers failed to draw 1,000,000 at home that season. All season, McCarthy received letters to the effect that he was ruining the league. "You'd think it was wrong to win ball games and to win pennants. Some of the letters are vicious. 'Do I want to win 'em all?'" Relaying this to a reporter, McCarthy fixed his tie, grew a bit calmer, smiled ever so slightly, and honestly asked: "Who doesn't want to win them all?"[14]

On September 1, Nazi Germany invaded Poland. Americans immediately began debating the questions of war involvement and isolationism. While opinions varied among ball players as much as they did among the public at large, baseball would provide a symbol of innocence and comfort, a relief from the war issues, and a reminder of national values. The work of McCarthy's Yankees that season reinforced the ideals of dedication and their success allowed many fans to wrap themselves in a focus on baseball. Their dedication to such a teammate as Gehrig symbolized that even within such a discreet realm as sports competition, there are higher issues which need not, should not, and cannot be avoided. Other Yankee team choices underscored this sort of dedication. In 1937, for example, a Yankee pitcher named Johnny Broaca abruptly left the team in midseason. He also abandoned his wife. That fall, the Yankees voted Mrs. Broaca a full share of World Series money. McCarthy never wanted to advertise such moves. The point was to do what was right, not to brag about it.

The 1939 Yankees wrapped up the pennant on September 16. They were 17 games ahead of the Red Sox. Joe DiMaggio was batting .408 on September 2. Two days later he twisted his knee, not too badly, but enough to slow him down a bit. At the same time he caught a cold that gave him continuously watery eyes. Hoping all season that DiMaggio might hit .400, many fans and reporters wondered why, with the pennant a foregone conclusion, McCarthy did not give DiMaggio a rest. McCarthy never offered; DiMaggio never asked. DiMaggio likely wanted to protect his average, but he knew better than to inquire with McCarthy. McCarthy later told DiMaggio that he didn't want the fans to think of him as "a cheese champion." "Can you believe it?" DiMaggio later reflected. "But that's the way Joe was; he wanted you to play." DiMaggio still led the league in hitting, but by the end of the season his average had dropped to a mere .382. He had hit .266 in the last 25 games. The nation was facing the possibility of taking on a whole new set of heavy burdens. McCarthy's ways that relegated personal ambitions and glory to the cause of something bigger seemed the right way of doing things. A good soldier did not let his buddies go into battle while he stayed behind nursing an eye infection. Gehrig always personified this, and everyone else would learn it more and more. At the end of the season, with the Yankees having performed so perfectly, a reporter at last came up with a criticism of McCarthy that people thought was valid. His uniform was too baggy. Drawing upon the contemporaneous popularity of Walt Disney's movie *Snow White*, the *Daily News'* Jimmy Powers said McCarthy looked like one of the Seven Dwarfs. McCarthy paid no heed and never altered his uniform. Given some things that Jimmy Powers would later write, this was one of his more perceptive columns.[15]

With a record-shattering fourth straight American League pennant, McCarthy had yet another National League champion to face. This year it was the Cincinnati Reds. Cincinnati had been touted as the one team that could possibly beat the Yankees. The National League was more of a pitching and defense league. But the past three Series had proven that Yankee power was just too much for that sort of baseball. Cincinnati had great pitching and defense, and they had good power too with outfielder Ival Goodman, first baseman Frank McCormick, and catcher Ernie Lombardi. Their biggest asset was their duo of starting pitchers, Paul Derringer and Bucky Walters. Together that year they had won 52 games. With the succession of the three previous World Series margins having gone from 4–2 to 4–1 to 4–0, it seemed this year the Yankees would at least have some decent competition. That's what various sports reporters were saying anyway. McCarthy had no comment. He "said" he had not scouted the Reds. He added, however, "if I do have a man [scouting Cincinnati] I won't tell you." He had actually compiled some reports on the Cincinnati batters and put Bill Dickey and the pitchers to work on them.[16]

McCarthy did not need to do a thing with his starting lineup. He used the same eight men for the entire series. Charlie Keller had hurt his ankle in September, but by the time of the Series, he was well enough to play. Mrs. McCarthy said she made special prayers in Church for a quick mending of Keller's ankle. The prayers worked and then some. McCarthy's pitching choices were key matters. In game one, the Reds started their 25-game winner Paul Derringer. McCarthy sent out Red Ruffing. Ruffing had been having arm trouble late in the season, and one reporter, Dan Daniel of the *World-Telegram*, concluded that McCarthy's choice of Ruffing indicated he was "either playing a shrewd game or ... in a state of confusion." McCarthy always trusted his hunches, especially, as he relayed to told Dan Daniel, the ideas that come to him in the wee hours of the morning. The choice of Ruffing certainly confirmed McCarthy's self-confidence. Ruffing pitched very well, but so did Derringer. Cincinnati scored once in the fourth inning. In the fifth inning Joe Gordon was on first. Babe Dahlgren then doubled. Outfielder Wally Berger retrieved the ball and threw to second base. Third base coach Art Fletcher saw where the throw was going, and he kept Gordon going home. McCarthy later said Fletcher's call was "the outstanding play." The play was close, but Gordon was safe. The score remained 1–1 until the bottom of the ninth. Then Charlie Keller tripled, and Bill Dickey singled him home. The Yankees won 2–1. Cincinnati Manager Bill McKechnie walked out to congratulate Selkirk and Dickey. He called over to McCarthy: "You coming out tomorrow, Joe?" McCarthy responded: "Yeah, I'll be out Bill, and I guess you will too." The Reds had lost the game, but McKechnie's words exemplified what his men now knew — they could play quite well with those much-heralded Yankees, or so they thought.[17]

Buoyed by the strong showing in game one, Cincinnati felt even more confident with 27-game winner Bucky Walters starting the next day. McCarthy again played a hunch. Monte Pearson had had a respectable, but hardly Walters-level, season of 12 wins and 5 losses. But McCarthy remembered it was Pearson who had stood in and beat none less than Carl Hubbell in game four against the Giants in 1936. On this day, Pearson pitched his greatest game. He had a no-hitter through seven innings. The Reds scratched two hits from there, but they amounted to nothing. The Yankees jumped on Walters with a three-run rally in the third inning, and Dahlgren added a solo home run the fourth. The Reds knew the Yankees were tough. They did not know that when McCarthy's hunches were on target they were unbeatable. After the close game one, the Reds felt "up." As they traveled back to Cincinnati for game three, having seen both of their two marvelous aces lose, they were decidedly downcast.[18]

Lefty Gomez had been out of action for two weeks, but McCarthy again felt he "certainly deserves a chance." It was another McCarthy hunch, only this one was not on the money. The Yankees gave Gomez a cushion, scoring two runs at the top of the first, but Gomez was ineffective. He gave up a run in the first. In the second, he gave up two. McCarthy was on edge. He lost his temper over a two-strike foul tip he believed Dickey had caught. The umpire did not alter his decision, naturally. McCarthy was at least not ejected. Later that inning Gomez injured himself fielding a grounder. McCarthy lifted him and put in Bump Hadley. This proved a good choice. Hadley pitched a shutout from there. Meanwhile, against the lower ranks of the Reds pitching staff, DiMaggio homered, Dickey homered, and Keller homered twice. Mrs. McCarthy's prayers had apparently been well received. The Yankees won 7–3 and were up three games to none. The team was ready to begin celebrating in the locker room, but McCarthy put a stop to it with the simple words: "better wait until tomorrow." As for the game, McCarthy shrugged to reporters: "There's nothing much to say. Keller, DiMaggio, and Dickey did all the talking." Then he added with a wry smile: "They were kind of noisy too, weren't they?"[19]

Oral Hildebrand was a veteran pitcher who had had good years with both the Indians and the Browns. McCarthy had traded for him for the '39 season, but he had proved a bit disappointing, winning only ten games. McCarthy continued to believe in him, however, and he decided to try him for game four. Cincinnati had no choice.

They sent Derringer back out, with Walters in the bull pen. Both Derringer and Hildebrand pitched well. With a scoreless tie in the fifth, McCarthy relieved Hildebrand, who he felt was weakening, and brought out Steve Sundra. Sundra was effective, but in the seventh inning, after the Yankees had scored two at the top of the inning, the Reds scored three unearned runs. McCarthy then turned to his ace reliever Johnny Murphy. Murphy gave up one in the eighth, but the Yankees tied the game with two in the ninth, on a fatal error by the Reds shortstop. This set up extra innings. In a now famous inning of baseball lore, the Yankees scored three runs in the top of the tenth on a play known as "Lombardi's snooze."

In the inning, Crosetti walked, Rolfe sacrificed, and Keller was safe on an error. DiMaggio then singled, and when the ball got away from Ival Goodman in the outfield, both Crosetti and Keller scored. Keller was nearly out, and when he was attempting to score, he slammed hard into Reds catcher Ernie Lombardi. The ball rolled away from Lombardi, and he appeared to rest, as one paper put it, "brooding over the futility of it all." Lombardi was actually a touch dazed from the bang of big Charlie Keller crashing into him. Some said that Keller had kicked Lombardi in the testicles. By the time Lombardi was recovering, Joe DiMaggio was trying to score, and his perfect slide was safe, just under Lombardi's tag. Johnny Murphy shut down the dispirited Reds in their half of the tenth, and that was it.[20]

Now the Yankees could celebrate. Indeed, for the first time it was McCarthy who led in the singing of "Roll Out the Barrel." His singing voice was described as "a throaty baritone," further proof of why it was good that he never tried the theater professionally. "I'm tickled beyond words," he effused. "It's great to have a ball club like this winning the way it does." Euphoric as he was, and with all the players and reporters whizzing by and congratulating him, when Charlie Keller shook his hand for the second time, McCarthy cracked: "Charlie, that's the second time you did that. Now I guess you want me to kiss you?" As everyone knew, McCarthy never missed a thing. McCarthy and the Yankees each received $5,542 shares for their World Series win, slightly less than the $5,783 they had earned in their sweep of Chicago the year before. By the standards of subsequent generations, the sum appears paltry, but a cruise from New York to Miami then cost $81, meals included (to Havana, the cost was $105). Some players used the money for such vacations. Mr. and Mrs. McCarthy simply went back to Gates Circle.[21]

The four-game sweep of Cincinnati was the final exclamation point on the dynasty McCarthy had built. The year 1939 marked the 100th anniversary of baseball's "invention." (In the early 20th century, Albert Spalding had claimed that Abner Doubleday had started baseball in Cooperstown, N.Y., in 1839; it was a myth.) Although no one could fully determine when the game actually emerged out of sports like cricket and rounders, baseball's scions and the press had fastened upon the "1839" story as the starting point, so McCarthy and the Yankees' fourth consecutive championship had the added symbolism of cap-stoning the national pastime's century mark. The '39 victory marked the fifth time the Yankees had swept a World Series. Aside from the Boston Braves' sweep of Philadelphia in 1914, no other team had ever accomplished a four-game sweep even once. McCarthy's Yankees were proving conclusively they were the best ever. By 1939, with the wide margins of the four straight pennant victories and the succession of World Series opponents from the Giants to the Cubs and the Reds, it was clear that it did not matter what team stepped up to challenge the Yankees. There would be only one result.

In five World Series, McCarthy had accumulated a record of 20 and 3! Some fans, both for the Yankees and against them, grew almost bored. Some said it was like rooting for U.S. Steel, but the point was that during the Great Depression many were doing just that. As with respect to U.S. Steel, calls again came forth to break up the Yankees, but anti-trust was not so popular in the Depression. It seemed better to favor what continued to work and to join it, if that was possible. For Yankee haters, boredom and derision were natural defenses, and for even the most rabid of Yankee fans, it was difficult not to be at least a little blasé. When the Yankees returned from Cincinnati there was but a small crowd at Grand Central Station to greet them, and it was a good thing too, because most of the troupe had gotten off at 125th Street to head to their homes in Westchester County. Even Mayor LaGuardia left the train there. When some players had tried to whoop it up a bit on the train, McCarthy told them to "cut that kid stuff out," scoffing, "I thought I was managing professionals!" Frankie Crosetti later recalled, "You didn't dare fool around afterwards or Joe McCarthy would send you packing." "Like any clubhouse," Tommy Henrich recalled, "ours had its cutups and good times, but ... there wasn't a whole lot of hell-raising. ... McCarthy simply wouldn't allow it." This was simply another World Series victory, and like anything else in the day-to-day routine of a New York year, the best thing to do was take the shortest route home and avoid the traffic. McCarthy's only comment was that he wanted to take Mrs. McCarthy to the World's Fair in Queens, as through the summer months he "couldn't find the time for it."[22]

For New Yorkers, and many other Americans, the sense of absolute perfection being achieved with an unruffled, lithe confidence was ennobling. The Depression had been traumatic. An excess of hoopla over any achievement smacked of the audacity of the 1920s, whose revelry and hedonism seemed to have been a chief part of the failure of an adolescent society to see oncoming dangers before it was too late. Babe Ruth's rise and fall had symbolized such immaturity in baseball; McCarthy's Yankees thus presented a new, and indeed, as their unequaled record showed, a better formula, one that achieved more because it had risen above the childish roar and pizzazz of past times.

A McCarthy team could achieve all it could and plan safely for the future too. In May, when McCarthy put in an appearance at the New York World's Fair's Court of Sport, a boy asked him who would succeed him as manager. McCarthy blanched for a moment, then he recovered and said, "I hope ... when it comes time for me to quit managing the Yankees, I have the choice of naming my successor [and] recommend you for the job." This was a bit like Roosevelt seeking a third term, unthinkable in past times but completely acceptable following the Depression. As Babe Ruth had symbolized a previous era, McCarthy's quiet, utterly overwhelming grey-flannel suit success thus caught the fancy of 1930s fans, not just because he won, but because of how he won. The drunken audacity of Babe Ruth had had a romantic appeal. McCarthy's way was anything but romantic, but oh how it worked! As Lefty Gomez put it: "He was a tough guy ... he really knew the game. We went through a lot of schooling with him. He was always trying to be perfect in everything."

A safety-conscious America of the Depression era certainly understood this outlook, and when it worked they could not give it more respect, however begrudgingly. McCarthy's players had to be teachable. They behaved with maturity; no bed checks, always dressed in coats and ties. As McCarthy said, "You don't go into a bank and see people with shirts unbuttoned and hairy chests." The emotional players like Ben Chapman and Johnny Allen had been weeded out. Any other such jarring influences were not welcome. Bench jockeying and swearing had declined; so did on-field fights (and they did not rise in frequency until the 1980s and beyond). At times McCarthy encouraged his players to get on an opponent from the bench, but he was intelligently selective about it. He had nudged his men to jump all over the Giants in the '37 World Series, but he knew in other times when silence served better. Gerry Walker, a strong hitter with the White Sox, and a very easy-going personality, was someone to whom McCarthy wanted little said: "Gerry is sleeping; let's not wake him up." On another occasion, when one Yankee tried to razz Detroit's star second baseman Charlie Gehringer, McCarthy snarled: "Leave him alone; don't wake him up. He hits .340 as it is. Get him mad and he's liable to hit .800!" McCarthy's was the controlled, rational way to succeed, a formula the country felt they should have had more of before the economy went sour.[23]

To Yankee supporters, the success could be likened to the work of FDR and the New Deal. To Yankee-haters it was more akin to what Meyer Lansky and Lucky Luciano had succeeded at creating with the mafia, causing greater fear and depression around them. Hated or loved, matters of control and domination had won the day, and in baseball one figure seemed most responsible. When a reporter asked Bill Dickey what the secret of the Yankees' success was, he simply pointed to McCarthy and said "that man."[24] Who could argue? St. Louis's Gas House Gang had symbolized a nostalgic clinging to old ways which a depression era rendered compelling, at least for some. A St. Louis reporter asked Coach Art Fletcher why there was no singing or highjinks on the Yankee bench. Fletcher calmly replied: "We say it with base hits, pitching, and fielding."[25] McCarthy's Yankees were the new, completely organized juggernaut, the way to success that a terribly harsh reality demanded. Command of detail, perception of talent, development of new players, a psychological understanding of each of his men, assembling a team of dependable coaches and assistants, mastery of game tactics, needling opponents, not suffering fools—whatever aspect of managing one could raise, McCarthy was the master. And he did it all with a outwardly calm, utterly self-contained confidence that unflinchingly took on all the burdens of the tasks at hand as a matter of course.

In the true Socratic sense, the late 30s Yankees were a team which "did its job," with their only diversion coming in regard to such truly higher matters as their undisputably noble care for a fallen hero. McCarthy and the Yankees had triumphed amidst Depression. To many the victories appeared cold and arrogant. But winning amidst the losses of Gehrig and Ruppert, the triumphs had to be seen as more than products of something more deeply humane. Of course, many a Yankee-hater, of the day and since, would resist any such praise.

28

The Sun Can't Shine
All the Time

With the coming of the baseball season in 1940, the sports pages were of course full of predictions about more Yankee triumphs, all to the chagrin of the rest of the American League. Joe McCarthy's utter domination was hardly a point of joy among the other managers in the league. Thoughts about breaking up the Yankees were still present among American League managers. The AL passed a rule forbidding the pennant winner from making intra-league trades, but McCarthy had such a solid core of young talent, there was no reason to worry. McCarthy always laughed at his league rivals who wanted to embargo the Yankees. "That's the wrong strategy for the opposition," he declared. When he was with Chicago, he procured Riggs Stephenson, Kiki Cuyler, and Rogers Hornsby in trades. "If I were running behind I'd move heaven and earth to break down the strength of the winner with trades. But," he sighed, "I am the only manager in our league who has that angle on the situation."

McCarthy's success seemed to have driven rival managers to distraction, literally so in that they had diverted one another onto the notion that non-commerce would solve their problems. They could not beat the Yankees, and their response was to pretend they were not there. McCarthy would never let himself feel, let along display, any such sense of futility or fear. And his Yankees came to mirror him. Reporter Harry McLemore of United Press wrote that "in talking with any American League manager other than Joe McCarthy, I always try to keep from mentioning the New York Yankees." It was, he mused, "the same sort of politeness that prevents one from talking about Thanksgiving to a turkey."

When interviewing the wisecracking White Sox Manager Jimmy Dykes, McLemore's strategy failed, however. "I know what you really want to talk about," snapped Dykes, "so let's talk about the Yankees." McLemore immediately shifted his tone to accommodate the sarcastic Dykes. "They can't be such a tough team," McLemore inquired, "you beat them 4 out of 22 last year." Dykes smiled: "It isn't the Yankees as a team that bothered us. It's their key man. Let them lose their key man and the result would be a mad scramble for the pennant." "Who's the key man," asked McLemore. Dykes thought a few seconds and nodded: "Well, Bill Dickey, or if not Bill Dickey, Joe DiMaggio, or let something happen to Joe Gordon, then where will they be? And don't overlook Red Rolfe at third base as a key man, and if you don't think Crosetti is a great shortstop and vital to the Yankees, you're crazy." McLemore inserted: "Red Ruffing?" Dykes agreed: "Now you're talking. There's a real key man." "In all," McLemore tabulated, "Dykes named nine key men." Conclusion: "If something happened to these nine men simultaneously, it would make it pretty tough for the Yankees." Life would actually get pretty tough for the Yankees in 1940, and it indeed required something to happen to most of their key nine players, and to several others besides.[1]

A few American League players and some reporters tried to show they were not so terribly awed by the Yankees. The Tigers' Hank Greenberg predicted a pennant, not for Detroit, but for Boston. He pointed especially to the improvement that had come to the club with the addition of rookie Ted Williams in 1939. He saw Williams and the Red Sox only getting better. The Yankees had certainly come to respect Williams as quickly as anyone. In an early season meeting with the pitchers, McCarthy and Dickey had gone over tendencies, strengths, and weaknesses of various hitters in the league. With Williams, the Yankees had tried the usual tests of pitching him high and tight then low and away. The pitchers reported: "High and tight is ball one, and low and away is ball two." After a few minutes on Williams, Dickey closed the discussion: "I think he's just a damned good hitter." Learning of Greenberg's words, McCarthy commented when making a dinner speech in Elizabeth, New Jersey: "No one man can win a championship for a ball club. Hornsby couldn't; Cobb couldn't. But just the same," McCarthy concluded with a rueful twinkle, "I certainly hope nothing happens to Joe DiMaggio." McCarthy knew that Cleveland, Boston, and Detroit could give him trouble that season, but, while knowing how the fickle matter of injuries can debilitate anyone, he remained guardedly confident.[2]

McCarthy had spent another quiet winter in Buffalo. For five weeks that winter he sat for over three hours a day for an artist, Tony Sisti, who painted his portrait. Sisti later commented on how pleasant and interesting a subject Mr. McCarthy was. "I could see his power and quality of leadership," Sisti vividly recalled. "He had kind eyes and was very observant, ... modest, meticulous, sensitive, and very artistic." The impatience and distance that members of the press regularly encountered was never present, as was so with his friends and with his best players. At one point during weeks of the sitting, the flow of work did have to stop for several days. Lou Gehrig called. His condition had taken a turn for the worse, and he wanted to see McCarthy again while he still had some strength. McCarthy went to New York at once. When the portrait was completed, Mrs. McCarthy felt Sisti had drawn her husband's mouth a bit to one side. Joe was pleased with the portrait, however. In regard to the mouth, he explained to Babe: "That's the way I talk. That's the only way I can talk to players in the dugout and still watch what's going on in the field. No. Tony's got it right. That's me, all right." McCarthy eagerly offered to buy the painting, but Sisti liked it so much that he kept it for himself.[3]

As the season approached, injuries proved to be a problem for the Yankees. Lefty Gomez twisted his ankle and could not pitch properly. In his first season start against Washington he sprained his back. Up to that point in the game, he had not been effective anyway. In the annual April exhibition series against the Brooklyn Dodgers, Jake Powell had a collision with the outfield wall and suffered a fractured skull. Red

Ruffing was hit in the right elbow by a line drive during batting practice. Bill Dickey had a pulled muscle in his left thigh. Buddy Rosar suffered a bad cut on his throwing hand. Pitcher Marvin Breuer was ill. Red Rolfe had a sore throat and an eye infection. On a single play, Joe Gordon had hurt his leg, although he did not leave the lineup, and Joe DiMaggio twisted his knee. Something had now kept DiMaggio out of the opening day lineup in five consecutive seasons. As Lefty Gomez mused: "Nothing ever seems to happen to DiMaggio—in the winter."

As of May 1, the whole Yankee team was batting .161. DiMaggio came back on May 8, just in time to lose to Detroit, Cleveland, and Boston. Usually DiMaggio's injuries ended with a splashy first appearance. In 1940, people were expecting the same thing, but this time, alliterated the *Daily News*, "DiMaggio didn't matter." On May 11, the Yankees lost their eighth game in a row. No Joe McCarthy-managed team had ever lost like that. Some of the losses were especially hard to swallow. In a 3–2 loss to Boston, all three Red Sox runs were unearned. The eighth consecutive loss, also to Boston, saw the Red Sox tie the game in the ninth, go ahead in the top of the eleventh, with George Selkirk then grounding to the pitcher with the bases loaded to end the game. Matters had deteriorated to such an extent that the *Daily News* felt perfectly justified headlining the next day, "Just think the Yankees almost won!" The *Daily News* would be out of line with some of their articles that season, but this time they caught the mood of many fans. McCarthy had to bench George Selkirk, Charlie Keller and Frankie Crosetti for poor hitting. On May 21, the New York Yankees, champions of baseball since 1936, were in last place. In the previous two weeks they had lost 10 of 13.[4]

Nothing was going right that May. Gomez couldn't pitch. When the team headed West on a road trip, they stopped in Akron, Ohio for an exhibition game. McCarthy had Gomez try pitching there, and he was ineffective even against the minor leaguers. At that point, McCarthy sent Gomez back East, first to his doctors in New York, and ultimately to Johns Hopkins hospital in Baltimore. Dizzy Dean was there seeing the same doctor. Dizzy Dean was through, and lots of people feared the same was true for Gomez. Rumors were again circulating about Joe DiMaggio being in cahoots with a mob-connected boxing promoter, Joe Gould. Gossip had it that a percentage of DiMaggio's salary was going straight to Gould. With Britain and France battling for their lives against the Nazis, it was not a good time for Americans to read more about the failures of expected winners. Commissioner Landis cleared DiMaggio of any transgressions. Throughout the problems, McCarthy had little to say to the media. There was nothing unusual there. On DiMaggio's situation he said: "What money Joe DiMaggio makes from outside sources is his own business. We are satisfied with Joe's denial that no one shares his baseball salary." In regard to the team losing, McCarthy said nothing publicly, but he did call the team together. He spoke to them only one time about the losing streak: "You've been champions, and you've always conducted yourselves like champions. Now let's prove to everyone that we can take it as well as dish it out. No alibis. No beefing. Just go along and bear down and do your best. I know you'll snap out of it soon."[5]

To show his confidence, McCarthy reinserted Selkirk, Keller, and Crosetti into the lineup in late May. The team was in the cellar, and while this was tremendously symbolic, it was not as dire a situation as "last place" implied. The fifth through eighth place teams were tightly bunched. In the last week of May the Yankees suddenly won six in a row, and just like that they had jumped from the cellar to fourth place. Boston, Detroit, and Cleveland were ahead of them, however, and hopping over them would take much more work, as well as a certain measure of luck. A crowd of 82,437 came to watch the Yankees on Memorial Day, so no one could say the fans were not loyal. After a 4–3 victory over Cleveland on June 9, the Yankees were still in fourth place, but they were only three games behind league leading Boston. McCarthy was right, they did snap out of it.

Throughout, he was still tenaciously tending to the details. Reserve outfielder Mike Chartak made a fine play one afternoon, fielding a single and throwing out a runner trying to go from first to third on the hit. "I came in the bench all pepped up, quite satisfied with myself," Chartak recalled: "McCarthy called me over and whispered in my ear, 'Fine throw. But why didn't you get the ball on the first bounce. If you had got[ten] it on the first, there would have been nothing close about the play at third. As it was, the man wasn't out by very much. Maybe he wasn't out at all.'" Chartak admitted that McCarthy was right, and later reflected as so many others did — that McCarthy saw everything. If the Yankees could come back, it would not be for any inattention to detail from their manager. The big question, especially with Gomez still ailing, was whether the pitching could sustain the team through the summer.[6]

Always one to see well past the short term highs and lows in a season, Connie Mack judged, after the Yankees had climbed out of the cellar and back into contention, that New York was going to come up short. "I still think the Yankees will not win the pennant. They are in a winning streak, but I am sure they will not come out on top." McCarthy had been juggling players in strange positions to compensate for the team's injuries, and he was relying on a less than distinguished pitching staff. He moved Babe Dahlgren from first base to third. He switched Tommy Henrich from outfield to first base in a game against Cleveland. As often occurs in such situations, the infielders took extra care when throwing to Henrich. As Henrich remembered, "they tried to help me. They began to aim at me and started making bad throws. ... I remember the last one hit the dirt eight feet in front of me." Ernie Bonham was pitching a shutout before Henrich went to first. With several throws to first getting by Henrich, Cleveland came back to win. "After the game," Henrich recalled, "McCarthy gave me time to cool off. Then he said 'I thought you were a first baseman.' 'Yes,' I said, thinking of those low throws, 'but not a coal miner.'"

McCarthy had some new infield talent out in Kansas City, Johnny Sturm, Jerry Priddy, and Phil Rizzuto. He went out there with George Weiss during a Chicago to St. Louis travel day to take a look at them, but he decided the three were not yet ready. The team continued to struggle with inconsistent pitching and unsure fielding, and when the hitting fell off, the losses started piling up again. After winning eight straight in early June and pulling to within three games of the lead, the Yankees lost nine out of ten in late June and found themselves ten games out. The team batting average was only .248. Even DiMaggio was under .300.

Rumors were flitting about that club was going to be sold, with various names coming forth like Jim Farley, actor Joe E. Brown, and Ambassador Joseph Kennedy. Possible sales were going to depend on the resolution of the war question, and of course that only provided more confusion. Rival teams no longer felt fear when playing New York. It seemed the past glory was over. In New York City, the more brash style of the resurgent Brooklyn Dodgers under their new leaders, President Larry MacPhail and Manager Leo Durocher, seemed a better pathway to success in a time dominated now more by war than depression. McCarthy's ways suddenly seemed of a older era.[7]

From July 15 to August 9, the Yankees' record was nine and seventeen. They slipped to fifth place. It may have been in the generally downward tone of the month that led McCarthy to decide not to manage the American League All Star team that summer. McCarthy never fully explained his reasons. That month, the Yankees' injuries and illnesses continued. Charlie Keller was ill with stomach troubles and tonsilitis. The first day Jake Powell could practice after his fractured skull, he took a line drive in the knee. Selkirk sprained an ankle, and DiMaggio twisted his back and later his ankle. Bill Dickey was spiked on a play at the plate and suffered a gash in his left foot. He needed stitches and was lost for several weeks. Dickey's replacement, Buddy Rosar, was hit by a pitch on his right wrist and could barely hold a bat for a few days. Red Ruffing pulled a tendon in his left leg, and pitchers Monte Pearson, Marv Breuer, and Marius Russo were also down in July and August. Meanwhile, Lefty Gomez never regained his form. In mid August, amidst these many maladies, weak hitting, and poor play, reporter Jimmy Powers of the *Daily News* wrote what can probably be called *the* most tasteless article in the history of sports journalism. They Yankees have collapsed, he wrote, and the question is "why?" He wondered:

> Has the mysterious polio germ which felled Lou Gehrig also felled his former teammates, turning a once great team into a non-contender? ... Poliomyelitis, similar to infantile paralysis, is communicable. The Yankees were exposed to it at its most acute stage. They played ball with the afflicted Gehrig, dressing and undressing in the locker room with him, traveled, played cards, and ate with him. Isn't it possible some of them also became infected? It is hard to believe mere coincidence can explain away the wholesale failure of the individuals. In Gehrig's case, one of the most prominent symptoms was the loss of muscular power. The same symptoms can be found in many of the Yankees today. ... Are the Yanks infected?

Powers was not even attempting a sick joke here. He was in deadly earnest, and he was totally out of touch with medical facts. (When Gehrig was first diagnosed in 1939, some of the Yankees were indeed skittish about sitting near him on the bench for fear of contagion. Bill Dickey, Gehrig's roommate, was quite scared and underwent several medical examinations, fearing the worst as his play was definitely off in 1940.) Gehrig's disease, ALS, was not polio or infantile paralysis, although some newspapers and magazines had cast it as such. Gehrig, slipping away, but working on appointment by Mayor LaGuardia to the New York Municipal Parole Commission, was greatly disturbed by the article. He later had court papers served to sue Powers and the *Daily News* for $1 million. Bill Dickey and other Yankees considered suits too. (Can one imagine the light in which a jury of New Yorkers would have seen Powers and his paper?) Fortunately for Powers and the *Daily News*, Gehrig withdrew the suit after Powers wrote a long article of withdrawal and apology. Although he hardly needed it, McCarthy's opinion of the news media received further confirmation.

Other reporters shunned Powers, as did the players, more than a few of whom wanted to take Powers out and prove to him, on his face and ribs, that they still possessed plenty of the "muscle" Powers thought to be deteriorating. McCarthy would have not objected.[8]

Powers' article actually came out at the very time the Yankees started to get over their injuries. His article may have spurred the Yankees into a state of greater determination. Healthy from August 9 to September 2, and with young Ernie Bonham pitching especially well, they won 20 of 23. Boston had faded from the race, but Cleveland and Detroit were still ahead. The Yankees' revival had brought them right back into the pennant chase. On September 11, Detroit and Cleveland were virtually tied, with the Yankees but one half game behind and headed out on a Western trip.[9]

Detroit won two key games from the Yankees in the next week. Horribly wrenching was a subsequent loss of three straight games in St. Louis to the lowly Browns. Babe Dahlgren made a key error in one of the losses. He missed a sign. Mental errors were unacceptable to McCarthy at any time, let alone at that point in September, perhaps even more so from the man who had replaced Lou Gehrig. The day after the Yankees snapped out of that little slump, DiMaggio pulled a groin muscle and had to sit out a few games. On the trip West, the Yankees won only five of twelve. They could not recover. Detroit won the pennant. Cleveland, full of dissension over their former Newark manager, Oscar Vitt, was one game behind them, the Yankees two.[10]

The Cleveland Indians' situation involved a number of their players rebelling against their tough manager. Vitt was ultimately fired. McCarthy reacted angrily: "The owners of the Indians should have backed up Vitt with a new two-year contract. Do you know what's wrong?" he fumed. "The parents of the United States obey their children. In that way we breed a race which does the sort of thing those Cleveland men did to Vitt." McCarthy seemed more upset about Vitt's lot than his own. Of course, he had not been fired. As for the Yankees' finally missing the pennant, he lamented, "We lost it out West on our last trip where we dropped a couple of close decisions. ... But I must say for the boys, they never quit on me."

Another factor was a pitcher named Johnny Babich. After two mediocre seasons with the Dodgers and one with the Braves, Babich had been in the Yankee organization, but he got no higher than Kansas City. McCarthy's scouts concluded he was not good enough for the majors. The Yankees traded him to Philadelphia. In two seasons with the A's he would win but 16 games, 30 in his entire career. But 1940 was Babich's "career year." He won 14 that season, and five of those wins came against the Yankees. "Johnny Babich!" blurted McCarthy, "Who ever heard of Johnny Babich?" In October, the day before the season ended, with the pennant gone, another mishap occurred. While playing in Washington, George Selkirk had to be rushed to St. Elizabeth's Hospital with a burst appendix. No matter their sudden rush in September, it seemed the baseball fates wanted to leave their final mark on McCarthy and the Yankees that season. Injury after injury, they could not help but feel a little snake bit. As for the failure to win five straight pennants, McCarthy did snap to one reporter: "What's the matter? Has everyone forgotten the other years? What do we have to do, win them all?" The irony of that was obvious, in view of what led McCarthy to trade Roy Johnson. McCarthy later gathered himself and simply shrugged, "Well the sun can't shine on the same dog's back all the time."

With all the injuries, the fact that he had kept the team in the thick of the race was quite an achievement. Even some reporters were willing to acknowledge that. After the final game, one reporter had the gall to ask McCarthy if he knew the difference in the World Series share between the second and third place team. McCarthy glared at the reporter for a long moment. Then he just lowered his head, took off a shoe and clipped a toenail. "I dunno," he muttered, "I never bothered figuring it out." Cincinnati beat Detroit in the World Series that year, and the third place Yankees' share came to $600. Newark won the Little World Series anyway; they beat Louisville.[11]

In addition to Newark's victory, the year was not a total loss for McCarthy in at least one other respect. McCarthy learned a valuable bit of baseball history, the learning of which sharpened his political skills. Back in May, amidst a series with the Senators, McCarthy had actually been invited to visit the U.S. Senate, where he had a meeting with none less than Vice President John Nance Garner. Garner gregariously held forth, asking McCarthy if he knew who devised the Texas leaguer. McCarthy confessed that did not know, whereupon the Vice President informed him "the fellow who invented it" was none other than himself. As a lad playing ball in Texas, he drawled, he could not hit the ball very far and had not enough speed to beat out balls to the infield. So, Garner intoned, "I figured the best thing for me to do was just to meet the ball and tap it over the infield. ... it was very successful," he smugly concluded, embellishing: "After that all the young fellows around our town were doing the same thing, and it spread throughout the State, and finally somebody called that kind of hit 'a Texas leaguer.'" McCarthy certainly knew better than to question any such rodomontade, especially from a political figure of no lesser stature than the Vice President. He nodded, cleared his throat, and sagely replied, "Well, I've finally caught up with the man who was responsible for a lot of my headaches, because as a second baseman I spent half my time chasing Texas leaguers."[12] Garner was happy, and thanks to McCarthy's acquiescence, Garner was able confidently to hold onto his story about inventing the Texas leaguer. His hold on the Vice Presidency could not be similarly sustained that fall, however, and there was nothing McCarthy could do for Garner about that.

29

Lou Was a Fine Man

After such a frustrating season as 1940, McCarthy and the Yankees were out to prove something the next spring. Barrow showed the American League that he was not the least bit ruffled by the events of 1940. That November, he signed McCarthy for another three years, maintaining his salary at $35,000. With Ruppert gone, there was talk of the Yankees being sold to new owners, with a syndicate led by Postmaster General Jim Farley being mentioned most often. McCarthy stayed out of all such front office matters. He spent an intentionally quiet winter at Gates Circle. The time there was always restorative to McCarthy, and after the 1940 season he was especially in need, and he knew it. "I stayed out of the banquet league as much as possible this winter," he noted, "and I feel better for it. This is the best rest I have had in a long time."

Just as McCarthy always had total concentration and devotion to his duties as manager, he had the necessary ability to "turn it off" completely. The life he had in Buffalo was particularly helpful here. He tended to his proverbial garden. He loved a simple dinner of corned beef and cabbage, with ice cream for dessert. He enjoyed hunting, although the 1940–41 season was not good. Mrs. McCarthy and he took in stage shows when they came to town. (McCarthy always lamented the decline of vaudeville.) He loved to watch magic shows and could perform a good few tricks himself. Most evenings the McCarthys spent simply at home, McCarthy usually enjoying a good cigar, especially that winter as he had bought a red leather chair, which described as "the sittin'est chair ever." As far as Buffalo's infamous winters were concerned, he had but one simple comment: "I like the winter weather." He knew the stresses he faced from March to October, and once he was home he had to do anything but force himself to slow down. He only wished the winters were longer. "Time always goes so fast between seasons. You just seem to get home when you're packing to go away."[1]

Once assembled in Florida, McCarthy and the Yankees could not help but express optimism about the upcoming season. The law of averages indicated that they could not possibly have another such year of injuries and illnesses as they had just gone through, and any reasonably healthy Yankee team would have to be a contender. What McCarthy faced in 1941 was another embarrassment of riches. There were no major contract disputes, and some new talent was coming up. In 1940, McCarthy's three Kansas City infielders, Johnny Sturm, Jerry Priddy, and Phil Rizzuto, had each hit over .300, and they turned 194 double plays in 154 games, a statistic former second baseman McCarthy particularly liked.

Knowing what he had "coming up," just before the opening of spring training, McCarthy sold Babe Dahlgren to the Boston Bees (Braves). It was strictly a cash deal. The motive here may have been a matter of his confidence in his new alternatives, but McCarthy may have also been prodded by the memory of Gehrig. It is always hard to be the one who succeeds a legend. Bob Shawkey's year managing the Yankees proved that to New York baseball fans. Dahlgren had filled in at first base reasonably well in 1939 and 1940, although in late 1940 he missed a throw in a September loss to Cleveland and committed the key mental error of missing a sign in an important late-season loss in St. Louis. Tommy Henrich recalled that McCarthy was particularly peeved at the missed sign. Dahlgren was never a great hitter, .235 and .264 in '39 and '40, but his fielding often appeared spectacular, and the fans took to him.

McCarthy rarely made comments about players he traded or sold. He had pontificated about the emotional unreliability of hotheaded Southerners when he dealt away Ben Chapman and Johnny Allen. Otherwise he was sensibly quiet and wished any former Yankee well. With Dahlgren he was uncharacteristically disparaging. Reporters accounted for Dahlgren's tenure with the Yankees with phrases like "an excellent fielder, [but] Dahlgren never could hit." McCarthy thus needed to say nothing about Dahlgren's weak batting, but rather than letting it go at that he actually went on to comment about Dahlgren's fielding. McCarthy said that Dahlgren "makes easy plays look hard" because "his arms are too short."

Dahlgren bristled. "That was a mean remark," he said. "McCarthy tried to make me out a freak. I would not have minded so much if he had said I did not hit enough. But he should not have made a personal remark like that." Dahlgren said his arms were normal in every way. With the Braves in March, he even had his arms measured to prove his point. (Only one player on the team had longer arms.) McCarthy may have noticed a tendency in Dahlgren not to extend his arms from the elbow or the shoulder. Some ball players do inadvertently "short arm" plays for that very tendency. What McCarthy once said about DiMaggio's fielding was the reverse of what he saw in Dahlgren: "You never saw DiMaggio make a great catch. You never saw him dive for a ball. He didn't have to. He was already there to catch it. That's what you're expected to do—catch the ball—not make exciting catches." With Boston, Dahlgren again gained a reputation as one of the more exciting fielding first basemen in the league, but again some of his many spectacular plays may have been the sorts others handled less dramatically. No mean judge of talent himself, Boston Braves Manager Casey Stengel switched Dahlgren to third base that year at mid-season, much to the surprise of many Boston fans. Beyond the fact that McCarthy and Stengel likely saw what the cheering fans missed, McCarthy's obvious fondness for Gehrig and his lament over Gehrig's fate may have been in back of the oddly vocal way with which he handled the deal.[2]

McCarthy had what he first thought was an inspired idea when he began sorting out the question of his infield. In everyone's estimation, Joe Gordon was certainly one of, if not the best, second basemen in the American League. McCarthy prided himself as being the one who both spotted Gordon's talent and had sufficient faith in him to see him through a bad patch of playing in early 1938. McCarthy was especially fond of the fact that Gordon could never recount his own offensive statistics and was concerned only with the team's numbers. Given that sort of ability and spirit, McCarthy had a hunch he could make a first baseman out of Gordon while giving a full chance to young Jerry Priddy at second as well as to his mate Phil Rizzuto at shortstop. "We don't want to break up Rizzuto and Priddy," he said. Naturally, Priddy was enthusiastic, but he strutted a bit too much for most of the team's taste. He actually told Gordon, "I'm the better second baseman. I can make the double play better than you. ... I can do everything better than you."[3] McCarthy did not react and went on with his experiment.

While McCarthy was working on Gordon at first, there was another and much bigger cloud hovering over the team, and all the teams. The United States War Department had instituted a military draft, and of course many ball players were of age and of sound mind and body. When a reporter told McCarthy that Rizzuto might be drafted, he only shrugged. "What can you do about it?" he asked. "We're no worse off than any other ball club." Steadfastly, that would be McCarthy's view about his players and military service. As long as baseball was to be played, he would do his job as manager the very best he could. When vitally more important matters took players from his midst, he fully accepted it, and just as fully expected everyone else connected with the game to feel exactly the same way. "No matter how many are called," he proudly asserted, "baseball won't squawk." In the spring of 1941, McCarthy, of course, had no idea how fully the military needs of the nation would overtake him. But his attitude would never waver.[4]

The Yankees looked generally sound in practices and in exhibition games. Tommy Henrich was looking much improved. Red Rolfe's health was 100 percent, and he hit .364 in the spring games. Reporters were doubting Lefty Gomez, but McCarthy was enthusiastic. After an exhibition game against Brooklyn, McCarthy offered reporters an insight about why he felt positively about Gomez. It was indicative of the depth of McCarthy's grasp of baseball and how he could see things that others could not. In the game, some Dodgers hit the ball hard against Gomez. This made reporters doubt, but McCarthy differed: "I don't care if they hit him. I wanted to see him throw hard, and he did. The tip-off was on some of those foul ticks that went flying back to the grandstand. Did you see the way they took off from the bat? That's the tip-off. When a fellow is fast, I'm very satisfied. Now if he doesn't come up with a sore arm after that I'll be better satisfied."[5] How many other managers draw anything from the speed of those seemingly meaningless foul balls that go straight back to the screen?

While Henrich, Gomez, and others were looking up, Joe Gordon was "struggling painfully around first base." McCarthy believed Gordon simply needed more time. It made for a very frustrating spring for Gordon and the rest of the infield. As when Henrich played some first base in 1940, the other fielders could see Gordon was not quite at ease. They grew slightly more tentative in their throws. Split-second timing on various plays thus fell off. At that level of baseball, anything just shy of perfection becomes noticeable, especially to the players themselves, and even more to a man like McCarthy. The consciousness of such a problem often further aggravates matters, and the cycles compound. McCarthy determined that Gordon was such a good athlete that matters could work out for the best, and he made no adjustments during the exhibition season. A month after the "short arms" controversy had died down over Babe Dahlgren, McCarthy told some reporters, "Gordon [at first base] was not anything sudden with me. I had that idea in my mind all through last season. Babe was a good first baseman, but I saw a lot of things sitting on the bench you fellows did not see up in the press box. There were a lot of things he could not do. I knew then, and I know now, that Gordon would be a better first baseman."[6] McCarthy continued the experiment with Gordon.

Even though Gordon was struggling at first, the Yankees were strong that spring. They won 20 of 25 exhibition games. One game was a trifle tense. It was a 10–4 drubbing of a team in Oklahoma City. The tension was due to the fact that the Oklahoma team was managed by Rogers Hornsby. A happier reunion came for McCarthy that spring in Memphis where got reacquainted with his old Cubs pitcher Guy Bush, now managing a filling station and running a farm. The day before opening day, Jerry Priddy sprained his ankle. McCarthy had to put Gordon back on second and inserted rookie Johnny Sturm at first. The opening weeks of the season went well. Memories of the terrible beginning of the 1940 season faded. After nine games, Priddy's ankle had healed, and McCarthy went back with Gordon at first.

Sturm had only hit .240, but Priddy's hitting would be even less potent. After starting seven games, he was batting only .176. Given the way he had popped off at Gordon, he was not getting much sympathy or encouragement from anyone. The team was in the race with Cleveland and Detroit. Out in Detroit for their first series there, the Yankees lost all three games, but then Detroit suffered its biggest loss of the season — Hank Greenberg was drafted into the Army. Detroit's Mayor John W. Smith had secured him a one-day deferment so he could play in the third game of the series with New York. Greenberg responded with two home runs. But now he was gone.[*] Without Greenberg, Detroit fell to a fourth-place tie that season. The Yankee losses in Detroit triggered a slump that made some fans fear a May, 1940 repeat. From April 22 to May 14, DiMaggio hit but .194. The Yankees lost five games in a row in the second week of May. Their record was a mere 14 and 13, and they had slipped to fourth. McCarthy decided to make some changes. He benched Priddy, who was still hitting only .204. Priddy would never by a Yankee regular again. His pride/arrogance never abated, however. He finished the '41 season and stayed with the Yankees in 1942, playing fewer than 60 games each year and complaining regularly that McCarthy was underutilizing him. In January, 1943, the Yankees traded him to Washington.[7]

When McCarthy benched Priddy, he also sat Rizzuto down. Rizzuto had been hitting .246, but he had made several key errors during the losing streak. McCarthy had him work on his fielding. "You jam your spikes into the ground when you go deep for a ball," McCarthy advised. "Let your right foot slide to a stop. That way you're better balanced to make the play and throw." No one else had ever caught this tendency in Rizzuto. A taller or larger shortstop could not make such an adjustment, as his sliding momentum would likely be too strong, but it was just the right adjust-

---

[*]Hank Greenberg's tour of duty officially ended on December 5, 1941. He could have avoided further service from that point. But within a week after Pearl Harbor, he reenlisted voluntarily and would not play baseball again until the second half of the 1945 season.

ment for the diminutive Rizzuto. For the moment, Crosetti was back at shortstop, and Gordon was again his second baseman. A month later Crosetti was spiked and Rizzuto came back in, this time fielding much more sharply. Despite his weak hitting, Johnny Sturm played first. McCarthy conceded that his attempt to switch Gordon to first base might have been a mistake. The real point was that he recognized his error and did not let his ego get in the way of making any sensible adjustments. (Several years later, when he was managing in Boston, McCarthy was moving Johnny Pesky from shortstop to third base, and he tried to assert that Gordon was fine at first, and that he only moved Gordon back to second base because Priddy was hurt. It was not true, but the expressed memory was convenient in regard to his desire then to put a positive face on his shifting of Pesky, which in that case was quite successful.)[8]

Phil Rizzuto became a fixture in the lineup, and, like others, he quickly learned how exacting, and inspiring, a taskmaster McCarthy could be. One afternoon that year, Rizzuto was up with two out and a man on first. He signaled the runner a hit and run. "I got a base hit," Rizzuto recalled, "and the guy went to third." Rizzuto was feeling very proud of himself. Then, "after the game, he [McCarthy] called me over and said, 'You know that's a bad play.'" "Geez," Rizzuto responded, "I got a base hit." McCarthy then tutored: "with two out it's a bad play. With one out it's a great play; with two out if you miss the ball and the guy's thrown out, the inning's over." McCarthy always wanted to play percentage baseball. There was nothing deflating in his lesson. He knew the level of baseball he wanted, mental as well as physical, and he knew how to get it. "Oh," concluded Rizzuto, "he was a great teacher."[9]

McCarthy's switching of the lineup may have helped perk the Yankees up that May. With Gordon back on familiar ground and Sturm handling first base comfortably, the infield situation was settled. Sturm, McCarthy acknowledged, "is playing much better ball now than he did down South. I don't know what the trouble was with him down there," he said. Speculating that it may have been just a case of nerves, McCarthy was now reasonably satisfied. And in May, Sturm batted .270. McCarthy was comfortable enough to joke with Sturm. In a game with Boston on May 25, Ted Williams cracked four consecutive hits between first and second. After the fourth one, McCarthy looked at Sturm and ruefully noted: "The least you could have done was wave at it."

Elsewhere, the team was secure too. In the outfield George Selkirk had a bad ankle, but with Charlie Keller and the improved Tommy Henrich, McCarthy had no problem sending the two young fielders to accompany DiMaggio. Bill Dickey did have some knee trouble, but Buddy Rosar filled in capably where needed. McCarthy solved Dickey's knee problem when he spotted the fact that his shin guards were a bit too short. With the pitchers, McCarthy was not getting many complete games out of them. From May 18 to June 1, the staff produced none. But he kept eight pitchers rotating regularly and seemed to have the touch for calling upon the right one at important times. The team was rolling, but in June, two matters overrode everything as far as the attention of the Yankees and their fans was concerned. One was tragic, the other spectacular.[10]

On June 1, the Yankees swept a double-header from Cleveland to pull within a game and a half of the league lead, then shared by Cleveland and surprising Chicago. Joe DiMaggio then had a hitting streak going of eighteen games. He had several such streaks of sixteen to twenty-two games in 1939 and 1940. Each began to receive press notice around the fifteenth game, and this one was no exception. He got a hit the next day in Cleveland off Bob Feller, although the Indians won the game. That evening the Yankees headed off to Detroit, and when they arrived at the hotel they received the news— Lou Gehrig had died that afternoon. McCarthy and Bill Dickey, Gehrig's roommate, left for New York immediately. "Joe McCarthy," recalled DiMaggio, "took the news as though he had lost a son."

Out in Detroit the next day, the rest of the Yankees assembled under Coach Art Fletcher. The flag at Briggs Stadium flew at half-staff, as it did at all ball parks that afternoon. A minute of silence was observed. Then the game went on. Detroit scored four runs in the first inning; McCarthy likely knew why. The Yankees shut them out from there but could only score two. McCarthy knew why here as well. (Joe DiMaggio got a hit to extend his streak to twenty games.) McCarthy and Dickey arrived in New York for the funeral on June 4. The funeral, at Christ Episcopal Church in Riverdale, was understated and dignified, a perfect embodiment of the modesty that Gehrig and McCarthy shared. The Reverend George V. Barry simply read the Episcopal order for burial. That was enough. There was no eulogy. There was no ball game either, as it rained in both New York and Detroit that day. McCarthy and Dickey served among the pallbearers.* McCarthy's statement to the press could not have been sweeter. Without a reference to baseball, he simply said: "Lou was a fine man." At his home in Buffalo, McCarthy had a photograph of Gehrig on which his favorite player had written "May I Always Deserve Your Friendship." He always did. McCarthy had a special room in his house for all the treasured baseball memorabilia and trophies. He always kept the picture of Gehrig separately in his living room. Years later McCarthy remembered: "Gehrig was a wonderful fellow; always hustled. Never gave a manager a moment's trouble. 'Just went out every day and played his game and hit the ball. I'll say he hit the ball, and in all directions. ... I never asked him to bunt, not once in eight years. I don't think that would have been very good strategy."[11]

The evening after Gehrig's funeral, McCarthy and Dickey rejoined the team in St. Louis. The American League race was very close at that point. As of June 6, five games separated the first six teams. Only Washington and St. Louis were out of the running. First-place Cleveland had been in a bit of a slump. In the previous ten days they had won no games other than those pitched by Bob Feller. The way was open for one of the teams to streak ahead. Returning to the team, McCarthy adopted his usual all-business attitude. He held no team meeting, and everyone got the message. By this time Joe DiMaggio's hitting streak was getting plenty of media attention, but the pennant race was certainly on everyone's mind too. With McCarthy's return, the Yankees won five in a row over St. Louis and Chicago. Then they went into Cleveland for a series with the first-place Indians. As always, McCarthy fully rested one

*The other pallbearers were New York Deputy Mayor Rufus McGalen, who represented Mayor LaGuardia, Francis J. Kear, N.Y. Deputy Police Commissioner, John C. Maher and Mary Fraschi, Gehrig's two colleagues on the Parole Commission, Dr. Caldwell B. Esselstyn, Gehrig's physician, John Kiernan, a journalist and friend, Andy Coakley, a former major league pitcher and Gehrig's baseball coach at Columbia, Bill "Bojangles" Robinson, the famous dancer, and Timmy Sullivan, the Yankees' bat boy.

of his pitchers, in this case Atley Donald, to face Bob Feller. Donald held Cleveland to one run. The Yankees scored four. DiMaggio extended his streak to 27. Now the papers were sensing something special in the works and were raising the details of the various records DiMaggio was approaching. In 1931, Earle Combs had hit in 29 straight games for a Yankee team record. As far as all-time streaks were concerned, Ty Cobb had once hit safely in 40 straight games; George Sisler in 41.[12]

The Yankees swept the series in Cleveland, and through the month they kept winning. From June 6–30, New York's record was 17 and 4, and they had taken first place. In addition to DiMaggio's streak, the Yankees set another record, hitting at least one home run in 25 straight games. That streak ended on July 1. The attention on that streak had taken a little attention off DiMaggio, and placed some pressure on the whole team. Still the pressure on DiMaggio was enormous. McCarthy understood the growing tensions for DiMaggio, and he eased the burden where he could. When DiMaggio was up, McCarthy never gave the take sign. "I was up there a lot of times when Joe McCarthy could have given me the take sign," DiMaggio recalled. "He didn't, though. He let me hit whenever I wanted to." Then DiMaggio paused and nodded: "Don't ever think that didn't help." A key example here came in game #40. Even though he had won five games from the Yankees in 1940, Philadelphia's Johnny Babich was still steamed at the Yankees for keeping him in the minors. Against DiMaggio in 1941 he bragged the press how he was going to pitch around Joe and spoil his streak. This riled the Yankees, who expected pitchers to say they were going to bear down extra hard against DiMaggio. Babich's rant could not be respected. In game #40, DiMaggio had a 3–0 count against Babich. McCarthy gave him the go ahead, and DiMaggio lined the next pitch through Babich's legs for a hit. (Babich was white as a sheet.) In another instance, during a home game against St. Louis on June 24, Tommy Henrich was up in the eighth inning with a man on first and one out. Henrich called "time." He went to McCarthy, suggesting that he bunt. DiMaggio was hitless to that point. The Yankees had a lead, and if Henrich hit away and grounded into a double play the streak would likely end. McCarthy pondered the matter a second and agreed; Henrich bunted, sacrificing the runner to second. DiMaggio stepped up with two outs and got a hit. McCarthy would always listen to a good idea. The streak was a major part of what kept the team going that summer. The Yankees won 42 of the 56 games. McCarthy knew that bending a little to help the streak would be good for morale as well as for winning.[13]

The war was raging in Europe and in the Pacific. Hitler had conquered France and had just invaded the Soviet Union. Many in the nation knew it was only a matter of time before the US would become involved. Others held strongly to isolationist sentiments (a *Daily News* poll showed that 71.3 percent of New York State residents were anti-war, and such sentiments were at least as strong in the Midwest). The excitement of the DiMaggio and the Yankees' 1941 season served as a temporarily unifying diversion. In effect, the Yankee team was saying with their performance: this is the best example of that world that may soon be forced to put behind, an example to which isolationists could cling or one in which interventionists could find nostalgia.

Joe DiMaggio was on everyone's mind all over the country. That summer "Did he get one?" was as specific as anyone had to be when asking about the streak.

Reporters heard such words at road stops in rural Montana. With hits in both games of a doubleheader sweep of Washington, DiMaggio tied and surpassed George Sisler's 41-game mark. At the point when DiMaggio was about to pass Sisler's mark, the fact of a 44-game record set by Willie Keeler in 1897 came to light. Until 1900, foul balls did not count as strike one or strike two (and being hit by a pitch counted only as a ball), so Keeler's streak had come under different circumstances. But the papers held it up as a record just the same. At that very moment, the elements of nature appeared to add to the pressure as DiMaggio sought to secure an all-time record. An intolerable heat wave hit New York in late June/early July. Air conditioning was unheard of at that point. Several people drowned trying to cool off in the Hudson River. Others collapsed inside buildings, but DiMaggio and the Yankees kept playing. Amidst the 100-degree swelter, on July 1, New York swept a doubleheader from the Red Sox. DiMaggio got a hit in each game to tie Keeler's mark, and when he got his hit in game two, fully half the crowd at the second game left the steamy stadium.

McCarthy never gave DiMaggio any late-inning rest even under such circumstances. He was still thinking about the pennant race. When asked about DiMaggio possibly breaking Keeler's record, McCarthy was gruff with reporters, even by McCarthy standards. (It may have been the heat, and he may have also had a nip of whiskey in him.) "Nuts!" he yelled. "I got a lot of records. What do they mean?" As for DiMaggio himself, McCarthy only shrugged: "He's great. Everyone knows it. What do you want me to say it for?" DiMaggio never took offense. He liked the press about as much as McCarthy did, besides DiMaggio was concerned about the pennant race too. The Yankees' lead in the league was now three games, and the next day, with a dramatic home run, DiMaggio broke Keeler's mark. Then an even greater miracle occurred in New York. It rained. The heat wave and Keeler's record were broken. The needed rain did cancel the traditional July 4 doubleheader with Washington. This one was to have been special, as a monument to Lou Gehrig was scheduled to be unveiled in the left center field of Yankee Stadium, next to ones to Col. Ruppert and Miller Huggins. The ceremony occurred instead on July 6, with Bill Dickey and McCarthy serving as the official unveilers.[14]

Whether it was as much DiMaggio's streak that lifted the Yankees or excellent Yankee play that helped buoy DiMaggio, New York pulled ahead of the American League in June and July. DiMaggio's streak, of course, ran for 56 games. Within that stretch, the Yankees ran off a 14-game winning streak and won 40 of 43 consecutive games. They also hit at least one home run in 35 of 37 straight games. DiMaggio's streak ended in a game with second-place Cleveland. The Yankees won the game 4–3, and the victory put them a full seven games ahead. They would never be headed or even approached. After the Cleveland game, DiMaggio hit safely in his next 16 games.[15]

"Joe and Ed [Barrow] really took the Yankee machine apart and then put together again hitting on all cylinders," wrote Jimmy Powers. One feature of this, which was quintessential McCarthy-style management, involved the team not getting too low or too high amidst the events of a season. With Gehrig's death, the winning streaks, the home runs, and of course with DiMaggio's 56-game streak, one could have expected some sort of let-down or even a major slump. This is what McCarthy always sought to avoid. He continued to emphasize crisp fielding in practice. (A less known record the Yankees appeared on their way to setting that year was the number of executed double plays—they eventually tied the mark of 194.) After DiMaggio's streak ended, the team did lose a game to Bob Feller. Then they reeled off nine straight wins, and their lead grew to eleven and a half games. Of the 16 games in which DiMaggio hit safely after his 56-game streak ended, the Yankees won 13 of them. Jimmy Powers raised one criticism: "The team lacks color. Joe McCarthy can't, or won't, talk entertainingly enough to break into the sports pages." McCarthy likely paid no heed of the comment. If anything he may have considered it a compliment, particularly given Powers' comments about Lou Gehrig in 1940. As for DiMaggio, the fact that he reeled off a 16-game hitting streak after the "56" came to an end was a great source of pride to McCarthy. It was the best illustration of his idealized player, and team, that not only achieved utter excellence but kept that highest level on an absolutely even keel.[16]

The great Yankee teams of the Babe Ruth era jauntily loaded up on the second-division clubs and held their own with the other top teams. In 1941, McCarthy's team regularly clobbered the best in the league. The Yankees' old trainer, Doc Painter, was asked to comment on the '41 team. Aside from Barrow, no one in the organization had been there longer. Oddly, Painter said this was "not a great team, but they do great things." This appeared similar to saying that Henry Ford was not a rich man, he just has a lot of money. But there was a point there, albeit a trifle strained. Recognizing that DiMaggio was great in any era, Painter felt, perhaps with a bit of nostalgia, that the likes of Ruth, Gehrig, Combs, Koenig, Meusel, Combs, Lazzeri, and Pennock stood higher than Henrich, Keller, and Sturm, or even Dickey and Gordon. The difference was the fiery nature of 1920s teams, while a fond memory for Painter, was something for which McCarthy had little use, and he was apparently not thrilled with Painter for his comments. If the Yankees inspired more awe than affection, that was fine with McCarthy. In any case he did not want comments from within the organization stirring up any sort of controversy in this regard. On August 3, the Yankees were up by 12 games, and they had just held their opponents to 30 consecutive scoreless innings.[17]

If any of the Yankees did suffer some sort of letdown in 1941, it came in early August. But the insignificance of the slips further revealed how impenetrable a machine McCarthy had set forth that season. Bill Dickey had been beaned by a pitch on July 24, and he was not wearing a helmet. He had to stay out for several games. (McCarthy had ordered a shipment of helmets, but he remained ambivalent about them, still letting the players make up their minds for themselves.) DiMaggio went through several hitless games. Since hitting in 71 of 72 consecutive games, he got only 10 hits in his next 48 at bats, and his average dropped 25 points, but the rest of the team would not be affected unduly. They kept winning, and no other team made a run at them. By August 18, the Yankees' lead was 17 games. No team had ever had that big a lead so early in the season.

A few injuries began to creep in. DiMaggio twisted his ankle and was out for over a week. After recovering from his beaning, Dickey was hit in the shoulder by a foul tip. Rolfe had some stomach troubles. Gordon banged his knee in a double play collision. Keller hurt his heel. McCarthy grew a trifle edgy. No lead was ever safe with him. He used the injury situation to give some playing time to others like Rosar,

Crosetti, and Priddy. But, even with a big lead, his tense mood was apparent. He bristled even more than usual at some reporters who were pressing him on the point that the team might be in some sort of difficulty. Describing McCarthy as being "in extra bad humor before a game," one scribe asked McCarthy about his apparent shakeup of the lineup. McCarthy yelled back: "Why don't you fellows let a man work?"

If McCarthy had not let all the downs and ups from Gehrig's death to DiMaggio's streak affect the team, they built up within him more than he knew. On August 30, after a victory in Washington, McCarthy had to be taken from the Shoreham Hotel to Georgetown University Hospital. The problem was described as a return of his gall bladder difficulties. Likely, it was also another time when the scotch consumption, to which he treated himself in the evenings, got out of hand. McCarthy was one to bear all burdens and share with no one, and it would catch up with him from time to time. Still, McCarthy's system ran on, as the Yankees continued to win with Coach Art Fletcher in charge. As happened before, perhaps the only discernible result of McCarthy's absence could be seen in the behavior of Lefty Gomez. In a game with Boston on September 3, Gomez was tossed for his bench jockeying of the plate umpire. As he was leaving the dugout, Gomez grabbed a bat and began to walk while tapping the bat on the ground like a blind man with a cane. He would never have dared do that under McCarthy's glare. (The trouble was, as Art Fletcher later recalled, McCarthy was quietly sitting in the stands that afternoon.)[18]

Just after Labor Day, McCarthy returned to the team. He said nothing to Gomez about his ejection/performance. Besides, on September 5(!), the Yankees clinched the pennant. No one had ever wrapped up a season so early, not even the '36 team. On May 24, New York's won-loss mark was 14 and 15. The day before, McCarthy put Gordon back at second base. From there, the Yankees won 75 percent of their games. DiMaggio towered over everyone with his performance that year. His mark of .357 led the team in batting by far. At .307, Phil Rizzuto was the only other Yankee to break .300 (Red Ruffing did, but he only batted 89 times; Keller was close, batting .298 and knocking in 122 runs). Still, Doc Painter may have been right. Aside from DiMaggio, the '41 Yankees were not a team of great individual players. Their pitching was similar. Ruffing and Gomez each had but 15 wins, and they led the team. But McCarthy had five other pitchers each with nine or more wins. Generally, he pitched each with a full week's rest. Meanwhile, McCarthy had his ace reliever, Johnny Murphy, who won eight and saved a league leading 15. Everyone could do a particular job, and, as Bill Dickey had said: "that man" made the whole thing work. The Boston Red Sox were a team somewhat like the Yankees that year—a slate of decent pitchers, a solid starting team, and several, not just one, outstanding stars—Joe Cronin, Jimmie Foxx and Ted Williams. But they didn't have McCarthy.

Phil Rizzuto recalled how McCarthy once "outmanaged" Joe Cronin in an unusual way. One Sunday morning, McCarthy and Rizzuto went to mass in Boston. They went to the same church as Cronin. "Mr. McCarthy noted that Joe Cronin … went up to the altar afterwards. Marse Joe nudged me in the ribs and said, 'Phil, find out what he's doing up there.' I came back and said, 'Cronin lit two candles.' Joe said, 'Phil, here's two bucks; go up there and light three candles.' Which I did. … That afternoon we won the game 3–2." Perhaps the only complaint about the team from those near the Yankees was that the players were not generous in their tipping of the railroad station "redcaps." Joe McCarthy was the exception here too. When the Yankees won the pennant just after Labor Day, it was so early in September that few were prepared to feel much excitement. It seemed almost other-worldly. After the pennant clinching game was over, one reserve outfielder, Stanley "Frenchy" Bordargaray stood up in the locker room and began to sing "Roll Out the Barrel." No one joined him. Babe Dahlgren did send McCarthy a telegram of congratulations. When the Yankees arrived back in New York with the pennant wrapped up, no one was there to greet them. Bordagaray said he "couldn't even find a redcap to carry my bag." Word must have been out — about Bordagary's singing, about the Yankees' tipping, or both.[19] In any case, the Yankees clinching the pennant was news to no one.

No team ever had such time to prepare for a World Series as the '41 Yankees. For the remainder of September, McCarthy juggled his lineup, giving some playing time to the bench while still keeping everyone sharp. Phil Rizzuto bruised his wrist, and Charlie Keller went down with a bone chip in his right ankle. At first Keller appeared doubtful for the World Series. The team did tie the all-time record for double plays, but the big excitement for baseball fans that month concerned two matters: whether Boston's Ted Williams could sustain his .400 batting average and who would win the National League race. Throughout the month of September, the Yankees received virtually no significant newspaper coverage. Williams hit .400 of course. In the National League, Brooklyn had the lead, but they faced strong pressure from the St. Louis Cardinals, sparked by a youngster just brought up from the minors late in the season named Stanley Musial who hit .426 in twelve games. With Musial, St. Louis made it close, but Brooklyn won in the final week.[20]

War appeared to be drawing closer to America that October. Japanese aggression in the Far East was receiving more world censure. The War Department issued "shoot on sight" orders to the Navy. Hitler was menacing Moscow and London. But for a few weeks, there was something extra-exciting happening in New York. It was the first time that the New York Yankees would face the Brooklyn Dodgers in a World Series. The world's problems were of monumentally greater significance. But until the U.S. declared its stance, the nation remained full of questions and debates. When people's attention can then turn temporarily to something that reaffirms a common ground and provides a bit of nostalgia, interest will be heightened. For New Yorkers, and their fans elsewhere, this was part of the excitement that surrounded the 1941 series. There had been five previous Yankees-Giants World Series, and these had certainly stimulated a lot of pride, as well as conflict.

The Brooklyn Dodgers added an edge to the intra-city rivalry. The Dodgers had been "in the wilderness" for a generation. They had not won a pennant since 1920. The Yankees and Dodgers saw one another as rivals. In the week before opening day in April, they always played one another in two or three exhibition games. The Yankees and Giants never did that, and throughout the 1920s and 1930s when the Yankees and Dodgers faced each other in April exhibitions, there was a kind of David and Goliath character to the matches. Although they had plenty of working-class fans, especially among Italians, the Yankees, with the legacy of Ruppert's and Huston's money, symbolized uptown patrician New York. The Dodgers, in contrast, were clearly "da bums." Many wealthy New Yorkers loved them, but they belonged most deeply in the hearts of working-class Brooklynites, people who still preferred to think and say they did not even reside in New York City. The feelings were intense, and nowhere did they manifest themselves more strongly than in regard to baseball allegiances.

Although more image than reality, it seemed that in every business in the city the employers were Yankee fans while the workers rooted for Brooklyn. Brooklyn's brash managerial pair, President Larry MacPhail and Manager Leo Durocher, embodied that bumptious, stand-up-to-the-big-shots attitude, although the alcoholic MacPhail was rude to rich and poor alike. Under MacPhail, the Dodgers also tried to cultivate their popular, plebian image. To titillate the average fan, MacPhail and Durocher invited lots of show business personalities to the locker room. McCarthy would stand for no such stunts. Even Ed Barrow was still not allowed in the Yankee clubhouse. Amidst the buildup to the Series, McCarthy remained typically laconic. He said he had no plans for the Series other than to win. Durocher was trying all the rhetorical ploys he could. Hoping to stir up memories of Howard Ehmke, he made a special point of saying he was not going to name his starting pitcher for the first game. McCarthy was not jarred and had an especially good reply to Durocher. In regard to Brooklyn's starter he simply said "What difference does it make?" Otherwise, he cautioned his team against any Yankee bravado causing an underestimation of Brooklyn. "Any team that wins 100 games is a great ball club," he maintained. "We are making no mistake in our estimation of the Dodgers."

Away from reporters' eyes, McCarthy prepared the Yankees meticulously. Here his phenomenal memory was in evidence. The Dodgers had a first baseman named Jimmy Wasdell. Red Ruffing asked if anyone knew anything about him. McCarthy immediately recalled Wasdell from an exhibition game in Chattanooga several years before. He told Ruffing that Wasdell could not hit a changeup. He was right. Wasdell batted .200 in the Series. Tommy Henrich once exclaimed: "I still don't believe a man can have that kind of memory." While McCarthy was respectful and circumspect as the Series approached, other Yankee rooters were vocal. When former Yankee pitcher George Uhle was sent out by MacPhail and Durocher to scout the Yankees, names were hurled about him like "jellyfish," "Mata Hari," and even "Gestapo." Emotions throughout the city ran high. Before the Series, Commissioner Landis took the unusual step of called Durocher and McCarthy to a meeting. He told them to behave "in a proper manner." Landis was chiefly concerned with Durocher.[21]

As in past Series, McCarthy went with one lineup. In this case: Dickey, Sturm, Gordon, Rolfe, Rizzuto, Keller, DiMaggio, and Henrich. Selkirk pinch-hit twice, and Bordagaray ran once. There were no slick personnel moves here. The managerial keys again lay in the pitching decisions. McCarthy's season-long nurturing of his pitching staff proved a vital factor. Lefty Gomez had not won a game since September 15 and did not look strong in his last outing. Even though he had a phenomenal record in the World Series, McCarthy did not start him, or even use him in relief. He chose 37-year old Red Ruffing for game one. Led by a Joe Gordon home run, the Yankees built up a 3–1 lead after six innings. The Dodgers scored one in the seventh and were threatening more when their young shortstop Pee Wee Reese tried aggressively to sneak over from second to third on a popup. He failed; McCarthy said the double play was a key point in the game. Ruffing held the Dodgers from there.[22]

Led by Leo Durocher, the Dodgers were predictably aggressive in game one, both on the field and with their mouths. This continued in game two. Dodger starter Whit Wyatt threw bean balls at Joe DiMaggio. Dodger catcher Mickey Owen slid hard into Rizzuto in the fifth inning, and the Yankee bench was ready to take the field and fight. In that inning the Dodgers scored two to tie the game. They added one more in the sixth, when a double play throw from Gordon pulled Sturm off the base. At that point, McCarthy relieved starter Spud Chandler with Johnny Murphy. One run down, the Yankees threatened in the bottom of the sixth. In that inning Murphy was due up, with two runners on. McCarthy did not pinch hit for him. Murphy did not come through with a hit, and neither team scored from there, giving the game to Brooklyn.

McCarthy had been magnanimous after the first game, conceding that the game could have gone either way and that the Yankees had gotten some breaks. After the loss in game two he was a steamed. Brooklyn's pitcher, Whit Wyatt, he declared, "was no better than Chandler or Murphy." McCarthy was especially incensed at Wyatt having thrown "dusters" at DiMaggio. He saw this as part of MacPhail's and Durocher's ways, of which he did not approve one bit. "Anybody who tells you a bean ball or a duster is part of the game is crazy. Good pitchers don't have to play that way. You never saw Walter Johnson throw a duster, did you? It's a bad thing. How can you say it's part of baseball when you're liable to hurt or kill the father of a couple of kids."

McCarthy would encounter more and more of this style of baseball in future years, and his views would never change. As for the second game of the Series, he felt as well that without the errant throw from the usually dependable Gordon, the Dodgers would not have scored their third run. Asked why he did not pinch hit for Murphy in the sixth, McCarthy glared: "you just don't do those things. You don't sacrifice your good pitchers for a hit that early in the game when your club is only one run behind. You'd run out of good pitchers all the time if you did." Since Murphy held Brooklyn from there, it proved a wise move to keep him in. He felt he was wise to bank on the team scoring from there. It was the percentage move, and that was how McCarthy always played it. It was the first World Series game McCarthy had lost since 1937, the first at Yankee Stadium since 1936.[23]

Game three shifted to Brooklyn, and after two 3–2 games, everyone believed the Series would be close. For game three, McCarthy sent out Marius Russo. He pitched a four hitter. Brooklyn's "Fat Freddie" Fitzsimmons proved Russo's match at first. The game was scoreless through seven innings. In the Yankee half of the seventh, Fitzsimmons again held them, but the final out, by Russo, was a line drive that hit Fitzsimmons on the knee. Reese fielded the ball and threw out Russo, but Fitzsimmons had a fractured kneecap. Now facing relief pitching, the Yankees rallied for two runs in the eighth. The Dodgers could counter with but one, and Russo completed the win.

When a Series stands at two games to one, the fourth game is crucial for the team behind, as after the next game they are either even or virtually gone. How well McCarthy remembered that from 1929. Game four showed more offense, with the Yankees jumping out 3–0 in the top of the fourth. The Dodgers came back with two in the fourth and two more in the fifth. McCarthy lifted his fourth starter, Atley Donald. Marv Breuer held the Dodgers from there. In the eighth McCarthy brought in

Murphy again, the only pitcher to see action for McCarthy in more than one game that Series. Murphy also held the Dodgers scoreless. But the Dodgers' pitcher Hugh Casey, who had entered the game in the fifth inning, had shut down the Yankees too. It was Casey who had replaced Fitzsimmons in game three and could not save the game for him, so this day he was determined to win. Up 4–3 in the ninth, it looked like Casey and the Dodgers were going to even the Series.

Then came one of the most famous plays in the history of baseball; "Flatbush's Darkest Hour," the *New York Times* called it. With two out, Tommy Henrich swung and missed what appeared to be strike three. The ball got by Dodger catcher Mickey Owen, however, and Henrich made it safely to first base. Then came the barrage: DiMaggio singled, Keller doubled, Dickey walked, Gordon doubled, Rizzuto walked. Murphy finally grounded to short. In all, four runs crossed the plate after Henrich had swung and missed at strike three. Murphy held the shell-shocked Dodgers in the ninth, and the usually quiet Yankees were jubilant. No one asked McCarthy why he did not pinch hit for Murphy in the ninth.[24]

Of the Henrich third strike, Lefty Gomez wise cracked: "We've been working on that play for months." To a reporter, Joe DiMaggio laughed "Well, they say everything happens in Brooklyn!" Tommy Henrich recalled Joe DiMaggio then chortling "no one comes back from that!" Henrich was stunned: "DiMaggio *never* talked like that," he said. With the close games, and having lost in 1940, DiMaggio and the Yankees were obviously less arrogant than they had been against the Cubs and the Reds. With the aggressiveness of the Dodgers, they knew they had gotten the greatest break against a formidable foe and were letting off a little steam. When some had started to celebrate after the third victory over Cincinnati in 1939, McCarthy had cut them off. He wisely made no such effort this time. Emotions were high, and he knew it best to let them run a bit.

McCarthy may have recalled another time when he seemed about to bring a World Series back to a 2–2 tie — game four, 1929, and that awful eighth inning. He always believed things have a way of evening out. Perhaps a bit humbled by the memory of what had happened to him twelve years before, McCarthy was blandly philosophical about the Owen play: "That just goes to prove what has been said for a long time, the game isn't over until the last man is out." Then he added with a little more twinkle, in praise of his players: "it's not the break itself that counts, but what follows. We just followed that one through." That was what McCarthy's Yankees always prided themselves on, making the utmost of an opponent's lapse. Brooklyn would certainly never forget it.[25]

McCarthy had yet another well rested starter for game five — Ernie Bonham. The *New York Times* snidely referred to McCarthy's "inexhaustible supply of mound talent," but it was McCarthy who kept and cut the right pitchers, trained them, and cagily rested them. The success just looked too easy, and writers were not unlike a lot of fans, and opponents, in their willingness to underestimate what McCarthy had done. In game five, the Dodgers were snarling throughout. In the fifth inning the benches nearly cleared. McCarthy was swept up in the mayhem a bit himself. He actually appeared from the dugout in the fourth inning and disputed an umpire call. He never appeared on the field otherwise. The Yankees had jumped out 2–0 in the second. Bonham gave up one run in the third inning, but he was invincible from there.

The Yankees scored one more. Brooklyn was frustrated. They were beaten, and they knew it. The *Brooklyn Eagle* found what optimism they could with their subsequently famous headline the next morning: "Wait Til Next Year!"[26] Meanwhile, with the victory, McCarthy had set a record winning his sixth World Series. John McGraw, Connie Mack, Miller Huggins, no one had ever done that. Joe McCarthy was number one.

Again the Yankees were on top. The '41 victory made the 1940 season appear all the more aberrational. With the Series triumph, phrases like "Bronx Bombers" returned to the baseball lexicon. Washington's Clark Griffith pushed again for a ban on any trades with the American League champion. Resentment of the Yankees' success was not unlike Republican resentment at the utter domination of national affairs by the Democrats. In that respect, McCarthy was thus resented and admired like President Roosevelt. It looked like nothing could keep McCarthy and the Yankees from continuing to roll along as they had. They would, but the subsequent triumphs would come under very different circumstances.

Victory in the '41 World Series did pose one major hardship on McCarthy that autumn. Back in the spring, McCarthy and a reporter had been commiserating with one another about their respective toothaches. Both acknowledged that they would likely have to get their molars extracted, but McCarthy said he wanted to wait on his dental work until the Yankees had won the World Series. To that implicit cockiness, the reporter could not help but wisecrack: "Well, you'll have to wait a long time." His honor thus challenged, McCarthy made an agreement with the reporter — that he would indeed win the Series that season and get his bad teeth pulled immediately after the victory. It was part of a wager, in which the reporter would have to attend a party hosted by McCarthy after a Yankee victory, while McCarthy would attend the reporter's party if any other team won the Series that year. With the molars in mind, either affair was to be called a "coming out party." True to his word as always, on October 8, just two days after the triumph over Brooklyn, McCarthy paid a visit to his dentist, who yanked no fewer than sixteen of McCarthy's teeth![27] (Dentists were more radically surgical in those days.) Mr. and Mrs. McCarthy then hosted a party. The reporter attended, and Joe did not eat very much.

30

And the War Came

I honestly feel that it would be best for the country to keep baseball going.
— President Franklin Roosevelt
(letter to Commissioner Landis)

McCarthy was always meticulous about training camp, and not simply because he wanted to impose rules and habituate players to observing his system. That risked mere order for its own sake, something which many other managers cherished but which was never that important a matter to McCarthy. McCarthy knew what training was needed to prepare a team for the season and to evaluate prospects properly. So thorough was he in the sense of the outcomes he wanted that he recognized the limitations for his judgments within the context of what training camps provided. The playing fields of Florida had their limits to him, for example. The visual backgrounds were different than players would see in the regular season. The nature of the sun fields, "the glare of the white sun," as he put it, was different in Florida. Some Florida infields were shorter than normal. The sandy nature of some of them yielded different hops and required different timing than many regular season parks. Some who then looked great in the South did not pan out in the regular season, while others never showed their best in Florida. Over the years, McCarthy had constructed the best system he could, but he knew the limits and quirks of its people and components.[1]

With the United States' entry into World War II, so many elements of his system would be strained. All other teams suffered too, but few had built such a sophisticated system as the Yankees. For New York, there was more to deteriorate. Just before he left Buffalo for spring training in 1942, McCarthy was already anticipating one matter. Many people were going to enlist or be drafted. In no way did McCarthy ever criticize any one who joined to fight, but he did comment "You can't tell what a man is going to do in these times." His comment was not negative, but indicative of how much he valued predictability and consistency. Lesser managers left more matters to the fates when accounting for successes and failures. McCarthy fully grasped where chance played its role, but no one took better care of the details that could be addressed before the fates took over. In 1942, his job was still to manage a baseball team. President Roosevelt had told Commissioner Landis that playing baseball was an altogether fitting and proper thing to do during the war. Until he was told otherwise, McCarthy would devote his thinking to the goal of his hired task of managing a ball club the best he could.

McCarthy knew the new difficulties that would present themselves to him with the war on. Among the first things on his mind were personnel demands. With so many going into the service, McCarthy noted that "many youngsters who otherwise would be seasoned for a year or two in Double A will step right into a big league lineup." The unpredictability of who could then find themselves with an excellent new player, he said, "could make [for] quite a topsy-turvy race."[2] For the '42 Yankees there was an added problem involving some of the players being late for camp, held over in Hollywood where they were taking part in the making of *Pride of the Yankees,* the MGM movie starring Gary Cooper about the life of Lou Gehrig. A bigger problem concerned a number of players engaged in salary disputes with Ed Barrow. They were all resolved, but the negotiations with DiMaggio took several weeks, and, naturally, they received a great deal of publicity.

The salary gap between Barrow and DiMaggio was ultimately $45,000 vs. $40,000, with DiMaggio signing for $42,000. Barrow repeatedly tried to use the issue of the war in his negotiations. True, he acknowledged, the Yankees had won the World Series, but the war situation made everything different. He regularly pointed out that Hank Greenberg had gone from a $50,000 contract in 1941 to the Army's pay of $21 a month. Amidst the jockeying and posturing, one newspaperman intelligently suggested that DiMaggio take his previous year's salary of $37,500 plus $3000 in War Bonds, with the Yankees putting an equal proportion of their gate receipt profits into War Bonds too. No one listened. When Barrow referred to Greenberg's Army salary, people could have countered that Barrow and the Yankee management were not reducing their own salaries, but somehow in the minds of the fans, the dickering over salaries reflected worse upon the players. After he began playing in the exhibition games and during the early season games, DiMaggio was often greeted with boos when he stepped up to the plate. While he had occasionally intervened with some star players during contract time, McCarthy nervously stayed out of all salary matters and tersely snarled at any reporters when asked to comment on DiMaggio's or any others' contract talks.[3]

McCarthy was always a nervous manager, but that March he had good reason. Towards mid-month he still did not have DiMaggio, Keller, Gordon, and Ruffing. Johnny Sturm was in the Army. Red Rolfe was ill with colitis. Selkirk was hitting only .100 in the spring games, and McCarthy had to wonder about Bill Dickey. Dickey was 35 years old and had caught over 100 games a season since 1928. It simply stood to reason that he could begin to break down physically. In a Florida series with the pennant hopeful St. Louis Cardinals, the Yankees lost six of nine games. With respect to the losses in Florida, McCarthy was actually reassuring. Accounting for what was apparently less than precise play against the Cardinals, McCarthy noted: "It is hard to drive a world championship club. How could I give the boys a pep talk before, let us say, a game with Newark? Tell the fans not to worry. The Yankees will come along." The team was leaving Florida at that very point, and they were soon to play Newark. McCarthy thus knew very well how to give a pep talk in such a situation, and the newspapers were happy to relay it.[4]

McCarthy had to leave the Yankees for a few days in early April. One of his step-brothers, John Cassidy, had died. Cassidy had been a boyhood companion, and the loss was genuine. McCarthy returned to the club in three days. As when his mother died, any expressions of condolences were met with a simple nod and with a clearly implied message — let's go to work. Everyone was picking the Yankees to repeat. Hank Greenberg's enlistment would keep Detroit down. Bob Feller had enlisted, so Cleveland's prospects fell away. One poll showed 73 of 76 sports writers picking the Yankees. In another, every manager in the American League picked them. McCarthy agreed, but he knew well the problems of injuries that can always arise, and now there was the added possibility of players going into the service.[5]

McCarthy had some early experiments at first base to work out. With Johnny Sturm in the Army, the position was open. McCarthy decided not to try Gordon there again. Henrich would play there a few games that season, but he was so much better in the outfield, and McCarthy did not want to frustrate and waste him. There were several prospects from Newark. One was Buddy Hassett, the other, a big 6'5" kid named Ed Levy. With all the Jewish fans in New York, Levy's appearance with the Yankees prompted cheers, much as Lazzeri, Crosetti, DiMaggio, and Rizzuto had among Italians. Ed Barrow certainly did not object to any such ethnic concerns leading to greater attendance. For years the Giants had tried to tap New York's Jewish fan market, but they could never land a standout Jewish player. They had a second baseman named Andy Cohen, but he did not pan out. They once had a strong young first baseman from the Bronx named Hank Greenberg, but they already had Bill Terry and did not think enough of the youngster's speed, so they released him. Levy looked good in Florida, and he got the first shot at the position when the season opened. Levy did not work out with the Yankees, however. In the first place, regarding Barrow's concerns with ticket sales, Levy was not Jewish. (His mother was Irish and his biological father was a gentile named Whitner. His stepfather was Jewish, hence the adopted name. In one plate appearance with the Phillies in 1940, Levy had actually played under the name Whitner.) More important, and of singular importance to McCarthy, Levy simply could not hit. At the end of April, he was batting .122. Buddy Hassett got the job. He hit well as soon as he stepped into the position, and he held it through the season.[6]

Joe Gordon had only batted .177 in Florida. He was one of McCarthy's early concerns. But when the season started, Gordon was suddenly the hottest hitter in the league. At the end of April he was batting .487. With Gordon the leading the team, the lineup was fairly well set. Rolfe's illness continued to keep him sidelined, but McCarthy moved Crosetti to third base, with Jerry Priddy in reserve, leaving Rizzuto at shortstop. Henrich, Keller, and DiMaggio remained the outfield. Dickey caught, with Buddy Rosar giving him regular breaks.

The Yankees and Cleveland vied for the early lead. Cleveland had a first-year manager, Lou Boudreau. The first time the Yankees played the Indians, in the first inning McCarthy went on the offensive — a fake bunt, a hit and run, a bunt, another hit and run. In all, the Yankees scored five runs in the first inning. McCarthy described his thinking: "I knew they [Cleveland] would not expect us to play a base running game, and I though I would confuse them. The boy is in his first year managing ... and I thought I would put the fear of God into them early." It sounded ruthless. It was; and Boudreau would prove the sort who would not want it any other way.

In mid/late May, the Yankees ran off 20 wins in 23 games. They took the lead. Gordon continued to hit, in May and early June he ran off a 29-game hitting streak. Hassett had a 20-game streak. DiMaggio was hitting only .263, and with some fans still booing him over his salary demands, many leapt at the notion of Gordon being their new hero. The Yankees lead was 11 games by mid June. The games were all beginning at 4:00 P.M. to accommodate the war workers, and the Yankees donated over 1,000 baseballs for the soldiers' recreational needs at nearby service camps. Soldiers were always admitted free to Yankee Stadium, too.[7]

When Joe Gordon's hitting streak ended his average began to "slump," as he dropped from .394 to a mere .370. McCarthy immediately saw what was causing the slip. "He's going after bad balls again." McCarthy knew each of his players so well that he could anticipate and spot tendencies almost immediately and try to correct them before they compounded. Still, Gordon's slight dropoff seemed to affect others. Hassett and Henrich had been hitting well, but they also fell back in June. Meanwhile DiMaggio and Keller continued to disappoint. Keller's average was only .245 in June. DiMaggio's held around .260. In a game against Philadelphia, DiMaggio hit four consecutive line drives. Each one went right at an outfielder for an out. After the fourth one, DiMaggio returned to the dugout and kicked a bucket of ice. "Psychologist" McCarthy attempted to step forward. "What the hell do you think you're doing?" he snarled. DiMaggio uttered a few expletives, and then McCarthy changed his tone: "I was just worried you might hurt your foot." DiMaggio did not laugh, however, and his slump did not abate. Lefty Gomez used to be able to needle DiMaggio with some success, but at this point no one could, not even McCarthy. No one seemed able to step up. With a June record of merely 17 and 13, New York's eleven-game lead fell to a mere three, over Boston. The pressure of it clearly affected McCarthy. Outwardly he was positive: "I'm not worried at all. ... We hit slumps the same way as any other ball club, and we come out of them too." But he had another "gall bladder ailment" and spent a week away from the team from June 28 to July 6. Some reporters were speculating in generalities about a decline of "team pride," how "they have lost the drive [and] the cohesion that held them together." McCarthy hated such idle nonsense from reporters. He knew it had no merit; besides, it did anything but contribute to his own disposition.[8]

McCarthy was back to manage the All-Star Game. While he was away, the Yankees, under Art Fletcher, took a critical series from the Red Sox. Upon returning, McCarthy said he felt fine, but reporters said he appeared "pallid." In the all-star game he was criticized, as he had been in the past, for playing too many of his Yankees, but his squad won. The next day he managed the same all-star squad against an all-service team that included Mickey Cochrane, Bob Feller, and Ben Chapman. McCarthy's team won that one too. Pestered by reporters as to whether he was planning to make any major changes in view of the Yankees' June slump, McCarthy snapped at them: "when I change ... nobody will know it till the afternoon of the game." At least reporters then understood that McCarthy was feeling better. His players learned it too.

The next day one of his pitchers, Hank Borowy, developed a blister on the middle finger of his pitching hand and asked to be taken out. McCarthy told him to forget about it and keep pitching. The next batter doubled, so McCarthy took him out.

"I saw that Borowy still had that blister on his mind and it was causing him to let up. So I yanked him." McCarthy expected toughness, and when he reminded people of this, they often responded. Borowy may not have gotten the message, but the rest of the team sure did. After the All Star game, DiMaggio went on an 18-game hitting streak (and 26 of 28) during which he batted .378; the Yankees won 11 in a row. The fans were cheering DiMaggio now, and the Yankees' lead was back up to 12 games.[9]

McCarthy had said that in the new circumstances of the war that "you can't tell what a man is going to do." He remembered the completely unsettled time of World War I when people ended up in the trenches or working in mills and shipyards. People responded to the pressure in any number of ways. McCarthy's second catcher, Buddy Rosar, had been a useful backup to Bill Dickey. That July, Dickey was out with a shoulder injury, and Rosar was starting. With the Yankees in their 11-game winning streak, Rosar suddenly went to McCarthy on July 17, asking for a few days off to go to his home in Buffalo to take a civil service examination with the hopes of becoming a policeman. Policemen were exempt from the military draft. When he asked McCarthy for the time off, McCarthy refused him, and did so rather tersely. "Absolutely not," he admonished, "not even if you were my brother." Given that his brother had just died that spring, McCarthy's response may have been more heartfelt than Rosar realized. In any case it was firm, but Rosar was not really hearing it. What Rosar did not mention, and what was clearly contributing to his frantic behavior, was that his wife was about to give birth to their second child. (Had McCarthy known, he would likely have refused him anyway. Many ball players had gone on playing while their wives gave birth.) Rosar persisted, but McCarthy was hardly one ever to be swayed into changing his mind. Rosar finally told McCarthy: "I'm going anyway." He told reporters, "This is a sane desire for protection. Baseball is my meat and drink right now, but no one can say when I'll go out there and meet with an accident that will end my baseball days." Clearly the pressures of family and war were mounting on Rosar, and, as McCarthy had said, one could not predict how a person will react under such circumstances.

When Rosar told McCarthy he was defying orders and leaving for Buffalo, McCarthy calmly responded: "That's up to you." Rosar then asked a bit nervously: "If I go, what are you going to do?" Even more calmly, McCarthy replied: "That's up to me." The Cincinnati Reds had just cut a veteran catcher named Rollie Hemsley. McCarthy knew Hemsley well. He had played with the St. Louis Browns and the Cleveland Indians for nine seasons. Hemsley was 35 years old, but McCarthy had phoned his friend, Cincinnati Reds Manager Bill McKechnie, and received assurances that Hemsley was in sound physical shape. It must have been quite a turn of events for Hemsley. In one day he was released by the Reds, then he received a long distance phone call from Joe McCarthy. At first he actually thought someone was playing a cruel joke on him. But after he was persuaded that the call was genuine, he quickly agreed to terms. On Saturday, July 18, Hemsley packed his belongings and headed for New York. He caught both games of the next afternoon's doubleheader against Chicago. The Yankees won both games, and Hemsley got a hit in each game. White Sox Manager Jimmy Dykes protested Hemsley's presence in the lineup, claiming that the Yankees must be over the 25-player limit. McCarthy had just optioned a player, Ed Kearse, to Newark, so there was no infraction. McCarthy was never so imprecise.

Late in the second game, when Hemsley was about to go out to the on-deck circle before his turn at bat, McCarthy counseled him to go easy, that he need not run too hard down the first base line. It was undoubtedly the only time that Joe McCarthy ever advised a player to do anything but go all out on every play. (On the next play, Hemsley laid down a bunt and beat it out.) Hemsley remained with the team, backing up Dickey in 29 games over the next two months. As for Rosar, McCarthy would actually be a bit lenient, perhaps because he learned of the issue of Rosar's wife giving birth. He fined Rosar $250, but he merely threatened to suspend him indefinitely if he did not report to the team when they were to play in Cleveland on July 20. Rosar did report in Cleveland, so there was no suspension. The Yankees beat the Indians, and the Cleveland fans cheered loudly for Hemsley. He got a hit in every game of that series. Rosar was confined to the bench. (His wife had given birth to a healthy eight-pound son.) Rosar played in 16 more games that year. He suffered a spiking on his foot in August and was down for several weeks. As for the Civil Service examination, 1034 took the exam; 190 made the eligible list. Rosar was not among the 190. In other words, after all the fracas, he flunked the exam. Rosar had told the Civil Service Commission in Buffalo that he "doesn't believe there will be any baseball next year and that he wants to get a job to protect his wife and family." As it turned out there would be baseball, and Rosar would have a job playing ball — in Cleveland.[10]

Throughout the summer, teams were losing players to the military. In July, the Yankees learned that Tommy Henrich was to be inducted on September 1. The Pirates announced that with the drain of talent, they were going to test some "colored players." With the Pittsburgh Crawfords and the Homestead Grays in their midst, they knew well of the quality of players around them. They looked at Sam Bankhead, Willie Wells, Leon Day, and Josh Gibson. The Phillies announced they were going to try out a "colored catcher" of the Baltimore Elite Giants named Roy Campanella. (Commissioner Landis made each of them abandon the idea.) McCarthy never made any moves or any comment about the issue of segregation, then or at any other time. His Yankees were generally never in the state of need of other teams, whose non-commerce with African-American talent perversely held them in their second-rung status. The war years showed the greatest strain for personnel in baseball, but the racial bar held even then. As long as old Judge Landis was the Baseball Commissioner, there was no chance of any change there.[11]

McCarthy's team sustained a lot of bumps and bruises that summer. It was, he described, "as long a list of injuries as any team in either league." Rosar had been spiked. George Selkirk, Buddy Hassett, Jerry Priddy, Red Rolfe, Phil Rizzuto, Tommy Henrich, and Joe Gordon were all out for some days in the summer. So were three pitchers, Marius Russo, Atley Donald, and Spud Chandler. With so many infielders sidelined, Rollie Hemsley even played a little third base. His was an enthusiasm that McCarthy liked a lot. With so many icing down their injuries, McCarthy had to juggle effectively, and he held onto first place, although the twelve-game lead of July dropped to five. "Sure looks like we have the pennant iced," he quipped, "but we might run out of ice before the season ends." Boston had been in some disarray earlier in the season, but, led by young Ted Williams, they had regrouped into the best hitting team in the league and were closing fast. Amidst the pressures and injuries, on August 30, another Yankee was on the "out" list — Joe McCarthy. The night before, he had fallen in his bathroom, hitting his head and back, suffering a concussion. The papers made no reference to "gall bladder trouble" this time. It was just a "fall," but he was out for a week. Sadly, he missed Tommy Henrich's last game, an emotional event with the stadium announcer noting his imminent departure and the crowd giving him a huge ovation when he stepped up to bat for the last time. The opposing pitcher, Dizzy Trout, deliberately delayed his delivery so Henrich could enjoy the adulation. Henrich yelled for a pitch. "Not yet, Tommy," the normally mean Trout shouted back, "this kind of moment happens once in a lifetime. Take time and enjoy it." He did.[12]

Art Fletcher did his usual capable filling in for McCarthy during his recovery. The Yankees lost no ground to Boston. McCarthy returned on September 7, with a noticeable bump on his head. He suffered several more dizzy spells that month, and once the season was over he cut back on many previously planned public engagements. Back with the team, McCarthy headed out West for the Yankees' final road swing. In Cleveland on September 14, they clinched their sixth pennant in seven years. The blasé reactions to Yankee championships were more in evidence than ever in that summer of 1942. Ever more, the war was overshadowing all such achievements. With the drain of talent into the services, fans perceived a diminution of quality, real or imagined, and they certainly sensed that there were bigger issues in their midst than the AL pennant.[13]

While the war was diluting some of the intensity about the baseball season, the existing fan interest was more on the National League anyway, for there the Cardinals and the Dodgers again battled closely through September. Now with Stan Musial playing full time, the Cardinals got the better of it, winning on the second to last day of the season. Odds makers made the Yankees a 2–1 favorite in the Series, and the first game of the Series confirmed everyone's ho-hum expectations. McCarthy said "in a game like this you want a fellow out there who won't get flustered." He sent out Red Ruffing. He was now 38 years old, but McCarthy had been resting him for two weeks, and he had started several World Series for the Yanks. For 7 ⅔ innings, Ruffing pitched a no-hitter. He weakened, giving up one hit in the eighth, but St. Louis did not score. Meanwhile, the Yankees had scored 5 runs, and they got two more in the top of the ninth. The Cardinals jumped up and scored four runs in the bottom of the ninth, but McCarthy relieved Ruffing with Spud Chandler, and he closed the Cardinals out. The Yankees appeared to accept the victory and Ruffing's performance with "matter-of-fact calmness, as if they had it coming," and people expected another championship in short order. The Cardinals, however, had reason to be hopeful. Their ninth inning rally could have easily turned the game their way.[14]

Game two was a troublesome one for McCarthy and the Yankees. Ernie Bonham started for New York. He gave up two runs in the first inning but was strong from there. In the seventh inning, Cardinals third baseman Whitey Kurowski tripled in their third run with a line drive that left fielder Charlie Keller (and Joe McCarthy) yelled was a foul ball. The umpire's call stood, of course, and the Cardinals were then up by three. Meanwhile, the Yankees hit but could not score. On the day they had ten hits. They scored three runs to tie the game in the eighth inning, but St. Louis scored again in the bottom of the eighth. In the final inning, the Yankees threatened, but good fielding by the Cardinals snuffed out the potential rally. With none out, the Yankees had a man on first. Buddy Hassett connected for a long single to right field. A decade later, McCarthy recalled vividly,

> the drive came on a perfect hop to [Enos] Slaughter. He didn't have to bend; he didn't have to reach. He could handle the ball on the dead run, and he had the arm and the ability to make a perfect throw to third base.... It was only the first out, but it smothered our rally. I'll always remember that perfect throw. The fact is, after that throw we weren't the same club.

The allegedly foul-ball triple also rankled McCarthy. After the loss he was asked for a comment, and he shot back: "Yes, I've got a lot to say, but not before all you news-papermen."[15] Even if he could dispute the game, however, McCarthy and the Yan-kees knew full well that the Cardinals were not pushovers.

With the Series tied 1–1, the teams moved to New York. In game three, Enos Slaughter and Stan Musial each made leaping catches of balls that would have oth-erwise cleared the fence. Otherwise, Cardinal pitcher Ernie White pitched a strong game, as did McCarthy's starter Spud Chandler. The game was a tense affair. Frankie Crosetti had to be restrained when he shoved an umpire over a disputed call. (Films showed Crosetti to have been right about his dispute, but obviously not about shov-ing the umpire.) The Cardinals squeezed over a run in the third, and added one in the ninth, while the Yankees were shut out. With the loss, the Yankees were in a tight spot. The fourth game would be the first game in which the Cardinals got more hits than the Yankees. Each team hit well, and going into the seventh inning the score was 6–6. McCarthy later lamented that Johnny Murphy was injured, and he could not relieve Atley Donald at that moment for a pinch hitter. "We had no other pitcher to use." The Cardinals scored three runs from there, while the Yankees' hitting went lame.[16] Now the Cardinals were in command. As in '29 and '41, the last innings of game four meant the difference between being all even or down 3–1.

Perhaps remembering 1929, McCarthy was getting testy. The Cardinals had a diminutive equipment manager, Butch Yatkeman. He was popular with the team. Some of his hidden contributions to the team were his barbed comments that his shrill, piping voice turned into effective bench jockeying. Yatkeman had apparently irked McCarthy and some of the Yankees, so much so that at the beginning of the fifth game, Coach Art Fletcher came out to turn in the lineup card and demanded that Yatkeman be ordered to leave the bench and remain in the clubhouse. The Cards protested, but since Yatkeman was not a uniformed player or coach, Fletcher (and obviously McCarthy) was within his rights. The umpire upheld the Yankees' protest. The little move proved to be a case of winning the battle and losing the war. The protest smacked of whining. With Yatkeman having to listen to the game on the clubhouse radio, the Cardinals knew ever more certainly how the Yankees were feel-ing on the ropes. Their jockeying grew more intense. McCarthy's hope here was that if the Yankees could grab a lead, the Cardinals' confidence would be shaken. For the fifth game, he turned back to Red Ruffing to start. Despite less rest than normal, Ruffing pitched a good game, as did his opponent Johnny Beazley. Up 2–1 in the fifth, the Yankees had a chance to break the game open when they loaded the bases, but they could not score. Now the Cardinals' verbal taunts grew more intense. St. Louis tied the game in the sixth. In the top of the ninth, Kurowski homered with a man on. In the bottom of the inning, the Yankees put the first two men on base. Then, inexplicably, the Yankees' runner at second was picked off. After that, Cardinal second baseman Jimmy Brown made a great play on a line drive for the second out and then fielded a harmless grounder for the final out.

The Cardinals had done what the Yankees usually did. They made key plays in the field to snuff out rallies. They pushed over runs when they needed them. They gained the psychological edge, and they left their opponent feeling they had been outgunned. It was an odd feeling for New Yorkers—McCarthy's Yankees, 24 and 4 in the postseason to that point, had actually lost a World Series. Lefty Gomez could only sniff: "Victory party at the Horn and Hardart!" (the Horn and Hardart being a chain of cheap New York coffee shops). It was a great day for Yankee haters everywhere. Late in the afternoon, as McCarthy finally left Yankee Stadium, two boys approached him. One handed McCarthy his game program, and McCarthy signed it for him. Walking away, one boy asked: "Who's that?" His buddy responded excitedly: "Joe McCarthy!" McCarthy heard it and smiled at a reporter: "It ain't so bad. They still want my autograph."[17]

As he had been in 1929, McCarthy was outwardly magnanimous in his World Series defeat. He went to the Cardinals' locker room to congratulate the St. Louis team. "The Cards," he said "had good speed, good spirit, and a really fine manager in Billy Southworth. They won, and there is nothing we can take away from them." Having raised the "speed" issue, McCarthy proceeded to knock it back down, noting "they didn't steal any bases during the Series." He was indeed a little taut about the defeat. Some had been criticizing him, and the outcome of the Series added to the felt sense of legitimacy here. Amidst the war-time struggles, McCarthy had released long-time team trainer Earl Painter, a man who had been hired by Miller Huggins. McCarthy replaced him with Eddie Froelich. Froelich had worked for the White Sox, but he had earlier been McCarthy's batboy with the Cubs. McCarthy's move seemed self-indulgent, an inappropriate motive at any time, let alone during the war. Some said McCarthy felt "Doc" Painter was the last of Babe Ruth's clique. When Painter once said something flattering about Babe Ruth, McCarthy had snarled at him, "Knock it off and get back to work." McCarthy may have held onto misgivings about Painter ever since Joe DiMaggio blistered and infected his ankle with a Diathermy lamp in 1936. Whatever the motive, McCarthy was abrupt and edgy about any such criticism as came with his firing Painter, and within the year Froelich was in the Army anyway.

Now that McCarthy had lost a "big one," and with obviously bigger issues all around them, those who wished to criticize the great man sensed both legitimacy and leverage. The glory years of 1936–1939 certainly now seemed long ago. Reflecting upon how matters had fallen, Connie Mack commented: "This is not a Yankee team, not like the Yankee teams we used to know. It is a good team, good enough to win in our league, but you would not want to talk about them in the same terms as we used to talk about some of the great Yankee teams of the past." For McCarthy there was indeed a saddening sense of matters slipping from his grasp. It was not just the loss in the World Series. It was the circumstances of the war that was turning his world into something more petite. He would not have dreamed about complaining, as he fully appreciated the greater issues at stake. When he lost he endured the jeers that no one receives but those who have been on top for a long time. With McCarthy, particularly, the jeering was strong, as his success always seemed so purely a matter of being so lucky to be in the position in which he found himself. As the baseball world shrank amidst war pressures and with the taunts over losing, McCarthy tucked away a resolve. He would certainly do the best he could with what befell him for the war's duration, but his goal was to get back to that supreme level he had once attained. Trying to re-attain any past glory can prove a most frustrating endeavor.[18]

31

Can't Push Buttons Any More

In the winter of 1942–43, McCarthy did little traveling, even by his standards. This was not only due to the war. Mrs. McCarthy caught the flu, twice in three weeks that winter. Joe also got hurt. On Christmas Eve, McCarthy's handyman was finishing some holiday chores, and he had his son deliver the McCarthys a load of firewood. The boy was only thirteen, and the logs were too heavy for him. As he was lugging some of the load into McCarthy's home, he staggered. McCarthy intervened, and as he tried to take some of the load from the lad, one log fell right on his big toe. For over a week, McCarthy stubbornly refused to go to a doctor. Finally on January 2, he had his toe examined, and then only because a doctor had come to check on Mrs. McCarthy. The toe was broken, so Joe stayed off his feet for a few weeks.[1]

As the United States entered into its second full year on full war footing, the government was making more detailed demands. There were still plenty of rumors that baseball would be cut out entirely for the war's duration. That did not occur, but the government imposed many new limitations. The rules came forth sporadically and caused some confusion. Deftly reflecting both confusion and patriotism, Ed Barrow acknowledged: "I don't know what the government wants, but whatever it is, I am for it." McCarthy felt exactly the same way. One thing the War Department saw as a must was the saving of fuel by cutting out all excessive travel. Without complaint, major league baseball teams accepted orders not to travel below the Mason-Dixon Line when they met to train for the 1943 season. The Washington Senators could stay in the area around the District of Columbia (they trained at the University of Maryland), and the Cardinals and the Browns could venture a bit south of St. Louis. Everyone else had to stay in the North.

If anyone in 1943 needed further emphasis that the traditional world of baseball was gone, on February 8, Daniel Casey died. He was the New York player in 1887 who struck out in the bottom of the ninth with two out and the bases loaded in a game against Philadelphia, inspiring baseball's most famous poem by Ernest Thayer. The world of old baseball was indeed over. The same day that Casey died, Joe McCarthy traveled to Asbury Park, New Jersey, to lay out a baseball diamond amidst a storm of snow and ice. There was to be his site for "spring" training.[2]

Former Philadelphia A's pitcher George Earnshaw noted that the steam heating systems of most college fieldhouses where baseball teams would train were not going to be nearly as good as the warm outdoors of Florida and Arizona. He predicted many sore arms would develop. Out at Asbury Park, McCarthy and the Yankees would have access to such an indoor arena; good training was indeed going to be difficult. A week after McCarthy set up the field in New Jersey, Joe DiMaggio enlisted. "He was a good boy and a loyal boy," said McCarthy. "God bless him, he'll make a good soldier." Several other Yankees were also gone. Tommy Henrich was already in the service. By March, 1943, Red Ruffing, Phil Rizzuto, Buddy Hassett, George Selkirk, and Lefty Gomez* were all in uniform too. Red Rolfe had retired and was coaching at Yale. McCarthy still had Joe Gordon, Bill Dickey, Frankie Crosetti, and Charlie Keller, although as of mid-March, none of them had signed. Even though Gomez and Ruffing were gone, McCarthy still had a strong pitching staff. A few of the pitchers, Spud Chandler, Johnny Murphy, and Atley Donald, had been living in Florida during the winter, and McCarthy had them stay there and train in the warm weather for the first few weeks of March while he and the rest labored up in Asbury Park.

The New Jersey camp was crude in every way. Despite the cold, McCarthy wanted the team to train outside whenever possible. "The sport is essentially an outdoor one, and indoor training is of little help," he said. "Rubber sneakers are dangerous for ball players. Wood floors impose muscle strains a ball player is not accustomed to. I want no basketball court exercises." (He had learned of the dangers of basketball training back in Louisville in 1920.) Then he quickly added, "We are willing to do all in our power to cooperate with the war effort, and do not let this be analyzed in the slightest way as any sort of beef. It is just a technical diagnosis of training." No one accused McCarthy of complaining, but the New Jersey site was depressing nonetheless. McCarthy may have been reminded of the training conditions he had endured with the Wilmington Colts back in 1907. Reporters in New Jersey noted that McCarthy appeared taciturn — even by McCarthy standards! McCarthy reminded himself and others that one season when he was with Buffalo, the team had trained in Massachusetts. Still, the conditions were hard, and there was no denying it. The Yankees were lucky to get rooming accommodations.

Asbury Park was near the ocean, not too far below New York, and British Navy convoy officers and crews used the hotels there when they were on layover between voyages. The hotel the Yankees used was unfinished. McCarthy's was the only room with a phone. Meals were minimal, and the hotel's heating system did not work well, as McCarthy described: "the heat doesn't reach my room until it's time to be in bed and then I don't need it." The weather did not cooperate. Reporters would call the camp "the Asbury Park freeze." With McCarthy still wanting as much outdoor work as possible, many players developed colds. On March 14, only five players were able to suit up and work out.[3]

Until Gordon, Dickey, Crosetti, and Keller arrived, McCarthy was working with essentially a new team. In the first exhibition game, against Newark, the names on

---

*Gomez had been sold to the Braves anyway. He was no longer effective. McCarthy had frankly said to him: "You're not throwing as hard as you used to." Gomez responded: "You're wrong, Joe. I'm throwing twice as hard, but the ball isn't going as fast." After the war, Gomez went to work for Wilson Sporting Goods. When filling out the Wilson Company's employment form, he came to the section marked "Reason for leaving last employer?" Gomez wrote: "I couldn't get anybody out." (During the war Gomez remarked that he wished, in hindsight, that he had beaned a few batters in the 1930s when he toured Japan with Babe Ruth.)

the lineup card read: Stirnweiss, Weatherly, Metheny, Etten, Lindell, Johnson, Robinson, and Grimes. None had played on the '42 Yankees, except for Johnny Lindell, and in '42, Lindell had been a pitcher; now he was playing in the outfield. The whole roster was "more or less of an experiment," shrugged McCarthy, "and will remain so until I find out more about them." In late March, Dickey, Gordon, and Keller signed, but McCarthy held them out of the exhibition games. Trying to do too much too soon in training, Dickey and Keller injured themselves anyway. With the "new" lineup, the Yankees lost every one of their exhibition games in April. Crosetti signed in mid-April, but because of the shoving incident with the umpire in the '42 World Series, he was not going to be allowed to play in the first 30 games of the '43 season anyway.

Other teams were at similar loose ends, so pennant picking among reporters amounted almost to random selections. McCarthy actually declared the Washington Senators to be the team to beat. They had come in a distant seventh in '42, and some reporters laughed. But McCarthy always knew the personnel of the league. The Senators would contend all season and finish in second place, much to the surprise of all but one.[4]

Roy Weatherly looked like one of the stronger newcomers. He had played seven seasons in Cleveland, but he had a notoriously bad temper. After one outburst, McCarthy took him aside and had a very simple talk with him. There were to be no more such outbursts. There were none. With people like Johnny Allen and Ben Chapman, McCarthy felt the problem was not so much that they had tempers but that they could not control their tempers. Weatherly kept control and played a good season. Shortstop George "Snuffy" Stirnweiss was the best of the new arrivals. He had played well in Newark the previous year, and he showed considerable speed. McCarthy had not had a speed-oriented team since the heyday of Ben Chapman. But this season, McCarthy said "I am going to let George run." Just before the season began, Stirnweiss received official word that he would not be drafted because of stomach ulcers. New York fan interest was high on Stirnweiss; he was Jewish and a native of the Bronx. The question was whether he could adequately handle the position of shortstop. He would certainly have his chance, for Crosetti's suspension would not end until late May.[5]

The season began with meager attendance. On Easter Sunday only 18,005 came to Yankee Stadium to watch New York play Boston. Al Simmons, the man whose home run had opened the awful 8th inning of the 4th game of the '29 World Series against McCarthy's Cubs was now back playing left field for the Red Sox. McCarthy could have picked up some other old veterans, but he preferred to go with youth and do the best he could teaching and molding them. With no stars of yore, with slightly nervous young players, with the remaining stars like Gordon, Dickey, and Keller all being quiet sorts, and with McCarthy's usual taciturn ways with the press, the '43 Yankees struck some as more than a bit dull. Wrote one reporter: "Joe [McCarthy] offers no more information about his ball club than FDR does about the placement of troops or equipment on the war fronts. ... The Yanks are the dullest and most colorless ball club we have ever run across." In earlier times, McCarthy would have privately nodded approvingly at such a description, but now the papers could take the point in more earnest, as baseball was supposed to be a happy diversion for a war-weary nation. McCarthy could hardly respond, let alone adjust to such criticisms. He simply had to be himself, but the sense wore on him of a world appreciating him less and less.[6]

The Yankees may have been colorless, but they pushed themselves ahead in May. They took the lead for good on May 30. Switching Johnny Lindell to the outfield proved a wise move, as he became an excellent fielder and hit over .300 in the early part of the season. Having acquired catcher Rollie Hemsley in the previous season, McCarthy kept him. This also proved wise, as Bill Dickey was hurt several times and missed over half the games in the season. Ken Sears was another catcher McCarthy groomed who contributed well that summer. Another newcomer, Billy Johnson, proved a capable successor to Red Rolfe at third base. Nick Etten had played mediocre ball with the Phillies in previous seasons, but McCarthy saw something, traded for him, and his judgment proved to be on target. Etten had a strong season, the leading hitter among the Yankee regulars for much of the year. Bud Metheny was another McCarthy "find" who played well. McCarthy again proved his mastery at rotating and keeping healthy a roster of solid pitchers. Spud Chandler was his ace, with 20 wins and a 1.64 ERA (he was voted league MVP). Four other pitchers each won twelve or more. George Stirnweiss proved to be the only disappointment. He did not handle his position at shortstop terribly well. Crosetti played the majority of games after his suspension was over. McCarthy still believed Stirnweiss had a bright future, but knew that benching the rookie could be devastating. So, as he had done years before with Joe Gordon, he had Stirnweiss sit next to him on the bench to absorb as much information as he could. Stirnweiss later acknowledged: "I learned more sitting next to Mr. McCarthy on the bench ... than in all the other years I played baseball."

McCarthy tried Stirnweiss at third base, claiming, somewhat boorishly, "anybody can [play third]. It's the easiest position in the infield. [Ossie] Bluege played it for years in Washington and never uncrossed his legs." In a more sober mood, McCarthy saw that Stirnweiss would not work out there either. McCarthy would later move Stirnweiss to second base, and there he would be an all-star. Of note here with Stirnweiss is the fact that he felt it completely natural to refer to his manager as "Mr. McCarthy." Gehrig, Dickey, DiMaggio, Gordon, and the others had all held McCarthy with no less respect, but they always called him "Joe." While McCarthy was waiting for the days to return when he could manage under normal circumstances, the ground was shifting beneath him in ways he did not fully grasp.[7]

Further reflecting his sense of a team with less experienced men, and knowing the temptations from lengthy road trips, McCarthy made a point of absolutely forbidding any gambling on the team. He had always had such a rule, but in normal seasons he looked the other way with small games among his stars. With the new players, McCarthy knew more control was needed. He exercised it and proved he was still able to do a superb job of choosing and managing younger and lesser talent. Bill Dickey was the only player to hit over .300, and he was out a lot. Writers pointed to the "McCarthy luck," in regard to his knack for putting the right man in to get the key hit or strike out the key opponent. The uncanniness of his instincts was such that many writers of lesser talents could not but see it as mere luck. McCarthy and the Yankees won another pennant, by thirteen games.[8]

There were some embarrassingly comic moments that made some wonder "Can

this be the Yankees?" A slump in late June and early July saw the Washington Senators come to within percentage points of the lead. (By the end of July, however, the
Yankees reeled off twenty wins in twenty-five games, and their lead was back up to
ten games.) The Yankees were caught batting "out of order" in one game. They were
actually in proper order, but Art Fletcher had miscopied McCarthy's lineup, and
Fletcher's copy was the one turned in at the game's outset. A New York reporter asked
a rival manager about the Yankees. "They're not the same Yankees," nudged the
reporter. "They look bad." The manager responded: "Don't worry, nothing can happen to 'em with McCarthy around." It was a job of managing that proved to the
observant that McCarthy, having managed the finest, could go back and make a more
mediocre team play well too.

The jealousy was still there, however. In past years, especially '37 and '39,
McCarthy had been jealously criticized for playing his Yankees at the expense of others in the All-Star Game. (He usually won, however.) So in the summer of 1943, after
first inviting any other pilot in the league to manage, he deliberately played no Yankees in the All Star game in Philadelphia. His squad won anyway. Some reporters were
miffed at the fact that he had not let on to them of his plans. McCarthy took some
delight in their distemper. The easy grace of many great players regularly makes the
untutored fan think the tasks of playing well are easy. All who know the game to any
depth know this to be untrue. McCarthy's winning over so many years prompted
the same sort of cavalier sense, and because the nature of good management is so
much more subtle a matter than hitting or fielding, and because most observers have
played but never managed, the sense of how managing is not so easy does not so readily dislodge an "anybody can do it" outlook. McCarthy's continued distance from,
and at times disdain for, the press prompted relatively few to express much contrasting admiration. Dan Daniel of the *New York World Tribune* and Frank Graham
of the *New York Sun* were exceptions here. But their voices were not enough to offset
the envy-driven desire to find fault. This would never abate.[9]

At the season's end, there came an announcement of tentative plans for American and National League stars to tour the South Pacific. The players and managers
were chosen by the sixteen managers from the two leagues. Six Yankees were selected
for the squad. But the American League manager chosen was Boston's Joe Cronin.
McCarthy never commented, but reporters sensed that he was disappointed. Everyone chosen was naturally excited and honored to go and help the morale of the soldiers, and McCarthy felt he had certainly earned the honor of managing the team.
He knew he had the respect of all his colleagues, and he could not understand why
this respect was not enough to guide the choices. Some may have felt that "Jolly Joe"
Cronin would lend a lighter tone to the tour, with having fun being a primary concern. What was clearly present among some involved was a certain envy, a sense that
here, at least, was an opportunity to see McCarthy *not* win one. Four days after the
team selections had been announced, the War Department cancelled the trip. Even
with the issue moot, ill feelings from the selections lingered. Symbolically, on September 8, McCarthy suffered a black eye after being struck by a ball during fielding
practice. He was winning, but there was not much fun in it.[10]

After winning the '43 pennant, McCarthy was eager for the upcoming World
Series. St. Louis had again won the National League pennant, and McCarthy deeply

wanted revenge for the previous year's loss. Both clubs had changed drastically because of service inductions. Nevertheless, the occasion seemed like history repeating itself, especially after the Yankees once again won the first game and the Cardinals took the second. As he typically did in a World Series, McCarthy used the same starting lineup and made judicious choices in pitching. His ace Spud Chandler won the first game. In the second, his starter Ernie Bonham weakened in the fourth inning, as the Cardinals built up a 4–1 lead. Some criticized McCarthy as he left Bonham in the game. But Bonham steadied from there, yielding no more runs. The Yankees did no scoring, however, until the ninth when they scored two with none out. They could do nothing from there, but the choice to leave Bonham in the game proved correct.[11]

When the Series was tied 1–1 in 1942, the Cardinals went on to win the next three, so there was more than a little nervousness when the same situation presented itself in 1943. But this time it was McCarthy's team that seized the initiative. His pitchers gave up but three runs in the next three games. Down 2–1 going into the eighth inning of game three, the Yankees broke open both the game and the Series with a five-run barrage, highlighted by a triple from rookie Billy Johnson. The Yankees were in a mood to celebrate, but McCarthy held them in check. When reporters looked for McCarthy to praise Johnson, he judiciously waved them off: "Let's don't talk about it. I just don't like to start talking about a young fellow like that and how well he's doing. Sure he's doing well, but let's talk about it after the Series, not now." When he had a DiMaggio or a Keller, McCarthy knew the pressures of the limelight would not affect them. With a little-known figure like Billy Johnson, McCarthy knew it best to be more protective. It was not a new policy, it was always the same policy — do what is best for the character of the situation and people on hand at the time.[12]

The important fourth game was a close one. The Yankees won 2–1. Marius Russo pitched an excellent game. The Cardinals' only run was unearned, coming via two Yankee errors. When the game was over McCarthy pointed out the key moment of the game. The Yankees had just gone up 2–1 in the top of the eighth. The Cardinals' Stan Musial led off their half of the inning with a single. Then catcher Walker Cooper hit a hard bouncer past shortstop. Frankie Crosetti knocked it down, but both runners were safe. The St. Louis fans began to whoop it up as they sensed a rally was about to occur. McCarthy pointed out to reporters that Crosetti's knockdown was the key in the Yankees win. Reporters scratched their heads. McCarthy explained: had Crosetti not knocked the ball down, Musial would have gone to third. From there, said McCarthy, Musial would have likely scored, and "it might very well have been a different ball game." Noting the key which "most experts seem to have overlooked," McCarthy smiled broadly. He was still smiling when he left the stadium and a young girl gave him three scorecards and asked him to sign each of them. McCarthy gently chided her, "Is that all you have?"

The next day, Spud Chandler scattered 10 hits and pitched a shutout, giving the championship back to New York. "Beating any other National League club," reflected McCarthy, "would never have given us the same amount of satisfaction. They made us look bad last year. This time I think we repaid the compliment." McCarthy and the Yankees unanimously voted $500 shares from the World Series money to each of the Yankees in the armed forces. Many baseball people had been eager to criticize

McCarthy on the basis that anyone could win with the sorts of teams he had in the late 1930s. Beyond the point that McCarthy was the one who had formed these teams, the 1943 season showed that he could win with what one writer called many players who were "second violins on something less than championship teams."

Many sports writers still preferred to praise the Washington Senators' Ossie Bleuge for having done the best job of managing that season. The Senators had indeed contended and come in second, just as McCarthy had predicted back in March. McCarthy won the Manager of the Year Award, however. Ten players with the '43 Yankees had been minor leaguers the previous season. To those who had loved to criticize McCarthy's success as a mere extension of the personnel, the system, and the money at his disposal, his work with the 1943 Yankees proved he could truly "manage," not that he had not already proven that in Chicago, Louisville, and Wilkes-Barre. McCarthy was now back on top; nine pennants, seven World Series victories— it was quite an achievement. Who would have guessed that the '43 Series, won with lesser players amidst all the turmoil and diversions of the war, would be Joe McCarthy's last championship?[13]

Once again, people were free to envy McCarthy. One writer pointed out that a reason that McCarthy gets less recognition than he deserves was that he gets completely away from baseball once off the field. That was his way. Back home in Buffalo, McCarthy spent a completely quiet winter. He and Mrs. McCarthy still lived at Gates Circle, but that winter they bought a small 61-acre farm outside Buffalo on South Ellicott Creek Road, east off Niagara Falls Boulevard, in the town of Amherst. They began tending to all the details of fixing up the house to their liking. It was a good preoccupation for McCarthy, as he worried a great deal about his Yankees who were off fighting. After 1942 he had lost DiMaggio, Ruffing, Henrich, Selkirk, and Hassett to the service. By the time of training camp, 1944, Charlie Keller, Joe Gordon, Billy Johnson, Marius Russo, Spud Chandler, Joe Glenn, and Bill Dickey were all in uniform. The McCarthys had no children, and McCarthy's affection for his players was indeed strong. The induction of Dickey affected him particularly. Dickey had been with McCarthy since his first day as manager of the Yankees in 1931. "The Navy has landed a marvelous man," he proclaimed. "For me, personally, it is a tough day." McCarthy gave emphasis to the "personally" as, of course, he never put his feelings above the great tasks facing everyone at that moment. Still, as he noted, "losing two great clubs in two years is an experience." It "would be a complete knockout if we did not know that all the other clubs were being hit just as hard." Hit hard they were.[14]

President Roosevelt had said that baseball should go on, but some teams were finding it hard to find players. Below the level of major league baseball, some teams combined. In professional football Philadelphia and Pittsburgh merged in 1943 (they were the "Steagles"). The following fall, Pittsburgh merged with the Chicago Cardinals. In baseball one out of three "Double A" leagues closed entirely, and all the "Single A" leagues shut down completely. The major leagues would go on as best they could. 58-year old Ty Cobb, perhaps half-seriously, announced "I'm ready … to get back in harness myself to help preserve the game if the worst comes to worst." It was in the context of such massive drains on personnel that predictions for 1944 were completely up in the air. It's so bad, noted Grantland Rice, "even the St. Louis Browns might win the '44 flag."[15]

As in 1943, the training camps were again ordered to convene only in nearby confines. McCarthy did not want Asbury Park again. He was able to secure quarters in Atlantic City, where he had played indoor ball in the winter of 1909–10. With tourism reduced to nil, there were sufficient accommodations. Some outdoor fields were available, and on cold days the Yankees were able to share the use of some indoor Army arenas. As in 1943, there were many foul days. The Yankees trained outside for only six of the days they were in Atlantic City. While outdoors, McCarthy suffered much exposure, and, as he was older and not moving around as much as his players, he began to feel the effects more than anyone.[16]

As the camps were opening, reporters interviewed the various managers. Here Chicago White Sox Manager Jimmy Dykes made a little wisecrack that would become oh so famous. Things were going to be different for Joe McCarthy this season, Dykes quipped. "Joe McCarthy will really have to go to work this season. He won't be able to sit back as in other years and simply push buttons to win pennants." Dykes' statement was a meaningless little aside, but it became a huge issue. Reporters seized upon it, as it seemed to resonate among all those who did not fully appreciate or wanted to deprecate McCarthy's managerial genius. Many had previously raised the point that McCarthy's teams were so superb that they were virtually self-starting. The words "push button manager," however, seemed somehow the perfect reification of what everyone with McCarthy-envy wanted to believe — that they could do the same thing with the kind of talent he had always had at his disposal. It was impossible to dislodge such views, as success could only prompt more envy while the slightest failure would only invite derision. Even the obvious example of what McCarthy had accomplished in 1943 quieted no one.

McCarthy's reaction to Dykes stirred the pot even more. He was indignant. Dykes said McCarthy hit the ceiling. He certainly had a right to be mad, but the sense that Dykes' wisecrack had gotten under his skin naturally made his opponents want to rub it in more. Since they could not beat him, they sure loved to irritate him. Dykes later admitted that he was always a bit of a wise guy, and the statement's significance had been blown way out of proportion. (He said he never dreamt that his words would take such proportions, but he still maintained the quip "was to be sure an amusing exaggeration, but not without some truth.") At a dinner of baseball writers that spring, McCarthy was asked to sit in the front and push a button as each speaker was to come to the front. He angrily refused; it probably would have been better for him if he had agreed, but that would have been totally out of character. During his early seasons with the Yankees, McCarthy certainly had not liked it when New York writers dubbed him with the name "Second Place Joe." But "Push Button Manager" angered him to distraction. When he first learned of the comment, one reporter said "he jumped to his feet, fire in his eye: 'I had no push-buttons in Louisville, and I won pennants there,' shouted Marse Joe, as he stormed from the scene." Over and over, reporters in one city after another asked him about it. He would always bristle. Even before Dykes' famous remark, McCarthy had been queried about how easy it must be to manage with such a collection of great players. "Yes," he snapped, "I spend all my summers in Atlantic City and only come back for the World Series." For a long time reporters had been frustrated with the minimal information and emotion they had gotten out of McCarthy. Now they had something that seemed to get a rise out of the great man. They stayed with it.[17]

A few reporters clacked out words to the contrary. Joe Williams of the *New York World-Telegram* wrote of how McCarthy had been "reduced from caviar to corn pone." For years, he said, many had been raising the call "Break up the Yankees. It took another world war to do it," but, Williams acknowledged, "the job is being done thoroughly. ... We have read his managerial ability will be put to the test this year. What, may we ask have they been testing all these previous years?" Williams concluded, "the point seems so obvious, it scarcely merits attention." Williams was being logical. But the key was that he was a Yankee fan. Fans, players, and managers of the seven other American League teams had gone through so many years of futility that they could hardly be expected to behave logically. When they could come up with a rhetorical ploy that somehow seemed to work, like any other form of effective bench jockeying, they would use it. Use it they did. Were any sort of verbal wedge available to him, McCarthy would have instructed his players to do the very same thing. In 1932, for example, his Yankees had been merciless with the Cubs about the "half-share" of World Series money voted to Mark Koenig. McCarthy himself always chided Giants Manager Bill Terry about his pipe smoking. Now he had to take it. "Push-Button Joe" was a nickname that would stay with McCarthy for the rest of his career. He did not like it one little bit, and he never really forgave Jimmy Dykes.[18]

To the degree that there was a kernel of legitimacy in Dykes' wise crack, McCarthy was indeed compelled to manage differently with the players left to him during the war. With a roster of names like Etten, Johnson, Robinson, Zuber, and Grimes, McCarthy had to do a lot of teaching of fundamentals. It was truly like going back to AAA-level baseball. McCarthy could manage at that level at well as anyone, but returning to such a level was a trifle depressing. Some said he began to drink more, especially on the road. Tommy Henrich had pointed out that with the great Yankee teams before the war, McCarthy "did not tell us *what* to do." When McCarthy wanted a player like Henrich to do certain things, "he didn't tell me how," remembered Henrich. "That would be up to me. ... he was telling me to exercise the discipline to figure out how to carry out his orders."[19] To the untutored, and to the wise guys like Dykes, who never did better than third place, the privilege of managing from such a position as McCarthy had held seemed ridiculously easy (very much in the literal sense of inviting ridicule). The point was that McCarthy had built up his managerial loft to such a position that he could operate this way. When he managed in Wilkes-Barre, Louisville, and Chicago, and in his leaner years with the Yankees, he had had to be more of a teacher, and he did this very well indeed. His eye for talent, combined with Ruppert's and Barrow's money and management, was such he built up a team of excellent players, with coaches he had judiciously picked who had the talent to tend to the mechanics of teaching where needed. Then, and only then, did he dare elevate himself to a level no other manager ever saw, one that invited envy and brought on Dykes' wisecracks.

In this regard, McCarthy's running of the Yankees was like another leader of a revered New York institution, Arturo Toscanini of the NBC Symphony. Toscanini also had the best players, and when he told violinists "a bit more legato," he did not have to tell them how; he knew they would do it, and he would dismiss them if they did not. He could then put his energies into making the kind of music he wanted and not worry about teaching the mechanics of how properly to produce it. Conductors of lesser orchestras could immaturely entertain themselves with the notion that if they had an orchestra like "the NBC," they could conduct just as marvelously as Toscanini. No one ever called Toscanini a "push-button conductor," but he had his detractors, and his position certainly invited envy. A few conductors of the day were certainly close to if not as good as Toscanini, and an equally few managers may have done nearly as well as McCarthy with the talent and organization he had helped build around him.

The point was that both Toscanini and McCarthy had each previously done all the work with the mechanics wherever it was necessary. They had done it so well, indeed, that with the right financial backing (RCA President Robert Sarnoff, who underwrote the NBC Symphony, was even wealthier than Col. Ruppert), they could build organizations that eclipsed all former levels of playing. In neither case was there any leaping to the elite levels by the mere luck of falling into a rich spot. To the untutored it only seemed that way, and their sense of "anyone can do what he does" provided the fertile ground in which such a seed as Dykes' little joke could implant itself.

As in 1943, McCarthy again had a virtually new lineup that spring. At Yankee Stadium, everyone on the ground crew was under the age of eighteen. McCarthy had a lot of "basic" work to do, and the logistical imperatives of wartime made this even harder. Before the season, the Yankees were only allowed to play the teams that were training nearby — the Phillies, A's, Dodgers, Giants, and Newark. McCarthy switched Stirnweiss to second base, and here "Snuffy" played exceptionally. Stirnweiss had been an all-American football player at the University of North Carolina. In his baseball career, since high school in the Bronx, he had been a shortstop. But at the major league level, even that of the war years, he could not handle the position, especially the throws. McCarthy had once said that football players, like Riggs Stephenson and Stirnweiss, often take too many blows to the chest and shoulders. This, he believed, affected their throwing muscles and motions. McCarthy was very good at shifting personnel. Trying to make Joe Gordon a first baseman proved a less than spectacular innovation. Otherwise, no manager ever showed such wisdom, and risk-taking, as McCarthy in successfully shifting players into new, sometimes radically different positions. Infielder Ben Chapman became an outfielder. Shortstop Red Rolfe became a third baseman. Pitcher Johnny Lindell became an outfielder. Stirnweiss became a second baseman. Compared to such moves, perhaps the only more significant shift ever in baseball came when the Red Sox manager shifted Babe Ruth from pitcher to outfielder, and that was done by McCarthy's boss— Ed Barrow.[20]

With everyone in the league fielding so many new, untested players, the pennant situation was anybody's guess. As Grantland Rice had said, even the St. Louis Browns could win the pennant. Whether or not Rice's words had motivated them, St. Louis indeed jumped ahead at the start, winning 12 of their first 15. New York held second place, two games back. McCarthy spoke of how "my boys have the spirit and heart of champions," predicting "they'll start digging in ... and go all the way." The trouble at first was that the Yankees were first going to have to do it without their Manager. The exposure to the bad weather in Atlantic City in March had given McCarthy a cold he could not shake. It grew steadily worse, and on April 10, just as the season was about to begin, he had to leave the team. He was diagnosed with influenza complicated by neuritis. Mrs. McCarthy took him home to Buffalo. "I don't

know when I'll be back," he confessed. "I just feel all in." He was feverish, had shoot-
ing pains in his shoulders and legs, and had lost 15 pounds. Speculations began to
circulate that McCarthy was going to retire. That was not going to happen. When a
reporter asked him about retiring and taking up farming on his new property, he
mused: "Farming? That's a losing proposition. If I want to indulge in a farm, I'll certainly have to stay in baseball to afford it." At least his spirit was back up. His physician and Mrs. McCarthy wanted to keep him in Buffalo to regain his strength. "He
should have more rest," Mrs. McCarthy told the papers, "but he's anxious to be back
with the team."

He returned on May 9. With the Browns ahead, McCarthy was asked for a comment, and this time he was cooperative, obviously wanting to instill fight in his team:
"Do I fear St. Louis. Heck no, let them fear us. We're still the champions!" He went
out of his way to compliment Coach Art Fletcher for the job he did in his absence,
and then went right to work. He did concede one point to his doctor, Arthur Burkel:
for much of the spring he was drinking only milk in the evening. With the war and
the decline of player quality, reporters were less deferential towards McCarthy. They
peppered him with questions, including request after request for any comment about
the "push button" label. The Yankees were not as good, and the bigger issues of the
war made the press see McCarthy in a different light. With all this, McCarthy often
wanted something besides a glass of milk, and apparently, as the '44 season wore on,
he began to drink more.[21]

In the late spring and early summer, the Yankees and St. Louis went back and
forth with one another for the American League lead. The Yankees would occasionally falter. One writer said "the Yankees' fielding was so bad it was funny, [mean-
while] the pitching was strictly 4F," 4F being the Army Draft Board's label for men
found physically unfit for service. In one four-game stretch in July, the Yankees committed twelve errors. In a doubleheader with Chicago, they committed ten errors.
"Box seat customers [back of 1st base]," noted one scribe, "are starting to flinch every
time an infielder heaves the ball." When Buddy Hassett was on leave from the Army,
he came to the Stadium and proclaimed that he would keep coming to games "as long
as the Yankees continued to win." Dick Young, newly hired with the *New York Daily
News*, wise cracked that Hassett would then not need to ask for an extension of his
leave. "If McCarthy wins with those lugs," wrote an exasperated Jim McCully of the
Daily News, "he CERTAINLY will be a miracle man [emphasis his]."

On May 31, the Browns held first place, as the Yankees were skidding with five
straight losses, and nine losses in eleven games. In the summer, St. Louis built its
lead to nine and one half games. Detroit and Washington vied with the Yankees in
the first division. At one point in August, New York was in fourth place. Joe Trimble of the *Daily News* complained "this Yankee team is the saddest ... since the pre-
Miller Huggins days. All the genius of McCarthy's management," Trimble wrote,
"cannot overcome the mental and physical confusion the players exhibit on the field,
and there are no worthwhile replacements for the shabby regulars." In June, Newark
was indeed floundering in last place in the International League.[22]

Throughout the struggles, McCarthy did nothing but keep the team hustling.
He did admit once in June "I just don't have the players." But he never let up. Tac-
tically he went away from the McCarthy-ball of the late 1930s. He could not wait for

powerful bats to produce a big inning. He did a lot of running, bunting and "inside baseball." Here he used Stirnweiss's speed to good advantage. "Stirny" would lead the league with 55 stolen bases. To try to keep the defense as strong as possible, to "keep stepping," as McCarthy put it, he drilled endlessly. McCarthy held practices every day the team had a day off. (The only exception was on June 6, when all baseball came to a halt, and everyone prayed for the invasion of Normandy.) McCarthy's experiment with Stirnweiss worked perfectly. Stirnweiss proved to have found his rightful place at second base. The others struggled, but McCarthy would not let them quit. Despite the many errors and miscues, McCarthy never lost his temper or yelled at one of his players that entire summer. Noting their youth and inexperience, McCarthy pointed out, "What sense would there be in bawling them out?" He would be stern at a Gehrig or DiMaggio, but this was different. One marginal infielder, Oscar Grimes, made three errors in one inning, costing the Yankees the first game of a double header. When he got to the locker room after the game, McCarthy approached him. Grimes thought to himself, "Uh Oh; this is it." Surprisingly, McCarthy gave him a slap on the back and told him how he had once had a worse inning than that in Louisville. "Now get out there and win this second game for me," McCarthy urged. "You know," Grimes concluded, "You've got to play your guts out for a man like that."

Amidst the weak play there were actually some rumors that Joe DiMaggio was going to get an early discharge and be back with the team in September. (DiMaggio was in Honolulu that summer, being treated in a hospital for a stomach disorder, and he was able to return briefly to San Francisco, but he never applied for a medical discharge and fully expected to return to duty, which he did.) Ed Barrow told the press that he preferred to let the wartime squad do what they could anyway. McCarthy was up to the challenge. After being nine and a half games behind St. Louis, McCarthy's "lugs" scrambled their way back into the race. On September 2, one and one half games separated the top four teams of the league — St. Louis, Detroit, New York, and Boston. On September 5, after successive doubleheader sweeps of Washington and Philadelphia, and having won 14 of their last 18 games, the Yankees were in first place, knocking St. Louis out of the lead for the first time since May. No set of pushed buttons did that.[23]

Jim McCully, one of the reporters who was so exasperated with the Yankees' play that summer, accounted for New York's resurgence. "The big root of the Yankee tree which grows pennants in the Bronx," he extolled, "is Joe McCarthy, and don't let anyone tell you differently." Amidst the season-long desperation over personnel, one McCarthy acquisition that summer was 41-year old Paul Waner. With over 3000 hits to his credit, Waner was well past his prime in 1944 and under normal circumstances would not have even been playing on a major league club. He only did a little pinch hitting for McCarthy that September, producing but one hit in nine at bats. When the season was over he had a comment about his first acquaintance with Joe McCarthy:

> I have been around quite a bit, and as a National Leaguer I used to be skeptical of a lot I had heard about him [McCarthy], but, since sitting on the bench with him, I want to tell you his work has been a revelation to me. [John] McGraw was great, but even McGraw had his flaws. I can remember many a time, on certain plays, I could

have closed my eyes and guessed what McGraw's next move would be. With
McCarthy, his opponents never have the faintest idea what he is going to do next, yet
his every move is sound.

Waner said he made a point of sitting close to McCarthy, "at first to make sure he
knew I was around." After a few games, Waner noted, "I would not have missed it
for the world — I got such a belt out of watching him operate!"

McCarthy kept the Yankees in the race until the end. Perhaps the only manager
with the wiles of McCarthy was old Connie Mack. And it was Mack who bested the
Yankees three straight in mid September. He used two lesser pitchers— 38-year old
Luke Hamlin and Don Black — to sweep a doubleheader. Reporters and fans were
reminded of Howard Ehmke besting the Cubs in 1929. McCarthy always held the
deepest respect for Mr. Mack. Including the fateful series with last-place Philadelphia, the Yankees lost 7 of 8 in mid September, and their contention faded. Led by
pitcher Denny Galehouse, St. Louis won their key games down the stretch, giving
the Browns their only pennant in the franchise's long history at that locale. The U.S.
government officials were happy in one respect. The Cardinals won again in the
National League, so there was no unnecessary travel in the Series, not even across
town. The Cards and Browns used the same ballpark. It was the first World Series
since 1921 and 1922 to occur in one stadium. The Cardinals won in six games. New
York fans were saddened, of course, but no one could fault the team's heart, or their
manager's. With all the obstacles, Ed Barrow noted, it was McCarthy's finest job of
managing. "I learned more about baseball from Joe McCarthy," said Paul Waner,
"than I learned all that time in the National League."[24]

After so many seasons at the absolute summit of baseball, the war years took a
toll on McCarthy. Never did he utter a word of complaint, for he grasped the larger
issues at stake as well as anyone. But the winning years had allowed him to become
an utter perfectionist. It was a perfectionism driven in part by his years in places like
Wilkes-Barre, Toledo, Wilmington, and Franklin. He hated the haphazard ways of
the minors, the bone-jarring bus rides, the dirty hotels, the bad food. With the Spartan times of the war, he felt his venue slipping back to this sort of level. He then
became more meticulous and demanding in regard to petty matters over which he
could attempt to exert control. This was symptomatic of a more depressed state, in
response to which he regularly imbibed his White Horse Scotch. This would wear
on him deeply.

32

One War Ends and Another Begins

The fall and winter of 1944–45 were a most eventful series of months. The big changes in the marches toward victory in the wars in Europe and the Pacific dwarfed every other piece of news. By the time McCarthy's Yankees and other's teams were beginning to assemble for the 1945 season, talk about victory in the war had gone from hope to expectation. For sports fans and professionals this brought the added expectation for their own little worlds that the ranks of players would at long last be refilled with all the stars who would soon be discharged from military duty. After the rough times of '43 and '44, McCarthy was certainly looking forward to the return of DiMaggio, Gordon, Dickey, and Keller. Meanwhile, he still had to form a team with what was available, and he had to do so under decidedly new circumstances.

Within the Yankee organization, the off-season was eventful. Since the death of Col. Ruppert in 1939, the ownership of the Yankees had been somewhat in abeyance. Control of the Yankees rested with a team of bank executors. Uncomfortable with low wartime revenues, the executors put the team up for sale. A new team ownership formed in late January 1945 with two new principal owners, Dan Topping and Del Webb. Of greatest importance to all Yankee personnel here was the third man who bought in with Topping and Webb and who in February became the club's new president and business manager — Larry MacPhail. Ed Barrow was 76 years old. When Judge Landis passed away in November 1944, baseball owners asked him to help with the affairs of the Commissioner's office until a successor to Landis was selected. After that he retired. His long association with the New York Yankees, and with Joe McCarthy, was over. It was a new era, and the key question on the minds of all concerned with the Yankees focused on what kind of impact MacPhail would have.

Views about MacPhail's possible impact upon the Yankees fell into two groups. One hoped that MacPhail would jazz up the Yankees. The other feared that MacPhail would jazz up the Yankees. McCarthy was not a big fan of jazz, literally or figuratively. Musically, he liked George M. Cohan–style show tunes; he liked his baseball straight, the old-fashioned way too. Larry MacPhail had made his first impact in baseball when he ran the Cincinnati Reds organization in the late 1930s. There he made a winner out of a failing franchise. He was the first to bring lights and night games to the major leagues. From Cincinnati, he moved on to the Brooklyn Dodgers, who had been down for twenty years. Again, he produced a pennant winner. He did

301

so with a flourish of showy promotional activities. For Yankee fans, the question was whether the Barnum and Bailey manner with which MacPhail bulldozed so much tradition in Cincinnati and Brooklyn was based on the desperation to which he felt he needed to resort to pump life into dead clubs, or whether it was an inextricable part of his personality. If it was the latter, people expected trouble, for the New York Yankees were hardly a moribund outfit. Furthermore, Joe McCarthy was hardly a manager who needed any advice on the running of a baseball team, and MacPhail was notoriously meddlesome along these lines. Events would prove "Loud Larry" to be incapable of being anything but an abrasive promoter. Department store promotions, automobile sales, banking, baseball; it was all the same to him.

At that very time, organized crime was moving into new areas of activity. One of their greatest new enterprises involved the development of Las Vegas, Nevada, into a big-time vacation spot. In this endeavor, one of the mob's leaders was Ben "Bugsy" Siegel, a man of brains, vision, violence and psychoses. If baseball ever had a "Bugsy," it was Larry MacPhail, smart, full of ideas, occasionally violent, always rude. (During World War II, Bugsy Siegel developed a scheme to kill Benito Mussolini; during World War I, MacPhail was in the service and was serious about a plot, for which he once went AWOL, to kidnap and kill the Kaiser. MacPhail always claimed the ashtray he kept on his office desk had previously belonged to Kaiser Wilhelm.)[1]

When former Postmaster General James Farley was reported to be forming a syndicate of investors to buy the Yankees (and there was some effort in this regard), he was asked about how much personal control he would desire over the team. Farley responded, "what a sucker I would be to try to take over a job being handled by a man like Barrow." Many other owners had a similar view as Farley's. Wading into a new situation and feeling one knows absolutely what is best is hardly a good way to manage an organization, especially one with a highly successful record. MacPhail's view was just the opposite. Former New York Giant Manager Bill Terry called MacPhail "a brilliant screwball." MacPhail had no sense of what others had done before him. Nor had he any such cares. His ego-driven ways were everything to him. There was no middle ground.

Friction would soon begin between MacPhail and McCarthy, as well as between MacPhail and Topping and Webb. Less than two months on the job, for example, MacPhail announced that Yankee Stadium was going to be expanded to hold 100,000 people and that he was going to gain a full third of the shares of Yankee stock. The tensions all around would never abate. MacPhail always browbeat everyone around him. He liked it when people like Leo Durocher yelled back at him. McCarthy and the Yankees were accustomed to other ways. Before a game back in September 1942, McCarthy was sitting on the bench. His coach Art Fletcher handed him the lineup card. A reporter, Arthur "Red" Patterson of the *New York Herald Tribune*, was seated nearby. McCarthy began filling out the card, and there were no surprises in the lineup. Nevertheless, with Patterson still close, McCarthy felt uncomfortable and began to yell: "How can a man get his work done around here with everyone sticking his nose where it doesn't belong?" Larry MacPhail made this same Red Patterson the Yankees' new traveling secretary and publicity man. Patterson then began dutifully and regularly pumping McCarthy for news for MacPhail's publicity office. This galled McCarthy to distraction, and further to drink.[2]

No matter the hopes and expectations in the nation in March 1945 baseball teams had to obey the same war restrictions as they began preparations for the new season. Asked whether major league baseball could survive further war pressures, McCarthy sounded like he was predicting an outcome for the Yankees in a pennant race: "If we get a break on the Western front, and it looks like we are, baseball will be safe." Like the rest of the country, McCarthy was upbeat. He added about himself: "I didn't have a cold all winter. 'never felt better leaving for spring training." But then when asked about specific plans for the composition of the team, he had to contend with the realities of wartime personnel. "I have no plans. I have no plans," he fretted. "How can any manager? You['ve] got to improvise from day to day." The wartime reality was still there. Personnel were scarce. Travel was restricted.[3]

The Yankees again trained in Atlantic City. A type of organizational scheme emerged with respect to the training sites of the major league teams. Half trained in New Jersey, Delaware, and Maryland. The other half were in Indiana, Illinois, and Missouri. They set up exhibition games within their discrete regions, thus keeping travel to a minimum. On March 13, however, all travel for exhibition games was cancelled. The Yankees had to scratch ten of their sixteen scheduled games. All the other teams were set back similarly. The teams out in Indiana, Illinois, and Missouri had to contend further with massive flooding hitting the Midwest that spring. In Atlantic City, the Yankees had to scramble for training sites. The Atlantic City Armory was being used as an Army hospital and rehabilitation center. The Army was also using the city's massive Boardwalk Coliseum, sometimes called the Convention Hall, for troops on rehabilitation. MacPhail persuaded officials to let the Yankees hold a few of their practices there, as they could provide the troops both entertainment and uplift. Otherwise, the Yankees had to make do with the Atlantic City High School Gym and with a hangar at the Municipal Air Field, a building with a cement floor, heated by a single wood-burning potbelly stove. Such were the contrasts between the hopes for the return of old glories and the ongoing reality of wartime restrictions.[4]

A twist of fate added a cruel edge to the spare conditions under which McCarthy and the Yankees chafed. One soldier assigned to Atlantic City to serve as a physical training instructor was none other than Joe DiMaggio. In his off-duty time, DiMaggio was allowed to visit the Yankee camp. But as far as his availability to the Yankees was concerned, he may as well have been stationed in New Zealand. DiMaggio went further. "I would give anything to be able to take the field with the Yankees," he stated with more than a little ache. But, with a sense of duty and, even more, of personal protection and resentment, he added, "if I were discharged tomorrow I would not return to the club. I would not play ball with the war still on. You say the fans would not hoot a man with a medical discharge. Well, I would not take the chance. I will never forget the going-over some of the boys in the stands gave me before I went into the service."

There had been resentment at ball players seemingly "fiddling" at baseball while others were off fighting, but there was a fickleness in the way fans singled out some players. Ted Williams and Joe Gordon played the full 1942 season and were not booed. DiMaggio did the same and was. All were in uniform in 1943. McCarthy had never involved himself in the decisions his players made about the armed services, and DiMaggio certainly felt absolutely no resentment or disrespect towards McCarthy.

But he would reenter baseball his way. Here McCarthy would again not even so much as drop a hint to try to entice DiMaggio to return as soon as possible. Of course, he greeted DiMaggio when he visited the training site and was sincerely cordial, but that was it. Meanwhile, McCarthy would do his best with the ragged outfit that was no better than the one he fielded in '44.[5]

Like the rest of the major league managers, many of McCarthy's players in 1944 and at the outset of the '45 season were 4F's, men who had been ruled in some way physically unfit for military service. As training camps started, some leaders in Washington were grumbling about 4F athletes. Illinois Congressman Melvin Price wanted a special review of the 4F's who had been rejected at induction centers but were playing professional baseball. Future Baseball Commissioner, Kentucky Senator Albert Chandler was also critical of too many 4F's. The War Department was sensitive and wanted to avoid any criticism about "favoritism." Many of the 4F's, like Yankee second baseman George Stirnweiss and pitcher Joe Page, had ulcers, and it was deemed that all men with such a condition would largely be spending their service years in sick bay if forced to eat Army chow. But the specter of any such effort as one to induct as many 4F's as possible put ball teams on even thinner ice. McCarthy could only shrug: "I won't go out on the field in Washington on April 16 [opening day] without someone at first [base]." With few exhibition games under their belts and starters with names like Buzas, Grimes, Crompton, and Savage, McCarthy opened the season against equally strapped opponents. With such depleted personnel on all teams, the *Cleveland Plain Dealer*, frustrated with the Indians' poor performance that year, declared at midseason that war baseball was "a joke" and that "no one would care if [it was] discontinued." No one else showed that much disdain, but frustrations were certainly widespread. Given what New York had left, one reporter noted only one basis for any Yankee fan holding onto thoughts of a pennant: "Yankee flag backers base their hopes more on the magic of Manager Joe McCarthy than on the power of their players."[6]

New York's opening game in Washington was originally to have been played just four days after President Roosevelt died. The game was postponed, of course. Just three weeks after the opening games came the victory over Nazi Germany. V-E day did bring a halt to the grumbling about and potential review of all the 4-F ball players, and more generally it took some pressure off baseball. McCarthy had said that the Yankees "should do all right, if we can keep what we have." After a month of playing, however, fans were a trifle leery, and McCarthy was feeling nervous. The Yankees were competitive among the league leaders, but they were leading the league in two categories that were particularly disturbing to McCarthy — errors and runners left on base. Other than Stirnweiss, no one hit well. Johnny Lindell had hit decently, but he was inducted in June. (No one knew how much longer the war was going to last in the Pacific.) When Lindell left, McCarthy told a reporter: "There goes the only big league outfielder on the squad." At one point in May, three of McCarthy's early regulars, Herb Compton, Bill Drescher, and Mike Garbark, had combined for 2 hits in 52 at bats. "We just can't hit," mused McCarthy, joking, "Must be the meat shortage." One paper even rhapsodized with a short poem:

> With Lindell gone down to Fort Dix
> The Yanks are in a helluva fix.

With Lindell in the army, McCarthy had four outfielders. As the anemic hitting and the errors continued, McCarthy saw no more utility in treating the men harshly than he had in 1944. But the poor play and the frustration at not being able to put runners across ate at him. One of his pitchers, Bill Zuber, a native of a German farm community in Iowa, did not speak good English. Several times he did not do what McCarthy told him because he misunderstood his words. Such frustrations marked quite a fall from the teams that executed for him so flawlessly in the late 1930s. Aggravating all this, Larry MacPhail regularly held forth to the press about how the team was not hustling. MacPhail actually elaborated, claiming he saw more hustle when he was with Columbus in the American Association! He did not know what he was talking about. MacPhail was simply a self-absorbed, narcissistic drunk who somehow felt that he was saying something profound and insightful whenever he mouthed off (and who was accustomed to a surrounding of sycophants who marveled at the profundity of his words). McCarthy had long heard such nonsense spew from ignorant reporters. Hearing it from the loud lout who had succeeded his friend Ed Barrow would get increasingly unbearable. Mr. Barrow never made any such public statements.[7]

By early July, McCarthy had used 101 pitchers in 60 games. He had one good starter, Hank Borowy. The others were less dependable. The Yankees continued to lead in errors (94) and left on base (509, nearly one per inning). With Lindell gone, the hitting was showing no improvement. Meanwhile, one rival team was getting stronger. Hank Greenberg received his discharge and was back with the Tigers in July. He hit a home run in his very first game. With Greenberg's return, Detroit, already a contender, began to play the best baseball in the league. In mid–July the Yankees were three and one half games behind. (The only player New York had gotten back from the service was 41-year old Red Ruffing.) On July 15 and 16, the Yankees were on the road, having just split a pair of games in Detroit. From there they traveled to St. Louis, where it rained steadily for four days. The Yankees then lost a doubleheader and fell to fifth place. They had lost seven of their last ten games, seventeen of their previous twenty-six. During the depressing layover in St. Louis, the weather, the frustrations of the poor hitting, the errors, the left on base figures, the behavior of Larry MacPhail, the endless, repetitive questions from reporters, and the "push button" charges all piled up and proved too much. McCarthy was not eating, he had not slept well in three days, and his "gall bladder" was acting up on him again. He spent two days never leaving his St. Louis hotel room. He was drinking. On July 20, McCarthy called MacPhail and told him he was going home to Buffalo. Art Fletcher took charge of the team.[8]

"I am sorry to have had to leave the ball club at this time," McCarthy apologized, "but under the circumstances there was nothing else for me to do." Arriving in Buffalo, McCarthy pleaded with the press: "I'm tired, really concerned about my health. I just want to go out to my home and rest — alone, away from everyone. No newspapermen, no photographers, not for a while, please. Give me a chance to get back on my feet." One of the things McCarthy liked about Buffalo was the fact that the press and people there did respect his privacy. In New York rumors began to fly again that McCarthy was going to resign. "It's a fairly safe bet that he's not coming back," opined one. Babe Ruth told a New Jersey newspaper that he would consider being McCarthy's replacement: "I definitely would be interested and feel I am entitled to at least one chance." After the 1944 season, McCarthy had discussed the possibility of retirement with Ed Barrow. He and Barrow had apparently agreed that such a move would look bad for the new Yankee leadership. With this new episode in St. Louis, McCarthy did offer his resignation. MacPhail refused to accept it and responded with outward magnanimity: "I won't accept your resignation. I know that you are feeling rotten, physically and mentally, but I don't want you to quit.... Go home to Buffalo and see what you can get straightened out. Meanwhile don't worry about the ball club. Just get well. That is the important thing."[9]

McCarthy went home. Mrs. McCarthy scoffed at the rumors about her husband resigning. Mrs. McCarthy and their family doctor and friend, Arthur Burkel, understood what was wrong and what needed to be done. McCarthy had described his life during the regular season: "You have no regular hours. You forget about meals. ... Most of the time I'd have just coffee, perhaps a glass of orange juice in the morning. Then I'd forget about meals until 7 or 8 o'clock at night. You're too busy with the actual games to think about yourself." When such a routine combines with the depressing pressure of losing, and when a person regularly drinks whiskey on top of it, the results can be dangerous. McCarthy admitted his regimen "tears a man down. Then," he added, "there's that blazing New York heat which doesn't help. These things gradually add up and spell breakdown. They did for me."

The solution was the life he enjoyed at his farm outside Buffalo— no phone calls or pressures, rest, moderate exercise (walking), sunshine, and a regular diet of healthy food. The rest cure worked. At first, people close to the Yankees were predicting that McCarthy would need at least a month to recover. Some said that, for sure, he would not be back that season and that Art Fletcher would be in charge the rest of the way. MacPhail told some reporters that McCarthy had "mentioned the possibility of quitting." McCarthy denied all reports that he was resigning, and he must have bristled at MacPhail's indiscretion with the press. Barrow always kept such matters in confidence. With MacPhail he realized more and more that he could not speak so freely. MacPhail notwithstanding, in three weeks, McCarthy was feeling better. MacPhail pocketed a bit of pride and went up to Buffalo and talked with McCarthy. He wanted him back. If he had not known how valuable McCarthy was, he sure learned. On August 8, Dr. Burkel somewhat begrudgingly confirmed McCarthy is "well enough to go if he wants to." One Buffalo reporter wrote: "Eyes that had been dulled with pain for the greater part of a month were fresh again. Some of that old Irish humor was back." McCarthy joked that no one should worry about him coming back, as the team had done well without him. They had won nine of fifteen games under Fletcher.[10]

McCarthy rejoined the team in Cleveland on August 9. With him, the Yankees proceeded to win two games from the Indians, the first of which was Red Ruffing's third straight win since his Army discharge. Prospects for a pennant charge looked good. The victories over Cleveland, combined with their wins under Fletcher, put New York back up in third place, only two and one half games behind leading Detroit. Washington was just ahead in second place. McCarthy assured people he now felt fine. He praised Fletcher for his work, and he went on to emphasize, as he had when he first took his leave in July, that he had "not had any trouble or interference from

Larry MacPhail." He stated emphatically, "We've gotten along fine." MacPhail had said much the same. Of course, it was a all obfuscation. MacPhail had gone to Buffalo and met with McCarthy on August 7. Neither went into any specifics of the meeting, but both said things were fine.

But additional problems had arisen during McCarthy's rest. On July 27, MacPhail sold pitcher Hank Borowy to the Chicago Cubs. Borowy was McCarthy's best pitcher. He was from New York, had graduated from Fordham, and was very popular with the fans. Borowy had pitched well in the previous two seasons and been a star in the '43 World Series. MacPhail told the press that McCarthy had favored the move. McCarthy did no such thing, and he felt that MacPhail's selling of Borowy (for $100,000) while he was away was a typically underhanded MacPhail move. Some said the deal was MacPhail's way of returning a favor to Cubs owner Philip K. Wrigley. When MacPhail was running the Dodgers in 1941, he had been able to procure Billy Herman from the Cubs during Brooklyn's pennant drive. Now the Cubs were close to a pennant, and they got Borowy from MacPhail. Beyond its underhandedness, the Borowy sale indicated that MacPhail had given up on the Yankees' 1945 season and was building resources for the future. As the Yankees were less than three games out of first place on August 10, the time hardly seemed right to forfeit any pennant prospects. Borowy was not to be pitied. He won eleven games for Chicago that summer, and with him the Cubs won the National League pennant. McCarthy returned to the Yankees with the loss of his best pitcher slapped right in his face. So much for the posture of good Manager/General Manager relations.[11]

After the Cleveland series, the Yankees' next stop was Detroit. Due to rainouts earlier in the season, they had to play two doubleheaders in two days. The Yankees lost all four games! Extra galling to McCarthy was that in the four games, the Yankees committed eleven errors. The last two errors came on one play. Detroit outfielder Roy Cullenbine, a former Yankee, was up with two runners on base. He bunted to pitcher Ken Holcombe. Holcombe elected to throw to first, but he threw wildly. Second baseman George Stirnweiss ran the ball down and threw home. The throw got away from the catcher, and Holcombe was still standing in the middle of the field, not backing up home. Result: two runners scored on a thirty-foot bunt. (Holcombe would not be back with the Yankees next season.)

Larry MacPhail may have been wrong in conceding the season when he traded Borowy in July, but after the Detroit fiasco, everybody was throwing their hands up. (Even Yankee fans could not feel too much despair, however. The day of the second doubleheader loss to Detroit, Japan surrendered.) Then came four more losses to St. Louis. "If Joe McCarthy should suddenly up and quit the Yankees again," lamented one reporter, "no one could really blame him. ... The only pennant these guys will get will be the one they buy at the Army-Notre Dame game." McCarthy did not quit, but he was hardly elated. In the third loss to St. Louis he blew his stack at an umpire and was ejected from a game. This was only the second time he had been ejected in his fifteen years as the Yankees' manager. In Detroit in early September he was ejected again. His grip was slipping, and the Yankees had fallen all the way down to sixth place.[12]

Newspapers were lamenting the Yankees fortunes with phrases like "the hollow shell of what was once a great baseball dynasty." McCarthy would have none of it, however. He had been through such troughs before, and he had often made a come-back. He would do it with this Yankee team too. After the losses to St. Louis, Char-lie Keller rejoined the team. There were rumors that DiMaggio would return. With Keller, Stirnweiss, and Frankie Crosetti back on board, the Yankees seemed again to have the nucleus of a decent team, especially on days when Red Ruffing pitched well, as well as on the good days of another pitcher, Bill Bevens. Spud Chandler was also back. People lamented; if only MacPhail had not sold Borowy. McCarthy quietly agreed. With scores of players being discharged from the service, all teams were going through gyrations of personnel. Some said the pennant race was turning into a mat-ter of who would get more of their best players released from the Army.

In late August, early September, the Yankees seemed resupplied and came back again. They won eleven of fourteen and drew to four games behind Detroit. At that point they had seven games coming up with the Tigers, and optimism was return-ing. Right then came a rash of injuries, however. Outfielder Bud Metheny, catcher Aaron Robinson, and George Stirnweiss all went down. Several pitchers had bad arms. McCarthy once had to use reliever Joe Page as a starter with just two days of rest. In one of the Detroit games, his pitcher, Al Gettel, was in difficulty, and McCarthy had no one to insert. Gettel had to stay in and was hit hard. McCarthy finally pulled him, sending in his batting practice pitcher, Paul Schreiber. Schreiber was nearly 43 years old and had not pitched a major league game since 1923. Detroit won that day 10–0, and they went on to win five of the seven. Then the Yankees had to face Cleveland, losing two games, one to their young ace Allie Reynolds, the sec-ond to their other ace just out of the Navy — Bob Feller. This stretch of injuries and losses did knock the Yankees out of the race. Five days after the losses to Feller and Reynolds, Joe DiMaggio announced he was not returning to the Yankees until 1946.[13]

McCarthy remained at the helm, but this time Coach Art Fletcher felt the pres-sures. Fletcher was 60 years old and had had heart troubles. On September 12, he felt some chest pains. The next day he had to be rushed to a hospital. Doctors advised Fletcher to get out of the game completely, and they urged him to do so at least for the rest of the season. Fletcher chose to leave the game for good. This was a blow to McCarthy. Fletcher had been his assistant since 1931. They made a terrific team, and there was no replacing him. Meanwhile, Detroit nosed out Washington for the pen-nant on the last day of the season. The Yankees were six and one half games behind.[14]

When McCarthy returned to the Yankees in August, he told reporters that he would finish the season, but "1946 will depend upon my health." After some rest, McCarthy contemplated his future that winter, he could not but think optimistically about the Yankees' chances in 1946. The war was over. Everybody would be back. As the Yankees had fallen the farthest, the "return to normalcy" certainly meant they had the most to gain. There would be questions and adjustments, but that was what managing a baseball team always involved. With everything he had once achieved, he could hardly bear the thought of bowing out at such a low point. McCarthy never let on, but he was thinking about one last hurrah. He deserved to go out a cham-pion. Such giddy thoughts made the specter of Larry MacPhail, the Hank Borowy trade, and other frustrations fade a bit. McCarthy would be back, and the search for "one more" would come oh so close, and be *oh* so frustrating.[15]

33

And Now He Wasn't There

If anyone wondered whether "Loud Larry" MacPhail was going to make significant changes in the Yankees' way of doing things, the opening of 1946 training camp left no doubts. In February, eighty Yankees boarded planes and headed off to Panama. No major league baseball team had ever before gone off to such a distant place to train. Whether there was anything inherently better about training in Panama as opposed to Florida apparently seemed not to matter to MacPhail. The key was that he could brag that the idea was his. It certainly stamped the new style of business management within the Yankee organization. MacPhail was image-conscious. He sought pizzazz for its own sake in an effort to generate excitement and increase fan interest and ticket sales. McCarthy and Barrow were never against things that stimulated the fans' excitement, but they always felt this was something to be done within the context of what made the team play better baseball. With MacPhail the matter of the quality of baseball was more tangential.

The Yankees started camp much earlier than normal. They took off for Panama on February 7. But other teams were starting early too. The Brooklyn Dodgers convened in Vero Beach, Florida, on February 4. Everyone realized there was much to "sort out" with the established players, the returning war players, and the rookies. For McCarthy there was, indeed, much to organize. A big question here involved second base. George Stirnweiss had been one of the few Yankee stars during the war. In 1945 he had led the American League in both batting and stolen bases, and second base was the position where he played well. At the same time, Joe Gordon was back from the service. He had been the American League MVP in 1942. In previous times, McCarthy had tried Gordon at first base and Stirnweiss at shortstop. Neither experiment worked. Both could only play second. Elsewhere he simply had lots of talent. In the outfield, Keller, Henrich, and DiMaggio were back, so were George Selkirk and Johnny Lindell. At catcher, Dickey was back, along with Ken Sears, Rollie Hemsley, Aaron Robinson, and Ken Silvestri. Although he was still in the Navy, the Yankees also had a highly touted youngster named Lawrence Berra. Scouts said he could hit as well as Charlie Keller. Rizzuto and Crosetti (now 35) presented an old problem at shortstop. The only hole was at third base because Billy Johnson was still in the Army.[1]

The team fared well in the warmth of Panama. They played some local teams and some squads connected with nearby U.S. Army and Naval installations. Lefty Gomez was now managing a team in Caracas, Venezuela. He wanted to arrange for a game with the Yankees, but the scheduling could not be worked out. McCarthy and the players had to adjust to a diet of corbina, chayotes, plantain, and papaya, but no one came down with any sort of stomach illness. Phil Rizzuto did suffer a bout of malaria, however, and he lost a considerable amount of weight. The otherwise healthy Yankees were given a tour of the Canal, and they attended several lavish receptions, including one hosted by the President of the Republic, Enrique A. Jimenez. The excitement pleased MacPhail, as he received invitations for similar spring training excursions from the governments of Venezuela, Colombia, Puerto Rico, and Cuba. Learning of these invitations and recalling the Navy's wartime recruitment slogan,

McCarthy in 1946, his last season with the Yankees. The seasons of managerial stress, the war years, and dealings with Larry MacPhail had worn on him (as had a little drinking). After leaving the Yankees, McCarthy would come back to manage the Boston Red Sox and come achingly close to two pennants, losing each on the final day of the season. (National Baseball Hall of Fame Library, Cooperstown, N.Y.)

the *New York Sun* chortled: "Join the Yankees and See the World." To McCarthy it was all very nice, and as long as the ball fields were good and the weather cooperated. He did not mind the extra plane ride. DiMaggio proved he was ready to play again. He hit .526 in the games in Panama. This certainly made McCarthy happy. Later that spring when DiMaggio's son stood in the dugout with a catcher's mask, McCarthy called out to the boy's father: "Get that mask off him and stick a bat in his hand, Joe. A DiMaggio doesn't look right unless he has a bat in his hands." That was about as jovial as McCarthy would be during practice.[2]

The Yankees arrived in Florida on March 4. Here another MacPhail "innovation" did not sit well with McCarthy. In order to show how "grand" the Yankee organization was, MacPhail signed many more players than normal and set up two training sites, one at Miller Huggins Field in St. Petersburg, the other across Tampa Bay at Bradenton. McCarthy obviously wanted to oversee the entire training enterprise, so how was he supposed to be in two places at once? MacPhail had an "answer," one that added to the luster he earnestly wanted to advertise to the press: McCarthy would travel by air between the two sites. Here was a case of pizzazz for its own sake, not merely irrespective of the needs of actual field management but very much counter to them. "MacPhail's flying circus" was the new joke in the New York papers. How does the use of an airplane make for better management? How does wasting time flying between sites overcome the problem of the sites' needless separation? It was marginally less inefficient than a slower mode of transportation, but it was not a solution. To McCarthy, MacPhail's nonsensical methods seemed akin to a Federal government administrator claiming he was treating the problem of starvation in Europe by disseminating photographs of lavish banquet tables, now with an added bureaucratic justification that the photographs were of the highest quality. McCarthy wanted a single site. When MacPhail made that impossible, he preferred to shuttle between sites on a bus. He found even that service unreliable. MacPhail had left the running of that service to his son Bill. McCarthy utterly detested everything about MacPhail, what he did and how he did it. He felt in anything but good hands and certainly missed Ed Barrow. As for all the hoped-for publicity that March, Larry MacPhail did not get his wish anyway, as much of the baseball press attention in Florida that month focused on the Brooklyn Dodgers because of their signing of Jackie Robinson. McCarthy never appeared to show any concern about players' religion, politics, or race. He just cared how well they played, although some of his name-calling could be coarse. MacPhail was too image-conscious a publicity hound to take such a risk as the Dodgers had in the signing of Robinson. (Robinson would train with the Dodgers in 1946, amidst enormous press attention, but, by design, he played a season with Brooklyn's AAA team in Montreal before "breaking the color line" the next season.)[3]

Shuttling between ball fields wore a bit on McCarthy. When he learned that MacPhail had arranged for the Yankees to travel almost exclusively by air that season, he was not enthused. Flying from New York to St. Louis made sense, of course, but flying many of the shorter hops hardly seemed logical. MacPhail had also originally planned to schedule seven night games at Yankee Stadium. That spring he suddenly announced there would be fourteen lighted games. Other teams were doing much the same. McCarthy's regimen of checking on the players at breakfast before heading off to the ballpark would be all awry under such circumstances. It was a new era in which he was entering. Additionally, he no longer had the same team of assistants upon which he once relied so happily. Earle Combs had left after 1944. Art Fletcher retired in 1945. He still had Johnny Schulte, who had been with McCarthy since 1934, and in Florida McCarthy left him in charge of the Bradenton site. Elsewhere he now had Johnny Neun and Red Rolfe.

McCarthy made his way through the Florida training. He solved some of his personnel issues, at least at catcher, by trading Rollie Hemsley to the Phillies and Ken Sears to the Browns. Buoyed by post-war optimism, fan attendance and enthusiasm at exhibition games was larger than ever. Perhaps feeling a sense of camaraderie of personality with MacPhail, the *Daily News* reporter Jimmy Powers, the man who had speculated in 1940 that some of the slumping Yankees may have caught some of Lou Gehrig's malady, rhapsodized that the Yankees "are throwing off their colorless, lackluster ... airs that distinguished them under the Barrow regime." MacPhail was pleased with that. McCarthy was not. Powers had shown gross disrespect to Gehrig and the Yankees, and now he was defaming the retired Barrow. McCarthy said nothing, however. The question was whether the team could win, not how the press perceived the players' individual or collective personalities.

Several days later, Powers made his views even more explicit. He praised a former manager of the Boston Braves and Brooklyn Dodgers, Casey Stengel, because he "never flew into a tantrum and fired a man for the picayune reasons Joe McCarthy, Ed Barrow and others we know have used as a basis for summarily disposing of a player who acted like a man and not a brow-beaten mouse." Powers never said of whom McCarthy or Barrow had allegedly disposed. He was likely referring to Roy Johnson, Johnny Allen or Ben Chapman, none of whom went on to terribly distinguished careers after New York. To McCarthy, Allen and Chapman were indeed the ones who "flew into a tantrum." But the debatability of the issue was of no concern to a man like Jimmy Powers. He believed he had his finger on the kind of spirit that MacPhail wanted to spread — that the war was over, that the Depression-era conformity was a distant memory, and that this was a time for greater individuality.

To McCarthy, it was all so very much beside the point. Powers was serving the role of an ad man for MacPhail, trying to sell people on the idea of vacationing in a place like Las Vegas. To McCarthy, an ideal vacation was time spent tending his farm outside Buffalo. The times were changing. A man who the Yankees and the other reporters shunned in 1940 was now the favorite press lapdog of the team's loud-mouthed GM.[4]

Detroit Manager Steve O'Neill made the prediction that the Yankees' choice to begin to train so early would backfire on them. They could start well, he conjectured, but they will likely peak too soon and fade. McCarthy showed not the slightest respect for that. He believed trained professional athletes could keep up a stiff pace with no trouble. The beginning of the season went extremely well for New York. "Good Times Again in the Bronx," headlined the *Daily News*. They were in first place in much of the early weeks. But in early May, the Boston Red Sox reeled off 15 straight wins and zoomed into the lead. The Yankees were playing well. In their first 31 games, they hit 30 home runs. Along with Boston's Ted Williams, Joe DiMaggio and Charlie Keller were leading the league in home runs. As of May 13, New York's record was 16 and 9, thus a winning percentage of .640. The trouble was the Red Sox record was an incredible 22 and 4. A team compiling wins at that clip will not be caught, and indeed that season the Red Sox would not be.[5]

McCarthy was having his problems. There was talk of the players forming a union. McCarthy was dead against it. "Our players are well treated and don't need it," he asserted. "I have not heard of anyone on this team being interested in a union." That would be a problem for managers and owners, but not for many years. Another matter that looked like a bigger problem in the short run concerned a new baseball league forming in Mexico. Phil Rizzuto and George Stirnweiss had received offers, and Mexican League agents were often seen in many major league parks, as well as at Negro League games. The Mexican League never proved to be a major threat to the American and National Leagues, but in early 1946, many baseball people were taking serious note. McCarthy worried about these matters. Neither Rizzuto nor Stirnweiss jumped to Mexico, however. Meanwhile, the Red Sox were McCarthy's biggest problem. They would win 40 of their first 50 games. By the end of May many of the other AL teams appeared to be conceding Boston the pennant. McCarthy could never do that. He had hoped a victory in 1946 would be a "last hurrah" from which he could retire on top. Now he was frustrated and a bit depressed.[6]

McCarthy was never terribly graceful in either victory or defeat. He was never one to charm reporters. Those veteran New York reporters who respected him knew it best largely to leave him alone and to expect little from him in an interview. With age, with MacPhail, and after the difficult war years, all of McCarthy's crusty tendencies were growing, as was his drinking. He would snap not just at players, coaches, and reporters, but at waiters, bartenders, baggage porters, hotel maids, and even fans. After a defeat in the pre-season, a waiter in Florida attempted a bit of small talk with McCarthy. McCarthy barked at him, "You take care of the food around here, and I'll take care of the ball games." When the breaks went against him, he seemed to take it as a personal affront. His insolence and insulting remarks constituted ways to seal himself off from a world in which he was less and less comfortable and over which he felt less and less control. He was still a great manager, but an ever more petty man. For a media just beginning to tilt into the banalities of "up close and personal" stories, such a devolving personality would be difficult to ignore.[7]

On May 16, the Yankees headed out on their first trip around the West. They split two games in both St. Louis and Chicago, and then they headed for Cleveland where they won a doubleheader with two well-pitched games by Spud Chandler and the now venerable Red Ruffing. McCarthy was mad at Cleveland Manager Lou Boudreau. He felt earlier in the season Boudreau used some lesser pitching talent against the Red Sox while sending out his best against the Yankees. The next day's game against Cleveland on May 20 proved a hard loss for McCarthy. Before the game, McCarthy was barking abusively at his players during infield practice. A Cleveland fan sitting near the Yankee dugout heard it all and began shouting taunts at McCarthy. McCarthy ordered his players to "get on him," but they could do little. Then McCarthy called for the police to silence the fan or remove him from the park.

In the game, the Yankees were down 3-1 going into the ninth inning. Nick Etten and Bill Dickey then hit home runs to tie the game. In the bottom of the ninth reliever Bill Zuber was pitching. Zuber had been one of the Yankees' wartime pitchers. He was not one of McCarthy's all-time great relievers, but he had, what Zuber used to describe with his thick Iowa-German accent, "*meine gut* 'zidearm zinker' ball." In the bottom of the ninth, with one out, the Indians third baseman Ken Keltner caught one of Zuber's "zinkers" for a home run to win the game. Cleveland had a short right field line, yet Zuber threw the righthanded Keltner an outside pitch that he could more easily pop to right. One newsman observed, "When Keltner went bing, McCarthy was fit to be tied." McCarthy asked Zuber what he threw to Keltner. When Zuber said Keltner had hit his curve ball, McCarthy sarcastically congratulated Zuber for saving his best pitch for another time. McCarthy had seldom resorted to sarcasm. Long after the stands had emptied, McCarthy sat in the dugout fuming. It would be his last time managing in a Yankee uniform. That evening he tied into a little White Horse Scotch.[8]

The next day, McCarthy was said to be suffering from a cold, and with the raw, rainy weather in Cleveland at the time he was advised by a doctor to remain in his hotel room. It was a good game to have missed, anyway. The Indians scored four runs in the first inning, and Bob Feller throttled the Yankees from there. With that loss in Cleveland, the Yankees were to head up to Detroit. McCarthy was in a foul mood. He had been drinking. He was angry about Zuber's ninth-inning loss. He was frustrated with the sense that Boston was not going to be caught, thus ending his hopes that '46 could be his career-ending championship. Now he had to get on a plane to go to Detroit. This made his frustrations with MacPhail surface all the more. With the time it took to leave downtown Cleveland, get to the airport, fly to Detroit, and drive from the airport to downtown Detroit, there seemed no advantage in flying. And the conditions were hardly commodious. On trains, McCarthy was usually able to travel in a private compartment. In those compartments, McCarthy often held private talks with players, for if he had some sensitive criticisms to raise with someone, he always wanted to do it away from any reporter's or teammate's ears. On a plane he could not do this. This particular evening, rather than wait until getting to the hotel in Detroit, he decided to scold someone anyway.

Relief pitcher Joe Page had not been observing good disciplinary habits, and McCarthy felt it was affecting his pitching. Page had a reputation for being a fast-lane party boy. He certainly liked to socialize, but Page was actually anything but a devil-may-care sort of person. Joe DiMaggio, Page's roommate, grasped this about Page. DiMaggio commented: "I wonder if he'll ever understand himself. He's got everything to make good, but he goes to bed every night wondering if he can win. He acts smart and fresh, but he's not. He tries to make you think he's indifferent, but he's really worried all the time. He tries to be friendly with people, but he only gets them mad at him." Page's active social life served as a compensation for the fact that he had grown up in the poor mining country of Western Pennsylvania and had, only two years before, lost three members of his family (his mother, father, and sister) in a period of less than eleven months. His insecurities were great, but McCarthy was only concerned about the fact that Page was keeping poor hours and not performing up to his ability. He remembered that Page had lost some key games in late 1944, never letting on that he was injured. McCarthy wanted no repetition of any such ineffectiveness. With the increasing frequency of night games, players like Page were starting to keep different hours. Older managers' ideas about curfews and early breakfast requirements made less sense, and some had trouble adjusting. On the plane to Detroit, McCarthy was not interested in Page's psychological issues or the changing organizational circumstances of baseball teams. On the plane McCarthy found Page seated next to a window. He sat down next to him and began a tirade:

McCarthy: You're going to sit and listen to what I have to say.

Page: Sure.

McCarthy: When are you going to settle down and start pitching? How long do you think you can get away with this?

Page: Get away with what? I'm not trying to get away with anything. I'm doing the best I can. What do you want out of me?

McCarthy: Who the hell do you think you're kidding?

McCarthy's voice grew more shrill. He then threatened Page: "I'm going to send you down to Newark," he warned, "and do you know what you'll make there? Peanuts! PEANUTS!" The shouting went on, and everyone on the plane, the Yankees, the reporters, and all the other passengers could not help but hear it. Page was completely humiliated and basically told McCarthy to go ahead and send him down. Everyone on the plane was stunned. McCarthy had never treated a player like that. Phil Rizzuto said "the thing I remember about McCarthy was how he never told any player off in public — all problems were settled behind closed doors." It was, Tommy Henrich recalled, "something I never expected to see." It made no sense for him to do it. Page himself later reflected quite maturely: "If anyone else had talked to me like that I would have hit him, but I could not do that to a man like Joe." Even if he was sick, drunk, hung over, depressed, or all these and more, McCarthy was failing as a decent manager. No one had ever seen him behave like this.[9]

When the plane arrived at Detroit's Wayne County Airport, McCarthy's ranting continued. The Boston Red Sox happened to be leaving Detroit that evening to go to Cleveland, and the teams crossed paths at the airport. McCarthy eyed Boston owner Tom Yawkey and yelled out: "You're riding a winner now, Tom; you're sitting on top of the world, so enjoy it while you can because when we meet in June, the Yankees will move up, and by July the Red Sox will be lost in our dust and you'll be fleeing to your South Carolina plantation to get away from it all." McCarthy's phrase "getting away from it all" was perhaps a slip, Freudian or otherwise, indicating what he knew deep down he desperately needed. McCarthy had always demanded mature decorum from his players as they traveled — proper dress, good manners. Now he was yelling like a drunken fraternity boy at a football game. One of the coaches muttered to him: "You oughtn't to try to discourage a nice guy like Yawkey." McCarthy immediately snapped: "Maybe I was just trying to encourage myself." Again, his admission that he was in need of self-encouragement was revealing of his depression, and his tone certainly betrayed his drinking. McCarthy never spoke openly of his own needs for self-motivation. He always quietly bore all. This night he was grossly out of character. He turned back to Yawkey: "Hey Tom, you can relax during your next stop; Feller won't be pitching again for a few games. We wore him out making five hits off him today." When had Joe McCarthy ever abused and disrespected his entire team, let alone in front of their biggest rival, and with sarcasm to boot? (If the late Lou Gehrig had always wanted to "deserve" McCarthy's friendship, McCarthy was hardly acting accordingly himself.)[10]

McCarthy still was not through. With a few coaches and reporters, McCarthy shared a taxi into Detroit. In the cab, he continued to complain about the loss in Cleveland: "I'm glad I did not have to look at that thing today. It was a break that my cold kept me from the ball park in Cleveland." A few minutes later, egged on by his sense of the silliness of flying from Cleveland to Detroit, he growled at his coach John Schulte: "Have a look over on the right; that is the municipal airport, the place I thought we were going to land." The driver interjected: "Pardon me, that's the Ford River Rouge Plant. The Municipal Airport is way on the other side of town." McCarthy raised his voice at the driver: "So what; they're all built too far out. We might as well have come the whole way from Cleveland by car instead of flying." McCarthy may have realized how wrong he was dressing down Joe Page as he had and was venting his anger, fastening onto the notion that had the team traveled by train he could have talked to Page privately. His abusive rambling about flying continued:

> Funny, every time we have a flight scheduled we lost. We lost the get-away game in New York to the Red Sox before taking off for St. Louis. ... Then we lost the finale of the series with the Browns just before we had to grab our plane for Chicago. In Chicago we lost the last one before we flew into Cleveland; and now we've just lost the last one in Cleveland before winging over the lake to Detroit. It must be psychological or something.

He turned to Red Rolfe and sputtered: "You figure it out, you went to Yale." Like everyone else, Rolfe was nervously embarrassed at the specter of his revered manager's behavior, and he gently corrected: "I went to Dartmouth. I just coached at Yale." Not the least bit calmed, McCarthy went on: "Well I still think it is odd, losing the particular games we did. It's one of those deep problems that might floor a Harvard man even. [suddenly changing focus] Where are we now? Oh it must be getting near downtown Detroit from the lights over there." The driver clarified: "Pardon me, that's the Pontiac plant." McCarthy immediately barked at him: "The hell you say. Well let me tell you that we don't want any industrial tour of this town. We want to get to the hotel and in time for one of the dining rooms still to be open." From there, the driver sensibly stayed mute. McCarthy went back to his fuming about flying:

> I was just thinking that it's funny how we win every time we're just in off a flight. We copped the first one in St. Louis, the first one in Chicago, and the first one in Cleveland. And so maybe we'll win the first one here. Hurrah! Hurrah! I got it now. It must be because the pitchers are just a bit jittery about flying, and thinking about it in advance makes them lose the day they're taking off. They win the first one in each town because they are relieved and relaxed because the flight is over. Yes that may explain it. I'm glad I figured that out and all by myself too. A lot of help you coaches are to a busy manager. Well here we are at last at the hotel. It was a great flying trip. Twice as much time traveling on land as in the air.

It was so painfully obvious to everyone that McCarthy was in a horrible state. The newspaperman who was in the cab from the airport reported that "On top of the cold he caught in Cleveland, ... [McCarthy's] old gall bladder trouble began acting up here yesterday." Something was acting up, anyway. The next day, McCarthy did not come down for breakfast, and he did not go to Briggs Stadium for the ball game, which the Yankees won. Johnny Neun managed the club in McCarthy's absence. A physician was called to McCarthy's hotel room. He gave him injections for pain and nausea. The next day, May 23, McCarthy left for Buffalo.[11]

To some people, McCarthy's departure for Buffalo looked like the mid-season break he took in July of 1945. Still, no one had seen such behavior as he had shown during the trip from Cleveland to Detroit. Chewing out Page, hollering at Yawkey, sarcastically insulting his team in front of rivals, verbally abusing a cab driver, snarling his coaches— he had never done any one of these, let alone all of them in a mere matter of hours. The next day, Larry MacPhail sent George Weiss up to Buffalo to meet with McCarthy. MacPhail likely knew better than to go himself. Weiss was a trusted colleague of McCarthy. For years he had run the Yankee farm system for McCarthy and Barrow, and the new Yankee management team wisely held onto him. (Some rumors had it that McCarthy was about to be fired and was being presented with a "jump or be pushed" ultimatum.) Weiss told McCarthy that MacPhail did not want him to resign and that he should take some time off as he had the previous summer.

McCarthy would not hear of it, however. He was fed up. He told a doctor that he simply felt "awful." (His regular physician and friend, Arthur Burkel, happened to be in Boston that week.) Reporters tried to phone him, but Mrs. McCarthy would not let anyone speak to him. Asked herself whether her husband was resigning, Mrs. McCarthy said "I don't know anything about it. There's no truth to it as far as I know." MacPhail phoned him twice that day as well. He and Joe did speak. After consulting with his wife and doctor, McCarthy was firm. This time he was tendering his resignation, and no one was going to change his mind. Mrs. McCarthy cancelled his railroad reservation to Boston. McCarthy wrote a letter to MacPhail who dutifully, some said gleefully, released it:

> It is with extreme regret that I must submit my resignation as manager of the Yankee ball club, effective immediately. My doctor advises me that my health would be seriously jeopardized if I continued. This is the sole reason for my decision, which, as you know, is entirely voluntarily on my part. I have enjoyed our pleasant relations, and I was happy it could continue until we won a championship. I am going to miss the team very much, and I am sure that they are going to continue on to win the pennant and the world's championship.

MacPhail responded: "As you know, I have been extremely reluctant to accept your resignation. Regretably, you are not going to continue. We will miss you." To the press MacPhail simply, and not very sincerely, said "McCarthy was the most cooperative manager with whom I have ever been associated in baseball." Meanwhile MacPhail bragged to some of the players that he fired McCarthy, and with deliberate indiscretion he spoke to some reporters about McCarthy's drinking. The veteran players were upset. "Joe was gone," recalled Tommy Henrich,

> and I was crushed. All of us were in a state of shock. McCarthy was the only manager many of had ever played for in the big leagues. I may have been more disappointed than any other player on our team because of my unlimited respect for him and confidence in him as our leader and strategist. Besides it was the wrong time to lose McCarthy. No manager ever handled a team or its individual players better in troubled times than McCarthy did, and these were definitely troubled times. We needed his mother-hen understanding and patience as we struggled to fight our way through this thing, and now he wasn't there.[12]

The Yankees named Bill Dickey to manage the Yankees. Symbolically, the lights went on for Yankee Stadium's first night game just days after McCarthy resigned. (The day after McCarthy resigned, the Chicago White Sox fired Jimmy Dykes. McCarthy was too ill to enjoy it.) Bill Dickey managed the Yankees for 105 games. The team did not do as well under him. It was hard for someone who has been playing with the team suddenly to have to make the managerial decisions and moves. "Dickey," remembered Tommy Henrich, "didn't solve a thing. Dickey didn't want the job. ... It was impossible for him to transform himself overnight into an authoritarian figure over the same men who were his buddies only the day before." If Dickey called for DiMaggio to bunt, DiMaggio would readily show that he was not pleased.

Such little dissensions would keep arising. McCarthy's winning percentage that season had been .629. Dickey's would be only .543. There was no catching Boston with that level of winning. Dickey resigned in September. Johnny Neun finished out the last two weeks of the season. It was unlikely that any team, even one led by McCarthy, could have caught the Boston Red Sox that year anyway.[13]

When McCarthy wrote in his resignation how he was "happy" to "continue [as manager] until we won a championship," he could not have made clearer the fact that he was staying on as manager to win one more World Series and go out on top. Obviously, he hoped that 1946 would be the year, and when it was clear that the season belonged to the Red Sox, he grew depressed. The war had left him with a feeling that he was leaving a legacy that ended on an unacceptably sour note. The victory over St. Louis in 1943 was empty; the '44 and '45 seasons amounted to AAA level baseball. Before the war, McCarthy seemed invincible. With the war, he was reduced in what he did. Before the war, he and the Yankees had symbolized what greatness could be in the nation. The war, however, called not for mere symbols of heroic action in sports but for the real thing. With such real heroes returning to the game, old men like McCarthy appeared ever more antiquated, respected to be sure, but only in regard to the smaller bier that was a mere game.

What the Yankees had built in the 1930s was something McCarthy believed he could resurrect, if only for one year. With all the years he had put into baseball, he wanted to leave the game at the high level that he alone had attained. With more than a touch of overweening ego, he did not grasp how much the ground had shifted under him. He did not like some of the obvious changes—flying, night games, MacPhail. He simply felt he could push on regardless. By not adjusting, he paradoxically created a different environment than he had established in the glory days. A manager cannot dress a player down on an airplane as he used to in a private compartment on a train. With Ruppert, Barrow, Combs, and Fletcher all gone, it was not the same world. The new players regarded him differently than they had in the glory days. Younger stars like Stirnweiss were calling him "Mr. McCarthy." For many of the young prospects there was something beyond respect or even awe. They feared him. His drinking may not have impaired his baseball judgment. (Even if it had, a McCarthy with a nip of scotch during a game was still probably the best manager in baseball.)

But he was certainly handling personnel in a different manner that could readily appear petty. When he saw pitcher Frank Shea wearing his cap twisted slightly to one side, McCarthy jumped all over him: "Straighten that hat. You're a ballplayer not a clown." There was no one to help compensate and adjust amidst this new climate. Star players like DiMaggio would only glare at anyone who was not performing, and the always-affable Art Fletcher was not there. Three days after McCarthy had resigned, one veteran player sadly acknowledged: "That incident on the plane [with Joe Page] was just the climax of a long series of one-way conversations. In the past, if Joe called you in, you got your chance to talk. This season he refused to let the player cut in. Much as I hate to say this, Joe got the youngsters scared." (Joe Page did not go down to Newark; he stayed with the Yankees through 1950, and McCarthy would see him again.) So it was time to go. The shame of it was that by staying and wanting to go out a winner, McCarthy's end with the Yankees was all the more tainted. As Dan Daniel of the *New York World-Telegram* lamented: "He should have walked out of the Stadium with music playing and banners flying."[14]

Upon Joe's resignation, Mrs. McCarthy predicted "Joe will be back before long. ... He could no more quit baseball than a priest could leave the church."[15] Mrs. McCarthy may have wanted her husband to see the broader issues of health and family, but she knew better than anyone how much the game meant to him. McCarthy would regain his health and would indeed find another opportunity for the very sort of ending Dan Daniel envisaged. Here, however, the fates of the game would be so tantalizingly cruel.

34

Will They Love Him in September as They Didn't in May?

For the rest of 1946, McCarthy stayed at his ever-more beloved home outside Buffalo. He named it "The Yankee Farm." His health returned, as it always had before. The drinking, which he never gave up, was not a problem at home. It was always a horribly aggravating factor amidst the sleepless nights, poor diet, and overwhelming pressures he endured while managing. That was when it always got the better of him. By late June of that year, away from the game, the road pressures, the sleepless nights, and the haphazard diet, he felt better. He was tanned, fit, and clear-eyed. Still, he never attended a game, fearing his presence anywhere would spark immediate speculations that someone was going to hire him. As he preferred, reporters and everyone else in Buffalo did not bother him for interviews. In the fall, operatives in New York's Erie County Democratic Party were actually entertaining the idea of having Joe McCarthy run for County Sheriff. McCarthy "Sherman'ed" that idea, intoning firmly: "I have no political ambitions." Baseball was another matter, however. By September he admitted, "There's no denying I'd like to be back." At first, he later admitted:

> I didn't miss baseball. I built a new barn. ... Game time would come along ... and I just didn't care. I wouldn't even listen in on the radio. I only glanced at the box scores in the papers while turning from the front page to the comics. Then the barn was finished. I started building the fence ... out in the backyard. That took up most of the ['47] season, but I found myself tuning in to the night games. I began to get a kick again reading and studying the box scores. ... When the fence was finished, I guess I knew I was ready to get back into baseball.[1]

McCarthy always liked Boston Manager Joe Cronin. Cronin was a great player with both Boston and Washington, and McCarthy respected his talents as a manager. Of course McCarthy was rooting for the Yankees in 1946, but he was happy for Cronin when Boston won the pennant. Sadly, Boston had limped home with the pennant that year. They had played wonderfully through the summer, but in early September they went into an awful tailspin just as they were wrapping up the league title. When their "magic number" was one, they took five days to secure the pennant. For

320

the rest of the month, their play was largely mediocre. The National League race, meanwhile, ended in a tie between St. Louis and Brooklyn. National League rules then required a best of three series. (St. Louis won.) While that playoff was occurring, Cronin arranged a practice game for the Red Sox with an assortment of American League players. During the game, Ted Williams was hit by a pitch on his right elbow. Although he never raised the alibi, Williams could not hit as well with the injury and the resulting swelling. He hit a disappointing .200 in the Series, and the Red Sox lost a heartbreaking World Series to the Cardinals in seven games. As the 1946 season was ending, Cronin privately told owner Tom Yawkey that he wanted to step down as manager after the next season. They contacted Joe McCarthy about managing the Red Sox after 1947. Yawkey told this to a Boston sports writer. Out of respect for Yawkey, these discussions and agreements were not made public.[2]

The year 1947 was a momentous year in baseball. The Dodgers' Jackie Robinson broke the color line at long last. Several months later, Larry Doby did the same with Cleveland in the American League. Brooklyn had other controversies besides Jackie Robinson's entry into the game. As the 1947 season was about to commence, a war of words opened between the Dodgers and the Yankees. Always rivals for fan support in the city, the rivalry grew in 1945 when Larry MacPhail, a former Dodger administrator, had joined the Yankee organization. In 1939, MacPhail had been responsible for hiring the brash former Yankee, Leo Durocher, as the Dodgers' manager. When they found one another on opposite sides of the New York baseball wars, their two similarly abrasive personalities made for quite a conflict. During spring training that year, Durocher had accused MacPhail of consorting with gamblers.

That March, the Yankees and Dodgers had held an exhibition game in Havana, Cuba, and Durocher said that known professional gamblers were seated with MacPhail in his private box. MacPhail denied this, and he accused Durocher (and Dodger owner Branch Rickey) of lying and defaming his character. For baseball people, any charge of gambling was the absolute worst thing, as the taint of the 1919 World Series scandal had never left the sport, nor would it. Durocher's reckless charges led to an avalanche of publicity. The matters went to the office of the new Commissioner Albert "Happy" Chandler. As he investigated, Chandler ordered all parties to be silent about the subject with the press. After reviewing the record of charges and counter-charges, Commissioner Chandler fined the Yankees and the Dodgers $2000 each. Charlie Dressen, a Yankee coach who had been quite vocal in criticisms of the Dodgers, was suspended for 30 days. As for Durocher, Chandler met with him personally. The Commissioner reviewed the MacPhail controversy and some other actions involving Durocher, including a fight he had gotten into with a fan in 1946. For what Chandler termed "an accumulation of unpleasant incidents detrimental to baseball," he banned Durocher from baseball for a full year.[3]

What McCarthy's opinion was of all the name calling and publicity, he never said, but the Yankee-Dodger events did encroach upon his Yankee Farm. In January of 1947, reporters asked him how he felt about not going to spring training for the first time in over thirty years. He said he felt completely relaxed about it. Then Durocher was suspended on April 10, just as the season was to open. The first thing Branch Rickey then did was call McCarthy to see if he would be willing to manage the Dodgers in Durocher's absence. It would have been quite a sight — Joe McCarthy in a Brooklyn Dodger uniform. McCarthy took the offer seriously. He was completely healthy. The sore spot was that he did not want merely to serve as a one-year care-taker. He knew how good a club Brooklyn had and was certainly intrigued at the possible challenge of building a new dynasty there. But Rickey wanted to give Durocher the option of getting his job back in 1948. As Rickey and McCarthy were conferring, the season began. Dodger coach Clyde Sukeforth managed, and won, the first two games. McCarthy ultimately turned down the one-year offer. Rickey hired Burt Shotton. Many later speculated bemusedly about what the results could have been had McCarthy taken the job. The Dodgers won the National League pennant that year. The Yankees won the AL pennant under their new manager Bucky Harris. The Dodgers/Yankees World Series that October was one of the best ever, and one of the most tension-filled. McCarthy's presence in a Dodger uniform would have only added to a Series that was a classic anyway. The Yankees won, with their pitching star being none other than Joe Page. Despite all the excitement throughout 1947, McCarthy never came to a Yankee game, except on "Old Timers" day at the Stadium in September.[4]

Later that year, one development in the Yankee organization buoyed McCarthy's spirit. Dan Topping and Del Webb got rid of Larry MacPhail. After the World Series victory, MacPhail had gotten into an argument with Branch Rickey, and he allegedly punched one of Rickey's associates, John MacDonald, who had been on MacPhail's staff when he worked for the Dodgers. Then MacPhail attempted to fire the Yankee Farm Director, McCarthy's friend George Weiss, and got into a big fight with Dan Topping over the matter. Topping and Webb would not have Weiss removed. They bought out MacPhail's shares and removed him from the Yankee organization. George Weiss himself was named the new General Manager. When MacPhail left, he tried to part amicably with Del Webb. He stuck out his hand and said "Del, you've been a good partner to me." Webb icily replied: "I don't want to shake your hand." McCarthy had certainly not forgotten all the frustrations he had been through with MacPhail, so the end of the alcoholic "Loud Larry's" tenure with the Yankees was not a story he minded hearing.[5]

An incident during the Yankees' failed pennant drive in 1948 reinforced the legacy McCarthy had left with New York, a legacy that ran infinitely deeper than the behavior in Cleveland and Detroit that immediately preceded his resignation. In one tight game, with runners on base, Tommy Henrich was at bat. He looked down to the third base coach for a sign. The coach relayed nothing. He looked again — same result. He called time, and went to talk to Manager Bucky Harris. Harris told Hen-rich that he would let him use his own judgment in this important situation. Hen-rich certainly felt flattered at the confidence Harris was showing in him, and he recognized that Harris would never trust an untested rookie's judgment at such a juncture, but the main thing that struck him was, as he said, that

> nothing like that would ever have happened under Joe McCarthy. He was firmly in charge at every moment, and he, not the players, ordered the strategy to be followed. ... McCarthy led us firmly and confidently, and we, as his players, responded well to his leadership. Under Bucky [Harris] we were a relaxed ball club — too relaxed in my opinion. We didn't have that fire in our bellies that McCarthy kept stoking all season long.

After the 1948 season, Harris lost his job.[6] As Bob Shawkey had found out 18 years before, it is hard to follow a legend. (And as Casey Stengel would learn, just as McCarthy had before, it is better to be the one who follows the one who follows the legend.)

Everyone knew that McCarthy was indeed the very sort of complete leader that Henrich said he was. Joe Cronin knew this as well as anyone, so did Tom Yawkey, no matter the taunting incident at the Detroit airport in 1946. In 1947, the Red Sox pitchers came down with a rash of sore arms, and they were unable to defend their American League championship. Some blamed Cronin, claiming he mismanaged the pitching staff.[7] The day after the Red Sox season ended in September, 1947, they announced to the public: Joe Cronin was now the General Manager of the Boston Red Sox. Former General Manager Eddie Collins, now ill, would be the team Vice President and advisor to Cronin. Taking Cronin's place as the new Manager of the Boston Red Sox would be Mr. Joseph Vincent McCarthy.

McCarthy had received offers from other teams. In addition to the Dodgers wanting him to replace Durocher in 1947, Detroit had offered him the job of managing the Tigers. Pittsburgh wanted him too. McCarthy made all matters clear to the Boston newspapers—"I could have gone with other clubs, but I chose the Sox." His salary of $40,000, while excellent, was a bit lower than other offers, and he likely could have asked for more. The key was that he was back managing, and clearly with a contender. "When you've been in baseball as long as I have," he confessed, "it gets in your blood." The attraction of managing the Red Sox lay in their obvious potential to become a truly outstanding team. What also lay ahead was the famed Boston press, who many predicted would be ready to engage in epistolic duels with the acerbic McCarthy. Apropos of McCarthy's anticipated arrival in Boston, New York writer Milton Gross warned: "When a Boston writer sits down, he puts on his spurs before opening his typewriter case." Scarcely a month after his appointment as Red Sox manager, McCarthy did fire Boston's popular trainer Win Green. He also cut sinker ball pitcher Bill Zuber, who had been released by the Yankees and ended up with the Red Sox in '47. McCarthy likely wanted no reminders of those depressing war years, as well as the losses in Cleveland that immediately preceded his '46 resignation.* Zuber's presence would have recalled all that.[8]

Among the Boston press, Zuber's departure caused no ripples, but Green's sure did. Green was an icon, and with his departure, some scribes had their knives out. Milton Gross warned, "the ink-stained wretches of the Hub [Boston] may not have invented the second guess, but they have certainly refined it to an incisive art." The city had not won a World Series since 1918. The press thus felt both the utmost of entitlement in being critical and absolutely no reason for deference. As likeable a manager as there was in baseball, Joe Cronin had been anything but immune from the press's knives. One Boston writer, Huck Finnegan of the *Boston American*, confronted Joe Cronin in Cleveland on the very day the Red Sox clinched the 1946 pennant. Cronin, smiling over Boston's victory, called out to Finnegan: "Well, what do

---

*McCarthy may have felt disdain for Bill Zuber, but Zuber felt nothing but enthusiasm and admiration for McCarthy. After his pitching career was over, Zuber went back to his native German-Iowa community where he opened Bill Zuber's Dugout Restaurant. On the wall of the dining room, he proudly displayed a copy of McCarthy's "Ten Commandments of Baseball."

you say now, you _____ bastard?" Finnegan growled: "Don't be so damned cocky, Cronin. You weren't so cocky last year and you won't be next year. I'll be around to remind you of it." After an exchange of "F" words, the two parted and took separate trains back to Boston. Tom Yawkey had a similar exchange with another scribe. Already full of self-importance, the Boston press now had Joe McCarthy to add to their subjects to be put under their microscopes.[9]

The Boston press of these years possessed an extraordinary sense of entitlement. The Red Sox had indeed not won a World Series in almost 30 years. The sense was present of the team being "cursed" as a result of the selling of Babe Ruth to the Yankees in 1919. The narrow loss of the 1946 World Series deepened it. The significance of "the curse" would not fully emerge for another two years, however. At the outset of the 1948 season, Boston fans, players, and writers were of the belief that their hour had at long last come around.

Until Tom Yawkey bought the team in 1932, the Boston press often gave more coverage to the Braves. Then Yawkey began to spend lavishly, and the Red Sox built up a potent team. A belief in Boston was that the talent Yawkey had assembled by the late 1930s— Jimmie Foxx, Lefty Grove, Joe Cronin, Heine Manush, Wes Ferrell, Rube Walberg, Ted Williams, Johnny Pesky, Bobby Doerr, and Dom DiMaggio— would have been enough for several World Series wins but for the War. The 1946 season proved Boston's superiority, and the loss that October to St. Louis was just a bad break. Now was the time for Boston. The Yankees had had their day in the late 1930s, now the true "Yanks" were going to step forth and displace them as the game's premier team.

For the Boston media, these lofty expectations prompted them to see their role as watchdogs. The city expected championships, and anything that would appear to be detracting from that was more than fair game for a reporter. In 1939, for example, Ted Williams seemed to loaf a bit in the outfield, and the fans booed him. He yelled and spat at them and snarled at reporters who questioned him about it. Thereafter, he was terse with the press and refused to speak to two young reporters in particular, Dave Egan of the *Boston Record* and Duke Lake of the *Boston American*. He also never again tipped his cap to the Boston fans. (He finally did so in retirement, a full 60 years later.) Tom Yawkey sided with Williams over the 1939 incidents, neither fining nor even reprimanding him. Lefty Grove had often sulked similarly, and reporters accepted it. Older reporters had generally acquiesced to Yawkey, but the younger ones would not, indeed they came to see older reporters, Red Sox management, and players like Williams as a veritable cabal they righteously needed to oppose. Yawkey had added to this buddy-buddy image, having previously paid many reporters' traveling expenses and having maintained an open bar for them at Fenway.

As the older scribes retired, and many did during the War, the Boston press was increasingly dominated by those "with their knives unsheathed." Meanwhile, the public seemed to have an appetite for sports muckraking. Pressure on newspapers' circulation figures from the new medium of television added to the sense of urgency among Boston reporters to do all they could to get a good story, and along with these pressures young, sports reporters also entered the Boston arena from such locales as Springfield, Lowell, Worcester, Manchester, New Hampshire, Portland, Maine, and many others. Yawkey no longer picked up press expenses, and the open bar was gone. It was a completely different atmosphere.

After being away during the war, Ted Williams may have expected more respect upon his return. He got just the opposite. In a game in New York in early 1946, he took a strike three with two on and missed a fly ball. The same ole' Egan banged away at him again, and many others were now asking him tough questions. Since Egan would not change, neither would Williams. For Williams, the issue was that he wanted to focus on, and not be diverted from, what made him the best hitter he could be. For reporters, paradoxically, the issue was much the same. They felt an obligation to pinpoint and perhaps correct anything that appeared to be diminishing the Red Sox pursuit of that elusive championship. In 1946 one Red Sox official, Larry Woodall, told every rookie, as he had apparently done before, "Don't talk to the Boston writers; they can't be trusted." When opposite sides in a struggle each feel a sense of moral righteousness it is difficult if not impossible for the conflict to do anything but grow more and more intense.

Egan and Lake, and others, like the pugnacious little (5'1") Hy Hurwitz of the *Boston Globe*,* never let up on Ted Williams or on many of the other players. The disappointing 1947 season only added to the pressures. The sports journalism world of 1948 Boston was a bit like a 17th-century New England village. Everyone not only knew everyone else's business, they felt entitled to know it, and they felt something must be wrong with anyone who wished to keep anything private. It was into this atmosphere of self-righteousness, name calling, and high expectations that Joe McCarthy stepped when he became the Red Sox manager. Early into his tenure with Boston, McCarthy began to answer lots of reporters' questions with the refrain that New York reporters had endured season after season: "Let me worry about that." The fight was on.[10]

When McCarthy signed with Boston, they already had infielders Bobby Doerr and Johnny Pesky, catcher Birdie Tebbetts, and outfielder Dom DiMaggio. And of course there was Ted Williams. McCarthy's pitching staff had three pitchers who had posted great years in 1946, Boo Ferriss, Mickey Harris, and Tex Hughson. They also had two strong newcomers, Maurice McDermott and Mel Parnell, plus two veteran starters, Joe Dobson and Denny Galehouse. McCarthy especially remembered Galehouse who, with Cleveland and St. Louis, had pitched numerous strong games against McCarthy's Yankees and was instrumental down the stretch in the Browns' 1944 pennant drive. Over the winter of 1947–48, Boston improved themselves even further. They cut a major deal with the St. Louis Browns. Boston gave up six players plus what was then a huge figure of $375,000. In exchange the Red Sox received two more pitchers, Ellis Kinder and Jack Kramer, shortstop Vern Stephens, and utility infielder Billy Hitchcock. Newspapers called it "The Missouri Purchase." (St. Louis was originally going to trade Kinder, Kramer, and Stephens to Cleveland for player-manager Lou Boudreau, but when Cleveland President Bill Veeck learned that St. Louis was then going to trade Boudreau to Boston he cancelled the deal.)

In September, 1946, the Globe *had asked Williams to write his thoughts about the pennant-winning season, with Hy Hurwitz to ghost-write for him. Reporters would soon hear Hurwitz complaining about having "to go down and listen to that big SOB." Meanwhile, Williams regularly sighed to his teammates about having "to talk to that no good little bastard."*

Ellis Kinder was 33 years old, and he had won his first major league victory only two years before. But Cronin and McCarthy recognized his talent. McCarthy was famous for taking a large staff of good pitchers and getting ten to fifteen wins out of virtually all of them. Barring injuries, he now clearly had the material to do that with his pitchers in Boston, and his lineup, however he would configure it, was going to look impressive. At the time of spring training, players standing around the batting cages of various American League teams were all commenting, both to reporters and to one another, on how tough Boston was going to be. They now had such a depth of talent at the plate, in the field, and on the mound, and they had best manager. When McCarthy signed with Boston, Tommy Henrich said "It looks to me as though the Red Sox will be the team to beat next year." Joe DiMaggio said at spring training in 1948 "we talked only about the Red Sox. We figured Boston was the team to beat. With McCarthy managing and the tremendous amount of talent Boston had picked up ... we thought the Red Sox were the most dangerous contender."[11]

Under "Jolly Joe" Cronin, the Red Sox had a reputation for being a fairly loose, easy-going outfit; "a country club" some described it. The players certainly knew McCarthy's reputation for toughness, but they did not know fully what to expect. Cronin obviously hoped that McCarthy could mold the talent he had assembled into a cohesive unit, just as he had done with the Yankees all those years before. The players all knew the stories about no telephoning, card playing, or smoking in the clubhouse. They knew his general reputation for toughness. Bobby Doerr commented: "He didn't say much. He was a very sharp guy. I didn't quite know how to take McCarthy. I [had] played for Cronin my whole career. He was a wonderful guy to play for. McCarthy was very reserved, never said anything to you. It was a little harder to me to play for him, but I respected him for his brilliance as a manager." What Doerr and the Red Sox found in McCarthy was, as Ted Williams put it, a man who "was all business." From the moment everyone arrived at the Red Sox training camp in Sarasota, Florida, that was the atmosphere — business.[12]

McCarthy presented no "you're playing for the great McCarthy" cult of personality. He never did that before (although he may have inadvertently done so in his final months with the Yankees in '46). As with the Yankees, he did not impose any major "system" of discipline. In New York his discipline was simple — "there are players in Newark who can easily take your place." That was his attitude in Boston, although the Red Sox minor league teams in Birmingham and Louisville (the latter team bought by Yawkey in 1938) did not have quite the talent of the Yankees' network. At the Sarasota training camp he did impose one rule — that players were not to carry laundry through the hotel lobby. "You're at the top of your profession," he said. "Act with dignity."

More than anything else, McCarthy brought to Florida that spring a fully systematic sense of how the club was going to train. Players had never before been part of practices that were so organized and so taxing of their physical reserves and their talents. Everyone was in motion amidst what one reporter called "the fast, business tempo of a McCarthy workout." No one rested for a second. Any lapses were immediately noticed. When one player sat down during practice, a reporter commented: "It must have been a broken leg." One Boston writer nodded with satisfaction: "It did not take long to discover how thorough a person Marse Joe is." When a reporter asked when practice would start, McCarthy responded with unexpected detail: "I was out on the field and noticed the grass was soaked with dew. I've got to check upon the field for two or three days to see just when the dew disappears before setting a time for the start of practice." Reporters were amazed with such specificity. Most managers simply decided upon a time — 10:30 — and thought little about it. McCarthy was different. What threw some reporters was the normally laconic nature of McCarthy on many other matters. Asked if he was satisfied with the Sarasota ball field, McCarthy nodded "yes." That was it.

McCarthy's new trainer, Eddie Froelich, who had worked with him in New York, and who had been his bat boy with the Cubs, tried to counsel the press here: "If Joe McCarthy is satisfied and says everything is satisfactory, then you should know that things are perfect. Joe does not say much, but when he is satisfied with conditions then you can be sure that no improvements are necessary." "Yes" meant yes. Many newspapermen did not grasp this, but the players sure did.[13]

Joe Cronin had generally given reporters and photographers full access to the locker room and to the sidelines of the practice field. When McCarthy held meetings with the team, which he did regularly that spring, the reporters were asked to leave the room. Some took this as an intentional slight. Here the reporters were unduly elevating their sense of their own importance. McCarthy and the players simply knew that there were certain matters that were only for their ears. If the press did not understand that they were not central to the Red Sox play, it was not something McCarthy was going to spend any time proving to them.

Ted Williams was one who seemed to delight in the new tone McCarthy created. For one thing, of course, he had had his troubles with the press. For another, perhaps more importantly, he recognized that what McCarthy was doing was not a matter of tone for its own sake. Rather it was a product of McCarthy's complete focus on the matter of training for a season. Williams had a well-established reputation for misbehavior, particularly with newsmen, and sometimes with fans. Again, perhaps elevating their own significance, newsmen and others had then been speculating all winter how the quixotic Ted Williams and the tough Joe McCarthy would get along with one another.

When McCarthy was first hired in Boston, veteran pitcher Bobo Newsom quipped: "I sure hope Williams has a good winter, because he's going to have a bad summer with McCarthy." Many felt that Joe Cronin had babied Williams, and hence the tougher McCarthy would be cause for sparks. McCarthy added to the all the questions when he predicted "I'll treat Ted Williams just like any other ballplayer." There was no issue in the first place. Williams' and McCarthy's respective rows with the press proved that they shared one common trait of not suffering fools gladly. The only overt concession to the issues upon which the reporters were dwelling came with the matter of McCarthy's usual demand that players wear coats and ties in the hotel lobby and at dinner. Williams never cared to wear a tie, anywhere, and reporters were sure that sparks would fly over that. Much to some reporters' disappointment, at the first breakfast at Sarasota, McCarthy arrived wearing a nice, open-collar Hawaiian shirt. The message was obvious. McCarthy's only comment: "Any manager who can't get along with a .400 hitter ought to have his head examined."

Williams told a reporter: "You know, I think Mr. McCarthy has the greatest system of getting a team in shape there is. [He] has got everything systematized perfectly." To another writer Williams exclaimed: McCarthy is "a wonderful manager who knows how to get the most out of his players. All he wants is hustle all the time." Years later McCarthy commented on the anticipation of problems with Williams: "Some people thought I might not get along with Williams. I don't know where they got that idea from. ... Williams was no problem. ... He played. He hustled; followed orders. He followed orders perfectly. Of course I only gave him one order — hit. No insubordination there. He hit." A trifle miffed at seeing no fireworks erupt, reporters tried to seize upon any inkling of a problem between Williams and McCarthy. The following spring, Williams waved off a photographer and was alleged to have said that "Nobody, not McCarthy or anybody else, can tell me when I could or could not have my picture taken." Later that day, the same photographer was nearing Williams and was being detained by a Red Sox official. Williams called out: "Come on in and take as many pictures as you want." The main thing that reporters took from this sequence of events was that Williams had supposedly expressed defiance of McCarthy. It was untrue, and McCarthy made no issue of the story.

On another occasion during spring training in 1948, Williams had contemplatively walked through the hotel lobby with his head down, and failed to hear a greeting from Mrs. McCarthy. Again the press jumped on this, but Williams had simply been preoccupied with something, and he went out of his way to apologize to Mrs. McCarthy as soon as he learned of the matter. Thereafter, Williams and Mrs. McCarthy always had warm dealings. Williams' daughter was born that spring, and Mrs. McCarthy chided him that it would not be long before his daughter was bossing him around. "So I've heard," smiled Williams, "but that will be the day."[14]

With respect to the Red Sox' possible lineup for the 1948 season, McCarthy was faced with several questions. The purchase of Vern Stephens complicated the infield. He had two first basemen, Jake Jones and Stan Spence, although Spence was primarily an outfielder. Bobby Doerr was clearly the starting second baseman. Billy Goodman was more than capable there too, but the job was Doerr's. For some reason, nevertheless, Doerr remained a little tense around McCarthy. Goodman could also play shortstop, but that had been the position of Johnny Pesky, and now they had Stephens, another shortstop, plus Billy Hitchcock, although there was little doubt that he was to be a reserve player. Billy Goodman wondered: "I sure would like to know just where Mr. McCarthy would like to have me play this season." Pesky and Stephens were each established shortstops, and everyone wondered what McCarthy would do. Many reporters expected that Stephens would be switched to third base. On March 8, McCarthy's decision was front page news in the *Boston Post*: Johnny Pesky was to play third base. McCarthy recognized Pesky's quickness. Always a team player, Pesky expressed nothing but delight with the move. "McCarthy is a fine man, and he doesn't make any mistakes," he proclaimed. With both conviction and encouragement on his mind, McCarthy held "to me he can't miss at his new position." After two days, it was clear that Pesky could handle hard hit balls and all other tough chances. McCarthy smiled: "I knew he could do it; his play doesn't surprise me." Embellishing, McCarthy recalled "a pretty fair shortstop by the name of Red Rolfe [who] was switched by me and became one of the top third basemen," adding references to the switches he had made with Ben Chapman and Johnny Lindell.[15]

Any references McCarthy made to the Yankees irritated some Boston reporters, of course. As he did not like to talk to reporters about matters still in abeyance in his mind, McCarthy was always willing to reminisce. New York reporters could always get stories out of him about the Cubs. He first used recollections about the Yankees for similar reasons, but many in the Boston press reacted to this with suspicion. McCarthy had been with the archrival Yankees so long that some fans feared he might harbor divided loyalties. Some newsmen reminded him of this. McCarthy seemed instinctively to know that any sort of direct denial would only confirm matters among the suspicious, so he tried to keep it light. It's silly, he said, after all: "New York wore white in practice; we wear gray." Suspicions remained, but McCarthy knew it was best to ignore them. None of his players believed any such nonsense, but some journalists kept the thought tucked away in their mental files.

McCarthy brought Earle Combs out of retirement to be one of his coaches. (Combs had left the Yankees after 1946 and coached for a year with the St. Louis Browns. When asked in 1947 why he would not return to New York he had said, "The fact is, as I see it, the Yankees are not the Yankees anymore. No sir, not without Joe." Combs did not like MacPhail either.) Another coach he hired to work with the pitchers was Johnny Murphy. To the suspicious, these Yankee links looked sinister. Everyone else recognized that McCarthy simply wanted a staff that could help him win a pennant. Indeed when the Red Sox played two exhibition games with the Yankees that spring, everyone could not help but notice how intensely played they were. They split the games. McCarthy made two pitching changes in one inning, something he had never done in an exhibition game. Yankees manager Bucky Harris played Joe DiMaggio for the full nine innings of both games. Most of the other regulars on both sides played the entirety of both games as well. "You would have thought it was a World Series game," DiMaggio recalled. DiMaggio and McCarthy did smile at one another before the game, but during the game it was all business. There were no divided loyalties.[16]

McCarthy's players encountered anything but divided loyalties. Indeed they had never witnessed such undivided intensity of focus. "Joe McCarthy knows what he is doing," noted Bobby Doerr, "and whatever he does must be the right thing. That man has been right all the time he's been in baseball." McCarthy drilled everyone endlessly on specifics. The truth in the old adage "the devil's in the details" was never more apparent than it was to McCarthy's Red Sox players that spring. Catcher George "Birdie" Tebbetts had always recognized that his hustle and not his ability was what kept him in the majors. "I didn't realize," he later admitted, "that I was giving the [mere] physical appearance of a hustler. It was just a kind of an act. I was putting on a show, but I wasn't really giving Joe the little extra he wanted. He got it after that. But how many mangers do you know who ever cut anything so fine?"

The rest of the team also learned they would have live up to higher expectations. With such high-level players as he had, McCarthy knew better than to confront many directly when he detected a slight drop-off in hustle. As he had with some of his Yankees, McCarthy would often tell another player about hustle when he knew the player about whom he was really concerned was within earshot. It worked, so much so that the players quickly caught on to their new manager's tactic. During intra-squad games, McCarthy was also constantly quizzing the players on the bench to see if they were alert as to what was occurring on the field. McCarthy worked with Jack Kramer, correcting the delivery motion he used while holding a man on first. He improved Billy Hitchcock's pivot at second base on double plays. He worked with Hitchcock and Billy Goodman on how best to tag a runner coming into second base. During one exhibition game, on a hit to the outfield with a runner on second, Vern Stephens ran into the outfield to take the relay which he then threw slightly wide of the plate. McCarthy quietly corrected him in the dugout. "You could have gotten that man at the plate." Stephens asked how. "You went too far into the outfield," advised McCarthy. "Let the outfielder make a long throw to you. Your throw must be accurate, and it won't be if you have a long throw." Stephens later acknowledged: "I've been playing ball for ten years, and nobody ever told me that."

Billy Hitchcock, later himself a manager, sat near McCarthy as he saw a Red Sox player be thrown out sliding into second. "Billy," he noted, "that man wasn't thrown out at second base. He was out at home. If he would have run the first twenty steps as fast as the last twenty, he would not even have had to slide." When another player scored from second on a hit, McCarthy immediately saw that "we would never have made it if the shortstop had been playing six feet deeper." Hitchcock and the Sox were learning what the Yankees knew — McCarthy saw everything everyone else saw, and he saw things no one else could see. One reporter was impressed. "The players," he wrote, "were discovering some of the reasons that McCarthy has such a great record." As Stephens' relay plays showed improvement, McCarthy was asked to account for it. He smiled: "I pushed a button, and that's what happened." The old nickname was still on many lips, and McCarthy knew it. There were also those who felt that McCarthy only wanted to manage teams destined to be frontrunners, so he would not have to work hard. The players knew better, and some reporters were grasping it too. One wrote: "After watching McCarthy give instructions, we incline to the belief that … Marse Joe is a natural teacher."[17]

While the players were responding positively, McCarthy's image still continued to sit poorly with some fans and reporters. There was a group of Boston fans known as the "Royal Rooters," who came down to Sarasota every training season. When Joe Cronin was the manager, he had always made a point of ingratiating himself to the group. He and some players regularly met with them for drinks for an hour or so before dinner. McCarthy did not spend any time socializing. He was never hostile to the group, but glad-handing was just not his way. Cronin was gregarious and mixed easily. Away from a baseball field, McCarthy was shy. Some of the fans did not like it. They felt they were being snubbed. A few reporters reacted negatively too, and when McCarthy was his usual laconic self, especially with silly questions, the negatives grew. By April some Boston reporters were already writing about a "Cold War," and not just the one between the U.S. and the U.S.S.R. After the first few weeks of training camp, McCarthy had stopped meeting with the press every day. When McCarthy held a substantive meeting with Boston reporters, one paper sardonically headlined in their sports section: "Extra! McCarthy Talks Baseball!" *Time Magazine* reported the hostility. Milton Gross, a writer for *Colliers Magazine,* wrote that spring of how McCarthy regarded the press as a bunch of "parasitic busy bodies." "Despite an enviable record," read the article,

> McCarthy is neither a graceful winner nor a good loser. On the occasion of more than one victory celebration, Joe has told off certain newspapermen who did not treat him with adjectives becoming his record. The fact is Joe cannot abide criticism or even conversation on a losing day, as innumerable players, writers, bartenders, Pullman porters, hotel maids, and waiters have discovered to their humiliation. An inconsolably lonely man, with small grace for conversation [or] the whimsies or vagaries of life, McCarthy regards every bad break as a personal affront. When his club is not going right, he takes refuge in insolence and insulting remarks.

Such a characterization of the press as "parasitic" obviously did not sit well, although some players agreed, especially Ted Williams. Tensions grew. "I don't talk to him unless absolutely necessary," sulked one *Boston Post* scribe. McCarthy did not attempt to address the matter. To him it was a variation of the same theme he had heard in New York and Chicago. But Boston had a different press atmosphere. They had nearly as many scribes as New York in a community not even half as big, and with a more aggressive spirit. Boston had been a loser for so many years that the players and manager did not command the same respect. McCarthy expected respect; the press was used to acting with an aggressive disrespect. It was a lethal combination. McCarthy did not fully grasp that this was a new era of media scrutiny, in a post-war environment which, unlike that of the Depression era, did not augur for as much respect for authority in general. McCarthy took comfort in the point, which some discerning reporters understood too, that success in the upcoming season would solve everything, just as the lack of success would make any good feelings, even if they had arisen, turn sour.[18]

Ted Williams had to leave the team just as the preseason tour of the South was beginning. He feared he had appendicitis and would require surgery; he was OK but he stayed in Boston and was ready when the season began. The opening of the season was not a happy one. The Red Sox lost three in a row to the Philadelphia A's. At a key moment in the third loss, right fielder Sam Mele lost a fly ball in the sun, reminding people of McCarthy's Cubs' loss in Philadelphia in game four of the 1929 World Series. McCarthy did think about Mele in comparison to his regular Yankees right fielder, Tommy Henrich. Here Mele did not fare well. ("Henrich would have stuck that ball in his ___," McCarthy yelled.) Henrich certainly was a better fielder and hitter. Some said McCarthy came to hold a personal grudge against Mele, even more after he had engaged in some horseplay with Ted Williams later that summer. The wrestling put Williams out of the lineup for several games. Right field would be the weak spot in the Sox lineup that year. After the Philadelphia games, the Red Sox lost two of three to the Yankees. In one game, they committed three errors. In another loss, the Red Sox were shut out for eight innings by Eddie Lopat. Down 5–0, they then scored four runs in the ninth inning. They lost the game, but the fact that they did not merely go through the motions in the ninth inning and nearly won gave some writers and fans a hint of the new ways of the team. Boston fans were famous for their defeatism. McCarthy would have none of it.[19]

It was certainly difficult for McCarthy to maintain an optimistic spirit on the team that spring. The Red Sox got off to a disastrous start. In mid May, Ted Williams was hitting .385, but the next highest average was Vern Stephens' .267. No one else was even above .240. Dom DiMaggio was batting .175. Among the pitchers, Ellis

Kinder was hurt, and Tex Hughson had severe arm trouble and had to be sent down to the minor leagues. Hughson did not agree and was resentful. Even McCarthy badly banged his head on a steel girder that hung over the dugout in Philadelphia. He had done that in Shibe Park before, on the day that Hack Wilson lost the ball in the sun in 1929. On May 23, Boston lost a doubleheader to Chicago. Their record stood at 12 and 17. McCarthy, noted one writer, "is now managing one of the most astounding fall downs in history."[20]

The Red Sox were in seventh place. Only the hapless Chicago White Sox were worse. New York, Cleveland, and surprising Philadelphia were battling one another for the league lead. McCarthy was his usual testy self with the reporters. Fans and writers were speculating about possible shifts in the lineup. Reporters tried to goad McCarthy, criticizing him for believing he was alone in his agonizing over the Sox' woes. McCarthy, sarcastically noted one scribe, "is not the only one worrying about his Red Sox. A few million local residents are sweating it out with him." Asked whether he was considering any switches in the lineup, McCarthy always gave his standard response: "I'll worry about that. You'll know in plenty of time." In mid May when the roster had to be cut, McCarthy sent pitcher Ellis Deal down to the minors and kept young Maurice McDermott. Asked why, McCarthy pointed to his earlier choosing to keep Johnny Broaca and Lefty Gomez in seasons when neither had started well. Again, he was irritating people when he was silent, and if he talked about the Yankees of old as a way of avoiding discussions of the '48 Sox there was more irritation.

Sardonically, one writer, Harold Kaese, came to McCarthy's defense. "How could McCarthy expect the everlasting support of the press," he asked, "while telling Boston writers to let him run his own team? Such an outrageous request has not been heard since Dad asked the kids if he might use the family car one evening." Kaese's message was not heeded, and it would not be, not at least until the Red Sox started to win. McCarthy kept faith. Again asked what he would do with the 1948 Red Sox, he finally opened up a bit: "Nothing," he snorted. Then he elaborated. "That's right; a great ball club will find its own level. This is a great ball club, and its own level is the top." This seemed but vaporous nonsense that Memorial Day when the Red Sox seemed but one more death to commemorate.[21]

Johnny Pesky was down with a pulled muscle for a few games in May. Billy Goodman took his place at third base and played well, in the field and at bat. When Pesky returned to the lineup, McCarthy had to consider more fully what he could do with the valuable Billy Goodman. He had played well in spring training, shown great willingness to take direction, and complained to no one about any time spent on the bench. Meanwhile, first baseman Jake Jones had been hitting but .200. On the day of a doubleheader loss to Chicago, a Jones error had cost the team the second game. The picture looked bleak for Boston, mired in seventh place after so much pre-season hype, seemingly out of the race before Memorial Day, with no trade possibilities in the offing. Reporters knew it was futile to ask McCarthy what he had in mind. Again and again, he intoned "Don't you fellows worry about things. I'll run the ball club." Two writers had clacked out the idea of Billy Goodman being shifted to first base. McCarthy hardly took the idea from them, but on May 25, he started Goodman at first base and batted him in the leadoff position against St. Louis. Jake Jones sat on the bench for much of the rest of the season.

Although Goodman hit a home run, the Red Sox lost the game to the Browns, and the dark speculations about the team's future continued. Among these musings were rumors that McCarthy was going to resign. Relations with the press were bad, and this was coloring reportage of everything else. Some newsmen later claimed that the Red Sox' poor showing in April and May 1948 stemmed from the players being "too much in awe" of and intimidated by McCarthy. No player ever corroborated this. They were all impressed with him. They had total confidence in McCarthy and wanted to win for him. The sense of intimidation was something many in the press felt, and they readily projected this into their analysis.[22]

In late May, the experiment with Billy Goodman leading off and playing first base was foremost on McCarthy's mind. In order to protect Goodman, he was going to stiff-arm the press even more than normal, no matter the resulting gossip. A major league player taking on a whole new position, during the regular season no less, is hardly akin to trying a new place in the field in a sandlot game. There was much to learn. More importantly, there was much that needed to be grasped to such a point that it could become instinctive so that teammates could feel confident. McCarthy knew that any undue press focus and hyper-analysis could disrupt the delicate process at work with Goodman's change of positions. The press felt fully entitled to involve itself, and McCarthy felt just as entitled to shut them out. "You've got plenty to write without writing about that," he scolded. Wanting Goodman to feel no extra pressure, McCarthy tried to downplay the significance of the switch. He told a reporter the switch "doesn't mean a thing." The reporter asked why he would say that. McCarthy barked at him: "You fellows want to know everything, don't you?" Admitting some had guessed correctly about his putting Goodman at first, he defensively chided: "You didn't guess he was going to lead off, did you?" Sensing the obvious tension in the situation, a reporter tried a more gentle tactic, raising the general point about Goodman being "a pretty good ballplayer." McCarthy still reacted defensively: "Well, you don't have to go into any detail do you?" Here was where McCarthy was clearly not at all skillful at the very managerial tasks that were increasingly needed with the growth of media everywhere in baseball and in the general news. With game tactics and strategies against other managers, McCarthy could be as subtle and nuanced as anyone in the business. With reporters he was just the opposite. In this case, a few nips of White Horse Scotch were likely rendering the jabs even more blunt.[23]

Through the end of May, the Red Sox continued to struggle. Their record as of Memorial Day was an anemic 14 and 28. Several writers had openly declared themselves "feudists" in regard to Mr. McCarthy. Now the stories were even bigger. On May 28, the *Post* headlined, not in the sports section but on page one of the entire edition: "Sox Pilot to Quit Team." (They likely chose not to name McCarthy in the headline not purely out of disrespect, because the baseball coach at the Massachusetts Institute of Technology, Henry T. McCarthy, did resign the same day.) Boston was just completing a long road trip, during which they had won but two of thirteen games. A standard refrain among Boston fans of the day, as well as before and since, was: "What's the matter with the Red Sox?" That May millions of New Englanders sang that chorus, and now they were apparently learning that their manager was leaving them. Other Boston papers were placing Red Sox matters on their front pages too. The normally silent Mrs. McCarthy spoke up here about her husband's resignation: "Ridiculous! I can't understand why anyone would get such an idea. Joe's had too many winners to let something like this bother him." Joe Cronin also scoffed at the story of McCarthy quitting. Noting the team had played just over 30 games, Cronin counseled "wait until we've played 154."

At that point on the disastrous road trip, the Sox were in Washington, D.C., and Cronin went to the Shoreham Hotel in Washington to see McCarthy. Some said he spent the evening talking McCarthy out of quitting and getting him to ease off on the whiskey. No one would ever know for sure, as there was no third party with them. McCarthy's only comment to the rumors was "I may have jumped a winning team, but I never jumped a loser." McCarthy was not leaving, although over the next three days the Red Sox lost four games to the Senators.[24]

McCarthy was trying all sorts of lineup combinations. Four different leadoff hitters started in four straight games. McCarthy even put Jake Jones back at first base for a game; they still lost. In the final game of the road trip, June 1, Ellis Kinder did pitch a complete game, and Boston beat Philadelphia 8-1. Now they were heading home. One writer likened McCarthy and the Red Sox' return to New England to Napoleon and the French Army's return from Russia. Kinder's strong outing in Philadelphia appeared to have no significance. This team had apparently tossed away the season. They were ten games out of the lead. Ted Williams was the only one swinging a bat with any authority. The first game at home was another loss, this time to the lowly St. Louis Browns, and all Boston's fandom shrugged even more. All that money on the "Missouri Purchase," the hiring of McCarthy, what a waste it all seemed. Old Bostonians figured maybe the Puritans had been right all along. The near miss in the 1946 World Series could now be seen as the first sign. There was predestination at work here, and all the efforts of Yawkey, Cronin, and McCarthy could deter the team's calamitous fate, as an 18th–century New England preacher once put it, no better than a spider's web could stop a falling rock.[25]

Then came a remarkable turnaround. Boston started to win, and it did not matter who they played. From June 3 to 29 they won 16 of 19 games and stood only five and one half games out of first place. No one was griping about McCarthy anymore. His press critics went mum. One morning the *Post* answered the old "What's the Matter?" question with a simple headline on page one: "Nothing's the Matter!" Ted Williams was leading the league in hitting, and when he went down for two weeks with some strained cartilage on his left side, "Little" Billy Goodman led the team. At the All-Star break Goodman was batting .312. He had worked out splendidly at first base. He was fielding well. (He was shaky at first, but McCarthy had spotted that he needed a better fitting glove.) His hitting was strong, too. In regard to Goodman's contribution, McCarthy recalled his scripture, Isaiah, chapter 11, verse 6: "And a Little Child Shall Lead Them." Goodman was actually not that "little." He stood 5'11", but he weighed only 165 pounds. He was also quite young, only 22, and the poetics of his preferred Christian name, "Billy," added to the sense of this "little child" somehow destined to lead the team. Goodman was a McCarthy-type of player, very quiet, easily coached. About the only problem McCarthy ever found with him was that he dressed somewhat casually.[26]

While McCarthy's mind turned to the book of Isaiah, some of New England's Puritan descendents may have preferred Deuteronomy 33: "Their Foot Shall Slide in Due Time," but like most people, baseball fans in 1948 drew from scriptures as their mood dictated. Boston was winning. The Boston Braves were in first place in the National League to boot. From June 1, the day Ellis Kinder beat the A's, until July 26, Boston compiled a record of 40 and 13. One of the defeats was a bitter 2–0 loss to Cleveland on June 8. Here Mel Parnell pitched a great game, as did Cleveland's Gene Bearden, who was in the midst of the one great season of his career.

Cleveland's runs came with one on and a curving line drive by Lou Boudreau, thought foul by every partisan fan in right field, but which the umpire ruled to have passed the foul pole in fair territory. Literate Bostonians dubbed it "the King Lear home run." ("Fair is Foul and Foul is Fair.") The loss snapped a five-game winning streak, and, as the season turned out, the "King Lear" play would be long remembered. Despite that game, but with their 40 wins in less than two months, the Red Sox had moved from seventh to first place! Having headlined his "resignation" less than two months before, the *Post* proclaimed "Joe McCarthy, once again the miracle manager in baseball." To the team, the *Post* cheered: "Well done, lads."[27]

When McCarthy was losing, the newspaper reporters wanted to know exactly why. When he won, they were generally content to marvel. "There is some kind of genius connected with the present condition of the Sox," wrote one. "Exactly what kind of magic it is that McCarthy employs is not clear." But "Sox fans are too busy buying tickets to heckle." The question in late July was, varying the first line of an old popular song, one that was actually a McCarthy favorite: "Will They Love Him in September as They Didn't in May?" (The actual song was "Will You Love Me in December as You Do in May?" written by the same Jimmy Walker who became mayor of New York.) The answer to the semi-musical question would have to be seen, but they sure did love McCarthy in July.

A particularly endearing incident came on July 24. That afternoon, McCarthy was ejected from the first game of a doubleheader with rival Cleveland. McCarthy stood in the runway between the dugout and the clubhouse for the rest of the game listening to the radio. One of his pitchers, Mickey Harris, stood at the runway entrance to the dugout and relayed signs from McCarthy out to catcher Birdie Tebbetts. With the winning run on base at the top of the ninth inning for Cleveland and pinch hitter Allie Clark stepping in, Harris relayed to Tebbetts that McCarthy wanted his pitcher, Dave Ferriss, to throw Clark side-arm fastballs. McCarthy screamed his orders, nervous about whether Ferriss got the sign. Ferriss struck out Clark with a sidearm fastball. The crowd went crazy, as the win brought them even closer to the league lead. With the game over, McCarthy could come back to the field. As he did, the crowd roared even louder. McCarthy waved his cap and danced a jig. When the story hit the papers, Boston's working-class Irish smiled and cheered. Back in September, when he first signed with Boston, McCarthy had said: "I'm going up with the real Irish now." Now he was certainly regarded fully as one of them. To hell with some reporters, and to hell with any Puritan predestination, Mac and the Sox were a winnin' bunch o' lads.[28]

If the baseball gods had predestined the 1948 American League winner, they were certainly concealing matters. On the morning of August 4, short of a flat-footed tie, the race could not have been tighter. The first four teams stood as follows:

	Wins	Losses	Percentage	Games Behind
Cleveland	56	38	.596	
New York	57	39	.594	—
Boston	58	40	.592	—
Philadelphia	59	41	.590	—

Ted Williams was down with a twisted right knee. His hitting was not impaired, but he could not run well in the outfield. McCarthy used Williams as a pinch hitter, and he left it to Williams to tell him when he could return to the lineup. In mid–August, Billy Goodman had to go into the hospital with appendicitis for several days. In late August, Doerr was also injured. Two of McCarthy's best pitchers, Joe Dobson and Jack Kramer, were hurt, as was Mickey Harris. His bullpen was weak all year, but veteran Denny Galehouse put in several good outings. He shut out Chicago on July 22. In a game against Cleveland on July 30, the Indians jumped on young Mel Parnell for six runs in the first. Galehouse relieved him with one out. He pitched the next eight and two thirds innings, giving up but one run and two hits, enabling the Red Sox to come back and win.

McCarthy was proud of Galehouse's performance. The Cleveland papers were gnashing their teeth over his showing: "When an old man like Galehouse [36 years old] … could hold them to two hits in one put-out shy of a full nine," they growled, "the Indians must have choked up." Twelve days later Galehouse beat the Yankees. McCarthy and everyone else smiled broadly at that. The Philadelphia Athletics faded a bit in August, but New York and Cleveland did not. It was an American League pennant race unlike any ever seen. After the disastrous month of May, Boston had chinned their way back into it, but their impressive showing had not made the other two AL powers fold their tents. At the end of August, a mere game and a half separated the three of them.[29]

McCarthy showed all his outstanding managerial qualities during the incredible heat of the pennant race that summer. With all the winning, the media complaints about McCarthy ill-treating the press completely vanished. Now people realized that his refusals to comment on the bad weeks were part of his patient approach to his players. He did not want any hint of a signal to his players that he was growing impatient with them, for that, he knew, would only compound the troubles. The counterpoint was equally important — that when events turned around, it would then sink into the players that even in the bad patch they had their manager's confidence. When the players realized that, it meant a great deal, and the winning spurt became more than a flash in the pan. For business leaders, politicians, teachers, or sports coaches, the same lessons of psychology and leadership apply in all cases, and nobody understood and practiced them like McCarthy.

A sense of McCarthy's human priorities beyond even the pennant race came forth that August, too. On August 16, Babe Ruth died. (He was only 53.) Players and fans were well aware of how Ruth had made managing the Yankees more difficult for McCarthy in his first years in New York. But McCarthy showed no hint of anything but genuine affection and respect: "Babe was a great guy. He was a great man for baseball, probably one of the greatest there ever will be. Everybody who ever played with him or was associated with him in the game will mourn his passing." McCarthy was as tough a manager as the game ever saw, but his simple human touch was never absent, and it was part of his success—a component of personality that cannot be learned from a manual or by mere imitation. What McCarthy once said of Dizzy Dean, pointing to his heart, "he has one of these," McCarthy's players knew to be true of their manager too. It made them want to win for him very, very much.[30]

Cleveland lost a bit of ground in early September, and the Red Sox pulled ahead. At the same time the Boston Braves inched ahead of the Dodgers for the lead in the National League. Bostonians felt ever more convinced that they indeed resided in "the Hub" of the universe. The prospects of an all–Boston World Series looked as bright among New Englanders as the emerging fall colors. One *Boston Post* cartoon depicted two men talking on the street. "Howz things with you?" asked one. "Great," the other responded, "my wife left me, my house burned down, but the Braves 'n Sox are in." With Cleveland apparently fading, a crucial series loomed with the Yankees on September 9. The demand for tickets was so strong that people joked about owner Tom Yawkey sleeping in his office so he would make sure he could get into Fenway Park on the day of the game. Other than season passes, tickets could only be purchased on game day and at the ball park. By sunrise, the line at the window went around the block and headed out towards Newton. By noon, scalpers were getting $50 a ticket.

McCarthy made his managerial presence felt in the game. The Yankees opened with four runs. Amidst the groans to pull starter Earl Johnson, McCarthy paid no heed and patiently stayed with him. From there he held the Yankees scoreless into the sixth inning. Boston countered with five runs in their half of the first, driving out starter Spec Shea. With the game in doubt in the seventh, the Yankees had put in Joe Page. Although McCarthy was ready to send Page down to Newark when he resigned from New York in May of 1946, the Yankees had kept him. He became their (and the game's) best relief pitcher, and he bore down especially hard whenever he faced McCarthy's Red Sox. He never forgot the dressing down he had received from McCarthy on that plane from Cleveland to Detroit. He also harbored a grudge against Bobby Doerr, as the two had gotten into a fight earlier in the season. Boston fans loved the usually unflappable Doerr. Of course they sided with Doerr in the altercation and loudly booed Page whenever he subsequently appeared in Fenway Park.

With Page pitching in the seventh inning, Dom DiMaggio doubled, and Johnny Pesky sacrificed him to third base, nearly beating out the bunt himself. With DiMaggio on third, the Yankees brought their infield in, and Page faced Ted Williams. Williams hit a high bouncer to second baseman George Stirnweiss. He fielded it cleanly but just missed nabbing DiMaggio at the plate. Vern Stephens then singled, with Williams stopping at second base. When Stephens was batting, McCarthy began his psychological/tactical moves. He sent reserve catcher Matt Batts to the on-deck circle as an apparent pinch hitter.

As Batts was heading for the plate, McCarthy recalled him. In Batts' place he sent out Bobby Doerr, who had been hurt and out of action since August 31. McCarthy knew the crowd would react to the appearance of Doerr, especially when it was to face Page, and he wanted to maximize its intensity, hoping it would have an effect on Page. It seemed to do just that. With the crowd growing louder with every pitch, Doerr worked the count to 3 and 2; then he fouled off three pitches, and finally drew a pass to load the bases. McCarthy sent in a runner for Doerr, and naturally the crowd cheered him again. Billy Goodman was next up, and Page had apparently been rattled. His control went awry. He walked Goodman, scoring Williams. Page had to be relieved.

McCarthy had won a psychological skirmish. Boston scored three more that inning and won the game 10–6. McCarthy's team was now two and a half games in front. They won the next day 9–4, scoring eight runs in the third inning and breezing home from there. Their three and a half game lead was their largest of the season. McCarthy had done it. New Englanders had not felt such confidence in any leader since Nathaniel Hawthorne's Reverend Dimmesdale.[31]

The very day after the first, dramatic victory over the Yankees, one writer, Al Hirshberg of the *Boston Post*, published an article claiming the real credit for the Red Sox remarkable performance should go to— Joe Cronin! He asserted that in late May the team was indeed falling apart, and that McCarthy's putting Billy Goodman in the lineup at first base had not stopped the losing. When the team was at its nadir, losing four games in Washington, Hirshberg said it was Cronin who came to Washington and "quietly … took control not of the ball club but of McCarthy. He spent," Hirshberg alleged, "almost every waking moment with his idol, soothing him, assuring him that everything would straighten itself out. By the time the series with the Senators was over," said Hirshberg, "McCarthy was himself again." While Cronin was a great GM for McCarthy, and while he did help McCarthy get through a rough patch in Washington, it was quite a stretch to claim that Cronin deserved the real credit for the Sox' turnaround. It would have been like claiming that Ed Barrow was the real reason the Yankees won four straight World Series in the late 1930s. Most important was the question of why someone in the Boston press felt it appropriate at that point in the season to opine so obnoxiously as to who was really responsible for the Red Sox' comeback. Cronin and McCarthy made no comment, and no one would question the right of a sports writer to say what he wants. It was just typical of the milieu in which McCarthy and the Red Sox were playing. If all seemed blissful, someone would make sure to find a way to dampen spirits. Hawthorne's Roger Chillingworth was a likely role model here.[32]

Hirshberg's column did not cause any team letdown, but the Red Sox lost the third game of the Yankees series, and people questioned McCarthy on a major call. The Red Sox were down 6–2. They battled back to tie the game and send it into extra innings. In the tenth inning, McCarthy had a reliever in the game, Earl Caldwell, a 43-year-old veteran he had picked up from the White Sox in midseason. McCarthy's bullpen ranks were depleted, and the Yankees were starting the end of their order. McCarthy thus felt he could get another inning out of Caldwell and turn to another pitcher later if he needed one. But Caldwell walked the eighth batter, catcher Gus Niarhos. Then he hit pitcher Spec Shea with a curve ball. Fans stirred, but Caldwell struck out leadoff man Charlie Keller. Then he walked Tommy Henrich and struck out Hank Bauer. With two out and the bases loaded, up stepped Joe DiMaggio. McCarthy stuck with Caldwell. DiMaggio worked the count to 3 and 2. Caldwell then threw a changeup; DiMaggio crushed it, but it sailed foul by a foot. McCarthy waved wildly at Caldwell. He did not want him, or anyone, to try to put a "cute one" past DiMaggio. DiMaggio then hit Caldwell's next pitch, a fastball, for a grand slam home run. The Red Sox went quietly in their half of the tenth.

The *Boston Post* was actually sarcastic. "Don't forget the other DiMaggio," they snorted. No other city had such a heel-nipping sports press as Boston's. The Yankees were now two and a half games out. Another Red Sox win would have put them four and one half games ahead. Meanwhile, Cleveland beat Detroit, and with the Red Sox loss the Indians were only three and one half games out. Fans were now arguing with one another about why McCarthy chose to leave Caldwell in the game. McCarthy never responded to any second-guessing, and he certainly never gave a second of notice to charges of divided loyalties. Boston would win many other encounters with the Yankees that September, but the fans and reporters seemed to remember most the loss to Joe DiMaggio's dramatic grand slam. Why did McCarthy stay with Caldwell? Why didn't he turn to someone like the underused Mickey Harris? The most paranoid were asking whether McCarthy wanted to give DiMaggio an opportunity for drama. His scowl at Caldwell for trying to fool DiMaggio with a change-up belied that. Still, denial only confirms most conspiracy thinking. Five days later Caldwell gave up another grand slam, and the muttering continued.[33]

After the Yankee series, Denny Galehouse and Mel Parnell pitched two good victories over Philadelphia, but neither New York nor Cleveland wavered, and Vern Stephens came down with a case of the flu. Then McCarthy's weakened bullpen let him down again, as the A's beat Boston 10–4. Two days later, out in Chicago, much the same happened. On September 14, Ellis Kinder pitched a strong five-hitter for a 4-1 win. The next day, Boston's pitching collapsed again, as Chicago won 17-10. The following day, the lowly St. Louis Browns won 3-1. Bobby Doerr was finally back in the lineup. (Billy Hitchcock had played well in his absence — 15 hits in 35 at bats in 9 games.) The game felt especially anemic as the Red Sox could do nothing for eight innings. Their one meaningless run came in the ninth inning. The frustration from there was even worse. With the one run in, two runners on base, and two outs, Birdie Tebbetts hit a hard line drive. The runners were sprinting, of course. Browns' shortstop, Ed Pellagrini (formerly with the Red Sox) leaped for the ball. The ball hit his glove and popped out, but Pellagrini caught it with his bare hand just before it landed. Game over, as it would likely have been had he dropped it. The Yankees were now one game out. One writer reported that McCarthy "has not been bearing up too well in the rocky going" and was especially "not feeling well after the 3-1 loss" to the Browns. Another paper announced that McCarthy was probably going to miss the next day's game in St. Louis. McCarthy missed no games, but he was drinking, and amidst the extreme September pressures this was never good.[34]

Some said that no one but Ted Williams sat close to McCarthy on the bench because of fear. Others said his drinking made his breath so bad that no one wanted to be near him; only Williams' weak sense of smell allowed him to sit close. How often the drinking was problematic was not something anyone systematically catalogued, but there was no denying its presence. Generally McCarthy's players were loyal to him. A few felt he held grudges and treated them unreasonably. Pitcher Tex Hughson, who had pitched so well in Boston's 1946 pennant year, was one who felt McCarthy never gave him a good chance. Some said this was due to Hughson drilling Joe DiMaggio in the ribs with a pitch. When DiMaggio was struck, he flipped the bat away in disgust. As DiMaggio trotted down to first base, McCarthy turned to the Boston bench and said "Look at him. He won't rub it." Indeed, DiMaggio didn't.

Most chalked the incident up to the respect in which McCarthy held Joe DiMaggio; others saw more evidence of McCarthy's divided loyalty.

In any case, McCarthy seemed not to like Hughson. For Hughson there was an added psychological factor. He had been successful in 1946, but largely with his fastball. He knew the fate of many one-pitch wonders, so in 1947 he tried to master a curve, sinker, and knuckleball. He was not successful. He developed a sore arm, and his record fell. At the same time his father passed away. For the deepest of reasons, he then dearly wanted to make a comeback. He sincerely felt he had the "stuff" to do it and never relinquished the belief that a closed-minded Joe McCarthy prevented him from doing so. Hughson became a very bitter man for the rest of his life.[35]

Outfielder Sam Mele was another player against whom McCarthy seemed to maintain a grudge. After Mele had lost a fly ball in the sun in Philadelphia early in the season and later gotten into the good-natured joust with his friend Ted Williams, bruising one of Williams' ribs, McCarthy kept Mele on the bench for much of the summer. Still, Mele was hitting only .233, so it may not have been just personal. In Boston's next game in September against St. Louis, McCarthy was indeed drunk when he arrived at the clubhouse. Coach Del Baker slipped Mele's name onto the lineup card he always recopied for McCarthy. McCarthy was apparently too drunk to notice. Mele came through with a bases-loaded double that won the game for Boston that afternoon. After Mele had doubled, the next batter walked. McCarthy signaled for a double steal; whether he knew or cared if it was Mele on second base no one knew. Mele twisted his ankle sliding into third. The Boston bench rushed onto the field to check on Mele. Left alone, McCarthy wandered inexplicably up the first base line in front of all the bemused St. Louis fans. "When are you going to switch to wine, Joe?" yelled one. McCarthy then wandered over to third base and berated Mele: "Get up you f___in' Dago!" Then he turned his ire to Baker and demanded to know why the double steal. Baker calmly responded, "You called for it." McCarthy backed off.

The abusiveness of the scene was similar to the cab ride from the Detroit airport in 1946. The whole specter was embarrassing, yet the team continued to win. To what extent McCarthy's alcohol consumption was a problem to the team, or to himself, remains a vexing question. Certainly the sensibilities and microscopic press inspections of subsequent eras make his drinking appear loathsome, but the question of McCarthy's own effectiveness and the team's performance are hard to judge, as all matters turn on the question of what would have occurred if the drinking had not been there. Some players, like Paul Waner, always said they played a bit better with a nip in their system. Waner always said it made the ball appear fuzzier and easier to hit. One of McCarthy's pitchers, Ellis Kinder, pitched well when drinking, and less effectively when sober. In that era, drinking did not have the stigma it has subsequently carried. Most players simply shrugged and shouldered on. Their faith in their manager never appeared to waver.[36]

Boston won their next two games in St. Louis. From there they lost a doubleheader to Detroit. The first of the two losses was especially painful. Boston had come back to tie the game in the ninth inning. Then in the twelfth inning, Detroit doubled with a man on. The throw from right field looked good, but, inexplicably, relief pitcher Earl Johnson cut the throw off. Game over. In game two, relief pitcher Boo

Ferriss gave up a home run, hit the next two batters, then gave up a walk and a single. McCarthy's bullpen staff was so depleted that he had to could not relieve Ferriss. Detroit's winning runs scored that inning. McCarthy needed more than a shot of scotch to cure his relief pitching problems. The only silver lining that day was that the Yankees lost too, but Cleveland had swept two from Philadelphia. Now the Indians were a half game behind Boston, and the Yankees were one game out.

The next day, McCarthy gambled, starting Mickey Harris in order to give Mel Parnell an extra day's rest. Harris had not pitched since August 9, but McCarthy's instincts were good this day, as Harris pitched a four-hitter. Harris's difficulty here was that he was usually nervous around McCarthy. From this McCarthy had concluded that Harris could be timid in tight games, so he used him less. Some reporters criticized this, contending that Harris could contribute if given more opportunity. McCarthy paid no heed to the reporters, of course. On this day in September, Harris came through, and with the added rest, Parnell won the next day.[37]

Now one game up on Cleveland, the Red Sox had to play one game in Cleveland before heading East. Before a crowd of 76,772 Indian fans, the Red Sox ran into a three-hitter from Bob Feller. There was nothing McCarthy could do that day. The Indians' victory put them in a tie with Boston. The Yankees lost the next day to Chicago. The Red Sox and the Yankees then returned to New York for a series. New York won the first game, as Detroit beat Cleveland. The result: for the first time in the history of major league baseball, outside of the meaningless first weeks of a season, there was a flat-footed three-way tie for first place. Everyone's record stood at 91 and 56. The American League office had no idea what could be done if the season ended that way. On September 27, the League did have three official coin flips to see who would get home field advantage for a playoff game should any pair of the three teams finish tied for first. Meanwhile, over in the National League, the Boston Braves clinched the pennant on September 26, so all baseball eyes were on the AL. The Yankees and Red Sox split the next two games. Cleveland won. Now the Indians were in first place.[38]

Boston had five more games to play, all at home. On September 28, they lost to Washington. The Yankees lost too, but Cleveland did not. New York and Boston were now two games out. The next day all three won. Cleveland had won 18 of their last 21 games. On September 30, with Cleveland idle, New York and Boston each won. The next day, October 1, Cleveland lost to Detroit, as New York and Boston had the day off. With their loss, Cleveland was one game up with two more games to play in Detroit. Meanwhile, New York and Boston also had two more games—with each other! "The Boston prayer right now," wrote the *Herald*, "is that the Tiger pitching will be at its peak against Cleveland and that their Denny Galehouse and Mickey Harris ... will be hot as firecrackers." Boston or New York had to sweep the other to have a chance. Splitting the games would eliminate both. With a sweep, either would need two Cleveland losses to win the pennant or one loss to cause a tie and a playoff. (The *Herald* did not know how prescient was their call for prayer for Galehouse.) The paper cartooned Joe McCarthy as a condemned man in a jail cell eating his last meal and saying to himself "Maybe I'll get a reprieve via Detroit." The Boston-based Gillette razor company purchased 100 television sets and placed them all over Boston Common for people to watch the Red Sox-Yankee games that weekend.[39]

In Boston's Saturday game with New York on October 2, Johnny Pesky singled in the bottom of the first inning. With one out, Ted Williams stepped up and hit a home run. Boston never looked back. They scored two more in the third and one in the fourth. Jack Kramer pitched a five-hitter. The Red Sox won 5-1. The Yankees were eliminated. Gerry Hern of the *Boston Post* pronounced, "Today ends an era in sport — the end of Yankee dominance of the American League." (They would win 14 of the next 16 pennants.) McCarthy said nothing about the Yankees, but he did have some words for the reporters. "Well it's the closest American League race in history, and I am glad to be in on it," he reflected. "But it does not surprise me that we're still in on it on the last day of the season. You fellows [reporters] gave up on us back there [in May] when we were 13 games behind. ... We were all counted out, but here we are back again with one game to go." This was an essential feature of McCarthy. So often, when speaking to reporters, he could not get himself to focus on anything other than the fact that he was speaking to reporters. They became his target rather than his go-between with the baseball fans. With players, the subject for him baseball, but with the press it was often the press itself. His outlook only magnified the already well-entrenched tendencies of some reporters to put themselves unduly at the center of their own foci. Here it was, the high point of the pennant race, yet the media remained an issue for him.[40]

Cleveland had beaten Detroit that Saturday, so the situation on Sunday was simple. Any result would give Cleveland the pennant except one: if Boston won and Cleveland lost. In that case, the season would end in a tie with a one-game playoff the next afternoon. Boston won. Their offense came through with five runs in the third inning and four in the sixth. Boston fans figured McCarthy would start either Ellis Kinder or Mickey Harris. Instead, McCarthy had turned to Joe Dobson. Dobson pitched well enough through four innings, and from there the relief was effective. The final score was 10-5, with Dom DiMaggio hitting a key home run. The Red Sox were jubilant. They went into the clubhouse clapping and shouting. This was the first time the Red Sox had ever beaten the Yankees at the end of the season with everything on the line. Once the team had all entered the clubhouse, McCarthy stood at the door and barked at the reporters trying to enter: "No press! When we get finished you can all come in." Many of the players may have appreciated the gesture, but the reporters were miffed. McCarthy was true to his word. The door opened to the reporters in five minutes. Players in the showers were singing, to the tune of "O Tannenbaum," "Who's better than his brother Joe, Dominic DiMaggio!" Reporters asked McCarthy to pose with Saturday's winner, Jack Kramer and with other players. "Never mind me," snapped McCarthy. "Take their picture. They played the game." To the team he spoke simply: "You're the gamest bunch I ever coached." During the postgame celebration, happiness turned to delirium when the news came in from Detroit. The Tigers had beaten the Indians. The season had ended in a tie, the first in the history of the American League. Nine years later Cleveland's Bob Feller reflected: "I'll tell you what kind of manager Joe McCarthy was. ... Back in 1948 we led the league in everything except stolen sweatshirts and yet he tied us on the last day of the season and forced a playoff." On the basis of the previous week's coin tosses, the Indians-Red Sox game was to be in Boston. Many fans who left Fenway Park after the Sunday Yankee game simply walked directly to line already forming at the ticket window and never went home that evening. With game tickets selling only at Fenway Park, Monday's Cleveland game still sold out in three hours.[41]

With the news arrived of Detroit's victory, the press in the Boston clubhouse converged on McCarthy asking him about what pitcher he was going to start in the next day's playoff against Cleveland. A *Boston Post* headline simply presumed: "Parnell to hurl playoff." The *Post* was hardly out in left field predicting a Parnell start for Monday. The young lefthander had won 15 games that year. He was 3-1 against Cleveland, with the one loss in June due to the "King Lear home run." He did have a bad outing against Cleveland on July 30. That day McCarthy had relieved him with one out in the first inning, with Denny Galehouse going the rest of the way and winning with a one-hitter. Parnell had last pitched against Washington on Thursday. He had thrown in the bullpen during the Yankee series, as had virtually everyone else. During the clubhouse celebration on Sunday, Parnell asked some reporters, "Did he name him yet?" He was obviously referring to McCarthy's naming of the playoff game starter, and even more obviously he wanted the ball. Reflecting the even keel on which he always kept his important managerial decisions, McCarthy begged off answering the reporters about the next day's starter: "I don't know who I'll pitch tomorrow," he honestly answered, elaborating: "I'm too excited; I'm too happy. I haven't had a chance to get my thoughts together. I had everyone in the bullpen today because we had to win this one. I've got to think about it. There's no sense in making up my mind [now] and then have to change it tomorrow." With an Irish twinkle he quipped: "Maybe I'll get the word tonight in a dream, or better still, just find some nice little man and rub his curly head for inspiration."[42]

McCarthy's words "have to change it tomorrow" are important, because his decision as to who would start the game against Cleveland became the stuff of legend in Boston, and it remains one of the most second-guessed decisions in the history of baseball. All sorts of stories cropped up recounting how and why McCarthy came the decision he made about the starting pitcher. Of significance is the fact that virtually all of the stories emerged many months later, during the following spring training and later, when reporters and players conferred with at least six-month old memories and with lots of time pondering over and embellishing upon what had happened.

Some stories have had it that McCarthy asked his catcher, Birdie Tebbetts, to see who wanted to pitch the game, with Tebbetts then allegedly telling McCarthy: "You won't believe this, but none of the guys wants to pitch," except for "the only one who really wants the ball." Other stories had it that the night before the game McCarthy told the one pitcher Tebbetts had named that he was going to start. Others have speculated that McCarthy, believing himself (or posturing that he believed himself) to be psychic, came up with the idea at 4:00 in the morning as he often did with regard to many important matters. The ideas about McCarthy's choice have taken on all sorts of wild proportions. The story that "none of the guys wants to pitch" certainly seems utterly preposterous. What major league pitcher worth his salt would not leap at the chance to pitch in such a situation?

The idea of McCarthy going through any sort of screening process also contrasts utterly with the solitary way he had made all key baseball decisions for the previous quarter century. Mel Parnell said bluntly: "McCarthy would never ask anybody if they wanted to pitch a ball game. He *told* you [emphasis his]." Parnell always said he wanted to pitch, adding that other pitchers on the team would have leapt at the opportunity as well. Years later, after McCarthy had passed away, Tebbetts refused to corroborate the story about him asking the pitchers: "There are only two people who know what happened. One of them is Joe McCarthy and he's dead, and I'm not going to say anything." Tebbetts claimed that McCarthy had asked him to talk to the pitchers, bragging that "Joe McCarthy and I were very close." The fact was that no player ever had that kind of closeness with McCarthy, not even Lou Gehrig, Bill Dickey, or Joe DiMaggio. The 4:00 A.M. idea obviously has no evidence. As for telling someone the night before, McCarthy had never done this; why would he want to endanger the sleep of someone he wanted well rested the next day?[43]

The press, fans, and players (on both sides) expected Mel Parnell would start. McCarthy may have been uneasy about using him with just three days' rest. He liked his pitchers to have more. But at this point in the season, he had few reserves. Parnell came to the park not just hoping to pitch, but expecting to. "I went to the ball-park," he remembered. "I looked under my cap, and sure enough, there was the ball." That was McCarthy's way of tapping a pitcher to start. There was a breeze that day at Fenway, however, one that blew out to left field wall, the notorious "Green Monster" that turns so many fly balls into doubles and home runs. In the history of the Red Sox, that left field wall has hurt many a left-handed pitcher. Indeed aside from Babe Ruth, perhaps the most effective left-handed pitcher the Red Sox have ever had was Mel Parnell, so good was he at spotting his pitches low and away from right-handed hitters. With the wind blowing out to left field, and with Cleveland's three best hitters—Lou Boudreau, Ken Keltner, and Joe Gordon—being right-handers, McCarthy began to think seriously in the hours before the game. Back in 1938, his Yankees had a key game in Fenway. The wind was blowing out to left field that day, and the Red Sox were starting a right hander, Jim Bagby. Rather than going with a string of lefties in the lineup, McCarthy benched George Selkirk and Tommy Henrich for righties Myril Hoag and Jake Powell. Powell hit a game-winning home run, and reporters were lavish in their praise of McCarthy's wiliness. The wind was up again this day, and McCarthy decided it best to make a switch.

In contrast to those who spoke of McCarthy deciding the day or the night before, the fact was that under McCarthy all the Boston pitchers were required to shag fly balls in the outfield during pre-game batting practice—all pitchers that is but the day's starter. He was not to run and risk tiring himself. As all the other pitchers were dutifully practicing, Parnell was in the locker room. McCarthy went to him: "Son, I've changed my mind. I'm going with the right-handed pitcher today. The elements are against the left-hander." Parnell obviously did not like the change. "Hell," he recalled, "I'd pitched a lot of games with the wind blowing out." Parnell thought McCarthy was going to turn to Jack Kramer. He was less rested, but he had won 18 games that year, the most on the club. As Parnell headed for the outfield, everyone asked him: "What are you doing out here?"[44]

The pitcher Joe McCarthy called in from the outfield was not Jack Kramer but Denny Galehouse. Galehouse's record at that point in the year was only 8–7. He had won some key games in June and July, including the eight and two thirds inning stint in relief of Parnell that beat the Indians on July 30. McCarthy certainly remembered that outing. He also remembered Galehouse's strong games for Cleveland and St. Louis in previous seasons against the Yankees. Perhaps even more, McCarthy remembered Galehouse winning down the stretch to help the Browns secure the pennant in 1944. McCarthy may have been thinking again about the effectiveness of Connie Mack's starting Howard Ehmke against his Cubs in the first game of the 1929 World Series. Whatever McCarthy's motive, Galehouse was the starter. Birdie Tebbetts had said that he had told McCarthy that Galehouse was the only starter that wanted to pitch. His story of going to McCarthy with that news has come down in several forms. One has it that when Tebbetts came to McCarthy with the news, McCarthy already had Galehouse's name written down. Yet another story says that McCarthy had written down "Kinder and Galehouse." Galehouse later gave some credence to Birdie Tebbetts' story about being asked the evening before. But here *he* was inconsistent. He said he knew the night before, but here he merely said that Tebbetts had told him he was "pretty sure." Elsewhere Galehouse said he only told Tebbetts of his willingness to pitch but did not know of McCarthy's choice until game time.

The obvious question, in regard to Galehouse's claim that he knew that he was going to start the night before, was why did he go out with the other pitchers to chase fly balls? The only logical answer here could be to deceive the opposition. Tebbetts supposedly told him to go along as though he was not starting. McCarthy may have wanted to conceal his choice from the Indians for as long as possible, but would he really risk tiring out a 36-year-old just to hide the fact of his starting role for a few extra minutes? Such a claim of trying to deceive the opposition puts the whole matter in the realm of conspiracy thinking. Hence, the evidence does not fully add up, and this shows just how devious the plot was. When advocates reach that level of argument and claim that the evidence to the contrary proves their point, there can be no resolution. Denials only confirm suspicions. From the newspaper accounts at the time of the game, the only indication of any jockeying by McCarthy with Galehouse came in the *Boston Globe*. Just hours after the game, the *Globe* reported that just before the game began, "the Red Sox Manager held a private meeting with Galehouse before the right-hander took his bat and ambled for a little hitting practice." That does indicate that if he was then informing Galehouse he was starting, McCarthy may have been trying to conceal things from Cleveland, but it certainly limits any claim of Galehouse or Tebbetts knowing anything the night before.

Parnell later said that "Denny turned white as a ghost" when McCarthy told him, indicating no prior knowledge, but how could Parnell have seen this if he was already in the outfield with people asking him "what are you doing out here?" On and on such muddled stories have raged. In the end: the wind was blowing out, and McCarthy changed his starting pitcher choice from Parnell to Galehouse. Noting all the tired arms on the staff, Billy Goodman concluded, "I think no matter who McCarthy started in that game he would have drawn criticism." Johnny Pesky put it simply: "McCarthy was just a fine man and knew baseball. He figured Galehouse had plenty of rest."[45]

The chief question remaining from the Galehouse controversy is why the many, sometimes bizarre, stories cropped up. A region filled with cultural elements that romanticize failure and look for supernatural signals of intervention (elements certainly present among other baseball people anyway), such a key situation as the 1948 playoff game will prompt endless gossip. What fully fueled all the controversies, of course, was the outcome of the game. In the first inning, Galehouse got the first two batters out. Then Lou Boudreau stepped up and hit a home run, and from that point Galehouse struggled. Perhaps a more important question than why he started Galehouse was why McCarthy chose to leave him in the game as long as he did. Galehouse was ineffective. He gave up three runs. In the fourth inning, he yielded to Ellis Kinder with runners on base and none out; two more Indians scored that inning.

The Red Sox, meanwhile, were also surprised by Cleveland's choice of pitcher. They expected Bob Feller or Bob Lemon. Instead they faced Gene Bearden. Bearden was a knuckleball specialist, having an excellent year, the best of his career, and on this day he was superb. Cleveland President Bill Veeck and General Manager Hank Greenberg said the Cleveland trainer was slipping Bearden shots of brandy between the early innings. Lemon and Feller were warming in the bullpen in most of the early innings, but they were not needed. Cleveland won in a thirteen-hit rout, 8–3. Bearden was a hero. Boston was glum.

That night a killing frost hit the city, literally too. The next morning, the *Boston Post* had no word about the game on page one. Their sports section started on page 21. Coverage of the Cleveland game did not come until page 38, after the hunting and fishing section. Thoughts about the playoff game were certainly not buried in the back pages of Red Sox fans' minds that Tuesday morning, and the thoughts have never left the backs of their minds. A few months later, one *Post* reporter predicted "long after McCarthy has retired from the game, he will still be asked how he happened to select Galehouse to pitch that day." This proved oh so true. McCarthy lived another twenty-nine years, and in his last days mentioned "I still hear from second guessers." Then he went on:

> [The] truth was I didn't have anybody else. My starters were all used up from getting us into the playoff. And Galehouse pitched a great game for me against the Indians the last time we were in Cleveland. [If I had started Parnell or Kinder] I would have been second-guessed for starting a tired pitcher. No matter what you do, you get second guessed.[46]

McCarthy's claim here does not accommodate the fact that he apparently intended to start Parnell but switched because of the wind. On this point, the stories have gone round and round for years. Baseball is the national game, as such it is also the nation's second-guessing game.

When the game was over, McCarthy asked the press for a short reprieve before they entered the clubhouse. This time they honored his request without complaint. McCarthy had the look of Frank Skeffington in *The Last Hurrah*, having just lost the mayoral election. He shrugged at the loss. "These things happen," he mused. "We played Cleveland even all year; they just got the odd game. That young fellow [Bearden] pitched well. I've been whipped before, and I can take it. I just feel sorry for the boys." There was little else to say to the press. To Mel Parnell he did say "I made a mistake. I'll just have to live with it." Reporters of the day did not overhear this. Boston fans were disconsolate. It was the strangest feeling, for while the Red Sox had just missed the pennant, the very next day the city hosted the opening of the World Series with the Braves facing Cleveland. Cleveland won the Series in six games.[47] For a self-styled Puritan, the Cleveland loss could certainly be cast as further punishment for the hubris of fancying an all–Boston World Series as an event that would somehow reinforce a sense of the city being the Hub of the universe. "The City Upon the Hill" could be a dangerously prideful concept to those who truly believed in its religious underpinnings.

When a team appears to run into a barrier of some inexplicable sort, analysts will go to any length and draw upon all resources of their cultures in attempts to explain the problem. After narrowly losing the World Series in 1946 and coming oh, so close in 1948, Red Sox fans began to think ever more of the supposed "Curse of the Bambino." New Englanders seemed to be living out a Greek tragedy. Trading Babe Ruth was the unpardonable sin which cursed the team and its fans. The Sox were a terrible team until the late 1930s. They emerged into a strong contender, but World War II depleted their great players. Then they bounced back into contention but could not win it all. There had to be a reason. In addition to "the curse," the notion of some sort of Puritan predestination also continued to resonate. Hoping for the Red Sox to win a championship was somehow akin to 17th-century New Englanders' hope for redemption through their prideful certainty of the goodness of such figures as Hawthorne's Dimmesdale. Now many reporters and saloon-goers fancied themselves as Roger Chillingworths. And if anyone was thought to be doing the work of the devil, folks could certainly look to the man who chose to start Denny Galehouse.

What James Joyce once called "the Irish romance of failure" was another perversely appealing means of accounting for another significant ethnicity in the city, and one of their own, Mr. Joseph Vincent McCarthy, now seemed quite the failure. More sinister-minded folks looked at McCarthy's history with the Yankees, implying that his heart was never fully with Boston. Here one writer even pointed to the fact that Galehouse was warming in the bullpen for many innings during the weekend games with the Yankees, implying that McCarthy's excessive fear of DiMaggio and the Yankees led him to tire Galehouse unduly before the game with Cleveland. McCarthy certainly respected the Yankees in every way, but to say he was "scared" of them to the point of hurting his managerial effectiveness is quite a stretch. He had certainly never shown any such tendencies in the previous 40 years he had been in baseball. Like any such theory that blends psychology and conspiracy, there is never any hard evidence unless the accused admits that the theory is right. Denials only confirm the suspicions that those who are not in accord just do not understand. After the loss to Cleveland, Red Sox fans would prove an ever more suspicious lot.[48]

While Bostonians were pondering the loss to Cleveland (some would say they have never stopped), McCarthy had a different way of dealing with it. He told reporters he felt lousy about it, and he did. Then he went into his office, closed the door, and tended to matters on his desk. After all the press and all the other players had left, Ted Williams still sat there. He felt so down he just could not shower and dress. Finally he did. Then, as he trudged alone through the training room, he recalled, "I heard this voice behind me. [The voice said:] 'Well, Ted, we fooled 'em, didn't we.' It was McCarthy." Williams turned and asked, "What do you mean, Joe?" McCarthy drew a slight smile and explained: "Well they said you and I couldn't get along, but we got along pretty good, didn't we?" Williams nodded with a bit of a grin, "Yea we did, Joe." Lou Gehrig had called McCarthy "that smart student of psychology," and here McCarthy was showing exactly what Gehrig meant. The game was over. McCarthy obviously knew what Williams was feeling. He needed to bring Williams around and knew just how to do it. It was a pretty smart ploy, reminding Ted Williams how wrong he and McCarthy had proven various members of the press to be. Twenty-one years later, Williams remembered, "How could I ever forget those kind words? They were the kindest words ever spoken to me in baseball."

Beyond defying the press, the Red Sox also had every reason to feel proud. The team had played magnificently. Williams himself had led the league in hitting again as well. His playing for such a manager was a great reward too. Williams had already known this. Now he knew it more than ever. "I'm lucky to be playing for such a man," Williams noted.

Ted Williams was indeed a difficult personality to many people in the game. He had had a most problematic childhood and compensated by developing an utter perfectionism with which he pressured and drove all around him, as well as himself. He could feel comfortable with nothing less. Anything but perfection would disconcert him, and his reactions could be incendiary. Never once did McCarthy set Williams off. He succeeded not by "handling" Williams (for that did not signify any striving for perfection and would itself be a great irritant) but by simply being so utterly proficient at every aspect of managing that Williams could not but feel himself in the best of hands. Williams was far too intelligent to be mollified by any manager who tried to cater to him especially. McCarthy's superbly honed, utterly competent, "all-business" ways gave Williams the balance in life that he had rarely experienced. Thus when McCarthy took the unusual step of reaching out to him at such an awful moment as befell them that Monday afternoon in October, Williams could only grasp the humanity of it. He later reflected, "Joe McCarthy was something special. I loved Joe McCarthy. I cried when he died."[49]

As the loss sunk in, a few in the press reflected positively. Considering the season, one *Herald* reporter declared the day after the game: It's "not the World Series, but it's a considerable accomplishment, and how McCarthy even did it with what he was forced to consider his pitching staff is a miracle to rank beside the [then ongoing] Berlin airlift." Elsewhere in Boston, the grousing was noticeable, and with it came panicky thoughts of heads rolling. Reporters had asked "Will they love him in September...?" They did love him in September. October was another matter, however. On October 5, the *Globe* reported McCarthy was "out as manager." Four days later, the *Post* reported the same thing. The *Post* also reported that Bobby Doerr and Johnny Pesky were to be traded. There were even rumors that Ted Williams was going elsewhere. McCarthy was soon home in Buffalo, and he made no comment on the trade stories. On October 14, the *Globe* announced that the Red Sox had released Del Baker as a coach hired Kiki Cuyler in his place. Baker was a holdover from Cronin's days as manager. Cuyler had played for McCarthy in Chicago. Only one man would make such a decision for the Red Sox. So much for the stories of McCarthy leaving, and so much for any felt need for house cleaning. Ted Williams already knew the truth anyway.[50]

35

A Marvelous Little Fella'

In the autumn of 1948 McCarthy was home at the farm outside Buffalo. Just before Thanksgiving, on November 24, he received a phone call. Hack Wilson had died. McCarthy had always had a soft spot in his heart for little Hack. He knew Wilson had behavior problems. He knew the problems as well as anyone in baseball, yet no one seemed able to bring out the greatness in Hack despite these problems better than Joe McCarthy. Wilson had been a good but not great ball player under John McGraw. Then came his terrific years with McCarthy and the Cubs. After McCarthy left the Cubs in 1930, Wilson never played as well again. For a year under the overly tight managerial reins of Rogers Hornsby, Wilson chafed. Hornsby suspended him for breaking training rules and fighting with a reporter. Eventually he traded Wilson to Brooklyn. Wilson came back with a decent season for the Dodgers in 1932, batting .297, but he fell off from there with one and a half mediocre years in Brooklyn, followed by a few games with the Phillies. Then he was out of the major leagues for good.

Although he was born in Ellwood City, Pennsylvania, Wilson had come to consider Martinsburg, West Virginia, his home. Martinsburg was where Wilson first played organized baseball. After the Phillies released him, Wilson returned there and tried managing the semi-professional team for whom he had first played, the Martinsburg Blue Sox. He also tried his hand at running a sporting goods store. With the Depression, and with his continued drinking and fighting, Wilson did not do terribly well at managing either the team or the store (or himself). No one in the major or minor leagues would hire him. Virtually broke, he went to Chicago to try to cash in on the name he still had there from his career with McCarthy and the Cubs. In 1938, a downtown nightclub hired him to be a master of ceremonies. One evening that October, during the Yankees-Cubs World Series, McCarthy took in his show. This job did not last, however; Wilson's drinking and generally delinquent behavior ended it.

When the war came, Wilson drifted to Baltimore and found work in a plant of the Glen L. Martin Company. The plant job ended in 1945. Then Wilson could only find odd jobs, mainly tending bar. None of these jobs lasted either. The Baltimore City Parks Department gave him work, mowing lawns, tending to foliage, and managing a public swimming pool in the city's Druid Hill Park. Wilson still never learned to manage his life or control his alcoholism. By 1948 the years of drinking had worn him down. He began to suffer fainting spells. In October he had to be hospitalized for head wounds due to a fall, the details of which were never fully known. He may have been in another fight. The head wounds were soon complicated by internal hemorrhages and pneumonia-like symptoms. With these complications he began to decline. In November, fearing the end and wanting to do something positive, Wilson spoke on a program called "We the People Radio." He advised young people to heed their elders and save their money, obviously hoping he could to steer a few away from the life he had led. Just a few weeks after the radio program, Hack Wilson died.

Upon Wilson's death, his second wife, Hazel, claimed his corpse and had it shipped back to Martinsburg. The office of the National League stepped in to make the arrangements and pay the expenses. After a simple funeral at Martinsburg's Rosedale Cemetery, McCarthy and some others from the Cub days pooled some money to commission a monument. It was completed in September, 1949. It stood thirty inches at its base and ten feet high. On it, beneath an insignia of a baseball and crossed bats, were the words: "One of baseball's immortals, Lewis R. (Hack) Wilson rests here."

That September, McCarthy and the Red Sox would be in a frenzied pennant race. Nonetheless, McCarthy took time out to come to the ceremony. The Sox were playing in Washington, and he, along with former Cub Kiki Cuyler, made a day trip out to Martinsburg. At the unveiling, with a small gathering that included Cuyler, Charlie Grimm, John Schulte, and players from the old Martinsburg team with whom Wilson had first played. McCarthy spoke: "To me, along with the sorrow I experience in thinking of Hack, comes the pleasing memory of happy days with him. This monument we unveil to his memory recalls great accomplishments in baseball. His record speaks for itself, and it will be long remembered by millions of youngsters and the men he played with." When he finished his speech, McCarthy gave a sigh. Then a twinkle crossed his eyes. He looked at the gathering, shook his head slightly, and added with a wry smile: "He was a marvelous little fella'."[1]

36

Good to the Last Game

And so the Red Sox would again convene and try to win that elusive championship to which they had come so close. No sooner did they gather in Sarasota than discussions began to whirl of the Cleveland game, and especially of McCarthy's choice of Denny Galehouse. Reserve catcher Matt Batts later claimed that the players "lost some respect for McCarthy [and] got kind of down on him because of it." No one else reflected that way, however, at the time or later. McCarthy would say nothing. That was last year. His focus was on 1949. With reporters he continued to be opaque. The main way Boston writers could get him to talk was again to drop the name of one of his old New York or Chicago players. About the only topics of conversation McCarthy would initiate concerned such recent Broadway musicals as *South Pacific*.[1]

McCarthy had specific issues in mind. Would the pitchers be healthy? What was best to do with Williams in 1949? In 1948 he had shifted Ted Williams a bit, having him hit more to left field and not pull the ball all the time. Williams had batted .369, but his home run production had dropped to 25, which was certainly low for him, his lowest playing year total since 1940. McCarthy also wondered why presumably intelligent ball players develop foot blisters as a result of wearing new spikes. "They will get a new glove and spend most of the winter punching it. ... You'd think," he sighed, "they'd start wearing their baseball shoes ... during the winter and break them in, but they won't." Another concern was at first base. The Red Sox had an allegedly great prospect named Walt Dropo. McCarthy had seen him in camp in 1948. The question was whether the big first baseman could hit a curve ball. The year before, McCarthy thought "not yet," and Dropo spent the season at the Sox farm team in Birmingham, Alabama. There he hit .359, so some thought Dropo was now ready for Boston. That raised the question of what then would be done with Billy Goodman.

Another issue concerned the "hole" the Red Sox had in right field. None of the right fielders of 1948 — Sam Mele, Stan Spence, Wally Moses — had been strong. McCarthy wanted more quality play there. That spring, one of Joe Cronin's scouts, Larry Woodall, had an opportunity to grab one promising outfielder. Across town from where the team's Birmingham Sox played was an eighteen-year old who reportedly did everything spectacularly both at bat and in the field. In the spring of 1949, Woodall was going to go watch the kid play, but it rained and he decided not to stay an extra day in Alabama to scout him. Besides, the kid was African American. He had been playing for the Negro League Birmingham "Black Sox," and it was highly questionable whether owner Tom Yawkey or others in the Red Sox management would go along with the idea of signing him. Yawkey was, through and through, an elite South Carolinian, and he did not appreciate such teams as Cleveland integrating the American League. Neither did the Texan Larry Woodall. With Yawkey's sensibilities at the helm, the Red Sox would indeed be the last American League team to integrate (with Elijah "Pumpsie" Green in 1959).

In 1945, Boston had rudely turned away from the possibility of hiring Jackie Robinson after a reporter, Wendell Smith, and the Boston City Council had pressured the Sox to give tryouts to three Negro Leaguers, one of whom was Robinson. Some in the City Council had made noises about withholding their vote, required annually by local law, to allow baseball on Sunday unless the three were given a tryout. The tryout went well, but the Red Sox were merely going through the motions and never seriously considered retaining Robinson or any other African American. In 1949 they passed on giving a look at this kid in Birmingham too. His name was Willie Mays. McCarthy never knew until later.[2]

In 1948, reporters had written how McCarthy seemed to intimidate some of the players. To a large extent, this may have been a projection from the media, but to the degree there may have been anything to that point in 1948, fears or anxieties about playing for the great McCarthy were not present in 1949, except, of course, among the rookies. (When McCarthy called any rookie's name, he came on a gallop and was usually taking his cap off by the time he was within 30 feet of the dugout.) In 1948, some players first considered it odd that McCarthy only held one practice per day. They quickly realized that, with the way McCarthy ran his practices, one session was plenty. In 1949 they were ready for the regimen. Everybody was moving; no one could loaf. They now had a sense of pride in the knowledge that they were experiencing the very best. With that, the veterans made the newcomers and the rookies "snap to." The Yankees had always felt and done much the same.[3]

Some reporters also expressed the sense that relations in the new year were better between McCarthy and the press. In 1948, the press corps was presented with a man they immediately contrasted with Joe Cronin. Almost anyone would have seemed aloof and distant compared to Cronin, and McCarthy's personality made the difference ever more stark. "He gave the impression of swaggering and considering everyone who was not connected with the Yankees as minor leaguers," reflected one reporter, adding "it could be that the reputation of the great McCarthy had something to do with that." In 1948, reporters were spending a lot of time reporting on their perceptions of McCarthy and the press as opposed to their perceptions of McCarthy as manager of a baseball team. In 1949, with some notable exceptions, reporters seemed more determined to be supportive and not go out of their way to find fault. Then or since, players did not perceive any change in McCarthy. His nature and age were such that major changes were highly unlikely. He was still "all business" and still one who steadfastly kept his own counsel. It just was not such a shock any more.[4]

Manifestations of "arrogance" came forth, but they tended to do so in ways that were less offensive to self-styled Boston insiders. With Williams, DiMaggio, Stephens, et. al., McCarthy's team was a gate attraction on the Florida exhibition circuit, especially among National League fans who would not see them during the regular season. The Philadelphia Phillies hosted the Red Sox one afternoon at their training site in Clearwater. They advertised the game heavily, and 2,000 turned out. McCarthy came, but without Birdie Tebbetts, Bobby Doerr, Vern Stephens, Dom DiMaggio, or Ted Williams. Phillies owner Robert Carpenter was furious. He yelled at McCarthy, and McCarthy bluntly told Carpenter that nobody tells him how to run his club. The Phillies beat the Sox remnants, 9–7, and Carpenter loudly and sarcastically announced to the crowd: "Due to the fact that the *mighty* Red Sox, led by their *great manager* Joe McCarthy, have not brought their stars, the Phillies will gladly refund admission[emphases his]." (Only twenty-five people asked for their money back.)

The story, merely of a Grapefruit League game, made the front page of the *Globe*, but it was not tinged by any outrage. Bostonians' sense of the situation was insular. If McCarthy was being arrogant and imperturbable, he was doing so in the interests of Boston, and the only victims were mere Philadelphians. While some were still gnashing their teeth over the outcome of the 1948 season, the sense was that, after coming so close, 1949 could be different. This yielded more than the usual baseball fan spring optimism among Bostonians. One writer, noting that fully fifteen of the team's losses in '48 were one-run affairs, mused with a certain Puritan pathos: such ill-fortune "could not happen two years in succession — or could it?"[5]

"This is the best Red Sox team since the great teams of the years before the First World War," wrote one veteran reporter. At the end of the pre-season schedule, McCarthy pronounced "the Red Sox are ready." Boston had come within an ace of hosting an "All-Hub" World Series. As opening day of the season approached, the hopes for such an October in '49 naturally bloomed, and with the quality of the two clubs, there was a certain degree of expectation too. As it turned out, the Braves would disappoint. They played sub-.500 ball. Their fine manager Billy Southworth left during the season, and they barely finished fourth. The Red Sox, meanwhile, would add another line in their infamous history of quests for a World Series championship. They would have a spectacular season with some wrenching ups and downs all the way to the very last day.[6]

Here and there in the early season, the optimism of the Sox fans popped up. After three wins in a row over Washington and Philadelphia in late April, the *Post* confidently declared "We're on the Way!" But hopes faded somewhat in early May. Walt Dropo had played well enough in spring training to earn a shot with the Red Sox. But by May 1, he was batting .151. McCarthy cut Dropo again and sent him back to the minors. "Who's on first?" was a popular comedy routine at the time, but it was no joke in Boston. McCarthy's "right fielders," Sam Mele, Tommy O'Brien, and Stan Spence were not performing, and McCarthy had still not forgiven Mele for his horseplay that injured Ted Williams in 1948. Respectively, Mele, O'Brien, and Spence were batting .192, .143, and .000. Veteran pitchers Joe Dobson, Mickey Harris, and Ellis Kinder had been ineffective. Catcher Birdie Tebbetts was ailing with a bad back and shoulder. Ted Williams was insisting on pull hitting to right field. All teams were "shifting" on him, and rather than adjusting and hitting to left, he was stubbornly continuing to pull the ball.

Personal matters were also intervening. Dom DiMaggio lost his father on May 3. McCarthy's brother, Maurice, also passed away that spring. McCarthy left the team for two days to attend the funeral in Philadelphia. Maurice was not a stepbrother from his mother's second marriage. He was the last member of the original family Joe had helped his mother struggle to support with his work in yarn mills back in the 1890s. This was not a loss McCarthy could simply take in stride. It was part of why he could honestly look at such a loss as the '48 playoff and from the heart simply say "that's baseball." Like many of his background, he knew what real sacrifice and loss were. Earle Combs managed in McCarthy's absence.[7]

In New York, Joe DiMaggio was injured. All spring, he was suffering from a painful bone spur on his heel that made it difficult for him to walk, much less play baseball. Doctors operated on it and told him that it would get better, but they could not predict when. DiMaggio would miss the Yankees' first 65 games. For the Yankees' new manager, Casey Stengel, the absence of DiMaggio and other player injuries placed added pressures on him. He was constantly juggling his lineup. Stengel proved to be quite the magician, holding the league lead and selecting the right lineup for each moment. Still, players and managers around the league kept figuring the Yankees were vulnerable. For the Red Sox, this was an added incentive, as the pennant seemed that much more theirs for the taking. When the early season did not go well, an added sense of unfulfillment hit them hard. On May 12, just as in May, '48, the Red Sox found themselves in seventh place. Exemplifying the year-old frustrations that were adding to the current woes, the same day the Red Sox found themselves in seventh place, they released Denny Galehouse. He had pitched two ineffective innings in '49; no team would even pay the paltry $10,000 to pick up his waiver rights.[8] Galehouse's release sharpened the questions so many had about McCarthy's judgment, about the '48 playoff, and about the current state of the team. Back came the same refrain: What's wrong with the Red Sox?

Amidst the second consecutive year of May troubles, some reporters complimented McCarthy for maintaining his composure. "Even a Job would find it difficult being patient," wrote one, but McCarthy was. A week earlier he had made an important move. It did not bear fruit immediately, but McCarthy was confident that it would. The Red Sox completed a deal with the St. Louis Browns, trading Stan Spence, who was playing poorly, and paying $100,000 for outfielder Al "Zeke" Zarilla. In 1948, Zarilla had hit .329 with St. Louis. He was not hitting as well in early 1949, but McCarthy believed in him. "Zarilla," McCarthy declared the day he traded for him, "is a hustling, lively type of ball player who can run, throw, and will be tickled to play in Boston." Zarilla certainly was delighted. Who would not be enthused about going from the Browns to the Red Sox in 1949? His slump continued in his first weeks with Boston, but he was McCarthy's right fielder.[9]

The Red Sox had been on the road in mid–May. They lost nine of 14 and were twelve games out of the lead. Then they came home and ran off ten victories in 13 games. By the end of the month, they had climbed from seventh to second place, with the Yankees in first. Back on the road in early June, they proceeded to lose nine of ten, 12 of 15. Amidst the new losing streak, McCarthy called a team meeting and, uncharacteristically, spoke loudly and harshly to the players. He rarely enforced discipline. He had always been able to demand his players be of such maturity that they did not need any collegiate-level oversight. This was one of the reasons reporters regularly felt snubbed; on the road managers usually held forth to reporters in the hotel lobby. McCarthy did not want to linger in the lobby and appear to be checking up on the hours his players were keeping. Now he felt he had to be more explicit with them, and he did not mince words. He never did.

McCarthy's remonstration made the front pages in Boston. Pitchers Mickey Harris, Ellis Kinder, and Tex Hughson continued to disappoint. Ted Williams' and Dom DiMaggio's hitting had dropped, and the others were not measuring up to expectations. As the American League trade deadline was approaching in mid–June, there were actually rumors that Williams would be traded. On June 17, after a loss to Cleveland, the team was under .500 and in sixth place. With great fanfare, Winston Churchill had just spoken at the Massachusetts Institute of Technology, and the Red Sox' poor showing prompted one scribe to remark, in Churchillian style, of the well-paid team: "Never have so many been paid so much for doing so little." (Thirteen Red Sox owned Cadillacs.) The intermittently effective and not terribly brilliant pitcher Tex Hughson declared of the Red Sox, "They're just snake bit." That was much too simple for McCarthy.[10]

Then, inexplicably, came yet another turnaround: 10 and 1 in mid/late June. McCarthy had made two changes. He traded Sam Mele to Washington. Mele had been batting only .196, and McCarthy never liked him. McCarthy also recalled pitcher Mickey McDermott from Louisville. Otherwise, McCarthy had held steadily to his lineup, and it was now producing for him. DiMaggio and Zarilla were hitting again. Zarilla had raised his average forty points. Ellis Kinder was starting to pitch effectively. He lost a game in relief on June 9, but he would not lose another through the rest of June, July, August, and September. As of June 27, the spurt of victories had left the Sox five games behind the first-place Yankees, and the Yankees were due into Boston the next day for three games. While the standings and the Red Sox' hot streak made for enough excitement, an announcement from the Yankees added immeasurably to the drama. Joe DiMaggio's heel was feeling better. He was going to play his first game of the season in Boston. Boston fans were usually gracious towards Joe DiMaggio. In the final two games of the 1948 season he had played gamely, although greatly weakened by pneumonia-like symptoms. He withdrew himself toward the end of the last game, and the Fenway Park fans cheered him.[11]

When DiMaggio appeared in Fenway on June 28, the fans again greeted him warmly. A small airplane circled Fenway with a banner that read "The Great DiMaggio." In the game young Mickey McDermott outpitched the Yankees' Allie Reynolds, but Joe DiMaggio made the difference with a timely home run. The Yankees were up 5–4 in the ninth, and Casey Stengel brought in Joe Page, who delighted himself shutting down McCarthy's team. The next day, Boston seemed to have exacted revenge as they were up 7–1. Then, boosted by Joe DiMaggio's two home runs, New York came back to win 9–7. The Boston fans still cheered DiMaggio, *and* some were actually booing Ted Williams, even though he went three for five that afternoon. In the third game, New York cruised to a 6–3 win. This time DiMaggio did not hit one or two home runs, he hit three. The *Post* headlined "Smelling Salts, Please!" Another writer surveyed the Red Sox' dressing room after the third loss and noted "only the playing of a funeral march was needed to complete the scene." Some fans and writers had held onto the suspicion that McCarthy held such fondness for and fear of his

Yankees, and for Joe DiMaggio, that it affected some of his decision-making. To this end, when some speculated that DiMaggio would not be able to run because of his heel, McCarthy took exception. "Just watch him," McCarthy warned. Some seized upon this as evidence that McCarthy was indeed rooting for DiMaggio and hurt his own team. More cogently, the simple point was that McCarthy was giving sound advice (and indeed DiMaggio could run).

Beyond the dubious questions about McCarthy's allegedly divided loyalties, in these games it was the reporters who were clacking out new chapters of the Joe DiMaggio legend and the Boston fans who were cheering him. McCarthy would obviously acknowledge his former player's greatness, but his managerial ways were not discernibly affected. If anything, those accusing McCarthy of fearing DiMaggio and the Yankees may have been projecting their very own fears and anxieties. In game two of the series, for example, when the Yankees overcame a 7–1 deficit, DiMaggio hit his first home run off Ellis Kinder. McCarthy relieved Kinder with Earl Johnson, who fared no better. Some argued that McCarthy should not have relieved Kinder, but was too fearful to leave him in, adding that Kinder's drinking may have also been a factor in McCarthy's choice to take him out. One problem here was that earlier in the season Kinder had tried to behave more soberly. Several times, Joe Cronin had tried to influence Kinder toward sobriety, with $50 at each inducement. Each time Kinder's pitching weakened, and to correct his ineffectiveness, McCarthy himself gave Kinder a $20 bill (some said Cronin gave him $100) and told him to go out and get drunk. The "remedy" worked, as a drunker Kinder was a terror the rest of the season (as well as for the rest of his life; he died of cirrhosis of the liver at age 55). That day in June, however, McCarthy took Kinder out, not because of alcohol but because of DiMaggio.[12]

No matter the fuzzy thinking in the accusations about McCarthy fearing his old team, the suspicion lingered. One writer angrily asserted "McCarthy spoke of Yankees with pride, thus implying the Sox could never take the place of the Yankees in his heart." The trouble was that no player on the Red Sox corroborated the suspicion. McCarthy did not want to talk about current plans in the works and always diverted nosy reporters with stories about the Yankees, just as he had told Cub stories to New York scribes, but members of the Boston press could not see past their own projections. As one wrote, "The old skipper could not seem to shake his conviction that the Yankees were somehow tougher than his boys. McCarthy's fear did his ball club no good. But in those days, it hovered in the air around him, along with a vaporous hint of Scotch." It is hard to argue with notions of hovering vapors, for if someone believes in ghosts it is impossible to dislodge the beliefs with mere facts and reason.[13]

After the dramatic Yankee series, the papers were making their usual death pronouncements. McCarthy was thinking about how to rebound. He did not come up with anything immediately. W.C. Fields' gravestone allegedly says "On the whole, I'd rather be in Philadelphia." The shell-shocked '49 Red Sox came to disagree, as after the three losses to DiMaggio they proceeded to lose three more in Philadelphia. Then they headed to New York where the Yankees swept them in a July 4 doubleheader. That made eight straight losses. Amidst the tailspin, the Red Sox seemed to be fighting nature as well as the Yankees. On July 4, it was dry and windy in New York, and in the Stadium infield dirt was flying everywhere. In the ninth inning the Red Sox had the bases loaded. Johnny Pesky was on third base. Al Zarilla lofted one to right field. Amidst the dust, Pesky could not see if the ball was caught or had landed for a hit. So he ran from his lead back to third, tagged up just in case, and then sprinted to the plate. He slid into home and the umpire signaled safe. Catcher Yogi Berra and the rest of the team screamed. As it turned out the Zarilla's drive had not been caught, and the umpire reversed his call since Pesky had indeed been forced out at home. The umpire could see the outfield no better than Pesky, but Pesky was the one who was out. Game, Yankees. With the eight straight losses, the pennant hopes really did look bleak. Boston was back below .500, in fifth place, twelve and one half games off the lead.[14]

While Mickey McDermott threw a four-hitter the next day and beat the Yankees, the victory seemed meaningless. After the doubleheader loss, Casey Stengel opined: "They'll never recover from this blow." Rumors were flying that McCarthy was going to be fired. Others were sure that he would simply be eased out after the season. McCarthy said not a word about the rumors. Throughout July, however, he always winked at one reporter, Arthur Sampson, whenever he saw him. Sampson would then ask of any news, and McCarthy would always smile and say: "Nothing, I'm still here." With the losses to the Yankees, McCarthy had said nothing remonstrative to Pesky. He could not get angry about a player being blinded by a dust storm. "Keep your chin up, Johnny," he reassured. "Anybody could have made that mistake. You're a great ballplayer in my book. You just keep satisfying your boss." It was great wording, for it not only encouraged Pesky to keep plugging, it also encouraged him to pay no heed to critics. Lou Gehrig had said it best — "that smart student of psychology." In New York after the doubleheader loss, McCarthy opened briefly to the press. "They think the race is all over. Well, we finish the season here October 1 and 2 ... very likely the pennant won't be decided until that last day." (It wouldn't be.)[15]

With McCarthy's calm leadership, the Red Sox started to win again, and the press was suddenly bugling something besides "Taps." Boston won 17 of their next 22 games, mostly on the road. Dom DiMaggio went on a hitting streak that extended to 34 games, including every game in July. DiMaggio, Williams, Pesky, Goodman, Tebbetts, and Stephens were all batting over .290. Bobby Doerr would soon reach that level too. McCarthy had him stop trying to pull outside pitches, and his average rose from there. There was no soft touch in the starting eight. By the end of July, the Yankees were still ahead by eight games, but everyone in the American League knew Boston was the team they least wanted to face that summer. If fans thought Boston was simply in a hot streak in mid and late July, they forgot who was managing them. McCarthy always endeavored to keep a team on an even keel to sustain winning rather than just go through a series of peaks and valleys.

His magic was working in August. From July 31 to August 22, now largely at home, the Red Sox won 20 of 23. The word "pennant" began to reappear in the papers. All eight players in the regular lineup were hitting .300. Afternoon games at Fenway were selling out. In a tight game with Washington, McCarthy called a steal of home. It worked for the go-ahead run in a victory that put Boston in second place. The manager "soon to be fired" had once again become "a genius." On August 27, Boston was one and one half games out of first place. The top two RBI and home run leaders in the American League were Vern Stephens and Ted Williams. The top two in batting were Dom DiMaggio and Ted Williams. The top two in hits were Dom DiMaggio and Johnny Pesky. Ellis Kinder was unhittable. Mel Parnell was almost as formidable, as was Mickey McDermott, to whom McCarthy several times referred as "Gomez." McDermott came down with back spasms in August, however, and doctors wanted to inject his back with Novocain. McDermott was willing, but McCarthy would not let the doctors do it. "Nobody wants to win a pennant more than I do," he affirmed, "but I am not going to take any chances with that boy's future or with Tom Yawkey's investment in him. No pennant is worth that." McCarthy's words did not injure morale; quite the contrary. Players knew ever more that he always had their best interests in mind.[16]

By September, the pennant race was simply a question of whether New York could hold on against the incredible onslaught from Boston, 42 and 15 since July 4. Ellis Kinder said he would pitch every other day if necessary. He had not lost since June 9. Between them, Kinder and Parnell pitched in 82 of the Red Sox games that year. The team was batting .281. The Yankees were a distant second at .269. Two games with the Yankees that week yielded a split. Joe Page happily slammed the door on them in the first game, striking out four of the last five Red Sox batters. The victory put the Yankees up by two and one half games. Another loss would be disastrous. Ellis Kinder pitched the next day. He gave up but one hit through six innings. In the seventh he gave up two walks and a single, scoring a run. McCarthy called for two pitchers to warm up in the bullpen. He called time and stepped out to the mound himself, something he rarely did. "What's the matter, Ellis. You in trouble?" he asked. Kinder replied: "No I'm cold, that's all. The wind's blowing in on my back. Let me stay in. I'll get this guy out." McCarthy nodded: "OK, you've got it." Kinder then walked Gene Woodling to load the bases, but he struck out the next batter and went the distance from there.

The Red Sox again pulled to a game and a half behind the Yanks. An easy victory came the next day in Philadelphia, while the Yankees split a doubleheader with Washington. After the loss to Boston, Connie Mack called his team together and gave them a little talk, gently humiliating some and nudging others as only he could. The A's swept a doubleheader from Boston the next day, pushing the Yankee lead back up to three. Connie Mack seemed always to save his managerial best for Joe McCarthy, and McCarthy would not have wanted it any other way. Newspapers again wrote of the end of Boston's pennant chances. This was something McCarthy did want another way. He knew there was still time.[17]

Boston proceeded to win its next seven games, but their efforts gained them all of one game on New York. Two games out on September 24, Boston had New York coming to town for two games. In the first game, Kinder came through again. His opponent, Eddie Lopat, was the first opposing left-hander to complete a game against the Red Sox at Fenway all year. But Williams hit his 42nd home run, and Kinder threw a shutout. The margin was now one game. Mel Parnell pitched a four-hitter the next day, and the race was tied. In the game, Al Zarilla threw home as Tommy Henrich was trying to score. Catcher Birdie Tebbetts held his hand up, signaling Henrich "relax, no play at the plate." Then he caught Zarilla's throw, and Henrich was out. McCarthy enjoyed the play and was chortling in his office afterward when an assistant reminded him he had to get to South Station. He had to catch a train for the next day's game, in New York. En route to Yankee Stadium, McCarthy ordered Yankee Pot Roast for the team dinner.

The Yankee game was tense. The Yanks were up by three runs in the seventh. Al Zarilla recalled how McCarthy kept saying, "Hang in there. We'll get 'em. Keep pluggin'." On the surface, the words sound like mere cliches, but Zarilla said that coming from McCarthy they meant a lot. They helped the team's confidence. "Nobody got panicky." (Paranoid rumors about McCarthy's divided loyalties certainly cannot be reconciled with such facts.) Johnny Pesky meant the difference in the game with aggressive base running. People had blamed Pesky for his running lapse amidst the dust storm of July 4. This time there was no swirling dust, and Pesky slid under catcher Ralph Houk on a McCarthy-called squeeze play to take the lead. The Yankees screamed at the plate umpire again, as they had on July 4. But this time the umpire, Bill Grieve, did not change his call. (Stengel and Houk both shoved Grieve and another Yankee, Cliff Mapes, accused him of accepting a bribe. The league fined each of them $500.) Pesky's was the winning run. The Red Sox had won their tenth straight, and for the first time in the 1949 season, the Boston Red Sox were in first place.[18]

The Yankees and Boston were slated for two more games the next weekend, October 1 and 2. Before then, Boston had to play three games in Washington while New York had to play Philadelphia. It was as the team headed for Washington that McCarthy and Kiki Cuyler traveled out to Martinsburg, West Virginia, to dedicate a memorial monument to Hack Wilson. Even at such a juncture in the '49 season, McCarthy would never miss such an occasion. Hack's memory was too important. Back in Washington, Boston won, as New York beat the A's.

The next day Boston lost a 2–1 heartbreaker to the Senators. McCarthy had started a 19-year-old, Chuck Stobbs, who pitched a shutout for eight innings. The Red Sox only scored one run, however. In the ninth, Stobbs gave up the tying run. McCarthy immediately relieved him. Given the pennant situation, all his pitchers were in the bullpen, and he brought in Ellis Kinder. The first batter he faced singled, putting runners on first and third. With a left-hander coming up, McCarthy relieved Kinder with the left-hander Mel Parnell. Washington countered by trying a steal of home on Parnell. The surprise did not work as planned. Parnell reacted but, in effect, too quickly, as the runner never made it close to home. He was so short of the plate that he was able to stop and try to go back to third. Caught in a rundown, he was tagged out. Amidst the rundown, Johnny Pesky was drawn off third, however, and no one else covered the base. This allowed the other Washington runner to advance to third. The play may have left Parnell a bit tired, excited, or both. In any case, his next pitch was wild. It rolled to the screen, and the winning run scored from third base. It was a horrible way to lose. That same day, the Yankees beat Philadelphia, tying the league race again. The next afternoon Washington's pitching staff yielded fourteen walks, allowing the Red Sox to get away with a weakly played 11–9 win. The win was as lucky as the previous day's 2–1 loss had been unlucky. Later in the day, the big news came: the A's had beaten the Yankees 4–1. Now the Red Sox were again a game up, and they headed for New York for the last two games, needing to win only one to clinch the pennant.[19]

It was hard for the Red Sox not to feel a little cocky about the upcoming series. McCarthy did not mind such attitudes anyway. Their record since July 4 was an amazing 61 and 20. They had won better than three of every four games they played. Few teams had ever played that well for a half season, let alone do so with all the pressure Boston had fighting the Yankees. Now they merely had to win one out of two. On the surface that did not seem too hard. All the pressure seemed to be on the Yankees, although they were playing at home. Harold Kaese of the *Globe* ruminated: "Unless some heartless tragedian gets his slimy paws on the script, the 1949 baseball season is about to have its fairy tale ending for Boston baseball fans." Still, the Sox had not hit well in their last two outings in Washington.[20]

Before the Saturday game, the Yankees held a ceremony honoring Joe DiMaggio, then weak with a viral infection. In his "thank you" address, DiMaggio went out of his way to praise his former manager McCarthy. McCarthy came out to shake DiMaggio's hand. A few Boston writers scowled. Then it was back to business. In the game, McCarthy started Mel Parnell, who had won 25 games already. Casey Stengel countered with Allie Reynolds. Boston jumped on Reynolds for four runs. Stengel relieved him with Joe Page. He had been relying on Page all year; this was his 59th appearance of the season. Stengel asked him how long he could go. "All the way," Page smiled, "this is my long one." Boston had four runs, but from there Page allowed them but one harmless hit. He seemed always able to rise to the occasion against McCarthy. Boston was up 4–2 in the fifth inning, but Parnell weakened from there, and McCarthy put in Joe Dobson. Dobson pitched nearly as well as Page, allowing just four hits after the fifth inning, but one of the hits was a home run in the eighth inning by Johnny Lindell. "The whole thing is Joe McCarthy's fault," Lindell chortled. "In 1942, I came up from Newark, and Joe switched me from pitcher to outfield." Lindell's home run put New York ahead, and Boston could do nothing against Page. McCarthy had few extra hitters to insert in such situations. His starting eight were clearly his best, and if they were stymied, there were few offensive options. His pitching situation was similar, as it had been in 1948. In Kinder and Parnell, he had two great starters in '49, but the ranks grew thin from there. The game was lost. The race was again tied. At this point, at least, McCarthy had Kinder for the next day. He had not lost since June.[21]

There could be no tie this season in the American League. The last game of the season would decide it. McCarthy made no speech to the team. At this point any sort of "rah-rah" would have been ridiculous, especially with such veterans as McCarthy had. Ellis Kinder made the statement that if the Red Sox could score three runs, he would win the game. Kinder's confidence was no mere bluster: he had been pitching sensationally for months, and he was supremely confident, confident enough to have been out drinking all Saturday night. This was nothing unusual. Kinder had shown he could not pitch well when he tried to go on the wagon, and McCarthy gave him money to go out and get drunk. Kinder pitched better, so he kept drinking. Having lost none since June, he was not about to change his regimen the night before the final Yankee game. McCarthy would not have wanted him to. Vern Stephens and Al Zarilla persuaded a reporter friend, Arthur Richman of the *New York Mirror,* to take Kinder out the night before the game. Kinder got back to the Red Sox hotel at 4:00 A.M., quite drunk and with a lady.[22]

The next day, Kinder was out there throwing hard. In the Yankee half of the first inning, he yielded a hit to Phil Rizzuto. Some said it was a hard hit that got by Pesky and Williams. Others said Williams lost it in the sun. Still others believed Williams could have held it to a single. No error was charged. Rizzuto ended up standing on third base. The next batter, Tommy Henrich, choked up on the bat and touched Kinder for a little grounder that enabled Rizzuto to score. McCarthy had ordered the infield back, conceding the run. The choice seemed a good one in that Kinder gave nothing from there. "We could never hit him," recalled New York's Jerry Coleman, "and he showed no sign of tiring." Stengel's pitcher Vic Raschi proved equally tough that day, however. In seven innings, the Red Sox had gotten only one legitimate hit, a single to center by Al Zarilla. Otherwise they chalked up but a roller past Raschi which Rizzuto could not handle. (Ted Williams walked twice but had no hits.) Into the eighth inning, the Yankees' one run in the first stood as the game's sole tally.

In the Boston half of the eighth, Tebbetts led off. Tebbetts was playing in his 122nd game at catcher, a very high number for any catcher, let alone for a 36-year-old. He was quite worn down, but McCarthy could certainly not spare him this day. He grounded out. Due up next was Ellis Kinder. Kinder thought himself a good hitter. One Boston writer, Al Hirshberg, always contended that Kinder was a good hitter, but that season he had but 12 hits, and was batting a mere .130. He definitely wanted to stay in the game, but McCarthy made his move. McCarthy believed that a manager should always make the percentage move. The situation called for a pinch hitter, and he sent up a young player named Tom Wright who had been up with the team from Louisville for only a few weeks and had been at bat but three times. The Yankees had no "book" on him. Given the way Kinder was pitching, Jerry Coleman remembered, "we gave full approval to McCarthy's decision." Wright drew a walk, so the move did not seem too bad. Raschi certainly would not have walked Kinder. This gave the Red Sox a man on with one out and the top of the order coming up, not a bad situation for a rally. The next man up, Dom DiMaggio, hit the ball hard but right into a double play. DiMaggio was so fast that he rarely hit into double plays, but here he did, and the inning was over.[23]

McCarthy now had to turn to his very tired pitching staff. He brought in Parnell, even though he had pitched over four innings the day before. Parnell had little in reserve. The Yankees jumped on him. Tommy Henrich homered, and the game seemed over. Yogi Berra singled, and McCarthy then pulled Parnell. Tex Hughson came in. He had not pitched in many weeks and continued to believe that McCarthy had it "in" for him. Hughson believed he could have held New York had McCarthy first turned to him rather than to Parnell. Hughson got Joe DiMaggio to hit into a double play. But then Lindell singled; Hank Bauer ran for him. Billy Johnson singled to left. Ted Williams juggled the ball, and Bauer ended up safe at third. Mapes was walked, loading the bases. Jerry Coleman then hit what looked like an easy pop to short right field. The ball, however, fell in just between Bobby Doerr and a diving Al Zarilla, who was playing deep. All three Yankee runners scored. That made four runs for the Yankees that inning, leaving the Red Sox facing a five-run deficit going into the ninth.

So many times that season, when the Red Sox hit a bump, people counted them out. Now all seemed truly lost, but McCarthy's teams did not quit. In the top of the ninth, Pesky was first up, and he fouled out. The Yankee crowd started to stir and cheer. But then Williams walked, Vern Stephens singled, and Bobby Doerr hit a blast over Joe DiMaggio's head that rolled into deep center field. Williams and Stephens scored. (The ailing DiMaggio then removed himself from the game.) Al Zarilla flied to right center, and Billy Goodman singled, scoring Doerr. Birdie Tebbetts was then up with a man on and Boston down 5–3. Page and Reynolds were warming in the bullpen, but Stengel stayed with Raschi. Tebbetts hit a fly down the first base line that stayed in play. From first base Tommy Henrich ran back and caught it easily, and the Red Sox lost the pennant. Ellis Kinder had said that if the Red Sox scored three runs, he would win the game.[24]

When the game was over, McCarthy went to the Yankees clubhouse to con-gratulate Casey Stengel. "McCarthy was graceful," Ted Williams remembered, "He had to be in terrible pain, but he went over to the Yankee locker room." When McCarthy arrived he told Stengel: "You did a great job all summer." "Thanks Joe," Stengel replied, "I couldn't've beaten a better man. Everything Joe DiMaggio said about you yesterday goes for me too. Men like you taught me all I know about this game, and if you'd won we'd all've been rooting for you in the Series. And Joe," Casey added, "you've won so many that it was nice of you to let us have this one." Several Yankees honestly told McCarthy they were sorry he didn't win this one. Casey later admitted: "If the tables had been reversed, I doubt if I could have done that. That took a big man." So much for *Colliers'* claim that McCarthy was a poor loser. Mean-while, of course, McCarthy's good sportsmanship here served those who wanted to believe he harbored divided loyalties. Such a mentality would have held the New York Giants suspect for sending Lou Gehrig a gift on July 4, 1939.[25]

No team ever lost two pennants in a row in such aching ways as the Red Sox did in 1948 and 1949. Up in Lawrence, Massachusetts, some townspeople held a mock funeral, complete with a casket marked "Red Sox." Some 5000 fans had lined up at Fenway Park to buy World Series tickets. All went home grumbling, many of them about McCarthy's decision to lift Ellis Kinder for a pinch hitter. There would be no end to the analyses as to what had gone wrong. There was one simple notion: that when there are equally strong teams in the league, as the Sox faced with the likes of New York and Cleveland, the only legitimate hope is to be in the thick of the race, make the percentage moves, and hope the breaks fall your way. The notion that the Red Sox just did not get the necessary breaks was, for Bostonians, too easy an expla-nation; it was insufficiently brooding. The Irish romance of failure and Puritan notions of predestination and the pitfalls of pride all augured for more wrenching accounts. The lousy teams of the '20s and '30s now assumed a place of less conse-quence in the team's legacy. The suffering of that generation was nothing compared to what happened in 1948 and 1949. "The Curse of the Bambino" earned even greater credence. The fates were now truly conspiring to tantalize. Speculations of a more practical sort also flew that the team had developed and truncated itself in too much regard for the peculiarities of Fenway Park. (In '49, Boston was spectacular at home, 61 and 16, but only 35 and 42 on the road.) Ted Williams received more than his share of barbs for not hitting to left field, for taking too many walks, and for not fielding well enough.

Meanwhile, Manager McCarthy was anything but immune. Like barroom philosophers, reporters penned such prattle as the notion that under McCarthy the Sox "were entirely lacking in that needed determination." (There was never any elaboration as to what the deuce that meant, and never any corroboration from any player.) The most paranoid raised again the views that McCarthy still harbored loyalties to the Yankees. In the first Yankee game, why did he relieve Parnell so quickly and put in the ineffective Joe Dobson? Was McCarthy's "fear" of the Yankees causing his undue haste? The critical choice to hit for Kinder received the most inspection and took on the most sinister dimensions. Again, McCarthy was supposedly motivated by his excessive fear of the Yankees. Or he secretly favored them. Or he was a manager unable to win in a close race. He won many times by wide margins with the Cubs and Yankees, but (and here the "push button" label resonated among many barroom conversations) it now seemed McCarthy could not win the close ones—'49, '48, '44, '40, '33, '30, '13(Wilkes-Barre). Some people felt they had discovered a pattern. Any defenders could retort how he managed the teams into contention, but that he, like any manager, can't control the quirks of the game. Back and forth the arguments went. The only hard fact anyone could safely deduce from it all was something that became a journalistic refrain that was almost as common around Boston as "What's wrong with the Red Sox?": "No one's neutral about McCarthy."[26]

As the team returned to Boston, Ellis Kinder drank a few more beers and yelled about being taken out in the eighth inning. "Goddammit, if that old man McCarthy had let me stay in," Kinder growled to a reporter, "we would'a won it all." Ted Williams said the train ride back to Boston felt even longer than the ride all the way back from St. Louis after losing the 1946 World Series. Then and since, Boston fans discussed McCarthy's Kinder decision hour upon hour. It became almost as infamous a part of Red Sox lore as "Denny Galehouse." As late as 1973, when the American League instituted the "designated hitter" rule, Harold Kaese of the *Boston Globe* wrote that "the new rule is 24 years too late for Joe McCarthy." Few Red Sox fans needed any clarification there. In '49, everyone had an opinion about the Kinder call. Given the Sox rally of the ninth inning, some held Kinder would have won the game. Yogi Berra disputed that point. Kinder left the game trailing 1–0, and, Yogi declared: "If Raschi had had to win one to nothin', he would'a won one to nothin'."

Besides Kinder himself, Matt Batts was the most critical of McCarthy: "We were some kind of hot about him pulling him [Kinder] out. We couldn't understand it. Two outs. Why?" Of course, there was only one out. Zarilla, Doerr, and Tebbetts defended McCarthy's choice. Tebbetts was firm: "Why he had to. You're scoreless in the eighth; you're one run behind, one out and the pitcher's up. You've got to use a pinch hitter." Doerr added: "One thing McCarthy was sharp at — knowing the situation of pulling pitchers. He didn't miss much on that." Newsmen reported that all the Yankees believed McCarthy had made a wise move, but of course they were all glad to see Kinder out of the game. One *Globe* writer used the press's bad relations with McCarthy to mount a defense of McCarthy's decision: "Considering McCarthy's lack of sympathy for baseball writers, I don't know why I should be defending him, but I think he made the right move — the percentage move." Back in 1933 McCarthy had written: "Always play the percentages."[27]

The loss to the Yankees propelled many Bostonians into perpetual baseball despair. When the team arrived back at South Station, however, 1000 people and a six-piece band were there to greet them. Signs said "We Love You" and "You're Still Our Team." The players stayed and mingled with the people. Al Zarilla, having hurt his leg in the game, was limping. Several hundred fans wanted to assist him. Some even wanted to carry him. Ellis Kinder was greeted with big cheers. Ted Williams was so mobbed he could not reach his wife. They had to leave in separate cabs. The papers noted, "The cheer for Joe McCarthy surpassed all others." The turnout visibly affected McCarthy. A reporter noted "a genuine grin on his face and just as genuine tears in his eyes." He shook many hands. Tom Yawkey was there, of course. He gave McCarthy a friendly pat and simply said "Tough luck Joe." Some reporters had cynically expected McCarthy to leave New York and go directly to Buffalo, but McCarthy had said "I'll be on the train with the boys."

For the reporters who were surprised, it showed how little they understood him. In the past years, when McCarthy's Yankees won a World Series on the road, the team would disperse immediately. This was a different situation, and McCarthy grasped it as well as anyone. "We never had a reception like this when I was with the Yankees," he noted. "How 'bout next year?" someone asked. "If you want me back," McCarthy responded, "you write it." Reporting McCarthy's words, one Boston correspondent then noted in his next day's article: "This is to write it."[28]

Joe Cronin and Tom Yawkey told McCarthy that they were completely satisfied with his work and that he was welcome to come back as manager. The matter was entirely in his hands. McCarthy said he would make up his mind, but first he would head to his farm. Once there, he said he would "possibly" be back, adding, "right now, I'm trying to relax." Then he turned to his land and said, "Say, isn't this the most beautiful weather. It's great to be home." Joe relaxed, and in 1950 he was back.[29]

37

It's Later Than You Think

You certainly could not blame Joe McCarthy. He got us right to the brink, to the very last day, two years in a row. One victory would have meant the pennant both times. I think it proves how much he got out of the club.
— Ted Williams[1]

It should be no surprise that baseball fans come with the same array of psychological coping mechanisms as does any large cross section of people. During the off-season after 1949, many Boston baseball fans got over the utter shock of having missed two consecutive pennants by the narrowest possible margins. Meanwhile, others utterly engrossed themselves in it. By the time the Red Sox were ready to reconvene in Sarasota in March of 1950, the questions of 1948 and 1949 were still reverberating, so the press was still asking some of the same old questions. Meanwhile, several other things had happened to McCarthy and the Red Sox. On February 11, McCarthy's third base coach and former Cub, Kiki Cuyler, died of a heart attack. As with the death of his brother Maurice in April, this was the kind of loss that truly meant something to Joe McCarthy. Along with Hack Wilson, Kiki was one of McCarthy's first great players. Now both had died, scarcely over a year apart from one another.[2]

Another development involved a trade, fallout from which prompted more gnashing of teeth in regard to the two pennants so narrowly lost. Just before the convening of training camp, the Red Sox traded pitcher Jack Kramer to the New York Giants. They had originally dealt Tex Hughson, but Hughson then chose to retire, so the Red Sox traded Kramer as a replacement. Hughson always believed that McCarthy had underutilized him, and he held a grudge for a long time. Kramer was not happy about the deal and said so. His open complaints fed those reporters and fans who were obsessively preoccupied with the '48 and '49 failures. Given that a change of any single game could have conceivably altered the outcome of either season, such preoccupations were easily jogged. In regard to the trade, Kramer claimed he had been "railroaded out of the American League," because he had "told off Joe McCarthy a couple of times last season," justifying his impertinence by saying "he had it coming to him." Kramer went on, saying McCarthy held a personal grudge against him and was "just plain vindictive. When you're winning he's all for you," Kramer noted, but "when you're not going so well, he avoids you like you['ve] got a disease."[3]

Kramer alleged one problem with the Red Sox involved McCarthy's removal of their long-time trainer Win Green. Green had been with the Red Sox since the days of Tris Speaker. He was an icon, and when Kramer raised his removal as a significant matter, some seized upon it as an excuse for further rumination as to how this had "made the difference" in the two lost pennants. Here one reporter nostalgically described how Green's role with the Sox encompassed so much beyond merely that of trainer. Green had been "a friend, a personal counselor, and 'one of the gang.'" At the outset of the '48 season, one writer had mentioned "what the Red Sox will miss most is Win Green's smile." The implication was that McCarthy had then taken some of the heart out of the Sox, hence they lost. While they all certainly liked Green, other Red Sox players did not corroborate the sense of importance Kramer and some writers were attaching to his dismissal.

Some players had been willing to confide in Green, even about problems they felt with the Red Sox management. Everyone knew that was not a good thing to do with McCarthy's man, Eddie Froelich. Some felt this rendered the Sox less loose; others said it made them be more mature. Kramer was not always known for maturity. He did have complaints about Froelich and McCarthy. While Boston's best pitcher in 1948 (18 wins), Kramer came down with a sore arm in 1949, and his record fell to a mere 6 and 8. He said Froelich had not helped him, implying that Green probably could have. He went on, claiming that McCarthy was a manager who played favorites with his "fair-haired boys," namely DiMaggio, Pesky, Williams, Stephens, Goodman, Doerr, Tebbetts, and Zarilla. Here, of course, Kramer had named McCarthy's starting lineup. Naturally, McCarthy "favored" them.

In regard to his trade to the Giants, Kramer claimed that the Yankees had offered several players for him, but that McCarthy had nixed the deal because he wanted him out of the league. Both McCarthy and Cronin denied that, Cronin adding that he had tried to trade Kramer to several American League teams, with none showing interest, and that every American League team elected to pass Kramer on waivers. Boston players also took exception to Kramer. Several said he "dogged it" during the '49 season. One reporter added that Kramer's impressive 18 and 5 record in 1948 had been a bit lucky, as his ERA was 4.35, one of the highest among the regular pitchers on the team.[4]

Some teammates had described Kramer as a "grand opera," and his reaction to being traded certainly reinforced this characterization. His was an example of the very personality-type among the fans and press that was dramatically seeking scapegoats for the outcomes of the '48 and '49 seasons. Amidst the back and forth over the issues in the press, Kramer undercut much of his credibility when he blurted: "All you Boston writers are on McCarthy's side." No one could possibly buy Kramer on that point. But the whole brouhaha was an example of how any issue at that time would rekindle the anger over the loss of the pennants, with much of the anger focusing on McCarthy's management. One reporter was hardly helpful (and likely did not want to be) when he closed the book on the Kramer controversy by concluding: "McCarthy may have muffed two pennants for the Sox … but hardly because of his handling of Kramer."

Not all writers were as obsessive about the past two seasons as some of the fans, but even the reporters who did not fully share in the city's baseball anger were usually smart enough to write about what they knew many people were eager to read. Like Southerners always wanting to read about the Civil War, people will always be drawn to traumatic episodes in their collective, and personal, histories. And in a nation just then reacting hysterically to what appeared to be less than 100 percent success in a Cold War with the Soviet Union, scapegoating was rampant, infecting even fundamentally trivial matters like sports. Insular Bostonians' variation on these themes simply recast *their* Joe McCarthy as a witch rather than a witch hunter. To many Americans, Mao Ze Dong and his cohorts did not take over his country; instead "We lost China," and to many Bostonians, Casey Stengel and the Yankees did not win the pennant; McCarthy and the Sox lost it.

While some Boston reporters had sensed a slight warming of relations between McCarthy and the press in early '49, as training camp was about to open in 1950, many sensed the opposite. The pressures on the press were growing, as television was eating away their popularity. The *Boston Transcript* had folded, and reporters could not but fear that others were soon to follow. So their willingness to go after any sports figure would be boundless if there was a story to be written that could boost circulation. With Kramer gone, McCarthy added a new catcher to the squad to back up Tebbetts, something that was sorely needed in 1949. He landed Buddy Rosar from Philadelphia in exchange for Billy Hitchcock. (Hitchcock did not react like Kramer; he just moved on to Philadelphia.) Rosar was the catcher who went AWOL from the Yankees in 1942 to take a civil service examination in hopes of becoming a Buffalo policeman and avoid military service. He played the '49 season for McCarthy. If Kramer had been right about McCarthy holding grudges, Buddy Rosar would never have been given a chance with the Red Sox.[5]

McCarthy's aloof, solitary ways had always made him a target for reporters, many of whom confusedly considered their getting a story as much a Constitutional matter as their right to write a story. Public figures' rights not to speak were not respected, any more than were the rights of some accused of political crimes given any respect when they asserted their right to remain silent. Boston's Joe McCarthy never "took the Fifth," he just remained his reticent self. One *Boston Herald* writer complained that very season how he had seen

> Casey Stengel, often naked as a jailbird ... [with] a can of beer in one hand and gesticulating with the other, while answering questions, delivering opinions, and acting out anecdotes. [Meanwhile with McCarthy,] I sat one day in the Red Sox clubhouse with some fifteen other scribes for fourteen minutes on my watch, and nobody said a thing but "How've you been?" and "Lend me a match." Mr. McCarthy sat facing us like a House Un-American Activities witness standing on his constitutional rights ... [One would] have thought the whole scene had been painted.

McCarthy's new rival, Casey Stengel, had shown a better way to handle reporters—talk a blue streak at them, sometimes to the point of nonsensicality. Casey's humorous ways deflected all other motives of inquiry. He made himself the issue, and it gave the media a story that sold copies. Everyone was then happy, particularly with Yankees winning. McCarthy could never behave like Casey. Baseball, not McCarthy, was always the issue to him. This was one of several reasons why Joe DiMaggio never much liked Casey Stengel. Certainly, other factors added to this situation. DiMaggio's career was in decline at this point, and Casey had taken him out of the cleanup spot, but even before then DiMaggio often rolled his eyes and shook his head at the way Stengel pontificated and circumlocuted to reporters. He preferred his former manager's silent ways. But with the ever-expanding and intrusive behavior of the media, the predilections of McCarthy and Joe DiMaggio were decreasingly tenable, ever more so in the political/ baseball culture of Boston which had among all major metropolitan areas, the greatest number of papers and reporters in proportion to its population.

Beyond the growing quantity of media, the nature of many of the individuals in the Boston press added to the tension. While he was certainly one of the most sensitive and controversial figures in the Red Sox relations with the press, Ted Williams did say in this regard:

> I think without question that Boston had the worst bunch of writers who ever came down the pike in baseball. I think any professional sport has to have press coverage, has to have color written about the teams, but can you do all that without being unfair, without picking on somebody, without making a damned mountain out of a molehill, without putting somebody on the spot?[6]

McCarthy tried to maintain the perspective that media matters were utterly peripheral. Reporters asked him many questions about the 1949 season and the final games with the Yankees. Here he was as reticent as he had been the previous spring about the Cleveland playoff. One reporter cried in frustration: "McCarthy would never talk about the decisions he made. You couldn't get McCarthy to say anything. Nothing. You'd look in and he'd be smoking a cigar and you'd say 'Hi, Joe' and that was it. He wouldn't tell you a f___ing word. Nothing." In his most generous moods, in the off-seasons after his successive World Series wins in the late 1930s, for example, McCarthy acknowledged that second guessing was part of the game, for it extended from baseball's essential non-scientific aspects that made it so fascinating. Yet when pressured by the relentless media, McCarthy felt that any yielding would only invite demands for more information he was not prepared to give.[7]

Paying little heed to the swirls of the petty concerns around him, McCarthy got down to business in Sarasota. Several things were on his mind. While the paranoid were scouring for demonic reasons for the outcomes of 1948 and 1949, McCarthy read some important lessons from the two seasons, lessons with which he still would have wanted to contend even if he had won two pennants. He knew the team lacked depth in two areas—relief pitching and bench strength. The Yankees won in 1949, despite a rash of injuries, because Casey Stengel had reserves (and knew how to use them). In addition to DiMaggio, Rizzuto, Henrich, and Berra, the Yankees had Cliff Mapes, Hank Bauer, Gene Woodling, George Stirnweiss, Charlie Silvera, Johnny Mize, and Johnny Lindell. Aside from Joe DiMaggio and maybe Henrich, none of these Yankees could clearly crack McCarthy's starting lineup in Boston.

But beneath his starting eight, McCarthy had little—Merrill Combs, Tom Wright, Lou Stringer; it was not much, although in 1950 many were again pinning hopes on young Walt Dropo. The lack of a bench loomed ever more hauntingly as all of McCarthy's regulars except Billy Goodman were fairly old. Vern Stephens was 29. Bobby Doerr, Johnny Pesky, Al Zarilla, Dom DiMaggio, Birdie Tebbetts, and Ted

Williams were all over 30. Such a situation usually means injuries will more likely occur, and McCarthy knew it. In pitching, McCarthy still had two ace starters Parnell and Kinder, but Kinder was (an old) 34. Meanwhile the Yankees had Eddie Lopat, Allie Reynolds, Vic Raschi, and promising newcomer Ed "Whitey" Ford. Most important, the Yankees had Joe Page in the bullpen. McCarthy had no such "fireman." Bucky Harris said if the Red Sox had had Joe Page, they would be champions. Cleveland had released Satchel Paige, but Cronin was not interested in him. Of course, Paige was forty-two years old.[8]

The other key matter on McCarthy's mind involved averting another such disastrously slow start as the team had gone through the previous two seasons. (Although McCarthy never said explicitly, the bad weeks of early '48 and '49 were to him the big reasons for Boston not winning either pennant.) With these points in mind, he spent spring training doing all the normal things to round his team into playing shape. He had the same starting eight set in his mind, but he kept an especially sharp eye out for new talent. He also played the regulars more fully in the exhibition games. To those concerned with ticket sales in the Florida ballparks, this was great. For McCarthy, the goal in the Florida games was to make sure the team would "hit the ground running" when the season began. Even more than usual, the players then found the regimen of McCarthy practices to be quite stiff, and they encountered more storming and fuming than usual at any dropped balls, missed cut offs, or wild throws. As in '49, now ever more so, the players were also hounded by reporters as to their takes on the reasons for the outcome of the previous season. When they beat the Yankees on March 13, the *Post* explained "Finally did it!" Back came more memories and gnashing analyses from the obsessive and more questions from reporters. Whether he was concerned with the added pressures, or just acting spontaneously, McCarthy did add a little levity one day when he grabbed a bat and stepped up to the plate, the last hitter that day at batting practice. He had not done this since Louisville. The spectators enjoyed it. At that juncture, the players definitely remained on their toes. Johnny Pesky crowded him at third base, and McCarthy tried to go down the line to keep him honest.[9]

Ellis Kinder took a line drive in the side at one practice in early March and cracked a rib. He had to sit out much of the month and ease back into condition. Otherwise, McCarthy was satisfied with training: "I don't know how anybody could ask for more than we have in the way of conditioning." The tour of Southern cities went well, especially the traditional stopover in Boston's top minor league city, Louisville. It had then been 30 years since McCarthy had first managed the Colonels. McCarthy joked about it: "I've been all around and now I'm just one step from returning to Louisville." The crowd loved it. They organized a ceremony for him. Wathen Knebelkamp, Jr., son of McCarthy's old boss, was there to make the presentations. On hand were many players from the Louisville days. McCarthy had been back many times over the years, but folks in Louisville perceived this visit was somehow special.[10]

While the day in Louisville was touching, in the game Birdie Tebbetts was hit by a foul tip on his throwing hand and split a finger. It had to be splinted, and he would be out for at least a week. Backup Buddy Rosar had strained his back. Now, all of a sudden McCarthy was left with only Matt Batts. The catching situation plus

Ellis Kinder's rib condition cast some gloom over the spring optimism. Still, writers and other managers were picking Boston. Connie Mack said "I doubt whether the Boston club can be beaten." The pressure was on to have a good start. "No excuse for a slow start," opined the *Globe*. "We've just GOT to start fast this time," yelled Dom DiMaggio. McCarthy himself was open about the point too. "All we need to get rolling is a flying start, and this year," he noted, "the schedule favors us because we will be at home for a considerable stay at the outset." A fast start would have certainly been a comfort in itself. More important, it would have erased most of the "here we go again" anxieties.

Opening day came to Fenway Park on April 17. The Red Sox' opponent was none other than the Yankees. The fans were happy and relaxed at first. The fast start, for which everyone including McCarthy hoped, indeed came to be—for six innings. At the end of six, the Red Sox had a lead of 9–0. The final score: 15–10 Yankees! New York scored nine runs in the eighth inning. "Short season, wasn't it?" quipped one Boston paper. Joe DiMaggio said, "That was the strangest game of baseball I have seen, played in, or heard of." The Red Sox had other ways of describing it, most of which were unprintable. McCarthy may have been reminded once again of the eighth inning in game four of the 1929 World Series. After the debacle, having endured so much pressure from the newsmen for so long, McCarthy, with the unanimous consent of the team, banned the press from the Red Sox clubhouse for a full half hour after each game.[11]

With the horrible loss to New York on opening day, reporters naturally had a lot of questions. They were free to ask them, but only after the 30-minute interlude. During that time, some players left. Reporters wanted the emotional reactions of players. They did not want them to have time to give more reflective thoughts. The loss to the Yankees kicked up the bad memories. The simultaneous closing of the clubhouse door made suspicions and ill feelings grow even more. One writer with the *Globe* voiced the opinion that Casey Stengel had outsmarted McCarthy by using left-handers Henrich and Mize against McCarthy's left-handed starter, Mel Parnell. McCarthy likely wondered how a reporter could label "smart" a tactic so utterly obvious as using left handed–hitters against a left-handed pitcher. Reading such pablum made McCarthy want to keep the doors shut longer. Others in the press brought back some of the same old characterizations about McCarthy's reticence. "Interviewing Joseph Vincent McCarthy," whined one, "is like removing the teeth of a bucking bronco with an oyster fork. The man is so cautious he does not dare say 'Good Morning' for fear the weather will change."

With the loss and with the new press rules, writers were going to vent their unhappiness, and as long as Boston was not winning, reporters bet that most of their readers would share their frustrations. Some early complaints about McCarthy's aloof manner had been points of humor among many press and fans, as was the case in Chicago and New York. By 1950, there was little humor about it in Boston. Later that April, on McCarthy's 63rd birthday, reporters sent him a telegram that said: "Do not read this telegram until 30 minutes after you have opened it. Happy Birthday." McCarthy chuckled, but he did not change the press rule. He seemed ever more crusty. Al Hirshberg of the *Boston Post* searingly called him "a sour, disillusioned man who looked upon the world with the jaundiced eye of a violinist about to change a tire." At least that criticism contained an element of respect. Many were just nasty. Rumors were also flying that McCarthy was drinking more. His trusted trainer, Eddie Froelich, was apparently keeping a flask from which he could take a nip during games.[12]

On April 22, Birdie Tebbetts was catching batting practice for the first time in the regular season and seemed ready to go back in the lineup. Rosar was still out, however. Meanwhile, Ted Williams was down with a fever, missing his first games since August of 1948. Dom DiMaggio pulled a calf muscle. Billy Goodman chipped an ankle bone. (McCarthy brought Walt Dropo up from Louisville.) Ellis Kinder's pitching was not effective; neither was the bullpen's. McCarthy himself showed frustration and irritation. On April 23 he actually bumped an umpire during an unusually loud argument. He was ejected of course. The Sox' "start" was 4 and 6, and once again the refrain was all about Boston: "What's the matter...?" Indeed the old adage — "Boston, where Cabots speak only to Lowells, and Lowells speak only to God"— had reportedly gone through a metamorphosis. The new adage: "Boston, where the Cabots and the Lowells both speak to the Ginsbergs and the Murphys about that all engrossing question, 'What's the Matter with the Red Sox?'" The *Boston Post* began to print fans' letters. Few were flattering.

> Birthday Greetings, Marse Joe. Don't you wish you stayed in Buffalo? I do.
>
> Is McCarthy looking for a coaching job with the Yankees, ordering Coleman passed twice? [In the opening Yankee game, McCarthy twice ordered Jerry Coleman intentionally walked. Each time he subsequently scored.]
>
> What's the matter with McCarthy? Last year you could not get him to lift a pitcher until the damage was done. The final day, to the amazement of all, he pulled Kinder. This year it is just the same. There is never any bullpen activity until it is too late. What the Sox need is a new manager.

Some fans had asserted that McCarthy had kept the bullpen too active at times, hence that the relief pitchers to whom he turned were needlessly tired. As usual, the composite of fan complaints left little but a pattern of contradictions. But any cogent countering of illogic or pointing out of contradictions would not change the fans' spirit. "They hanged me in effigy from every lamp post in Boston," McCarthy remembered only half-jokingly. Meanwhile, with the media noting almost every day how they were still unable to get into the team's clubhouse, the clouds only thickened. On April 23, 40,000 people gathered on Boston Common at noon for a prayer meeting led by the young evangelist Billy Graham. The prayers were for world peace and national repentance. Some said many of the assembled Bostonians that hour were also praying for the Red Sox. That was the afternoon McCarthy was thrown out of a game for bumping an umpire; so much for the power of prayer.[13]

The press continued to complain about being barred from the clubhouse. Even here, conspiracy-minded paranoia crept into reporters' analysis. "A few [players] may have asked for it, but it is inconceivable that it could have been voted unanimously," earnestly asserted one scribe. Again, the press revealed its ego here, thinking they knew the team and were closer to some of the Sox than the players were to one another. On May 2, the team voted to retain the half-hour rule. The margin was made public: 23 to 3, plus 3 abstentions. Tebbetts was the only starter to vote "no." Reporters could (should) have been chagrined about their doubting the solidarity of the team's stance in regard to the 30-minute rule. Maybe if some reporters had admitted that some of their rude ways might have been part of the problem, there could have been a bit of reconciliation. Instead reporters just hammered away at their "rights" to what one called the "reasonable information" that can only come immediately after a game. Harping upon their victimization, they even bandied about trendy terms like "iron curtain" and "cold war."

Casey Stengel may have been good at what subsequent generations would call "spinning," but McCarthy was not, and other players, notably Ted Williams, were not interested in adjusting to the pressures of expanding media. Williams was one of the most enthusiastic supporters of the press bar. After one game he stood near the clubhouse door and snapped, "not yet, you chowder heads, not yet!" Joe Cronin expressed support for the team's decision. Some reporters actually hinted at a threat of taking the matter to Baseball Commissioner Chandler. Nothing came of this, but as long as the Red Sox floundered on the field, reporters were going to be anything but charitable. The *Post* did show some integrity, printing one letter from a fan in Brockton, Mass., which read: "Ed Barrow said 'Make no mistake. McCarthy is a great manager.' I place more confidence in the opinions of Mr. Barrow than I do in some of the writers who are continually needling him." As is normal in such situations, however, the sanest people usually keep silent.[14]

McCarthy's drinking was certainly adding to the bad feelings that were all about Boston baseball circles in 1950. While no one could prove that a sober Joe McCarthy could have won pennants, or whether a different, sober manager could have done a better job, the sense that McCarthy was indulging himself at the team's and the city's expense was hard to dislodge. Ellis Kinder was quite the drinker himself. One afternoon he arrived at Fenway to start against Chicago and threw wildly in his warmups. McCarthy did not notice. He hit the backstop and bounced several pitches to the first Chicago batters, and Tebbetts had to yell "Get him out of there, he's drunk." McCarthy finally lifted Kinder, promising to fine him, but never collected the money. While his 1949 performance (more precisely, his second half of '49 performance) had been fantastic, Kinder was through as a starter. His drinking had caught up with him, and while alcohol may not affect the nuances of managing as obviously as it destroys as the physical powers of a pitcher, people could legitimately wonder whether McCarthy needed to reform or get out. Still, with alcohol not having quite the same stigma it would come to have, reporters did not note any great dissension among the Red Sox *vis à vis* their manager, and given how angry the scribes were about being held out of the locker room, they were clearly ready to pounce on any such problem if they perceived even a hint of it.[15]

In early May, while the press was continually complaining, Boston actually began to win. After their 4 and 6 start, the Red Sox ran off a 10 and 1 spurt, and they took first place on May 10. Williams had recovered from his fever and got a hit in each of the eleven games. The next day, however, came a disastrous doubleheader loss to Detroit, with the first game being a rude 13–4 blowout. The Yankees immediately reclaimed the league lead. On the afternoon, the Red Sox committed six errors. When Ted Williams miscued in the second loss, fans booed him. He responded by spitting and making several hand and finger gestures at them. Already disposed to be negative, reporters were very critical: "His actions recall the rowdyism in baseball's early days before clergy dared attend games." Some players defended Williams—"I'd do it too if I was booed." McCarthy would not discipline Williams. Between the fans, the press, Williams, the rest of the players, and Manager McCarthy, there seemed to be a choosing of sides all around. The sourness did not abate, as the Red Sox started no new winning streak that May. On a Western tour they merely split 10 games, losing many close ones. One newspaper cartoon depicted McCarthy as a fisherman and Tom Yawkey as a cook; McCarthy handed Yawkey some tiny minnows, saying "You shudda seen th' big ones that got away."

Reporters pounded away at the fact that McCarthy never let them in on any of his strategies. For the third year in a row, the end of May saw fans and reporters beating up on the Red Sox. As before, everyone had expected big things. The team had held first place one day. Now, after losing a Memorial Day doubleheader to the Yankees, they were five games back. Even McCarthy was willing to philosophize a bit: "Sometimes I think I'm in the greatest business in the world, and then you lost four straight and you want to change places with a farmer." At this point, the pounding did not come from just the Boston writers. Even New York reporters were slamming them. Red Smith of the *New York Herald Tribune* called them "a beaten team." Arthur Daley of the *New York Times* wondered: "Maybe they just don't have it." Joe Williams of the *New York World Telegram* asked "Do the Red Sox quit under pressure?" Dan Parker of the *New York Daily Mirror* quoted Birdie Tebbetts as declaring "there is not enough spirit in the whole lot of them to provide one flickering flame for a cigarette lighter." Parker excused McCarthy here, citing the spirit he had instilled in the old Yankee teams. He blamed Ted Williams, and Jimmy Cannon of the *New York Post* added to this sentiment, claiming he "knew" that Williams wanted to be traded, preferably to Detroit.[16]

The bad mouthing, the incessant questions, the boos—everything was piling up, although Williams emphatically denied all the rumors about wanting to be traded. Throughout it all McCarthy was calm, his demeanor aided at times with a nip of whiskey. He did sarcastically comment to one reporter: "And they wonder why baseball managers get ulcers and bad dispositions." His focus was still on the team's woes on the field, not on the locker room, and certainly not on the press. On June 4, Dom DiMaggio reinjured his leg. He would be out for another two weeks. Meanwhile, the Red Sox fans did rally to the team's side. When the team returned from the road on June 2, they greeted Ted Williams with a great ovation. The Red Sox burst forth with an extended week-long offensive display unlike any ever shown in the history of baseball. They won six of their next seven games, their one bad game an 8–4 loss to Chicago on June 6. Otherwise, they scored in double figures every day, totaling an incredible 104 runs in seven games. Included in the streak was a record 29 runs in one game against St. Louis, the record coming the day after they had scored 20 runs against the same hapless Browns. 49 runs in two straight games marked another record. (The previous day was the 8–4 loss to Chicago, nevertheless the three-day run total of 53 still marked another new record.) The unprecedented spurt of offense excited the fans, of course.

Some analysts then wondered why such an obviously talented, explosive team could not channel its energies more consistently. This harkened people back to the same myriad of questions asked of the Red Sox since the fall of 1948. And when the team lost the next two games by scores of 12–7 and 18–8, the euphoria started to evaporate. When they lost a doubleheader the very next day in Detroit, the enthusiasm was all gone. (The scoring of seven runs in the first loss set a new three-day run record, but no one found any comfort there.) The offensive splurge and subsequent letdown left the Red Sox still five games behind New York, with Detroit in second place. When teams win and lose by a run or two, managerial decisions and game tactics can make the difference. When the wins and losses are by huge margins, there is little for a manager to do. McCarthy indeed felt powerless. The collective personality of his team, as it handled the various peaks and valleys with the press and fans, was something he could only lead by an example of calm focus. Whether he could have done that better without a regular nip of Scotch is a matter of conjecture. Like a good physician, a manager should do more than merely no harm.[17]

The club headed out for a Western tour on June 11. McCarthy left the team for a day's visit to his farm while the club stopped in Scranton, Pa. for an exhibition game. He rejoined them for an 8–1 victory in Cleveland. Young Chuck Stobbs pitched and looked strong. It was McCarthy's 2125th victory, his last. Cleveland won the next two, pushing the Red Sox back, six and one half games behind Detroit, who had passed New York for first place. Detroit was Boston's next stop. Detroit had the bases loaded with one out when Boston pulled off what appeared to be an inning-saving double play. But the umpire ruled the runner at first safe. The two lead runners had crossed the plate, and, with the umpire's ruling, the two runs counted. McCarthy was so angry that coach Earle Combs had to get between him and the umpire. It is possible that McCarthy was calculating that a display of temper would put some fire into the team. On the other hand, he may have been simply depressed, drunk, and very angry.

Detroit won the next two games, sweeping the series. Detroit certainly brought ill to McCarthy. Gehrig withdrew himself from the lineup there in 1939. The Yankees were in Detroit when they learned that Gehrig had died in 1941. McCarthy left the Yankees in 1946 when they were in Detroit. Detroit had just derailed Boston's high scoring streak. At least this series was over. Matt Batts later said that "for several days they looked for him in Detroit. They found him in the gutter, skid row. He was in real bad shape." McCarthy was drinking, but he was at the ballpark for each game that series, so the notion of people looking for him for several days does not quite square with the record. Boston seemed to be heading down again, but Detroit's new manager, Red Rolfe, still warned everyone: "Don't count the Sox out yet."[18]

The team moved on to Chicago. McCarthy was not seen up and about during the entire train ride. And the next day, June 20, he was confined to his room in the hotel. Matt Batts said the confinement was involuntary. Otherwise, it was just like the events in Detroit with the Yankees in May, 1946. This time the stated reason was an attack of pleurisy and influenza. He did not go to the ballpark. He went home to Buffalo. When he arrived at the airport, the cameramen and reporters were all there flashing bulbs and peppering him with questions about whether he was quitting. McCarthy actually took a swing at one cameraman, although rather half-heartedly. Then he relented. He shrugged to Babe: "Let him get his picture and let us be on our way home." When he got to his car, his dog gave him a lick. McCarthy faintly smiled: "At least somebody still likes me."

Rumors were everywhere in the baseball world that McCarthy was going to be asked to resign. Mrs. McCarthy spoke, first insisting that he was going to rejoin the team soon. "He won't quit, and he hasn't been fired." After a day at home, Joe McCarthy told the Buffalo papers: "Sure I'll be back with the Red Sox. I'm just sick and ache all over. And I feel wobbly." Joe Cronin announced: "McCarthy can manage for the Red Sox as long as he wants." Cronin spoke with McCarthy and advised him not to make a quick decision: "Why don't you wait a few days before making up your mind. You may feel differently about it when you get fully rested."

McCarthy had made a decision, however, and was firm with Cronin. "That's not fair to Tom Yawkey," he said. "The club needs definite direction right now. It would be fatal to delay this decision. I think an announcement of a new manager should be made at once." McCarthy did heed Cronin's advice in one respect. He spoke with Yawkey before making any announcement. To Yawkey he could express nothing but gratitude:

> I don't want you to think that I'm letting you down. I sincerely appreciate the consideration you have given me since I came out of retirement to join the Red Sox. I honestly had hoped that I could win a pennant for you before I was forced out of action. But I simply don't feel up to it. I get too tired physically [when] traveling. I assure you I make this decision only after considerable thought for all parties concerned. It is for the best interests of everyone.

The next day, June 24, came the headlines: "McCarthy Quits as Red Sox Pilot."[19]

Joe Cronin's summation of the situation was simple: "Joe was just weary and wanted to quit." Cronin named Steve O'Neill, who McCarthy had hired to replace Cuyler, to manage the team. Obviously the disappointment with the team's start, the troubles with the press, and the pressures of age and drinking all piled up. Mrs. McCarthy said "He's just physically exhausted," adding, "It's later than you think." Joe McCarthy said he had been contemplating resigning for some time; he concluded:

> I just could not go on anymore. My physician had advised me that it would be a big help to my health if I discontinued my baseball job with its demanding periods of travel, press, and irregular diet. My first consideration is [to] my health and to my family, and I reached the conclusion that it would be best for the team and myself if I retired. When a man can't help a ball club anymore, it's time to quit, and a sick man can't help a ball club. I feel much better now that the strain is off. ... I wish Steve O'Neill the best of luck. I believe he can do a good job.

McCarthy dearly wanted to win one for Joe Cronin and Tom Yawkey, and he wanted to go out on top. But despite the goals, the romance had gone out of the game for him. Mrs. McCarthy reflected that Joe had often told her "there was romance connected with baseball for almost everybody in it and when that romance died, a fellow should quit."[20]

The Red Sox players were all saddened by the news. Pitcher Mickey Harris had noted the extreme tension under which McCarthy had operated: "Every time a guy got on base against you, he acted as if it would cost the Red Sox the pennant." Birdie

Tebbetts, perhaps in cognizance of the drinking issues, was a trifle opaque about McCarthy's departure. "This is a strange business," he said. "This is a ticklish situation for a ball player to be in. The less said the better." Tex Hughson, always bitter in his belief that McCarthy had grossly misused him, had left the team, but he later contended that Joe Cronin had put McCarthy on a kind of probation about drinking, so when McCarthy continued to drink, he had to quit. Cronin never corroborated this.

Everyone else who was actually with the team was open and simply wished McCarthy well. Matt Batts had certainly been critical in noting McCarthy's drinking difficulties, but he recalled: "Even so, when McCarthy quit, I didn't like it. He was the reason I got to the big leagues. He gave me the chance. I would fight for him, and he knew that. I was upset." When he learned of McCarthy's resignation, Billy Goodman smiled: "I hope he lives to a ripe old age, and this may do it for him. He was always nice to me." Bobby Doerr said "I'm a little surprised. But then this is a nerve-wracking business, and I guess it was getting on Joe's nerves." Dom DiMaggio lamented "I am very sorry to hear about it. He was tops in my book." Vern Stephens showed empathy: "He was a good manager, no doubt about it, but he was getting old and maybe it was a good time to step out." Buddy Rosar blamed himself and the team: "It wouldn't've have happened if we hadn't gone into a slump." Ted Williams bared a bit of soul: "I'm awfully sorry to see him go, but perhaps it's the best thing because you could see it was killing him. There was never a harsh word between us, and there were times when he could have spoken harshly to me." Seven years later, Williams said, "My years of playing under [McCarthy] were really the happiest of my career."

Perhaps the only harsh words came from St. Louis Browns President Bill DeWitt. With the 29–4 drubbing less than two weeks old, DeWitt snorted: "I'm sorry McCarthy stepped out. We were going to pour it on him. He had something coming to him. I'm sorry he's not here to get it." (When the Red Sox left Chicago, their next stop was St. Louis, where they swept all four games of their series with the Browns.) After all the years of harshness in the press, reporters proved largely charitable. The *Boston Herald* noted, albeit ungrammatically: "Nothing but vultures are indelicate enough to rattle their wattles before a potential casualty actually becomes a *corpus delicti*." McCarthy's critics turned simply maintained their focus on the Red Sox and their quest for that elusive championship.[21]

Days after his resignation, McCarthy had expressed to a reporter his frustration "that he just couldn't seem to do anything right for the ball club." The Red Sox had one of the greatest assemblages of talent, a team which could score 29 runs in one game. Yet they inexplicably fell into horrible slumps. After McCarthy left, the 1950 Red Sox rebounded and went through another heartbreaking stretch run. Ellis Kinder returned to form, and Parnell pitched well. The team hit solidly all summer. The day McCarthy left, all eight starters, the three major subs, and two pitchers were hitting above .295. That summer the Sox again clawed their way back into contention. On the morning of September 20, Boston was a half game behind the league leading Yankees. Pennant fever was again gripping Boston. Then, inexplicably, came a doubleheader loss to Cleveland and two critical losses to New York. The Red Sox fell back, and the Yankees kept winning. A week later the Red Sox were mathematically eliminated with a loss to Washington. The Senators' winning pitcher that day was Gene Bearden, the man who had beaten them in the 1948 playoff.[22]

The feeling of being cursed continued to haunt Boston. McCarthy could not lead them over the top, and no one else could either. One answer to the failures in that era was the simple point that the Yankee (and Cleveland) teams of the day were some of the greatest ever. Like the McCarthy juggernauts of the late '30s, the '49–'53 Yankees were some of the greatest of all time, often overlooked among those who sing the praises of the N.Y. teams of the late '20s, early '60s, and late '90s. For Bostonians such an answer did not come close to exorcizing "the Curse." After '48, '49, and '50, and after such painful losses as those in '67, '75, '78, '86, and 2003, fans concluded that if there was a "curse," however, it was at least a great deal bigger than Joe McCarthy. And after the victory in 2004, all was forgiven.

38

A Pleasant Good-Bye

When Joe McCarthy celebrated his 60th birthday on April 21, 1947, he had been away from baseball for nearly a year. He had left the Yankees the previous spring, and just that month he had turned down an offer from Branch Rickey to manage the Brooklyn Dodgers for the year Leo Durocher was in Commissioner-ordered exile. Mrs. McCarthy then spoke with a Buffalo reporter, telling him that out at their farm in Amherst, NY, Joe "likes the life out here. It's made a new man out of him," she said. "It's given him back his health. ... He has new hobbies now. He is interested in flowers."[1] Mrs. McCarthy was convinced, and certainly hoped, that her husband would not go back to managing. Of course, McCarthy would go back and spent the next two wonderfully awful seasons with the Boston Red Sox. But when McCarthy left the Red Sox in 1950 it was final, and then his farm in New York proved the very tonic that Mrs. McCarthy said it was. Buffalo was always a happy town for McCarthy, and the farm outside Buffalo was even more restorative. He would spend the rest of his life there. McCarthy had invested his money wisely, and he never needed additional income.

In 1950, while still the manager of the Red Sox, McCarthy did do an advertisement for B.F. Goodrich tires. Beneath his picture, he was quoted: "If you can tell which *athletes* are best, you can tell which *tire* is best. Teamwork helped me win seven world championships, and it's teamwork that makes B.F. Goodrich the best tire value"[emphases his]. It was the only such endorsement he ever did.[2] Otherwise, he and Babe settled into their farm, and he was not budging. Feelers about other managerial jobs came forth from the Dodgers, the Tigers, and the Phillies, but soon all baseball people accepted that McCarthy's retirement was indeed genuine. He received many invitations to attend spring training with the Yankees, and to do so with TV and radio networks. He turned down every offer. "I can't leave with the lilacs in bud, the forsythia in golden bloom, the apple and pear trees about to cast their splendor. The ducks are back. It's the best time of the year. My world is here."[3] And there he stayed.

On February 3, 1957, McCarthy received word that he had been elected to the Hall of Fame across the state in Cooperstown, quite a present for his upcoming 70th birthday. Just the week before, *New York Times* columnist Arthur Daley had criticized the Hall not yet placing McCarthy "where he belongs. ... Common sense

Mrs. Elizabeth "Babe" McCarthy. Joe and Babe were married in 1922. She was from Buffalo, New York. They met when McCarthy played for the Buffalo Bisons in 1914–15. They had no children. Other than when he was involved in baseball matters, McCarthy never went anywhere without her. In 1965, Mrs. McCarthy suffered an incapacitating stroke. Joe hired nurses and tended to her every need for the rest of her life. She died in 1971. (National Baseball Hall of Fame Library, Cooperstown, N.Y.)

demands his immediate admission." Lefty Gomez had also spoken about what an injustice it would be if McCarthy was not named to the Hall: "He was the best we ever had." In 1957, McCarthy was voted into the Hall, and the reporters' ballots were unanimous. McCarthy's old Chicago newspaper friend Warren Brown was then the acting chair of the Hall's Veterans Committee. He phoned McCarthy and told him, "We got you to the end of the trail, and this is the happiest day in my baseball life." Since 1950, the McCarthys had visited the Hall every summer. In 1955 they were present for the induction of Joe DiMaggio and Gabby Hartnett, two of his favorite players. When McCarthy's turn came two years later he joked that "if they didn't put me in the Hall soon I was going to move here so I could be close to it."

He may have agreed with Arthur Daley, but he never explicitly voiced anything close to a complaint about deserving induction. While his comment sounded offhanded, he was deeply touched when the phone call came from the Hall. "It's nice to walk in the garden while you can still smell the roses," he said. He had told Warren

In retirement. McCarthy bought property outside Buffalo and lived out his years on his "Yankee Farm." He kept up with the sports scene, entertained visitors, personally answered all his mail, advised members of the Yankee scouting organization, and tended to his land. Clear-eyed and lucid to the end, he lived to the age of 90. (National Baseball Hall of Fame Library, Cooperstown, N.Y.)

Brown, in deadly earnest, that he was concerned "that in being named I didn't keep some ball player from getting into the Hall of Fame. After all, I think there are a lot of former major league stars who deserve it more than me." This was no false modesty. It went to the core of what made McCarthy such a great leader. He always held his players in such respect. At the ceremony he told the gathering that up to that time his three greatest thrills in baseball had been being hired for his first major league job in 1925, winning his first pennant in 1929, and winning his first World Series in 1932, but being elected to the Hall of Fame was now his greatest moment.

"When a player is elected to the Hall of Fame," he noted to the crowd on induction day, "he has no one to thank. He reached there on his bat or his arm. But a manager has everyone to thank, and I want to do that today." He actually then enumerated no list of names, fearing that he might leave one off and offend someone. But he did single out two people — Mrs. McCarthy and Mrs. Eleanor Gehrig. Mrs. Gehrig had come for the occasion. The crown applauded Mrs. McCarthy. When Mrs. Gehrig rose, a rapt silence came over the gathering. With the reaction to Mrs. Gehrig, McCarthy smiled just a bit and noted: "Many a sad memory but a lot of happy ones are brought back by seeing you." Even for such an occasion as that, the crowd was unusually moved. Less than a month after the Hall of Fame induction, Yankee Stadium held a ceremony honoring McCarthy during their annual Old Timers Day. The intensely private Joe DiMaggio interrupted his vacation in Europe to fly back for the occasion.[4]

The life on the "Yankee Farm" remained a pleasure for McCarthy for many years. In an age before many electronic devices, the McCarthys worked out a wonderful system to communicate about the property. If Joe was out on the land somewhere and he received a phone call, Mrs. McCarthy would sound a horn and write a note. At the sound of the horn, Joe's golden retriever "Colonel" (named for Jacob Ruppert) would run to the back door. Mrs. McCarthy would attach the note to Colonel's collar, and he would run it out to Joe. There, at last, was a system of McCarthy signals an opponent could decipher, at least on the surface. Other signals remained secret. When Colonel died, other dogs could not be trained so well. McCarthy's only regular departures from the farm came when he went to Yankee Stadium for old-timers games. In his retirement, McCarthy kept up with the game but largely through the newspapers and television. He watched with displeasure the growing tendencies of managers to yell at umpires with great histrionics. McCarthy remained proud that he rarely argued with umpires, and then usually over a matter that concerned a specific rule, rather than a judgment call. (He never commented about the fact that when he did argue with a stubborn umpire, it could certainly be a corker.) He felt excessive arguing with the umpires was the purview of second division clubs, and when he saw it infecting the game more and more he did not like it. "A lot of those things I see I can't believe. Those managers," he ruefully noted, "must think they're actors." (He did see Billy Martin manage on many occasions.)[5]

McCarthy's other chief way of keeping in touch with the game was to handle his own correspondence. When anyone wrote him, especially young people, he responded personally, on his own manual typewriter. Young people were especially important to him. Like everyone else, he knew that the future of the game depended on them. In 1971, when some said the game was in decline, he commented: "There's nothing wrong with baseball. Just provide the boys with bats and balls and a place to play and the country will continue to develop top players."[6] One day McCarthy was walking with his friend Ralph Hubbell, a local sportscaster. They were strolling near his old Gates Circle neighborhood in downtown Buffalo, and a genuine anger came over him when he saw a sign at the entrance to a park: "No ball playing allowed." Hubbell recalled, "It was the only time I ever saw Joe get really mad."[7] (It has only been in the early twenty-first century that baseball's scions have started to take full and serious note of the fact that American cities now provide little to no space for young people to play baseball.) McCarthy corresponded with everyone who wrote him, and, with an honest consternation that reflected the lack of ego he brought both to his managing and to his life, he drew great joy in the fame that his mail revealed he maintained, especially among young people. "I get more mail [and] more requests to sign pictures and cards to autograph than I did when I managed." People actually writing who had not even been alive when he managed the Yankees—"Imagine that," he smiled. One letter came from a fan in St. Louis who had written McCarthy in 1928. He had then asked McCarthy for an autographed baseball. McCarthy wrote back promising a ball at a future date. In 1957, the fan returned McCarthy's letter of promise; McCarthy sent back an autographed ball. The fan gave it to his son.[8]

In his honest surprise at his ongoing fame lay a clue as to what made McCarthy so successful. He had total command of the details of the game, of course, yet he sought the knowledge and exercised authority with no real force of ego. No one had a stronger sense of his own command of every facet of the game, yet no one required fewer protocols and constructed less of a cult of personality in their management than did Joe McCarthy. "John McGraw," wrote the *New York Times* Arthur Daley, "won ... with dictatorial pugnacity. Connie Mack did the same through sheer paternalism. McCarthy did it with phlegmatic unobtrusiveness."[9] The press would then develop any number of negative images about him to fill in the blank here, and their inventions were largely an extension of their inability to get McCarthy to bare his soul and help create the juicy stories they hoped to write. McCarthy could never accommodate. Unlike many managers, he had no need for such histrionics, and his reticence was never a mere act. Unable to see past their own egos, many reporters could not grasp that.

While McCarthy studiously answered all the mail he received from fans, he never accepted a deal with any publisher to write a memoir. Again, the ego-less fastidiousness he brought to his profession manifested itself. He had offers of as much as $250,000 to write a book of his baseball memories, but he would never do it, nor did he take up any similar offers for magazine articles or movies. The only way he could have written such an autobiography would have been to do it with complete honesty, and he told friends that there were several players about whom he would have to say some very negative things. He did not wish to do that. It was clear to those who knew him, that he was referring here specifically to Rogers Hornsby and Babe Ruth, as well as to the little foibles and weaknesses of many people he admired. McCarthy had complete faith in his own convictions, but he did not have any pressing need to have his views enter the public domain.[10]

Once, while with the Yankees, McCarthy was speaking with several reporters. The flow of the conversation jogged a memory, and he said "that reminds me of a great story." The reporters all leaned in, of course, ready for a great bit of baseball lore, but just as quickly McCarthy pulled back. "No," he declared, "I guess I'd better not tell it. ... The fellow is still in baseball, and it might reflect on him." He noted that even if everyone agreed to keep the matter private, it would eventually get out, and he did not want that. "It's so good that you'd tell it to someone else, and he'd use it. Sorry fellows, I'd better not." The story was never told.[11]

McCarthy was always that way about private matters. He was a public figure, but he maintained in his own mind a strict distinction between what belonged in the public realm and what did not. This was part of why various members of the press had difficulties with him. In an age when the media were growing larger, more intrusive, and feeling an ever-increasing sense of entitlement, it made for many clashes, but McCarthy had never wavered, nor would he in retirement. Whatever the particulars about the likes of Babe Ruth and Rogers Hornsby, or about the many players of whom he thought so highly, McCarthy never said. Nor did he ever answer one question he was asked *so* many times: "Since you managed both, who was better, Joe DiMaggio or Ted Williams?" McCarthy had had only one reply here: "How the hell do you answer a question like that?" Whatever his thoughts on the subject, they doubtlessly would have interested everyone connected with the game and justified any such publisher's advance as a quarter of a million dollars, but McCarthy felt it was not something posterity needed to know.

This was the way McCarthy ran his life, and the way he insisted on managing his teams. No one but the coaches needed to know the signals he sent. Everyone could see and know what he wanted in terms of performances by his men, but no one needed to know what his opinions were of the men about whom he was making management decisions. The composer Aaron Copland was once asked to name his favorite work among his many compositions; he responded by noting that a wise mother may have a favorite among her children but knows never to reveal it. McCarthy would have concurred. The convictions, feelings, analyses, or emotions he held about his men were not for display. Such discussions were not his way. "I always figure the truth comes out in the end," McCarthy once told a reporter. If the truth ended up being an ambiguous matter of debate and conjecture, like the reasons the Red Sox did not win the pennants in 1948 and 1949, perhaps that *was* the truth. After all, the wisdom in accepting such ambiguities in life is one of the things that baseball teaches.[12]

Referring to the desire to refute any misinformation in the media, McCarthy mused, "If I make a fuss, I just give the writer more publicity, 'probably just what he wants. When somebody writes something bad about me, and I know it is not true, well I just figure I do not want anything more to do with that fellow, that's all." Once McCarthy retired from the game, he could live in accordance with that outlook and at last feel no undue pressure for it from the media. "Now that the parade has passed my by," he acknowledged, "I don't mind it [media inquiries] much any more." Reporters were naturally less and less aggressive around him as well. Among the sports scribes in the Buffalo area, McCarthy's relationship with them came to be as warm and friendly as his relationship with some Boston writers had been icy and hostile. Perhaps in his later accommodation, McCarthy was eager for a bit of the publicity he missed more than he had first anticipated. In any case, the nature of the stories was now less urgent, so the give and take in the process of forming the story had none of the old tensions McCarthy had so detested.[13]

While Joe McCarthy never wrote a memoir, he did clarify a few matters. At an Old Timers gathering Tommy Henrich asked him to explain the signs he relayed to his coaches. He still would not do it. His authority was still clear. At another reunion, Lefty Gomez told him of the night he and Joe DiMaggio went out to a Philadelphia nightclub called Palumbo's. DiMaggio dared Gomez to go up on stage. Of course Gomez took the dare and joined the girls in the chorus line. Gomez knew that McCarthy saw through virtually all his antics, but here he confessed: "That's the only thing I ever put over on you, Joe." McCarthy's only comment to Gomez and the rest of the gathering: "I was sitting in the back of Palumbo's that night."

As far as who his greatest players were, in 1948 he had named an all–McCarthy team. There had been a few surprises, more of omission than commission, for all of his named "favorites" like Gehrig, DiMaggio, and Williams were hardly marginal players. His choices of pitchers were Charlie Root, Lefty Gomez, Spud Chandler, and Red Ruffing (no Ellis Kinder or Mel Parnell, but he was then new with the Red Sox). His catchers were Bill Dickey and Gabby Hartnett. His infielders: Lou Gehrig, Joe Gordon, Frankie Crosetti, Red Rolfe, and Bobby Doerr (no Phil Rizzuto, *or* Rogers Hornsby). And his outfield: Joe DiMaggio, Tommy Henrich, Charlie Keller, and Ted Williams (no Riggs Stephenson, Hack Wilson, *or* Babe Ruth).[14]

Meanwhile, on other such all-time lists, everyone naming the game's all-time managers never omits Joe McCarthy. When McCarthy retired from the Red Sox in 1950 he had already carved a place for himself among the greatest managers in baseball. Connie Mack, John McGraw, Miller Huggins, and Joe McCarthy — in one order or another they are always the names atop the manager lists when baseball enthusiasts survey "the greatest." A few have come along since then who make most "lists," like Casey Stengel, Walter Alston, Sparky Anderson, Earl Weaver, Tony LaRussa, and Joe Torre, but McCarthy has remained, and will in all events remain, a standard against which all great managers are evaluated. Among many baseball analysts, Bill James simply says that McCarthy was the greatest.[15]

As far as who was the greatest manager, McCarthy himself actually had a slightly different view than Bill James. In the summer of 1969, Ted Williams paid a visit to McCarthy's farm. He was accompanied by a Buffalo reporter and by Ed Doherty, public relations director for the Washington Senators. Shortly after his guests arrived, McCarthy served drinks and Williams toasted: "To Joe McCarthy, the greatest manager baseball ever knew." McCarthy was deeply touched, again reflecting his genuine lack of ego: "Ted," he responded, "that was the nicest thing anyone ever said about me." Williams replied, "I've been saying you're the greatest for years." They chatted a bit more. Doherty reminded McCarthy that he had been a bat boy for Providence in the International League in 1915 when Joe played second for Buffalo. Doherty and Williams listened in wonderment as McCarthy then calmly named every player on the 1915 Providence team and pinpointed many of their strengths and weaknesses. (When Dartmouth and Exeter graduate Red Rolfe left McCarthy's tutelage and managed the Tigers in 1949, he kept an organized set of charts, detailing all such points with regard to the players of every team in the league. McCarthy never needed such charts.)

When Ted Williams generously toasted his host, his words sparked something in McCarthy's mind, and after a bit more conversation McCarthy offered to take Williams on a tour of his house, which Williams of course accepted. McCarthy kept a separate room in his home for his baseball memorabilia. In his living room there was nothing about baseball, except for two pictures. One was a picture of Lou Gehrig, with the words: "May I always deserve your friendship." The other was a picture of Connie Mack. On it Mr. Mack had penned a simple inscription: "To a great manager and a great friend." As Williams looked at Connie Mack's picture, McCarthy said, "You are wrong about me, Ted. *There* was the greatest manager of all time." Bill James is usually thoroughly considered and precise in his judgments, but here the baseball world may yield to Joe McCarthy's view. Connie Mack agreed with Bill James, however.

There was one other picture McCarthy kept in a special place in his house, separate from the rest of his baseball memorabilia. That picture was of Ted Williams, and McCarthy kept it in his bedroom. (As Williams and the others were driving back to Buffalo, Williams asked how McCarthy was fixed financially. McCarthy was paying for Babe's round the clock nursing care, and Williams was concerned. Such was the loyalty and love Williams felt for his former manager.)[16]

At the time of his visit to McCarthy, Williams had recently been appointed manager of the Washington Senators. One of his first moves was to ban all card playing in the clubhouse, although no card tables were axed to bits. Birdie Tebbetts was another McCarthy player who became a manager. His first post was in Indianapolis, and when he was hired, the first thing he did was telephone McCarthy to seek his counsel. (Tebbetts got his nickname because he was a high-pitched chatter-box behind the plate. McCarthy advice to Birdie was thus: "stop talking so much; shut your mouth and you'll be OK.") Both Tebbetts and Williams proved to be good managers, but not great ones. They certainly knew the game, and each knew all of McCarthy's methods, but McCarthy's management was not something that could be merely copied.[17]

One key matter in McCarthy's success involved the special nature of the organizations of which he had been a part. Unlike many sports clubs, and other corporations, McCarthy was never part of an institution with any excessive front office bureaucracy. He realized this himself, noting that he managed for four men who fully owned their own clubs— Bill Knebelkamp in Louisville, William Wrigley in Chicago, Jacob Ruppert in New York, and Tom Yawkey in Boston. "I never had to contend with a Board of Directors," he noted both with thanks and perhaps with a touch of anger, as the one time in which such upper management was messy for him — with Dan Topping, Del Webb, and Larry MacPhail — the results were not good.[18]

In Plato's *Republic* comes the dictum that the greatest justice comes in a world in which all people do their own jobs, implying that justice is diminished when people seek to do the job of someone else. McCarthy's teams always followed that idea. McCarthy rarely meddled with business and contract matters, leaving that to Wrigley and Veeck, Ruppert and Barrow, and Yawkey and Cronin. They, in turn, left him alone. Within his realm, he would do absolutely everything, and outside that world he would do virtually nothing. He would judge talent, but not the purchase it. He would train, place, and replace his men. When players had problems, whatever the level, he would handle them, unless they intruded upon the club's business arrangements. And of course all field matters, strategic and tactical, were his purview alone. To build such a structure and make it work was not a mere matter of outer architecture. McCarthy thrived when he could trust those above and beneath him to do their jobs well and to leave him alone to do his. This was more a matter of character than structure. When others, usually of lesser character, crossed lines and meddled in his business he withdrew.

McCarthy spent years building his ability from player, to base coach, to instructor, to field manager, and his basic ingredients— an eye for talent, patience, and a steel-trap memory — never matters for mere copying. He also hired people to do his assistant work, all tasks he could do himself, and did so with the same great talent-spotting ability that he displayed in the eyeing of the talent of a prospective player. One cannot summarily toss together the pieces of such an arrangement, hop up to the capstone and expect it all to work. The years of careful, patient planning were

apparent and ennobling when McCarthy put it all on display. For a nation of baseball fans, especially in a traumatic era like the Great Depression, McCarthy and the
system he represented provided an example of something that could succeed. It was
more than a mere soothing fireside chat, it was an actual working example of an organization that systematically built itself and succeeded in the very era in which so
many others were failing.

A sad paradox here was that the late '30s Yankees were so successful that other
Depression era clubs ended up being financially worse off. It was McCarthy's success
that indeed cemented the tradition of "Damn Yankees" among his opponents. Therein
lay another irony: McCarthy's unprecedented success helped inspire a successful
Broadway musical, Joe McCarthy's favorite venue of entertainment. *Damn Yankees*
was not his favorite show, however. Even among the legions of Yankee-haters that
McCarthy helped inspire, there was no lack of respect. (Many of the detractors of
the famous 1930s fireside chats did not hold such respect.) For McCarthy's players,
the sense of the carefully drawn world, requiring thoroughness and sanity from all
those involved at upper levels, came forth in the form of a system to which they had
to adhere but in which they felt complete fairness. On them it placed but one essential demand — do your absolute best at all times. Phil Rizzuto grasped that when he
commented upon McCarthy's passing: "He was very, very strict, but very, very fair."
Paul Waner commented that all his tactical decisions were uncannily on the mark.[19]
Players said that any dressing down was done in private (except Joe Page's). McCarthy
commanded respect to such a degree that he did not need any protocols of leadership. Usually his players did not call him "Skipper," "Sir," or even "Mr. McCarthy."
They called him "Joe." He needed nothing else, as one writer had noted with pride
in 1932: the fewest rules, the most discipline.

As in so many walks of life, the best organization is that which requires the
fewest outer limitations but is able to elicit from its participants the greatest willingness to contribute their utmost to the team. When it worked, as it did so well for
McCarthy, it took a world war to stop it. It all seemed so effortless that opponents
derided him as a mere pusher of buttons. This envy and need to deride was so strong
that successful managers of later eras like Casey Stengel, Walter Alston, and Earl
Weaver also endured the same "push button" label. In the late 1930s, Yankee haters
said that rooting for McCarthy and New York was like rooting for U.S. Steel. When
some are so successful as to invite that kind of envy, such detraction is ultimately
complimentary, and when the verbal particulars of the derisive rhetoric carry on to
similar situations in later generations and other walks of life, the compliment runs
even more deeply.

When sports books and magazines cover the topic of "dynasties," no matter
how people may praise the Montreal Canadiens, the Boston Celtics, or Notre Dame
football, no one ever puts any team dynasty but the New York Yankees at the top of
the list, and no one was more responsible for the establishment of that dynasty than
Joe McCarthy. Babe Ruth and Miller Huggins won the first championships. But they
could not sustain the winning, nor do it quite so consistently. Jake Ruppert and Ed
Barrow provided the money and organization, but others like Tom Yawkey did as
much and brought forth as many resources. Casey Stengel and Ralph Houk certainly
sustained the Yankee dynasty, and under lesser figures it may have fallen away sooner.

But the establishment of the Yankees as a true, and reviled, dynasty was, more than of anyone else, the work of Joe McCarthy. For those who then claimed that he won because he had the best material, there is the simple point that he was the one who put the materials together. Critics further point out that McCarthy won with great material but tended to lose when pressed, coming so close but failing to win in 1930, '33, '35, '40, '44, '48, and '49. To say that McCarthy won nine pennants and came close in seven others is hardly a criticism. The key is to be in position to win. The final outcomes from that point often hinge on chance. Indeed one of the greatest points of praise for the golfer Jack Nicklaus is the fact that he not only won 18 major tournaments but came in second place 19 other times. McCarthy would doubtlessly be happy with such a comparison, as would Nicklaus.

The retired life on the farm remained a pleasure for Mr. and Mrs. McCarthy for many years. Joe would normally eat a large breakfast, then eat lightly at lunch and dinner. He usually enjoyed one drink before dinner and sometimes had one before bed. The scotch problems of his later managing years never reappeared in retirement. All the newspapers' references to "his gall bladder acting up again" may certainly have been kind cover-ups, as McCarthy never had any gall bladder trouble later in life. In 1965, life began to change for the worse. That year, Mrs. McCarthy suffered a stroke, and she lived thereafter as an invalid. "I don't celebrate anything now," McCarthy grimly nodded in 1970. "After you reach my age you don't want to celebrate. My wife's been very sick, and I don't get around. We don't have any birthday parties now — used to years ago, of course. Not anymore." More ruefully, McCarthy mused to Ted Williams, "You know, Ted, I never quit managing. Since Babe became an invalid, I'm managing five women — three nurses, a housekeeper, and a cleaning woman. I'm glad I have managing experience."[20] It was like being the $6.50 a week "head tender" at the Germantown Yarn Mill again. On October 13, 1971, Joe McCarthy had to enter a Buffalo hospital for cataract surgery. The surgery was successful, but three days after he left the hospital, on October 18, Mrs. McCarthy passed away.[21] McCarthy was devastated with Babe's passing, and as it came at a point when he felt so physically weak and vulnerable after his cataract operation, the blow was especially harsh. His friends said that Joe never really recovered. His joy for life never fully returned.[22]

With Babe's passing and with the creeping infirmities of age, McCarthy grew less interested in tending to his property. He leased the use of his land and ultimately sold 80 of his 87 acres. A couple, Fred and Marie Richards, came daily to look after matters. Marie Richards had been Babe's primary care taker in her last years. Fred Richards tended to all house maintenance and ran the acreage. They took him shopping, to the barber, to the optician, and to church. "I am lucky to have such devoted friends," McCarthy sincerely acknowledged. He went out less and less. In 1972, he did attend the dedication of a complex of four Little League baseball fields in Buffalo. It was named "Joe McCarthy Field." "I am happy to repeat," he intoned: "Give a boy a bat and a ball and a place to play and you'll have a good citizen." Phil Rizzuto came to the dedication. He was casually dressed, and McCarthy gently reminded him that he used to require a coat and tie.[23]

Admirers came from time to time, and various local newspapermen interviewed him. But generally he lived a quiet life, at times, it seemed, in virtual anonymity. On an ABC Monday night baseball broadcast, Howard Cosell referred prematurely to "the late Joe McCarthy."[24] On April 21, 1976, a plaque to McCarthy was placed in Yankee Stadium. It was McCarthy's 89th birthday. McCarthy could not attend. "I'm not feeling good enough to go any place any more," he shrugged. In 1976 and 1977, as the Yankees reattained greatness, and as McCarthy approached his 90th birthday, several newspapers contacted him. Joe Garagiola interviewed him before a national audience on NBC. McCarthy had commented to friends how he had grown so old that he was like the proverbial cow's tail; his clothes had outgrown him. But while he was physically infirm, his mind was still razor-sharp, and it showed with all who spoke with him. Managers, he told to several interviewers, now take too many trips to the mound. It slows the game down. Two and one half hours he felt is about the right length of time for a game. Recalling Grover Alexander pitching a game that scarcely lasted an hour, McCarthy laughed about the food concessionaire complaining that he didn't have enough time to cook the hot dogs. McCarthy told Garagiola and others that the designated hitter rule was a terrible idea. "I like to see the pitcher come to bat. If they get the designated runner on top of the designated hitter, they can do without the manager. The batboy could manage the club then." When asked who would have been the DH on his great Yankee teams of the 1930s he quipped: "They were all designated hitters in those days." He noted that the hitters are not brushed back as often as they used to be, and that with the protective helmets they are not as easily intimidated, all revealing how much more accepted and common-place brush-back tactics were in the past.

When Henry Aaron surpassed Babe Ruth's all-time home run mark in 1974, McCarthy asserted that Ruth was the superior player on the basis that he hit his home runs in many fewer at bats. He greatly respected such modern greats as Aaron, but felt that Ruth was their superior. He freely conceded that, as among boxing fans, each generation of baseball people favors its own. The extremely high salaries of the modern game, he feared, take away some of the incentive to play well. With such salaries as modern baseball had developed, McCarthy also saw no need for a union: "The game isn't made for a union because of the great difference in salaries. There are enough smart players today to run their own affairs." Contrasting the modern game with the play of his day, McCarthy thoughtfully noted that players "seem to have more speed now." Perhaps he was delicately implying that there was more power in the game when he managed Ruth, Gehrig, DiMaggio, and Williams. When Joe Garagiola asked him: "How do you manage the likes of Babe Ruth and Ted Williams?" McCarthy replied without a second of hesitation: "You don't. You don't call pitches for the greatest of home run hitters, and you don't try to manage a .400 hitter." Turning to Ted Williams in particular, he added, "the secret of Williams' success was that he always hit strikes. I never saw him hit a bad ball." The wisdom of ultimately knowing when it was his job to stop managing was something he never lost, and many others never had. With the Yankees back in the World Series in 1976, McCarthy was finally asked if he was still a fan. Again he was unhesitating: "Sure I'm pulling for them," he nodded. "Once a Yankee, always a Yankee."[25]

On July 27 that summer, McCarthy suffered a fall and fractured a hip. The surgery to repair the fracture was successful, but, as is often the case with such injuries at an advanced age, McCarthy's general health soon began to deteriorate. He was able to go home after the hip healed, but he was quite weak, and later that November he had to be rehospitalized. He had reinjured his hip, and pneumonia soon complicated matters.[26] Despite a regimen of antibiotics, McCarthy continued to weaken. From his fourth floor window at Millard Filmore Hospital, McCarthy could see his old home on Gates Circle. As he steadily weakened, a nurse called one of McCarthy's friends, sportscaster Ralph Hubbell. "Mr. McCarthy seems to be slipping away," she said. Hubbell rushed over. He sat with McCarthy, but Joe was now too weak to speak. Hubbell then took McCarthy's hand, and said "Hi Joe, it's me, Ralph. I'm back again." Hubbell felt a slight squeeze from McCarthy's right hand, so he knew Joe had heard him. "Then," wrote Hubbell, "he went on his way. Babe had been waiting for him a long time. I said, 'So long, Joe .' ... It was a pleasant good-bye."[27]

McCarthy died on Friday, January 13, 1978, just three months shy of his 91st birthday. There were big doings in the sports world that weekend — the Dallas Cowboys and the Denver Broncos were about to play in the Super Bowl. Meanwhile, in the nation's general news, former Vice President Hubert Humphrey had died the same day. The death of old Joe McCarthy up in snowbound Buffalo thus passed with little notice. And it snowed so hard that week in Buffalo that few former ballplayers or officials from Major League Baseball could make it to the January 17 funeral. Two representatives from George Steinbrenner's New York Yankees did make it up to St. Christopher's Church in Tonawanda that snowy day, as did Monte Irvin from Baseball Commissioner Bowie Kuhn's Office and Ken Smith, a former New York reporter, from the Hall of Fame. Vincent MacNamara was also present. He was the President of the New York–Pennsylvania Baseball League with whom McCarthy had played and first managed in Wilkes-Barre. The New York State Legislature passed an official resolution of sorrow. Otherwise, all mourners present were from Buffalo. For years folks had come to call McCarthy "Buffalo Joe," and the city's infamous winter had truly taken him as one of its own. It was a warm feeling. McCarthy was buried in Mount Olivet Cemetery, a site very close to his Yankee Farm. The bulk of his estate ($721,200.91) went to Marie Richards for "devoted service to my late wife, Elizabeth McCarthy." Other bequests went to his parish in Buffalo, to John Schulte, a surviving coach from the Yankee days, and to Eddie Froelich, his batboy in Chicago and trainer in New York and Boston. "My parents were dead when I met him as a 14-year-old bat boy," Froelich eulogized. "Joe McCarthy was like a father to me." It was McCarthy who helped Froelich get an education and become an athletic trainer. Once with the Yankees, Froelich never left McCarthy's side. As with Colonel Ruppert, McCarthy always valued loyalty.[28]

Several years after McCarthy had died, Joe DiMaggio strode into the lobby of Buffalo's Hyatt Regency Hotel one afternoon. As always, everyone in the room riveted their attention on him. Instantly, he was surrounded by people eager for autographs and conversation. Most of the reporters in the room knew better than to try to approach Joe DiMaggio for any reflections or information. DiMaggio had long made it clear to the media that he was not to be bothered. Nevertheless, one young local writer dared to approach him. Instantly, DiMaggio reacted. "Are you a reporter?" he snapped. When the young writer acknowledged that he was, DiMaggio calmly waved him off and began to walk away, sniffing: "I don't want to talk." The reporter pressed lightly, however, and asked DiMaggio if he could ask him some questions about Joe McCarthy. The reporter recalled: "DiMaggio took a few more steps, then suddenly stopped. 'Wait a minute,' DiMaggio asked, 'are you from Buffalo?'" The reporter nodded yes, and DiMaggio's entire countenance and tone changed. "Joe was from Buffalo," he smiled, "go ahead and ask your questions." The young man got his interview right on the spot, and the rest of the press in the room were absolutely shocked at the sight of this youngster being able to get Joe DiMaggio to talk to him. In the interview, when asked "What did Joe McCarthy do for you?" DiMaggio was quite sincere and not the least bit sarcastic when he replied, "He didn't do anything; he just managed."[29]

"I played under three great managers," reflected Tommy Henrich, "Joe McCarthy, Bucky Harris, and Casey Stengel, and I have to put McCarthy at the top. For my money he wrote the book."[30] That was the only "book" that Joe McCarthy needed to write. Some lesser managers are too easygoing, their teams decline and then respond to martinets. Other managers put too much pressure on their teams; they decline and respond, for a time, to a more relaxed atmosphere. The Yankees' ups and downs in the 1970s, '80s, and '90s under Billy Martin, Bob Lemon, Dick Howser, and Yogi Berra exemplified this all too well. Only a few managers are able to strike the balance here that works for a long time. The forces of Connie Mack's paternalism or John McGraw's sheer pugnaciousness were extraordinary here. McCarthy did it by sheer force of calm ability and utter confidence in himself. McCarthy projected no particular personality, not that his approbation was not enlivening or that his anger was not feared, far from it. Indeed one reason both had such an impact was that they were so rarely expressed. When any emotional expression came forth it was an exception, usually logical and necessary, extending from a system he had constructed which demanded adherence because of its inherent validity. That was "the book." "A good memory, patience, ability to recognize ability ... [and] know what to do with it" — those were the key ingredients as far as McCarthy was concerned. Otherwise he was genuinely modest: "There was no secret. I had good ballplayers. And I worked with good organizations."[31] It sounds so simple, but no one could execute it all better than McCarthy. Above all, perhaps, no one had a keener knack for understanding and respecting the personalities of each of his players and knowing how then to motivate each of them in a different way whenever he felt it was needed. McCarthy once said that he never read a book on psychology.[32] The fact was that he did not need to.

All who played for McCarthy recognized they were playing for the master of the game. His mistakes were there, but there were certainly not many of them. Meanwhile his triumphs were utterly astounding. Perhaps his real triumph lay not in the winning but in the spirit he created with his teams that led to the winning. Way back in 1927, when McCarthy was merely in his second year managing the Cubs, a local stage actress who went by the stage name of "Mitzi" wrote an article about him. She confessed to have known nothing about baseball, but said she had become a huge fan of the Cubs as she witnessed McCarthy quickly turning the team from last place into a contender. From her utterly unmuddied, naive perspective, there was only one cause for the turnaround: "the miracle man." If he had not been such a miracle man in baseball, "Mitzi" wrote,

> Joe McCarthy would be a magnificent man of the theatre. ... In the theatre it is one
> thing to develop an individual star; many managers have done that much; but to pro-

duce a company of stars, acting together in perfect harmony — that takes genius. ...
Here is a personality that any person connected with the theatre can watch and study,
and come away from stimulated and inspired.

When I first met Mr. McCarthy, ... I was a little bit afraid of him. I had heard he
was strong in discipline — ooh! — had little time for social chatter — booh! — and spent
all his time thinking about baseball. He sounded like a machine, but as soon as I took
a real look at him I recognized an intensely human being. Mr. McCarthy has the
paternal complex developed to a remarkable degree; as soon as he begins to talk I saw
that his players were his children; he gave them more than the spark to light up their
different talents; he gave them the great human response that parents give their young
folk for honest effort. He has what psychologists call "the spirit of cosmic father-moth-
erhood."

As Mr. McCarthy spoke to me of his players I saw ... real modesty. ... This "master
mind" has never yet been known to say "I" with any ego. It only amuses or antagonizes
him when he reads about his own "master strategy" or "mystery man" qualities. ...
"It's ridiculous, that's all," he scoffed. "I like to see credit placed where it belongs, and
on this team it certainly belongs to the boys."[33]

The intense passion for the game and for his work combined with a genuine modesty about himself — that was exceedingly rare for a manager in any field. What
"Mitzi" saw in 1927 changed not one bit over the next 50 years, especially that intan-
gible concept of genius. The combination of ability and humility explains why winning never changed Joe McCarthy and Joe McCarthy never changed any player; he
just made them be the utmost of what they could be.

For McCarthy, the greatest joy came not in the winning, but in regard to the
men he affected with his hard work. With the notable absence of any reference to
anything about baseball, he reflected late in his career, very much indeed like a proud
father: "When you know in your heart you've helped some of these young fellows
make good, when you know you played a part in their success, that's when you know
you're accomplishing something, you're not wasting your time. When I think of the
fellows, ... and I see what they've made of themselves, and they come to me and tell
me I helped them do it, why, I feel I've done something important."[34] No one could
argue with that call.

Appendix:
Joe McCarthy's Major
League Managerial Record

Year	TM/L	G	W	L	PCT	Standing
1926	Chi-N	155	82	72	.532	4
1927	Chi-N	153	85	68	.556	4
1928	Chi-N	154	91	63	.591	3
1929	Chi-N	156	98	54	.645	1
1930	Chi-N	152	86	64	.573	2
1931	NY-A	155	94	59	.614	2
1932	NY-A	156	107	47	.695	1*
1933	NY-A	152	91	59	.607	2
1934	NY-A	154	94	60	.610	2
1935	NY-A	149	89	60	.597	2
1936	NY-A	155	102	51	.667	1*
1937	NY-A	157	102	52	.662	1*
1938	NY-A	157	99	53	.651	1*
1939	NY-A	152	106	45	.702	1*
1940	NY-A	155	88	66	.571	3
1941	NY-A	156	101	53	.656	1*
1942	NY-A	154	103	51	.669	1
1943	NY-A	155	98	56	.636	1*
1944	NY-A	154	83	71	.539	3
1945	NY-A	152	81	71	.533	4
1946	NY-A	35	22	13	.629	2
1948	Bos-A	155	96	59	.619	2*
1949	Bos-A	155	96	58	.623	2
1950	Bos-A	59	31	28	.525	4
24		3487	2125	1333	.615	

Source: John Thorn and Peter Palmer, eds., *Total Baseball: The Ultimate Encyclopedia of Baseball,* 3rd Edition, (New York: Harper Perenial, 1993), p. 2195.

Chapter Notes

Chapter 1

1. Dan Daniel, *New York World-Telegram*, May 25, 1946, p. 12; Ed Fitzgerald, "Nobody's Neutral About McCarthy," *I Managed Good, But Boy Did They Play Bad* (New York: Playboy Press, 1973), p. 254; Edwin Pope, *Baseball's Greatest Managers* (Garden City, N.Y.: Doubleday, 1960), pp. 136–7; Charles B. Cleveland, *The Great Baseball Managers* (New York: Thomas Y. Crowell, 1950), pp. 118-19.

2. Interview with Mrs. Susan McCarthy, *Chicago Herald and Examiner*, June 15, 1926, p. 13; *New York Times*, January 28, 1937, p. 35, Clippings File, National Baseball Hall of Fame and Museum, Cooperstown.

3. Eddie Gold and Art Ahrens, *The Golden Era Cubs, 1876–1940* (Chicago: Bonus Books, 1985), p. 108; *New York Times*, January 28, 1937, p. 35, Clippings File, Cooperstown.

4. Quoted in Donald Honig, *The Man in the Dugout: Fifteen Big League Managers Speak Their Minds* (Chicago: Follett, 1977), p. 81.

5. *Buffalo Evening News*, August 4, 1969, section C, p. 2; January 14, 1978, p. 11.

6. See, for example, Edwin Pope, *Baseball's Greatest Managers*, p. 136; Ed Fitzgerald, "Nobody's Neutral About McCarthy," *I Managed Good, But Boy Did They Play Bad*, p. 254; *New York Sun*, April 21, 1943, p. 13; and Dan Daniel, *New York World-Telegram*, October 1, 1938, p. 23, May 25, 1946, p. 12.

7. *New York World-Telegram*, May 25, 1946, p. 12

8. *Philadelphia Evening Public Ledger*, October 13, 1932, p. 22; *New York Sun*, April 21, 1943, p. 13; Interview with Mrs. Susan McCarthy, *Chicago Herald and Examiner*, June 15, 1926, p. 13.

9. *Buffalo Express*, March 28, 1914, p. 13; "Down Memory Lane with Joe McCarthy," July 23, 1936, Clippings File, Cooperstown; Associated Press Biographical Sketch, No. 3002, November 15, 1942, Clippings File, Cooperstown; Pope, *Baseball's Greatest Managers*, p. 139.

10. *The Illustrated Buffalo Express*, April 8, 1906, p. 9.

12. *Buffalo Evening News*, November 19, 1942, p. 22; *The Illustrated Buffalo Express*, May 21, 1906; May 28, 1906, p. 9.

13. *Buffalo Express*, March 28, 1914, p. 13.

14. "Down Memory Lane with Joe McCarthy," July 23, 1936, Clippings File, Cooperstown; *Wilkes-Barre Record*, March 8, 1913, p. 9.

Chapter 2

1. *Wilmington Evening Journal*, April 1, 1907, p. 2; *Wilmington Every Evening*, April 4, 1907, p. 6.

2. *Wilmington Evening Journal*, April 5, 1907, p. 6; April 11, 1907, p. 8; *Wilmington Every Evening*, April 6, 1907, p. 6;

3. *Wilmington Every Evening*, April 8, 1907, p. 6.

4. *Wilmington Evening Journal*, April 11, 1907, p. 8.

5. *Wilmington Every Evening*, April 9, 1907, p. 6.

6. See Pope, *Baseball's Greatest Managers*, p. 137.

7. *Wilmington Evening Journal*, April 15, 1907, p. 8; *Wilmington Every Evening*, April 15, 1907, p. 6.

8. *Wilmington Evening Journal*, April 23, 25, 27, 29, 30, May 1, 2, 3, 4, 1907, p. 8; *Wilmington Every Evening*, April 19, 26, 29, 30, May 1, 2, 6, 1907, p. 6.

9. *Wilmington Evening Journal*, May 11, 1907, p. 8; *Wilmington Every Evening*, April 27, 1907, p. 6.

10. *Wilmington Evening Journal*, May 13, 1907, p. 7.

Chapter 3

1. Quoted in Maury Allen, *Where Have You Gone, Joe DiMaggio* (New York: North American Library, 1976), p. 20.

2. Class D Contract, Franklin Baseball Club, and Joseph V. McCarthy, June 2, 1907, Copy from Kenneth Jacklin, grandson of L.L. Jacklin, Clippings File, Cooperstown.

3. *Pittsburg Post*, May 20, 1907, p. 7. (In the 19th and early 20th century, Pittsburgh spelled its name without an "h").

4. *Ibid.*, May 16, 1907, p. 13, June 3, 1907, p. 6, June 24, 1907, p. 7; *Pittsburg Dispatch*, June 9, 1907, section 6, p. 2, June 18, 1907, p. 8; *Oil City Derrick*, June 8, 1907, p. 3; Maury Allen, *Where Have You Gone, Joe DiMaggio* (New York: E.P. Dutton, 1975), p. 39.

5. *Pittsburg Post*, June 17, 1907, p. 7; *Oil City Derrick*, May 17, 1907, p. 3.

6. *Pittsburg Dispatch*, July 1, 1907, p. 6, July 7, section 4, page 5, July 15, 1907, p. 12, July 18, 1907, p. 6, July 20, 1907, p. 6.

7. *Ibid.*, July 20, 1907, p. 6, August 5, 1907, p. 6, Aug. 25, 1907, p. 13.

8. *Ibid.*, August 27, 1907, p. 9, Aug. 29, 1907, p. 6, Aug. 30, 1907, p. 6, September 2, 1907, p. 6, Sept. 3, 1907, p. 6, Sept. 5, 1907, p. 6, Sept. 8, 1907, p. 6, Sept., 18, 1907, p. 7.

9. *Ibid.*, September 17, 1907, p. 6; "Down Memory Lane with Joe McCarthy," July 23, 1936, Clippings File, Cooperstown.

Chapter 4

1. *Toledo News Bee*, March 21, 1908, p. 8.

2. *Ibid.*

3. *Ibid.*, March 28, 1908, p. 8.

4. Clippings File, Cooperstown.

5. *Chattanooga Daily Times*, March 26, 1908, p. 10, March 27, p. 12, March 28, p. 10, March 29, p. 10; *Toledo News Bee*, March 26, 1908, p. 10, March 27, p. 12, March 29, p. 6, March 30, p. 6.

6. *Toledo News Bee*, April 1, 1908, p. 8.

7. *Ibid.*, April 4, 1908, p. 8, April 6, p. 6, April 7, p. 10, April 8, p. 8, April 10, p. 12, April 10, p. 10, April 11, p. 12.

8. *Ibid.*, April 17, 1908, p. 12, April 21, p. 8, April 22, p. 8, April 23, p. 10, April 24, p. 12.

9. *Ibid.*, April 25, 1908, p. 8, April 27, p. 7, April 28, p. 8, April 30, p. 10, May 2, p. 6.

10. *Ibid.*, May 6, 1908, p. 8, May 7, p. 10, May 8, p. 12, May 9, p. 6, May 11, p. 8, May 13, p. 8, May 16, p. 6, May 18, p. 6.

11. *Ibid.*, May 23, 1908, p. 6.

12. *Ibid.*, May 25, 1908, p. 6, May 26, p. 8, May 29, p. 3, June 2, p. 8, June 5, p. 6, June 6, p. 8, June 11, p. 10.

13. *Ibid.*, June 13, 1908, p. 6, June 16, p. 8, June 22, p. 6, June 26, p. 12, June 27, p. 6, July 1, p. 8, July 2, p. 12, July 4, p. 3.

14. *Ibid.*, July 11, 1908, p. 6, July 17, p. 10, August 1, p. 6, Aug. 8, p. 6, Aug. 10, p. 7, Aug. 11, p. 8, Aug. 15, p. 6, Aug. 18, p. 6, Aug. 24, p. 6.

15. *Ibid.*, August 29, 1908, p. 6, September 2, p. 6, Sept. 5, p. 5, Sept. 12, p. 6, Sept. 17, p. 6.

Chapter 5

1. *Toledo News Bee*, May 19, 1908, p. 8, September 15, 1908, p. 8, March 23, 1909, p. 8.

2. *Ibid.*, March 23, 1909, p. 8.

3. *Ibid.*, March 19, 1909, p. p. 12, March 29, p. 6; Clippings File, Cooperstown.

4. *Toledo News Bee*, April 22, 1909, p. 10.

5. Ibid, April 26, 1909, p. 6, April 30, p. 12, May 1, p. 8, May 3, p. 3, May 4, p. 8.

6. *Ibid.*, May 24, 1909, p. 8.

7. *Ibid.*, May 26, 1909, p. 10, May 29, p. 8, June 8, p. 10, June 26, p. 10.

8. *Ibid.*, July 3, 1909, p. 12, July 5, p. 5., July 31, p. 8, September 2, p. 8; Ed Fitzgerald, "Nobody's Neutral About McCarthy," p. 255.

9. *Toledo News Bee*, September 16, 1909, p. 8.

10. *Ibid.*, September 18, 1909, p. 8, Sept. 28, p. 9.

11. *New York Sun*, April 21, 1943, p. 13; *New York Daily News*, September 19, 1944, p. 30; Edwin Pope, *Baseball's Greatest Managers*, p. 139. (Other than an occasional reference to a few associates, McCarthy left little record as to his involvement in the fight game. Whether he fully managed one or several fighters, worked as a corner man, or anything else, cannot be fully determined. The public records about the fight scene in early twentieth-century Philadelphia, or elsewhere, contain no systematic coverage of managers or corner men of the hundreds of journeymen boxers. In September, 1944, prior to a ball game, McCarthy did briefly reminisce to a *New York Daily News* reporter about a fighter in Milwaukee, Ad Wolgast, on whom he had successfully wagered. He added in passing: "I had a fighter myself at the time," meaning he was managing one.)

12. *Toledo News Bee*, March 19, 1910, p. 11.

13. *Ibid.*, March 11, 1910, p. 12.

14. *Ibid.*, March 24, 1910, p. 11, April 5, p. 12, April 12, p. 12; Clippings File, Cooperstown.

15. *Toledo News Bee*, April 14, 1910, p. 12, April 15, p. 12, April 16, p. 8, April 22, p. 12, April 26, p. 8.

16. *Ibid.*, April 30, 1910, p. 10, May 6, p. 12, May 16, p. 10, May 19, p. 8, May 21, p. 10, May 31, p. 10, June 14, p. 12.

17. *Ibid.*, June 4, 1910, p. 8, June 29, p. 8, July 1, p. 12, July 2, p. 8, July 9, p. 8, July 16, p. 8, July 18, p. 6, July 23, p. 8, July 30, p. 8.

18. *Ibid.*, August 6, 1910, p. 8, August 13, p. 8, September 8, p. 10, Sept. 10, p. 8, Sept. 28, p. 10.

19. *Ibid.*, March 8, 1911.

20. *Ibid.*, March 30, 1911, p. 12, April 1, p. 10.

21. *Ibid.*, March 28, 1911, p. 12.

22. *Ibid.*, April 27, 1911, p. 12, April 29, p. 10, May 13, p. 8, May 31, p. 12.

23. *Ibid.*, May 31, 1911, p. 12; *Indianapolis Star*, May 30, 1911, p. 10, May 31, p. 10, June 4, p. 2; *Indianapolis News*, May 31, 1911, p. 14; Clippings File, Cooperstown.

24. *Indianapolis Star*, June 5, 1911, p. 6, June 7, p. 8, June 10, p. 8, June 12, p. 8, June 19, p. 8.

25. *Ibid.*, July 30, 1911, p. 2, August 12, p. 8, Aug. 14, p. 6, Aug. 21, p. 7, Aug. 26, p. 8, Sept. 3, p. 1, Sept. 11, p. 8, Sept. 17, p. 2, Sept. 23, p. 8, Sept. 25, p. 9, Sept. 27, p. 8, October 8, p. 4; *Indianapolis News*, August 14, p. 10, August 31, p. 8.

26. *Wilkes-Barre (Pa.) Record*, March 8, 1913, p. 9.

27. *Indianapolis Star*, March 28, 1912, p.11, April 18, p. 10, May 7, p. 10, May 9, p. 10, May 13, p. 9.

28. "Down Memory Lane with Joe McCarthy," July 23, 1936, Clippings File, Cooperstown.

Chapter 6

1. *Syracuse Post-Standard*, July 9, 1912, p. 13.

2. *Wilkes-Barre Record*, May 14, 1912, p. 17;

3. Ibid, April 27, 1912, p. 9, May 12, p. 9, June 17, p. 16, May 22, p. 17; *Troy Record*, July 3, p. 11.

4. *Wilkes-Barre Record*, June 17, 1912, p. 16.

5. *Syracuse Post-Standard*, July 18, 1912, p. 12; *Albany Evening Journal*, July 18, p. 6; *Wilkes-Barre Record*, July 13, p. 9.

6. *Wilkes-Barre Record*, July 17, 1912, p. 9, August 5, p. 9, Aug. 6, p. 19, Aug. 27, p. 9.

7. *Syracuse Post-Standard*, August 15, 1912, p. 9, August 21, p. 9, August 28, p. 9, September 2, p. 11, Sept. 3, p. 11.

8. *Ibid.*, August 29, 1912, p. 9; *Albany Evening Journal*, August 29, p. 6; *Wilkes-Barre Record*, September 3, p. 9.

9. *Wilkes-Barre Record*, March 10, 1913, p. 9.

10. *Syracuse Post-Standard*, September 5, 1912, p. 14, Sept. 9, pp. 16–17; *Wilkes-Barre Record*, Sept. 9, p. 9.

11. *Albany Evening Journal*, September 9, 1912, p. 6, Sept. 11, p. 6, Sept. 12, p. 6, Sept. 13, p. 6; *Wilkes-Barre Record*, Sept. 10, p. 9, Sept. 11, p. 17.

12. *Wilkes-Barre Record*, September 11, 1912, p. 17.

13. *Ibid.*, February 9, 1912, p. 7.

14. Ibid, September 12, 1912, p. 15, Sept. 13, p. 17, Sept. 14, p. 22; *Albany Evening Journal*, Sept. 14, p. 6, Sept. 16, p. 6, Sept. 26, p. 6; *Wilkes-Barre Record*, Sept. 14, p. 22, Sept. 22, p. 20, Sept. 24, p. 17.

15. *Wilkes-Barre Record*, March 8, 1913, p. 9.

16. Ibid; *Albany Argus*, March 8, p. 10.

17. *Syracuse Post-Standard*, April 12, 1913, p. 18.

18. *Ibid.*, May 5, 1913, p. 10, May 12, p. 11, May 13, p. 12, May 26, p. 12, May 30, p. 9; *Albany Evening Journal*, June 9, p. 6, April 8, p. 9, April 19, p. 24, April 26, p. 24.

19. *Albany Evening Journal*, June 10, 1913, p. 6, June 13, p. 6, June 20, p. 6, June 27, p. 6, June 30, p. 6.

20. *Syracuse Post-Standard*, August 1, 1913, p. 13, August 8, p. 12, August 11, p. 14; *Albany Evening Journal*, July 22, p. 6, August 26, p. 6; *Albany Argus*, July 27, p. 8; *Wilkes-Barre Record*, May 2, p. 9, July 24, p. 9.

21. *Syracuse Post-Standard*, September 9, 1913, p. 11, Sept. 15, p. 12; *Albany Evening Journal*, Sept. 15, p. 6; *Wilkes-Barre Record*, August 15, p. 9, Aug. 18, p. 9, Aug. 21, p. 9, Aug. 25, p. 9.

22. *Albany Evening Journal*, September 15, 1913, p. 6; *Wilkes-Barre Record*, Sept. 15, p. 11; "Down Memory Lane with Joe McCarthy," July 23, 1936, Clippings File, Cooperstown.

Chapter 7

1. *Buffalo Express*, March 28, 1914, p. 13, March 31, p. 12, April 12, p. 60, April 16, p. 13, April 22, p. 15.

2. *Ibid.*, April 23, 1914, p. 15, April 24, p. 11; see also Lawrence Ritter, *The Glory of Their Times*; Marshall Smelser, *The Life That Ruth Built: A Biography* (Lincoln: University of Nebraska Press, 1993), 45; Ed Linn, *The Great Rivalry: The Yankees and the Red Sox, 1901–1990*. (New York: Ticknor and Fields, 1991), p. 62.

3. *Buffalo Express*, May 5, 1914, p. 5, June 7, pp. 53, 60.

4. *Ibid.*, August 12, 1914, p. 11, September 1, p. 12; *Buffalo Evening News*, April 17, 1971, section C, p. 2.

5. *Buffalo Express*, July 9, 1914, p. 13, July 11, p. 11, July 26, p. 56, August 2, p. 53, Aug. 4, p. 13.

6. *Ibid.*, August 14, 1914, p. 9.

7. *Ibid.*, March 30, 1915, p. 13.

8. *Ibid.*, April 17, 1915, p. 10, April 23, p. 13, May 31, p. 15.

9. *Ibid.*, June 23, 1915, p. 13.

10. *Ibid.*, May 23, 1915, p. 64, August 5, p. 13.

Chapter 8

1. Eddie Gold and Art Ahrens, *The Golden Era Cubs, 1876–1940* (Chicago: Bonus Books, 1985), p. 108; Will Wedge column, *New York Sun*, April 4, 1932, p. 34; *New York Evening Post*, February 23, 1931, p. 29; Frank Graham, *The New York Yankees: An Informal History* (New York: G.P. Putnam's Sons, [1943] 1951) p. 174.

2. *New York Journal-American*, March 3, 1944, p. 18; "Down Memory Lane with Joe McCarthy," July 23, 1936, Clippings File, Cooperstown.

3. *New York Sun*, April 4, 1932, p. 34; *Brooklyn Eagle*, October 17, 1915, p. 4; *Buffalo Express*, October 29, 1915, p.15; Edward Grant Barrow, *My Fifty Years in Baseball* (New York: Coward-McCann, 1951), p. 66.

4. *Buffalo Express*, November 27, 1915, p. 11, December 15, p. 11, December 16, p. 13; Hy Turkin and S.C. Thompson, *The Official Encyclopedia of Baseball, Jubilee Edition* (New York: A.S. Barnes, 1951), p. 401.

5. *Buffalo Evening News*, April 18, 1964, section C, p. 1; *The Sporting News*, April 25, 1964, p. 7; *New York Sun*, June 23, 1943, p. 13; *Buffalo Evening News*, April 18, 1964, section C, p. 1.

6. *Louisville Courier-Journal*, March 14, 1916, p. 7, March 17, p. 7, April 1, p. 9, April 7, p. 7, April 11, p. 7; *Louisville Times*, March 24, p. 12, April 5, p. 12.

7. *Louisville Courier-Journal*, April 20, 1916, p. 9.

8. *Brooklyn Eagle*, June 1, 1916, p. 8.

9. *Louisville Courier-Journal*, May 12, 1916, pp. 7–8, May 18, p. 8, May 21, section 3, p. 8, May 28, section 3, p. 9.

10. *Ibid.*, June 16, 1916, p. 8, June 17, section 3, p. 9, June 22, p. 8, July 25, p. 7, July 28, p. 7, August 18, p. 6, Aug. 20, section 3, p. 10, August 23, p. 6, August 30, p. 8.

11. *Ibid.*, September 8, 1916, p. 6, Sept. 20, p. 6, Sept. 26, p. 6, Sept. 30, p. 6, October 1, section 3, page 9; *The Sporting News*, November 10, 1954, p. 16, February 13, 1957, p. 6.

12. *Omaha World Herald*, September 27, 1916, p. 7, October 5, p. 10, Oct. 6, p. 10, Oct. 7, p. 17, Oct. 8, p. 1, Oct. 9, p. 7; *Louisville Courier-Journal*, Oct. 5, p. 8, Oct 6, p. 9, Oct. 7, p. 8.

Chapter 9

1. *Louisville Courier-Journal*, April 15, 1917, section 1, p. 9.

2. *Ibid.*, March 10, 1917, p. 7, March 24, p. 9, March 27, p. 7, April 1, section 5, p. 8, April 8, section 5, p. 2, April 17, p. 6, September 2, section 3, p. 7.

3. *Ibid.*, April 2, 1917, p. 7.

4. *Ibid.*, March 24, 1917, p. 1, April 3, p. 1, April 5, p. 1, April 6, p. 1, April 7, p. 8.

5. *Ibid.*, April 10, 1917, p. 7, April 29, p. 1, May 1, p. 7, May 7, p. 7, May 18, p. 6, June 7, p. 1.

6. *Ibid.*, July 10, 1916, p. 7.

7. *Indianapolis Star*, May 4, 1917, p. 1; *Milwaukee Journal*, May 4, p. 18.

8. *Louisville Courier-Journal*, June 8, 1917, section 3, p. 9.

9. *Ibid.*, July 15, 1917, section 3, p. 7, July 16, p. 7, July 18, p. 6, July 20, p. 6, September 2, section 3, p. 8.

10. *Ibid.*, August 10, 1917, p. 6, Aug. 22, p. 7, Aug. 24, p. 6, Aug. 29, p. 7, September 3, p. 7.

11. *Ibid.*, September 12, 1917, p. 7, Sept. 13, p. 8, Sept. 18, p. 6.

12. *Ibid.*, Sept. 21. p. 6.

13. *Ibid.*, April 3, 1918, p. 7.

14. *Ibid.*, March 1, 1918, p. 7.

15. *Ibid.*

16. *Ibid.*, April 1, 1918, p. 6.

17. *Ibid.*, May 11, 1918, p. 8, May 24, p. 8, June 1, p. 6.

18. *Ibid.*, May 17, 1918, p. 8.

19. *Ibid.*, June 16, 1918, section 3, p. 3.

20. *Ibid.*, June 19, 1918, p. 6.

21. *Ibid.*, July 18, 1918, p. 6.

22. *Louisville Times*, July 18, 1918, p. 5.

23. *Louisville Courier-Journal*, July 19, 1918, p. 8.

24. *Ibid.*, July 21, 1918, section 3, p. 2, July 22, p. 8, July 23, p. 8; *Louisville Times*, July 22, p. 6.

25. *Louisville Courier-Journal*, July 23, 1918, p. 8, August 1, p. 6.

26. *Ibid.*, August 19, 1918, p. 6, Aug. 21, p. 6, Aug. 25, section 3, p. 4.

27. *The Patriot* (Harrisburg, Pa.), July 18, 1918, p. 9.

28. *Ibid.*, July 5, 1918, p. 9, July 16, p. 9.

29. *Ibid.*, August 15, 1918, p. 7.

30. *Ibid.*

31. *Ibid.*, September 3, 1918, p. 7, Sept. 5, p. 7, Sept. 6, p. 7, Sept. 14, p. 13, Sept. 16, p. 5.

32. *Ibid.*, September 27, 1918, p. 13.

33. *Louisville Courier-Journal*, March 17, 1920, p. 3.

Chapter 10

1. *Louisville Courier-Journal*, March 5, 1919, p. 10, July 23, p. 8.

2. *Ibid.*, March 3, 1918, section 3, p. 6.

3. *Ibid.*, April 14, 1919, p. 7, May 6, p.8.

4. *Ibid.*, May 20, 1919, p. 10, May 29, p. 9, June 13, p. 9, June 16, p. 9, June 23, p. 6, July 1, p. 11, July 9, p. 8.

5. *Ibid.*, July 23, 1919, p. 8.

6. *Ibid.*, July 31, 1919, p. 8, August 1, p. 7.

7. *Ibid.*, August 3, 1919, section 5, pp. 4–6, Aug. 17, section 4, p. 2, Aug. 18, p. 6, Aug. 22, p. 8.

8. *Ibid.*, September 3, 1919, p. 6, Sept. 20, p. 4, Sept. 27, p. 7, March 8, 1920, p. 7.

9. *Ibid.*, October 14, 1919, p. 8, Oct. 19, section 5, p. 3.

Chapter 11

1. *Louisville Courier-Journal*, March 12, 1920, p. 7, March 14, section 3, p. 2; see also Dan Shaughnessy, *The Curse of the Bambino* (New York: E.P. Dutton, 1990), *passim*.

2. *Louisville Courier-Journal*, March 8, 1920, p. 7.

3. *Ibid.*, March 17, 1920, p. 3.

4. *Ibid.*, March 26, 1920, p. 7, April 3, p. 7, April 5, p. 6, April 8, p. 7, April 9, p. 7, April 10, p. 8, April 11, section 6, p. 10.

5. *Ibid.*, April 12, 1920, p. 7.

6. *Ibid.*, April 14, 1920, p. 7, April 15, p. 7.

7. *Ibid.*, May 3, 1920, p. 6, May 7, p. 11, May 22, p. 6, May 30, section 3, p. 2.

8. *Ibid.*, June 5, 1920, p. 6, June 11, p. 8, July 28, p. 6.

9. *Ibid.*, June 16, 1920, p. 6, June 23, p. 9, June 28, p. 6, June 30, p. 9, July 4, section 4, p. 2, July 16, p. 6, July 19, p. 6, July 23, p. 7, July 25, section 4, p. 2.

10. *Ibid.*, July 30, 1920, p. 6.

11. *Ibid.*, July 31, 1920, p. 6, August 3, p. 6, Aug. 4, p. 6.

12. *Ibid.*, August 6, 1920, p. 6, Aug. 8, p. 6, Aug., 10, p. 8.

13. *Ibid.*, August 13, 1920, p. 6, Aug. 14, p. 6, Aug. 16, p. 6, Aug. 15, section 4, p. 1, Aug., 29, section 4, p. 5.

14. *Ibid.*, September 14, 1920, p. 8, Sept. 18, p. 7, October 4, pp. 6–7, Oct. 17, p. 6, Oct. 26, p. 10, Oct. 31, section 5, p. 2.

Chapter 12

1. *Sporting News*, July 5, 1950, p. 6; Joe Williams, "Busher Joe McCarthy," *Saturday Evening Post*, vol. 211, April 15, 1939, p. 12; Charles B. Cleveland, *The Great Baseball Managers* (New York: Thomas Y. Crowell, 1950), p. 119; Frank Graham, *The New York Yankees: An Informal History* (New York: G.P. Putnam's Sons, [1943] 1951), p. 170; *New York Sun*, April 5, 1933, p. 30; *New York Times*, January 14, 1978, section 3, p. 24; Ed Fitzgerald, "Nobody's Neutral About McCarthy," *Sport Magazine*, vol. 9, no. 2, August, 1950, p. 20; McCarthy letter to David Alper of West Hempstead, N.Y., 1969, Clippings File, Cooperstown.

2. *Louisville Courier-Journal*, March 9, 1921, p. 6; Herman Masin, *Speakers Treasury of Sports Stories* (New York: Prentice Hall, 1954), p. 124; Fred Lieb, *Comedians and Pranksters of Baseball* (St. Louis: Charles C. Spink, 1958), p. 30.

3. *Louisville Courier-Journal*, March 9, 1921, p. 6, March 10, p. 7, March 18, p. 8.

4. *Ibid.*, March 9,1921, p. 6, April 10, section 6, p. 4.

5. *Ibid.*, April 10, 1921, section 6, p. 2, April 12, p. 8, April 13, p. 8, April 19, p. 11.

6. *Ibid.*, May 13, 1921, p. 8, June 4, p.7.

7. *Ibid.*, June 14, 1921, p. 8, June 26, section 5, p. 2, June 27, p. 6.

8. *Ibid.*, July 12, 1921, p. 6, July 13, p. 6, July 14, p. 6, July 26, p. 7, July 29, p. 8, July 31, section 5, p. 3; *New York Sun*, April 5, 1932, p. 11.

9. *Louisville Courier-Journal*, August 4, 1921, p. 6, Aug. 6, p. 7, Aug. 7, section 5, p. 3, Aug. 8, p. 7, Aug. 9, p. 6, Aug. 11, p. 6, Aug., 14, section 5, p. 3.

10. *Ibid.*, August 16, 1921, p. 6.

11. *Ibid.*, August 30, 1921, p. 8, Aug. 31, p. 6, September 1, p. 10, Sept. 2, p. 8.

12. *Ibid.*, September 21, 1921, p. 8, Sept. 22, p. 8, Sept. 23, p. 8, Sept. 26, p. 8, Sept. 29, p. 10.

13. *Ibid.*, September 29, 1921, p. 10, October 1, p. 6, Oct. 3, pp. 6–7.

14. *Baltimore Sun*, September 28, 1921, p. 10, October 2, section 3, p. 1; *Louisville Courier-Journal*, October 5, 1921, p. 9, October 17, pp. 8–9.

15. *Louisville Courier-Journal*, October 6, 1921, p. 11.

16. Ibid; *Baltimore Sun*, October 6, 1921, p. 10.

17. *Louisville Courier-Journal*, October 6, 1921, p. 11, Oct. 7, p. 9.

18. *Ibid.*, October 9, section 5, p. 3, Oct. 10, 1921, p. 9; *Baltimore Sun*, Oct. 8, p. 8, Oct. 9, section 3, p. 1.

19. *Louisville Courier-Journal.*, October 10, 1921, p. 6; *Baltimore Sun*, Oct. 10, p. 8; *Philadelphia Inquirer*, February 4, 1938, p. 15.

20. *Baltimore Sun*, October 12, 1921, p. 6, Oct. 13, p. 10, Oct. 14, p. 1, Oct. 17, p. 1, Oct. 18, p. 1; *Louisville Courier-Journal*, Oct. 14, p. 7, Oct. 16, section 5, p. 2, Oct. 17, pp. 8–9, Oct. 18, p. 1, 13.

21. *Louisville Courier-Journal*, October 18, 1921, pp. 1, 10, 13.

22. Lee Allen, *The Hot Stove League* (New York: A.S. Barnes and Co., 1955), p. 223.

Chapter 13

1. Quoted in Harry J. Rothgerber, Jr., "Joe McCarthy's Ten Years as a Louisville Colonel," from *A Celebration of Louisville Baseball in the Major and Minor Leagues* (Cleveland: Society for American Baseball Research, 1997), p. 7.

2. *Louisville Courier-Journal*, March 16, 1922, p. 11; *Buffalo Evening News*, October 19, 1971, p. 28; *New York Times*, April 1, 1933, p. 31; Ed Fitzgerald, "Nobody's Neutral About McCarthy," *Sport Magazine*, vol. 9, no. 2, p. 76.

3. *Louisville Courier-Journal*, October 19, 1921, p. 8, March 3, 1922, p. 8, March 8, p. 8.

4. *Ibid.*, March 19, 1922, section 5, p. 2, March 23, p. 9, March 25, p. 8, March 27, p. 6, April 1, p. 10.

5. *Ibid.*, March 27, 1922, p. 9, March 30, p. 10, April 2, section 6, p. 2.

6. Frank Graham, *The New York Yankees, An Informal History* (New York: G.P. Putnam's Sons, [1943] 1951), p. 171.

7. *Louisville Courier-Journal*, March 17, 1922, p. 8, March 24, p. 8, April 21, p. 8, October 17, p. 8.

8. *Ibid.*, March 22, 1923, p. 8.

9. *Ibid.*, April 13, 1922, p. 9, April 26, p. 9, April 30, p. 8, May 5, p. 9, May 7, section 6, p. 3, May 15, p. 8, May 18, p. 8, May 21, section 6, p. 3, June 16, p. 8, June 21, p. 9.

10. *Ibid.*, July 12, 1922, p. 8, July 13, p. 6, July 17, p. 6, July 31, p. 6, August 8, p. 8, August 20, section 6, p. 3, August 28, p. 6.

11. "Down Memory Lane with Joe McCarthy," July 23, 1936, Clippings File, Cooperstown.

12. *Ibid.*, October 6, 1922, p. 10, May 5, 1923, p. 8.

13. *Ibid.*, November 20, 1922, p. 1.

14. *Ibid.*, March 13, 1923, p. 8, March 21, p. 8, March 30, p. 9, April 9, p. 8.

15. *Ibid.*, April 20, 1923, p. 9, April 28, p. 10, May 1, pp. 9, 12, May 2, p. 1, May 3, p. 8, May 4, p. 13, May 5, p. 8, May 8, p. 10.

16. *Ibid.*, May 8, 1923, p. 9.

17. *Ibid.*, May 9, 1923, p. 8, May 20, section 6, p. 4, June 17, section 6, p. 2, June 18, p. 8.

18. *Ibid.*, May 16, 1923, p. 13, June 18, p. 8, June 19, p. 10, June 21, p. 11, July 4, p. 8, July 11, p. 9, July 13, p. 9, July 14, p. 8.

19. *Kansas City Journal*, July 17, 1923, p. 8.

20. *Louisville Courier-Journal*, August 4, 1923, p. 8, Aug. 17, p. 8, Aug. 26, section 5, p. 1, Aug. 27, p. 8; Pope, *Baseball's Greatest Managers*, p. 140.

21. *St. Paul Dispatch* note published in the *Louisville Courier-Journal*, September 23, 1923, section 6, p. 2.

22. *Louisville Courier-Journal*, September 30, 1923, section 6, p. 3, October 1, pp. 8, 10,

23. *Ibid.*, October 1, pp. 8, 10.

Chapter 14

1. *Louisville Courier-Journal*, March 2, 1924, section 6, p. 4.

2. *New York World-Telegram*, April 4, 1933, p. 24; Donald Honig, *The Man in the Dugout: Fifteen Big League Managers Speak Their Minds* (Chicago: Follett, 1977), p. 87; Honig, *The New York Yankees: An Illustrated History* (New York: Crown, [1981] 1987), p. 41.

3. *Louisville Courier-Journal*, March 25, p. 11.

4. *Ibid.*, October 8, 1923, p. 10, Oct. 9, p. 11, March 5, 1923, p. 6; Harry J. Rothgerber, Jr., "Joe McCarthy's Ten Years as a Louisville Colonel," p. 1.

5. *Louisville Courier-Journal*, March 15, 1924, p. 10, March 16, section 7, p. 1.

6. *Ibid.*, March 24, 1924, p. 7, March 26, p. 9, April 2, p. 9, April 5, p. 6.

7. *St. Paul Dispatch*, April 12, 1924, p. 7, *Toledo Times*, April 12, p. 6, *Louisville Courier-Journal*, April 12, p. 6, April 13, p. 6, April 14, p. 9, April 15, p. 11.

8. *Louisville Courier-Journal*, April 16, 1924, p. 9, April 21, p. 9, April 22, p. 9, April 29, p. 9.

9. *Ibid.*, May 2, 1924, p. 13, May 16, p. 13, May 27, p. 9.

10. *Ibid.*, June 2, 1924, p. 10, June 4, p. 7, June 19, p. 11, June 23, p. 10, June 27, p. 9, June 30, pp. 9–10.

11. *Ibid.*, July 9, 1924, p. 9, July 11, pp. 9–11, July 12, p. 6, July 18, p. 9; *Kansas City Journal*, July 25, 1924, p. 7.

12. *Louisville Courier-Journal*, July 29, 1924, p. 8, August 3, p. 7, August 21, p. 6, September 13, p. 6.

13. *Ibid.*, September 12, p. 9, Sept. 27, 1924, p. 8, Sept. 29, p. 6, Sept. 30, p. 9.

Chapter 15

1. *Louisville Courier-Journal*, March 7, 1925, p. 11, March 21, p. 11, March 13, p. 13, March 14, p. 9, March 16, p. 9.

2. *Ibid.*, April 12, 1925, section 6, p. 3.

3. *Ibid.*, April 22, 1925, p. 8, April 25, p. 9, April 30, pp. 11–13, May 2, p. 14; *Minneapolis Journal*, May 1, p. 15.

4. *Ibid.*, May 16, 1925, p. 11, May 20, p. 11, May 30, p. 11.

5. *Ibid.*, June 3, 1925, p. 10, June 4, p. 11.

6. *Ibid.*, June 10, 1925, p. 13, June 11, p. 11, June 12, p. 15, June 13, p. 9, June 14, section 6, p. 2.

7. *Ibid.*, June 18, 1925, p. 13, June 21, section 6, p. 4, June 22, p. 12, June 23, p. 11, June 25, p. 11, June 26, p. 10, June 29, p. 6, June 30, p. 11.

8. *Ibid.*, July 1, 1925, p. 11, July 5, section 6, p. 4, July 7, p. 9.

9. *Ibid.*, *Chicago Tribune*, July 8, 1925, p. 9, July 10, p. 10; *Louisville Courier-Journal*, July 8, p. 8; Peter Bjarkman, ed., *Encyclopedia of Major League Baseball Team Histories — National League* (Westport: Meckler Publishers, 1991), p. 149; *Christian Science Monitor*, 1965, Clippings File, Cooperstown.

10. *Louisville Courier-Journal*, July 16, 1925, p. 11.

11. *Ibid.*, July 18, p. 11, July 20, p. 6; Herman Goldstein, "Bounced Up, Recalling How the Cubs Hired and Fired Joe McCarthy," Clippings File, Cooperstown.

12. Tom Meany, *The Yankee Story* (New York: E.P. Dutton and Co., Inc., 1960), p. 99.

13. *Louisville Courier-Journal*, July 24, 1925, p. 11, July 28, p. 10, September 13, section 6, p. 2.

14. *Ibid.*, September 12, 1925, p. 9, Sept. 13, section 6, p. 2, Sept. 21, p. 11.

15. *Ibid.*, August 9, 1925, section 6, p. 2.

16. *Ibid.*, June 4, 1924, p. 7.

17. Eddie Gold and Art Ahrens, *The Golden Era Cubs, 1876–1940* (Chicago: Bonus Books, 1985), p. 109.

18. *Louisville Courier-Journal*, October 1, 1925, p. 13, Oct. 3, p. 11, Oct. 4, section 6, p. 2, Oct. 5, p. 9.

19. *New York Daily News*, April 8, 1942, p. 56.

20. *Louisville Courier-Journal*, May 30, 1925, p. 11, August 25, p. 8, October 6, p. 15.

21. *Ibid.*, October 6, 1925, p. 15.

22. *Ibid.*

23. *Ibid.*, October 8, 1925, p. 1, Oct. 9, p. 1, Oct. 10, p. 11; *Chicago Tribune*, Oct. 10, p. 21; *Chicago Daily News*, Oct. 10, p. 20; *Chicago Herald and Examiner*, Oct. 10, p. 19.

24. *Louisville Courier-Journal*, October 10, 1925, p. 13, Oct. 11, p. 1, Oct. 12, p. 9.

25. *Ibid.*, October 15, 1925, p. 9, Oct. 16, p. 14, Oct. 31, p. 17.

26. Harry J. Rothgerber, Jr., "Joe McCarthy's Ten Years as a Louisville Colonel," from *A Celebration of Louisville Baseball in the Major and Minor Leagues* (Cleveland: Society for American Baseball Research, 1997), p. 7; *New York Evening Post*, April 6, 1933, p. 11.

Chapter 16

1. Quoted in Donald Honig, *The Man in the Dugout: Fifteen Big League Managers Speak Their Minds* (Chicago: Follett, 1977), p. 81.

2. *Chicago Tribune*, October 5, 1925, p. 27.

3. Warren Brown, *The Chicago Cubs* (Carbondale: Southern Illinois University Press, [1946] 2001), p. 93; Ed Burns, "The Chicago Cubs," *Sport Magazine*, September, 1950, p. 76; Frank Graham, *The New York Yankees: An Informal History* (New York: G.P. Putnam's Sons, [1943] 1951), p. 173.

4. Quoted in *Chicago Herald and Examiner*, October 13, 1925, p. 2.

5. *Chicago Herald and Examiner*, October 10, 1925, p. 19; *Chicago Daily News*, Oct. 13, p. 26; *Chicago Tribune*, Oct. 13, p. 29.

6. Quoted in Honig, *The Man in the Dugout*, p. 81; see also Hank Newer, *Strategies of the Great Baseball Managers* (New York: Franklin Watts, 1988), p. 76; Maury Allen, *Where Have You Gone, Joe DiMaggio?*, p. 81.

7. *Chicago Daily News*, October 15, 1925, p. 25; *Chicago Tribune*, Oct. 13, p. 29.

8. *Chicago Herald and Examiner*, April 26, 1926, p. 11, May 7, p. 17.

9. Quoted in Honig, *The Man in the Dugout*, p. 85.

10. Quoted in Ed Burns, "The Chicago Cubs," *Sport Magazine*, September, 1950, p. 82; see also *New York Sun*, August 11, 1934, p. 28; *Chicago Tribune*, September 23, 1932, p. 12; Bill James, *The Bill James Guide to Baseball Managers From 1870 to Today*. (New York: Scribner's, 1997), p. 97; Robert W. Creamer, *Stengel: His Life and Times* (New York: Simon and Schuster, 1984), p. 173.

11. *Chicago Tribune*, February 15, 1926, p. 19, Feb. 22, p. 25, April 6, p. 21; *Chicago Daily News*, March 2, p. 21.

12. *Chicago Herald and Examiner*, March 1, 1926, p. 13, March 10, p. 13, March 16, p. 13, March 17, p. 15, April 12, p. 17; *Chicago Tribune*, February 12, p. 19, March 4, p. 17, March 16, p. 21; *Chicago Daily News*, March 3, p. 21; Ed Fitzgerald, "Nobody's Neutral About McCarthy," in Jim Bouton, *I Managed Good, But Boy Did They Play Bad* (Chicago: Playboy Press, 1973), p. 256; *Saturday Evening Post*, April 15, 1939, p. 13; Ed Burns, "The Chicago Cubs," *Sport Magazine*, September, 1950, p. 76.

13. *Chicago Tribune*, March 10, 1926, p. 23, March 23, p. 21; Jim Enright, *Chicago Cubs* (New York: Macmillan and Co., 1975), p. 97; *Boston Globe*, May 25, 1948, p. 38; Ed Fitzgerald, "Nobody's Neutral About McCarthy," p. 256.

14. *Chicago Herald and Examiner*, March 31, 1926, p. 13, April 1, p. 21, April 5, p. 15.

15. *Ibid.*, April 13, 1926, p. 9.

16. *Chicago Tribune*, March 12, 1926, p. 21.

17. *Ibid.*, April 9, 1926, p. 31, April 10, pp. 21–23; *Chicago Herald and Examiner*, April 6, p. 12; *Buffalo Evening News*, September 8, 1969, p. 11.

18. *Saturday Evening Post*, vol. 211, April 15, 1939, p. 14; *New York Journal-American*, December 19, 1953, p. 18; Jack Shea, "The Ups and Downs of Old Pete," *Sport Magazine*, April, 1950, p. 54; *New York Times*, January 14, 1978, section 3, p. 14.

19. *Chicago Herald and Examiner*, April 13, 1926, p. 9

20. *Ibid.*, April 22, 1926, p. 11, April 23, pp. 11–12, April 24, pp. 9–11, April 26, p. 11, April 30, p. 9, May 1, pp. 9–11, May 2, section 2, p. 3; *Chicago Daily News*, April 21, p. 1, April 30, p. 21.

21. *Chicago Herald and Examiner*, May 7, 1926, p. 17, June 8, p. 11; *Chicago Tribune*, June 8, p. 25; *New York Herald Tribune*, October 1, 1937, p. 28.

22. *Chicago Herald and Examiner*, May 20, 1926, p. 13, May 28, p. 11, May 29, p. 11; Warren Brown, *The Chicago Cubs* (Carbondale: Southern Illinois University Press, [1946] 2001, p. 95.

23. *Philadelphia Inquirer*, June 14, 1926, p. 19; *Philadelphia Public Ledger*, June 15, p. 17; *Philadelphia Record*, June 15, p. 11; *Philadelphia Evening Bulletin*, June 14, p. 29; *Chicago Herald and Examiner*, June 15, p. 13; *Chicago Tribune*, June 15, p. 23; *The Sporting News*, November 25, 1938, p. 3.

24. *Chicago Tribune*, June 16, 1926, p. 21, June 27, section 2, p. 2; *Chicago Herald and Examiner*, June 16, p. 11, June 18, p. 14; Wrigley's statement is also quoted in the *New York Times*, January 14, 1978, p. 24, in *The Saturday Evening Post*, April 15, 1939, p. 12, and in *The Sporting News*, January 28, 1978, p. 40; Donald Honig, *The Man in the Dugout*, pp. 84–85.

25. Donald Honig, *The Man in the Dugout*, pp. 84–85.

26. *Chicago Tribune*, February 22, 1926, p. 21, June 28, p. 15.

27. *Ibid.*, July 1, 1926, p. 21; *Chicago Herald and Examiner*, July 1, p. 11.

28. *Chicago Herald and Examiner*, July 8, 1926, p. 9, July 18, section 2, p. 6, July 21, p. 9; *Chicago Tribune*, July 18, section 2, p. 1.

29. *Chicago Herald and Examiner*, July 30, 1926, p. 13, August 1, section 2, p. 3, Aug. 2, p. 13.

30. *Ibid.*, September 2, 1926, p. 18, Sept. 3, p. 17, Sept. 15, p. 19, Sept. 16, p. 18, Sept. 17, p. 19.

31. *Ibid.*, September 29, 1926, p. 21.

32. Bill James, *The Bill James Guide to Baseball Managers*, p. 98.

Chapter 17

1. *Chicago Tribune*, February 28, 1927, p. 17

2. *Chicago Herald and Examiner*, March 2, 1927, p. 17.

3. *Ibid.*, March 3, 1927, p. 15, March 12, p. 15, March 14, p. 23.

4. Ed Fitzgerald, "Nobody's Neutral About McCarthy," *Sport Magazine*, IX, 2, August, 1950, p. 78; Warren Brown, *The Chicago Cubs*, p. 96.

5. Charlie Grimm, with Ed Presley, *Jolly Cholly's Story: Baseball, I Love You* (Chicago: Regnery, 1968), p. 57.

6. *Chicago Tribune*, April 3, 1927, section 2, p. 1, April 4, p. 27.

7. *Ibid.*, April 13, 1927, p. 23, April 14, p. 19, April

21, p. 19; *Chicago Herald and Examiner*, April 12, p. 17.

    8. *Chicago Tribune*, May 19, 1927, p. 15, May 20, p. 22, May 22, section 2, p. 1; *Chicago Herald and Examiner*, May 15, section 2, p. 3, May 18, p. 17, May 22, section 2, p. 1.

    9. *Chicago Herald and Examiner*, May 28, 1927, p. 15, May 31, p. 17, June 2, p. 17, June 12, section 2, p. 4, *Chicago Tribune*, May 29, p. 19, June 1, p. 17, June 8, p. 23, June 11, p. 17, June 13, p. 25, June 17, p. 19, June 19, section 2, p. 1, June 20, p. 18, June 21, p. 19; Warren Brown, *The Chicago Cubs*, p. 94.

    10. *Chicago Tribune*, June 22, 1927, p. 19, June 23, p. 17, June 25, p. 15, June 26, section 2, p. 1, June 30, p. 19, July 7, p. 17, July 8, p. 17, July 9, p. 1, July 10, section 2, p. 4, August 8, p. 23.

    11. *Ibid.*, August 2, 1927, p. 17, Aug. 11, p. 13, April 18, 1928, p. 25.

    12. *Ibid.*, August 17, 1927, p. 19, Aug. 18, p. 17, Aug. 19, p. 18, Aug. 20, p. 13, Aug. 21, section 2, pp. 1–2, Aug. 23, p. 18.

    13. *Ibid.*, September 1, 1927, p. 19, Sept. 2, p. 22, Sept. 4, section 2, p. 1, Sept. 5, p. 15, Sept. 6, p. 29, Sept. 7, p. 23, Sept. 8, p. 21, Sept. 12, p. 23, Sept. 14, p. 19; *Chicago Herald and Examiner*, Sept. 12, p. 19, Sept. 13, p. 15.

    14. *Chicago Tribune*, September 22, 1927, p. 27.

    15. *Chicago Herald and Examiner*, April 6, 1928, p. 19.

Chapter 18

    1. *Chicago Herald and Examiner*, October 6, 1927, p. 15, Oct. 7, p. 17, Oct. 9, section 2, p. 2.

    2. *Ibid.*, April 6, 1928, p. 19; *Chicago Tribune*, August 11, 1927, p. 3, October 11, p. 17.

    3. *Chicago Tribune*, February 16, 1928, p. 15, April 11, p. 25; *Chicago Herald and Examiner*, April 6, p. 17, April 10, p. 17.

    4. *Chicago Tribune*, April 12, 1928, p. 19, April 14, p. 21, April 30, p. 20; *Chicago Herald and Examiner*, April 10, p. 17, April 11, p. 19, April 12, p. 13, April 13, p. 14.

    5. *Chicago Tribune*, April 19, p. 15, June 22, p. 17; *Chicago Herald and Examiner*, April 19, p. 13, June 22, p. 15, July 27, p. 14, July 7, 1929, section 2, p. 3; Eddie Gold and Art Ahrens, *The Golden Era Cubs, 1876–1940* (Chicago: Bonus Books, 1985), p. 118. (Gold and Ahrens state that the jury awarded Young $1.)

    6. *Chicago Herald and Examiner*, May 4, 1928, p. 17, May 10, p. 19, May 15, p. 13, May 18, p. 15, May 22, p. 15, May 25, p. 17, June 3, p. 11, June 6, p. 16; *Chicago Tribune*, May 15, p. 19, May 16, p. 21, May 24, p. 21, June 2, p. 19, June 3, section 2, p. 2.

    7. *Chicago Herald and Examiner*, August 30, 1928, p. 15, September 1, p. 15, Sept. 11, p. 19, Sept. 15, p. 19, Sept. 16, section 2, p. 8, Sept. 23, section 2, p. 11; *Chicago Tribune*, Sept. 2, section 2, p. 1, Sept. 3, p.

13, Sept. 6, p. 15, Sept. 28, p. 19, Sept. 29, p. 17, Sept. 30, p. 29; Eddie Gold and Art Ahrens, *The Golden Era Cubs, 1876–1940*, p. 109.

    8. *New York Times*, March 25, 1938, p. 31.

    9. *Chicago Tribune*, October 11, 1928, p. 22, November 8, 1928, p. 23.

Chapter 19

    1. *Chicago Herald and Examiner*, March 6, 1929, p. 17, March 8, p. 21, March 19, p. 17; *Chicago Tribune*, February 17, section 2, p. 1, Feb. 18, p. 21.

    2. *Chicago Herald and Examiner*, March 12, 1929, pp. 15–16, March 24, section 2, p. 1, March 26, p. 15.

    3. *Chicago Herald and Examiner*, April 2, 1929, p. 15, April 3, p. 17, April 17, pp. 19–20, April 18, p. 15, April 19, p. 17.

    4. *Chicago Tribune*, February 17, 1929, section 2, p. 1; *Chicago Herald and Examiner*, April 8, p. 19.

    5. *Chicago Herald and Examiner*, April 25, 1929, p. 19, April 27, p. 17, April 28, section 2, page 3, April 29, p. 19, April 30, p. 19.

    6. *Ibid.*, May 9, 1929, p. 21, May 10, p. 25, May 12, section 2, p. 1, May 14, p. 19, May 16, p. 17, May 31, p. 19, June 8, p. 15; *Chicago Tribune*, May 24, p. 27, May 25, p. 27, May 27, p. 27, May 29, p. 17, May 31, pp. 23–4.

    7. *Chicago Herald and Examiner*, June 23, 1928, p. 15, June 20, 1929, p. 17, June 22, p. 15, June 30, section 2, p. 1, July 1, p. 19, July 3, p. 15, July 4, p. 17.

    8. *Ibid.*, July 5, 1929, pp. 1, 25, July 6, p. 15, July 13, p. 15; *Chicago Tribune*, July 5, p. 1, July 6, p. 15.

    9. *Chicago Tribune*, July 12, 1929, p. 22.

    10. *Ibid.*, July 8, 1929, p. 25; *Chicago Herald and Examiner*, July 7, section 2, pp. 1–3; Donald Honig, *The Man in the Dugout: Fifteen Big League Managers Speak Their Minds*, p. 85.

    11. *Chicago Herald and Examiner*, July 8, 1929, p. 21, July 9, p. 13; *Chicago Tribune*, July 8, p. 25, July 9, p. 23, July 10, p. 21.

    12. *Chicago Herald and Examiner*, July 11, 1929, p. 15, July 12, p. 15, July 13, pp. 15–17, July 14, section 2, p. 1; *Chicago Tribune*, July 12, p. 21, July 13, p. 15.

    13. *Chicago Herald and Examiner*, July 16, 1929, p. 13, July 25, p. 19, July 27, p. 17, July 31, p. 15, August 6, p. 15; *New York Herald Tribune*, October 1, 1937, p. 28.

    14. *Ibid.*, August 15, 1929, p. 15, Aug. 16, p. 19, Aug. 21, p. 17, Aug. 22, p. 17.

    15. *Ibid.*, August 25, 1929, p. 15, Aug. 27, p. 17, Aug. 29, p. 19.

    16. *Ibid.*, August 29, 1929, p. 19, September 1, section 2, p. 1, Sept. 19, p. 17; *Chicago Daily News*, October 3, p. 32; *Chicago Tribune*, Oct. 4, p. 25, Oct. 7, p. 25; *New York World-Telegram*, March 5, 1931, p. 35; Charles Cleveland, *The Great Baseball Managers* (New York: Thomas Y. Crowell, 1950), p. 121; Clippings File, Cooperstown.

    17. *Chicago Herald and Examiner*, September 20,

1029, p. 17, October 1, p. 19, Oct. 4, pp. 17, 20, Oct. 8, p. 21.

18. Donald Honig, *The Man in the Dugout: Fifteen Big League Managers Speak Their Minds*, p. 83; Leonard Koppett, *The Man in the Dugout: Baseball's Top Managers and How They Got That Way* (Philadelphia: Temple University Press, 2000), p. 61.

19. *Chicago Daily News*, October 8, 1929, p. 1; *Chicago Herald and Examiner*, Oct. 9, p. 15; *Chicago Tribune*, Oct. 9, p. 24; Donald Honig, *The Man in the Dugout: Fifteen Big League Managers Speak Their Minds*, p. 83; Leonard Koppett, *The Man in the Dugout: Baseball's Top Managers and How They Got That Way*, p. 61.

20. *Chicago Daily News*, October 8, 1929, p. 1; *Chicago Herald and Examiner*, Oct. 9, p. 15; *Chicago Tribune*, Oct. 9, p. 24.

21. *Chicago Daily News*, October 9, 1929, p. 1; *Chicago Herald and Examiner*, Oct. 10, p. 17, *Chicago Tribune*, Oct. 10, p. 23.

22. *Chicago Daily News*, October 11, 1929, p. 1; *Chicago Herald and Examiner*, Oct. 12, p. 17

23. *Chicago Daily News*, October 11, 1929, p. 18.

24. *The Sporting News*, November 10, 1954, p. 15.

25. *Chicago Daily News*, October 12, 1929, p. 1; *Chicago Tribune*, Oct. 13, section 2, p. 1; *Philadelphia Evening Public Ledger*, Oct. 13, 1932, p. 22; *Baseball Digest*, April 1948, pp. 7–8; Edwin Pope, *Baseball's Greatest Managers* (Garden City, N.Y.: Doubleday, 1960), p. 142; Joe McCarthy, "How Pennants Are Really Won," *Liberty Magazine*, September 30, 1933, p. 4.

26. *Chicago Herald and Examiner*, October 13, 1929, section 3, p. 1, Oct. 14, p. 17; *Chicago Tribune*, Oct. 13, section 2, p. 1; Warren Brown, *The Chicago Cubs*, p. 117.

27. Donald Honig, *The Man in the Dugout*, p. 281; Harvey Frommer, *Baseball's Greatest Managers* (New York: Franklin Watts, 1985), p. 192.

28. *Chicago Daily News*, October 14, 1929, p. 1, Oct. 15, p. 29; Honig, *The Man in the Dugout*, p. 281.

29. *Chicago Tribune*, October 15, 1929, p. 31, December 5, p. 28; *Chicago Herald and Examiner*, Oct. 15, p. 17, Oct. 18, p. 17; Ed Burns, "The Chicago Cubs," *Sport Magazine*, September, 1950, p. 82; Honig, *The Man in the Dugout*, p. 82; Clippings File, Cooperstown: January 2, 1930; Cancelled check, National City Bank, New York, June 7, 1930.

Chapter 20

1. *Chicago Tribune*, October 15, 1929, p. 31; February 17, 1930, p. 24; *Chicago Herald and Examiner*, March 11, 1930, p. 19; Eddie Gold and Art Ahrens, *The Golden Era Cubs, 1876–1940* (Chicago: Bonus Books, 1985), p. 118.

2. *Chicago Herald and Examiner*, April 14, 1930, p. 23, July 20, section 2, p. 1; Gold and Ahrens, *Golden Era Cubs*, p. 119.

3. *Chicago Herald and Examiner*, April 23, p. 14.

4. *Ibid.*, April 27, 1930, section 2, p. 5, April 28, p. 13, May 5, p. 21, May 9, p. 19, May 10, p. 19.

5. *Ibid.*, May 22, 1930, p. 17, May 27, p. 19, May 29, p. 17, June 5, p. 19.

6. *Ibid.*, May 31, 1930, pp. 19–21, June 1, section 2, p. 3, June 2, p. 21, June 4, p. 17.

7. *Ibid.*, June 7, 1930, p. 17, July 1, p. 19; *Minneapolis Tribune*, July 1, p. 18.

8. *Chicago Herald and Examiner*, July 9, 1930, p. 11; *Cincinnati Enquirer*, July 8, p. 10.

9. *Chicago Herald and Examiner*, July 25, 1930, p. 17, August 25, p. 21, Aug. 27, p. 19; *Chicago Tribune*, Aug. 27, pp. 19–20.

10. *Chicago Herald and Examiner*, August 29, 1930, p. 21, Aug. 30, p. 21, September 2, p. 21, Sept. 4, p.17, Sept. 6, p. 17, Sept. 7, section 2, p. 1, Sept. 8, p. 19; *New York Daily News*, August 5, 1940, p. 35.

11. *Chicago Herald and Examiner*, September 10, 1930, p. 17, Sept. 14, section 1, p. 2, Sept. 16, p. 19; *Chicago Tribune*, Sept.16, p. 23; see also Jim Enright, *Chicago Cubs* (New York: Macmillan, 1975), p. 97; William Curran, *Big Sticks: The Batting Revolution of the 20s* (New York: William Morrow, 1990), p. 253.

12. *Chicago Herald and Examiner*, Sept. 17, p. 19, Sept. 19, p. 19; *Chicago Tribune*, Sept. 17, p. 21, Sept. 19, p. 23.

13. *Chicago Herald and Examiner*, September 20, 1930, p. 17, Sept. 21, section 2, p. 1; *Chicago Tribune*, Sept. 20, pp. 1, 18, Sept. 21, section 2, pp. 1–2.

14. *Chicago Herald and Examiner*, September 22, 1930, p. 1; Herman Goldstein, "Bounced Up, Recalling How the Cubs Hired and Fired Joe McCarthy," Clippings File, Cooperstown.

15. *Chicago Herald and Examiner*, September 22, pp. 1, 19–21, Sept. 26, p. 19; *Chicago Tribune*, Sept. 22, p. 21, Sept. 26, p. 33; Charles C. Alexander, *Breaking the Slump: Baseball in the Depression Era* (New York: Columbia University Press, 2002), pp. 33, 50.

16. *Chicago Herald and Examiner*, September 23, 1930, p. 19.

17. *New York Daily News*, August 14, 1932, p. 58; Hank Newer, *Strategies of the Great Baseball Managers* (New York: Franklin Watts, 1988), p. 77.

18. Red Barber, *Walk in the Spirit* (New York: Dial Press, 1969), p. 152.

19. *Chicago Herald and Examiner*, September 28, 1930, section 2, p. 6; *Chicago Tribune*, Sept. 24, p. 22; Donald Honig, *The Man in the Dugout: Fifteen Big League Managers Speak Their Minds*, p. 85; *New York Times*, September 25, 1977, p. 35.

20. Warren Brown, *The Chicago Cubs*, pp. 118–120; Tom Meany, *The Yankee Story*, p. 104–05; Ed Hurley, *Managing to Win* (New York: A.J. Pollicino, 1976), pp. 42–44; Ed Fitzgerald, "Nobody's Neutral About McCarthy," pp. 260–61; Will Wedge, *New York Sun*, April 4, 1932, p. 34; Edward Grant Barrow, *My Fifty Years in Baseball* (New York: Coward-McCann, 1951), p. 165; Barrow, "The Greatest Manager," *Colliers*, June 24, 1950, p. 28; Frank Graham, *Lou Gehrig:*

A Quiet Hero (New York: G.P. Putnam's Sons, 1942), p. 139.

21. Warren Brown, *The Chicago Cubs*, p. 120; Honig, *The Man in the Dugout*, p. 178; Honig, *The New York Yankees*, p. 90; Ed Fitzgerald, "Nobody's Neutral About McCarthy," pp. 260–61; Tom Meany, *The Yankee Story*, p. 106; Robert W. Creamer, *Babe: The Legend Comes to Life* (New York: Simon and Schuster, 1974), pp. 351–52; Ed Barrow, "The Greatest Manager," *Collier's*, June 24, 1950, p. 28; Frank Graham, *The New York Yankees*, p. 174; *The Sporting News*, October 23, 1930, p. 3.

22. *Chicago Tribune*, October 2, 1930, p. 21, Oct. 3, p. 35, Oct. 8, p. 19; Charles B. Cleveland, *The Great Baseball Managers*, p. 115; Joe Vila, "Setting the Pace," 1931, p. 24, Clippings File, Cooperstown; Edwin Pope, *Baseball's Greatest Managers*, p. 135; *The Sporting News*, January 28, 1978, p. 40.

Chapter 21

1. Quoted in *Sport Magazine*, August, 1950, p. 78; Frank Graham, *The New York Yankees: An Informal History* (New York: G.P. Putnam's Sons, 1948), p. 176; Leonard Koppett, *The Man in the Dugout*, p. 95; Frank Graham, *Lou Gehrig*, p. 141.

2. *New York Times*, March 4, 1931, p. 24; *New York Evening Post*, February 23, 1931, p. 29.

3. Tom Meany, *The Yankee Story* (New York: E.P. Dutton, 1960), p. 109.

4. Milton Gross, *Yankee Doodles* (Boston: House of Kent Publishing Co., 1948), pp. 168–69.

5. *New York Times*, March 10, 1931, p. 28; *Philadelphia Record*, February 23, 1931, p. 17; *New York Daily News*, March 1, 1931, pp. 74, 77; Harvey Frommer, *Baseball's Greatest Managers*, p. 158.

6. *Chicago Tribune*, April 25, 1926, section 2, p. 4; *New York Sun*, March 9, 1931, p. 36, March 12, p. 36; April 11, p. 31, March 1, 1933, p. 30; Lee Allen and Tom Meany, *Kings of the Diamond: The Immortals in Baseball's Hall of Fame* (New York: G.P. Putnam's Sons, 1965), p. 231; Ray Robinson, *Iron Horse: Lou Gehrig and His Times* (New York: W.W. Norton, 1990), p. 143; Grantland Rice, untitled article, *Buffalo Evening News*, October 10, 1939, p. 24; Leonard Koppett, *The Man in the Dugout*, p. 96; Frank Graham, *The New York Yankees*, p. 177; Frank Graham, *Lou Gehrig*, pp. 142, 145; Clippings File, Cooperstown.

7. *New York Sun*, April 11, 1931, p. 31; Frank Graham, *The New York Yankees*, p. 178; Edwin Pope, *Baseball's Greatest Managers*, p. 143; Donald Honig, *The Man in the Dugout*, p. 86.

8. *New York Times*, March 4, 1931, p. 24; *New York Daily News.*, March 4, p. 50; *New York Sun*, March 16, p. 37; *New York World Telegram*, July 31, 1931, p. 9; Enright, *Chicago Cubs*, p. 100; Edwin Pope, *Baseball's Greatest Managers*, p. 144; Robert Creamer, *Babe*, p. 352; Dan Shaughnessy, *The Curse of the Bambino* (New York: Penguin Books, [1990] 1991), p. 77;

Marshall Smelser, *The Life that Ruth Built*, pp. 427, 432; *Philadelphia Public Ledger*, July 4, 1931, p. 14.

9. *New York Sun*, March 4, 1931, p. 41; April 1, p. 36; *New York Times*, March 22, section 10, p. 2; Herman Masin, *Speakers Treasury of Sports Stories*, p. 134; *New York Journal-American*, December 19, 1953, p. 18.

10. *New York Sun*, March 13, 1931, p. 36; *New York World-Telegram*, April 7, p. 28, April 8, p. 31, April 11, p. 8.

11. *New York World-Telegram*, April 8, 1931, p. 31; Edwin Pope, *Baseball's Greatest Managers*, p. 139; Leonard Koppett, *The Man in the Dugout*, p. 96; Joe DiMaggio, *Lucky to Be a Yankee*, p. 194; Harvey Frommer, *Baseball's Greatest Managers*, p. 155; Tommy Henrich, *Five O'Clock Lightning*, p. 20; Maury Allen, *Where Have You Gone, Joe DiMaggio*, p. 39; Richard Ben Cramer, *Joe DiMaggio: The Hero's Life* (New York: Simon and Schuster, 2000), p. 92; Edward Grant Barrow, *My 50 Years in Baseball* (New York: Coward-McCann, 1951), p. 155.

12. *New York World-Telegram*, April 14, 1931, p. 1, April 15, p. 34, April 16, p. 1, April 20, p. 24, April 22, p. 1, April 25, p. 8, April 30, p. 8; *New York Sun*, April 15, p. 40, April 16, p. 42, April 20, p. 35, April 23, pp. 40–41, April 24, p. 37, April 27, p. 33; Marshall Smelser, *The Life that Ruth Built*, p. 432.

13. *New York Sun*, April 27, 1931, p. 33.

14. *Buffalo Evening News*, April 17, 1971, section C, p. 2; *The Sporting News*, February 13, 1957, p. 6.

15. *New York Daily News*, April 8, 1942, p. 56.

16. *New York Daily News*, August 18, 1935, p. 76.

17. *New York World-Telegram*, May 4, 1931, p. 9; *New York Sun*, May 5, p. 30, May 7, p. 41, May 9, p. 16; *New York Daily News*, May 5, p. 43, May 6, p. 46, May 7, p. 50.

18. *New York Sun*, May 6, 1931, p. 39, May 12, p. 36; *New York Daily News*, May 10, p. 67, May 11, p. 44.

19. *New York Sun*, May 14, 1931, p. 41, May 15, p. 45, May 16, p. 34; *New York Daily News*, May 14, p. 42, May 15, p. 64, May 16, p. 34, May 18, p. 36, May 19, p. 42, May 22, p. 60, May 24, p. 74.

20. *New York Sun*, May 21, 1931, p. 41, May 25, p. 36.

21. Ibid, May 29, 1931, p. 34; *New York Daily News*, May 25, p. 38, May 26, pp. 46–8, May 28, pp. 53–4.

22. *New York Sun*, June 11, 1931, p. 36, June 13, p. 33, June 23, p. 42, June 27, p. 31, July 3, p. 31; *New York World-Telegram*, July 7, p. 27, July 10, p. 6; *New York Daily News*, June 20, p. 58, June 26, p. 52.

23. *New York Daily News*, June 22, 1931, p. 40, June 23, p. 42; *New York Sun*, June 23, p. 29, June 25, p. 36.

24. *New York Daily News*, July 5, 1931, p. 48, July 10, p. 44, July 11, p. 26, July 12, p. 56, July 13, p. 36; *New York Sun*, July 13, p. 28.

25. *New York Sun*, July 11, 1931, p. 27, July 13, p. 28, July 17, p. 14, July 21, p. 30, July 29, p. 28; *New York Daily News*, July 18, p. 26, July 28, p. 40, July 29, p. 36; *New York World-Telegram*, July 6, p. 22, July 9, p.

29, July 11, p. 8, July 13, p. 22, July 15, p. 25, July 20, p. 8.

26. *New York World-Telegram*, August 8, 1931, p. 11, Aug. 22, p. 4, Sept. 9, p. 25; *New York Daily News*, Sept. 10, p. 52, Sept. 21, p. 68, Sept. 25, p. 72; *New York Sun*, Sept. 10, p. 40.

27. *New York Daily News*, Sept. 26, 1931, p. 32.

28. *New York World-Telegram*, September 28, 1931, p. 28; Joe Williams, "Busher Joe McCarthy," *Saturday Evening Post*," April 15, 1939, pp. 12, 77.

Chapter 22

1. *New York World-Telegram*, July 25, 1931, p. 6; September 30, 1943, p. 34; *New York Times*, April 1, 1933, p. 31.

2. *New York World-Telegram*, February 22, 1932, p. 14, Feb. 23, p. 28, March 17, p. 35.

3. *Ibid.*, March 19, 1932, p. 6, March 21, p. 26; Tommy Henrich, *Five O'Clock Lightning*, p. 27.

4. *New York World-Telegram*, March 2, 1932, p. 27, March 7, p. 22, March 8, p. 23, April 4, p. 21, April 6, p. 23, April 8, p. 1; *New York Sun*, March 1, p. 31, March 4, p. 39, April 8, p. 38, April 12, p.34, April 19, p. 34.

5. *New York Daily News*, April 5, 1932, p. 42.

6. *Ibid.*, April 13, 1932, p. 42, April 21, p. 38; *New York World-Telegram*, April 20, p. 22, May 16, p. 16; *New York Sun*, April 21, p. 34, April 28, p. 34.

7. *New York Sun*, April 25, 1932, p. 30; *New York World-Telegram*, May 17, p. 27; May 23, p. 14; *New York Daily News*, May 7, p. 26, May 12, p. 46, May 15, p. 63, May 16, p. 34, May 18, p. 36, May 22, p. 62; Clippings File, Cooperstown.

8. *New York Sun*, May 19, 1932, p. 33; *New York World-Telegram*, May 16, p. 16, May 20, p. 1, May 21, p. 1, *New York Daily News*, May 31, p. 44.

9. *New York Daily News*, June 2, 1932, p. 40, June 3, p. 60, June 4, pp. 28–9; *New York World-Telegram*, June 2, p. 25; *New York Sun*, June 2, p. 38, June 3, p. 34, June 4, p. 38, September 14, p. 31; Frank Graham, *Lou Gehrig*, pp. 154–55.

10. *New York Daily News*, June 15, 1932, p. 38; *New York World-Telegram*, June 15, p. 13, June 28, p. 12; *New York Sun*, June 6, p. 31, June 10, p. 32, June 15, p. 30, July 2, p. 25, July 22, p. 16.

11. *New York Sun*, July 2, 1932, p. 25, July 5, p. 32, July 8, p. 15, July 12, p. 27, October 1, p. 29; *New York Daily News*, July 5, p. 42, July 10, p. 55; *New York World-Telegram*, July 5, pp. 1, 13, July 6, p. 13, July 7, p. 21.

12. *New York Daily News*, July 31, 1932, p. 52; *New York Sun*, July 26, p. 33, August 2, p. 21.

13. *New York World-Telegram*, August 3, 1932, p. 22; *New York Sun*, August 3, p. 22, August 10, p. 26, Sept. 9, 1931, p. 41; *New York Daily News*, August 14, 1932, p. 58; Ray Robinson, *Iron Horse*, p. 152.

14. *New York Sun*, August 2, 1932, p. 21; *New York Daily News*, August 13, p. 21.

15. *New York World-Telegram*, August 10, 1932, p. 22, August 12, p. 10, August 13, p. 7; *New York Daily News*, August 14, p. 60.

16. *New York Sun*, July 1, 1932, p. 23, September 6, p. 31, Sept. 7, p. 30; *New York World-Telegram*, July 1, p. 10, Sept. 6, p. 28.

17. *New York Herald Tribune*, September 14, 1932, p. 22; *New York Sun*, Sept. 14, p. 31; *New York World-Telegram*, August 9, p. 22; Press Release of American League Service Bureau, January 31, 1937, Clippings File, Cooperstown.

18. *New York Daily News*, September 8, 1932, p. 40, Sept. 9, p. 56, Sept. 16, p. 63; *New York Sun*, Sept. 8, p. 1; Sept. 9, p. 31, Sept. 16, p. 38; *New York World-Telegram*, Sept. 8, p. 26, Sept. 12, p. 22, Sept. 16, p. 31.

19. *New York Daily News*, September 25, 1932, p. 68.

20. *Ibid.*, August 18, 1932, p. 22, September 22, p. 48, Sept. 24, p. 22; *New York Sun*, August 11; *New York World-Telegram*, Sept. 15, p. 31, Sept. 23, p. 30; Clippings File, Cooperstown, Sept. 29, 1932.

21. *New York Sun*, September 27, 1932, p. 39.

22. *Ibid.*, October 1, 1932, p. 29; *The Sporting News*, October 23, 1930, p. 8; Robert Creamer, *Babe*, p. 357; *Buffalo Evening News*, May 21, 1956, p. 14; Frank Graham, *New York Yankees*, p. 183.

23. *Ibid.*, September 29, 1932, pp. 1, 28; *New York Daily News*, Sept. 29, p. 46, Sept. 30, p. 42; *New York World-Telegram*, Sept.28, p. 1

24. *New York Sun*, March 2, 1933, p. 30; Robert Creamer, *Babe*, p. 360.

25. *New York Daily News*, October 2, 1932, p. 56; *New York Herald Tribune*, Oct. 3, p. 17; Donald Honig, *The Man in the Dugout*, p. 86; Honig, *The New York Yankees*, pp. 91–2; *New York Times*, September 25, 1977, p. 35; McCarthy letter to William Kachulis of Forest Hills, N.Y., June 11, 1972, Clippings File Cooperstown; Robert Creamer, *Babe*, pp. 362–67.

26. *New York Daily News*, October 2, 1932, p. 56; *Buffalo Evening News*, May 21, 1956, p. 14.

27. *New York Daily News*, October 3, 1932, p. 34; *New York Sun*, Oct. 4, p. 39; *New York Herald Tribune*, Oct. 3, p. 17, Oct. 5, p. 29; *Buffalo Evening News*, May 21, 1956, p. 14; Donald Honig, *The October Heroes: Great World Series Games Remembered by the Men Who Played Them* (New York: Simon and Schuster, 1979), p. 249; *The Sporting News*, October 20, 1932, p. 4.

Chapter 23

1. *New York World-Telegram*, March 2, 1933, p. 24; Ray Robinson, *Iron Horse*, p. 147.

2. *Ibid.*, March 2, 1933, p. 24, March 15, p. 30, April 1, 1933, p. 21; *New York Sun*, March 23, p. 30; Clippings File, Cooperstown; Ed Barrow, *My 50 Years*, p. 167; Robert Creamer, *Babe*, pp. 372–74.

3. *New York Sun*, March 23, p. 30.

4. *New York World-Telegram*, April 17, 1933, p. 19; *Literary Digest*, December 23, 1933, p. 18, August 8, 1934, p. 23; Clippings File, Cooperstown.

5. *New York Daily News*, April 6, 1933, p. 46; *New York Evening Post*, April 6, p. 18; *New York World-Telegram*, April 18, p. 23; *New York Sun*, April 18, p. 27, April 22, p. 26.

6. *New York Daily News*, April 26, 1933, p. 42, April 27, p. 42; *New York World-Telegram*, April 26, p. 20; *Washington Evening Star*, April 26, p 12.

7. *New York Daily News*, April 28, 1933, p. 58, April 29, pp. 28, 29; *New York World-Telegram*, April 26, p. 1; *New York Sun*, April 26, p. 30

8. *New York Daily News*, April 29, 1933, p. 28, April 30, p. 70; Joe McCarthy, "How Pennants Are Really Won," *Liberty Magazine*, September 30, 1933, p. 4; McCarthy, "World Champs: What It Takes To Make 'Em," *Liberty Magazine*, September 13, 1937, p. 25.

9. *Ibid.*, May 12, 1933, p. 62, June 1, p. 48; *New York Sun*, May 3, p. 31, June 20, p. 30, June 21, p. 29, June 17, p. 26.

10. *New York Daily News*, May 21, 1933, p. 70, May 25, p. 52, June 20, p. 47; Robert Creamer, *Babe*, pp. 376–77.

11. *Ibid.*, June 11, 1933, p. 76, June 15, p. 46, June 23, p. 56, June 24, p. 25; *New York Sun*, June 16, p. 31, June 23, pp. 29–30, June 24, p. 28, June 27, p. 26; *New York Times*, June 24, p. 11; Ray Robinson, *Iron Horse*, p. 181.

12. *New York Daily News*, June 25, 1933, p. 72, June 26, p. 37, June 27, p. 39; *New York Times*, June 26, p. 18.

13. *New York Daily News*, July 5, 1933, p. 46, July 6, p. 50, July 7, p. 42; *New York Sun*, July 5, p. 31, July 7, p. 17; *New York World-Telegram*, July 5, p. 25, July 6, pp. 27, 33.

14. *New York Daily News*, July 19, 1933, p. 42, July 31, p. 66, August 1, p. 36, Aug. 26, p. 25; *New York Sun*, July 21, p. 15, July 24, p. 22; *New York World-Telegram*, July 24, p. 17, July 27, p. 26, July 29, p. 22, July 31, p. 19.

15. *New York Daily News*, August 4, 1933, p. 42, Aug. 8, p. 38, Aug. 9, p. 42, Aug. 10, p. 42, Aug. 14, p. 35; *New York Sun*, Aug. 2, p.33, Aug. 4, p. 15, Aug. 8, p. 27, Aug. 9, p. 23, Aug. 12, p. 25, Aug.14, p. 23; *New York World-Telegram*, July 28, p. 10; Frank Graham, *New York Yankees*, p. 195.

16. *New York Daily News*, August 15, 1933, p. 44.

17. *Ibid.*, August 16, 1933, p. 47, Aug. 17, p. 41, Aug. 18, p. 46, Aug. 19, p. 58, Aug. 20, p. 66; *New York Sun*, Aug. 16, p. 27, Aug. 17, p. 26, Aug. 18, p. 16, Aug. 19, p. 25, Aug. 21, p. 23, Aug. 30, p. 23.

18. *New York Daily News*, August 21, 1933, p. 33, Aug. 27, p. 66, Sept. 20, p. 47, Sept. 22, p. 62; *New York Sun*, Aug. 28, p. 23, Aug. 29, p. 23, Aug. 30, p. 23; *New York World-Telegram*, Aug. 18, p. 10, Oct. 2, p. 38; Jim Enright, *Baseball's Greatest Teams: The Cubs*, p. 100; Harvey Frommer, *Baseball's Greatest Managers*, pp. 155–56.

Chapter 24

1. *New York World-Telegram*, March 5, 1934, p. 21, March 27, p. 26.

2. *Ibid.*, March 23, 1934, p. 39, March 26, p. 21, March 29, p. 33; *New York Daily News*, April 18, p. 46; Frank Graham, *New York Yankees*, p. 195.

3. *New York World-Telegram*, April 2, 1934, p. 23, April 16, p. 20, April 20, p. 27, April 25, p. 28; *New York Daily News*, April 22, p. 72, April 25, p. 44.

4. *New York World-Telegram*, April 16, 1934, p. 20.

5. *New York Daily News*, June 3, 1934, p. 76, June 4, p. 43.

6. Leonard Koppett, *The Man in the Dugout*, p. 100; Ed Fitzgerald, "Nobody's Neutral About McCarthy," in Jim Bouton, *I Managed Good, But Boy Did They Play Bad* (Chicago: Playboy Press, 1973), p. 245; Ed Fitzgerald, "Nobody's Neutral About McCarthy," p. 18; Tommy Henrich, *Five O'Clock Lightning*, p. 87; *Sporting News*, February 25, 1978, p. 52.

7. *New York Daily News*, June 5, 1934, p. 46, June 11, p. 42, June 16, p. 33, June 17, p. 73, June 23, p. 33, June 27, p. 44, June 30, p. 28, July 14, p. 29, July 15, p. 65, July 16, p. 36, July 19, p. 44, July 23, p. 37, July 25, p. 40, July 31, p. 44; Donald Honig, *The Man in the Dugout*, p. 87; Frank Graham, *New York Yankees*, p. 195; Ray Robinson, *Iron Horse*, pp. 206, 209.

8. *New York Daily News*, August 1, 1934, p. 42, Aug. 9, p. 46, Aug. 21, p. 42, Aug. 24, p. 44; *New York Sun*, August 11, p. 28, Aug. 13, p. 23, Aug. 16, p. 23; *Buffalo Evening News*, February 15, 1938, p. 26.

9. *New York Daily News*, September 6, 1934, p. 52, Sept. 7, p. 68, Sept. 14, p. 70, Sept. 16, p. 99, Sept. 17, p. 44, Sept. 18, p. 48, Sept. 19, p. 38, Sept. 20, p. 59, Sept. 21, p. 75; *New York Sun*, Sept. 15, p. 29, Sept. 18, p. 26; Frank Graham, *New York Yankees*, p. 199.

10. *New York Sun*, September 12, 1934, p. 36, March 12, 1935, p. 26.

11. *New York World-Telegram*, January 1, 1934, p. 13.

12. "Baseball: Ruppert-McCarthy Battery Puts Ruth Out at Home," *NewsWeek*, July 27, 1935, p. 22; Edwin Pope, *Baseball's Greatest Managers*, p. 144; Leonard Koppett, *The Man in the Dugout*, pp. 95–6; Ed Barrow, *My 50 Years*, pp. 170–71; Marshall Smelser, *The Life that Ruth Built*, p. 498.

13. *New York Sun*, March 5, 1935, p. 30, March 15, p. 34; *New York Daily News*, April 1, p. 23, June 3, p. 44; Frank Graham, *New York Yankees*, p. 218.

14. *New York Sun*, March 15, 1935, p. 34; *New York Daily News*, April 1, 1934, p. 23, April 18, pp. 59–60, August 26, p. 39.

15. *New York Sun*, March 9, 1935, p. 38; *New York Daily News*, Sept. 29, 1934, p. 58.

16. *New York Sun*, March 20, 1935, p. 34.

17. *New York World-Telegram*, April 4, 1935, p. 39, April 5, p. 36, April 10, p. 29, April 12, p. 36; *New York Daily News*, April 4, p. 58, April 13, p. 32; Tommy Henrich, *Five O'Clock Lightning*, p. 32.

18. *New York Daily News*, April 4, 1935, p. 58, April 30, p. 44; *New York World-Telegram*, April 22, p. 24, April 26, p. 28; *The Sporting News*, November 10, 1954, p. 15; Tommy Henrich, *Five O'Clock Lightning*, p. 27.

19. *New York Daily News*, May 3, 1935, p. 72, May 16, p. 54, May 17, p. 66.

20. *Ibid.*, May 31, p. 58; *New York Sun*, May 1, p. 1; *Philadelphia Inquirer*, February 4, 1938, p. 15.

21. *New York Daily News*, June 21, 1935, p. 78, June 30, p. 73, July 13, p. 29, July 24, p. 44, July 25, p. 54, July 27, p. 28.

22. *New York World-Telegram*, August 6, 1935, p. 24, Aug. 13, p. 23, Aug. 16, p. 16; *New York Daily News*, Aug. 10, p. 24, Aug. 25, p. 78, Aug. 26, p. 39; *New York Sun*, Sept. 28, p. 33, March 3, 1936, p. 25, March 7, 1936, p. 36.

23. *New York Daily News*, August 18, 1935, p. 76; April 8, 1942, p. 56.

24. Edwin Pope, *Baseball's Greatest Managers*, pp. 135, 146.

25. *New York Daily News*, September 19, 1935, p. 66, Sept. 27, p. 56; *New York Sun*, Sept. 28, p. 33; *New York World-Telegram*, March 2, 1936, p. 20; December 8, 1937, p. 22.

Chapter 25

1. *New York World-Telegram*, September 4, 1935, p. 29, March 2, 1936, p. 20.

2. *Ibid.*, March 9, 1936, p. 24; Maury Allen, *Where Have You Gone, Joe DiMaggio*, p. 39; Joe Durso, *DiMaggio: The Last American Knight* (Boston: Little, Brown, 1995), p. 68; Joe DiMaggio, *Lucky to Be a Yankee*, pp. 66–8.

3. *Ibid.*, March 3, 1936, p. 24, March 5, p. 30, March 6, p. 32, March 12, p. 30; *New York Sun*, March 9, p. 24, March 12, p. 35; Tommy Henrich, *Five O'-Clock Lightning*, p. 47.

4. *New York Sun*, March 23, 1936, p. 28; *New York Daily News*, April 6, p. 38; Gene Schoor, *Joe DiMaggio: The Yankee Clipper* (New York: Julian Messner, 1956), p. 77; Richard Ben Cramer, *Joe DiMaggio: The Hero's Life* (New York: Simon and Schuster, 2000), p. 85; Joe DiMaggio, *Lucky to Be a Yankee*, p. 70.

5. *New York Daily News*, April 10, 1936, p. 61, April 16, p. 61.

6. *Ibid.*, April 20, 1936, p. 44, April 23, p. 32, April 28, p. 58; *New York Sun*, April 24, p. 34, April 30, p. 33, May 1, p. 32.

7. *New York Daily News*, May 4, 1936, pp. 46–48, May 6, p. 61, May 7, p. 60; *New York Sun*, May 4, p. 29, May 6, p. 37; *New York Times*, May 4, p. 23; *New York World-Telegram*, March 2, p. 20; Tommy Henrich, *Five O'Clock Lightning*, 1992), p. 23; Frank Graham, *The New York Yankees*, p. 226.

8. *New York Daily News*, May 2, 1936, p. 39, May 8, p. 64; *New York Sun*, May 8, p. 38; *New York Times*, May 8, p. 27, May 11, p. 38; Donald Honig, *Baseball Between the Lines*, p. 96; Gene Schoor, *Joe DiMaggio*, p. 80. Joe DiMaggio, *Lucky to Be a Yankee*, p. 75.

9. Anthony Violanti, *Miracle in Buffalo: How the Dream of Baseball Revived a City* (New York: St. Martin's, 1991), p. 62.

10. Maury Allen, *Where Have You Gone, Joe DiMaggio*, p. 51.

11. *New York Daily News*, May 18, 1936, p. 39, May 20, p. 58, June 15, pp. 42–44; *New York World-Telegram*, June 15, p. 23, *New York Times*, June 15, p. 26.

12. Edwin Pope, *Baseball's Greatest Managers*, p. 137; Frank Graham, *The New York Yankees*, p. 227; Donald Honig, *Baseball Between the Lines* p. 29; Ed Barrow, *My 50 Years*, p. 158; Richard Ben Cramer, *Joe DiMaggio*, p. 84; McCarthy letter to David Alper of West Hempstead, N.Y., 1969, Clippings File, Cooperstown.

13. *New York Daily News*, June 15, 1936, pp. 42–44, June 17, p. 60; *New York World-Telegram*, June 15, p. 23, *New York Times*, June 15, p. 26; Tom Meany, *The Yankee Story*, p. 102.

14. *New York Daily News*, June 17, 1936, p. 60; Maury Allen, *Where Have You Gone, Joe DiMaggio*, p. 40; Joe Durso, *DiMaggio*, p. 77.

15. *New York Daily News*, July 21, 1936, p. 45, August 3, p. 42, Aug. 25, p. 46, September 4, p. 61.

16. *New York World-Telegram*, March 11, 1936, p. 29; Marshall Smelser, *The Life That Ruth Built*, p. 496.

17. *The Sporting News*, September 17, 1936, p. 4; Joe McCarthy, "We'll Win the World Series," *Liberty*, October 3, 1936, p. 48.

18. *New York Times*, October 1, 1936, p. 1; *New York Herald Tribune*, Oct. 1, pp. 1, 26; *Philadelphia Inquirer*, Oct. 1, p. 17, Oct. 2, p. 24; *Buffalo Evening News*, Oct. 1, p. 36.

19. *Philadelphia Inquirer*, Oct. 2, p. 24; *New York Times*, October 3, 1936, pp. 1, 10; *New York Herald Tribune*, Oct. 3, pp. 1, 18; *Buffalo Evening News*, Oct. 3, p. 8.

20. *New York Times*, October 4, 1936, p. 1, and section 5, p. 1, September 13, 1937, p. 35; *New York Herald Tribune*, Oct. 4, p. 1 and section III, p. 1; *New York Sun*, March 24, 1937, p. 35; Frank Graham, *The New York Yankees*, p. 229.

21. *New York Times*, October 5, 1936, pp. 1, 26; *New York Herald Tribune*, Oct. 5, pp. 1, 22–3; *Saturday Evening Post*, April 15, 1939, p. 78.

22. *New York Times*, October 6, 1936, pp. 1, 30, Oct. 6, 1939, p. 22; *New York Herald Tribune*, Oct. 6, pp. 1, 31; *Philadelphia Inquirer*, Oct. 6, p. 19; *Buffalo Evening News*, Oct. 6, p. 26, May 2, 1956, p. 13.

23. *New York Times*, October 7, 1936, pp. 1, 34; *New York Herald Tribune*, Oct. 7, pp. 1, 28; *Buffalo Evening News*, Oct. 7, p. 35.

24. *Buffalo Evening News*, Oct. 8, 1936, p. 33; Frank Graham, *The New York Yankees*, p. 230.

25. Frank Graham, *The New York Yankees*, p. 231.

26. Ed Barrow, *My 50 Years*, p. 158.

Chapter 26

1. *New York Sun*, March 1, 1937, p. 28, March 6, p. 35, March 11, p. 34, March 18, p. 1.

2. *Ibid.*, June 4, 1937, p. 38, June 4, p. 31; *New York American*, May 19, 1937, p. 14; Clippings File, Cooperstown.

3. New York Daily News, April 19, 1937, p. 41; New York World-Telegram, April 17, p. 5B, April 19, p. 24; Tommy Henrich, *Five O'Clock Lightning*, pp. 10–15.

4. Edwin Pope, *Baseball's Greatest Managers*, pp. 135, 139; *New York World-Telegram*, July 1, 1942, p. 29; Harvey Frommer, *Baseball's Greatest Managers*, p. 157; Frank Graham, *New York Yankees*, 187–88; Ed Barrow, *My 50 Years*, p. 155.

5. *New York Daily News*, April 14, 1937, p. 62, April 20, p. 52, April 21, p. 67, May 2, p. 58; *New York World-Telegram*, April 17, p. 3B, April 20, p. 26, April 22, p. 32, April 28, p. 26, 28.

6. Joe DiMaggio, *Lucky to Be a Yankee*, p. 161–62; Ed Linn, *The Great Rivalry: The Yankees and the Red Sox, 1901–1990* (New York: Ticknor and Fields, 1991), p. xiv; Tom Meany, *The Yankee Story*, pp. 100–01.

7. *Buffalo Evening News*, October 2, 1937, p. 8.

8. *New York Daily News*, May 4, 1937, p. 48, May 6, p. 65, May 8, p. 37, May 10, p. 41, May 11, p. 49; *Buffalo Evening News*, October 2, p. 8; Joe Williams, "Busher Joe McCarthy," *Saturday Evening Post*, vol. 211, April 15, 1939, p. 80; Pope, *Baseball's Greatest Managers*, p. 140; Frommer, *Baseball's Greatest Managers*, p. 157; Tommy Henrich, *Five O'Clock Lightning*, pp. 8, 31; Donald Honig, *Baseball Between the Lines*, p. 17; Charles Alexander, *Breaking the Slump*, p. 135; Richard Ben Cramer, *Joe DiMaggio*, p. 92.

9. *New York Daily News*, May 26, 1937, p. 38, May 27, p. 62, May 31, p. 36, June 6, p. 94; *New York Sun*, May 26, p. 38.

10. *Buffalo Evening News*, October 2, 1937, p. 8.

11. *New York Daily News*, June 4, 1937, p. 62, July 2, p. 39, July 22, p. 53; August 1, p. 74; *New York World-Telegram*, June 4, p. 31, October 7, p. 30; Clippings File, Cooperstown, July 29, 1937, August 5, 1937; *The Sporting News*, July 1, 1937, p. 4; Charles Alexander, *Breaking the Slump*, pp. 140–41.

12. *New York Daily News*, September 12, 1937, p. 90, Sept. 14, p. 44, Sept. 24, p. 60; *New York World-Telegram*, October 2, p. 24; *St. Louis Globe-Democrat*, Sept. 23, 1943, p. 19; *New York Daily Mirror*, September 29, p. 34; Charles Alexander, *Breaking the Slump*, pp. 140–41.

13. *New York Times*, September 13, 1937, p. 35; *New York Daily Mirror*, September 29, p. 34; *New York World-Telegram*, October 7, 1937, p. 30, Oct. 11, p. 42.

14. *New York World-Telegram*, October 7, 1937, p. 30, Oct. 11, p. 42; *Buffalo Evening News*, October 6, 1937, p. 36, August 4, 1969, section C, p. 2; *The Sporting News*, February 13, 1957, p. 6; Tommy Henrich, *Five O'Clock Lightning*, p. 38.

15. *Buffalo Evening News*, October 7, 1938, p. 38, Oct. 8, p. 47, Oct. 11, p. 35, February 1, 1938, p. 27; *New York World-Telegram*, March 31, 1938, p. 24; Tommy Henrich, *Five O'Clock Lightning*, p. 87.

16. *The Sporting News*, November 3, 1954, p. 15.

17. *Ibid.*; *New York Journal-American*, December 19, 1953, p. 18; *Boston Herald*, April 26, 1948, p. 14; Harvey Frommer, *Baseball's Greatest Managers*, p. 157; Maury Allen, *Where Have You Gone, Joe DiMaggio*, p. 43; Joe DiMaggio, *Lucky to Be a Yankee*, p. 160.

18. *New York World-Telegram*, October 15, 1937, p. 21.

19. *Buffalo Evening News*, February 1, 1938, p. 27; *New York Times*, December 6, 1937, p. 31; Edwin Pope, *Baseball's Greatest Managers*, p. 145; Ed Fitzgerald, "Nobody's Neutral About McCarthy," p. 19; Tommy Henrich, *Five O'Clock Lightning* p. 20; Walter Winchell, "Joe Jumps on Jack,"*New York Mirror*, Clippings File, Cooperstown.

20. *Buffalo Evening News*, October 7, 1937, p. 38; *New York World-Telegram*, March 18, 1938, p. 18; *New York Times*, September 25, 1977, p. 35.

21. Edwin Pope, *Baseball's Greatest Managers*, p. 144; Harry Frommer, *Baseball's Greatest Managers*, p. 159; Hank Nuwer, *Strategies of the Great Baseball Managers*, p. 77; Dick Johnson, ed., *DiMaggio: An Illustrated Life* (New York: Walker, 1995), p. 250; *New York Sun*, October 14, 1937, p. 30; *New York World-Telegram*, December 8, 1937, p. 22.

22. *New York World-Telegram*, October 14, 1937, p. 21.

23. Donald Honig, *Baseball When the Grass Was Green* (Lincoln: University of Nebraska Press, 1975), pp. 223–24.

24. *New York World-Telegram*, October 12, 1937, p. 21, March 4, 1938, p. 31, March 8, p. 21, March 14, p. 9, March 26, p. 26; Richard Ben Cramer, *Joe DiMaggio*, pp. 116–17; Joe Durso, *DiMaggio*, p. 95.

25. *New York Daily News*, April 16, 1938, p. 27, April 17, pp. 75–6, April 19, p. 44, April 21, p. 56; Clippings File, Cooperstown; Gene Schoor, *Joe DiMaggio*, pp. 99–100; in his negative critique of Joe DiMaggio, Richard Ben Cramer (*Joe DiMaggio*, p. 123) claims that McCarthy held DiMaggio in a different status after the 1938 holdout; McCarthy made no statements indicating that; DiMaggio's return to the lineup occurred after a legitimate, and small, amount of preparation time; and the rest of the season went fine for each, as did subsequent seasons. It was later in 1938 that McCarthy took his admittedly favorite player, Lou Gehrig, out of cleanup and replaced him with DiMaggio, a matter Cramer himself notes (p. 127).

26. *Ibid.*, April 23, p. 26, April 24, p. 82, April 25, p. 39; Donald Honig, *Baseball Between the Lines*, pp. 29–30.

27. *New York Daily News*, March 3, 1938, p. 24, April 29, p. 54, April 30, p. 30, May 15, p. 2, July 5, p. 52; *New York Times*, February 18, 1939, p. 11.

28. *Ibid.*, May 10, 1938, p. 46, May 12, p. 48,

29. *Ibid.*, June 10, 1938, p. 48; Pope, *Baseball's Greatest Managers*, p. 140.

30. *New York Daily News*, June 1, 1938, p. 56, June 23, p. 49, August 1, p. 34; Hank Nuwer, *Strategies of the Great Baseball Managers*, p. 82.

31. *New York Daily News*, Aug. 6, 1938, p. 25, Aug. 7, p. 72, Aug. 8, p. 30, Aug. 22, p. 30; Joe Williams, "Busher Joe McCarthy," *Saturday Evening Post*, April 15, 1939, p. 78; Hank Nuwer, *Strategies of the Great Baseball Managers*, pp. 74, 77; Joe DiMaggio, *Lucky to Be a Yankee*, p. 165; Tom Meany, *The Yankee Story*, p. 104.

32. *New York Daily News*, September 18, 1938, p. 89, April 28, 1939, p. 62; Donald Honig, *Baseball When the Grass Was Green*, pp. 34–5; Donald Honig, *Baseball Between the Lines*, p. 30.

33. *New York Daily News*, September 29, 1938, p. 72; *New York Sun*, Sept. 21, p. 19.

34. *New York Daily News*, June 23, 1938, p. 49; *The Sporting News*, October 20, 1938, p. 1; Donald Honig, *Baseball Between the Lines*, p. 39; Richard Lally, *Bombers: An Oral History of the New York Yankees* (New York: Crown, 2002), p. 24; Ken Burns, "Shadow Ball," *Baseball*, part 5, PBS film series, Florentine Films, 1994; Robert Burk, *Much More Than Game: Players, Owners, and American Baseball Since 1930* (Chapel Hill: University of North Carolina Press, 2001), p. 61; Charles Alexander, *Breaking the Slump*, p. 166; Tommy Henrich, *Five O'Clock Lightning*, pp. 6, 43–44, 50.

35. *New York World-Telegram*, October 1, 1938, p. 23; *New York Sun*, September 20, 1938, p. 17; March 21, 1939, p. 25; Donald Honig, *Baseball When the Grass Was Green*, pp. 34–5; Curt Smith, "Farmer McCarthy Recalls Pennant Crop," *Rochester Democrat and Chronicle*, June 17, 1973, p. 18; Tommy Henrich, *Five O'Clock Lightning*, p. 29; *New York Daily News*, January 10, 1945, p. 39.

36. *The Sporting News*, November 24, 1938, p. 3.

37. *New York World-Telegram*, October 1, 1938, p. 23.

38. *Buffalo Evening News*, October 3, 1938, p. 21, Oct. 4, p. 22; *New York World-Telegram*, Oct. 6, p. 25.

39. *Buffalo Evening News*, October 6, 1938, p. 8, Oct. 7, p. 45; *New York World-Telegram*, October 7, p. 32.

40. *Buffalo Evening News*, October 8, 1938, p. 6; *New York World-Telegram*, Oct. 10, p. 20; *The Sporting News*, November 24, p. 11; Ray Robinson, *Iron Horse*, p. 239; Ed Fitzgerald, "Nobody's Neutral About McCarthy," p. 80; Donald Honig, *Baseball When the Grass Was Green*, p. 148; Charles Alexander, *Breaking the Slump*, p. 165.

41. *Buffalo Evening News*, October 8, 1938, p. 6.

42. Pope, *Baseball's Greatest Managers*, p. 144; Ray Robinson, *Iron Horse*, p. 237.

43. *The Sporting News*, November 24, 1938, p. 3; Red Barber, *Walk in the Spirit* (New York: The Dial Press, 1969), pp. 151–52.

44. Tommy Henrich, *Five O'Clock Lightning*, p. 55.

45. Lee Allen, *The Hot Stove League*, p. 223; Joe McCarthy, "World Champs: What It Takes To Make 'Em," *Liberty*, September 13, 1937, pp. 25–6.

Chapter 27

1. *New York Times*, January 14, 1939, p. 7, Jan. 16, p. 15, Jan 18, p. 23; Ed Fitzgerald, "Nobody's Neutral About McCarthy," p. 80; Richard J. Tofel, *A Legend in the Making: The New York Yankees in 1939* (New York: Ivan R. Dee, 2002), pp. 1–3.

2. *Buffalo Evening News*, October 14, 1938, p. 39.

3. James T. Farrell, "The Cultural Front," *Partisan Review*, vol. 7, no. 4, July/August, 1940, p. 311.

4. *New York Sun*, March 1, 1939, p. 29; *New York Times*, June 3, 1941, p. 26; Donald Honig, *The Man in the Dugout*, p. 93.

5. *New York Sun*, March 2, 1939, p. 27, March 18, p. 32, March 20, p. 21, March 23, p. 30, March 28, p. 23; *New York Daily News*, April 5, p. 60; Joe DiMaggio, *Lucky to Be a Yankee*, p. 106–07; Frank Graham, *Lou Gehrig: A Quiet Hero* (New York: G.P. Putnam's Sons), 1942, p. 199; Tommy Henrich, *Five O'Clock Lightning*, p. 65; Donald Honig, *The New York Yankees*, p. 95; Frank Graham, *The New York Yankees*, p. 248–50.

6. *New York Daily News*, April 11, 1939, p. 46; *New York Times*, April 3, p. 28.

7. *New York Daily News*, May 1, 1939, p. 40, May 3, p. 58; *New York World-Telegram*, May 2, pp. 1, 23, *New York Times*, May 3, p. 28, June 3, 1941, p. 26; see also C. Einstein, *The Second Fireside Book of Baseball* (New York: Simon and Schuster, 1958), p. 70; Donald Honig, *Baseball Between the Lines*, p. 70; Joe DiMaggio, *Lucky to Be a Yankee*, p. 107; Tommy Henrich, *Five O'Clock Lightening*, p. 65; Donald Honig, *The New York Yankees*, p. 95; Ray Robinson, *Iron Horse*, pp. 246, 252.

8. *New York Daily News*, April 30, 1939, p. 82, May 3, p. 58; *New York Times*, May 1, p. 27; Donald Honig, *The Man in the Dugout*, p. 88.

9. Honig, *Baseball Between the Lines*, p. 33; *New York Daily News*, May 4, 1939, p. 58, May 5, p. 60, May 6, p. 33; Harvey Frommer, *Baseball's Greatest Managers*, p. 159.

10. *New York Daily News*, May 10, 1939, p. 62, May 19, p. 52, May 28, p. 58, May 31, p. 52.

11. *Ibid.*, June 2, 1939, p. 62, June 10, p. 48, June 22, p. 54; *New York Times*, June 22, p. 26, June 3, 1941, p. 26.

12. *New York World Telegram*, June 22, 1939, p. 14.

13. *New York Times*, July 4, 1939, p. 18, July 5, p. 1; *New York Daily News*, July 5, pp. 4, 54; Ray Robinson, *Iron Horse*, pp. 262–63; Talmage Boston, *1939 Baseball's Pivotal Year: From the Golden Age to the Modern Era* (Fort Worth, Tx.: The Summit Publishing Group, 1994), pp. 16–17.

14. *New York Times*, July 5, 1939, p. 1; *New York Daily News*, July 5, p. 54, July 14, p. 44, July 30, p. 34, August 29, p. 43; Harvey Frommer, *Baseball's Greatest Managers*, p. 51; Ed Linn, *The Great Rivalry*, pp. 137–39; Arthur Siegel column, September 27, 1939, Clippings File, Cooperstown.

15. *New York Daily News*, September 2, 1939, p. 28, Sept. 17, p. 84, Sept. 26, p. 27; Anthony Violanti, *Miracle in Buffalo: How the Dream of Baseball Revived a City* (New York: St. Martin's, 1991), pp. 63–64; Joe Durso, *DiMaggio*, p. 111; Leonard Koppett, *The Man in the Dugout*, p. 98; Richard Ben Cramer, *Joe DiMaggio*, pp. 137–38; Tommy Henrich, *Five O'Clock Lightning*, p. 62; Ed Linn, *The Great Rivalry*, p. 141.

16. *New York World-Telegram*, October 11, 1938, p. 45, October 7, 1939, p. 21.

17. *Ibid.*, October 1, 1938, p. 23, Oct. 1, 1939, p. 20,

Oct. 5, p. 30; *New York Times*, Oct. 2, p. 22, Oct. 5, p. 29; Edwin Pope, *Baseball's Greatest Managers*, p. 145.

18. *New York Times*, October 6, 1939, pp. 1, 22.

19. *Ibid.*, October 8, 1939, p. 9.

20. *Ibid.*, October 9, 1939, pp. 1, 22–23; Richard Ben Cramer, *Joe DiMaggio*, p. 139.

21. *Ibid.*, October 9, 1939, pp. 22–23; Tommy Henrich, *Five O'Clock Lightning*, p. 78.

22. *Buffalo Evening News*, October 11, 1939, pp. 37, 39; Gordon Cobbledick, "Break Up the Yankees!" *Collier's*, February 25, 1939, p. 19; David Quentin Voigt, *American Baseball*, vol. II (University Park, Pa.: Penn State University Press, 1983), pp. 197–98; Lally, *Bombers*, p. 179; Joe DiMaggio, *Lucky to Be a Yankee*, p. 130; Tommy Henrich, *Five O'Clock Lightning*, pp. 20–21.

23. Joe DiMaggio, *Lucky to Be a Yankee*, p. 174; Clippings File, Cooperstown, May 21, 1939; Maury Allen, *Where Have You Gone, Joe DiMaggio*, p. 43–4; Tommy Henrich, *Five O'Clock Lightning*, p. 45.

24. *New York Daily News*, July 29, 1941, p. 35; Red Barber, *Walk in the Spirit*, p. 158.

25. *St. Louis Post-Dispatch*, July 26, 1937, p. 11.

Chapter 28

1. *New York World-Telegram*, October 15, 1937, p. 21; *Buffalo Evening News*, February 12, 1940, p. 19.

2. *Buffalo Evening News*, February 6, 1940, p. 23; Donald Honig, *Baseball Between the Lines*, p. 41; Tommy Henrich, *Five O'Clock Lightning*, p. 74.

3. *Buffalo News*, December 25, 1983, section E, p. 1.

4. *New York Daily News*, April 10, 1940, p. 60, April 11, p. 58, April 14, p. 82, April 20, p. 28, April 28, p. 78, May 3, p. 60, May 8, p. 60, May 11, p. 33, May 12, p. 80, May 13, p. 38; *New York Times*, May 12, section 5, p. 1, May 13, p. 22.

5. *New York Times*, May 16, 1940, p. 30, May 18, p. 19; *New York Daily News*, May 17, p. 54, May 23, p. 58; Gene Schoor, *Joe DiMaggio*, p. 117; Joe Durso, *DiMaggio*, p. 105.

6. *New York Daily News*, May 27, 1940, p. 46, May 31, p. 48, June 10, p. 38; *New York World-Telegram*, September 30, 1943, p. 35.

7. *Ibid.*, June 13, 1940, p. 58, June 18, p. 47, June 21, p. 52, June 25, p. 42, July 2, p. 42, July 8, p. 68; *Boston Globe*, March 15, 1950, p. 22

8. *New York Daily News*, July 13, 1940, p. 67, July 16, p. 57, July 21, p. 64, August 2, p. 38, Aug. 5, p. 35, Aug. 6, p. 40, Aug. 18, p. 70; *New York Times*, Aug. 20, p. 25, Aug. 21, p. 25, June 3, 1941, p. 26; Tommy Henrich, *Five O'Clock Lightning*, p. 112; Richard Ben Cramer (*Joe DiMaggio*, p. 160) mistakenly places the Powers article in 1941 adding, inexactly, that Gehrig's family sued Powers.

9. *New York Daily News*, September 2, 1940, p. 36, Sept. 8, p. 88, Sept. 11, p. 50, Sept. 26, p. 58; Joe DiMaggio, *Lucky to Be a Yankee*, pp. 102, 165.

10. *New York Daily News*, September 13, 1940, p. 58, Sept. 14, p. 32, Sept. 16, p. 38, Sept. 18, p. 66.

11. *Ibid.*, Sept. 28, 1940, p. 28, Sept. 29, p. 85, Sept. 30, p. 42; *New York World-Telegram*, October 10, p. 34; Clippings File, Cooperstown, June 27, 1940; Tommy Henrich, *Five O'Clock Lightning*, pp. 83, 87; Ed Fitzgerald, "Nobody's Neutral About McCarthy," p. 81; *New York Sun*, January 13, 1942, p. 24.

12. *New York Sun*, May 1, 1940, p. 36.

Chapter 29

1. *New York Times*, November 15, 1940, p. 32; *Buffalo Evening News*, February 21, 1941, p. 36; October 1, 1938, p. 23.

2. *New York Times*, February 24, 1941, p. 20, Feb. 26, p. 25; *New York Daily News*, May 30, p. 35; *New York Sun*, March 24, p. 23; Tommy Henrich, *Five O'Clock Lightning*, p. 87; Harvey Frommer, *Baseball's Greatest Managers*, p. 159; Richard Ben Cramer, *Joe DiMaggio*, p. 95; Tom Meany, *The Yankee Story*, p. 106.

3. Bill Madden, *Pride of October: What It Was to Be Young and a Yankee* (New York: Warner Books, 2003), p. 10.

4. *New York Sun*, March 7, 1941, p. 31; *Buffalo Evening News*, February 21, p. 36.

5. *New York Sun*, March 12, 1941, p. 35, March 18, p. 27, March 28, p. 31.

6. *Ibid.*, March 28, 1941, p. 31.

7. *New York Daily News*, April 3, 1941, p. 59, April 6, p. 88, April 13, p. 76, April 19, p. 29, May 2, p. 52, May 5, p. 35, May 6, p. 46, May 7, p. 63.

8. Richard Lally, *Bombers*, pp. 36–7; Tommy Henrich, *Five O'Clock Lightning*, p. 96; Gene Schoor, *The Scooter: The Phil Rizzuto Story* (New York: Charles Scribner's Sons, 1982), pp. 47–48; *Boston Globe*, March 8, 1948, p. 5.

9. Leo Trachtenberg, "Loved and Hated, McCarthy Worked as a Champion," *Yankees Magazine*, August 7, 1986, pp. 101–02.

10. *New York Daily News*, May 22, 1941, p. 52, May 31, p. 24, June 1, p. 78; *New York Times*, June 1, section 5, p. 6; Ed Linn, *The Great Rivalry*, p. 149.

11. *New York Times*, June 2, 1941, p. 21, June 3, pp. 1, 26, June 3, p. 26, June 4, p. 28; *New York Daily News*, June 2, p. 39, June 3, p. 1, June 4, pp. 57, 59, June 5, p. 59, June 6, p. 58; *Buffalo Evening News*, February 21, 1941, p. 36; Joe DiMaggio, *Lucky to Be a Yankee*, p. 193; Donald Honig, *The Man in the Dugout*, p. 87.

12. *New York Daily News*, June 6, 1941, p. 58, June 15, p. 76.

13. *Ibid.*, June 25, 1941, p. 58, June 30, p. 34, July 1, p. 46; *Buffalo Evening News*, April 19, 1975, section B, p. 2; Gene Schoor, *Joe DiMaggio*, p. 121; Joe DiMaggio, *Lucky to Be a Yankee*, p. 148; Richard Lally, *Bombers*, p. 40; Ed Linn, *The Great Rivalry*, p. 151; Joe Durso, *DiMaggio*, p. 131; Tommy Henrich, *Five O'-*

Clock Lightning. pp. 100–01, 112; Richard Ben Cramer (*Joe DiMaggio,* pp. 167–70) casts the Yankees as virtually catering to DiMaggio's streak. But McCarthy had done things for Gehrig's streak too, and with the Cubs he had also discarded the take sign for Hack Wilson. In all cases he never did so to the detriment of the club. On the contrary, he indeed knew that a failure to recognize the issues at hand could have been dispiriting to his players. Managing a team of outstanding players is never so simple a matter as either catering completely to the needs of the stars or ignoring the outstanding individuals completely.

14. *New York Daily News,* July 2, 1941, p. 46, July 3, p. 2, July 5, p. 24, July 6, p. 32, July 7, p. 36, July 10, p. 2; Milton Gross, *Yankee Doodles* (Boston: House of Kent Publishing Co., 1948), p. 57.

15. *Ibid.,* July 14, 1941, p. 37, July 15, p. 38, July 17, p. 47, July 18, p. 42.

16. *Ibid.,* July 19, 1941, p. 25, July 22, p. 41, July 29, p. 35.

17. *Ibid.,* July 29, 1941, p. 35, August 3, p. 74.

18. *Ibid.,* July 25, 1941, p. 28, Aug. 8, p. 54, Aug. 9, p. 24, Aug. 18, p. 33, Aug. 20, p. 57, Aug. 24, p. 80, Aug. 31, p. 49; *New York Times,* Aug. 23, p. 8, Aug. 24, section 5, p. 1, Aug. 25, p. 20, Aug. 31, section 5, p. 5; *New York World-Telegram,* March 20, 1943, p. 18.

19. *New York Daily News,* September 5, 1941, p. 56, Sept. 7, p. 87; *Buffalo Evening News,* July 8, 1972, section C, p. 3.

20. *Ibid.,* September 13, 1941, p. 29, Sept. 15, p. 36, Sept. 26, p. 60.

21. *Ibid.,* September 26, 1941, p. 66; Tommy Henrich, *Five O'Clock Lightning,* p. 21; Gerald Eskenazi, *The Lip: A Biography of Leo Durocher* (New York: William Morrow, 1993), pp. 133–4; Donald Honig, *Baseball Between the Lines,* pp. 29–30; Tom Meany, *The Yankee Story,* p. 102.

22. *New York Times,* October 2, 1941, p. 30.

23. *Ibid.,* October 3, 1941, p. 28; August 14, 1942, p. 43.

24. *Ibid.,* October 5, 1941, p. 28, Oct. 6, pp. 1, 21

25. *Ibid.,* October 6, 1941, pp. 1, 21.

26. *New York Times,* October 7, 1941, pp. 1, 28; *Brooklyn Eagle,* October 7, p. 1.

27. *New York Mirror,* October 16, 1941, Clippings File, Cooperstown.

27; *New York Daily News,* April 30, p. 48, May 3, p. 81.

7. *New York World-Telegram,* April 30, 1942, p. 15; *New York Daily News,* April 25, p. 24, May 14, p. 46, May 31, p. 74, June 9, p. 40, June 10, p. 60, June 15, p. 32; Frank Graham, *The New York Yankees,* p. 270; Tom Meany, *The Yankee Story,* p. 103.

8. *New York Daily News,* June 19, 1942, p. 44, June 22, p. 33, June 29, p. 37, July 1, p. 51; *New York Times,* June 28, section 5, p. 3, June 29, p. 19; Richard Ben Cramer, *Joe DiMaggio,* p. 201.

9. *New York Daily News,* July 7, 1942, p. 36, July 8, p. 58, July 9, p. 48, July 10, p. 42, July 23, p. 47, July 30, p. 41; *New York Times,* July 23, p. 23.

10. *New York Daily News,* July 19, 1942, p. 70, July 20, p. 32, July 21, p. 36, July 22, p. 50, July 23, p. 47, July 24, p. 38; August 12, p. 56; *New York Times,* July 19, section 5, p. 1, July 20, p. 17, July 21, p. 24, July 22, p. 24, July 23, p. 23, July 24, p. 14; Tommy Henrich, *Five O'Clock Lightning,* p. 134.

11. *New York Daily News,* July 26, 1942, p. 66, August 21, p. 47.

12. *Ibid.,* August 4, 1942, p. 39, Aug. 5, p. 54, Aug. 30, p. 78, September 1, p. 46; *New York Times,* Aug. 21, p. 22, Aug. 24, p. 19, Aug. 25, p. 26, Aug. 27, p. 23, Aug. 30, section 5, p. 1, Aug. 31, p. 21; Donald Honig, *Baseball Between the Lines,* p. 35; Tommy Henrich, *Five O'Clock Lightning,* p. 135.

13. *New York Daily News,* September 8, 1942, p. 43, Sept. 9, p. 62, Sept. 15, p. 44; *Buffalo Evening News,* November 26, 1942, p. 29, Clippings File, Cooperstown.

14. *New York Daily News,* September 28, 1942, p. 56, Sept. 29, p. 42; *Buffalo Evening News,* October 1, pp. 30–31.

15. *The Sporting News,* November 10, 1954, p. 16; *Buffalo Evening News,* October 2, 1942, p. 46.

16. *Buffalo Evening News,* October 3, 1942, p. 24, Oct. 5, p. 22; *New York Times,* November 13, 1943, p. 32.

17. *Buffalo Evening News,* October 6, 1942, p. 24; *St. Louis Globe-Democrat,* September 23, 1943, p. 19; Tommy Henrich, *Five O'Clock Lightning,* p. 136.

18. *Buffalo Evening News,* October 6, 1942, p. 25; Frank Graham, *The New York Yankees,* p. 275; Tommy Henrich, *Five O'Clock Lightning,* p. 32.

Chapter 30

1. *Buffalo Evening News,* February 21, 1941, p. 36.

2. *Ibid.,* February 19, 1942, p. 28.

3. *New York World-Telegram,* March 5, 1942, p. 25, March 7, p. 15, March 9, p. 21, March 13, p. 28.

4. *Ibid.,* March 13, p. 28, March 30, p. 15.

5. *New York Daily News,* April 6, 1942, p. 33; *Philadelphia Inquirer,* April 5, p. 6, April 7, p. 25, April 8, p. 29, April 9, p. 26.

6. *New York World-Telegram,* March 4, 1942, p.

Chapter 31

1. *Buffalo Evening News,* January 13, 1943, p. 17.

2. *Ibid.,* February 9, 1943, p. 18; Frank Graham, *The New York Yankees,* p. 279.

3. *Buffalo Evening News,* February 3, 1943, p. 35, Feb. 17, p. 37, Feb. 26, p. 34; *New York World-Telegram,* March 4, 1942, p. 27; March 2, 1943, p. 20, March 15, p. 20, March 17, p. 25, March 13, 1944, p. 17; *New York Times,* February 18, 1989, p. 11; *New York Herald Tribune,* April 3, 1943, p. 28; Tommy Henrich, *Five O'Clock Lightning,* p. 87; Richard Goldstein,

Spartan Seasons: How Baseball Survived the Second World War (New York: Macmillan, 1980), p. 102.

4. *New York Daily News*, April 1, 1943, p. 44, April 11, p. 78, April 14, p. 58, April 15, p. 54, April 19, p. 32; Frank Graham, *The New York Yankees*, p. 284.

5. *New York World-Telegram*, March 22, 1943, p. 22, March 24, p. 32; *New York Daily News*, April 20, p. 40; Ed McAuley, "The McCarthy Technique," *Baseball Digest*, vol. 3, no. 1, February, 1944, p. 24.

6. *New York Daily News*, April 23, 1943, p. 42, April 26, p. 39, May 5, p. 54, May 24, p. 41.

7. *Ibid.*, June 9, 1943, p. 58, July 8, 1944, p. 41; Milton Gross, *Yankee Doodles*, p. 57.

8. *New York Daily News*, May 31, 1943, p. 36, July 6, p. 44.

9. *Ibid.*, June 26, 1943, p. 23, June 27, p. 77, July 4, p. 60, July 6, p. 44, July 12, p. 40, July 14, p. 46, July 31, p. 24; *New York Times*, August 8, 1943, p. 33..

10. *New York Daily News*, September 9, 1943, p. 62, Sept. 30, p. 48; *New York Times*, October 1, p. 22, Oct. 3, section 3, p. 1.

11. *New York Times*, October 6, 1943, p. 27, Oct. 7, p. 29.

12. *Ibid.*, October 8, 1943, p. 23.

13. *Ibid.*, October 11, 1943, p. 25, Oct. 12, p. 31, Oct. 13, p. 31; *New York Daily News*, September 28, p. 44; Vincent Flaherty, "A Great Guy Even When He Hasn't Got It: That's Joe McCarthy," *Baseball Digest*, vol. 2, no. 8, Oct., 1943, pp. 34–5.

14. *New York World-Telegram*, March 15, 1944, p. 27, March 21, p. 17; *Buffalo Evening News*, April 22, p. 5, April 27, p. 24; *New York Daily News*, April 27, p. 34; Vincent Flaherty, "A Great Guy," p. 35.

15. *Buffalo Evening News*, February 4, 1944, p. 28, Feb. 19, p. 5.

16. *New York World-Telegram*, March 13, 1944, p. 17; Goldstein, *Spartan Seasons*, p. 113.

17. *New York Daily News*, May 16, 1944, p. 32; *New York Times*, November 10, 1943, p. 32; June 25, 1950, section 5, p. 2; *New York World Telegram*, April 13, 1944, p. 17; Arthur Daley, "McCarthy Could Manage," *Baseball Digest*, vol. 9, no. 9, Sept. 1950, p. 62; Associated Press Biographical Sketch, No. 3002, November 15, 1942; Edwin Pope, *Baseball's Greatest Managers*, pp. 134–35; Donald Honig, *The Man in the Dugout*, pp. 288–89; Harvey Frommer, *Baseball's Greatest Managers*, p. 156; Goldstein, *Spartan Seasons*, p. 157; Donald Honig, *Baseball Between the Lines*, p. 374.

18. *New York World-Telegram*, March 28, 1944, p. 20.

19. Tommy Henrich, *Five O'Clock Lightning*, p. 32; Ed Fitzgerald, "Nobody's Neutral About McCarthy," p. 81.

20. *New York Daily News*, April 2, 1944, p. 70. Other reference to football players like Steph. having throwing problems.

21. *Buffalo Evening News*, April 17, 1944, p. 6, April 18, p. 8, April 19, p. 34, April 22, p. 5, April 24, p. 8, April 27, p. 24; *New York Daily News*, April 18, p. 34,

April 19, p. 47, April 22, p. 23, April 27, p. 34, May 4, p. 44, May 8, p. 29, May 9, p. 35, May 10, p. 46; Tommy Holmes, "What You Learned from McCarthy," [*Brooklyn Eagle*] *Baseball Digest*, vol. 13, no. 9, pp. 65–66; Frank Graham, *The New York Yankees*, p. 283; Ed Fitzgerald, "Nobody's Neutral About McCarthy," p. 273.

22. *New York Daily News*, May 20, 1944, p. 22, June 10, p. 23, June 20, p. 24, July 3, p. 30, July 4, p. 30, August 13, p. 64, Aug. 16, p. 45, Aug. 21, p. 24.

23. Ibid, June 10, 1944, p. 23, August 16, p. 45, Aug. 17, p. 37, September 1, p. 41, Sept. 3, p. 48, Sept. 4, p. 28, Sept. 5, p. 33, Sept. 13, p. 51, Sept. 29, p. 42; *New York Times*, July 24, 1957, p. 31.

24. *New York Daily News*, September 8, 1944, p. 41, Sept. 17, p. 61, Sept. 18, p. 28, Sept. 29, p. 42; *New York Times*, October 1, section 3, p. 2; Frank Graham, *The New York Yankees*, p. 286; Tommy Holmes, "What You Learned from Joe McCarthy," *Baseball Digest*, vol. 13, no. 9, pp. 65–66.

Chapter 32

1. David Quentin Voigt, *American Baseball*, vol. II (University Park: Penn State University Press, 1983), p. 270; Bill James, *The Bill James Guide to Baseball Managers*, p. 125; John Lardner, "Mr. McCarthy Continues," *Baseball Digest*, vol. 5, no. 1, February, 1946, pp. 46–7; Maury Allen, *Where Have You Gone, Joe DiMaggio*, p. 118.

2. *New York Daily News*, April 14, 1945, p. 43; Milton Gross, *Yankee Doodles*, pp. 58, 164, 234.

3. *Buffalo Evening News*, March 12, 1945, p. 6.

4. *New York World-Telegram*, March 8, 1945, p. 21, March 10, p. 11, March 12, p. 15, March 14, pp. 21, 27, March 22, p. 21.

5. *Ibid.*, March 14, 1945, p. 29.

6. *Ibid.*, March 14, 1945, p. 29, March 27, p. 17; *New York Daily News*, April 15, p. 46, May 3, p. 44; *Cleveland Plain Dealer*, July 6, 1945, p. 13.

7. *New York Daily News*, April 12, 1945, p. 43, April 18, p. 52, May 7, p. 30, May 27, p. 67, June 8, p. 39, June 13, p. 53, June 20, p. 45; *New York Times*, February 7, 1946, p. 26; Milton Gross, *Yankee Doodles*, p. 143.

8. *New York Daily News*, June 13, 1945, p. 53, June 22, p. 38, July 1, p. 56, July 2, p. 36, July 3, p. 25, July 22, p. 80; *New York Times*, July 23, p. 22.

9. *New York Daily News*, July 24, 1945, p. 41, July 25, p. 49; *Buffalo Evening News*, July 24, p. 18, July 25, p. 30; *New York Journal-American*, July 24, p. 19; *New York Times*, July 23, p. 22; Ed Fitzgerald, "Nobody's Neutral About McCarthy," p. 273.

10. *Buffalo Evening News*, August 8, 1945, p. 30, August 16, p. 19; *Buffalo Courier-Express*, July 22, 1945, p. 18.

11. *New York Daily News*, July 28, 1945, p. 25, August 10, p. 36, Aug. 11, p. 22; *New York Times*, August 10, 1945, p. 22; Frank Graham, *The New York Yankees*, p. 288; Ed Hurley, *Managing to Win*, p. 64.

12. *New York Daily News*, August 13, 1945, p. 29, Aug. 14, p. 34, Aug. 16, p. 38, Aug. 17, p. 41, Aug. 18, p. 23, Aug. 19, p. 68.

13. *Ibid.*, August 13, 1945, p. 29, Aug. 27, p. 30, September 1, p. 22, Sept. 4, p. 38, Sept. 5, p. 56, Sept. 7, p. 41, Sept. 8, p. 22, Sept. 9, p. 75, Sept. 10, p. 29, Sept. 15, p. 22.

14. *Ibid.*, September 13, 1945, p. 49, Sept. 14, p. 48.

15. *New York Times*, August 10,1945, p. 23.

Chapter 33

1. *New York Times*, February 7, 1946, p. 26.

2. *Ibid.*, February 13, 1946, p. 27, Feb. 28, p. 26; *New York Sun*, Feb. 19, p. 29, Feb. 21, p. 22, Feb. 22, p. 18, Feb. 26, p. 28; Gene Schoor, *Joe DiMaggio*, p. 142; Schoor, *The Scooter*, p. 92.

3. John Lardner, "Mr. McCarthy Continues," *Baseball Digest*, vol. 5, no. 1, February, 1946, pp. 46–7; Richard Ben Cramer, *Joe DiMaggio*, p. 218; Tom Meany, *The Yankee Story*, p. 120.

4. *New York Times*, February 13, 1946, p. 27. *New York Sun*, March 26, p. 28, *New York Daily News*, April 1, p. 24, April 8, p. 37, April 11, p. 57.

5. *New York Sun*, March 14, 1946, p. 32; *New York Daily News*, April 20, p 25, April 28, p. 37, May 11, p. 25, May 13, p. 37.

6. *New York Daily News*, May 18, 1946, p. 25.

7. Milton Gross, *Yankee Doodles*, p. 60.

8. *Ibid.*, pp. 61–2; *New York Daily News*, May 19, p. 87, May 20, p. 36, May 21, p. 41; *New York Herald Tribune*, May 21, p. 28; Tommy Henrich, *Five O'-Clock Lightning*, p. 51; Milton Gross, *Yankee Doodles*, p. 62.

9. *New York Herald Tribune*, May 22, 1946, p. 27; *New York Daily News*, May 22, pp. 55, 57, *New York Times*, May 22, p. 26; Tommy Henrich, *Five O'Clock Lightning*, p. 164; Edwin Pope, *Baseball's Greatest Managers*, p. 147; Bill James, *The Bill James Guide to Baseball Managers*, p. 119; Harvey Frommer, *Baseball's Greatest Managers*, p. 160; Peter Golenbock, *Dynasty: New York Yankees, 1949–1964* (Chicago: Contemporary Books, 2000), pp. 19–22; Richard Ben Cramer, *Joe DiMaggio*, pp. 220–21; Milton Gross, *Yankee Doodles*. (Boston: House of Kent Publishing Co., 1948), pp. 20–21.

10. *New York Sun*, May 22, 1946, p. 35.

11. *Ibid.*, May 22, 1946, p. 35, May 23, p. 33; Harvey Frommer, *Baseball's Greatest Managers*, p. 160.

12. *New York World-Telegram*, May 22, 1946, p. 39, May 23, p. 33; *New York Herald Tribune*, May 24, p. 26, May 25, p. 16; *New York Times*, May 25, pp. 10, 19, 25; *New York Daily News*, May 25, p. 25; *Buffalo Evening News*, May 24, p. 41; Joe Durso, *DiMaggio*, p. 157; Tommy Henrich, *Five O'Clock Lightning*, p. 144.

13. Henrich, *Five O'Clock Lightning*, p. 145.

14. *New York World-Telegram*, May 25, 1946, p. 12, May 27, p. 25; Milton Gross, *Yankee Doodles*, p. 63;

Ed Fitzgerald, "Nobody's Neutral About McCarthy," p. 274.

15. *New York World-Telegram*, May 24, 1946, p. 20.

Chapter 34

1. Ed Fitzgerald, "Nobody's Neutral About McCarthy," p. 82; *The Sporting News*, October 29, 1947, p. 3.

2. Al Hirshberg, *What's the Matter with the Red Sox* (New York: Dodd, Mead, 1973), p. xi.

3. Red Barber, *Walk in the Spirit*, pp. 160–62; *New York Times*, April 10, 1947, p. 1.

4. *New York Times*, April 10, 1947, pp. 1, 31–32; *Buffalo Evening News*, January 21, 1947, p. 11; Ed Fitzgerald, "Nobody's Neutral About McCarthy," p. 82; Stanley Cohen, *Dodgers! The First 100 Years* (New York: Birch Lane Press, 1990), p. 83.

5. Tommy Henrich, *Five O'Clock Lightning*, p. 198.

6. *Ibid.*, p. 204.

7. Bill Cunningham, "The Boston Red Sox," *Sport Magazine*, vol. 9, no. 6, December, 1950, p. 75.

8. *The Sporting News*, October 8, 1947, p. 3; Harvey Frommer, *Baseball's Greatest Managers*, p. 192; Milton Gross, *Yankee Doodles*, p. 144; "Joe McCarthy's Ten Years as a Louisville Colonel," p. 7.

9. Milton Gross, *Yankee Doodles*, pp. 59, 62; Al Hirshberg, *What's the Matter with the Red Sox*, p. 18.

10. Al Hirshberg, *What's the Matter with the Red Sox*, pp. 8, 18, 123, 130, 133; *The Sporting News*, April 14, 1948, p. 6.

11. Ed Fitzgerald, "Nobody's Neutral About McCarthy," p. 277; Dan Shaughnessy, *The Curse of the Bambino*, p. 77; Joe DiMaggio, *Lucky to Be a Yankee*, p. 18; Ed Linn, *The Great Rivalry*, pp. 180, 184.

12. Dan Shaughnessy, *The Curse of the Bambino*, p. 77.

13. *Boston Globe*, February 25, 1948, p. 11, April 6, p. 13; *Boston Herald*, March 2, p. 7; *Boston Post*, March 9, p. 16; Ed Linn, *Hitter: The Life and Turmoils of Ted Williams* (New York: Harcourt, Brace, 1993), p. 309.

14. *Boston Post*, March 9, 1948, p. 16, March 17, p. 19; *Boston Globe*, March 6, 1948, p. 5; *Boston Herald*, March 3, p. 15; *New York World-Telegram*, October 15, 1947, p. 16; Donald Honig, *The Man in the Dugout*, p. 93; Peter Golenbock, *Fenway, An Unexpurgated History of the Red Sox* (New York: G.P. Putnam's Sons, 1992), p. 167; Ed Fitzgerald, "Nobody's Neutral About McCarthy," *Sport Magazine*, vol. 9, no. 2, August, 1950, p. 20; Ed Linn, *Hitter*, pp. 17, 309; Dan Shaughnessy, *The Curse of the Bambino*, p. 77; Milton Gross, *Yankee Doodles*, pp. 55–6; Ed Linn, *The Great Rivalry*, p. 182.

15. *Boston Post*, March 8, 1948, pp. 1, 12, March 19, p. 26, April 22, p. 21; *Boston Herald*, March 8, p. 11; *Boston Globe*, March 8, p. 5, March 10, p. 12; *The*

Sporting News, April 14, 1948, p. 6; *Time Magazine*, April 5, 1948, p. 48; Ted Williams, *My Turn at Bat*, p. 156.

16. *Boston Post*, March 9, 1948, p. 16; *Boston Herald*, March 15, p. 13; *Buffalo Evening News*, March 7, 1947, p. 36; Joe DiMaggio, *Lucky to Be a Yankee*, p. 18.

17. *Boston Globe*, March 9, 1948, p. 8, March 10, p. 12, *Boston Post*, March 16, p. 18; *Boston Herald*, April 2, p. 32; *Buffalo Evening News*, February 1, 1957, p. 29; Clippings File, Cooperstown.

18. *Boston Herald*, March 16, 1948, p. 17; *Boston Post*, April 15, p. 18, *Boston Globe*, April 8, p. 17; *Time Magazine*, April 5, 1948, p. 48; *Colliers Magazine*, April 24, 1948, p. 70.

19. *Boston Globe*, April 9, 1948, p. 1, April 10, p. 1, April 11, p. 1, April 19, p. 1; *Boston Herald*, April 21, p. 30, April 23, p. 42, April 24, p. 9, April 25, p. 42, April 26, p. 14; *Boston Post*, April 23, p. 26, April 26, p. 14; Pope, *Baseball's Greatest Managers*, p. 135; Ed Linn, *Hitter*, p. 310; Al Hirshberg, *What's the Matter with the Red Sox*, p. 89.

20. *Boston Post*, April 26, 1948, p. 14, May 9, p. 19, May 24, p. 15, May 25, pp. 14, 15; Dan Shaughnessy, *The Curse of the Bambino*, p. 78.

21. *Ibid.*, May 25, pp. 14, 15; *Boston Herald*, May 17, p. 11; *Boston Globe*, May 25, p. 38, May 26, p. 24; Al Hirshberg, *What's the Matter with the Red Sox*, p. 94.

22. *Boston Globe*, May 25, 1948, p. 38, March 4, 1949, p. 34; *Boston Post*, May 26, 1948, p. 24; *Boston Herald*, May 26, p. 25.

23. *Boston Post*, May 27, 1948, p. 20; *Boston Globe*, May 25, p. 38.

24. *Boston Herald*, May 27, 1948, p. 26, May 28, p. 1, May 29, p. 8; *Boston Globe*, May 30, p. 1, *Boston Post*, May 28, pp. 1, 22, May 29, p. 8, May 30, p. 9, May 31, p. 38.

25. *Boston Post*, May 30, 1948, p. 9, June 1, p. 20, June 2, p. 16, June 3, p. 18; *Boston Herald*, May 31, p. 36; Peter C. Bjarkman, ed., *Encyclopedia of Major League Baseball — American League* (New York: Carroll and Graf Publishers, 1993), p. 28.

26. *Boston Post*, June 7, 1948, p. 1, June 25, pp. 1, 19, 20; Ed Linn, *The Great Rivalry*, pp. 184–5; Tom Meany, *The Boston Red Sox* (New York: A.S. Barnes, 1956), p. 159.

27. *Boston Post*, June 9, 1948, p. 1, July 26, p. 14; *Boston Globe*, July 26, p. 1; Ed Linn, *The Great Rivalry*, pp. 184–5.

28. *Boston Globe*, July 24, 1948, p. 4, July 25, p. 26.

29. *Boston Globe*, July 28, 1948, p. 18; *Boston Post*, July 23, p. 12, July 31, p. 1, August 4, p. 20, Aug. 9, p. 13, Aug. 12, p. 18, Aug. 30, p. 10; *Cleveland Plain Dealer*, July 31, p. 11.

30. *Boston Post*, August 17, 1948, p. 1, Aug. 17, p. 18.

31. *Ibid.*, September 7, 1948, p. 19, Sept. 8, p. 20, Sept. 9, p. 18.

32. *Ibid.*, September 9, 1948, p. 19.

33. *Ibid.*, September 11, 1948, pp. 1, 8; Joe Durso,

DiMaggio, p. 173; Ed Linn, *The Great Rivalry*, pp. 185–87.

34. *Boston Post*, September 12, 1948, p. 32, Sept. 13, p. 16, Sept. 15, p. 20, Sept. 16, p. 21, Sept. 17, p. 26, Sept. 18, p. 6.

35. Tommy Henrich, *Five O'Clock Lightning*, p. 22; Al Hirshberg, *What's Wrong with the Red Sox*, pp. 70–71.

36. Ed Linn, *Hitter*, pp. 309–11.

37. *Boston Post*, September 18, 1948, p. 6, Sept. 19, p. 28, Sept. 20, p. 17, Sept. 21, p. 16, Sept 22, p. 22, Sept. 23, p. 21; Ed Linn, *The Great Rivalry*, p. 183.

38. *Boston Post*, September 24, p 30, Sept. 25, p. 6, Sept. 26, p. 30, Sept. 27, p. 1.

39. *Ibid.*, September 29, 1948, p. 19, Sept. 30, p. 18, October 1, p. 28; *Boston Herald*, Oct. 1, p. 1, Oct. 2, p. 9; *Boston Globe*, Oct. 1, p. 28.

40. *Boston Post*, October 3, 1948, p. 30; *Boston Herald*, Oct. 3, pp. 1, 27; *Boston Globe*, Oct. 3, p. 18; Ed Linn, *The Great Rivalry*, p. 190.

41. *Boston Post*, October 4, 1948, pp. 18, 19; *Boston Herald*, Oct. 4, p. 16; *Boston Globe*, Oct. 4, p. 4; *The Sporting News*, December 18, 1957, p. 18; Ed Linn, *The Great Rivalry*, pp. 191–92.

42. *Boston Post*, October 4, 1948, pp. 18; *Boston Herald*, Oct. 4, p. 16; *Boston Globe*, Oct. 4, p. 4; Dan Shaughnessy, *The Curse of the Bambino*, pp. 79–80.

43. Ed Linn, *The Great Rivalry*, pp. 193–98; Al Hirshberg, *What's the Matter with the Red Sox*, pp. 97–98; *Boston Magazine*, October, 1989, p. 88.

44. *Ibid.*, p. 198; Dan Shaughnessy, *The Curse of the Bambino*, p. 81; Peter Golenbock, *Fenway*, pp. 176–77; Dan Shaughnessy, *The Curse of the Bambino*, pp. 80–83; *New York Daily News*, September 29, 1938, p. 72; Clippings File, Cooperstown.

45. Ed Linn, *The Great Rivalry*, pp. 193–96; *Boston Globe*, Oct. 4, p. 16; Edwin Pope, *Baseball's Greatest Managers*, p. 135; Donald Honig, *Baseball Between the Lines*, p. 222; *Boston Magazine*, October, 1989, pp. 87–88.

46. *Boston Post*, October 5, 1948, pp. 38, May 20, 1949, p. 31; Donald Honig, *The Man in the Dugout*, p. 93; Bill James, *The Bill James Guide to Baseball Managers*, p. 118; Harvey Frommer, *Baseball's Greatest Managers*, p. 161; Hank Nuwer, *Strategies of the Great Baseball Managers*, p. 81; Dan Shaughnessy, *The Curse of the Bambino*, pp. 80–83; Ed Linn, *The Great Rivalry*, pp. 196–98.

47. *Boston Globe*, October 5, 1948, p. 21; *Boston Herald*, Oct. 5, p. 20; Peter Golenbock, *Fenway*, p. 177.

48. Richard Ben Cramer, *Joe DiMaggio*, p. 257.

49. Ted Williams, with John Underwood, *My Turn at Bat: The Story of My Life* (New York: Simon and Schuster, [1969] 1988, p. 153; *Buffalo Evening News*, September 8, 1969, p. 11; *Look Magazine*, July 4, 1950, p. 74.

50. *Boston Herald*, October 5, 1948, p. 1; *Boston Globe*, Oct. 5, p. 1, Oct. 9, p. 7, Oct. 14, p. 1.

Chapter 35

1. *Baltimore Sun*, November 24, 1948, p. 9, November 29, p. 9; *Chicago Tribune*, November 24, section 3, pp. 2–3; *Charleston* [West Virginia] *Gazette*, September 28, 1949, p. 18.

Chapter 36

1. Peter Golenbock, *Fenway*, p. 177; Ed Linn, *The Great Rivalry*, p. 183.

2. Peter C. Bjarkman, ed., *Encyclopedia of Major League Baseball—American League*, p. 30; *Boston Globe*, February 24, 1950, p. 10, Feb. 28, p. 13; *Boston Post*, March 3, 1949, p. 20; Dan Shaughnessy, *The Curse of the Bambino*, p. 90; Al Hirshberg, *What's Wrong with the Red Sox*, pp. 143–46.

3. *Boston Post*, March 9, 1949, p. 21.

4. *Boston Post*, March 4, 1949, p. 34; *Boston Globe*, March 5, p. 5.

5. *Boston Globe*, March 23, 1949, pp. 1, 16; *Boston Post*, March 27, p. 35.

6. *Boston Post*, April 8, 1949, p. 36, April 12, p. 21.

7. *Ibid.*, April 22, 1949, p. 20, April 25, p. 18, April 26, p. 20, April 30, p. 20, May 4, p. 26; *Boston Globe*, April 22, p. 31, April 25, p. 6, April 26, p. 10, April 29, p. 27; *Philadelphia Inquirer*, April 28, p. 12.

8. *Boston Post*, May 12, 1949, p. 26; Harvey Frommer, *Baseball's Greatest Managers*, p. 161.

9. *Ibid.*, May 6, 1949, p. 1, May 7, p. 8; *Boston Herald*, September 27, p. 22.

10. *Boston Post*, May 17, 1949, p. 18, May 31, p. 16, June 6, pp. 1, 18, June 11, p. 8; Al Hirshberg, *What's Wrong with the Red Sox*, p. 104.

11. *Boston Post*, June 28, 1949, p. 18.

12. *Boston Post*, June 30, p. 15, July 1, p. 16; Donald Honig, *Baseball Between the Lines*, p. 89; Peter Golenbock, *Fenway*, p. 180; Ed Linn, *Hitter*, p. 311; Dan Shaughnessy, *The Curse of the Bambino*, pp. 84–5; Joe DiMaggio, *Lucky to Be a Yankee*, p. 27; Richard Ben Cramer, *Joe DiMaggio*, pp. 266–68. (In his desire to demonize Joe DiMaggio, Cramer appeared logically compelled to criticize McCarthy, as the two had been cast as a perfect complement to one another—always mindful and seemingly without joys [Cramer, p. 93]. McCarthy and DiMaggio each had joys, and McCarthy had no divided loyalties when managing in Boston.)

13. Al Hirshberg, *What's Wrong with the Red Sox*, p. 91.

14. *Boston Post*, July 2, 1949, p. 6, July 3, p. 15, July 4, p. 35, July 5, p. 21; Dan Shaughnessy, *The Curse of the Bambino*, p. 85.

15. *Boston Post*, July 6, 1949, p. 18; *Look Magazine*, July 4, 1950, pp. 72–3.

16. *Boston Post*, July 29, p. 14, July 31, p. 22, August 1, pp. 1, 14, Aug. 2, p. 16, Aug. 13, p. 6, Aug. 27, p. 6; *Boston Herald*, September 16, p. 37; *Look Magazine*, July 4, 1950, pp. 73–4.

17. *Boston Post*, August 21, 1949, p. 16, September 1, pp. 1, 18, Sept. 8, p. 18, Sept. 10, pp. 1, 6, Sept. 11, p. 32, Sept. 12, p. 16.

18. *Ibid.*, September 24, 1949, p. 8, Sept. 25, p. 1, Sept. 26, pp. 1, 14, Sept. 27, pp. 1, 18; *Boston Herald*, Sept. 24, p. 11, Sept. 25, p. 1, Sept. 26, pp. 1, 16, Sept. 27, p. 22; *Boston Globe*, Oct. 5, p. 22.

19. *Boston Post*, September 28, 1949, p. 20, Sept. 29, p. 18, Oct. 1, p. 49; *Boston Herald*, Sept. 28, p. 25, Sept. 29, p. 24, Oct. 1, pp. 1, 10.

20. *Boston Globe*, October 1, 1949, p. 21; Dan Shaughnessy, *The Curse of the Bambino*, p. 85.

21. *Boston Post*, October 2, 1949, pp. 38–39; *Boston Herald*, Oct. 2, p. 51; Ed Hurley, *Managing to Win* (New York: A.J. Pollicino, 1976), p. 89.

22. Peter Golenbock, *Fenway*, pp. 178–80; Linn, *Hitter*, p. 311; Bill Madden, *Pride of October*, p. 116.

23. *Boston Post*, October 3, 1949, p. 18, *Boston Herald*, Oct. 3, p. 1, *Boston Globe*, Oct. 3, p. 8; Al Hirshberg, *What's Wrong with the Red Sox*, pp. 100–02; Bill Madden, *Pride of October*, p. 116.

24. *Boston Post*, October 3, 1949, p. 18, *Boston Herald*, Oct. 3, p. 1, *Boston Globe*, Oct. 3, p. 8; Al Hirshberg, *What's Wrong with the Red Sox*, pp. 100–02.

25. *Boston Post*, October 3, 1949, p. 1; *Look Magazine*, July 4, 1950, p. 74; David Halberstam, *The Teammates: A Portrait of Friendship* (New York: Hyperion, 2003), p. 167.

26. *Sport Magazine*, 1950; *Boston Post*, October 4, 1949, p. 20; Richard Ben Cramer, *Joe DiMaggio*, pp. 272–3.

27. *Boston Post*, October 3, 1949, pp. 1, 11, *Boston Herald*, Oct. 3, p. 14, *Boston Globe*, Oct. 3, p. 11, Oct. 5, p. 22; Harvey Frommer, *Baseball's Greatest Managers*, p. 162; Dan Shaughnessy, *The Curse of the Bambino*, p. 88; Peter Golenbock, *Fenway*, pp. 182–83; Ted Williams, *My Turn at Bat*, p. 159; *Baseball Digest*, April, 1973, p. 32; Al Hirshberg, *What's Wrong with the Red Sox*, p. 102; Harold Kaese, "Is the Designated Hitter Rule Good for Baseball?" *Baseball Digest*, vol. 32, issue 4, April, 1973, p. 36; Bill Cunningham, "The Boston Red Sox," *Sport Magazine*, December, 1950, p. 76; Joe McCarthy, "How Pennants Are Really Won," *Liberty Magazine*, September 30, 1933, p. 4.

28. *Boston Post*, October 3, 1949, p. 19; *Boston Globe*, Oct. 3, p. 1; Dan Shaughnessy, *The Curse of the Bambino*, p. 90.

29. *Boston Globe*, October 4, 1949, p. 36; *Buffalo Evening News*, Oct. 11, p. 40.

Chapter 37

1. Ted Williams, *My Turn at Bat*, pp. 155.

2. *Chicago Tribune*, February 12, 1950, section 2, p. 1; *Boston Globe*, Feb. 12, p. 49.

3. *Boston Globe*, February 27, 1950, pp. 1, 19–20, Feb. 28, pp. 30.

4. *Ibid.*, February 27, 1950, pp. 1, 19–20, Feb. 28, pp. 30; Peter Golenbock, *Fenway*, p. 187.

5. *Boston Globe*, February 28, 1950, p. 16, March 1, p. 26; *Boston Post*, March 24, p. 35; Al Hirshberg, *What's Wrong with the Red Sox*, p. 133.

6. *Boston Herald*, June 23, 1950, p. 18; Richard Ben Cramer, *Joe DiMaggio*, p. 273–74; Dan Shaughnessy, *The Curse of the Bambino* p. 61; Ed Fitzgerald, "Nobody's Neutral About McCarthy," p. 82.

7. Dan Shaughnessy, *The Curse of the Bambino*, pp. 76–7; Joe McCarthy, "World Champs: What It Takes to Make 'Em," *Liberty Magazine*, September 13, 1937, pp. 25–6.

8. *Boston Globe*, February 11, 1950, p. 4, March 14, p. 13, April 21, p. 27.

9. *Boston Post*, March 10, 1950, p. 28, March 11, p. 10, March 14, p. 19; *Boston Globe*, March 14, p. 12.

10. *Boston Post*, March 7, 1950, p. 23, March 27, p. 18, April 5, p. 22; *Louisville Courier-Journal*, April 12, section 2, p. 6.

11. *Boston Post*, April 14, 1950, p. 29, April 18, p. 1, April 19, pp. 36–37; *Boston Globe*, April 14, p. 24, April 17, p. 20; *Look Magazine*, July 4, 1950, p. 71; *Newsweek*, April 17, 1950, p. 62.

12. *Boston Globe*, April 16, 1950, p. 46, April 19, p. 28; *Boston Post*, April 22, p. 7; Edwin Pope, *Baseball's Greatest Managers*, p. 134; Harvey Frommer, *Baseball's Greatest Managers*, p. 162.

13. *Boston Post*, April 23, 1950, pp. 1, 37, 38, April 24, pp. 1, 19; *Boston Globe*, April 24, pp. 1, 8, April 25, p. 17; Bill Cunningham, *The Boston Red Sox*, p. 75; Clippings File, Cooperstown.

14. *Boston Post*, May 1, 1950, p. 15, May 2, pp. 20, 21; Ted Williams, *My Turn at Bat*, p. 127.

15. Ed Linn, *Hitter*, p. 311.

16. *Ibid.*, May 10, p. 22, May 12, p. 28, May 13, p. 1, May 31, p. 15, June 1, p. 17, June 2, p. 24; *Boston Herald*, June 12, p. 14; *New York Herald Tribune*, June 1, p. 24; *New York Times*, June 1, p. 13; *New York Daily Mirror*, May 31, p. 38; *New York World Telegram*, June 1, p. 19; *New York Post*, May 31, p. 27; Harvey Frommer, *Baseball's Greatest Managers*, p. 162..

17. *Boston Post*, May 19, 1950, p. 32, June 3, p. 8, June, 4, p. 33, June 5, p. 18, June 6, p. 22, June 7, p. 20, June 8, p. 20, June 9, pp. 1, 26, June 10, p. 8, June 11, p. 32, June 12, p. 18; *Boston Herald*, June 4, p. 54, June 5, p. 14, June 6, p. 13, June 9, p. 34, June 10, p. 6; Peter Golenbock, *Fenway*, p. 186.

18. *Boston Post*, June 13, 1950, p. 18, June 14, p. 23, June 15, p. 25, June 16, p. 21, June 17, p. 6, June 18, p. 35, June 19, p. 19; *Boston Herald*, June 14, p. 37, June 15, p. 29, June 16, p. 37, June 18, p. 47; Peter Golenbock, *Fenway*, p. 186.

19. *Boston Post*, June 21, 1950, p. 20; *Boston Herald*, June 21, p. 25, June 23, pp. 1, 19, June 24, pp. 1, 6; *Boston Globe*, June 21, p. 13, June 23, pp. 1, 28; *Buffalo Evening News*, June 22, p. 1, June 23, p. 45; *Chicago Tribune*, section 6, p. 1, June 23, section 4, p. 4; *The Sporting News*, July 5, 1950, p. 3; *Time Magazine*, July 3, 1950, p. 29; *Newsweek*, July 3, 1950, p. 62.

20. *Buffalo Evening News*, June 24, 1950, p. 5;

Boston Post, June 26, 1950, p. 18; Clippings File, Cooperstown.

21. *Boston Globe*, June 24, pp. 1, 6; *Boston Herald*, June 23, p. 18, June 25, p. 11; *The Sporting News*, December 18, 1957, p. 18; Pope, *Baseball's Greatest Managers*, p. 135; Peter Golenbock, *Fenway*, p. 186.

22. *Boston Post*, June 26, 1950, p. 18; *Boston Globe*, September 19, 1950, p. 1, Sept. 20, p. 14, Sept. 21, p. 23, Sept. 24, p. 1, Sept. 25, p. 1, Sept. 28, p. 12.

Chapter 38

1. Ed Fitzgerald, "Nobody's Neutral About McCarthy," p. 82.

2. *Life Magazine*, May 1, 1950, p. 1.

3. *Buffalo Evening News*, February 4, 1957, p. 23; April 18, 1964, section C, p. 1; April 21, 1977, section III, p. 38; January 14, 1978, p. 11.

4. *Ibid.*, February 4, 1957, p. 23; July 22, p. 24; *The Sporting News*, February 13, p. 5; *New York Times*, January 30, p. 34; February 4, p. 34; July 23, p. 33, July 24, p. 31; *New York Mirror*, February 4, pp. 33–34; *Chicago American*, February 6; *Washington Evening Star*, February 4, p. A-21.

5. *The Sporting News*, January 28, 1978, p. 40, April 25, 1964, p. 7; Ed Barrow, *My Fifty Years*, p. 66.

6. *Buffalo Evening News*, April 17, 1971, section C, p. 2.

7. Anthony Violanti, *Miracle in Buffalo*, p. 65; Harvey Frommer, *Baseball's Greatest Managers*, pp. 156–57.

8. *Buffalo Evening News*, April 21, 1973, section C, p. 1; *New York Times*, October 16, 1957, p. 32; September 25, 1977, p. 35; Edwin Pope, *Baseball's Greatest Managers*, p. 148.

9. *New York Times*, January 14, 1978, p. 24.

10. *Buffalo Evening News*, April 18, 1964, section C, p. 1; April 17, 1971, section C, p. 2; January 14, 1978, p. 11.

11. Arthur Daley, "McCarthy Could Manage," *Baseball Digest*, vol. 9, no. 9, Sept. 1950, p. 76.

12. Ed Fitzgerald, "Nobody's Neutral About McCarthy," p. 82.

13. *Ibid.*

14. *Buffalo Evening News*, April 17, 1971, section C, p. 2.

15. Bill James, *The Bill James Guide to Baseball Managers from 1870 to Today* (New York: Scribners, 1997), pp. 91–99.

16. *Buffalo Evening News*, August 4, 1969, section C, p. 2, September 8, p. 11; January 14, 1978, p. 11; Edwin Pope, *Baseball's Greatest Managers*, p. 135; *Suburban Press* (Buffalo), April 21, 1977, p. 14.

17. *The Sporting News*, March 8, 1969, p. 7; *Boston Record*, February 26, 1969, p. 11; Clippings File, Cooperstown.

18. *Buffalo Evening News*, April 21, 1977, section III, p. 38; Frederick John, "Baseball's Greatest," *Modern Maturity*, April–May, 1973, p. 15.

19. *New York Times*, October 1, section 3, p. 2.

20. *The Sporting News*, January 28, 1978, p. 40; *Buffalo Evening News*, August 4, 1969, section C, p. 2; April 17, 1971, section C, p. 2.

21. *Buffalo Evening News*, April 26, 1970, p. 21; October 19, 1971, p. 28; October 20, 1971, p. 78

22. Anthony Violanti, *Miracle in Buffalo*, p. 66.

23. *Buffalo Evening News*, April 17, 1971, section C, p. 2; July 8, 1972, section C, p. 3; April 21, 1973, section C, p. 1; April 20, 1974, section B, p. 2; January 14, 1978, p. 11; Clippings File, Cooperstown, June 18, 1972; *The Sporting News*, January 28, 1978, p. 40; Anthony Violanti, *Miracle in Buffalo*, p. 66.

24. *Buffalo Evening News*, April 21, 1977, section III, p. 38; *Suburban Press* (Buffalo), April 21, 1977, p. 14.

25. *Buffalo Evening News*, August 8, 1969, p. 11; April 17, 1971, section C, p. 2; April 21, 1971, section B, p. 2; April 21, 1973, section C, p. 1; April 20, 1974, section B, p. 2, April 19, 1975, section B, p. 2; April 21, 1977, section III, p. 38; January 14, 1978, p. 11; *New York Times*, August 29, 1976, section 3, p. 9; Frederick John, "Baseball's Greatest," *Modern Maturity*, April–May, 1973, p. 15; *Chicago Tribune*, January 14, 1978, section 2, p. 1; Clippings File, Cooperstown.

26. *Buffalo Evening News*, January 14, 1978, p. 11; *Boston Globe*, January 14, 1978, p. 22; *The Sporting News*, January 28, 1978, p. 40.

27. Anthony Violanti, *Miracle in Buffalo*, p. 67.

28. *Ibid.*, January 18, 1978, p. 8; State of New York Legislative Resolution, January 18, 1978, *Buffalo Evening News*, December 16, 1978, p. 14; *New York Times*, January 18, 1978; Clippings File, Cooperstown.

29. Anthony Violanti, *Miracle in Buffalo*, p. 62–63.

30. *The Sporting News*, January 28, 1978, p. 40.

31. Edwin Pope, *Baseball's Greatest Managers*, p. 137; Frederick John, "Baseball's Greatest," *Modern Maturity*, April–May, 1973, p. 15.

32. *The Sporting News*, November 24, 1938, p. 3.

33. *New York Telegraph*, September 11, 1927, p. 11, Clippings File, Cooperstown.

34. Ed Fitzgerald, "Nobody's Neutral About McCarthy," p. 83.

Bibliography

Newspapers

Albany Evening Journal
Baltimore Sun
Boston Daily Globe
Boston Herald
Boston Post
Buffalo Morning Express
Buffalo Evening News
Butler [Pa.] Eagle
Brooklyn Daily Eagle
Charleston [West Virginia] Gazette
Chicago Daily News
Chicago Herald and Examiner
Chicago Tribune
Cleveland News
Cleveland Plain Dealer
Detroit Free Press
Franklin [Pa.] Herald
Harrisburg Patriot
Indianapolis News
Indianapolis Star
Louisville Courier Journal
Louisville Times
Milwaukee Journal
Milwaukee Sentinel
Minneapolis Journal
Minneapolis Tribune
New York Daily Mirror
New York Daily News
New York Herald Tribune
New York Post
New York Sun
New York Times
New York World Telegram
Oil City [Pa.] Derrick
Philadelphia Inquirer
Philadelphia Public Ledger
Philadelphia Record
Sporting News
Syracuse Post Standard
Toledo News Bee
Washington Post
Washington Times Herald
Wilkes-Barre Record
Wilmington [Del.] Evening Journal
Wilmington Every Evening

Books

Alexander, Charles C. *Breaking the Slump: Baseball in the Depression Era*. New York: Columbia University Press, 2002.

Allen, Lee. *The Hot Stove League*. New York: A.S. Barnes and Co., 1955.

Allen, Maury. *Where Have You Gone, Joe DiMaggio*. New York: E.P. Dutton, 1975.

Barber, Red. *Walk in the Spirit*. New York: Dial Press, 1969.

Barrow, Edward Grant. *My Fifty Years in Baseball*. New York: Coward-McCann, 1951.

Bjarkman, Peter. *The Encyclopedia of Major League Baseball Team Histories — National League*. Westport, CT: Meckler, 1991.

Bok, Richard. *Casey Stengel: A Splendid Baseball Life*. Dallas: Taylor, 1997.

Benis, Charlie. *Mickey Cochrane: The Life of a Baseball Hall of Famer*. Jefferson, NC: McFarland, 1998.

Benson, Michael. *Ballparks of North America*. Jefferson, NC: McFarland, 1989.

Boone, Robert S., and Gerald Grunska. *Hack: The Meteoric Life of One of Baseball's First Superstars: Hack Wilson*. Highland Park, IL: Highland Publishers, 1978.

Boston, Talmage. *1939: Baseball's Pivotal Year: From the Golden Age to the Modern Era*. Fort Worth, TX: Summit Publishing Group, 1994.

Boudreau, Lou, and Russell Schneider. *Cover-*

ing All the Bases. Champagne, IL: Sagamore Publishers, 1993.

Bouton, Jim. *I Managed Good, But Boy Did They Play Bad.* Chicago: Playboy Press, 1973.

Brown, Warren. *The Chicago Cubs.* Carbondale: Southern Illinois University Press, [1946] 2001.

Burk, Robert F. *Much More Than a Game: Players, Owners, and American Baseball Since 1900.* Chapel Hill: University of North Carolina Press, 2001.

Cleveland, Charles B. *The Great Baseball Managers.* New York: Thomas Y. Crowell, 1950.

Cohen, Stanley. *Dodgers! The First 100 Years.* New York: Carol, 1990.

Conner, Anthony J., ed. *Baseball for the Love of It: Hall-of-Famers Tell It Like It Was.* New York: Macmillan, 1982.

Cramer, Richard Ben. *Joe DiMaggio: The Hero's Life.* New York: Simon and Schuster, 2000.

Creamer, Robert W. *Babe: The Legend Comes to Life.* New York: Simon and Schuster, 1974.

_____. *Baseball and Other Matters in 1941.* Lincoln: University of Nebraska Press, 2000.

_____. *Stengel, His Life and Times.* New York: Simon and Schuster, 1984.

Crepeau, Richard. *Baseball: America's Diamond Mind, 1919–1941.* Lincoln: University of Nebraska Press, 2000.

Curran, William. *Big Sticks: The Batting Revolution of the Twenties.* New York: Morrow, 1990.

_____. *Strikeout: A Celebration of the Art of Pitching.* New York: Crown, 1995.

Daniel, W. Harrison. *Jimmie Foxx.* Jefferson, NC: McFarland, 1997.

Dawidoff, Nicholas. *The Catcher Was a Spy.* New York: Pantheon, 1994.

DiMaggio, Dom, and Bill Gilbert. *Real Grass, Real Heroes: Baseball's Historic 1941 Season.* New York: Zebra, 1990.

DiMaggio, Joe. *Lucky to Be a Yankee.* New York: Grosset and Dunlap, 1947.

Durso, Joseph. *Joe DiMaggio: The Last American Knight.* Boston: Little, Brown, 1995.

Enright, Jim. *Baseball's Greatest Teams: the Cubs.* New York: Collier Books, 1975.

Eskenazi, Gerald. *The Lip: A Biography of Leo Durocher.* New York: Morrow, 1993.

Feller, Bob, and Bill Gilbert. *Now Pitching, Bob Feller.* New York: Carol, 1990.

Frisch, Frank, and J. Roy Stockton. *The Fordham Flash.* Garden City, NY: Doubleday, 1962.

Frommer, Harvey. *Baseball's Greatest Managers.* New York: Franklin Watts, 1985.

Gallagher, Mark. *The Yankee Encyclopedia.* Champaign: University of Illinois Press, 1977

Gehrig, Eleanor, and Joseph Durso. *My Luke and I.* New York: Crowell, 1976.

Goldstein, Richard. *Spartan Seasons: How Baseball Survived the Second World War.* New York: Macmillan, 1980.

Golenbock, Peter. *Dynasty: New York Yankees, 1949–1964.* Chicago: Contemporary Books, 2000.

_____. *Fenway: An Unexpurgated History of the Boston Red Sox.* New York: G.P. Putnam's Sons, 1992.

Grabowshy, John F. *The New York Yankees.* San Diego: Lucent Books, 2002.

Graham, Frank. *Lou Gehrig: A Quiet Hero.* New York: G.P. Putnam's Sons, 1942.

_____. *The New York Yankees.* New York: G.P. Putnam's Sons, 1948.

Greenberg, Hank. *The Story of My Life.* ed., Ira Berkow. New York: Times Books, 1989.

Gross, Milton. *Yankee Doodles.* Boston: House of Kent Publishing Co., 1948.

Halberstam, David. *Summer of '49.* New York: William Morrow, 1989.

_____. *Teammates.* New York: Hyperion Press, 2003.

Henrich, Tommy, and Bill Gilbert. *Five O'Clock Lightning: Ruth, Gehrig, DiMaggio, Mantle, and the Glory Years of the New York Yankees.* New York: Birch Lane Press, 1992.

Hirshberg, Al. *What's the Matter with the Red Sox.* New York: Dodd, Mead, 1973.

Honig, Donald. *Baseball Between the Lines: Baseball in the Forties as Told by the Men Who Played It.* Lincoln: University of Nebraska Press, 1976.

_____. *Baseball in the '30s: An Illustrated History.* New York: Crown, 1989.

_____. *Baseball When the Grass Was Real: Baseball from the Twenties to the Forties Told by the Men Who Played It.* Lincoln: University of Nebraska Press, 1975.

_____. *The Man in the Dugout: Fifteen Big League Managers Speak Their Minds.* Chicago: Follett, 1977.

_____. *The New York Yankees: An Illustrated History.* New York: Crown, [1981] 1987.

_____. *The October Heroes: Great World Series Games Remembered by the Men Who Played Them.* New York: Simon and Schuster, 1979.

Hurley, Ed. *Managing to Win.* New York: A.J. Pollicino, Inc., 1976.

James, Bill. *The Baseball Book, 1991.* New York: Villard Books, 1991.

_____. *The Bill James Guide to Baseball Man-*

agers from 1870 to Today. New York: Scribners, 1997.

Jordan, David M. *The Athletics of Philadelphia: Connie Mack's White Elephants, 1901–1954.* Jefferson, NC: McFarland, 1999.

Kashatus, William C. *Connie Mack's '29 Triumph: The Rise and Fall of the Philadelphia Athletics Dynasty.* Jefferson, NC: McFarland, 1999.

Katz, Lawrence. *Baseball in 1939: The Watershed Season of the National Pastime.* Jefferson, NC: McFarland, 1995.

Kavanagh, Jack. *Ol' Pete: The Grover Cleveland Alexander Story.* South Bend, IN: Diamond Communications, 1996.

Kelley, Brent. *The Early All-Stars: Conversations with Standout Baseball Players of the 1930s and 1940s.* Jefferson, NC: McFarland, 1997.

Kennedy, David M. *Freedom from Fear: The American People in Depression and War, 1929–1945.* New York: Oxford University Press, 1999.

Koppett, Leonard. *The Man in the Dugout: Baseball's Top Managers and How They Got That Way.* Philadelphia: Temple University Press, 2000.

Lally, Richard. *Bombers: An Oral History of the New York Yankees.* New York: Three Rivers Press, Crown Publishers, 2002.

Lieb, Frederick G. *The Boston Red Sox.* New York: G.P. Putnam, 1948.

_____. *Comedians and Pranksters of Baseball.* St. Louis: Charles C. Spink, 1958.

Linn, Ed. *The Great Rivalry: The Yankees and the Red Sox, 1901–1990.* New York: Ticknor and Fields, 1991.

_____. *Hitter: The Life and Turmoils of Ted Williams.* New York: Harcourt, Brace, 1993.

Madden, Bill. *Pride of October: What It Was to Be Young and a Yankee.* New York: Warner Books, 2003.

Masin, Herman. *Speakers' Treasury of Sports Stories.* New York: Prentice Hall, 1954.

Mayer, Ronald A. *The Newark Bears.* Union City, NJ: Wise Publications, 1980.

Mead, William B. *Two Spectacular Seasons: 1930— The Year the Hitters Ran Wild; 1968 — The Year the Pitchers Took Revenge.* New York: Macmillan, 1990.

Meany, Tom. *The Boston Red Sox.* New York: A.S. Barnes, 1956.

_____. *The Yankee Story.* New York: E.P. Dutton, 1960.

Murdock, Eugene Converse. *Baseball Between the Wars: Memories of the Game by the Men Who Played It.* Westport, CT: Meckler, 1992.

Nuwer, Hank. *Strategies of the Great Baseball Managers.* New York: Franklin Watts, 1988.

O'Connor, Anthony J., ed. *Baseball for the Love of It: Hall of Famers Tell It Like It Was.* New York: Macmillan, 1982.

Okrent, Donald, and Harris Levine. *The Ultimate Baseball Book.* Boston: Houghton Mifflin, 1984.

Pope, Edwin. *Baseball's Greatest Managers.* Garden City, NY: Doubleday, 1960.

Robinson, Ray. *Iron Horse: Lou Gehrig and His Time.* New York: W.W. Norton, 1990.

Rothgerber, Harry J., Jr. *A Celebration of Louisville Baseball in the Major and Minor Leagues.* Cleveland: Society for American Baseball Research, 1997.

Schoor, Gene. *Joe DiMaggio: The Yankee Clipper.* New York: Julian Messner, 1956.

_____. *The Scooter: The Phil Rizzuto Story.* New York: Scribner's, 1982.

Seidel, Michael. *Streak: Joe DiMaggio and the Summer of '41.* New York: Penguin Books, 1989.

Shaughnessy, Dan. *The Curse of the Bambino.* New York: Penguin Books, [1990] 1991.

Smelser, Marshall. *The Life That Ruth Built: A Biography.* Lincoln: University of Nebraska Press, 1995.

Thorn, John, and Pete Palmer, with David Reuther, et al. *Total Baseball,* 2d ed. New York: Warner Books, 1991.

Tofel, Richard J. *A Legend in the Making: The New York Yankees in 1939.* New York: Ivan R. Dee, 2001.

Tygiel, Jules. *Past Time: Baseball as History.* New York: Oxford University Press, 2000.

Van Riper, Guernsey. *The Mighty Macs: Three Famous Baseball Managers.* Champaign, IL: Garrard Publishing Co., 1972.

Violanti, Anthony. *Miracle in Buffalo: How the Dream of Baseball Revived a City.* New York: St. Martin's, 1991.

Voigt, David Quentin. *American Baseball, Vol. II, From Commissioners to Continental Expansion.* University Park: Penn State University Press, 1983.

Warfield, Don. *The Roaring Redhead: Larry MacPhail.* South Bend, IN: Diamond Communications, 1987.

Williams, Ted, with John Underwood. *My Turn at Bat: The Story of My Life,* 2d ed. New York: Simon and Schuster, [1969] 1988.

Articles

"All-Time Winning Managers," *Baseball Digest,* April, 1974, p. 82.

Barrow, Edward G., "The Greatest Manager," *Collier's,* June 24, 1950, p. 28.

"Baseball: Have an Aspirin," *Newsweek*, July 3, 1950, p. 62.

"Baseball: Ruppert-McCarthy Battery Puts Ruth Out at Home," *Newsweek*, July 27, 1935, p. 22.

"Baseball: the Red Sox Riddle," *Newsweek*, April 17, 1950, p. 80.

Boynton, B., "Managers and Close Games," *Baseball Research Journal*, 1995, p. 81.

Cannon, Jimmy, "Lessons from McCarthy," *Baseball Digest*, June, 1969, p. 62.

Cobbledick, Gordon, "Break Up the Yankees!" *Collier's*, February 25, 1939, p. 19.

Cumminsky, Joe, "The McCarthy Technique," *Baseball Digest*, February, 1944, p. 17.

Daley, Arthur, "McCarthy Could Manage," *Baseball Digest*, September, 1950, p. 29.

Daniel, Daniel M., "Meet Joe McCarthy," *Baseball Magazine*, September, 1932, p. 437.

Fay, Bill, "Baseball's Winner of 1949," *Collier's*, April 16, 1949, p. 20.

Fitzgerald, Ed, "Nobody's Neutral About McCarthy," *Sport*, August, 1950, p. 16.

Flaherty, Vincent, "A Great Guy Even When He Hasn't Got It," *Baseball Digest*, October, 1943, p. 34.

Graham, Frank, "The Joe McCarthy Method," *Baseball Digest*, October, 1943, p. 34.

Hirshberg, Al, "Joe McCarthy on the Pan," *Sport*, June, 1949, p. 10.

Holmes, Tommy, "What You Learned from McCarthy," *Baseball Digest*, October, 1954, p. 65.

Kaese, Harold, "Is the Designated Hitter Rule Good For Baseball?" *Baseball Digest*, April, 1973, p. 36.

Lane, Frank C., "Joe McCarthy, Baseball's Mysterious Man," *Baseball Magazine*, October, 1927, p. 483.

Lardner, John, "Mr. McCarthy Continues," *Baseball Digest*, February, 1946, p. 46.

Mann, Arthur, "Of McCarthy and Men," *Baseball Magazine*, October, 1943, p. 365.

McCarthy, Joe, "How Pennants Are Really Won," *Liberty*, September 30, 1933, p. 4.

_____. "We'll Win the World Series," *Liberty*, October 3, 1936, p. 48.

_____. "World Champs: What It Takes to Make 'Em," *Liberty*, September 18, 1937, p. 25.

McCauley, Ed, "The McCarthy Technique, II," *Baseball Digest*, February, 1944, p. 24.

"The New Leader of the Cubs," *Baseball Magazine*, August, 1926, p. 399.

Rumill, Ed, "He Hoops It Up for the Red Sox Now," *Baseball Digest*, March, 1948, p. 14.

Sampson, Arthur, "Joe McCarthy: He Hates to be Second," *Look*, July 4, 1950, p. 70.

Shaver, John W., "The Cubs: Baseball's Contribution to Successful Management," *Factory and Industrial Management*, October, 1929, p. 840.

Simons, Herbert, "A Good Joe — McCarthy," *Baseball Digest*, April, 1948, p. 3.

Stout, Glenn, "Pitching Puzzle," *Boston*, October, 1989, p. 85.

"This Is Final," *Time*, July 3, 1950, p. 29.

Williams, Joe, "Busher Joe McCarthy," *Saturday Evening Post*, April 15, 1939, p. 12.

Index